About Pearson

Pearson is the world's learning company, with presence across 70 countries worldwide. Our unique insights and world-class expertise comes from a long history of working closely with renowned teachers, authors and thought leaders, as a result of which, we have emerged as the preferred choice for millions of teachers and learners across the world.

We believe learning opens up opportunities, creates fulfilling careers and hence better lives. We hence collaborate with the best of minds to deliver you class-leading products, spread across the Higher Education and K12 spectrum.

Superior learning experience and improved outcomes are at the heart of everything we do. This product is the result of one such effort.

Your feedback plays a critical role in the evolution of our products and you can contact us - reachus@pearson.com. *We look forward to it.*

Governance in India

Basics and Beyond

GOVERNANCE IN INDIA

BASICS AND BEYOND

M. Karthikeyan

Chapter Opening Image: **Cara-Foto. Shutterstock.**

Senior Editor—Acquisitions: Sharel Simon
Editor—Production: M. Balakrishnan

ISBN 978-93-325-8803-5

First Impression, 2018
Second Impression , 2018

Published by Pearson India Education Services Pvt. Ltd, CIN: U72200TN2005PTC057128,

Head Office: 15th Floor, Tower-B, World Trade Tower, Plot No. 1, Block-C, Sector 16,
Noida 201 301, Uttar Pradesh, India.

Registered Office: 4th Floor, Software Block, Elnet Software City, TS 140, Blocks 2 & 9,
Rajiv Gandhi Salai, Taramani, Chennai 600 113, Tamil Nadu, India.
Fax: 080-30461003, Phone: 080-30461060
in.pearson.com, Email: companysecretary.india@pearson.com

Compositor: Chandraprabhu Enterprise Private Limited, Puducherry.
Printed in India at India Binding House, Noida.

BRIEF CONTENTS

CONTENTS

PREFACE

Dear Civil Services Aspirants,

The introduction of a separate Paper (Paper-II) in General Studies in the UPSC Civil Services (Main) Examination clearly shows the importance of understanding the concept of governance and its basics for the aspiring Civil Servants. There is certainly many lacunas in understanding the concept of governance, especially by the public servants who have been conferred power to govern the people. Introduction of such paper will help the future Civil Servants be adept and help them cater the needs of the citizens in a better manner. This book is thus an endeavour in helping the students to grasp the basics of Governance well and go beyond in getting transformed into agile and proficient Civil Servants.

In this context, it is pertinent that all civil services aspirants should be well equipped with this topic. Keeping the interest of vast segment of the student community and my close association with the aspirants for the past 10 years, I thought of coming out with this book, which will suit the requirements of Civil Services main examination participants.

Adequate care has been taken to make this volume as comprehensive as possible so that this will remain the major source of knowledge for all the topics with syllabus.

SPECIAL FEATURES OF THIS BOOK

1. This volume is written purely based on the requirement of the UPSC Civil Services Main Examination. This will cater collectively to all the topics included in General Studies Paper-II.
2. We have taken utmost care to keep the language of the contents very lucid and easily understandable so that the important aspects are comprehendible and retained by students to present a better answer.
3. Throughout the book, we have followed some unique patterns in the contents of all the chapters with learning objectives at the beginning of each chapter which will give the readers a clear idea about what the chapter is all about.
4. At the end of the each chapter, adequate numbers of practice questions have been included to make the preparation complete.
5. Wherever required, we have included relevant examples and illustrations to make the students effectively understand the basic concept of governance.
6. Important and useful reports of various committees and commission have been included wherever required in the chapters; this will be very useful in answering with quality and to make your answer to the point.

STRUCTURE OF THE BOOK AND UPSC SYLLABUS

This book has been developed in a magnificent way to include each and every aspect of the syllabus prescribed by the UPSC. Since these topics are introduced very recently in the UPSC syllabus and the source materials for these topics are very vast as the topic governance covers entire gamut of the subject of Public Administration and Political Science, I have, therefore, prepared this book to be the single-point ready resource material for Governance, which covers both basics and associated aspects.

Since the examination is of generalist in nature, I can assure you that you will be definitely be in a much better stand to answer all questions on this subject with the concepts discussed in this volume.

The very first edition of the book consists of various contents as briefly given here:

CHAPTER I: GOVERNANCE – AN CONCEPTUAL INTRODUCTION

This Introduction chapter covers all essential and important concepts to understand the basics of Governance. This chapter is quite elaborate so as to provide a strong basic to understand subsequent chapters better.

CHAPTER II: GENERAL FRAMEWORK OF INDIAN MODEL OF GOVERNANCE

This chapter provides an excellent depiction of how the Indian model of governance is devised and functioning. Discussions have been made pertaining to various organs and entities of Indian Governance (viz., the Indian democracy, basic structure and principles of the Constitution, Parliamentary system, Indian Federal dynamics, various independent constitutional bodies and the Indian innovation of the three-tier system of governance and the two-tier system of federalism).

CHAPTER III: INDIAN PARLIAMENT

Indian Parliamentary system is the fundamental institution concerning governance of the country. Hence, this chapter helps to understand the basics of Indian Parliament, why was it introduced, what are its important features, its powers and functions, and various other recent issues and concerns surrounding it.

CHAPTER IV: ISSUES CONCERNING THE JUDICIARY

Judiciary is the pillar which supports and holds the democratic setup from collapsing. Though it does not directly involve itself in the process of governing and governance, it does have a vital role to play. This chapter deals with the basics of Indian judicial system, the powers given to the judiciary as under the Constitution, the unique independent nature of the Indian Judiciary, various issues concerning the appointment procedures, importance of judicial review, the activism by the judiciary, and finally the reforms needed to make the judiciary function in a better manner.

CHAPTER V: ISSUES AND CHALLENGES PERTAINING TO THE FEDERAL STRUCTURE

Indian federalism in unique and it is indestructible Union of destructible States. This unique position has to be understood as per the Constitutional provisions and also how it actually functions in reality. This chapter gives a detailed look into what federalism is and what are the various issues surrounding the Indian federalism at present. Other aspects such as the emerging pattern of coalition governments, impact of the neo-economic policies, re-invention of the self-governing institutions, and issues of decentralization have been presented so as to give the readers better grasp on the subject at hand.

CHAPTER VI: CITIZEN'S PARTICIPATION IN GOVERNANCE

The participation of citizens in the governance process is important in the present scenario; as without their participation, the governance cannot be carried out. This chapter, in detail, deals with all the aspects concerning the citizen's participation. The concept and basics of civil society has been elaborated, theories of management relating to the citizens participation has been discussed, and other important issues has been given in a detailed manner to help understand the growing importance of role of citizen in the governance.

CHAPTER VII: COMPARISON OF THE INDIAN CONSTITUTIONAL SCHEME WITH THAT OF OTHER COUNTRIES

The Constitution forms the fundamental and basic law of all the countries. It provides the power, framework, and guidelines on the structure and functioning of the democratic institutions. Indian Constitution, though inspired from many others, has its own unique features. This chapter, therefore, compares the Constitution of India with that of other important Constitutions around the world. This helps understand the unique aspects of Indian Constitution in an effective manner.

CHAPTER VIII: STATUTORY, REGULATORY AND QUASI-JUDICIAL BODIES

The governance is carried out by various democratic institutions and the Constitutional, Statutory, Regulatory, and Quasi-Judicial bodies help in effectively and efficiently address matters related to governance. These bodies are the vital limbs of the democratic system, and without its able support the democracy will not function properly. This chapter gives an insight on various Statutory, Regulatory, and Quasi-Judicial Bodies present in India.

CHAPTER IX: REPRESENTATION OF PEOPLE ACT

Election process is the most important and vital in a democratic setup. Understanding the Electoral process and its laws is important

CHAPTER X: ROLE OF CIVIL SERVICES IN A DEMOCRACY

The role played by the Civil Services in a Democracy is the most important aspect of governance. The Civil Servants are the ones who implement the policies of the government, and therefore are the faces of the governance. Without their active and positive involvement, any reform in the governance process cannot be carried out. This chapter explains the role played by the Civil Service and various other issues involved in it. At the end of the chapters, certain important Administrative Reforms are also given which will be very helpful.

CHAPTER XI: E-GOVERNANCE

E-Governance is the latest facet in the field of governance. It is not a new concept, rather it makes the existing governance effective and more efficient. It harnesses the use of present Information and Communication Technology to take the process to the people and help involve various stakeholders in governing. This chapter elaborates upon the importance and present growth of E-governance and how more effective can it be made.

CHAPTER XII: RIGHT TO INFORMATION

Transparency, accountability, responsibility are becoming the watch word in a democratic system. People have the right to know everything the government is doing, there should be no secrecy in what a government does and every information should be shared with the people. The Right to Information Act sought to do this. This chapter clearly explains about the struggle undergone to bring to force this Act, various other important provisions of the Act, and the reforms needed to make in more effective.

CHAPTER XIII: CITIZEN'S CHARTER

Citizen's Charter is another important endeavour to make the governance system more effective. It helps in time-bound delivery of services to the people. This chapter effectively explains about the basics of Citizen's Charter, its importance, view from international perspective, and important reforms needed to make it function in a better manner.

CHAPTER XIV: WELFARE SCHEMES FOR THE VULNERABLE SECTION OF THE POPULATION

The State in the present era is considered to be a Welfare State, and therefore the State has enacted various legislations, constricted policies, and developed schemes to address the concerns of the citizens. In this context, it is important to know what has the government done for the vulnerable and the invisible section of the population (viz., the minorities, the schedules castes, tribes, disabled, and the women). This chapter elucidates various schemes, which the government has devised for the vulnerable section of the population.

ACKNOWLEDGMENTS

I would like to express my deepest and heartfelt gratitude to all the people who saw me through the first edition of this book *Governance in India: Basics and Beyond* for Civil Services (Main) Examination. I also individually thank all those who provided me constant support and assisted in the editing, proofreading, and design of this book.

Such an effort to bring out good-quality content focused exclusively for Civil Services Main Examination could never have been possible without a continuous and committed effort. I extend my sincere thanks to all those who supported me in this endeavour to complete this project.

I extend my sincere appreciation and deepest gratitude for the help and support extended by Mr S. Girissh, Mr T. V. Charan Tej, Mr Mohamed Yasar Arafat, Mr Simeon Vedamanikam, who contributed in every possible manner for the first edition of the book to come out successfully. I would also like to thank the assistance rendered by Mr P. Anbuselvan and Ms R. Swathi Ratnam.

I would also like to thank my students for their motivation and questioning minds which instigated me to come out with this compilation.

Finally, I express my sincere gratitude to Pearson India Education Services Pvt. Ltd. With their continuous support and efforts, the book has been published as per schedule.

My special thanks to Ms Sharel Simon and Mr Balakrishnan for their extended support and motivation throughout the project.

I take this opportunity to express my heartfelt wishes to all the readers of this book.

For more updates on Governance in India, stay tuned @ http://karthikeyan.net.in/governance

M. Karthikeyan

ABOUT THE AUTHOR

M. Karthikeyan holds B.Com. degree from University of Madras, Chennai, Tamil Nadu, India. Besides, he also holds a degree in Law from Dr. Ambedkar Govt. Law College, Chennai, Tamil Nadu, India. Presently he is a practising advocate in the High Court of Madras, Chennai, Tamil Nadu, India. Apart from his profession, he is actively involved in various institutions in the capacity of Director and visiting faculty to train students who appear for Civil Services Examination. He has also authored *Internal Security for UPSC* published by Pearson Education, India.

Stay tuned with his regular updates on Governance in India @ http://karthikeyan.net.in/governance

ANALYSIS OF PREVIOUS YEAR'S UPSC GENERAL STUDIES-II QUESTION PAPER

The UPSC completely revamped its mains examination syllabus and pattern in 2013. Moreover, General Studies-II covering the topics of Governance and International Relations was newly added to evaluate the conceptual understanding about the process of governance.

The important aspect of the book you are having in your hand is that, we have covered all the concepts till now asked by the UPSC in its General Studies-II Paper. The following is the analysis of the topics covered in the book and the questions asked by the UPSC.

Chapters	Years			
	2013	2014	2015	2016
Governance: An Introduction	1	1	1	2
General Framework of Indian Model of Governance	1	1	1	1
Indian Parliament	1	2	1	2
Issues Concerning the Judiciary	1	3	2	1
Issues and Challenged Pertaining to the Federal Structure	3	1	2	2
Citizen's Participation in Governance*	NA			1
Comparison of Indian Constitutional Scheme with that of Other Countries*	NA			
Statutory, Regulatory and Quasi-Judicial Bodies	1	2	2	2
Representation of People Act*	NA			
Role of Civil Services in a Democracy	NA	1	2	2
E-Governance*	NA			
Right to Information*	NA			
Citizen's Charter*	1	NA		
Welfare Schemes for the Vulnerable Section of the Population	6	3	4	2

It is clear from the above that all those questions pertaining to governance (General Studies-II) till now asked by the UPSC has been covered in this book. Apart from those topics which are regularly asked by the UPSC, this book has covered other topics given in the syllabus which has not been asked in the exams till now. This is in view of equipping and preparing the students to face the examination in a confident manner.

The topics such as **Representation of People Act, E-Governance, Comparison of Constitution, and Right to Information** are likely to be in focus in the coming years. These are of high relevance in the current scenario. These topics have been given an extensive coverage in this book to help equip the students for the exams to come.

HOW TO USE THIS BOOK

Since this book is different from those of other guides/books available in the market pertaining to Governance (General Studies-II), I would like to recommend the students using this book, on how to use this book in an effective way.

- I would suggest to the students first to go through the previous year's questions asked by the UPSC given in the Annexure. This will help the students understand the nature and pattern followed by the UPSC. This will also help the students understand the usefulness of this book they are having.
- Each topic is written as standalone and thus can be studied and understood individually.
- I would suggest the students to initially start by studying the first two chapters of this book, **Governance: An Introduction** and **General Framework of India Model of Governance**. These chapters will help the students to get introduced to the concept of Governance and understand its process and function.
- While studying each chapters, I would suggest the students to go through the Learning Objectives given in the beginning. It is the work plan of the Chapter and will help to get familiarised with the subject discussed in the chapter.
- Each chapter has been designed in such a way that the students are first introduced to the basics of that topic, after which in-depth explanation and analysis is presented. Students, therefore, will not face any hardship in comprehending a particular topic. Practice questions are also given in order to help the students to check their understanding of the topics.
- The intention of devising the book in this said manner is to make the students better understand all aspects of Governance. The aim is not just academic and to help students get prepared for the UPSC mains examination, the endeavour is to instil the values of public service and create public servants who are much knowledgeable in all aspects related to Governing and Governance.

Governance in India

Basics and Beyond

1 Governance – A Conceptual Introduction

LEARNING OBJECTIVES

In this Chapter, you will learn about:

- Governance
- Good Governance
- Kautilya on Good Governance
- Plato on Good Governance
- Aristotle on Good Governance
- Origin of the Modern Concept of Good Governance
- World Bank Prescription
- Elements of Good Governance
- Forms of Good Governance
- Reinvention of the Concept of Public Governance in the Light of Evolution of the Concept of Good Governance
- The Indian Story- Pre-1991 and Post 1991
- State, Market and Civil Society
- Public Choice Theory
- New Public Management
- Civil Society
- Governance as Networks and Collaborative Government
- Role of State in era of Governance

1.1 GOVERNANCE

"*Governance is the exercise of economic, political and administrative authority to manage a country's affairs at all levels. It comprises the mechanisms, processes and institutions through which citizens and groups articulate their interests, exercise their legal rights, meet their obligations and mediate their differences*".

(Policy Report, 1997, United Nations Development Programme (UNDP)).

The concept of Governance refers to the processes and structures that are intended to bring about accountability, responsiveness, transparency, stability, rule of law, equity and inclusiveness, empowerment and broad-based participation. Apart from this, Governance also represents the values, norms and rules of the system through which public affairs are managed in a transparent, responsive, inclusive and participatory way. In a broad sense, Governance can be defined as the institutional environment in which citizens and other stakeholders interact among themselves and participate in public affairs. Therefore, governance is more significant than just the organs of government.

The key distinction between government and governance underscored by many scholars is, the involvement of institutions beyond the state in the management of the public affairs. Deputy Secretary General of United Nations, in his speech said "*Governance is not something the state does to society, but the way society itself, and the individuals who compose it, regulate all the different aspects of their collective life*". The state thus is the wielder of power and the principal actor in the government. While in governance, whole society is involved in managing public affairs. The government still continues to play a key role in enabling and facilitating the participation of other elements in the society. The state, thus, as an enabler provides the important legal and regulatory framework and political order within which various organisations can act and function, and where the citizens act without fear.

The following is the key distinction between government and governance:

Government	Governance
Government is the structure which enables and facilitates the process of governance.	Governance is the process where-by various actors work for the welfare of the people.
It is the machinery and an organ which wields power of the State, it includes the Executive, legislature and the judiciary.	It is carried out by various entities including the State and other institutions existing outside of it, which includes the Civil Society, Non-Governmental Organizations etc.
It is a formal setup which interacts within itself and outside of it.	Though it evolves out of the formal setup of the State, it expands the scope of government and also intensifies the service delivery provided.

There are various entities which are involved in governance. Apart from the formal government and its institutions, the other actors are the NGOs, civil society, research institutes, financial institutions, educational institutions, lobbyists, MNCs, media, cooperatives, etc. All these institutions play a vital role in decision making and also influence the process of decision making.

1.2 GOOD GOVERNANCE

The World Bank defines the term Good Governance in one of its reports as *"Good governance is epitomized by predictable, open and enlightened policy-making, a bureaucracy imbued with professional ethos acting in furtherance of the public good, the rule of law, transparent processes, and a strong civil society participating in public affairs"*. Apart from this, Good Governance also refers to a participative manner of governing, which functions in a responsible, transparent and accountable manner based upon the notions of legitimacy, efficiency and consensus for the purpose of upholding the rights of individual citizens.

This idea of providing 'good' governance for the people has been in existence since ancient time. The concept of welfare state has been dealt by a number of world-renowned philosophers including Kautilya. The government is understood to bring the happiness and for the welfare of its subjects. In a democratic setup, it can also be associated with efficient and effective administration. So such an administration should be development oriented and committed to the welfare of the people.

1.2.1 Kautilya on Good Governance

Kautilya in his Arthashastra elaborating on the traits possessed by the king of a welfare state, he stated that the happiness of the king lies with the happiness of his subjects, their welfare is his welfare, he should not act for his own pleasure but for the pleasure of his subjects. Thus, 'The King' is just a title given to the one who governs, this titular role is thought to be the brain of the government and the people, who are governed, are considered to be the heart of the government.

The ultimate role of the king is, therefore to govern for the welfare of his people. Kautilya mentions the following imperatives of good governance of a king:

a. Guide the administration effectively
b. Take the middle path, avoiding the extremes without missing the goal
c. Maintain law and order of the state
d. Pay fixed salary and emoluments to the public servants
e. Lay emphasis on the writers
f. Lead a disciplined life with morality and ethics
g. Merge his individual personality with his duty
h. Display administrative qualities
i. Carry out strong measures against corrupt officials
j. Replace bad ministers with good ones

1.2.2 Plato on Good Governance

Plato is credited with creating the *Philosopher King* as an Ideal ruler. Plato believes that conflicting values in various part of the society can be harmonised. The rational and righteous political order as suggested by Plato leads to harmonious unity of society where every part flourishes, without the expense of the other. Such a political realisation is not possible without virtue. Plato in his book *Republic* calls for the rule a Philosopher King. The following are the important aspects of a Philosopher King theory as dealt by Plato.

a. The Philosopher king can be men or women.
b. Only the bright, stable and courageous people are chosen to be a king. Special intensive training should be provided to them covering a wide area ranging from music, gymnastics to military aspects and city management.
c. They should be imparted knowledge of being just, noble, good and advantageous.
d. Goodness is not just a concept but it is the ultimate state of their mind.
e. The aim of the rulers should be to spread happiness throughout the city by getting people close together in harmony.
f. An ideal state is not governed for private gain and is free from any civil strife.
g. The philosophers rule out of necessity and not for their benefit or pleasure. Hence, they should not have any attachment to the process of ruling and the power associated with it.
h. According to Plato, freedom is one of the important values of the society. Apart from this, other values include wisdom, courage, justice, moderation and friendship.

i. The rule of authority is not only rational but also moral and is based on the consent of the governed.
j. The underlying idea of governance by philosophers is based on the idea of welfare.
k. Philosophers rule calls for impartial and equal treatment of all citizens and social groups and the government exists for the benefit of all the group of citizens.

1.2.3 Aristotle on Good Governance

Aristotle can be considered to be the first person to deal with the term 'governance' when he classified political organisation based on the manner they are ruled as Dictatorship, Autocracy and finally Democracy. In his book *Nicomachean Ethics*, Aristotle describes that only when man lives with virtue, he can live a happy life as intended by the nature. In his other book *Politics*, he describes the role to be played by politicians and the political community in bringing about the life of virtue in the citizenry. Some of the important aspects dealt by Aristotle are as follows:

a. The end or purpose of politics is the best of the ends. And the main objective of politics should be to stimulate a particular character among the citizens of the state and to make them better beings who are prepared and willing to perform noble actions.
b. Aristotle calls for the citizens to directly participate in the assembly not just by voting for their representatives, but deliberately and willingly serve in the juries to help uphold the laws. So that the citizens can become part of a group which discusses the good and the bad, the advantageous and the disadvantageous, the just and the unjust and finally come to a decision and pass laws accordingly.
c. The state should exist for developing the virtue of its citizens. Those who are the most virtuous are fit to rule according to Aristotle; and they will be the best rulers, on behalf of the citizens, instituting laws which lead to a virtuous life.
d. According to Aristotle, no regime can exist if the laws do not rule them.
e. Every human life has a telos or purpose according to Aristotle. The purpose and function of the political community is to provide education and laws that will lead people to pursue and achieve their telos.
f. The best city according to Aristotle is one which is happy and acts nobly and such noble acts are impossible without noble ends.
g. According to Aristotle, the territory of a state should be large enough so that its inhabitants can live a life at leisure in liberal manner and at the same time with moderation. And the main concern of study of Aristotle is related about the life at peace and not at war, hence he elaborates upon the character of a peaceful state.
h. Aristotle calls for proper and effective education be provided to the young and it should be the main object of the legislator. Education should be same for all and common and should not be made privatized. The aim of education should be to empower the students to serve the common good of the city.

1.3 ORIGIN OF THE MODERN CONCEPT OF GOOD GOVERNANCE

The concept of 'good' governance emanated from the understanding of process of governance. Governance entailed participation from all sections of the society and the concept of good governance emerged at the end of 1980s, an era of tumultuous global political scenario. The collapse of Berlin wall on November 1989 triggered chain of events which ultimately led to the disintegration and collapse of Soviet Union and as a consequence the decay of alliances in the eastern bloc. These political changes brought about the serious discussion on how a state has to be devised in order to achieve- economic development, or in other words a discussion on good governance.

In the 1989 World Bank Study "Sub-Saharan Africa-from crisis to sustainable growth" scrutinized the development problems in Sub-Saharan Africa. For the first time, the term "governance" was used to define the need for greater institutional reform and a better and more efficient public sector in these countries.

This study defined governance as "the exercise of political power in order to manage the affairs of the nation". This concept of governance got further developed in the World Bank's 1992 publication "Governance and Development", and the term governance was defined as "the way in which power is used in the management of a country's social and economic resources for the purpose of development".

So governance emerged from the understanding of the government and 'good' governance from the understanding of the process of governance. This was done to help administrators understand the sound public sector management strategies. The governance cannot remain value neutral and hence the idea of 'good' governance is to qualify the process of governance. Because of its use by the World Bank and other International institutions, the concept of good governance gained impetus and is now at present widely welcomed and implemented in countries across the globe.

1.4 THE WORLD BANK PRESCRIPTION

The concept of governance has evolved and changed from time to time. Earlier it was only the process and then it changed to *governing by networks* during the cold war era. Finally in early 90's, the conditionality vested by the west on the developing nations was not restricted to economics alone, it also extended to social, political and administrative policies.

The third world countries, who got the development aid and assistance from the western countries had coined a concept of 'Good Governance'. This concept was officially highlighted in 1989 in a document from World Bank on the context of sub-Saharan countries of Africa. It identified four dimensions of good governance:

- Public sector management
- Accountability
- Legal framework for development
- Information and transparency

In 1992, the *World Bank* published a document titled "*governance and development*". In the document, it states 'good governance is central to creating and sustaining an environment which fosters strong and equitable development and it is an essential complement to sound economic policies'. It also identified three vital aspects of governance:

- The form of political regime exercised (parliamentary or presidential, military or civilian, and dictatorship or democratic).
- The process by which authority is exercised in the management of the country's economic, political and social spheres and the limit to which the citizens are involved and given responsibility.
- The capacity of government to design, formulate and implement policies and in general to discharge government function.

In short, good governance, according to World Bank, consists of:

- Political accountability
- Regular election to legitimize the exercise of political power
- Rule of law
- Participation of various social, economic, cultural and professional groups in the process of governance
- Bureaucratic accountability
- Independence of judiciary
- Freedom of information
- Transparency
- Effective and efficient administrative system
- Cooperation between the civil society and government.

The *Organization for Economic Cooperation and Development (OECD)* has also identified four major components of good governance:

- Legitimacy of the government
- Accountability of the political and official elements of government
- Competence of the government to make policies and deliver services
- Rule of law and respect for human rights.

As per the United Nations Economic and Social Commission for Asia and the Pacific (UNESCAP), Good governance has eight major features: participatory, consensus oriented, accountable, transparent, responsive, effective and efficient, equitable and inclusive, and follows the rule of law.

The *United Nations Development Program (UNDP)* in 1997 on its document entitled "Governance and Sustainable Human Development" enunciated a set of few principles that are grouped under five broad themes. They are:

1. **Legitimacy and voice:** It deals with the participation and consensus orientation of the society.
2. **Direction:** It explains the strategic vision of the government regarding good governance and human development.
3. **Performance:** The effectiveness, responsiveness and efficiency of the government are explained under this theme.
4. **Accountability:** It deals with the transparency and accountability of the government.
5. **Fairness:** The legal framework, Rule of law and equity among the citizens are explained in this theme.

Report on Human Development in South Asia (The Crisis of Governance, Human Development Centre, 1999)

This report lays emphasis on humane governance. It defines humane governance as good governance dedicated to secure human development. Governance must be:

- seen by people as participatory and in their own interest—'ownership';
- conducive to building of a society in which no one feels humiliated—'decency'; and
- embodied in structures which are transparent and accountable to the owners, that is the people—'accountability'.

Ownership, decency, and accountability are the bedrock principles underlying humane governance. While good governance must reduce transaction costs and enforce contracts, humane governance must be based on both real and perceived ownership, decency, and accountability for and by all citizens. People's active participation is the guiding force behind the concept of humane governance.

Humane governance is a powerful concept which, if implemented, can help in enriching the life of the common people and lay the basis for fairer and more just societies in which human, political, and economic rights of all people are protected and their freedom of choice expanded.

This Report on Human development in South Asia visualizes three dimensions of governance which brings about human development, they are political governance, economic governance and civil governance.

Political Governance

The characteristics of a good political governance are:

- Regular, free, and fair elections, with participation in form of multi-party democracy
- An impartial judiciary protected by constitutional separation of powers
- A constitution not easily amendable by any of the branches of government
- Accountability and transparency of elected representatives and public officials
- Full access of all citizens to justice that is prompt and affordable
- Elimination of all forms of discrimination against women and minorities
- Maintenance of peace and social cohesion within and between the states

Economic Governance

The definition of good economic governance seeks an equitable outcome to the economic processes. Of the set of available policies that will foster competition, the state must choose those which will be most beneficial to the poorest sections of the society. The following are the basis for economic governance:

- Macroeconomic stability (balanced budget, low inflation, stable exchange rate) with the help of an independent central bank
- Guaranteed property rights for the people
- Taxes and subsidies must be progressive
- Sufficient budgetary allocations to social priority areas, such as basic education, primary health care, safe drinking water, adequate nutrition, family planning services, and micro-credit schemes for the poor;
- Adequate job creation
- Efficient and well-targeted subsidies for the poor
- Equitable access to credit and land

Civil Governance

Good civic governance has several components. At its core is the determination and self-initiative of people to improve their capacity to govern their lives, by creating informal structures and processes to address the following basic concerns:

- Protecting basic human rights, particularly the rights of the disadvantaged members of society; and
- Securing fundamental political, economic and human rights for all.

Thus, from the above discussions we can deduce that governance is very dynamic and evolving in nature. It implies the following:

- Taking care of the functioning of the state for the well-being of its citizens
- Securing the citizens the fundamental rights guaranteed in the constitution
- Enrich and improve political, economic and social life of all the citizens
- Institutionalizing the system of governance
- Ensuring that the process of governance is transparent, responsive, responsible, accountable, action-oriented, ethical and accessible for all.

1.5 ELEMENTS OF GOOD GOVERNANCE

Good governance is a universally acclaimed, dynamic concept which is mainly associated with the effectiveness and efficiency of the administrative system in a governmental framework. The good governance is distinguished by the following aspects:

- **Participation:** Participation means that the people should be vested with the power to take part in decision making by participating in the organs of the government, that are Executive, legislative and Judiciary.

  The entire society should be involved in the governance as envisaged by good governance.

  The motive of good governance is, people should not only be the ultimate beneficiaries of the development, and they should also act as the active agents of development.
- **Transparency:** Transparency is another major attribute of good governance. Free flow of information, separation of powers, checks and balances between legislative, executive and judicial branches, check on bureaucracy etc., are the important features of transparency.

  Secrecy in governmental affairs leads to corruption, inefficiency and weakens the governance as a whole.

  Example: the unprivileged, marginalized and disadvantaged section of the society is affected to a large extent by not receiving the desired benefits from the socio-economic schemes of the government due to corruption or other malpractices of the officials.

  Good governance envisages on the need for the people to access quality information regarding the governance and make public all the transactions in which the public interests are at stake.
- **Accountability:** Accountability implies the key to good governance. It is an obligation or willingness to take responsibility or to account for one's actions.

Good governance ensures that both legislators and executives are answerable for their actions, performances and the use of public resources.

It is the responsibility of the officials to explain or justify their actions to the people of the country, because it is from them the officials derive their authority.

Accountability is closely related to participation, which ensures transparency.

- **Rule of law:** Rule of law is a principle that all people and institutions are subject to and be held accountable to law that is fairly applied and enforced.

  Good governance ensures that the legal framework should be fair, impartial, check excesses, protect human rights, secure justice etc.

In addition to the aforesaid aspects, good governance also includes the following:

- **Inclusiveness:** Good governance secures dignity and honour for all human beings, irrespective of their sex, colour, caste, and creed and provide them with opportunities for their well-being. No human being should be excluded from the mainstream functioning of the society.
- **Responsiveness:** All stakeholders in a society will have to be served within a reasonable time frame by the institutions and its process. This is one of the objectives of good governance.
- **Consensus oriented:** In a society, not all individuals are bound to have same interests. The aim of good governance is to mediate difference of interests has to be mediated through a broad consensus and arrive at a solution which is in best interest of the society as a whole.

Community participation is a necessary prerequisite for good governance.

- **Effectiveness:** According to good governance, the governmental institutions and processes, which are responsible for the administration, should make use of the resources available effectively in optimal level for the development and to meet the needs of the society. This will help the government economically.
- **Efficient:** The resource usage by the government should always be in an efficient manner, that is sustainable with no wastage and should also be environmentally conscious.
- **Responsibility:** Good governance holds the legislators responsible for keeping a constant vigil on the administration to maintain strong value and spirit to serve the people. It is also the duty of the legislators, as the people's representatives, to listen to the aspirations, political views and issues of the people and create law that satisfies the collective interests of the people.
- **Fair judiciary:** George Washington once quoted, "The administration of justice is the pillar of government".

  It is the aim of judiciary to protect the citizens from the wrongful acts of the government. The law and legal bodies should be the guardian of the rights available to the people and protector of these rights from being mishandled or misled. If dispute arises due to the encroachment of these rights, the law institution should serve justice for the people with equality and with no discrimination.
- **Empowerment:** The civil society should encourage and harness the political energy of the people by making them take part in the societal development. Good governance

generally empowers the marginalized and disadvantaged people in the society, by letting them be a part of decision-making process, since they are the victims of the government's inaction and apathy.

- **Clean bureaucracy:** The bureaucrats, who implement the policies of the government, should provide access to the people, all information they ask for, a genuine and easy mechanism for information sharing, effective grievance redressal mechanism and above all should be free from all kinds of graft and corruption. They should also be impartial, alert, dignified with ethical qualities imbibed.

1.6 FORMS OF GOOD GOVERNANCE

Famous American authors and consultants, David Osborne and Ted Gaebler have summarized how government can be reinvented. So according to them, the various forms of governments to make it more effective are the following:

Catalytic Government

The government should be steering rather than rowing. In other words, the government should bring in the public sector, private sector and non-governmental sector players into administrative action to solve the societal problems.

Community-owned Government

The government should empower rather than serve. In other words, the government should include communities, citizens and families in the service delivery, since they are the intended recipients of the services provided and should also empower them with more control in the services from the control of bureaucracy to improve government performance.

Competitive Government

Competition is perhaps the most important element for improving both the quality and cost-effectiveness of government services. The government, to increase performance and reduce cost, should inject competition among various service providers by rewarding efficiency and economy.

Mission-driven Government

Transforming rule-oriented government into goal-oriented government is the main motive. In other words, the government should be driven by its goals and not by its rules and regulations. If mission driven, the government seems to be more effective, efficient, flexible and innovative.

Results-oriented Government

The government should measure the performance of its service agencies mainly in terms of outcomes and not inputs. The government should find results by encouraging target achievement and mission-directed efforts. If the results are not measured, the government can't tell success from failure.

Customer-driven Government

Customer driven means the government should meet and work towards customers and not bureaucracy. The government should regard the people as their customers and offer them with choices, survey their attitudes, make service convenient and most important of all, allow them to make suggestions.

Enterprising Government

The government should emphasize more on earning money rather than spending it. For this the government should learn to recognize their assets and generate revenue from them. It should put its effort in resource mobilization by using fees, savings, enterprise funds, etc.

Anticipatory Government

Governments should prevent problems rather than trying to cure them once when they occur. Long-term strategic planning, foresight in management, investment and decision making, sorting preventive measures are some of the aspects of anticipatory government. The government should prevent the arising needs first and not just deliver services to meet ends.

Decentralized Government

The government should transfer the decision-making authority to those individuals and organizations at the bottom of the administrative hierarchy, who address problems on a regular basis, to get effective and innovative solutions. This is the dispersal of authority from higher to lower levels of governance to emphasize participation and teamwork.

Market-oriented Government

The government should utilize a market mechanism rather than a bureaucratic mechanism to provide service to the public. Government can use policy to leverage the decisions and behaviour of individuals, instead of attempting to directly control them through administrative programs.

By following the above said goals, governments across the world have formed many mechanisms. They are:

- Creating autonomous public organizations
- Reduction in the size of government
- Corporatizing government organizations
- Reduction in welfare expenditure
- Reforming bureaucratic structure
- Measuring and evaluating performance
- Privatizing public undertakings
- Decentralizing authority to lower levels
- Bringing in private agencies for providing service
- Promoting transparency in administration
- Encouraging people's participation in administration
- Declaration of citizen charter, etc.

1.7 REINVENTION OF THE CONCEPT OF PUBLIC GOVERNANCE IN THE LIGHT OF EVOLUTION OF THE CONCEPT OF GOOD GOVERNANCE

The characteristic feature of good governance as seen in the preceding paragraphs, require us to redefine and reinvent the fundamental understanding of the state. Since ancient times the state has performed functions pertaining to development, protection of sovereignty of the country and law and order. Gradually its functions started to increase and it became so enormous that it covered all aspects of the life a citizen, it thus became a leviathan. It got burdened with all these functions which only grew in intensity and density with time. Thus, as a result the state was unable to perform all these tasks by itself. This therefore resulted in neglect of several vital aspects of governance. Some of the important aspects of socio-economic development got ignored or overlooked. The administration worked from the ivory tower which was inaccessible and irresponsive to the needs and requirements of the people. Such a kind of system of governance cannot operate in the present era good governance. Thus, there is a need to redefine the state in the context of these.

Some of the important scholars studying these aspects have said that usually the state is understood to be composed of only three traditional integral components: the Legislature, Executive and the Judiciary. The aspects of local government, private sector and the civil society have been considered as components that exist outside the official mechanism. In the past these elements, that is civil society, private sector and the local government were considered to be existing within themselves without any links to other state machinery, or generally they were considered to be non-existent from the context of the state, as they had, if any, only a minor impact. But as time progressed their nature and role started to change. These 'informal' agencies started to raise and expand when they were officially given recognition by the formal agents, that is the government. Therefore, the private sector and the civil society were encouraged by the formal agencies to participate in the process of governance. Such a development gave rise to many 'new' organs of the state in terms of their social acceptance, autonomy and resources which called for the redefinition of the state itself. Thus, there has arisen the need to redefine governance which has now replaced the traditional system of governance, this is either because of the deliberate politics played by the state in an evolutionary way or because of enthusiastic private sector and expanding civil society including that of NGOs and other such similar agencies.

Therefore, the redefined role of state should be sustainable human development with inputs from the civil society and the private sector. The sustainable human development will ensure the following:

1. Develop cooperation, whereby everyone work together
2. Ensure sustainability, including the concern of environment for development
3. Empowerment of people, increasing the opportunity for the people to participate in governance and decision-making process
4. Provide security, creating a safe, harmonious and conducive environment for living.
5. Create equity, equal access to public services for all the citizens.

1.8 THE INDIAN STORY- PRE-1991 AND POST 1991

Pre-1991

This is the period when the birth of the new nation called India took place. After the recent freedom struggle, its leaders wanted to have a representative government which was answerable to the people, hence constitutional democracy was created. Since the country was still backward, the state took upon all the activities on itself. Even the private sector was underdeveloped due to lack of patronisation from the British. Hence, the only logical way forward during that initial period was to depend on the state to carry forward all the activities. The private sector and the civil society had no experience in governance process and they did not represent the diversified population in India, hence they were not taken on board. The state became the guardian of all the activities concerning the citizens, one could experience state from the cradle to the grave.

It was not long before the state became a leviathan. The state was not able to manage such an enormous burden. It became inefficient and inept. Moreover, the demon of corruption caught on and it further dragged down the state. This period was therefore called the license raj. The idea of state providing all services was taken more seriously by the later regimes. It came to such an extent that the state tried to prevent entry of well-established private players in areas they specialised, the government thus created a system of getting licences which tend to be a mammoth task in itself and apart from this the officials had to have their palms greased in order to make the file move a bit faster. This system prevented growth and entry of private players. Also the government reserved several key areas aimed at itself where such long-winding licences were not given. Combined with such policies and bureaucratic red-tapism, the country went further back into debt and which finally culminated in the year 1991, when the country had to pledge its gold in order to avoid default.

Planned growth in terms of five-year plans inspired from the Soviet Union was formulated and implemented. The socialistic pattern of society was sought by implementing such policies. The policy was called to be protectionist, and there was strong emphasis on import substitution and producing goods on our own. Economic interventionism became normal as state took over the control of the market.

Such policy resulted in balance of payment crisis, increased the national debt and created numerous problems in the public sector. In order to overcome this crisis, it was understood that the state has to be rolled back. This was also the view of international institutions like the World Bank and International Monetary Fund (IMF).

New Economic Policy-1991

The new economic policy formulated in 1991 reduced the scope and role of the government. The emphasis was laid on providing conditions wherein the public sector could function with competition from the private sector. This was sought to be achieved by deregulating industries and liberalising foreign investments. Presently the state has only a few strategic and key sectors under its control where the private players are not allowed, otherwise all other sectors have been liberalised and the state now functions parallel in competition with the private players.

Various other steps have also been taken in order to protect the public. Many acts have been amended in order to come to terms with the liberalised market scenario, pervious highly restrictive Monopolies and Restrictive Trade Practices Act (MRTP) which aimed to control the monopolistic and restrictive trade activities has now been changed. Apart from this, the state has sought to disinvest itself from various industries in order to give leeway for the management board of such industries to operate in a bureaucratic free environment. Such disinvested funds have been used for several development projects of the state. The state thus has not assumed the role of steering the economy from that of being the driver of the economy. Presently the role is to regulate the market, create environment conducive wherein no particular individual is preferred and the market competition takes over. Powers are sought to be given to the consumers of such services whereby they are free to choose any individual who is effective in providing them the services they need. The concept of minimum government and maximum governance has understood to be the way forward in the coming future.

- **Fiscal reforms:** The important element in the reform process was to bring back the fiscal discipline. The fertilizer subsidy was reduced, sugar subsidy was abolished and other rationalisation measures were carried out. Tax reforms as suggested by Raja Chelliah were implemented to raise revenue by bringing better compliance in case of income tax and customs and excise, it also tried to bring in transparency and stability in the tax structure.
- **Monetary and financial sector reforms:** The interest rate was liberalised, which ensured that the private players get better loans for their new and upcoming projects. Since the liquidity was freed it brought in investments. Greater competition was created between the private, public and foreign sector banks by eliminating various constraints.
- **Reforms in capital market:** Narasimham committee recommendations for reforms in capital market was introduced. The Securities and Exchange Bureau was given statutory recognition, the state officially took over the role of the market regulator. It sought to create a free, fair and competitive environment which would facilitate mobilization of resources.
- **Industrial policy reforms:** New industrial policy of 1991 was created. It aimed to deregulate to promote growth and competition. Hence, licensing was abolished except in some crucial sectors, areas reserved only for the public sector were restricted to only a few and other areas were opened for the private players to venture, disinvestment of the government share in public enterprises was encouraged, Memorandum of Understanding (MOU) was signed between the industry and the ministry in order to provide greater financial and administrative autonomy.
- **Trade policy reforms:** The main focus was to create openness. Policy was created to stimulate export and reduce licensing and regulation in the imports. Only certain items were kept in the negative list rest were opened for import, tariff restriction was removed and quantitative restriction was removed.
- **Promoting foreign Investment:** Government took several measures to bring in the foreign investment. Various sectors were initially partly and then subsequently fully opened up to full foreign investment. Foreign Investment Promotion Board was setup in order to bring in and regulate the foreign investments, various schemes to promote the foreign institutional investors were also carried out by the government from time to time.
- **Rationalization of the exchange rate policy:** The rupee was devalued. The difference between the nominal and real exchange rate was reduced. It was aimed to reduce the inflation and make the export more competitive.

1.9 STATE, MARKET AND CIVIL SOCIETY

The present era of neoliberalism demands a minimalist state. But the United Nation's Development Programme report portrays a worrying trend, human development indices in health, education, culture and environment have dropped significantly in countries where the state's role got shrunk. Thus, as per the understanding of good governance given by the World Bank in 1992, the state has a new and far more important role to play in bringing together the interests of public and private institutions while taking social actions.

Market has been traditionally outside the formal system of the state. Market is considered to be a force controlled by elements of nature, that is it does not follow fixed parameters, it is dynamic and uncontrollable. Economics has thus tried to understand the functioning of such market forces in order to device a pattern to it. State being a formal entity has been functioning based generally on written rules such as a constitution. The taking over the role of state by the market forces has been propounded by the scholars of economics around 1960s under the concept called the Public Choice Theory.

1.9.1 Public Choice Theory

Public choice theory refers to the use of tools of economy to deal with the traditional problems associated with political science. It is said to be the analysis of collective decision making. Thus, this evolution of public choice approach took place within the ambit of economics and basically focused on people's choice in selecting the public services. This theory envisages market-like competition in delivery of public services where the public are considered to be the customer, hence buyer of the best product. Public choice theory exerted major influence in giving a coherent understanding and interpretation of actual functioning of the politics and government. It lent hand in understanding the actual basis of functioning of the bureaucrats and the politicians. It also helped in creating an alternative to the formal setup, thereby empowering the citizens who were henceforth considered as customers or consumers of the public services.

This public choice theory is in strict opposition to the formal bureaucratic model of the state. It is in support of the market forces taking over the role of the bureaucracy, in this sense it is considered to be anti-bureaucratic. Such a theory developed because of the inefficiency and ineffectiveness of the bureaucratic system. The state seemed to function without any parallel system and they seemed to be the only provider of certain services to the people. Hence, the people had no choice but to be dependent on the government for all such services. Government barred with red-tape and corruption was not able to provide such essential services to the actual beneficiary. The state and bureaucracy as stated had taken all roles in the journey from the cradle to the grave of the citizen and the citizen had no other alternative but to be dependent on the government for anything and everything. The public choice theory reversed this idea.

1. This theory gave the power and choice to the people.
2. It tried to dilute the existing bureaucratic system and allow the market forces to penetrate whereby competitive environment is created.
3. When such free-market competition is created, it would ensure that the bureaucracy is faced with only choice that it either adapts to the market mechanisms or withers away.
4. Entry of market forces are a boon to the public in the sense that they now have option to choose who provides them the services they need, moreover in case they are dissatisfied with one provider they can always move to another, in this sense it creates a '*choice*' for the public.
5. The bureaucracy and the state in order to survive will try to bring in changes to its functioning, thus it would naturally become efficient and effective in the longer run.

Vincent Ostrom who is the supporter and proponent of the Public Choice theory, said that " *Perfection in the hierarchical ordering of a professionally trained public service accountable to a single centre of power will reduce the capability of a larger administrative system to respond to diverse preferences among citizens for many different public goods and services and cope with diverse environmental conditions.*" And "*A variety of different organizational arrangements can be used to provide different public goods and services. Such organizations can be coordinated through various multi-organizational arrangements...*"

Thus, the public choice approach opposes the traditional bureaucratic setup. It is in the favour of decentralisation whereby the monopolistic control by the state is broken down. The public thus should be allowed to participate in the administrative process. It also calls for institutional pluralism whereby a single service is provided by different operators hence creating a free-market scenario where the public is allowed to choose between them. In such scenario, the decision-making process is made democratic.

Thus, Public Choice theory calls for

1. Anti-bureaucratic measures
2. Diversified institutions for taking decisions
3. Bringing in the free market forces to operate the administration
4. Creating plural institutions, providing preferences for the consumers choices
5. Decentralisation of the power
6. Participation of the public in administrative process

The other essential aspect of the Public Choice theory is that it questions the very basis that is 'publicness' of the public administration. As per Niskanen the public administrators are 'budget maximisers' and the politicians are 'utility maximisers' who function for improving their vote banks. Thus, as per this understanding every individual and organisation not works for the public but rather to promote their own good and survival. The public is hence deprived of effective services. Thus, the central idea of Public Choice approach is to limit the government. 'Choice' to the public implies competition. This will ensure that the public administration becomes efficient and effective. The expansion of this theory can be seen by the development of the concept of New Public Management.

1.9.2 New Public Management

The reforms in the public sector were initially based on the theories of new institutional economics and managerialism. In the period of early 1970s, the conservative economists stated that the predominant presence of government was a hurdle to economic growth and freedom. They also advocated that the government should have a lesser role to play and the space created by withdrawal of the government in some areas has to be occupied by the market which alone can bring economic efficiency.

Moreover, the managerialists called for the adoption of principles of private sector which had the potential to solve the bureaucratic problems associated with the public sector. This measure of privatisation of public sector practices and services will change the values, culture of the public administrator. This would improve the performance of the government. In order to identify the best model, the scholars came up with the concept of New Public Management. The core themes for the New Public Management were the following:

1. Greater orientation towards the customer and increased responsiveness, providing and increasing the scope of non-public sector service providers.

2. A common and controlled mode of functioning whereby everything is effectively managed. Targets are identified and set and the performance is monitored.
3. Efforts to encourage entrepreneurial form of bureaucracy in deviation from its traditional form, and placing them with larger sense of accountability.
4. A strong focus is on to effectively control the finances, increase value for money and the efficiency.
5. Audits to be introduced at both professional and financial levels, transparent means are used to review the performance. Benchmarks are set and the professional behaviour is monitored.

The New Public Management approach brings together the public and private administration. It aims at making the public administration more effective, improving its efficiency and brining in economy. The basis of the public choice approach is taken and this approach laid emphasis on creating a process-oriented administration with more concentration on the performance indicators. The pay would be now linked to the individual's performance and quality improvement. The services offered by the administration are seen as product and hence the citizens are replaced by consumers. The public administration is just another provider of goods in the market, and hence they should not be given any kind of preference. All the functions of the state are broken down into separate, individual components whereby such individual entities are privatized or contracted out to competitive players.

The other major aspect is cost-cutting, whereby to do more or better with the same or less. Being seen as *budget maximisers* the public administrators are thus now under pressure to act efficiently. Thus, managerial aspects and understanding of the private sector has now been adopted for the public administration. As per Christopher Hood, the New Public Management has the following seven features:

1. Explicit standards and measures of performance are to be provided
2. Greater stress is laid on discipline and efficiency in utilisation of resource
3. Greater emphasis on output results than that of the procedure
4. Greater emphasis on professional management of the public services
5. Competition to the public sector by opening them up
6. Break down or disaggregation of units of the public sector
7. Take up the private sector management practices

The concept of New Public Management itself is in a state of transition and evolution and recent developments in public management has tried to make it more holistic and people-friendly. Thus, in the changing global scenario where market forces and individualistic goals often over run the social goals, the state and the markets are thus needed to be supplemented by the civil society organisations or the so called non-state actors for a democratic development administration.

1.9.3 Civil Society

A civil society is a collective of those social organisations of people who enjoy the distance and separation from the state, and are autonomous, they pressurize and influence the government on behalf of their people whom they represent. The markets being driven by profit and the bureaucracy generally considered to be inefficient and unresponsive. The civil society organisations have now gained prominence because of their very nature of being flexible, participatory, non-bureaucratic, non-official and cost-effective and also of their ability to reach the people untouched by the government.

The civil society aims to represent the people who are not or under-represented to the government. They represent the interests of those who find difficult to voice their opinion, the persons who are ignored and excluded from the system. The civil society thus gets involved in the activities of the state, they either contest or formulate alternate means of provision of service to the people. Some of the civil society organisations exist in order to aid the government and to help delivering the services by mobilising the people. Collaboration between civil society and the state happens when both sides are involved together in all aspects of policymaking, implementation and evaluation. Civil society is thus a reservoir of political, economic, social, cultural and moral resources which checks the authoritative behaviour of the state, promote pluralism, increase participation of the public and augment interest articulation, and finally provides alternate avenues of welfare services to the people.

1.10 GOVERNANCE AS NETWORKS AND COLLABORATIVE GOVERNMENT

The concept of governance can be understood in various ways. It can be understood as, first, to be an attempt to widen the scope of public administration by going beyond the formal setup of the government and second to be a democratic intensifying concept whereby it makes the administration more open, transparent and accountable.

The concept of governance ban can be defined as "the ability to get things done without having the legal backing to command that they be done". Thus, the concept expands the concept of governance and it therefore frees the administration from the conventional formalism. The important aspect of breaking of formalism is that it opens up various possibilities of using society's alternative collective problem-solving mechanisms and devices. Governance is thus understood to be more a network of multiple agencies and organisations than a fixed entity called government agency or department.

Governance in this aspect means establishment, operation and networking of various social institutions. In a concrete form it can be seen in the formal rules and regulations, various decision-making procedures and other activities that assist to outline social practices. In actual practice, there are numerous forms of community organisations, voluntary or other self-help approaches through which people organise themselves to achieve common purposes. This can be seen when people come together to solve problems like irrigation, water dispute, local dispute and taking community defence measures. Governance can be understood in such context as a way of shaping social institutions as a matter of public concern. To get the things done through the formally constituted system of government is hence not the only way to achieve the social goals.

Hence, governance becomes a network of numerous social organisations and there has to exist collaboration between these various organisations as it would avoid duplication of work. Governance being wider than government cannot be restricted to once single organisation. Even the civil society cannot alone be the provider of governance. Governance can happen only when the state, the private sector and the civil society comes together to provide services. There has to understanding and collaboration between these various players. To ensure this, there indeed has to be a formalised system of government, without the government the governance itself will lose its legitimacy. The civil society or the private sector cannot alone provide all such services to the people, hence governance is not a replacement of the government but rather expansion of the system, bringing together other participants into the formal system to enhance the service delivery ultimately benefitting the people.

The other aspect of governance highlights the importance of rule of law, human rights, the participatory development and system of democratisation. It goes beyond the managerial and technical aspect of the governance to the more fundamental ethical-normative dimension. The state as understood by the ancient Greeks stood for the providing good life to its citizens. Hence, it is not enough that the governance is carried out on managerial aspects. What is more important is the equity and legitimacy of the system. People from all corners of the society should be given opportunity to participate in the decision-making process and the fruits of development should invariably be shared with all without any discrimination. Also it must not get captured by an influential minority. People's perception about the governance process is also important. It serves as the measure of legitimacy of the governance. Empowerment is therefore a precondition of good governance.

In today's highly complex setup of governance, government alone cannot solve the various problems plaguing the society. A certain degree of networking with other organisations in the society will improve the capacity of governance as a whole. Moreover, this will also help in the development of 'social capital' in terms of the acceptance, involvement and co-sharing of problem-solving by various social groups.

1.11 ROLE OF STATE IN ERA OF GOVERNANCE

Though various theories and concepts such as the Public Choice approach, New Public Management, etc. call for a minimal government, the present understanding of 'good governance' reiterates the role of state in the era of governance. What needed is not lesser government but more governance that is the state should facilitate involvement of other participants into the act of government without itself going backstage. Only a formal state can ensure that a representative government is taken up, and people from all sections of the society get their voice heard. Thus, government cannot take a backstage, it should actively involve itself to ensure that the process of governance is carried out with equity and that underlying principles enshrined in the constitution be upheld.

The New Public Management has called for a democratic governance by means of reducing the role of government and increasing the role of private sector in providing services to the people. The main aspect is to expose the bureaucracy to competition and making the public administration adopt private managerial principles. These prescriptions sought to bring a market-regulated system of governance. The proponents of such concept assure that such a market-regulated system will help in better delivery of service for the development of society. But there are some flipsides to such measure:

- The market system itself is not perfect, and especially in developing economies it cannot be sustained to bring about development
- Markets decisions do not ensure that the resources are allocated optimally
- There is no system of ensuring equilibrium between aggregate demand and supply
- The fundamental ideal of equity is overlooked by the market mechanism

Because of all these shortcomings, the role of state has become more important in ensuring effective system of governance. Under New Public Management, the state is considered only to be a facilitator, but in reality the state has much more important functions to be carried out. The abovementioned New Public Management itself suggests that state should occupy all those areas which are overlooked or ignored by the market.

The essentiality of the role of the state in the present era can be understood by the following functions bestowed upon the state:

- Create a foundation of law based on which the private sector can play a pivotal role and help the government regulate such functions
- Ensure that the macro-economic stability is maintained for the purpose of attracting private sector investment because private sector cannot thrive when the economic conditions are fragile or instable.
- Invest in creating social capital. Investments have to be made in the sectors of social services and infrastructure development because the private sector will not venture into such acts as they are motivated by profit. The government is run for the public good and hence they can carry forward such functions. Moreover, investments in infrastructure involve huge cost and lost gestation period for getting returns. Hence, in order to attract effective investment in the economy the state should first ensure that it has all proper infrastructure in place.
- The state also needs to protect its vulnerable section. Not all the section of the society get representation by the private players, not all in the society has the ability or the power to make a choice, hence for all these disadvantaged sections of the society the government is the only hope for providing them means of livelihood. This cannot be entrusted with private sector, it can only be carried out by a representative and democratic government.
- The present concern about sustainable development and protection of environment can only be taken up by the state. The private sector will tend to overlook such aspects in pursuit of profit. The natural resources are wealth of the people and the nation, it has to be protected by the state and should not be allowed to get destructed in pursuit of attaining development. Hence, sustainable development can be achieved when the state creates proper legal checks and balances.

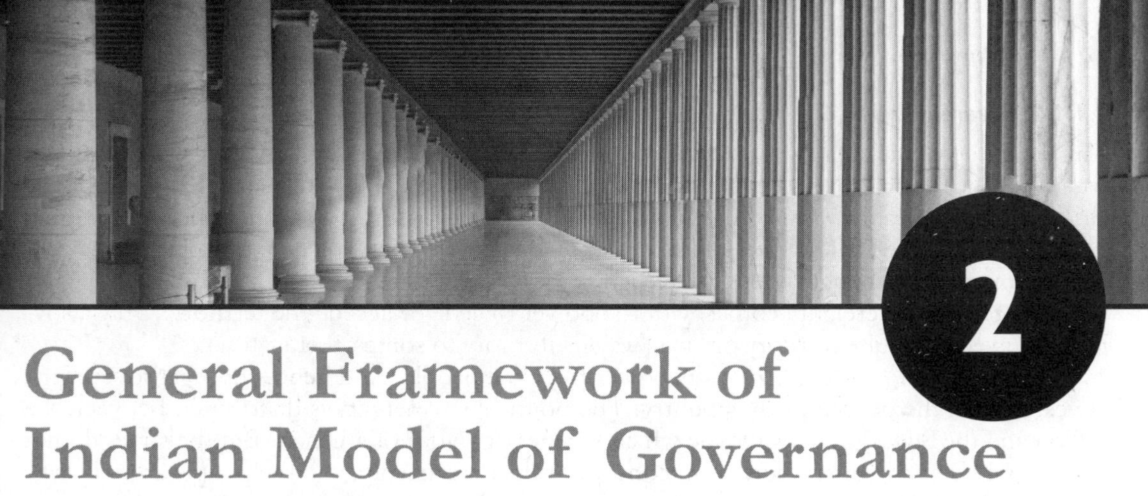

2

General Framework of Indian Model of Governance

LEARNING OBJECTIVES

In this Chapter, you will learn about:

- Basics of Indian Democracy
- Parliamentary Form of Government
- Representative Democracy
- Federal Form and its Dynamics
- Basic Structure of the Constitution
- Independent Constitutional Bodies for Effective Governance
- Three-tier System of Governance and Two-tier System of Federalism

2.1 BASICS OF INDIAN DEMOCRACY

2.1.1 Approach to Liberty, Equality and Justice

Preamble to the constitution is expected to imbibe the fundamental values and the philosophy based on which the Constitution is written. The fundamental rights, the Directive principles and even the fundamental duties arise and flow from the Preamble, and hence the Preamble declares the fundamental values and establishes the foundational principles of the Constitution. The Preamble is considered to be the most precious part of the Constitution; it is the soul and also the key to the Constitution. It is the quintessence of the Indian democracy as it exemplifies its basic philosophy and paves the way for growth of basic structure.

2.1.1.1 Source of the Constitution

The opening and the closing words of the preamble are 'We, the people of India…adopt, enact and give ourselves this Constitution'. This clearly conveys that the people are the source of origin of the Constitution. Thus, Constitution originated from the people, and the sovereignty under the Constitution lies with the people. The Constitution was an instrument of the popular will of the people of the country, and no one was opposed to the enactment of the Constitution. Dr. Ambedkar on the floor of the assembly in 1949 stated that, 'I say that this Preamble embodies what is the desire of every member of the House, that this constitution should have its root, its authority, its sovereignty from the people, and that it has.

2.1.1.2 Sovereignty

This signifies that the country is externally sovereign. It ceased to be part of the British Empire after passing of the Indian Independence Act, 1947. From 15 August 1947 to 26 January 1950, India was a British Commonwealth Dominion. And on 26th January, it became a 'Sovereign Republic' like other countries such as the United States of America, etc. But India is still a voluntary member of the British Commonwealth; though it does not recognise the sovereignty of the Queen of England.

Moreover, sovereignty comes with the power to cede or accede the territory. Only a sovereign state can acquire territory or give away its territory to some other state.

Constitution, as seen, derives its power from the people. And hence the legal sovereignty is vested with the people of the country. The political sovereignty is distributed between the Union and the States, a characteristic which inclines in favour of a Union. But the states do not have absolute sovereignty, there is no concept of dual-citizenship, and the people are only citizens of India and not of any states.

2.1.1.3 Socialist

This term was added to the Preamble by the 42nd Amendment. Its intention was to show that the country was a socialist state whose aim was to secure people with 'Justice-social, economic and political'. The Constitution does not define this term, but it is generally understood to be a state which ensures freedom from all forms of exploitation – social, economic and political.

2.1.1.4 Secular

This term was also added in the Constitution by the 42nd Amendment. It declares that the state shall have no religion of its own, and all the people in the country are free to profess, propagate and practice any religion and they are also equally entitled to freedom of conscience. The framers of the Constitution deliberately avoided mentioning it in the Preamble as they believed that the fundamental rights had clearly and effectively enshrined the principles of freedom of religion. Secularism is undefined in the Constitution. It can be generally accepted that all religions are equally treated with respect.

2.1.1.5 Democratic

This word has a comprehensive meaning. In a narrow sense it means the type of government. A responsible and representative system in which the people choose those who administer them, and such legislators are accountable and responsible to the electorate, that is, the people of the country. In a broad sense, it means in addition to the political democracy, it also includes the economic and social democracy. And this wider meaning is what used and meant in the Preamble of the Constitution.

2.1.1.6 Republic

This term implies to an elected head of the state. There is no hereditary head of the state. In a Republic the head is either directly or indirectly chosen. In India we follow indirect election system, as the role of President is merely ceremonial and symbolic. In a Republic, one among citizen is chosen as the head of the State.

2.1.1.7 Justice

It implies harmonious reconciliation of individual conduct with that the welfare of the society. The basic essence of justice is the achievement of common good. It embraces all the spheres, that is, social, economic and political.

The following elaborates on the wider aspects of concept of Justice:

- The concept of justice is very wide and is not confined to the justice administered by the courts.
- Social justice means that, all citizens are to be equally treated irrespective of their status, caste, creed, religion, sex, etc.
- Political justice implies that every citizen should have equal share and rights to participate in the political process without any form of discrimination or distinction made on basis of caste, creed, race, religion, etc.
- Economic justice ensures that the rich and poor are treated equally and alike. And efforts should be taken to bridge the gap between them.

2.1.1.8 *Liberty and Equality*

It is not just absence of arbitrary restraint on actions of the individual, but it also means creation of condition which enables full development of the personality of the individual. Liberty cannot be achieved without equality. Equality does not mean physical or mental equality; it means equality of status and opportunity. There has to be no restrictions based on caste, creed, religion, sex and region, etc. The concept of equality is supplemented by the prohibition of the practice of untouchability and also by the abolition of the titles. Rule of law, guarantees equality in opportunity, equality before the law and non-discrimination in relation to public employment.

- Liberty enshrined in the Constitution does not mean absence of restraint or domination.
- It is a positive concept, which means liberty of thought, expression, faith, belief and worship.
- The concept of equality embodies social, political and economic aspects. The equality is of status and opportunity.
- All citizens are equal before law and are to be treated equally, and enjoy equal protection of law.
- All citizens are entitled to enjoy political rights, such as right to vote and participate in the process of governance without any distinction.
- There can be no distinction based on caste, creed, religion, region and sex, etc. in matter of access to public employment and places.

2.1.1.9 *Fraternity*

The concept of fraternity is emphasised to ensure both the dignity of the individual and the unity of the Nation. It is a spirit of brotherhood, and its promotion will help in bringing together people from various religions and races etc. It places a moral obligation on the State to recognise individual personality of the citizens and help achieve human dignity and self-respect. Unity of the nation stands on the basis of dignity of the individual, and hence the role of state is to keep up the dignity of the individuals in the society. Unity and integrity tends to prevent the tendencies of provincialism, regionalism, communalism, linguism and secessionist and separatist activities.

2.1.2 Secularism – The Soul of the Constitution

The Preamble calls the State to be a sovereign, socialist, secular and democratic Republic. The term secularism has a special and significant meaning in the Indian context. As our Former Prime Minister late Smt. Indira Gandhi stated, 'Secularism and democracy are the twin pillars of our state, it is the very foundation of our society'.

The common understanding of secularism recognises that every citizen is equal, and there should be no stratification based on religion between them. Secularism also means tolerance of all religions and special emphasis on protection of the minorities and keeping up the communal harmony in the society. Thus, the essence of secularism is based on the following two basic principles:

- Acceptance of religion to be the private affair of the individuals and state has no concern over it.
- Religion is to be separated from politics.

2.1.2.1 Meaning and Nature

It has its origin in the West, meaning to separate the Church from the State. Secularism is not opposed to religion, rather it supports all religions and expects that all religions to be treated equally by the State.

To quote former President Dr. Radhakrishnan, who elaborately dealt with matters such as religion and secularism etc., that,

> *Secularism does not mean irreligion or atheism or even stress on material comforts. It proclaims that it lays stress on the universality of spiritual values which may be attained in variety of ways. We hold that no religion is to be given preferential status, or unique distinction, that no one religion should be accorded special privileges in national life, or international relations, for that would be violation of the basic principles of democracy and contrary to the interest of religion and the government. ... No group of citizens shall arrogate itself to rights and privileges which it denies to others. No person shall suffer any form of disability or discrimination because of his religion but all alike should be free to share to the fullest degree in the common life. This is the basic principle involved in the separation of church and state.*

Conception of a secular state, involves three separate and inter-related sets of relationship concerning the religion, individual and the state. The following are the three distinct aspects:

1. The State and the Religion – its separation from one another.
2. The State and the Individual – the relation between them, existence as a citizen.
3. Religion and the Individual – freedom to practice any religion.

The Western concept of secularism calls for an anti-religious ideology, and this is completely distinct from the practices carried out in the country. Our former Prime Minister, Late Smt. Indira Gandhi, had stated that, 'Secularism is neither a religion nor indifference to a religion, but it is equal treatment of all religions, not just mere tolerance, but positive respect – without this there is no future for the nation'.

2.1.2.2 Nehru's Approach to Secularism

Pandit Nehru was a true champion of the concept of a secular State. The conception of India as a secular country is his major achievement. He was averse to intrusion of religion into politics. He wanted to transform the 'caste-ridden Indian society' to a modern state. According to him, people from all religion have to be included in the governing process, only then the country can become a truly secular state. To quote, '*Religion is all right when it is applied to ethics and morals, but it is not good when mixed up with politics*'.

Nehru being an agnostic himself believed that, '*I have no desire to interfere with any person's belief*'. And thus, religion is ought to be a private affair of the individual where the state has no role to play, and likewise the sphere of religion too has no role to play in the activities of the state.

He desired a State that, 'protects all religions, but does not favour one at the expense of others and does not itself adopt any religion as the religion of the State'.

Nehru wanted that the free, independent India should be a non-communal and secular state. He declared that, '*The Government of a country like India, with many religions that have secured great and develop followings for generation, can never function satisfactorily in the modern age, except on a secular basis*'. He also added that, '*our Constitution is based on secular conception and gives freedom to all religions*'.

2.1.2.3 Secularism in the Constitution

1. The Preamble reflects the basic essence of the constitution, that the country is a sovereign, socialist, secular and democratic republic.
2. No State religion: There is 'no state religion' in India, the state does not follow any religion or confer upon its citizens any faith.
   - **Article 27 – Freedom as to payment of taxes for promotion of any particular religion**

     No person shall be compelled to pay any taxes, the proceeds of which are specifically appropriated in payment of expenses for the promotion or maintenance of any particular religion or religious denomination.
   - **Article 28 – Freedom as to attendance at religious instruction or religious worship in certain educational institutions**

     (1) No religion instruction shall be provided in any educational institution wholly maintained out of State funds.

     (2) Nothing in clause (1) shall apply to an educational institution which is administered by the State but has been established under any endowment or trust which requires that religious instruction shall be imparted in such institution.

     (3) No person attending any educational institution recognised by the State or receiving aid out of State funds shall be required to take part in any religious instruction that may be imparted in such institution or to attend any religious worship that may be conducted in such institution or in any premises attached thereto unless such person or, if such person is a minor, his guardian has given his consent thereto Cultural and Educational Rights.
3. Freedom of Conscience: The Constitution enshrines the freedom of conscience, whereby the people can propagate, practice any religion of their choice, and no one can stop an individual from doing so.
   - **Article 25 – Freedom of conscience and free profession, practice and propagation of religion**

     (1) Subject to public order, morality and health and to the other provisions of this Part, all persons are equally entitled to freedom of conscience and the right to freely profess, practise and propagate religion.

     (2) Nothing in this article shall affect the operation of any existing law or prevent the State from making any law.

       a. Regulating or restricting any economic, financial, political or other secular activity which may be associated with religious practice;

       b. Providing for social welfare and reform or the throwing open of Hindu religious institutions of a public character to all classes and sections of Hindus.

4. Freedom to manage religious affairs: The freedom is granted to various institutions and religious endowments to manage their own affairs, the state has no role in such activities, but all these activities have to be within the law of the land.
   - **Article 26 – Freedom to manage religious affairs**

     Subject to public order, morality and health, every religious denomination or any section thereof shall have the right
     a. to establish and maintain institutions for religious and charitable purposes;
     b. to manage its own affairs in matters of religion;
     c. to own and acquire movable and immovable property; and
     d. to administer such property in accordance with law.
5. Equality before law: No individual shall be discriminated on the basis of religion, and all people in the society are treated equally.
   - **Article 14 – Equality before law**

     The State shall not deny to any person equality before the law or the equal protection of the laws within the territory of India.
   - **Article 15 – Prohibition of discrimination on grounds of religion, race, caste, sex or place of birth**
     (1) The State shall not discriminate against any citizen on grounds only of **religion**, race, caste, sex, place of birth or any of them
     (2) No citizen shall, on grounds only of **religion**, race, caste, sex, place of birth or any of them, be subject to any disability, liability, restriction or condition with regard to
        a. access to shops, public restaurants, hotels and palaces of public entertainment; or
        b. the use of wells, tanks, bathing ghats, roads and places of public resort maintained wholly or partly out of State funds or dedicated to the use of the general public.
6. Cultural and educational rights: The interests of the minorities are protected, as they are given rights to manage their own affairs and also impart education on their own terms without any interference by the State.
   - **Article 29 – Protection of interests of minorities**
     (1) Any section of the citizens residing in the territory of India or any part thereof having a distinct language, script or culture of its own shall have the right to conserve the same.
     (2) No citizen shall be denied admission into any educational institution maintained by the State or receiving aid out of State funds on grounds only of **religion**, race, caste, language or any of them.
   - **Article 30 – Right of minorities to establish and administer educational institutions**
     (1) All minorities, whether based on **religion** or language, shall have the right to establish and administer educational institutions of their choice.
     (2) The state shall not, in granting aid to educational institutions, discriminate against any educational institution on the ground that it is under the management of a minority, whether based on **religion** or language.

In the leading case of Ismail Faruqui v Union of India (The Ayodhya Case), the Supreme Court interpreted the true concept of secularism as follows:

It is clear from the Constitutional scheme that it guarantees equality in the matter of all individuals and groups irrespective of their faith emphasising that there is no religion of the State itself. The Preamble of the Constitution read in particular with Articles 25 to 28 emphasises this aspect and indicated that it is in this manner the concept of secular is embodied in the constitutional scheme as a creed adopted by the Indian people has to be understood while examining the constitutional validity of any legislation. The concept of secularism is one facet of the right to equality woven as the central golden thread in the fabric depicting the pattern of the scheme in our Constitution.

2.1.3 Fundamental Rights

Indian Constitution is considered to be a social document. At core of the constitution are the fundamental rights and the directive principles. These act as the conscience of the constitution. The Part III of the Constitution guarantees each of its citizen's certain fundamental, basic substantive and procedural protections against the state.

The significance of including the chapter on fundamental rights in the Constitution is the recognition of the rights of humans. Every human is thought to have a set of inviolable rights which cannot be breached by anyone. And unless these rights are enumerated and explicitly mentioned, there is a chance that it might get violated, and people will have no remedy in such cases, and since significant sections of the population are illiterate, they would have no idea that they have these essential rights. And for centuries, a section of population has always been exploited, the practice of evil untouchability was practiced throughout, the women were not treated equal, and all these factors cannot coexist in a democratic setup.

Democracy calls for treating every citizen in the country with equality and respect. Rights of everyone, even a child, are important and such fundamental and basic rights have to be protected and guarded. Hence, the framers of the Constitution included this chapter right at the beginning in order to suggest its importance and fundamental nature. These rights are essential for a democracy to function effectively.

2.1.3.1 Meaning of Fundamental Rights

Without provision of rights no man can seek himself to be at his best, these rights are essential conditions of social life.

These are fundamental in the sense that these have been incorporated in the fundamental law of the land, that is, the Constitution. These are fundamental in the sense that they are justiciable rights, that is, they are strictly enforceable by the court of law and are available to all the citizens. They are also fundamental in the sense that they are binding on the public authorities in the country, that is, on central, state and even the local governments. Some of the rights, such as abolition of untouchability, are also available against the private individuals as well.

2.1.3.2 Salient Features of the Fundamental Rights

1. Integral part of the Constitution: These rights form the integral part of the Constitution and hence they cannot be altered or modified by ordinary legislation. These are fundamental in the sense that any law passed by any legislature in country should not violate these provisions, if they do, they are liable to be declared null and void, and get struck down by the courts as unconstitutional.
2. All rights are Justiciable: This is another important feature of this right. This means that if any of these rights are violated, the individuals have right to approach the courts, for protection and enforcement of their rights. The Supreme courts and the High Courts have the power to declare any law passed by legislature or executive to

be null and void, if they are inconsistent with these fundamental rights. Approaching the Courts for enforcement of these rights is itself made a fundamental right. The judiciary thus acts as the guardian of the fundamental rights.

3. Citizen's alone enjoy fundamental rights: This means that, the citizens of the country alone have the right to enjoy these rights. But some of the rights such as, Right of life, freedom of religion, right against exploitation are guaranteed to every person within the territory of the country, be it citizen or an alien. Hence, the Constitution distinguishes between citizens and aliens in matter regarding enjoyment of the fundamental rights.
4. Negative and positive rights: These rights can be divided into two distinct heads, those with negative character which impose restriction on the state without conferring special privileges on the people, and on the other hand there are positive rights which confer special privileges on the people, such as Article 18 which restricts conferring special titles to the citizens by the state. Similarly Article 17 abolishes untouchability. Right to equality, freedom of expression etc. fall under the second category.
5. No natural or unenumerated rights: This concept of fundamental rights is not based on the 'theory of natural rights', which says that 'Natural' rights belong to man by 'nature'. These are the rights which are possessed by man even before the state came into existence. Hence, the significant difference between the American Constitution and the India Constitution lies in the fact that, the American Constitution provides for enumerated rights which exist outside the constitution, while there is no such provision in India Constitution, as the Courts cannot enquire into any rights which are not enumerated in the Constitution.
6. Suspension of the rights: During the period of emergency the president may suspend all or any of the fundamental rights. He may also suspend the right to approach any court for infringement of fundamental right during such period.
7. Most comprehensive and detailed: This chapter is comprehensive and detailed, it treats each provision and Article in detail and every Article is elaborated with a set of limitations and reservations.
8. Fundamental rights are amendable: They can be amended without affecting or changing the basic structure of the Constitution.
9. Restrictive nature of rights: These rights are not absolute in nature. They are provided with limitations and reasonable restrictions. And these can be imposed in the larger interests of the community concerned. For example, Article 19 gives freedom of speech and expression, but this does not mean that anyone can utter anything, these have restrictions and limitations, and these rights are allowed within such limitations. Article 16 calls for equality of opportunity, but the State has been given the power to make reservations in favour of the scheduled castes and tribes.

2.1.3.3 Importance of Fundamental Rights

The chapter on the fundamental rights is essential in upholding the rights of the people. These protect the basic rights of an individual. They are not only a guide to the citizens, but also to the government, administrators in order to understand the limitations, and the areas to be covered to provide benefits to the people in the society. The following are the reasons why the fundamental rights are important.

- They act as a guide and inspiration to the policy makers to effectively make such policies which enhance the human life.
- They are used as checks against the arbitrary action of the government by the judiciary. The judiciary is the guardian of the fundamental rights of the people and whenever such rights are violated, the judiciary intervenes and provides relief to the people. And thus when policies of the government violate any of the essential rights, it can declare such act to be unconstitutional.
- The importance of the fundamental rights lies in the fact that they have been made as a 'basic feature' in the structure of the constitution. The fundamental rights consist of principles and values which are the basic essence of the Constitution. And hence these rights cannot be abrogated at all by the legislature, though the legislature has the power to amend the fundamental rights.
- The following are the six essential fundamental rights which are guaranteed by the Constitution of India.
  - **Right to Equality:** This right is provided in Articles 14-18. This are the essential right of equality among all people. It also includes the equality before the law, prohibition of discrimination on the grounds of religion, caste, race, gender etc., provision of equality of opportunity in relation to employment. It also abolishes the evil practice of untouchability. It also has exceptions whereby the state can make positive discrimination for the backward section of the society such as the tribal, scheduled castes and women etc. Right of equality is over looked in such cases.
  - **Right to Freedom:** There are the following six freedoms under Article 19:
    - Freedom of speech and expression
    - Freedom of assembly
    - Freedom of association
    - Freedom of movement
    - Freedom of residence and settlement
    - Freedom of profession, occupation, trade or business.

    The personal liberty is the most important fundamental right. All these articles under this section form the backbone of the fundamental rights. Other essential right is the right related to conviction of offences and protection against arbitrary arrest and detention in certain cases. Article 21 confers the most important right to life. It has been expanded by the judiciary to include plethora of rights which are essential to live a dignified human life. Right to receive Education has also been made a fundamental right under Article 21A. All these rights protect and uphold the freedom of the individual.
  - **Right against Exploitation:** Articles 23 and 24 of the Constitution call for this right. It prohibits all form of forced labour, child labour and bans trafficking of human beings. It was meant to abolish economic and physical exploitation of the weaker sections of the society.
  - **Right to Freedom of Religion:** Articles 25 to 28 elaborates about the provisions regarding to right to freedom of religion. These articles talk about the freedom of conscience and freedom to propagate and profess any religion. It also protects the religious institutions from certain taxes and gives freedom to manage them. This establishes the secular character of the state.

- **Cultural and Educational Rights:** Articles 29 and 30 talks about the cultural and education rights provided to the citizens. It gives freedom to every citizen to preserve his culture, tradition, language, script, etc. It also gives the rights to the minorities to establish and run educational institutions of their choice. The state shall not discriminate between various sections in the society.
- **Right to Constitutional Remedies:** It is given under Article 32. It gives the individual right to move to Supreme Court to enforce any fundamental right when it is violated. It is considered to be the heart and soul of the Constitution and holds paramount importance. The court thus is the guarantor and protector of the fundamental rights of the people.

- Thus the Part III of the Constitution contains elaborate provisions on the essential rights of the people. Most important aspect is that, within the fundamental right itself, is the provision/right of individual to move to court when such right gets violated. Thus, approaching court for enforcement of fundamental right is made a fundamental right. Nowhere in the world can we see such provision.
- The fundamental rights are based on the Universal Declaration of Human Rights. Hence, the provisions contained in these articles are of universal importance and have to be protected and upheld by the states concerned. Without these rights, the citizens can be treated less than humans. Hence, the fundamental rights fulfil the universal obligation of treating people with respect and dignity they deserve.
- The fundamental act as guidance force for the legislators and the executives. All the laws and rules, regulations, and policies should be for the development of the people and no act by the government should be in violation of these rights. It gives fundamental responsibility on part of the state to uphold and protect these indispensable rights.

Thus, fundamental rights have been made as the crucial 'basic structure' of the Constitution, which cannot be abrogated by the Parliament. These rights contain the provisions which are fundamental for the people to live in the society as a dignified human being.

2.1.4 Universal Adult Franchise – Principle That Made India the Largest Democracy of the World

Franchise means, the right of the people to vote and elect their own representative. This word evolved from the French word 'franc' which means free, hence it means the freedom to exercise their right to choose their representatives. And Adult franchise means that the right to vote should be provided to all the adult citizens in the country without any discrimination on the basis of caste, creed, class, religion, colour or sex.

It is based on the concept of equality, which is the basic democratic principle. It means that the right to vote should be available equally to all the people. To Denial of this right means violation of the right of equality. The spirit of democracy can only be maintained if the people are given the right to vote without any discrimination. This exercise of right to vote, adds to the individual's dignity, self-respect and the sense of responsibility. The universal adult franchise in other words, can be called as the foundation of democratic system of governance. Because of the power and right to vote-in and vote-out a government, the people are called as political sovereign.

As provided in the Constitution, the citizens cast their votes in the periodic election process to elect their representatives to the parliaments, assemblies and other such democratic institutions. These institutions are called the representative institutions as they represent the will of the people.

2.1.4.1 *Evolution of Concept of Universal Adult Suffrage in India*

Before Independence, only 13% of the population had the right to vote. Hence, there was a growing demand for the provision of universal adult suffrage before independence. The report submitted by Motilal Nehru in 1928 was the first one to call for 'unlimited adult franchise with equal rights for women'.

Dr. Ambedkar made a representation before the Simon commission to incorporate the provision of universal adult suffrage in the Constitution of the country. According to Dr. Ambedkar, these rights give the people politio-religious equality, and it is a 'most potent weapon in the hands of the most oppressed sections of the society'. Nehru was also keen in providing universal adult suffrage to the people after independence.

It was declared in the 1931 Congress session in Karachi that this concept will make the electoral process participatory and more inclusive. There were many numbers of debates during the framing of the Constitution and finally all agreed and enacted to provide for universal adult franchise.

2.1.4.2 *Age of Voting*

Initially the age was 21 years and 61st Constitutional Amendment reduced that to 18 years. There are certain qualifications prescribed to be a voter in India, they are as follows:

- He/She must be a citizen of India.
- He/She must have attained 18 years of age.
- He/She must not be of unsound mind.
- He/She must not have been declared bankrupt by a competent court.

2.1.4.3 *Constitutional Provision Ensuring Universal Adult Suffrage*

Article 326. Elections to the House of the People and to the Legislative Assemblies of States must be on the basis of adult suffrage.

The elections to the House of the People and to the Legislative Assembly of every state shall be on the basis of adult suffrage; but is to say, every person who is a citizen of India and who is not less than eighteen years of age on such date as may be fixed in that behalf by or under any law made by the appropriate legislature and is not otherwise disqualified under this constitution or any law made by the appropriate legislature on the ground of non-residence, unsoundness of mind, crime or corrupt or illegal practice, shall be entitled to be registered as a voter at any such election.

Thus, the Constitution of India itself grants the right of universal adult suffrage, this is a constitutional right and not a fundamental right, that is, one cannot approach the courts for its violation. But this concept does form the basic feature of the Constitution, and hence the Courts do intervene in case this right is infringed.

2.1.4.4 *Importance of Universal Adult Franchise*

- It made India the largest Democracy of the world.
- It legitimised the government, as it was elected by the will of majority of the people,
- It achieved gender equality as women were given right to vote and hence were considered equal to men in the political sphere.

- It also granted equality to the backward class people and the tribals who were considered as equal citizens.
- Universal adult suffrage with free and fair election, was considered to be the 'guarantor of minority rights.'
- It helped the representation of the unseen population, whereby such discriminated sections could elect those who can or willing to change their condition, thereby brining prosperity and development needed to alleviate their condition.
- This provides diversity in representation, whereby people from various section of the society get represented.
- It denotes the popular will of the people, and this will get reflected in the Parliament or in the Assembly or in any other local bodies.

2.2 PARLIAMENTARY FORM OF GOVERNMENT

The Constitution of India provides for a parliamentary system of government both at the centre and the states.

The Government is classified as parliamentary or presidential based on the relationship between executive and legislature. In the Parliamentary system the executives are responsible to the legislature for its actions. While in the Presidential form, the executives remain independent and separate and are not made responsible for the legislature.

The other names by which this parliamentary system is known are: the Cabinet System, Responsible government, Westminster model of government. Britain, Canada, Japan are examples of few countries which follow parliamentary form of government.

This is called a Cabinet system because the cabinet acts as the nucleus of the power in a Parliamentary system. This is called Responsible government as for every act and function it is made responsible to the legislature, who keep a check on them. This is also called Prime Ministerial form of government, as the Prime Minister plays a very important and vital role, and in present days, the Prime Minister is the face of the government, and his powers have risen significantly compared with his colleagues in the cabinet.

2.2.1 Features of Parliamentary Form of Government

The following are the features of the Parliamentary form of government.

2.2.1.1 Majority Party Rule

The political party which secures the majority in the Lok Sabha forms the government. Either the leader of the party is appointed as the Prime Minister, or some other member as chosen by the elected members is appointed by the President. The other ministers of the cabinet are appointed by the President on the advice of the Prime Minister. And, when no party secures a majority, the President can call upon the coalition of parties to establish the government.

2.2.1.2 Homogeneous Nature of Politics

The members of the cabinet belong to the same political party. And therefore they all share same political ideology. In case of coalition they are bound by the consent.

2.2.1.3 Prime Minister – The Leader

The Prime Minister is the leading figure in the government. He is the leader of the council of ministers, leader of the Parliament and leader of the political party which has the majority in the Parliament. He thus plays a very significant and crucial role both in the government and outside it.

2.2.1.4 Maintaining Secrecy

There is code of secrecy and hence the ministers cannot divulge any information outside in the discussions on policies, programs, proceedings, etc. They undertake the oath of secrecy before entering their office.

2.2.1.5 Dissolution of Lower House

The lower house – Lok Sabha, is dissolved automatically every five years after the end of tenure of the government. And in other cases the Prime Minister can submit recommendation for dissolution to the President. Thus, Lok Sabha is dissolved on the advice of the Prime Minister before the end of its term and fresh elections can be conducted. Thus, the executive has the power to dissolve the legislature in the Parliamentary system.

2.2.1.6 Collective Responsibility

This is the bedrock of the principle based on which the Parliamentary system works. The ministers are collectively responsible to the Parliament in general and Lok Sabha in particular (Article 75). The council of ministers act as a team, they swim or sink together. This collective responsibility to Lok Sabha means that they can remove ministry government by passing the vote of no confidence motion against them.

2.2.1.7 De jure and De Facto Executive

The President is the nominal head, the de jure, or titular executive head, meanwhile the Prime Minister is the real, de facto head of the government. Therefore, the President is the head of the State, while Prime Minister is head of the government. The Article 74 provides for the council of ministers headed by the Prime Minister to aid and advice the President in exercise of his functions. Such an advice rendered is binding on the President.

2.2.1.8 Double Membership

The ministers appointed are members of both the Parliament and the Executive. This means that a person cannot become the member of the Executive without him being the member of the Parliament. Hence, membership of the Parliament is an essential requirement. Further the Constitution provides that a minister who does not become member of the Parliament within months of his appointment ceases to be a minister.

2.2.2 Merits of Parliamentary System

The Parliamentary form of government has the following merits:

1. **Existence of alternative government:** In case the ruling political party loses its majority, the President can invite the opposition party to form the government. Time is given to the opposition to prove its majority on the floor of the house. Hence, In this system, there is a provision of ready alternative government, and there is no immediate need to conduct a fresh election. Hence, the leader of the opposition is called the 'alternative Prime Minister'.
2. **Extended representation:** In a Parliamentary system, the executive is made up of a group of individuals, hence there is a wide representation. The government can accommodate representations from various quarters of the society or from different regions.

Hence, the Prime Minister while formulating the ministry can take these considerations into account.

3. **Responsible nature of the government:** By its very nature, the Parliamentary system establishes a responsible system of government. The ministers are made responsible for the legislature for all their acts of omission or commission. The parliament exerts control over the executives through a number of devices like the question hour, adjournment motion, no confidence motion, discussions, parliamentary committees, etc.
4. **Congruence between the legislature and the executive:** This is the greatest advantage of the Parliamentary system. It helps in keeping harmony and cooperation between the legislature and the executive branches of the democratic system. The executive are part of the legislature and both are interdependent on each other. Hence, there is less scope for dispute arising between these two main organs of state.
5. **Prevents authoritarianism:** In this system the power is vested with a group of Individuals – the council of ministers and not on any one individual. Though the Prime Minister may seem powerful, the President as per Constitution acts on the aid and advice of council of ministers and not just of the Prime Minister. Hence, there is no scope for an Individual to assume authoritarian powers. Moreover, the Parliament in the form of passing no-confidence motion can also remove the executives.

2.2.3 Demerits of the Parliamentary System

Despite of numerous advantages, the parliamentary system suffers from the following disadvantages:

1. **In contradiction of the separation of powers doctrine:** In this system, the executives and the legislatures are together and cannot be separated. Hence, it goes against the concept of separation of powers. The cabinet here acts as the leader of both the executives and the Parliament. And in this system there is fusion of powers between the executives and the legislature.
2. **The Government is not stable:** There is no guarantee to provide a stable government in this system. The power to remove is vested on the Parliament and whenever it feels, even without any proper reason can pass no-confidence motion to remove the government in power, this scenario is more possible in case of coalition government, whereby the government hinges on the support of number of parties who if dissatisfied can withdraw their support thereby causing collapse of the government. Hence, there is no guarantee that the government will complete its tenure. Even defections can cause such instability in the government. Hence, there is no provision of stability in this system.
3. **Government by non-professionals:** Administrative efficiency cannot be attained as the ministers are not trained personnel. They lack the knowledge and the experience to govern. Hence, they are mainly dependent on their permanent executives or the bureaucrats for aid, advice and guidance. The Prime Minister has limited choice in selection of his cabinet colleagues and his choice is restricted to the Parliament alone. Apart from this, the ministers also devote their time to party activities, parliamentary work, cabinet meetings, etc.

4. **Policies of previous government not continued:** This system is not effective in creating and implementing long-term projects. This is because of the unstable nature of the government. The change in ruling party changes everything, even the policy is changed, and hence decisions taken by the previous regime are all reversed or modified. The Janata government in 1977 reversed or modified several policies of the previous Congress government. And the same was repeated by the Congress when they came back to power in 1980.
5. **The cabinet turning into despot:** Though an individual cannot become a despot in a Parliamentary system, there is possibility of the Cabinet, as a whole, becoming all powerful. When a party secures absolute majority in the Parliament, there is virtually nothing to stop the government to carry out any change to any law or rule. This was seen happening during the period of internal emergency in India during the 1970s. Thus, there is chance that the executive can assume tyranny.

2.2.4 Comparison Between Parliamentary System and Presidential System

Presidential System	Parliamentary System
The single executive is both the head of the State and head of the government.	There are dual executives, President being the head of the State and Prime Minister the head of the government
The Presidential election is separate and distinct from that to election to the legislature, both happens for a fixed tenure.	The head of the majority party which has won election in the Lok Sabha form the government. Hence, the elections are not separate for executives and the legislators.
The President and his office are not responsible to the legislature.	The entire executive are bound by collective responsibility to Lok Sabha.
There may not be the same party which has won the Presidential election be the majority party in the legislature. Hence, there is a lack of political homogeneity in this system.	It is the most politically homogeneous system. Only the party which has won majority in the legislature can form the government and hence be the executive. Hence, the executive and the majority in the Lok Sabha belong to the same political party.
This follows the doctrine of Separation of Powers. As seen the executives and the legislature are separate and distinct, and even the judiciary is kept separate.	There is fusion of powers between the two organs – executive and the legislature. They together create a responsible system of governance.
The lower house in this system does not get dissolved. The President has no power to do so, and even in case President demits his office before end of his term, the lower house completes its tenure separately.	The power to dissolve the house before the end of its term in in the hands of the executive. Recommendation to call for a fresh election can be put forth by the Executives to the President, which dissolves the house.
The President is the dominant head in this system, and every other body follows his leadership.	President in this system is just a nominal head. The authoritative leader is the Prime Minister on whose guidance the government functions.

In this system, the executives are members of executive alone, they are not members of the legislature Hence, there is existence of only a single membership.	Here the executives are also the members of the legislature. The ministers come from the Parliament. Hence, there exists dual membership, that is, being members of both executive and the legislature.
There exists a tension between the legislature and the executives. Since both are separate, there is difficulty in coordinating between them, especially in cases where executive and the legislature belong to different parties.	There is proper and effective coordination and cooperation between the executive and the legislature. The executives arise from the legislature and hence there is no conflict between these two organs of the state.
This system has a very narrow representation. The President can appoint anyone to be in his cabinet, and the government thus operate according to his wish.	The Prime Minister can appoint only those who are members of the legislature, even if not, they should become members within 6 months. Hence, there is wide representation.
The President is not made responsible to the legislature. Hence, the legislature has no control over the policies of the President.	All the actions of the Council of Minister have to be approved by the legislature in order for them to be made as a law, hence legislature keeps effective check and the government is made responsible to the legislature.
This system has the chance of transforming into a dictatorship by the President.	There is no such possibility as the executives are kept in effective check by the legislature.
This system provides the most stable government. The President and his government cannot be removed by the legislature, and it continues to finish its term without any hurdles.	The stability is not seen in this type of system, as there is chance for the lower house to pass no-confidence motion against the government, and thus vote it out of power. Hence, the government is not stable.
This system of government is run by experts. There is flexibility and freedom to choose any person or expert in that field to manage the particular office. It is the discretion of the President.	There are no experts as only the members of the legislature can be a minister. Hence, this system is a government run by amateurs.

2.2.5 Reasons for Adoption of Parliamentary System

There were a number of discussions in the Constituent Assembly, regarding the type of government to be adopted. There was the Presidential type of system followed in America under consideration, but that was overlooked to adopt the Parliamentary system. And the reasons behind the decision are as follows:

1. **Indian Society and its nature:** India is one of the most diverse and heterogeneous nations in the world, it has a complex and a plural society. Hence, this present system was adopted as it gives better scope for providing representation to interests of wider sections and regions in the government. This could therefore help in promoting national spirit and help build a united country.
2. **Being familiar with the system:** The system of Parliamentary form of government was much familiar to the makers of the Constitution. They had a first-hand experience in the functioning and operation of the Parliamentary system, as it was in action in India, being imposed by the colonial government. Hence, the Constitution makers felt that as the system was very well entrenched, the people were also familiar with the system, and hence there was no need to look for a new form of government.

3. **Preference to responsibility over stability:** When the choice had to be made between stability and responsibility, the Constitutional makers decided to choose the latter, as it would be beneficial for the people. During one of the debates, Dr. Ambedkar, stated that, 'a democratic executive has to satisfy two conditions: stability and responsibility. Unfortunately, it is not been possible to devise a system which can ensure both in equal degree. The American system gives more stability but less responsibility, while the British system offers more responsibility but less stability. The drafting committee on recommending the parliamentary system preferred more responsibility to more stability.
4. **In order to avoid legislative-executive conundrum:** The framers of the constitution wanted to avoid such conflict between the executive and the legislature. This was bound to occur in a Presidential system as seen in USA. It was thought that the newly emerged democratic country such as India cannot afford to have such conflicts between the two pillars of the State. It was desired to have a government which was free from such conflicts and could help in ensuring development of the people.

The Swaran Singh Committee was constituted to recommend whether the Presidential system could be adopted. It recommended that the present Parliamentary system itself was functioning effectively and hence there was no need to adopt another form of government.

2.2.6 Distinction Between the Indian and Westminster Model

This system of Parliamentary form is largely based on the British model. But it is not entirely similar, and there are crucial differences between the two, which are discussed as follows:

1. India is a Republic while Britain still follow monarchical system. This means that, the head of the State in India is elected, and it is not a hereditary office, and one among the citizen of the country is made the President, while in Britain, the Head is a hereditary post, and it continues to be so.
2. In Britain there is a system of 'legal' responsibility of the ministers where the ministers have to countersign any act or rule after being signed by the Head of the State. Such a kind of system is not followed in India.
3. The presence of 'Shadow cabinet' is unique to the British system. The Shadow cabinet is carried out by the opposition which mirrors the government, and formulates counter-legislations. It is the perfect training for the government in waiting. There is no such system in India and only the Head of the opposition party is accorded recognition.
4. The British system is established on the doctrine of sovereignty of the Parliament, where the Parliament is supreme. While in India, the Parliament is not absolute sovereign, it has restricted and limited powers because of a written Constitution, judicial review, fundamental rights and a federal system.
5. In Britain, the ministers can only be appointed from the Parliament. In India an outsider can be appointed, but for a period of 6 months, within which he should become member of either house of the Parliament.
6. The Prime Minster in Britain should be from the lower house, that is, from House of Commons. There is no such restriction in India, the Prime Minister can be from either house of the Parliament.

2.3 REPRESENTATIVE DEMOCRACY

The Indian Constitution not only provides political rights, being a social document it also protects the socio-economic fundamental right of the people. Dr. Ambedkar in the concluding speech in the Constituent Assembly stated that

> *Political democracy cannot last unless there lies at the base of it social democracy. What does social democracy mean? It means a way of life which recognises liberty, equality and fraternity which are not to be treated as separate items in a trinity. They form a union of trinity in the sense that to divorce one from the other is to defeat the very purpose of democracy.*

2.3.1 Concept of Representative Democracy

This is the type of democracy which is founded on the principle of people being represented by the elected officials. It is opposed to the Direct Democracy where the people are in total control of the system. Nearly all modern states, except a few, follow the ideal set by the representative democracy. For example, United Kingdom is a constitutional monarchy, India is a federal republic and United States is Presidential type.

In a society having a number of people, it is difficult for everyone to voice their view. The ideal of direct democracy where people directly represent themselves is possible when,

- The population is small
- The people are well educated
- System of democracy is well established.

Thus, in a mass-based society where the population is large, the most efficient form of democracy is the representative form. Even the developed and well-educated societies in West have not adopted the direct form of democracy, but rather have accepted to follow the representative form.

It allows for effective ruling by a small but well-established group on behalf of the other people in the society. This system is both time and cost effective. The decisions are taken quickly by a small group of people, and hence the view of entire population need not be ascertained, and as representatives they take the decisions knowing the pulse and need of the people.

This form of democracy originated from the idea of 'representative government' which arose after the French and American Revolution. Hence, it means that people elect their representatives – who make the law, and they are responsible and accountable to the people for their actions.

Generally the lower chamber in the democracies acts as the representatives of the people. For example, In India, it is called Lok Sabha – means the association of the people, in England it is called the House of Commons, in USA it is the Congress. Hence, in all democracies the lower house consists of the representatives directly chosen by the people themselves. Some of these countries may have an Upper house to keep a check on the lower house, these are democratic provisions in order to maintain the balance of the democratic system.

2.3.2 Powers of the Representative

They are elected directly by the people to the national legislature. They hold power for a specific period of term, at the end of which the process of election begins again. Hence, the representatives go back to the people, asking them to vote back to power, therefore the people in the democratic system have the power to change or make the same government continue to govern.

The powers of such representatives are not unlimited. They are checked by the following:

- They are bound by the Constitution, they have to abide by and follow the ideals of the Constitution. They cannot make any law which is in violation of the Constitution.
- The third Pillar of democracy, that is, Judiciary keeps an effective check on the legislature. They are the guardians of the Constitution, and when any law made by the legislature goes beyond the provisions of the Constitution, they are struck down as ultra vires.
- Other constitutional bodies such as the Election Commission, Union Public Service Commission, and the office of Comptroller and Auditor General are independent of the legislature. They keep an effective check on various aspects and hence make the representatives accountable to the people.
- The presence of Upper House is also meant to keep a check on the lower house. The Upper house understood to have people of wisdom and hence they act with prudence and try to curtail dictatorial tendencies of an absolute majoritarian lower house.

2.3.3 Representative Democracy in India

The Lok Sabha is directly elected by the people of the country, so the members of Parliament of Lok Sabha are the representatives of the people. The people elect their representatives from their own constituencies or locality. The whole country and each state is divided into different constituencies which are based on the territorial limit set by the Delimitation Commission. Hence, an individual stands for election in a particular locality/area from where the people living in that region vote to select the person who would give voice to them in the Parliament.

India have universal adult suffrage, hence any citizen who has completed the age of 18 years is eligible to vote. There is no discrimination in any manner to vote in the election process. This is the fundamental basis of representative democracy. The important aspects of representative democracy in India are as follows:

1. **President:** He is the head of the State. He is elected directly by Electoral College consisting of members of both house of the Parliament and the elected members of the state assemblies. He is an integral part of the Parliament though he does not take part in its sittings. Final approval to any bill has to be given by the President.

   He can promulgate ordinances when either house is not in session. It has the same effect as a law passed by the Parliament. It has to be noted that in all aspects the President should act in accordance to the aid and advice rendered by the Council of Ministers headed by the Prime Minister.
2. **Rajya Sabha and Lok Sabha:** Rajya Sabha is the council of State, and it represents the will of the people indirectly. They are elected by the members of the State assemblies by a system of proportional representation. Each state has a different number of representatives as it is decided on basis of the population of each state. It is a permanent body consisting of not more than 250 members, and among them 12 persons are nominated by the President.

   The lower house is directly elected by the people. It should not contain more than 530 members representing the states and not more than 20 representing the Union territories. The President has the power to nominate 2 members from the Anglo-Indian community if there are no other such representation.

The important aspect of the representative democracy is that the government should periodically obtain the mandate of the people through election in order to continue office legitimately.

Both the house share equal powers in all aspects, except a few, such as the Lok Sabha in the financial sphere, and the council of ministers are collectively responsible only to the lower house and not to the Rajya Sabha. Rajya Sabha too has some special powers assigned to by the Constitution, it has the power to dictate on matters related to items in the state list for the larger public interest concerned.

3. **Parliament and the executive:** The leader of the party which has secured majority in the election is called by the President and asked to form the government. The other ministers are appointed as per the recommendation of the Prime Minister. The Council of ministers are collectively responsible to the Lok Sabha and hold the office as long as it enjoys the confidence of the Lower House.

   There is harmony between the legislature and the Executive. This is because the executive is taken from the legislature. Hence, the ministers are members of both legislature and the executive. Thus, Parliament in India is to legislate, criticize, advice and air public grievances, while the executive is to govern, on behalf of the Parliament. The executive thus remain accountable and responsible to the Parliament.

4. **Parliament and Judiciary:** The Judiciary in India is integrated, where the Supreme Court is at the Apex, the High Courts are in the States, and District courts govern in the allocated districts.

   The court has a very important role to play in a representative democracy. They keep check on the acts, functions and laws made by the parliament. They are the guardians of the principles and ideals of the Constitution. If any law which is in violation of the constitutional values they are liable to be declared null or void by the Judiciary.

   Any illegal executive action which violates the fundamental rights of the people can be questioned by the courts on the basis of writ petitions. The fundamental rights of the people which are guaranteed under the Constitution are protected by the Supreme Court and the High Courts. Thus, the judiciary act as an effective check against illegal and unconstitutional acts of both the legislature and the executive.

The fundamental aspect of the representative government in the party politics and its recent evolution into the coalition system is dealt in the following sections.

2.3.4 Party Politics

The party system is the fundamental basis for the representative democracy. There is no other alternative to the party system than a dictatorship, hence the party system is very essential. They are essential in a democratic system. They link the people to the legislature and the executive. The nature of the representative government is determined on basis of the kind of party which governs it.

Though they are an informal entity, the party play a very important role in democratic setup. The important function is to organise and mobilise the electorate. They form the government if they get elected by the people. In a parliamentary system, the majority party which secures the vote of the electorate forms the government. During every election, the party releases a manifesto, in which it outlines its policies and ideas which they would implement if elected to power. And once they form the government they strive to implement those promises.

The minority party which loses the election takes up the role of the opposition in the Parliament or in the Assembly. They help in the breakdown of traditional barrier and help bind the diversified community which are divided based on caste, religion and region, etc.

2.3.5 Classification of Political Parties in India

In terms of geography, the political parties can be classified as national, regional or local parties, on basis of their ideology, they are differentiated into left, right or centre. And among the left, there are communist and socialist parties, and among the right there are traditional caste-based parties, etc.

Nehru made an observation regarding the prevailing party scenario in the country in 1953,

> *The Parties, as they exist in India today, apart from the congress, may be divided into four groups. There are certain political parties with economic ideology. There is the communist party with allied organisation. There are various communal parties under different names but essentially following a narrow communal ideology, and there are a number of local parties and groups having only a provincial or even a narrower appeal.*

Thus, further we may classify the political parties as follows:

1. **All India political parties:** As per the Election Symbols (reservation and allotment) Order, 1968, a party is recognised as a National Party only if it fulfils the following conditions:
   (i) The candidates set up by the party, in any four or more States, in the last general election to the House of the People or to the Legislative Assembly of the State concerned, have secured not less than 6% of the total valid votes polled in each of those states in that general election; and, in addition, it has sent at least four members to the House of the People in the aforesaid last general election from any state or states; or
   (ii) In the last general election to the House of the People, the party has won at least 2% of the total number of seats, any fraction exceeding half being counted as one; and the party's candidates have been elected to that House from not less than three states; or
   (iii) The party is recognized as state party in at least four states.

   These parties stand on the national platform and emphasise national issues for getting elected to the parliament. At the end of 16th Lok Sabha elections, six political parties were accorded National party recognition by the Election Commission.
2. **Regional parties:** They represent the regional-nationalism based on common language, history and culture of place which they are part of. Their strength is confined only to a particular area. According to the Election Symbols (reservation and allotment) Order, 1968, a party is recognised as a State Party only if it fulfils the following conditions:
   (i) In the last general election to the Legislative Assembly of the State, the candidates set up by the party have secured not less than 6% of the total valid votes polled in the state; and, in addition, the party has sent at least two members to the Legislative Assembly of that State in such general election; or

(ii) In the last general election to the House of the People from that State, the candidates set up by the party have secured not less than 6% of the total valid votes polled in the state; and, in addition, the party has returned at least one member to the House of the People from that state at such general election; or

(iii) In the last general election to the Legislative Assembly of the State, the party has won at least 3% of the total number of seats in the Legislative Assembly, (any fraction exceeding half being counted as one), or at least three seats in the Assembly, whichever is more; or

(iv) In the last general election to the House of the People from the State, the party has returned at least one member to the House of the People for every 25 members or any fraction thereof allotted to that State; or

(v) In the last general election to the House of the People from the State, or in the last general election to the Legislative Assembly of the State, the candidates set up by the Party have secured not less than 8% of the total valid votes polled in the State.

The privilege of being accorded recognition by the Election Commission is that, they can have their own permanent symbol for all their contestants, and they are given air time on All India Radio, Doordarshan to address the voters.

3. **Communal parties:** These are exclusive organisations open only to those who practice that particular religion or belong to that ethnicity. They seek to protect and promote interests of a particular community alone, hence their support base in small and confined to that region alone. The examples are Muslim League (Kerala), Akali Dal (Punjab) etc.
4. **Ad hoc parties:** These are temporary parties organised on the basis of a powerful personality. They only appear for a short period and does not have a mass base. Examples are Bangala Congress, Kerala Congress and the BKD of Charan Singh which were all short-lived ventures.

2.3.6 Salient Features of the Party System in India

1. **One party dominance system:** The Congress party was the fore front in the freedom struggle. It had the distinction of being the party of numerous illustrious freedom fighters. It was led by Gandhi, Nehru, and so many others. Hence, it became the only party leading the independent nation of India.

   And likewise it got elected with an overwhelming majority to the Parliament. And being a young country the people had first-hand experience of the British rule and they had seen the role played by the Congress during the struggle for Independence and hence the support to the party continued even after Independence.

   For a long time, no other party was able to establish a stable government at the Centre without the support from the Congress party. Even today, any possible alternative government is said to rest on the shoulders of the Congress party. Hence, in India there is domination of a single party, and even today its support base has not eroded.
2. **A multi-party system:** Credit should be given to the Congress party for not to convert its goodwill and convert into an authoritarian, despotic system. Hence, the basic necessity of a representative democracy got entrenched into the Indian system.

Though we could say that the Congress party is the dominant party, there is scope for existence for numerous other parties in the country. Though their recognition is subjected to the conditions provided in the Election Commission rules.

A number of parties are needed to represent the interests of various section of the population. No single party can satisfy needs and requirements of the entire population.

Presence of multi-party system also helps protect the democratic system, as they keep the government in check, by posing questions on their actions in the legislature, help people understand presence of alternative schemes, offer alternative thinking and ideology to the people. This system also helps in articulation and representation of the needs of a minor section of the population.

3. **Weakness of the non-Congress parties:** The non-Congress parties are not that well organised and does not have the mass base throughout the country. Even before the Independence, the Congress established and spread its association even to a remote village. But after independence, such measures were difficult to carry out, and hence no other political party could come close to congress in mobilisation of people and the resources. And also presence of dynamic leaders such as Nehru, Indira Gandhi etc. helped in sustenance of the party.
4. **Reliance on powerful personalities:** Most of the regional parties got formulated around the cult of a mass-leader. Down-south the cine personalities extended their on-screen image to the real-world and wooed the masses. The people too worshiped these personalities and hence accepted them as their leader. The formation of Anna Dravida Munetra Kazhagam (ADMK) around the personality of M.G. Ramachandran and creation of Telugu Desam Party around N.T. Rama Rao are the glaring examples of a single man shaped up these parties. Even today many such parties are run on basis of the goodwill of these powerful personalities.
5. **Lack of ideological commitment:** Another important aspect of political parties in India is that, apart from the leftist parties no other party has a concrete ideology. The Communist Party of India (CPI) has a socialist agenda, meanwhile even the Congress adopted the socialistic policies, but it brought in the neo-liberal reforms, most of the regional parties have a narrow vision, that is, development and protection of their own section of population. Hence, there is not much difference in electing a different party to power, more or less all these parties have committed to follow the ideology of development politics.
6. **Factions within the parties:** Some of the parties are not united and there are factions within them. The factions are based on personalities of different leaders within the parties. Sometimes these factions are dangerous for the party and may even lead to eventual breakup of the party. The break-away faction may join some other political party which may provide them with plum postings. This is because of lack of ideology in the political parties, which has made possible existence of various factions.
7. **Use of extra-constitutional means to power:** The parties apart from electioneering and campaigning might indulge in other means of getting into power. The breakaway faction might join the party in power and hence the party system has no proper value or ideology. They might tend to use unconstitutional means such as civil disobedience, strikes, mass demonstration and protest rallies to pressurise the party in power to accept their dictates.

2.3.7 Coalition Politics

The upper middle class elite played a dominant role in running the country after its Independence, and such scenario continued for a long time both in Centre and the States. This coordination and consensus was possible between Centre and State because of the one party dominance of the system, which is ruled in both by the Congress party. The consensual elite accommodation was possible because of the dominance of the political class by the powerful upper caste political elites, and hence similar view and line of thought was possible.

2.3.7.1 *Initial Phase of Coalition Era*

The scenario started to change after 1960s. There were some noteworthy changes in the political system such as rearrangement of the political forces, increasing role of rural elites in the system, rise of a particolored and complex elite structure. The year 1967 marked the coming of change, the Congress party lost elections in several prominent states and first phase of coalition governments with support from regional parties started to arise in the system. This could not be sustained for a long time because of the lack of initial experience, differences and contradictions among the parties. Indira Gandhi too played a significant role in curtailing the rise of coalition politics by centralising political and economic powers. But some states did challenge such unilateral and centralising tendencies of the Union government, they also questioned the veracity of the planning by the Centre. Though the initial phase of coalition politics was temporary and short lived, it indeed created some strong regional movements and state-specific parties in states like Tamil Nadu, Kerala, Orissa, West Bengal, Punjab etc.

2.3.7.2 *The First Phase of Coalition Era: The Late 1960*

The Congress party underwent noteworthy changes during the 1960s. It had lost its dominant status after the 1967 elections. By the end of 1960s, the Congress had polarized into two camps and split – one led by Kamaraj called as the Syndicate-Congress (Organisation) and another under Indira called as the Congress (Ruling). Indira Gandhi faced stiff opposition within her own party, she increasingly started to reject principle of consensus and ignored long standing and established leaders of the party. She dismantled the party's decentralized structure and restricted its functioning without any concern for regional and local sentiments. She practically took over the party operations completely. All senior members of the party had to fall in line with her dictates. This had not only changed working of the Congress party but it inadvertently also had significant impact on the Indian political federal system.

- This had led to growth of strong regional sentiment in the states. Strong case was made demanding decentralisation by sharing power of sovereignty by the states, especially Punjab and Assam during the second term of Indira Gandhi.
- Several prominent state-level parties came to power during Indira's second term in early 1980s – such as Assom Gana Parishad (AGP) in Assam, AIADMK in Tamil Nadu, Akali Dal in Punjab, Telugu Desam Party (TDP) in Andhra Pradesh etc.
- The state governments of West Bengal and Kerala led by the United Front of the Left parties, Swatantra party in Orissa, DMK-led government in Tamil Nadu had emphasised the need to restrain the authority of the Centre.
- In 1980s Jyothi Basu, N.T. Rama Rao and other opposition Chief Ministers came together to build a coalition of 'Non-Congress CMs' challenging the hegemony of the dominant Congress party and the so called 'centralized state'. Several conferences and conclaves were held to discuss these issues.

2.3.7.3 The Second Phase of Coalition Era: Late 1980's

The other major period of coalition era – the second phase – started in 1989, two years before the Economic Reform program. There was a transition from the dominant party system to a multi-party system and from a majoritarian government to a coalition government. Several unstable governments were formed in quick succession. The coalition politics got boost from the implementation of the Mandal commission reforms for reservation to OBCs by the V.P. Singh government and communalisation of the polity by the demolition of the Babri Masjid in Ayodhya. BJP emerged as a major force in the Centre, while in the states, caste-based, class-based politics of the SCc and OBCs took centre stage. Hence, the so called National parties had to align themselves with these state-level forces in order to win the elections as their powers had waned.

2.3.7.4 Present Era of Coalition Politics

In successive years the coalition government had become the norm in the Centre with support from the regional-state parties. Some of the dominant parties emerged in 1990s, such as Samajwadi Party (SP), Janata Dal (United) (JDU), Biju Janata Dal (BJD), Trinamool Congress, Samata Party, Nationalist Congress Party (NCP), etc.

1. It was impossible now to form a government at the centre without the support of these regional parties.
2. This had significant impact on the Federal system as states now played a dominant and decisive role in the coalition governments.
3. Though in 2014 elections BJP had won majority on its own, it still chose to form government with coalition of other parties.
4. Thus, states are now becoming increasingly assertive in centre-state federal bargaining as their dominance has increased in the National-level politics.
5. The coalition government and its effect is not restricted to National politics alone, it has a significant impact on the neo-liberal economic policies of the Centre.
6. Due to the opposition of the state governments, the Centre could not carry forward many decisive economic reforms. The states now have say in directing and modifying the economic policies.
7. The National parties too are now exploiting the coalition politics and thus the system has become more corrupt.
8. During the pre-liberalisation phase, there was a vertical competition between the national states, now it has become horizontal that is competition is now between the regional state governments themselves.
9. Hence, the policies of the Centre are now diffused across the states and it works on political considerations. Thus, the disintegration of the party system and unstable coalition has adversely affected the governance of the country.
10. There is now increased prominence of the state and regional parties because of the stability of the coalition government at the Centre.
11. The states hence now enjoy a greater degree of autonomy and they are trying to establish their own influence at the centre which is adversely impacting the polity.
12. The state-level parties are also in talks to create a United Federal Front to resist any centralization move.
13. Such 'centralization' measures invite condemnation not just from the regional and state parties but also from the National Parties themselves in order to preserve the federal

spirit and structure. Even the BJP-led government elected in 2014 has given greater emphasis on improving the dynamics of Centre-State relations at least on paper.

According to scholars the participation of the regional state parties in the coalition governments has led to 'refederalisation' of Indian democracy. Present era is moving towards increased decentralisation, refederalisation and regionalization of politics, and hence the institutions should also keep up with such changes in the political scenario for effective sharing of powers.

2.4 FEDERAL FORM AND ITS DYNAMICS

Although the Indian Constitution nowhere mentions the term 'federal', it has provided for a governance model, which is essentially federal in spirit. Federalism in India should be studied in the context of its pluralities of culture and its socio-economic conditions on the eve of Independence.

With a large population spread across a large pluralistic framework in terms of ethnic, linguistic, religious and other diversities, it was necessary to implement a system of polity that would accommodate these pluralities. This was to be done without compromising on building a unified nation. In order to serve the objective, the constitution makers decided on a democratic structure based on federal system of government with a unitary bias. While democracy ensures freedom to the citizens, a federation would ensure the protection of pluralities. This when managed by a strong union government, ensures the principle of 'unity amidst diversity' in order to march ahead to progress.

The perils of colonial rule made India as a land of severe economic disparities and chronic under-development. As the immediate goal for the newly born nation was to turn around the economic conditions, it was necessary to bring in an administrative system that would combine regional management and centralised supervision. It was thus decided that a federal polity with an empowered union government will best fit these requirements to achieve the goal.

2.4.1 Features of Indian Federalism

There are certain unique features in Indian federalism. They are as follows:

1. **Supreme and single constitution:** Constitution is the most supreme law of the land in India. It contains several components that together act as a rule of thumb in framing policies of the government. It guarantees a set of fundamental rights to the citizens. Similarly, it demarcates the domains of power of executive, legislative and financial powers of both the government of India and the states.
2. **Dual government:** The Constitution has distributed powers between the Union and the States. Through this distribution, it seeks to accommodate the diversity of India. By providing certain powers to the state governments, the constitution allows the states to take decision with flexibility according to local needs.
3. **Authority of the courts:** Legal supremacy of the constitution is an essential feature in the federal system. It helps in maintaining the division of powers between the union and centre. Courts have the final power to interpret the constitution and nullify actions on the part of the federal and state governments or their different units, which violate the provisions of the constitution.

4. **The mode of formation:** Unlike the United States, which was formed as a result of coming together of a group of states, Indian federalism was born out of the need for administrative convenience.
5. **Position of the states in the federation:** In the United States, since the states had existed much before the formation of federation, they held their own sovereignty vis-a-vis the federal government. Therefore, their constitution had several safeguards for the protection of state's sovereignty. Whereas in India, there was no such history of states holding a higher sovereignty. Thus, our states do not enjoy a higher authority in comparison to the union government.

2.4.2 Criticism of Indian Federalism

Though the founding fathers of the Indian Constitution have done their best to imbibe a federal character into our polity, there are a number of criticisms against it.

1. **Not a truly rigid constitution:** The amendment process to the Constitution of India follows a blend of rigidity and flexibility. Some of its provisions can be easily amended by the Parliament and some require ratification from the states. While it is challenging to pass amendments that affect the federal provisions, it is not as difficult as the amendment process in the United States.
2. **Powerful Union government:** The union holds more power as against the states. This can be understood by the number and importance of subjects under the Union list under Schedule 7 of the constitution. Even regarding the concurrent list, the constitution empowers the Parliament to override any law made by the state legislature in case of a conflict with a union law on the same subject. Additionally, all residuary powers are also vested with the Parliament. Besides this, it empowers the Parliament to legislate in certain cases on subjects in the state list.
3. **Unequal representation of states in the Upper House:** In bicameral legislatures of federal countries it is a basic feature to have equal representation for states in the upper house. India has deviated from this principle and has opted for proportional representation based on the population of the respective states.
4. **Executive is a part of legislature:** Separation of powers is yet another essential part of a federal polity. In India though, the political executive is an integral part of the legislature.
5. **Lower house enjoys greater power than Upper house:** The role of the Upper House in a federation is quite significant as it features representatives from the states. In the Indian Parliament however, the lower house enjoys greater powers compared to the Upper House. For instance, money bills can only be introduced in a Lower House; a no confidence motion against the government can only be initiated in the Lower House. Interestingly, the Upper House as well enjoys the unique power such as to initiate a bill for the creation of an All-India service. Such unequal distribution of powers among the houses of Parliament is contrary to the principle of federalism.
6. **Appointment process of Governor:** The power of appointing a governor lies with the President, who executes this power based on the advice of the council of ministers. As a result, the governor acts as an agent of the Union government.

7. **Destructible states:** A state's name, territory, or its very existence can be changed by the Parliament by passing a law to that effect. All of this can be done following the procedure of an ordinary bill.

2.4.3 Co-Operative Federalism to Competitive Federalism

- **Cooperative federalism** implies that the Union and states share a **horizontal relationship**, where they **'cooperate' in the larger public interest**. It's visualised as an important tool to enable states' participation in the formulation and implementation of national policies.
- **Sharing of powers and responsibilities** between the three levels of government is a key element of the concept, which involves participative policymaking. This is particularly important in areas of concurrent responsibility, where the Centre has had a tendency to ride roughshod over the States by occupying the common legislative space.
- A reform of the seventh schedule lists in the direction of greater empowerment of States would be consistent with the logic of increased financial transfers and cooperative federalism. Locating the right level for making and implementing policy is a central feature of the cooperative responsibility matrix.
- A key element in fostering cooperative federalism is the **respect for the mandate of elected governments, even those run by opposition parties**. In an era where the party system is fragmented along federal lines, the need is still felt to include State parties in federal coalitions, even when technically not necessary.
- **Competitive federalism** can refer to the relationship between the Central and state governments (vertical) or between state governments (horizontal). Post the 1990s economic reforms this idea of federalism gained prominence.
- The spirit of competition in a free-market economy is established through the provision of benefactions to states, their resource base available and their other comparative advantages. States has to compete not just with the Centre, but also with other states for gaining these benefits. Increasing globalisation, however, has made the already existing inequalities and imbalances between states much wider. Hence, there is concern about the states' freedom to formulate their own growth policies.
- With the onset of **globalisation**, there have been new economic roles for the government. There has been complex power sharing and multi-level relationship.
- Identity related issues (e.g, Telangana) and resource-based issues (like Cauvery and Narmada), so in multi-party system, need to forge federal coalitions is all the more important.
- Fiscal constraints of the states have led to the proliferation of central schemes and national missions.
- Because of responsive and participative democracy, we get **asymmetric federalism** (the acceptance of inequality of states) leading to decline in inequality, tensions and dis-satisfactions.

2.5 BASIC STRUCTURE OF THE CONSTITUTION

2.5.1 Basic Principles of the Constitution

The constitution is a set of laws and rules which sets up the machinery of the government, it also enshrines about the provisions regarding separation of various instruments of the state and about the role carried out by them. It also defines power of each organ of the state and establishes relations between them.

Every such structure of government is made up from some basic principles and these basic principles should be well established. Every such constitution around the world has such common features, apart from having their own exclusive feature. India is no exception, as it also has some of the basic principles in its foundation. These are not explicitly mentioned, rather the careful study of the Constitution would provide us with the following six essential features, which can said to be the foundation of democracy in the country. These are

- Fundamental rights
- Directive principles of state policy
- Federalism
- Cabinet form of government
- Judicial independence
- Popular sovereignty

The political freedom and the concept of civil liberty are said to lie at the base of our Constitution. The Constitution of India was created for the common man. The Constitution was meant not for those who rule, but was rather for the very people who are to be governed.

2.5.2 Emergence of Basic Structure of the Constitution

The emergence of the Basic structure doctrine can be traced from the judgements pronounced by the Courts, essentially the Supreme Court of the country.

1. **Amendment of fundamental right – Parliamentary supremacy in amendment-Shankari Prasad Case (1951):** The question whether the Parliament had the power to amend the fundamental right came up before the court within one year of the enactment of the Constitution. In the said case, the validity of First Amendment which curtained the right to property was challenged.

   The Supreme Court ruled that under **Article 368**, the Parliament had the power to amend even the fundamental right.

   The court interpreted that the laws given under Article 13, did not include Constitutional amendments.

   Hence, the Parliament had the power to take away, amend any of the fundamental rights by way of constitutional amendment under 368, as they did not constitute law.
2. **Amending of fundamental right – Curtailing of the Parliament – Golak Nath case (1967):** The above judgement given in Shankari Prasad case was reversed in this case.

   In this case, the constitutional validity of the seventeenth amendment Act was challenged which inserted some state acts into the ninth schedule.

The Court asserted that the fundamental rights have been given 'immutable and transcendental' position and therefore the Parliament cannot take away any of these rights.

Court said that, under Article 13, even a constitutional amendment is a law, hence it can be struck down as void in case it is in violation of the fundamental rights.

3. **Reaction of the legislature for on Golak Nath case – 24th Amendment Act:** The legislature reacted to the judgement of the Supreme Court, by enacting the 24th amendment act, which amended the Articles 13 and 26.

   It declared that, the power of the Parliament to amend the Constitution is supreme and it can take away any fundamental right under Article 368 and it will not constitute law as under Article 13.

4. **Doctrine of Basic Structure – Kesavananda Bharati Case (1973):** The 24th amendment act was challenged. The Court overruled its earlier judgement in the Golak Nath case. It held the 24th amendment to be valid, the Parliament had the power to amend the fundamental rights. But it established a new concept of 'Basic Structure' of the constitution.

   It ruled that the power to amend under Article 368 does not enable the Parliament to alter the 'basic structure' of the Constitution.

   This means that the Parliament cannot take away or modify any fundamental right which falls within the doctrine of basic structure of the Constitution.

5. **Reaffirmation of basic structure doctrine – Indira Gandhi case (1975):** The court invalidated the 39th amendment act of the Parliament, which had sought to keep the election dispute of the Prime Minister and the Speaker of the Lok Sabha out of purview of the courts.

   The Court held that this was beyond the amending power of the Parliament as it affected the basic structure of the Constitution.

6. **Reaction of the Parliament – 42nd amendment act:** This was in reaction to the judicial concept of the 'basic structure', which had invalidated the election of the Prime Minister.

   This act amended the Article 368, and declared that the power of Parliament is supreme regarding the question of amendment, there was no limitation to the power of the Parliament, and no such amendment can be questioned by any court for being contravention to the provisions of any of the fundamental rights.

7. **Finality of basic structure by the Judiciary – Minerva Mills case (1980):** The Supreme Court in this case struck down the provision which excluded the courts purview over the legislations.

   This was abrogation of power of judicial review which was a 'basic feature' of the constitution.

   Applying the concept of 'basic structure' to the Article 368, the court held that, 'Since the Constitution had conferred a limited amending power on the Parliament, the Parliament cannot under the exercise of that limited power enlarge that very power into an absolute power. Indeed, a limited amending power is one of the basic features of the Constitution and therefore, the limitations on that power cannot be destroyed. In other words, Parliament cannot under Article 368, expand its amending power so as to acquire for itself the right to repeal or abrogate the Constitution or to destroy its basic features. The donee of a limited power cannot by the exercise of that power convert the limited power into an unlimited one'.

In Waman Rao case (1981), the Supreme Court adhered to the doctrine of basic structure and held that it would only apply to constitutional amendments enacted after the Judgement of Kesavananda Bharati case (24, April 1973).

2.5.3 Elements of Basic Structure

The present position is that the Parliament has the power to amend the fundamental rights under Article 368. But this has to be carried out without affecting the 'basic structure' of the Constitution. Even now there is no proper clarification regarding what constitutes these basic structures. It is a dynamic concept and from various judgements of the Supreme Court we can identify the 'basic structure' of the Constitution as follows:

1. Secular nature of the Constitution
2. Federal character
3. Unity and integrity of the nation
4. Powers of Supreme Court under Articles 32, 136, 141 and 142
5. Limited power of the Parliament to amend the constitution
6. Judicial review
7. Supremacy of the Constitution
8. Separation of powers between the executive, legislature and the judiciary
9. Principle of equality
10. Independence of judiciary
11. Powers of High Courts under Articles 226 and 227
12. Effective access to justice
13. Welfare state
14. Sovereign, socialist, democratic and republic nature of the state
15. Harmony and existence of balance between the fundamental rights and the directive principles
16. Free and fair elections
17. The basic nature of the fundamental rights
18. Parliamentary system
19. Freedom and dignity of the individual
20. Welfare state

2.6 INDEPENDENT CONSTITUTIONAL BODIES FOR EFFECTIVE GOVERNANCE

The following bodies have been included in the Constitution as independent bodies. They have been accorded constitutional status and given power to take action for effective governance.

1. **Election Commission:** The Election commission has been granted permanent and independent status to carry out free and fair elections in the country. **Article 324** of the Constitution provides the power of superintendence, direction and control of elections to the Parliament, state legislatures and to the office of the President and the vice-president. Thus, the body of election commission is common to both Centre and the States.

Independence: Article 324 of the Constitution has made the following provision regarding the independence of the Election commission.

1. Security of tenure is given to the Chief Election Commissioner. He cannot be removed by any other manner except on the manner and grounds similar to that of a judge of the Supreme Court. Thus, he can only be removed by the President on the basis of a resolution passed in a special majority by both houses of the parliament, either on the ground of proved misbehaviour or incapacity. He does not come under the 'doctrine of pleasure of the president' even though he is appointed by him.
2. The service conditions of the chief Election Commissioner cannot be changed to his disadvantage after his appointment to the office.
3. No other Election Commissioner or a regional Election Commissioner can be removed except on recommendation by the chief Election Commissioner.

Powers and Functions: The powers and functions of the Election Commission are categorised into the following classifications:

1. Administrative
2. Advisory
3. Quasi-judicial

In detail the functions are as follows:

1. It has the power to register the political parties and it grants them the status of national or state parties on the basis of their performance in the poll.
2. It supervises the election machinery throughout the country to conduct free and fair elections.
3. It determines the code of conduct to be followed by the political parties.
4. It has the power to cancel polls and conduct by-polls in event of rigging, booth capturing, violence or any other such irregularities.
5. To render advice to the governor on matters relating to the disqualification of the members of legislature of the states.
6. To prepare the electoral rolls periodically and update them. It has the power to register all eligible voters.
7. It grants recognition to the political parties and provides them symbols to choose.
8. It also renders advice to the President in matters relating to the disqualification of the members of the Parliament.
9. It has the power to determine the territorial areas of the constituencies where election is about to take place based on the Delimitation Commission Act of the Parliament.
10. It notifies the date and schedules of elections and also scrutinises the nomination paper filed by the candidates.

2. **Union Public Service Commission:** The Union Public Service Commission is the agency for the central recruitment in the country. It is an independent constitutional body having powers under the Articles 315 to 323 in Part XIV of the Constitution. These Articles contain provisions regarding the composition, powers, independence regarding that of the UPSC.

Independence: The Constitution has made the following provisions concerning the independence of UPSC to ensure impartial and independent functioning of the body:

1. The chairman or a member enjoys security of tenure as they can only be removed on the grounds given in the Constitution by the President.
2. The conditions of service of the chairman or any other member cannot be varied to their disadvantage after their appointment.
3. The expenses of the salary, allowances, and pensions of both members and the chairman are charged on the consolidated fund of India. Thus, they are not voted upon in the Parliament.
4. The Chairman of UPSC after the end of his tenure is not eligible for any further employment in Centre or State.
5. The member of the UPSC after the end of their tenure is eligible to be appointed only as the Chairman of UPSC or any State Public Service Commission, but not for any other employment in either centre or state.
6. The Chairman or a member after the end of their tenure is not eligible for reappointment.

Functions: The following functions are performed by the UPSC:

1. Examinations for the all-India services, the central services and public services of centrally administered territories are conducted by the UPSC.
2. Assistance is provided to two or more states when such request is made by them, to frame, operate schemes for joint recruitment of eligible candidates in the required position.
3. When a request is made by the governor, the UPSC acts to fulfil them on approval by the President.
4. It is consulted on the following matters regarding the Personnel management:
   a. All matters regarding the recruitment to civil service or any other civil post.
   b. Regarding the principles to be followed while making appointments, in promotions and transfers from one service to other.
   c. The concerned department may formulate rules regarding promotion, transfer, suitability of candidates to particular posts etc. and UPSC then ratifies such rules devised.
   d. All such disciplinary issues which affects a person serving under the central government, such matters include
      - Withholding of promotion
      - Withholding of increment
      - Demotion
      - Removal from service
      - Dismissal from service
      - Compulsory retirement
      - Censure
      - Recovery of pecuniary loss
   e. Matters regarding to provision of extension of service and cases of re-employment of some retired civil servants.
   f. Any other issues regarding the personnel management.

Additional functions related to the centre can be conferred upon the UPSC by the Parliament by way of enactment. It can extend the jurisdiction of the UPSC by placing any public body, authority or any public institution. Thus, the jurisdiction of the UPSC can be expanded by an act of the Parliament. Annual report regarding its functioning is presented to the President who then submits it to the Parliament.

Role: The Constitution envisages a role of 'watch-dog of the merit system' in the country for the UPSC. It is concerned with recruitment to the top-most posts in the country, and it advices the government in such matters related to promotion, recruitment and transfers. But it is not concerned with other matters such as classification of services, cadre management, and training, pay and service conditions etc. These matters are handled by a separate department of Department of Personnel and Training. The role of UPSC is limited as the advice it renders is not binding on the government. It is the discretion of the government to accept or reject such recommendations.

3. **State Public Service Commission:** Parallel to the UPSC at the centre, there are State Public service commissions in the respective states. The Article 315 to 323 which govern the UPSC also governs the SPSC. These Articles contain provisions regarding the composition, powers, independence etc. regarding that of the SPSC.

   Independence: The Constitution has made the following provisions concerning the independence of SPSC, it ensures impartial and independent functioning of the body.

   1. The chairman or a member enjoys security of tenure as they can only be removed on the grounds given in the Constitution by the President.
   2. The conditions of service of the chairman or any other member cannot be varied to their disadvantage after their appointment.
   3. The expenses of the salary, allowances, and pensions of both members and the chairman are charged on the consolidated fund of the State. Thus they are not voted upon in the State assembly.
   4. The Chairman of SPSC after the end of this tenure is eligible for further employment as a member or chairman of the UPSC, but not for any other employment in either centre or state.
   5. The member of the SPSC after the end of their tenure is eligible to be appointed as the Chairman of SPSC or as a member or chairman of the UPSC, but not for any other employment in either centre or state.
   6. The Chairman or a member after the end of their tenure is not eligible for reappointment.

   Functions: The SPSC performs all such functions performed by the UPSC in the state concerned. These are as follows:

   1. It conducts exam for recruitment for any post in the state.
   2. Regarding the principles to be followed while making appointments, in promotions and transfers from one service to other.
   3. The concerned department may formulate rules regarding promotion, transfer, suitability of candidates to particular posts etc. and SPSC then ratifies such rules devised.
   4. All such disciplinary issues which affect a person serving under the state government, such matters include

- Withholding of promotion
- Withholding of increment
- Demotion
- Removal from service
- Dismissal from service
- Compulsory retirement
- Censure
- Recovery of pecuniary loss

5. Any other issues regarding the personnel management.

   The additional functions can be given to the SPSC by the state legislature. It can extend the jurisdiction of the SPSC by placing personnel system of any local body, corporate body or any other public institution. Hence, the jurisdiction of the SPSC can be extended by the act the concerned state legislature. Annual report is submitted to the Governor who the places this report before the state assembly for scrutiny.

   Role: The Constitution envisages a role of 'watch-dog of the merit system' in the state for the SPSC. It is concerned with recruitment to the top-most posts in the state, and it advices the government in such matters related to promotion, recruitment and transfers. But it is not concerned with other matters such as classification of services, cadre management, and training, pay and service conditions etc. These matters are handled by a separate department of Department of Personnel and Training. The role of SPSC is limited as the advice it renders is not binding on the government. It is the discretion of the government to accept or reject such recommendations.

4. **Finance Commission:** The Article 280 of the Constitution provides for creation of Finance Commission which is a quasi-judicial body. Every five year or at the discretion of the President the commission is constituted.

   Functions: The finance commission is required to make recommendations to the President on the following matters:

   a. The principles that should be basis for providing grant-in-aid to the states from the consolidated fund of India, by the Centre.
   b. Sharing of net-proceeds of taxes between the centre and the states and the allocation of shares between the different states concerned.
   c. Measures needed to be carried out to improve and enhance the consolidated fund of the state in order to supplement the needs of the panchayats and the municipalities as based on the recommendations from the State Finance Commission.
   d. Any other issues as referred to by the President in the interest of sound financial management.

   The report is submitted to the President who then lays it on the Parliament along with the explanatory note on the actions taken based upon its recommendations.

   Advisory Role: The recommendations of the commission are only of an advisory nature and hence government is not bound by it. It is up to the Centre to act upon the recommendations to share the resources with the states. As observed by the experts, that since the Finance Commission is a constitutional body, even though its recommendations may not be binding, the government should have a compelling reason to reject the same.

The Constitution understands that the commission will act as a balancing wheel of fiscal federalism in India. But its role has been undermined by the emergence of extra-constitutional body of the Planning Commission. And hence, the role of Finance Commission has been over shadowed by the Planning Commission which had taken over most of the roles provided to the commission.

5. **The National Commission for Scheduled Castes:** This body is directly established under the Article 338 of the Constitution of India. Other bodies such as the National commission for Minorities, the National Commission for Backward Classes, National Commission for Women, National Human Rights Commission, National Commission for Protection of Child Rights are all statutory bodies in the sense that they are created by acts of the Parliament.

Functions of the Commission: The following are the functions of the commission,

a. To investigate into and monitor all issues relating to the provisions made in the Constitution and other aspects for the SCs and to evaluate their functioning.
b. To take part and give advice in all matters concerning the planning process of socio-economic development for the SCs and to evaluate the progression of the group in the states concerned.
c. To inquire into specific complaints regarding the violation of the rights of the SCs.
d. To make recommendation to the Union or the State government to take measures in order to effectively implement the safeguards relating to the protection of the rights, welfare measures, and socio-economic development of the SCs.
e. To present annual report to the President and at any other time it seems necessary upon the working of safeguards provided to the SCs.
f. To carry out any other such function in relation to the protection, safeguard, welfare and development of the SCs as the President may recommend.

Powers of the Commission: The commission is given power to regulate its own procedure.

The commission while investigating into any matter related to any complaint received, has the power of a civil court in matters related to the following:

- To receive the evidence in an affidavit
- To summon any person from anywhere in the country and to examine such person under oath
- Requisitioning of any public record
- Issuing summons to examine documents or any witness
- Requiring the discovery and production of the necessary documents
- Any other matter which the President may specify

The centre and the state governments are requested to consult the commission before taking any major policy decisions concerning the SCs.

This commission is also vested with powers to discharge duties regarding issues concerning the other backward classes (OBCs) and the Anglo Indians. Thus, the commission has to investigate all constitutional or other legal issues for the OBCs and the Anglo-Indians and report such matter to the President about their functioning.

6. **National Commission for Scheduled Tribes:** Article 338-A establishes a separate commission for the Scheduled Tribes. Initially both the commission of SCs and STs were together under the Article 338. But they were separated by passing of the Constitutional 89th amendment Act, 2003. This amendment added the new Article 338-A to the Constitution.

   Functions of the Commission: The following are the functions of the commission,

   a. To investigate into and monitor all issues relating to the provisions made in the Constitution and other aspects for the STs and to evaluate their functioning.
   b. To take part and give advice in all matters concerning the planning process of socio-economic development for the STs and to evaluate the progression of the group in the states concerned.
   c. To inquire into specific complaints regarding the violation of the rights of the STs.
   d. To make recommendation to the Union or the State government to take measures in order to effectively implement the safeguards relating to the protection of the rights, welfare measures, and socio-economic development of the STs.
   e. To present annual report to the President and at any other time it seems necessary upon the working of safeguards provided to the STs.
   f. To carry out any other such function in relation to the protection, safeguard, welfare and development of the SCs as the President may recommend.

   Other functions of the Commission: These functions were added by the President to the commission in addition to its other functions. These are as follows:

   a. Measures to be taken to safeguard the rights of the tribal communities over the mineral resource, water resource etc. as per the law;
   b. Measures to be taken to ensure full and effective implementation of the provisions of the Panchayats (Extension to Scheduled Areas) Act, 1996.
   c. Measures to be taken to prevent the alienation of the tribal group from their land and help them effectively rehabilitate to a good location.
   d. Measures to be taken to see to it that the tribal are accorded ownership rights in respect to the minor forest produce.
   e. Measures to be taken to decrease and finally end the practice of shifting cultivation, which displaces the community and cause environmental degradation.

   Powers of the Commission: The commission is given power to regulate its own procedure.

   The commission while investigating into any matter related to any complaint received, has the power of a civil court in matters related to the following:

   - To receive the evidence in an affidavit
   - To summon any person from anywhere in the country and to examine such person under oath
   - Requisitioning of any public record
   - Issuing summons to examine documents or any witness
   - Requiring the discovery and production of the necessary documents
   - Any other matter which the President may specify

The centre and the state governments are requested to consult the commission before taking any major policy decisions concerning the STs.

7. **Comptroller and Auditor General of India:** The Constitution under Article 148 provides for an independent office of the Comptroller and Auditor General. He is the head of the audit and accounts department. He is considered to be the guardian of the public purse, and controls the entire financial system both at the centre and the states. It upholds the constitution and laws of the parliament in matters related to the financial administration. Dr. Ambedkar considered this office of CAG to be the most important office under the Constitution of India.

   Independence: The Constitution provides for the following provisions with respect to the independence of the CAG, they are as follows:

   a. He is provided with security of tenure, and can only be removed as per the provisions given under the Constitution. Hence, he does not hold the office as per the pleasure of the President even though he is appointed by him.
   b. He is not eligible to any other appointments after the end of this tenure, under the centre or the states.
   c. His salary and other emoluments are determined by the Parliament. He receives salary on par with the judge of the Supreme Court
   d. His salary or other aspects of his service cannot be varied to his disadvantage after he is appointed.
   e. The conditions of service of other officers serving in the office of audit and accounts department are prescribed by the President after the consultation with the CAG.
   f. All the administrative expenses of the office of the CAG is charged on the consolidated fund of India, hence it is not subject to vote by the Parliament.

   Further no minister can represent the CAG in the Parliament and no minister can be called to take up the responsibility of the actions carried out by the CAG.

   Duties and Powers: The Constitution under Article 149 authorises the Parliament to provide for duties and powers of the CAG in relation to accounts of the Union and the State or any other body. The Parliament has thus enacted the CAG's (Duties, powers and conditions of service) Act, 1971.

   The following are the duties and functions of the CAG as given in the Act and in the Constitution:

   a. He is given the power to audit the accounts related to all expenditure from the consolidated fund of India, the consolidated fund of the States, and consolidated fund of Union Territories having a legislative assembly;
   b. He also audits all the accounts relating to the trading, profit, manufacturing, balance sheets, profit and loss accounts or any other subsidiary accounts kept by any department of the centre or the states.
   c. To satisfy himself that the rules and procedures are followed properly by the government concerned he audits the receipts and expenditures, to have an effective control over the assessment, collection and proper allocation of the revenue.
   d. Apart from this, he also audits the accounts of contingency fund of India and public account of India, he also audits the contingency fund of the states and also public account of each state.
   e. He also audits the receipts and expenditure of the following:

- Government companies
- All bodies or corporations which receive substantial funding from either centre or the state
- Other entities concerned when required by the law

f. He carries out audit of any other department or entity, when such request is made by either the President or the Governor, for example audit of the local bodies.
g. As per **Article 150**, he advices the President on the matter of manner in which accounts have to be maintained by the government.
h. As per **Article 151**, he places the audit report before the President and the governor of the respective state concerned, who in turn places it before the Parliament or the Assembly.
i. As per **Article 279**, he determines and certifies the net proceeds of tax or duty. This certificate provided by him is the final.
j. He is considered to be the guide, friend and philosopher of the Public Accounts Committee of the Parliament.
k. He compiles and maintains all the accounts of the government. In 1976, the CAG was relieved of this duty of maintaining the account of the Central government which was handed over to the accounting department.

Three audit reports are submitted by the CAG to the President. They are, audit report on finance accounts, audit report on public undertakings, and audit report on appropriation accounts. The president places all these reports before the Parliament. The Public Accounts Committee of the Parliament then analyses and scrutinises these reports and places its findings to the Parliament.

Role: The important role is to uphold the Constitution and the laws of the Parliament in the sphere of financial administration. The accountability of the executive in the matter of finance is secured with help of the audit reports of the CAG. The CAG carries out audit on behalf of the Parliament, hence he is called as the agent of the Parliament. Therefore, he is responsible only to the Parliament.

The legal and regulatory audit is obligatory on part by the CAG, meanwhile propriety audit falls under his discretion. Propriety audit looks into the 'wisdom, faithfulness and economy' of the expenditure of the government, it comments on the wastefulness and non-essentiality of such expenditure.

8. **Attorney General of India:** Provision for office of the Attorney General is given under Article 76 of the Constitution. He is the highest law officer in the country.

Duties and functions: As the chief law officer of the country he is provided with certain essential duties, which are as follows:

a. Render opinion to the Government whenever President refers some legal issues
b. Perform other duties of legal character when it is assigned to him by the President
c. To carry out any other function as provided by the Constitution or any other law.

The President has devised the following duties for the AG:

a. To appear on behalf of the government in the Supreme Court on all matters where the government is involved.
b. To represent the government in instances where reference is made under Article 143 to the Supreme Court.

c. To appear, when requested, in any High Courts where the interests of the Government of India is concerned.

9. **Advocate General of the State:** Provision for office of the Advocate General is given under Article 165 of the Constitution. He is the highest law officer in the State, and thus he corresponds to the Attorney General of India at the centre.

   Duties and functions: As the chief law officer of the State he is provided with certain essential duties, which are as follows:

   d. Render opinion to the Government whenever Governor refers some legal issues
   e. Perform other duties of legal character when it is assigned to him by the Governor
   f. Carry out any other function as provided by the Constitution or any other law

   In course of his function, the Advocate General is entitled to appear before any court in the State.

   And further, he has the right to take part in any proceeding of both houses of the state legislature without the power to vote.

   He enjoys all the power and privileges as enjoyed by the member of the State legislature.

2.7 THREE-TIER SYSTEM OF GOVERNANCE AND TWO-TIER SYSTEM OF FEDERALISM

It is presently widely accepted that the system of local governance is essential for effective participation of the citizen's in the governance process. This system is indispensable and integral for the democracy to function effectively. This system strengthens the 'grassroots' democracy, whereby the system of government is taken to the hands of the people, and they get involved, this makes them to feel to be a part in the democratic system and it creates a sense of responsibility. Thus, in a vast, diverse and complex country like India, the system of local government and involvement of people in the governance process is administrative and political imperative.

The local self-governing institutions in India are called the Panchayats in villages and Municipalities in cities and towns. This was to enable the process of democratic decentralisation, and it was considered to be an instrument of popular participation. This was thought to bring in the people who were not touched by the formal system of government. It took the government to the door steps of the people. It wanted the people to be the part of the development process which concerned them. The following is based on the Report of the Working group on the Panchayati Raj and Rural governance, by the Planning Commission and Ministry of Panchayati Raj, Government of India.

2.7.1 Evolution of Local Governance in India

2.7.1.1 Pre-British Local Governance

India's old sacred books and historical sources mention village communities (councils or assemblies) across the sub-continent that were self-governing over millennia, serving as the main interface between the predominantly agrarian village economies and the higher authorities. Custom and tradition elevated these earlier councils or assemblies, called sabha, to a position of considerable authority. Slowly, they assumed the form of the Panchayat (an assembly of five respected elders). These panchayats became the pivot of administration, the focus of social solidarity and the principal forum for dispensation of justice and resolution of local disputes. During the medieval and Mughal periods these characteristics of the village panchayats remained unchanged.

2.7.1.2 Pre-Independence Panchayats

Several steps were taken during British rule in India towards setting-up formal local bodies. In urban areas, a municipal corporation came to be formed in Madras – on the British model of a town council – as early as 1687.

In 1870, Lord Mayo (Governor General-in-Council) secured the passage of a resolution for the decentralization of power aimed at bringing about greater administrative efficiency in meeting the demands of the people but primarily designed to augment imperial finances. At about the same time, a significant first step towards reviving the traditional village panchayat system in Bengal was taken through the Bengal Chowkidari Act, 1870, which empowered District Magistrates to set up Panchayats of nominated members in the villages.

- The Magna Carta of local democracy in British India was the Ripon Resolution of 1882 providing for rural local boards with two-thirds of membership to be composed of elected, non-official representatives and presided over by a non-official Chairperson.
- Actual progress in implementation was slow but the role of rural local administration was elevated; and the term, self-government gained currency.
- In 1906, the Indian National Congress, under the president-ship of Dadabhai Naoroji, affirmed self-government as the political goal for the country.
- In 1907, the government constituted a six-member Royal Commission on decentralisation with Shri R.C. Dutt as its only Indian member.
- The Report of this commission – released in 1909 – elaborated the principles enunciated in the Ripon Resolution and recognised the importance of Panchayats in the governance of India.
- In the same year (1909), the twenty-fourth session of the Congress at Lahore adopted a resolution urging the government to take early steps to make all local bodies from village Panchayats upwards elective with elected non-official chairmen and to support them with adequate financial aid.
- At its twenty-eighth session in December 1913 in Karachi, the Congress adopted a resolution regretting that decentralization had remained largely on paper.
- In her presidential address at the Congress session in Calcutta in 1917, Dr. Annie Besant blamed the inefficient bureaucracy for not doing even the little that was suggested in the Report of the Royal Commission on Decentralisation.

The Montagu-Chelmsford Reforms of 1919 made local self-government – under the proposed scheme of Dyarchy – a transferred subject bringing self-government under the domain of Indian Ministers in the provinces. To make local self-government both fully representative and responsible, the Montagu-Chelmsford reforms suggested that there should be (as far as possible) complete popular control in local bodies and the largest possible independence for them from outside control.

The Government of India Act, 1935 and the inauguration of provincial autonomy under it marked another crucial stage in the evolution of panchayats. With popularly elected governments in the Provinces, almost all provincial administrations enacted legislation for further democratization of local self-government institutions, including the village Panchayats.

2.7.1.3 Constitutional Provision in 1950

Following Independence, the first draft of India's Constitution did not include any provision for the Panchayats even though Gandhiji had sought to make village Panchayats the very foundation of democracy in independent India. President of the Constituent Assembly, Dr. Rajendra Prasad, drew attention of the Law Minister, Dr. B.R. Ambedkar, to this lacuna in a letter dated 10 May 1948, initiating discussion and debate both outside and within the Constituent Assembly. This eventually led to the passage of an amendment proposed by the well-known Gandhian, Shri K. Santhanam, on 25 November 1948 including village Panchayats in Part IV of the Constitution containing non-mandatory Directive Principles of State Policy. The amendment which was eventually numbered as Article 40 reads: **The state shall take steps to organise village panchayats and endow them with such power and authority as may be necessary to enable them to function as units of self government**.

2.7.1.4 Community Development Project, 1952 and the Panchayats

Community Development (CD) projects were inaugurated in 1952 and were modelled after the earlier experiments at Shantiniketan, Baroda (Vadodara), and Nilokheri. However, the dynamic driving force behind the CD movement, Minister S.K. Dey, was of the consistent view that CD projects could not achieve their full potential in the absence of effective institutions for people's participation.

Balwantrai Mehta Committee: In 1957, a historic breakthrough in establishing Panchayati Raj was effected through the Report of the Balwantrai Mehta Committee which recommended:

- Public participation in community works should be organized through statutory representative bodies.
- It was of the view that without an agency at the village level that could represent the entire community, assume responsibility and provide the necessary leadership for implementing development programmes, real progress in rural development could not come about at all.

Subsequently, National Development Council (NDC) endorsed the basic principles of democratic decentralization enunciated in the Balwantrai Mehta report and laid on the States the duty of working out the structures suitable to each state. It was during this period that the term Panchayati Raj gained currency as a process of governance organically linking the will of the people from the Gram Sabha to the Lok Sabha. Prime Minister Nehru inaugurated the three-tier Panchayati Raj in Nagaur, Rajasthan on 2 October, 1959.

Jayaprakash Narayan Committee: The Jayaprakash Narayan Committee spoke of the contradictory positions developing within the government in respect of Panchayati Raj, pointing out that: After having accepted Panchayati Raj as the agency responsible for planning and execution of plans…there is no longer any valid reason for continuing individual allocations subject-wise even to serve as a guide.

The Ministry of Community Development was brought under the Ministry of Food and Agriculture, and in 1971 the title 'Community Development' was dropped and replaced by 'Rural Development'.

Ashok Mehta Committee: By the early seventies, however, the Panchayats had gone from a phase of early ascendancy to one of decline and stagnation. The Asoka Mehta Committee (formed in 1978) made far reaching recommendations to amend the situation and recommended that Panchayati Raj be included in the Constitution. In keeping with the spirit of the Asoka Mehta Committee recommendations, some states – including West Bengal, Karnataka and Andhra Pradesh – revisited their respective Panchayati Raj systems and undertook several new initiatives to endow local bodies with more powers which served as a prime inspiration and example for subsequent reform.

The West Bengal Panchayat Act, 1973 (West Bengal Act XLI of 1973) brought some fresh air in the Panchayat system. Direct elections in all three tiers (through universal adult franchise) had to be held at regular intervals. They were made mandatory, without any discretionary power of any authority to postpone such elections indefinitely. Powers to collect tax and non-tax revenue were clearly defined. Functional domain of the Panchayats was more clearly delineated as compared to the earlier Panchayats. The new legislation empowered the Panchayats in various fields of activities encompassing rural life. Mandal Panchayats – as envisaged in the Asoka Mehta Committee – exist only in Andhra Pradesh, though, in addition to the Village Panchayats.

Constitution 73rd Amendment Act: The Congress government under Prime Minister P.V. Narasimha Rao introduced the 72nd (Panchayats) and 73rd (Nagarpalikas) Constitution Amendment Bills based substantially on the Bills moved in the Eighth Lok Sabha by Shri Rajiv Gandhi but also incorporating some of the changes wrought by the National Front Government. These two Bills were referred to a Joint Select Committee of the Parliament which effected some further changes but conforming considerably to the earlier 1989 initiative.

The Lok Sabha and the Rajya Sabha passed both Bills on the 22 and 23 December 1992, respectively. By the time the Parliament passed the two Bills, their sequence changed to 73rd and 74th, respectively. Following their ratification by more than half the State Assemblies, as required under the Constitution, the President of India gave his assent; the Acts came into force as the Constitution (Seventy-third Amendment) Act, 1992 on 24th April 1993 and the Constitution (Seventy-fourth Amendment) Act, 1992 on 1st June 1993. This added two new parts to the Constitution, namely, Part IX titled The Panchayats – and Part IXA titled The Municipalities.

Fifth Schedule Areas and PESA: The Fifth Schedule to the Constitution (Article 244) relates to administration and control of the scheduled areas and scheduled tribes other than those in North-East States. PESA was enacted in 1996 which extended Part IX of the Constitution to the Schedule V Areas. PESA promotes people-centric governance and provides a central role to the Gram Sabha. Chapter 10 of this document discusses in detail Sch. V and PESA.

Local self-governance in the NE states

The legal framework of LSG in North Eastern Region (NER) broadly comprises three typologies:

(i) Sixth Schedule Frame (Meghalaya, parts of Assam, Mizoram and Tripura)
(ii) State Legislation Frame (Nagaland and non-Council Areas in Mizoram)
(iii) National Frame (Arunachal Pradesh, Sikkim, Manipur excluding hill areas and non-Council areas in Assam and Tripura).

Each tribal area mentioned in Para 20 of the Sixth Schedule is designated as an autonomous district. The area inhabited by each of the tribes in a district may be carved out as autonomous region. Each autonomous district is governed by a District Council and autonomous region by a Regional Council. This unique Council frame comprises the third tier of legislature for Tribal Areas about Sixth Schedule matters. These Councils endowed with legislative, judicial and executive powers virtually function as a state within state.

State of the Panchayats Reports (SoPRs): The SoPRs (published in 2006, 2008 and 2010 respectively) show that, overall, the mandatory provisions specified in the Constitution have been implemented in the last decade and a half. All Part IX States (elections in Jharkhand held up till recently due to a court case) held regular elections through the State Election Commissions. All the states have implemented reservation for women, SCs and STs (the most have reservation for OBCs as well), bringing almost 1.6 million representatives from these groups into elected positions making the Panchayats the nursery of future leadership. State Finance Commissions have been constituted and in many States, their recommendations have been acted upon. All the states (excluding Uttarakhand & Jharkhand) have constituted DPCs and the most have initiated decentralised planning processes.

However, implementation of the Constitutional provisions – which were left to the discretion of the States – varies greatly. The most important aspect in strengthening of the Panchayats is the devolution of 3Fs (i.e., functions, funds and functionaries) related to the matters listed in the Eleventh Schedule of the Constitution. Another is the enablement of their function of preparing and implementing bottom up participatory plans for economic development and social justice. The states vary a great deal in both these respects. While some states have forged new paths, others are still to catch up. Of course, many states are trying out new approaches and mechanisms, and making corrections along the way.

Why are the Panchayats functioning sub-optimally?

The root cause is that the Panchayats are not seen as local governments with clear roles. This leads to:

Grossly inadequate devolution: Many states have not taken effective steps to devolve 3Fs to the PRIs to enable them to discharge their constitutionally stipulated function. Further, it is imperative that the PRIs have financial resources and manpower to match the responsibilities entrusted to them. While SFCs have submitted their recommendations, not many states have implemented these or taken steps to ensure PRI's fiscal viability.

Parallel systems: Parallel systems and organizations set up under various Central/State developmental programmes have further sapped strength of the Panchayats, pared away their legitimate functional space and even encroached upon their political space.

Excessive control by bureaucracy: In some states, the Gram Panchayats have been placed in a position of subordination: Gram Panchayat Sarpanches have to spend extraordinary amount of time visiting Block Offices for funds and/or technical approval. These interactions with the Block staff/office distort the role of a Sarpanch as elected representative.

Tied nature of funds: Activities permitted under the schemes are not always appropriate for all parts of the district. This results in unsuitable activities being promoted or an under-spend of the funds.

Reluctance to use fiscal powers: An important power devolved to GP is the right to levy tax on property, business, markets, fairs and also for services provided, like street lighting or public toilets, etc. Very few Panchayats use their fiscal power to levy and collect taxes. The argument pushed by Panchayat-heads is that it is difficult to levy tax on your own constituency, especially when one lives in the community. But when Panchayats do not raise resources and instead receive funds from outside, people are less likely to request a social audit.

Status of the Gram Sabha: Empowering the Gram Sabhas could have been a powerful weapon for transparency, accountability and for involvement of the marginalized sections. However, a number of the State Acts have not spelt the powers of the Gram Sabhas nor have any procedures been laid down for the functioning of these bodies or penalties for the officials.

Strategies to improve the functioning of the Panchayats

1. **Empowerment:**
   - Ensuring progressive devolution of functions, funds and functionaries (3Fs) upon the Panchayati Raj Institutions (PRIs).
   - Institutionalising GP-level dispute resolution mechanism.
   - Enhancing reservation for women PRIs and also their leadership quality.
   - Implementing PESA effectively.
   - Deepening decentralized governance in the 6th Schedule Areas.
2. **Enablement:**
   - Building the organizational capacity of PRIs and the professional capacity of Elected Representatives and Official Functionaries so that they can perform their mandated roles efficiently.
   - Institutionalising and using integrated decentralized participatory planning through the PRIs and DPCs for convergence of plethora of schemes and pooling of diverse resources for better outcomes.
   - Restructuring the Backward Region Grant Fund (BRGF) Programme to position the Panchayats as effective platform for mitigating regional backwardness.
   - Reviewing and upscaling the rural business hubs to promote the role of the Panchayats in economic development.
3. **Accountability:**
   - Positioning the Gram Sabhas at the core of PRIs for true self-governance and ensuring transparency and accountability of the Gram Panchayats.
   - Devising institutions, systems and processes for enhancing efficiency, transparency and accountability of the PRIs.
   - Implementing e-Panchayat in a mission mode.

By introducing these reforms the Panchayati Raj Institutions can be made effective and functional. It can help to bring about development of the people at the grassroots. It can also make the people participate in the governing process and thereby making the administration accountable to them.

3 Indian Parliament

LEARNING OBJECTIVES

In this Chapter, you will learn about:

- Basics of Indian Parliament
- Issues of Recent Concern in Parliamentary Functions

3.1 BASICS OF INDIAN PARLIAMENT

3.1.1 Introduction

> "*The people elect you to rulership, the wide glorious quarters elect you. Be seated on this high point in the body of the state and from there vigorously distribute the natural wealth and material prosperity to the people*"
>
> —Atharva Veda

The democratic governments across the world are majorly classified into parliamentary and presidential form, based on the nature of relation between the organs (i.e, the executives and the legislatives) of their government. In the parliamentary form of government, the executives take care of the legislature by framing the policies and acts and so can be held accountable by the legislature. Whereas, in the presidential form, the executive is not responsible to the legislature for its policies and acts, and thus independent of the legislature.

One of the most defining and distinguishing feature of parliamentary form of government is that the council of ministers are drawn from the legislature itself and the continuance of their office is contingent upon the support of the legislature. Thus, they should enjoy majority support from the legislature, and they are collectively held responsible to the lower house of the Parliament, which is directly elected by the people.

In the Parliamentary system of India, the leader of majority party in the Lok Sabha – or the House of the People – is chosen to head the government, and he becomes the Prime minister. Rest of the council of ministers are appointed by the President on the recommendation of the Prime Minister, and these ministers are members of either house of the Parliament, in case they are not, they have to become member of either house within 6 months from the date of appointment. The Prime Minister and his Council should enjoy the support of the Lower House, this house has the power to remove the government by passing a no-confidence motion against it. When such no-confidence motion is passed, it may lead to resignation of the government and paves way to the formation of a new government or fresh elections in case no party/coalition could form a stable government.

There is also a major difference in who heads the government and the state. In the parliamentary government, one heads the government and another person heads the state. On the other hand, both the government and the state are headed by the same person (the president) in the presidential government.

The parliamentary government is also called the Westminster model of government, cabinet government or responsible government and this form of government is being followed in Britain, India, Canada, Japan and many other countries. The parliamentary system originated in the British parliament which is located in Westminster and hence named 'Westminster model'. Parliamentary government is called a cabinet government because the cabinet (executive) is the main core of the parliamentary system. It is also known as 'responsible government', since the cabinet (executives) is held responsible by the legislature (parliament) and holds office as long as it enjoys the confidence of the latter.

The British system of government can be described as the 'prime ministerial government', because the power, influence and position of the prime minister have increased drastically off late. The same applies in the Indian context as well.

3.1.2 Why India Chose Parliamentary Government?

The Indian constitution provides for a parliamentary form of government both at the centre (Articles 74, 75) and in the states (Articles 163, 164). But while framing the Indian constitution, a dilemma whether to choose parliamentary or presidential system prevailed amongst the constituent assembly. Finally, the British parliamentary system was agreed upon by the founding fathers in consensus. The reasons were already dealt in the Chapter 'General Framework of Governance', it is explained in brief as follows:

1. Since the parliamentary system has been in operation in India since the British rule, the constitution makers felt the familiarity with the system.
2. A democratic executive must satisfy two conditions: stability and responsibility. The Draft constitution in recommending the parliamentary system of executive has preferred responsibility to stability, as stated by Dr B R Ambedkar. This point from Ambedkar, the father of Indian Constitution, shows the preference given to a responsible government which is provided by the parliamentary system.
3. The constitution framers thought that a just-born democracy could not afford to take the risk of a feud or conflict between its organ of government (executive v. legislative), which is prone to happen in presidential system, prevalent in USA. So they looked upon a government which would act conducive and supportive to its organs and go hand in hand for the development of the country.
4. The heterogeneity of Indian states proves to be one of the most complex plural societies in the world. Keeping this in mind, the framers of our constitution chose parliamentary system, as it gives greater possibility for representation of various sections, interests and regions of the country. They also sighted that this might promote a national spirit among the people and build a united India.

3.1.3 Features of Indian Parliament

Parliament is the supreme legislative body of India. The Indian Parliament comprises of the President and the two Houses – Rajya Sabha (Council of States) and Lok Sabha (House of the People).

The Indian parliamentary government has the following features:

3.1.3.1 De Jure and De Facto Executives

In India, there are both nominal and real executives. The President is the nominal (*de jure*) executive and the prime minister is the real (*de facto*) executive. The prime minister is the head of the government, while the president is the head of the State. The president exercises his power with the aid and advice provided by the council of ministers headed by the prime minister.

3.1.3.2 Majority Party Rule

In the Lok Sabha elections, the party which secures majority seats will be asked to form the government. A prime minister is chosen amongst the party members and he/she is appointed by the president. The council of ministers is also appointed by the president but on the advice of the prime minister.

When no single party can prove majority in the elections, the president can invite a coalition of parties to form the government.

3.1.3.3 Collective Responsibility

Collective responsibility is considered as the core principle of parliamentary government. Article 75 of the constitution states that the ministers are responsible to the Parliament in general and to the Lok Sabha in particular. It means that the Lok Sabha can remove the council of ministers including the prime minister (collectively called ministry) from the office by passing a vote of no confidence.

3.1.3.4 Political Homogeneity

In general, the members of the council of ministers belong to the same political party, so it is expected from them to share the same political ideology. If in the case of coalition government, the ministers are bound by consensus.

3.1.3.5 Dual Membership

The ministers enjoy double membership, that is, they are the members of both the legislature and the executive, meaning, a person cannot be a minister without being a member of the Parliament.

The Constitution states that a minister loses his ministership if he/she does not become a member of the parliament within six months from his appointment.

3.1.3.6 Prime Minister – The Leader

The Prime minister is the leader of council of ministers, leader of the party in power and the leader of the parliament. He plays the leadership role in the parliamentary system of government. He plays a crucial role in the functioning of the government.

3.1.3.7 The Dissolution

The executives in parliamentary system enjoy the right to dissolve the legislature. Before the expiry of the term of Lok Sabha (the lower house), the prime minister can advise the president to dissolve the lower house and hold fresh elections. Simply put, the Lok Sabha can be dissolved by the president on recommendation of the prime minister.

3.1.3.8 Secrecy

The ministers are asked to take an oath of secrecy, administered by the President, before entering their office. They operate on the principle of secrecy and cannot disclose information about their proceedings, decisions and policies.

3.1.4 Powers and Functions of the Parliament

Being the supreme legislative authority of India, the Parliament and the President hold several powers.

3.1.4.1 Office of The President

The President of India is a major component of Parliament. He/she is elected, from a group of nominees, by the elected members of the Parliament of India (Lok Sabha and Rajya Sabha) as well as of the state legislatures, and serves for a term of five years.

Historically, ruling party (majority in the Lok Sabha) nominees have been elected and run largely uncontested. A formula is used to allocate votes so there is a balance between the population of each state and the number of votes assembly members from a state can cast, and to give an equal balance between state Assembly members and national Parliament members.

If no candidate receives a majority of votes, there is a system by which losing candidates are eliminated from the contest and votes for them transferred to other candidates, until one gains a majority.

a. **Powers and Duties of the President**
   - He summons and prorogues the sessions of both houses of the Parliament.
   - He can even dissolve the Lok Sabha (under the recommendation of the Prime Minister).
   - A bill passed by the Parliament can become a law only after the consent of the President.
   - The President can use the power of **Pocket Veto** if he disagrees with a bill (the Indian Constitution does not specify a time limit for action to be taken by the President on a bill sent to him/her by the Parliament. Thus, by indefinitely postponing taking action on a bill, the president effectively vetoes it).
   - However, if a President receives a bill he/she had previously vetoed and sent back to Parliament, where such a veto has been overruled by another Parliamentary vote, then such a bill becomes an act within fourteen days of the President's receiving it – regardless of his/her subsequent action/inaction.
   - At the commencement of the first session after each general election of the Lok Sabha and at the commencement of the first session of each year, the president addresses both houses of the Parliament sitting together.
   - He can nominate two members to the Lok Sabha from the Anglo-Indian community if he or she feels that the community is not adequately represented.
   - He also nominates 12 members to the Rajya Sabha which consist of persons having special knowledge or practical experience in respect of such matters as the following, namely literature, science, sports, art and social service.
   - Articles 111 and 368 deal about the legislative powers of the President.
   - When a bill is passed by both the houses of the Parliament and is sent for the assent of the President, he can send back the bill for reconsideration to the Parliament unless it is a money bill or a constitutional amendment bill.
   - In case of the returned bill, when the Parliament again passes such bill with or without amendments, and sent to the President again for reconsideration, he has to pass such bill and cannot refuse to give assent.
   - Example of such an instance is when the Parliament Disqualification – Amendment Bill, 2006 as passed by both the houses and was returned by the President for reconsideration, it was again passed by both the houses and thus the President had to give

assent to the bill. But there is no time limit which has been specified within which the President has to give his assent in case of ordinary bills.

- Under Article 123, the President is empowered to promulgate ordinances when either of the houses is not in session. It has the same validity and power of a bill ordinarily passed by the Parliament.
- Such an ordinance ceases to operate if the Parliament does not approve it within 6 weeks of its date of sitting.

3.1.4.2 Lok Sabha (The Lower House)

Lok Sabha is also known as the 'House of the People' or the lower house. The Constitution provides that the maximum strength of the House be 552 members. The duration of the lower house, unless it is dissolved sooner, is for five years from the date of its first meeting and it cannot be extended in any case. As per Article 83, the Lok Sabha gets automatically dissolved at the end of five years.

The territorial constituencies from which the members are elected are fixed time to time by the Parliament subject to the condition that the number of such members is limited to 550 until the next census of 2026, as per Article 81.

All the members of the Lok Sabha (except two nominated members) are elected by citizens of India, anyone who is above 18 years of age, irrespective of gender, caste, religion or race, who is otherwise not disqualified to vote for the Lok Sabha.

To be eligible for membership in the Lok Sabha, a person must be a citizen of India and must be 25 years of age or older, mentally sound, should not be bankrupt and should not be criminally convicted. The total elective membership is distributed among the States in such a way that the ratio between the number of seats allotted to each State and the population of the State is, so far as practicable, the same for all states.

A total of 131 seats (18.42%) are reserved for representatives of Scheduled Castes (84) and Scheduled Tribes (47) only.

a. **Power and Duties of Lok Sabha**

Lok Sabha has certain powers that make it more powerful than the Rajya Sabha.

- In matters pertaining to non-financial (ordinary) bills, after the bill has been passed by the House where it was originally tabled (Lok Sabha or Rajya Sabha), it is sent to the other house, where it may be kept for a maximum period of 6 months. If the other House rejects the bill or a period of 6 months elapses without any action by that House, or the House that originally tabled the bill does not accept the recommendations made by the members of the other house, it results in a deadlock. This is resolved by a joint session of both Houses, presided over by the Speaker of the Lok Sabha and a decision is taken with a simple majority. The will of the Lok Sabha normally prevails in these matters, as its strength is more than double that of the Rajya Sabha.
- Money bills (a bill that involves government spending) can only be introduced in the Lok Sabha, and upon being passed, are sent to the Rajya Sabha, where it can be deliberated on for up to 14 days. If not rejected by the Rajya Sabha, or 14 days lapse from the introduction of the bill in the Rajya Sabha without any action by the House, or recommendations made by the Rajya Sabha are not accepted by the Lok Sabha, the bill is considered passed. The budget is presented in the Lok Sabha by the Finance Minister in the name of the President of India.

- The Lok Sabha shares equal powers with the upper house – Rajya Sabha in the following issues:
  - In initiating and passing any bill for constitutional amendment (by a majority of the total membership of the House and at least two-third majority of the members present and voting).
  - In initiating and passing a motion for the impeachment of the President (by two-third of the membership of the House).
  - In the impeachment of the judges of the Supreme Court and the state High Courts (by a majority of the membership of the House and at least two-thirds majority of the members present and voting).
  - Passing a resolution declaring war or national emergency (by two-third majority) or constitutional emergency (by simple majority) in a state.
- If the Lok Sabha is dissolved before or after the declaration of a National Emergency, the Rajya Sabha becomes the sole Parliament. It cannot be dissolved. This is a limitation on the Lok Sabha. But there is a possibility that president can exceed the term to not more than 1 year under the proclamation of emergency and the same would be lowered down to six-month if the said proclamation ceases to operate.
- Motion of no confidence against the government can be introduced and passed in the Lok Sabha. If passed by a majority vote, the Prime Minister and the Council of Ministers resign collectively. The Rajya Sabha has no power over such a motion, and hence no real power over the executive. However, the Prime Minister may threaten to dissolute the Lok Sabha and recommend this to the President, forcing an untimely general election. The President normally accepts this recommendation made by the Prime Minister, unless he is convinced otherwise that the Lok Sabha might recommend a new Prime Minister by casting a majority vote. Thus, both the executive and the legislature in India have checks and balances over each other.

3.1.4.3 Rajya Sabha (The Upper House)

The Rajya Sabha is also known as 'Council of States' or the Upper House. The first sitting of the Rajya Sabha was on 3rd April, 1952 with 216 members. Rajya Sabha is a permanent body and is not subject to dissolution. However, one third of the members retire every second year, and are replaced by newly elected members. Each member is elected for a term of six years. Its members are indirectly elected by members of legislative bodies of the states. Each member has a term of 6 years and elections are held for one-third of the seats after every 2 years. 238 members are to be elected from states and union territories and 12 are to be nominated by the President of India. The minimum age for a person to become a member of Rajya Sabha is 30 years. The fourth schedule governs the allocation of seats for the states and the union territories.

- Representatives of states are elected by the elected members of the Legislative Assembly of the state in accordance with system of proportional representation by means of single transferable vote.
- Representatives of union territories are indirectly elected by members of an electoral college for that territory in accordance with system of proportional representation. Except Delhi and Puducherry, no other Union territory has representation in the Rajya Sabha.

- As per Article 64, the Vice-President of India is the ex-officio chairman of the Rajya Sabha. But he is not the member of the house, and in case any member of the house is elected as the Vice-President he has to vacate his seat in the house.

The Council of States is designed to maintain the federal character of the country.

a. **Special Powers of Rajya Sabha**

Apart from sharing equal powers with respect to ordinary bills, initiating and passing of Constitutional amendment bill and other matters, the Upper house has some exclusive powers. Mainly it was created as a check against arbitrary nature of the lower house. It was called as 'Wise-Chamber' where it was believed that the Upper House with its wisdom and experience guides the lower house. The special powers of Rajya Sabha are as follows:

- As per Article 249, the Rajya Sabha has the power to authorize Parliament to legislate in matters given in the state list in nature of public interest.
- Under Article 312, the Rajya Sabha has the power to create a new All-India Service which is common to both the Centre and the States.

b. **The Need for the Second Chamber**

The system of Bicameral legislature was first set up in India in 1921 under the Government of India Act, 1919. The Government of India Act, 1935 retained the bicameral system. The need for having a second chamber was deliberated elaborately in the constituent assembly. And the overwhelming view of the members of the chamber was to retain in the bicameral system. The following are some of the key points of debate that took place in the constituent assembly:

- The Upper House was considered to be a house of deep reflection and revision which was to be unswayed by the election politics.
- Being a federal chamber and permanent house, that is, not being subject to dissolution, the council of state can effectively counter the direct representative of peoples in the lower house.
- Member of Constituent Assembly, Nazimuddin Ahmad, stated that the second chamber 'introduces an element of sobriety and second thought'. The Parliament of a sovereign nation has to deal with foreign and domestic matters of extreme importance which justifies the need for a second chamber.
- To quote Nazimmudin Ahmad, '*In these circumstances it will be wise for us to have two houses. A popular House is known for its vitality and vigour and that House will have the exclusive power in regard to money. But a second chamber introduces an element of sobriety and second thought, it would be wise for us, especially in view of many foreign subjects which are looming large in our minds, to have a second chamber*'.
- Other members of the Constituent Assembly were of the view that the second chamber would be a reflective and revising chamber.
- Speaking in the Constituent Assembly, Gopalaswami Ayyangar stated that the second chamber would '*hold dignified debates on important issues and delay legislations which might be the outcome of the passions of the moment and checkmate the hasty legislation*'.
- The second chamber was considered to represent the federal character of the country.
- Another member of the assembly, Loknath Misra, wanted the Council of States to be like that of the Senate in USA with equal representation of all states in it.

- Ananthsayanam Ayyangar contended that the second chamber would provide opportunity to people who are interested in politics but unwilling to join in the election process.
- Ultimately it was agreed that the Upper house would be the representative and protector of the interests of the State. With such provision, it would be impossible to represent the interest of the states in the Union legislature.

3.1.5 Role of Indian Parliament

Some of the major roles performed by the parliament are as follows:

3.1.5.1 Legislative Role

The Parliament makes laws on all subjects listed in the Union List. It can also make laws on subjects listed under the Concurrent List. In case there is any conflict or overlapping in the provisions existing in the Union and State enactment, the Union law prevails. In cases when an emergency has been declared, the Union Parliament can also make laws on subjects that fall within the State List. Thus, the legislative power of the Parliament is very wide and far-reaching, they are only curtailed by the Judiciary in case such legislations goes beyond the provisions of the Constitution.

3.1.5.2 Financial Role

The Parliament has been given exclusive powers to provide procedures through which revenue can be raised for the public services. And to achieve that, it imposes taxes and ensures that the money sanctioned for expenditure to various departments of the government has been used for the authorized purposes only. The Budget for the entire country is presented and passed by the Parliament, it includes almost all the important offices of public importance. And in every such budget there is increase or introduction of new taxes which affect the people.

The Parliament also takes decision of allocation of funds, grant-in-aid to the states based on the reports of the Finance Commission, and erstwhile Planning Commission. Thus, the Parliament through the committees like Public Accounts Committee, Committee on Public Undertakings, etc. scrutinizes the report submitted by the Comptroller and Auditor General to keep a check on the executive action. Hence, in the sphere of finance, the Parliament has a very important role to play.

3.1.5.3 Providing and Exercising Control Over Cabinet

Our Parliamentary system blends the legislative and the executive organs of the State in as much as the executive power is wielded by a group of Members of the Legislature who command majority in the Lok Sabha.

To be more specific, the government functions through various ministries under the charge of different ministries. The Parliament provides the ministers and holds them responsible to the elected representatives of the people. The Ministers could be a member of either of the two Houses of the Parliament. The actual execution of government policies as decided by the Parliament is carried out by the bureaucracy headed by a Secretary of the Department.

The Lok Sabha can also pass number of motions censuring the actions of the executives. The ultimate weapon in the hands of the Parliament is the no-confidence motion, which if passed will lead to the resignation of the government.

3.1.5.4 Assessment of the Work of the Cabinet

The Parliament provides the forum through which it ensures that the Cabinet remains in power only as long as it commands majority support in the Lok Sabha which comprises elected representatives of the people. It is one of the most important functions of the Parliament to bring about discussions and critical assessments of the performance of the government departments.

The debates ensure that the weaknesses in terms of performance are brought to light and the ministers and through them the entire executive machinery is kept on toes. There are also number of committees set up by the Parliament to keep check on the executive action, some of the committees are Estimates committee, Committee on Privileges, Ethics Committee, Committee on Subordinate Legislation, Business Advisory Committee, Rules Committee, General Purpose Committee etc.

3.1.5.5 Wide Representation

The parliament provides representation to all sections and regions in the country ensuring that the nation gets to know about various alternative points of view. Such representation ensures that the diversity of the nation is represented and the issues of all section of the society are effectively addressed in the Parliament.

3.1.5.6 An Organ of Information

Parliament is the most powerful organ so far as the information about the functioning of the government is concerned. The information provided in the Houses is authoritative and ministers are bound to provide information on matters of government when so desired by the members. Such information is made public through the media or under the Right to Information Act. Sharing of information is vital in a democracy as it will ensure transparency and will lead to the establishment of good governance, which will ultimately benefit the people.

3.1.5.7 Constitutional Role

The power to amend the Constitution vests with the Parliament. Constitutional amendments can be initiated by either of the house and have to be passed by each house by a majority of total membership as well as by two-third majority of members present in voting. In some cases amendments need ratification from half of the Legislative assemblies of the States. There are three types of bills for constitutional amendment which requires:

a. Simple majority: majority of members present and voting.
b. Special majority: two thirds of the members of the present and voting in each of the house.
c. Special majority with consent from half of all the state legislatures: Needs special majority in both the houses along with at least half of the state legislatures giving the consent for the bill.

Such an amending power of the Parliament is not ultimate and absolute. In the following matters, it requires the ratification of legislatures of half of the States.

- Election of the President
- Extent of the executive power of the Union
- Extent of executive power of the states
- Powers relating to Supreme Court and High courts
- Distribution of legislative powers

- Representation of the states in the parliament
- Provision relating to Article 368

Apart from these, the Parliament cannot amend the 'Basic Structure' of the Parliament. Based on the judgment of Supreme Court in *Kesavananda Bharati* case, it was held that the 'Basic Structure' of the constitution cannot be altered. Later when the legislature tried to override this judgment by enacting the 42nd Amendment, the Supreme Court came down again and declared such provision to be unconstitutional in the *Minerva Mills* case. The Supreme Court stated that the power of judicial review was one of the basic features and it cannot be taken away.

3.1.5.8 Judicial Role

Parliament has the exclusive powers to impeach the President and remove judges of the Supreme Court and the High Courts through a prescribed procedure. Parliament can also punish a person for contempt or defamation of the House. It can also punish its members or outsiders for the breach of privilege or its contempt. Thus, it plays a quasi-judicial role in such occasions and such powers have been conferred by the Constitution itself.

3.1.5.9 Elective Role

Elected members of the Rajya Sabha and the Lok Sabha constitute the electoral college for the election of the Vice-President. Along with elected members of the State Legislatures, they form the electoral college for election to the office of the President. Therefore, they have also such elective role to play apart from their other important roles. Election of President is of paramount importance, though not directly elected by the people, he is elected through their representatives. It thus places greater responsibility in part of the Parliamentarians to choose such person whom the people would choose. Parliament thus plays an important role in the electoral process.

3.1.5.10 Role in Creation of States

The Parliament can also by legislation create new states or make changes in the existing boundaries and alter the name of the states. Our Constitution though a federal entity, leans more towards the Centre. The federal system is considered to be 'destructible States of indestructible Union'. Thus, the boundaries, names, territorial extent etc. of a state can always be changed, and such a power is in the hands of the Parliament and not the states themselves. Even if the states are not interested or against such move, they have no power under the Constitution to challenge it. Thus, the Parliament has been bestowed with the ultimate power to create or alter boundaries of the States.

3.1.5.11 Role Played by the Parliament to Address the Grievances of the Public

The meaning of the term Parliament implies that it is a place of discussion of public affairs. The issues which are raised receive due consideration, and the government has to respond to such issues. There are number of devices available to the member to raise question, start discussion, seek information, and put forth the needs and aspirations of the people. The following are some of the devices used:

- Questions
- Motions
- Resolutions
- Short duration discussion

- Calling attention motion
- Special mention
- Discussion on Motion of thanks to the President which is addressed to both houses assembled together
- Motion of no-confidence and confidence in the Council of Ministers
- Discussions on bills
- Zero hour
- Half-hour discussion

All these enable the members to effectively redress the grievances of the people. There are also number of committees such as the Committee on Public Petitions, Finance committees, Welfare of OBCs, Empowerment of Women, Welfare of SCs and STs, on Subordinate legislation, and various Department-related Standing Committees etc.

Thus, all these devices help to highlight the needs of the public before the government. The government cannot ignore issues raised through such fora, because it will be adverse to public interest. Thus, parliament plays an important role to redress the grievances of the public.

3.1.5.12 Other Roles

- Discussion of various issues of national and international importance
- Imposing emergency
- Creation or abolition of state legislature, etc.

The Parliament is considered to the nerve-centre of the democratic politics in India. The Council of Ministers is drawn from the Parliament and they are collectively responsible to the Lower House – Lok Sabha. The Parliament has the sole power to amend the Constitution and legislate. Parliament articulates the needs, aspiration, pain, and the suffering of the people. The accountability of the executive is secured by the Parliament. They question the administrative actions and the wrong-doings. The Council of Ministers who are members of both the Executive and the Legislature, is considered to be 'a hyphen which joins a buckle which fastens the legislative part of the state with the executive part'. This organic connection between the executive and the legislature can also be described in the words of Woodrow Wilson, 'the ministers to lead the Houses – without dictating to them and, the ministers themselves be controlled without being misunderstood'. Hence, there exists close coordination between the executive and the legislature which is seen absent in the Presidential form of government.

3.1.6 Decline of Indian Parliament

India holds the unique distinction of being the largest democracy in the world. For the past 70 years it has shown its resilience and has stood strong against clandestine forces that have challenged its integrity. However, it has to be agreed that our parliamentary system is not immune to challenges and limitations. Though it has provided one of the finest constitutions and legislative systems in the modern era, experts feel that the Indian parliamentary setup is undergoing a steady decline in terms of its accountability and efficacy as the highest law making body in the country.

- Our founding fathers envisioned to create a democratic system in which the legislature, executive and the judiciary will have their own domains of operation.
- While they would have significant autonomy with their respective functions, a system of checks and balances, where one will be responsible to another, would ensure the credible functioning of each institution in this setup – the legislature would create laws,

which will be implemented by the executive, which will in turn be interpreted and enforced by the judiciary.

- In the meanwhile, the executive will be responsible to the legislature and the latter will have to be accountable to the judiciary regarding the constitutionality of the laws made.
- While the system provided for an ideal mechanism for a representative democracy, over the years the three organs have taken turns to ruffle feathers against each other, trying to manifest their importance or to restrict the others' sphere of influence.

On numerous occasions, the judiciary has had strained relationships with both the executive and the legislature. The judiciary has stepped many a times beyond its domain to direct the executive in the name of judicial activism. Passing orders to use CNG (M.C. Mehta v. Union of India, (1991)2 SCC 137) and cleaning of rivers (M.C. Mehta v. Union of India) are a few examples.

The executive on the other hand, doesn't do any less in pushing its powers on the other two organs. The executive has tried to pass laws against the rulings of the judiciary in order to provide relief on a stop-gap basis. Also, while lawmaking is a collective responsibility of the legislature, the past few decades have hardly seen a private member's bill being passed by the parliament or state legislatures. Moreover, the executive has made excessive use of the ordinance route to pass those laws that serve the government's interests and which are likely to be shot down by the legislature.

There are four vital responsibilities of the parliament,

Representation of citizens, law making, oversight of the executive and scrutiny of the budget.

The following briefly outlines the backseat that Parliament has taken over the years, some examples being the declining number of working days and the bills passed. If numbers are an indication of the performance of an institution then on the face of it, the Parliament has fallen short in discharging its constitutional obligation and reveals a steady decline in its functioning. The following shows how parliamentary functioning is declining over time.

1. **Loss of productive time:** Over the past few decades, the Lok Sabha has consistently lost a significant portion of its productive time to disruptions and petty political clashes – the 15th Lok Sabha has been marked as the most disrupted in the history of the Indian Parliament. Such hindrances slow down the law-making process and curb the effective performance of the legislature. The 15th Lok Sabha, passed only 179 out of the total 291 bills introduced. This is the lowest on record by a legislature that lasted a full five-year term.
2. **More ordinances:** The decline in parliamentary functioning has led to the government resorting to the ordinance route as an alternative. The weightage of ordinance as against conventional law creation has increased.

   In the famous D.C. Wadhwa v. State of Bihar (AIR 1987 SC 579), the unbridled use of ordinance by the Government of Bihar was challenged in the Supreme Court. The court observed that the excessive use of ordinance outside the domain of conventional lawmaking is a usurpation of the legislative process and thus a fraud on the Constitution. Nonetheless, governments still make use of ordinances to get laws into place.
3. **Member bill:** Private member bills are essential to ensure fail-proof governance. This is because such bills are likely to be drafted considering the gaps and loopholes in law and policy. Moreover, these members are free from the influence of the government or the cabinet. Despite their potential to serve as effective instruments to

regulate and refine government policies, they have been hardly given importance in our parliamentary system. Since 1952, only 14 private member bills have been passed till date. Though they get introduced before the Parliament, they are hardly given the importance that is given to a government bill.

4. **Debates on budget:** Having an oversight on the government's expenditure is yet another important task of the Parliament. Considering the number of hours being spent on discussing the budget in the recent past, it can be believed that even this function of the Parliament is on a decline. Conventionally, discussions on the Demand for Grants are made in the house following the examination of such demands by parliamentary standing committees. In the past 10 years or so, nearly 95% of the demands are being passed without proper discussion in the house.
5. **Fraud on exchequer:** The daily expenditure incurred by the parliamentary process is quite a burden on the public exchequer, considering the inconsistencies mentioned above. The salaries, office allowances etc., of members of parliament, amount to several crores every year. This is in addition to other perks that they get in kind. As much as it is expected of the government to be accountable, the highest law-making body should as well be equally accountable. The only way to ensure this is by bringing in reforms.
6. **Disruptions in the Parliament:** The Speaker described the constant disruptions of the Lok Sabha by the opposition members as 'Murder of Democracy'. Various incidents such as cash for votes, snatching away the papers when they were presented, hurling of torn papers at the chair, cash for query, displaying placards despite their prohibition, shouting of slogans, ambling the well of the house, defiance of rules, violation of rules of debate, and showing utter defiance to the chair have tarnished the image of the Parliaments before the public. And the most important aspect is that there remains an utter disconnect between the public needs and requirements and the debates and issues dealt with by the Parliament.

Thus, there has been a steady decline in performance of the Parliament. The following can be assessed as the **reasons for decline of Parliament:**

1. The authority which was initially rested on the Parliament has now been taken over by the Cabinet. The Cabinet now has been ultimate decider of important aspects such as summoning of the house, proroguing of the session, preparation of daily time table for the session, providing the inaugural speech to be delivered by the head of the state, and doing numerous other things which fall under the purview of the Parliament.
2. The role played by the members of the parliament has not been up to the level expected of them. The quality, competence, culture and commitment have significantly declined. Large number of MPs show very little interest in attending the Parliament. The attendance records show a dismal picture of nature of absenteeism of our members.
3. The quality of debates in the Parliament has gone down. In the previous era, the debates in the Parliament were characterized by wit, humour and wisdom but today they have been reduced to character assassination, insults and abuses.
4. In the Westminster system of government, the Prime Minister is the leader of the house. Such a person should command respect and should be dignified in his/her approach in the Parliament. Nehru was such a leader, he never missed to attend any

sessions, and he was present throughout in cases concerning important issues. But during the tenure of Rajiv Gandhi it was not so, he as very conspicuous of his absence especially when important issues came up for discussion. Thus, such behaviour of the leader of the house and the government sent out a bad message to both the members in the house and the people outside the house.

5. The virtual monopoly of a single political party for nearly 50 years after independence has made the legislature a rubber stamp authority. This is because all the bills, policies, acts are not effectively debated in the Parliament. The data shows that the Parliament spends very little time in sifting through the acts, bills, amendments which are to be passed. Hence, there is little accountability and the effective check to be kept by the Parliament is absent, here there is thus the dictatorship and dominance by the Cabinet. In the 2008, 14 important bills were passed in a single day, and numerous such voluminous legislations are passed without effective notice or debate, this shows the way in which the accountability of the parliament is bypassed by the government.
6. Even in finance bills the situation was the same. Crores of amount is granted when the Appropriation Bill is placed before the Parliament without any debate. In the 2004–2005 the Railway Budget was passed without any debate and discussion, and the same happened for the general budget also, which was passed without discussion.
7. There has been a steady decline in the number and duration of the sitting of Parliament after the first Lok Sabha. This decline is not only seen in number of hours or sittings, it is also seen in quality and length of debates and its outcomes. The highest recorded sittings were during the first Lok Sabha (1952–1957) which was for 3784 hours (677 sittings). In the year 2011 the Parliament totally sat for a meagre 73 days and 2008 was the worst recorded as the Houses sat for just 46 days. The Parliamentary affairs minister was quoted saying that each disruption to the Parliament cost the exchequer 2.5 lakh a minute.

Commenting on the second session of the 14th Lok Sabha, *The Hindu* observed that,

> '*Parliamentary misconduct has become so routine that it might appear a waste of effort even to discuss the whys and wherefores of it. Forget the daily adjournments and walkouts; in recent times disrupters have spared no occasion, not even the once sacrosanct presidential address. However, when confrontation reaches a point where the very existence of Parliament was questioned, then it is distress time as much for the democracy as for the institution itself*'.

Thus, there is seen a steady decline in nature and functioning of the Parliament. And this has resulted in monetary loss as well as social loss to the people. They have not only lost valuable time, but they have lost the train of development.

3.1.7 Suggestions for Improvement

Since the first day of independence, these pulpits of governance have served the purpose of being a forum for the vast population spread across a multiplicity of ethnic and linguistic diversities. But as discussed prior to this section, parliamentary culture in India has indeed taken a beating. What makes it worse is that without investing much effort on assessing the reasons for decline, the stakeholders concerned treat the situation with overt cynicism.

Over the past seven decades, the structure and functions of Parliament have grown on the principles of democratic socialism, economic democracy and distributive justice. Of late, due to the information explosion, technological revolution and challenges in administration brought about by LPG (Liberalization, Privatization and Globalization) reforms, along with the age-old principle of Welfare State, etc., have conferred upon the Parliament a larger spectrum of responsibilities. All of the above coupled with the inadequacy of time; limitations in terms of access to information and the sub-standard conduct of parliamentary proceedings have resulted in the creation of mediocre legislation and unsatisfactory parliamentary oversight on administration.

Minimal effort has been taken to develop the essential ingredients to achieve success in parliamentary polity. These include discipline, character, and a sense of public morality, ideologically oriented two-party system and willingness to listen to and to accommodate minority views.

Whenever the government of the day enjoyed a lean majority (that too with the aid of a coalition) and the opposition had little numbers to emerge as an alternative, the Parliament has performed less effectively. Examples of this situation were many a time visible during the 1989–1999 decade. The floor of the house hardly witnessed a constructive legislative process. There was little respect among the members and ministers to the institution, which could be understood by the alarming trends of absenteeism and defection.

- Parliamentary reforms have a decisive role in ensuring sustainable and equitable growth, especially in an era fueled by liberalization and globalization.
- Archaic processes have to be revised, control mechanisms on members should be strengthened, debating and decision-making procedures should be made efficient etc.
- For the Parliament, constant review and revamp should be done to prevent it from becoming obsolete.
- As much as efforts are being taken to do this, it shouldn't be restricted to mere administration of stop-gap measures.
- A full-scale review is essential to provide institutional, structural, procedural and organizational improvement.

What is needed is a full-scale review. We have to be prepared for fundamental institutional – structural, functional, procedural and organizational – changes. The overriding guiding norm and purpose of all parliamentary reforms should be to make both Government and Parliament more relevant to meet the challenges of the times and the changing national needs in the context of the objective of faster economic growth.

Both the Parliament and the Government should be collectively concerned with concurrent and contemporaneous monitoring and evaluation of the implementation of economic reforms, scrutiny of the overall performance of the economy, targets, achievements, shortfalls etc. The following are the reform measures which are needed to be carried out.

1. **Reforms in budget process:** Some serious thinking is called for in the matter of reforming the budget procedure in Parliament and bringing it closer to the needs and constraints of the new situation. The number of occasions on which voting by divisions may be needed during a budget session is very large. Also, the defeat of any demand for grant is deemed to be tantamount to expression of lack of confidence in the Government. There is every possibility of a division being asked for more often only to embarrass the Government. It would be unrealistic to expect all the Members to be present all the time through the session. It would, therefore, be wise to reduce to the barest minimum the number of days on which voting by division is considered imminent. Also, the time may be fixed by agreement and announced in advance with appropriate whips issued and attendance ensured otherwise.

2. **Nodal Standing Committee on Economy:** A Nodal Standing Committee on National Economy with subject-oriented study groups, assisted by scholars and experts, should be constituted to monitor economic policy formulation and implementation. The respective study groups would make performance evaluation on these areas and prepare internal study reports which will be produced to the Committee. These will be presented annually by the Committee to the Parliament. Besides being informative on policy measures of the government, it helps in keeping a constant vigilance and performing reviews on the system as a whole. The insights presented by the committee could be discussed effectively by the houses of Parliament every year.
3. **Better communication to improve public perception:** The Parliament serves as a link between the citizens and the government. But there is a perceived disconnect between the people and the parliament, whenever they discuss its proceedings. They are led to believe that there is hardly any contribution from them in the decision-making process. This was caused due to the ineffective management of public relations in the past. And it has resulted in a poor perception of the Parliament and its members.

   Systematic and conscious efforts are required to rebuild a good rapport between the people and the parliament. For this purpose, the potential of mass media, print publications, online media etc., should be harnessed to get the message across the board. The news channels such as DD News, RSTV and LSTV have to be exploited to the maximum in communicating about the parliamentary proceedings via electronic media. Live coverage of debates and sessions in the parliament will help in building a sense of credibility among the public.
4. **Panchayats and Parliament:** In an era where there are calls from different quarters to decentralize governance, the roles of an MP as against a local body member have to be clearly demarcated. Immense care has to be taken to avoid any conflict or overarching of powers among them. The scope of work for an MP, with respect to his/her constituency has to be restricted to issues of national importance. For effective implementation of those schemes which require the coordination of the two, as in the case of MPLADS, proper brainstorming and planning has to be done to avoid any implementation blunders.
5. **Improving the quality of participation of members:** Proper functioning of Parliament is dependent on the quality of participation of members. From good conduct, insightful questioning to sincere participation in constructive debates, every member should act beyond what his/her party requires. It should begin with proper training and orientation of newly elected members about the conventions, traditions, rules and regulations that determine parliamentary conduct. The curriculum should include things such as adequate knowledge of the constitution, the parliamentary system, the Rules of Procedure and Conduct of Business, etc. Insufficient training and orientation in the past has adversely affected the performance of the members and the parliament at large.
6. **Reducing the expenditure of the Parliament:** The costs involved in maintaining the parliamentary system in our country have always been increasing. One of the most commonly discussed aspects of parliamentary expenditure is the spending on salaries and emoluments of its members. The charges under this heading alone go up to several lakhs a year. This along with the ministerial salaries and that of the members of state legislatures put together would run into crores annually. Prudent fixing of salaries and emoluments is the immediate need of the hour. Moreover, this is one of the expenditures that

are not discussed in the budget. Therefore, it is a moral responsibility of the legislators to take salaries that are not disproportionate to the work they do.

7. **Improving information supply:** Any conversation becomes irrelevant if there is not a valuable sharing of information. Information is one of the essential instruments to have an effective functioning of a participatory democracy. Without this, it would be difficult to have a hold over the arbitrary nature of governance by the party in power. Unfortunately, most of the time, our members rely on official documents and data that have only been published by the respective ministries. More often than not, this information is likely to be inadequate. To address this situation, an independent national information repository, exclusively for the purpose of providing information to members of the parliament, should be created.
8. **Planning legislation and improving its quality:** The quality of our legislative products have been often turned down as haphazard. This is primarily due to the non-compliance in spirit to the process of law making adopted by our constitution makers. There is a need for a dynamic and comprehensive approach to law making

   This can be done by:

   (i) Streamlining the functions of the Parliamentary and Legal Affairs Committee of the Cabinet.
   (ii) Widening the roles of the Law Commission.
   (iii) Setting up a Legislation Committee to supervise and coordinate legislative planning.
   (iv) Referring all bills to the newly set-up Departmental Standing Committees for consideration and scrutiny, consulting concerned interest groups and finalization of the second reading stage in the relaxed atmosphere of Committees aided by experts thereby reducing the burden of the House without impinging on any of its rights and improving the quality of drafting and content of legislation.

9. **Setting up a Constitution Committee for Amendments:** The executive powers of the Union are collinear with its legislative powers. However, the constituent power should belong to the Parliament. This means that while the government can initiate and orient the legislature to make laws that suit its policies, the parliament has a bigger responsibility in terms of bills that amend the constitution.

   - At present, constitutional amendment bills are introduced just like any other ordinary bill in the Parliament.
   - While this encroaches on the time of the parliament for passing ordinary bills, it also gives very little time for discussing the need for and the pros and cons of the respective amendment bills.
   - Instead of clubbing it with regular business, if it can be put through a scrutiny by a specific committee on constitutional amendments or a body authorized by the Parliament, it would go a long way in ensuring a better standard of amendments.

The scrutiny should go deep into the cause and relevance of the proposed amendments and critically examine each and every provision, in order to produce an outcome, much better than what can be done through the conventional process of law making. This committee could include members of both houses of the parliament and judicial officers/legal experts such as the attorney general or solicitor general to provide insights and inferences about the bills. While it will make the amendment process much more robust, it will also reduce the possibility of the amendment being turned down by the judiciary as unconstitutional.

10. **Departmental Committees and Parliamentary streamlining:** The setting up of the 27 departmental standing committees has been a remarkable parliamentary reform in the past decades. However, what began as three committees in 1989 on an experimental basis has been increasing ever since, at a progressive pace. Having specific departmental standing committees does help in faster completion of business. However, the overall costs in running such a huge framework of committees necessitate a larger bill of expenditures.

    Parliamentary supervision of administration through committees is supposed to enable good governance and not act as a barrier at all times. For proper conduct of standing committees, the following measures can be adopted:

    (i) Proper closing of pre-budget scrutiny of budgetary estimates and demands for grants before they are voted in the House.
    (ii) Concurrent and contemporaneous examination of the activities of Government departments and matters of national concern in cool, non-partisan atmosphere.
    (iii) Monitoring of performance, relating to financial inputs to the policy objectives and actual outcomes to measure effectiveness and detailed examination of supplementary estimates.
    (iv) Feedback with valuable insights and information to the Parliament and to the Government to review economic proposals.
    (v) Closer and competent inspection of all legislative proposals.
    (vi) Review of the implementation of different laws passed by the Parliament across the respective subjects.
    (vii) Encouraging participation by backbenchers and creating a second level of leadership.
    (viii) Development of skill specialization and expertise in legislative processes among members.

    The committees could, strengthen the government by providing valuable insights for the better functioning of the government and the parliament. With a spirit of cutting-edge professionalism, thee committees could play a major role in accelerating the Parliament towards becoming a forum for meaningful body for multilateral dialogue.

11. **Control over borrowing:** While the budgetary proposals and estimates are reviewed by the several committees in the Parliament, there is no specific committee to oversee the function of public borrowing. A limit on public borrowing will instil a sense of responsibility and an idea and it leaves behind a smaller burden for the upcoming generations.
12. **Discussing committee reports on the floor of the House:** When a committee's report is not read on the floor of the house, it belittles the importance attached to the particular committee. This could result in some very useful recommendations going unnoticed or insufficiently discussed.
13. **Codifying parliamentary privileges:** While members of the parliament are justified in receiving certain privileges in view of exercising their duties, limitless powers or concessions should not be given to them. These privileges are given to the parliament by the people and hence should not be misused. A joint committee may be created to rationalize the extent of privileges offered and recommend appropriate regulations.

14. **Reforming the functions of parliamentary parties:** The parties that have their members as members of the parliament should have the responsibility to train them accordingly. Relevant briefing on the position of the party on specific issues, speech notes and write-ups etc. have to be given prior with proper training in order to avoid any miscommunication on the floor of the house. Free voting on issues shall be called for in case of most discussions on the floor of the house. This will create an environment in the house, free from the influence of parties. Such a measure would also change the way confidence on a government is tested. Only when a government is defeated through a no-confidence motion shall it be asked to resign.
15. **Reforms in quality of debates and discussions:** One of the areas where such a restraint should come in is with time management for discussions and debates. It comes as no surprise that sessions throughout the year have little significant business done, due to unnecessary discussions and resentment towards the party in power by the opposition and vice versa.

    - What begin as rational debates are more likely to end up as adjourned sittings, since political parties try to use the floor to show their wrath against each other instead of using the floors as constructive forums for policy management.
    - This situation can be addressed by having such discussions at the committee level.
    - Besides having enough time for such discussions, it also leaves the floor of the house for debating issues of national importance.
    - Members should be sensitized on the proper use of parliamentary devices such as *Question hour* and *Zero hour*.

    Several other items of business such as Adjournment Motions, Calling the Attention Notices, No-Confidence motions, etc. initiated by Private Members have to be taken up at a dedicated time on a weekly basis. Moreover, parliamentary business can be shared between the committees and the houses equitably, in such a way that neither organ is denied necessary time allotment.
16. **Reform in expression of opinion of the members:** Freedom of expression should be given to every Member of Parliament without compromise. It is one of the basic principles in representative democracy. It is accepted that unparliamentary or objectionable words spoken should be removed from the record of the house's proceedings on the speaker's advice. However, this should not be misused by the speaker to hold an unsolicited control on the opposition members. The same is applicable to television broadcasts of the sessions. As much as possible, proceedings should be telecasted without deleting or muting portions of the sittings.
17. **Reforms in Question hour:** Both houses of the Parliament demarcate an hour each during every day of the session for questions. Essentially, this should be a time where the government is questioned about its policy or a decision or some matter with significant importance. However, this has become a time where discussions are made and hardly five questions are covered in a time where around twenty questions are to be taken up for answering. A proper scrutiny of the list of questions will reveal that a lot of the admitted questions are trivial or ambiguous in nature. At times, some questions of top priority cause a serious dislocation of the proper functioning of ministries in the government. Such practices and processes of raising and admitting such questions must be reviewed and streamlined for effective conduct of business in the Parliament.

18. **Reforms in other motions:** Adjournment motions too are not immune from being ineffectively used. The purpose of this motion is to call the attention of the House for immediate discussion on a matter of urgent public importance, which has not been already included in the List of Business for the day. However, the discretion of admitting such a discussion lies with the speaker. When admission is refused, members keep storming the well and what follows is a tug-of-war between them and the speaker. The solution to this lies in the speaker expressing his/her genuine opinion on the urgent **importance of the issue and maintaining order in the house.**
19. **Other procedural reforms:** Either house of the Parliament has its own set of rules and procedures. All those rules except the ones which have been codified in the Rules of Procedure should be regularly reviewed and they should be removed if they are found to be obsolete. Conventions and procedures should be adapted according to the demands of time and should never be a hindrance to the proper functioning of the Parliament.
20. **Tackling absenteeism:** Yet another problem faced by parliamentary conduct is the increasing incidences of absenteeism among members. It is no less than a threat to democracy. A quorum of at least one-tenth is required for conduct of business in the Parliament. But this cannot be allowed to become a standard minimum attendance requirement for having sessions. As members who represent the people, they should have a moral inclination to attend parliamentary sessions except in cases when they have to attend other duties of high priority. Therefore, a minimum number of hours to be attended by a member can be added to the rules and procedure, in such a way that the member would contribute significantly. Those not complying can be given a deduction in their salaries throughout the session.
21. **Reform in Parliamentary Secretariat:** The success of the parliamentary system lies in the independent and impartial functioning of the parliamentary secretariat. The secretariat should be supplied with the best of the resources available. Besides, they should also be constituted with mechanisms to correspond freely with the ministerial secretariats.
22. **Decriminalization of politics:** The judgment given by the Apex court in the Lily Thomas case will go a long way in decriminalizing the election process, where only an individual without criminal background is fielded by the political parties. The media and the civil society have to distinguish between serious penal offences, financial irregularities and acts of violation of prohibitory orders. These different charges may not be equated with one another.
23. **Linkage between the People and Parliament:** The Parliament is the communication link between the government and public. There is a necessity to establish a good rapport between the two entities. The public and the government have to be brought together. The Parliament belongs to the people and not its members. The members are thus responsible to the public at large. The members should have access to the opinion of the public and the public should also have the access of the Parliament.
24. **Regular orientation programmes:** Improving the quality of the members is one of the most important aspect of the reform process. It is the bound duty of every member to uphold the dignity and decorum of the institution both inside and outside of it. The image of the Parliament will be poor unless the quality of its members is improved. A newly elected member is often lost in the number of traditions,

conventions, rules, regulations, formalities etc. of the parliamentary system. Hence, there is need to institutionalize the process of training for the newly elected members. The curriculum of such training should cover all aspects including, the Constitution, the knowledge about the political system, the Rules of Procedure and Conduct of Business, various other practices, traditions, precedents, do's and don'ts of members, and rules of Parliamentary etiquettes etc. There should also be periodic training imparted to the members on various issues so that the quality of the institution never falls.

3.1.8 Conclusion

The endurance of democracy and freedom in India are completely dependent on the successful functioning of the Parliament. Though we can take pride in the relentless working of this body for the past 70 years, we have to accept that the issues mentioned above are slowly eroding its stand as an institution of legitimacy and a watchtower of democracy. But it is also true that no reform can happen in a single blow. And no single reform can bring about a miracle change. The way ahead should be taken with utmost care and caution by setting up a parliamentary reforms commission, on the lines of a commission instituted in the United Kingdom for a similar purpose. The recommendations of this commission should be presented to the Rules Committee of the parliament, which will present it to the house and suitable reforms can be incorporated. Such periodical initiatives done with a sincere effort will increase the credibility of the Parliament and fortify its character as the watch tower of Indian democracy.

3.2 ISSUES OF RECENT CONCERN IN PARLIAMENTARY FUNCTIONS

3.2.1 Anti-Defection Law-intent and its Impact

Defection is defined as 'to abandon a position or association, often to join an opposing group' which essentially describes a situation when a member of a particular party abandons his loyalty towards that party and provides his support (in the form of his vote or otherwise) to another party.

The Anti-Defection Law was passed through the 52nd Amendment in 1985, which added the Tenth Schedule to the Indian Constitution which detailed the grounds of defections and also prescribes disqualification for the defectors of a house of Parliament/state legislature.

It was again amended by the 91st Amendment Act, 2003. Prior to this amendment, a 'defection' by one-third members of a political party in the legislature was considered to be a 'merger'. This amendment changed and made that, at least two-third of the members of the political party have to be in favour of such merger for it to be valid. It also made mandatory, that those who wish to shift party should resign their seat in the legislature, and hence they have to seek re-election if they wish to defect.

The main intent of the law was to combat **'the evil of political defections'** and to bring in stability to the government. The major unintended consequence of the act is hindering the elected members from voting on their own conscience when there is party whip issued on the matter. To overcome this issue of forced voting, many committees have been set up to modify the act by amendment and to provide freedom of expression of individual MPs.

3.2.1.1 Intent of Law

Assuming the right intent of lawmakers, the legislation was aimed

1. To reduce the power of money used for alluring elected members to make or break a government and strengthen parliamentary democracy by prohibiting floor-crossing.
2. To bring stability to the government and the political parties; and not let the government to be held at ransom by few elected members.
3. To make elected members responsible and accountable to the group of voters who have casted their vote because their loyalty and affinity to the party.
4. To make the elected member loyal to the political party on whose party symbol and support the person got elected to the house.

However, with hindsight, outlawing party defections invites observers to speculate about the framers' intentions. Was it to produce competitive party systems or to consolidate power within existing parties? It may be led to believe that the law was proposed with some erroneous intentions, and besides that it has led to unintended consequences including an autocratic party system, quelling of dissent and making of false leaders.

Grounds of disqualification by anti-defection act 1985

1. **Member belonging to political parties**
   a. If an elected member voluntarily gives up his membership of a political party.
   b. If he votes or abstains from voting in such House contrary to any direction issued by his political party or anyone authorized to do so (whip), without obtaining prior permission. As a pre-condition for his disqualification, his abstention from voting should not be condoned by his party or the authorized person within 15 days of such incident.
2. **Member elected otherwise than as candidate set up by any political party**
   a. If Independent member joins a political party post-election.
3. **Nominated members**
   a. If a nominated member joins a political party after six months of his nomination to legislature.

3.2.1.2 Authority Concerning Anti-defection

The law states that only the presiding officer, that is, Chairman or the Speaker of a House, can make decisions on disqualification of a member under this Schedule, and his/her decision is final. If a question arises on the presiding officer on the subject of disqualification, then the decision shall be made by a newly elected presiding officer (principle of natural justice). The law states that the Presiding Officer's decision is final and not subject to judicial review. The Supreme Court struck down this condition partly and held that no judicial intervention shall be made until the presiding officer gives his order. However, the final decision can be appealed in the High Courts and Supreme Court.

The Chairman or the Speaker of a House has also been empowered to make rules for giving effect to the provisions of the Tenth Schedule. The rules are required to be laid before each House and are subject to modifications/disapproval by the House.

3.2.1.3 Exceptions Provided in Tenth Schedule

a. **Cases of Split**

No member shall be disqualified for being member of a group which has arisen as a result of split in his original political party and such a group shall consists of not less than one third members of the legislative party concerned.

This provision (paragraph 3) has since been omitted from the Tenth Schedule by the Constitution (91st Amendment) Act, 2003, which came into force with effect from 1 January, 2004. Consequent upon the omission of Paragraph 3, it is not now permissible to claim a split in the legislature party.

b. **Cases of Merger**

At least two-thirds of the members of a party have to be in favour of a 'merger' for it to have validity in the eyes of the law. The tenth schedule states, 'The merger of the original political party or a member of a House shall be deemed to have taken place if, and only if, not less than two-thirds of the members of the legislature party concerned have agreed to such merger.'

The Dinesh Goswami Committee on Electoral Reforms, the Law Commission in its report on 'Reform of Electoral Laws' and the National Commission to Review the Working of the Constitution (NCRWC) all recommended the deletion of the Tenth Schedule provision regarding exemption from disqualification in case of a split.

c. **Exemption to persons elected to the office of Speaker/Chairman or Deputy Speaker/Deputy Chairman**

No disqualification is incurred by a person who has been elected to the office of the Speaker or the Deputy Speaker of the House of the People or of the Legislative Assembly of a State or to the Office of the Deputy Chairman of the Council of States or the Chairman or the Deputy Chairman of the Legislative Council of a State if he severes his connections with his political party after such election. Also, no disqualification is incurred if he, having given up by reason of his election to such office, his membership of the political party to which he belonged immediately before such election, rejoins such political party after he ceases to hold such office.

d. **Election to the Office of the President**

Election commission made it clear that political parties cannot issue any direction or whip to members to vote in certain way during the presidential election. Voting and not voting will not fall within the ambit of the anti-defection law

e. Obtaining prior permission before 15 days and not condoned by his party.
f. Voluntarily joining non-legislative party which does not have single member in the legislature.
g. Voting against the party in an ordinary bill for which whip is not issued and does not topple the government on its failure
h. If expelled by the party the person continues to be the member of the house until he/she voluntarily joins a legislative party (e.g. Sasikala Pushpa TN – MP Rajya Sabha)
i. Abstaining from voting due to proven health conditions subject to acceptance of presiding officer of the house.

Advantages and Disadvantages of Anti-Defection Law

Advantages	Disadvantages
The important advantage is that it prevents shifting of allegiance of the members of the party thereby providing stability to the government.	This reduces the accountability of the government to the people and the Parliament.
Importantly it promotes party discipline. It upholds party loyalty as the person who got elected from a particular party is prohibited from shifting to another party.	It interferes with the rights of the individual and his freedom of speech and expression against policies of his party. This effectively curbs dissent within the party.

Important Judgments of Disqualification and the Tenth Schedule by the Supreme Court

The Supreme Court took upon itself to effectively implement the anti-defection law. It in its various landmark judgments has upheld the Constitutional validity of this law. And in other subsequent cases, it established that the Court is the final authority, and it could even question the action of the Speaker, who according the law is the final authority to decide such. The following are the most important judgments of the Court and the main issues it decided upon.

Main Issue(s) in the Case	Judgement of the Court and the Name of the Case
Whether the right to freedom of speech and expression is curtailed by the Tenth Schedule.	The provisions do not subvert the democratic rights of elected members in Parliament and state legislatures. It does not violate their conscience. The provisions do not violate any right or freedom under Articles 105 and 194 of the Constitution. ***(Kihoto Hollohan v. Zachillhu and Others, AIR 1993 SC 412)***
Whether only resignation constituted voluntarily giving up membership of a political party	The words 'voluntarily giving up membership' have a wider meaning. An inference can also be drawn from the conduct of the member that he has voluntarily given up the membership of his party. ***(Ravi S. Naik v. Union of India, AIR 1994 SC 1558)***
Whether a member can be said to have voluntarily given up his membership of a party if he joins another party after being expelled by his old political party.	Once a member is expelled, he is treated as an 'unattached' member in the house. However, he continues to be a member of the old party as per the Tenth Schedule. So, if he joins a new party after being expelled, he can be said to have voluntarily given up membership of his old party. ***(G. Vishwanathan v. Speaker, Tamil Nadu Legislative Assembly, AIR 1996 SC 353)***

Main Issue(s) in the Case	Judgement of the Court and the Name of the Case
Whether paragraph 7 of the Tenth Schedule barring the jurisdiction of courts in cases of disqualification is constitutional.	The paragraph seeks to change the operation and effect of Articles 136, 226 and 227 of the Constitution which give the High Courts and the Supreme Court jurisdiction in such cases. Any such provision is required to be ratified by the legislatures of at least half of the states as per Article 368(2). The paragraph was, therefore, held invalid, as the Tenth Schedule had not received the above mentioned ratification. ***(Kihoto Hollohan v. Zachillhu and Others, AIR 1993 SC 412)***
Whether paragraph 6 of the Tenth Schedule granting finality to the decision of the Speaker/Chairman is valid.	To the extent that the provisions grant finality to the orders of the speaker, the provision is valid. However, the High Courts and the Supreme Court can exercise Judicial review under the Constitution. Judicial review should not cover any stage prior to the making of a decision by the speakers/chairmen. ***(Kihoto Hollohan v. Zachillhu and Others, AIR 1993 SC 412)***
Whether a speaker can review his own decision to disqualify a member under the Tenth Schedule	The Speaker of a house does not have the power to review his own decision to disqualify a candidate. Such power is not provided for under the Tenth Schedule, and is not implicit in the provisions either. ***(Dr. Kashinath G. Jhalmi v. Speaker, Goa Legislative Assembly, AIR 1993 SCC 703)***
Whether the speaker of a legislature is bound by the directions of a court.	The court cited the Kihoto Hollohan case, where it had been said that the speaker, while passing an order under the Tenth Schedule, functions as a tribunal. The order passed by him would, therefore, be subject to judicial review. ***(Ravi S Naik v. Union of India, AIR 1994 SC 1558)***
Whether judicial review by courts extends to rules framed under the Tenth Schedule.	Rules under the Tenth Schedule are procedural in nature. Any violation of those would be a procedural irregularity. Procedural irregularity in immune from judicial scrutiny. ***(Ravi S. Naik v. Union of India, AIR 1994 SC 1558)***
When can a court review the speaker's decision–making process under the Tenth Schedule.	If the speaker fails to act on a complaint, or accepts claims of splits or mergers without making a finding, he fails to act as per the Tenth Schedule. The Supreme Court said that ignoring a petition for disqualification is not merely an irregularity, but a vilation of constitutional duties. ***(Rajendra Singh Rana and Others v. Swami Prasad Maurya and Others. AIR 2007 SCC 270)***

Some recent orders on disqualification by the Speaker for defection.
The Speaker is the final authority to decide the cases related to defection. The law states that only the presiding officer, that is, Chairman or the Speaker of a House, can make decisions on disqualification of a member under this Schedule, and his/her decision is final. But this decision is subject to the final review by the Judiciary. He has also been empowered to frame rules. The following are some of the important decisions taken by the Speaker regarding defections.

a. **Final order of the Speaker requirements for proving an inability to obey a party whip due to external factors.**
   Shri Rajeev Ranjan Singh 'Lalan' v. Dr. P.P. Koya, JD(U), (January 9, 2009). Dr. Koya defied a party whip requiring him to be present in the House and vote against the Motion of Confidence for the government. He claimed he was too ill to be present in the House. The Speaker concluded that Dr. Koya abstained from voting by remaining absent, and the evidence of the 'illness' is not sufficient to conclude that he was so ill that he could not be present in the House.
b. **When can it be said that a party member has deliberately defied a party whip?**
   Shri Prabhunath Singh v. Shri Ram Swaroop Prasad, JD(U), (October 3, 2008). Shri Prasad defied a party whip requiring him to be present in the House. In his defence, he denied that any whip was issued or served. The Speaker held that in view of the fact that there is evidence to show that the whip had been delivered to Shri Prasad's house, and had been duly received, it cannot be said that Shri Prasad had no knowledge of the whip.
c. **Whether public criticism of one's political party amounts to defection?**
   Shri Avtar Singh Bhadana v. Shri Kuldeep Singh, Indian National Congress, (September 10, 2008). The INC alleged that Shri Bishnoi often dissented from, and criticized the Congress government publicly, and had demanded the dismissal of the government in Haryana. The Speaker held that a person getting elected as a candidate of a political party also gets elected because of the programs of the party. If the person leaves the party, he should go back before the electorate.
d. **Whether stories in the print or electronic media can be taken as evidence of defection?**
   Shri Rajesh Verma v. Shri Mohammad Shahid Akhlaque, BSP, (January 27, 2008). It was alleged that Shri Akhlaque joined the Samajwadi Party in a public meeting. It was alleged that at this meeting, Shri Akhlaque had said that at heart, he had always been a member of the SP. The Speaker reasoned that there is no reason why news clippings and stories in the media would be untruthful. The Speaker therefore held Shri Akhlaque disqualified for having voluntarily given up membership of the BSP.

Recommendations of various bodies on Anti-defection law

Body/Committee	Main Reforms Suggested/recommended
Dinesh Goswami Committee on electoral reforms (1990)	• Disqualification should be limited to cases where (a) a member voluntarily gives up the membership of his political party, (b) a member abstains from voting, or votes contrary to the party whip in a motion of vote of confidence or motion of no-confidence.

Body/Committee	Main Reforms Suggested/recommended
	• The issue of disqualification should be decided by the President/Governor on the advice of the Election Commission.
Halim Committee on anti-defection law (1998)	• The words 'voluntarily giving up membership of a political party' be comprehensively defined.
	• Restrictions like prohibition on joining another party or holding offices in the government be imposed on expelled members.
	• The term political party should be defined clearly.
Law Commission (170thReport,1999)	• Provisions which exempt splits and mergers from disqualification to be deleted.
	• Pre-poll electoral fronts should be treated as political parties under anti-defection law.
	• Political parties should limit issuance of whips to instances only when the government is in danger.
Election Commission	• Decisions under the Tenth Schedule should be made by the President/ Governor on the binding advice of the Election Commission.
Constitution Review	• Defectors should be barred from holding public office or any remunerative political post for the duration of the remaining term.
Commission(2002)	• The vote cast by a defector to topple a government should be treated as invalid.

3.2.1.4 Reforms Needed in Anti-defection Law

The step taken to curb the menace of defections was indeed a landmark decision. But much more needs to be done in order to cure the system of such issues. Reforms need to be continuous and concurrent in order to cleanse the political system. The following are few insights:

1. The decision-making power of presiding officers should be limited and should be altered on principle of natural justice, that is, no person shall be judged in his own case.
2. 'Voluntarily giving up membership' should be defined and needs comprehensive revision.
3. Political parties should limit issuance of whips to instances only when the government is in danger and not for other bills, that is, ambient of the law should be restricted to money bill and no confidence motion.
4. The Election Commission had recommended that the decisions under the Tenth Schedule should be made by the President/Governor on the binding advice of the Election Commission. A constitutional amendment vesting the power to decide matters relating to disqualification on the ground of defection with the President/Governor acting on the advice of the Election Commission would actually help in preserving the integrity of the Speaker's office.

3.2.2 Delegated Legislation – Necessary Evil

The legislature is considered to be the law-making organ of the State. But in the modern times, due to various factors such as complexity of legislation, paucity of time, and fast-changing environment, the legislature is unable to make requisite number of law needed. Hence, there is need for the legislature to delegate its law-making power to its subordinates to ensure smooth functioning of the administrative machinery, as it is not possible for it to deliver the quantity and quality required. And such a legislation, passed by the executive, on behalf of the legislature is called the **Delegated legislation**. The Committee on Minister's Powers stated that, '*the truth is, that if Parliament, were not willing to delegate law-making power, Parliament would be unable to pass the king and quantity of legislation which modern public opinion requires*'.

3.2.2.1 Definitions

The Delegated Legislation is otherwise known as Subordinate legislation. According to Salmond, '*Subordinate legislation is that which proceeds from any authority other than the sovereign power and is, therefore, dependent for its continued existence and validity on some superior or supreme authority. They may be regarded as having their origin in the delegation of the power of Parliament to inferior authorities, which in the exercise of their delegated functions remain subject to the control of the Sovereign Legislature*'.

The Committee on Minister's Powers in England defined delegated legislation, '*as the exercise of minor legislative power by subordinate authorities and bodies in pursuance of statutory authority given by the Parliament itself*'.

Sir Cecil Carr states the following, '*Delegated legislation is a growing child called upon to relieve the parent of strain of overwork and capable of attending to minor matters, while the parent manages the main business. The delegated legislation is so multitudinous that the statute book would not only be incomplete but misleading unless it be read along with the delegated legislation which amplifies and amends it*'.

3.2.2.2 Essential Characteristics of Delegated Legislation

The following are the essential characteristics of a delegated legislation:

1. There should be no extraordinary delay while framing of the subordinate legislation.
2. The administrative authority should not go beyond the powers given in the parent act.
3. Arbitrary and discriminatory rules should not be framed.
4. The rules thus framed should contain, short titles, explanatory notes, reference to earlier amendment, etc. to provide clear understanding.
5. The language used should be clear and simple.
6. Tax or financial levies, charges should not be imposed.
7. Sub-delegation, that is, delegation of a delegated legislation is not encouraged.
8. Essential and important legislative functions cannot be delegated.
9. The rules such framed should not act in retrospect, unless the parent acts provides so.
10. In cases as required, consultation should be made with concerned authorities to frame effective and efficient rules.
11. There should be wide and sufficient publicity to be given to such rules, so that the public gets to know about them.
12. The public interest should be kept paramount while framing these rules.
13. The final authority to interpret these rules are the Parliament and the Courts, the administrative authority themselves are not given such powers.

3.2.2.3 Reasons for Growth of Delegated Legislation

The executive has a very vital and essential role to play in the era of 'welfare state'. Hence, it has become imperative to delegate powers to the subordinate authorities for taking necessary decisions. The following are the pertinent reasons for the growth of delegated legislation:

1. **Pressure upon parliamentary time:** The Parliament is burdened with numerous issues that it does not have sufficient time to pay attention to all the matters. It cannot look into all day-to-day aspects of administration, which is therefore left at their discretion. Parliament does not have time to discuss all such matters in detail and hence delegation becomes necessary for better and effective administration.
2. **Flexibility:** The legislative procedures are long and cumbersome. Some of the administrative matters require quick and decisive action, for example bank rate, terrorist acts, foreign exchange, import and export policies etc. and only administrators with sufficient powers can deal with such matters expeditiously.
3. **Emergency:** During emergencies such as war, terrorist acts etc. the country requires immediate steps and actions. And this cannot be made through a legislative process as it will take more time, hence such aspects are delegated and dealt by authorities, hence the executives are empowered to deal with such scenarios.
4. **Technicality of the subject matter:** The Parliamentarians are generally amateurs and they do not have requisite knowledge and technical prowess to address all the issues that arise. Some matters such as, atomic energy, space science, drug and pharma policies, subjects relating to economy etc. are all specialised subjects and they have to be dealt by those people who are experts in these areas.
5. **Experiment:** The legislation procedure by the Parliament is very rigid, and the delegated legislation is flexible enough to make experiments. Certain situations and problems require experiments and this cannot be provided with help of the Parliament.

3.2.2.4 Advantages and Disadvantages

Advantages	Disadvantages
It saves the limited time available to the Parliament.	The Parliament has insufficient time to scrutinise these delegated legislations, the Parliament does not effectively review them.
They allow for rapid change	Such change is not effectively managed by the Parliament.
The Parliamentarians lack technical or detailed knowledge regarding the subject matter.	The sub-delegation of powers cause further problem of confusion because of its complexity.
It is effective in quick response to new developments.	The delegation legislation is enormous and it is nearly impossible to keep track about all such delegated powers and this leads to complexity.
It enables quick and minor necessary changes to the statute.	There is lack of publicity of such rules framed, hence public do not know about them.
Withdrawal or amendment of the laws are very easy and can be made without much hassle.	It is regarded as generally undemocratic as most of these rules and regulations are made by the public administrators who are not the elected representatives of the people.

3.2.2.5 *Necessary Evil*

As per the Committee on Subordinate Legislation, Subordinate Legislation is **a necessary evil**. The tendency to delegate legislative powers to executive agencies has become so wide-spread and dangerous that the very existence and utility of the legislature are at their vanishing point.

Clothing the administrators with legislative power is regarded by many as an act of denial of civil liberties in certain circumstances. It is one kind of surrender of Parliament to the Executive; and it has strengthened the bureaucracy, and may turn democracy into **despotism and arbitrary rule**. Lord Hewart, describes delegated legislation as 'The New Despotism'. He further states that, '*It is not merely that in this instance Parliament is being outmanoeuvred or in that instance the courts have been defied. It is that the whole scheme of self-government is being undermined, and that too in a way which no self-respecting people, if they were aware of the facts, would for a moment tolerate*'.

Sir John Marrott, who also agrees with the view of Lord Hewart, states that, '*It is my profound conviction that the prevailing and increasing disposition on the part of the British Parliament to confer upon the executive quasi-judicial and quasi-legislative functions is wholly mischevious and ought to be resisted. The old despotism, which was defeated, offered a challenge. The new despotism, which is not yet defeated, gives Parliament an anaesthetic. The strategy is different, but the goal is the same. It is to subordinate Parliament, to evade the Courts, and to render the will or the caprice of the executive unfettered and supreme*'.

Mary Parker Follet considered the concept of delegation as a mere myth of the administrative theory. She believed that, 'authority belongs to the job and stays with the job'. Hence, the person who does the job should have the authority to do it. And according to her, the authority belongs to the function (job) and hence it cannot be delegated. And thus the term 'delegation of authority' is an obsolete expression and has no meaning. She also states that, 'Authority must be functional and the functional authority carries with it responsibility'.

Again the speed at which the laws are made and amended through the process of subordinate legislation is likely to endanger the life, liberty and property of the citizens and what is worse 'multiplicity of rules and amendments may exhaust the patience and defy the endurance of those who would understand them'. Yet it has come to stay. The problem now is not how to abolish the system or find a substitute, but how to ensure legislative control over subordinate legislation.

3.2.2.6 *Safeguards, Controls and Suggestions*

1. **Spelling out the parameters:** It is necessary to spell out clearly the parameters within which the delegated legislation should function. It is important that the legislature do not pass any skeleton legislation which can be completed only through such delegated process. There is need for defining the parameters within which the delegated legislation should operate.

   The following are some of the limitations suggested by the Committee on Subordinate Legislation:

   (i) A financial power may not be delegated.
   (ii) Delegated legislation may not be allowed to have retrospective effect as it is the prerogative of the legislature.
   (iii) Power of judicial review may not be waived or curtailed by these rules.
   (iv) Language should not be ambiguous and be simple and easy to understand.
   (v) Blank delegation, that is, delegation involving rule-making on fundamental issues may be avoided.

(vi) Essential legislative functions, repeal of law and modification in acts may not be delegated.
(vii) Discriminatory rules may be avoided.

The Select Committee of Ministers' Power was appointed by the British Parliament in 1931, declared that the delegation of legislation is an essential aspect of the Public Administration, and if it is formulated properly will result in safeguarding the rights of the individual. The following are the recommendations made by the committee:

(i) The legislative power should be delegated to a trustworthy authority which commands general confidence and not to some officer of inferior status who is unfit to exercise the power.
(ii) If any particular interests are to be affected specially, the authority should consult them before making its laws.
(iii) There should be means of amending or revoking the delegated legislation.
(iv) The limits within which the delegated power is to be exercised ought to be definitely laid down.
(v) Adequate means should be taken to ensure publicity to rules.

2. **Legislative control:** Such control is sought to be achieved by laying the delegated legislation, along with the bill, in the Parliament. Rules in Lok Sabha No. 70 and Rajya Sabha No. 65 mention that a bill involving such proposal of delegation of power shall be '*accompanied by a memorandum explaining such proposals and drawing attention to their scope, and stating also whether they are of exceptional or normal character*'.

This process does not serve much purpose as it is just routine and much information is not shared. The real control over the delegated legislation can be achieved when the rules made by the government is laid before the Parliament. These rules can be amended, changed, modified or removed by the Parliament. But, this aspect is post-mortem, as in India, the rules come in immediately and only later it is laid before the Parliament for the approval. However, in UK it is scrutinised before it comes into force. And in India, even after laying before the houses, it is hardly discussed. Hence, the Committee on Delegated Legislation suggested the following to improve the legislative control:

(i) All acts of Parliament should uniformly require that the rule shall be laid on the table of the House 'as soon as possible'.
(ii) The rules will be subject to such modification as the House may like to make.
(iii) This period should be uniform and should be a total period of 30 days from the date of their final publication.

Committees on Delegated legislation

There are two committees one each in Lok Sabha and Rajya Sabha which extend the control over the delegated legislation. The Lok Sabha Committee was established in 1953 and the Rajya Sabha Committee was established in 1964. Both these committees consist of 15 members. The objectives of the Committee are provided in Rule 320 of the Lok Sabha which is to consider the following:

(i) Whether it is in accord with the general objects of the Constitution or the Act pursuant to which it is made.

(ii) Whether it contains matter which in the opinion of the Committee should more properly be dealt with in an Act of Parliament.
(iii) Whether it contains imposition of any tax.
(iv) Whether it directly or indirectly bars the jurisdiction of the courts.
(v) Whether it gives retrospective effect to any of the provisions in respect of which the Constitution or the Act does not expressly give any such power;
(vi) Whether it involves expenditure from the Consolidated Fund of India or the public revenues.
(vii) Whether it appears to make some unusual or unexpected use of the powers conferred by the Constitution or the Act pursuant to which it is made.
(viii) Whether there appears to have been unjustifiable delay in its publication or in laying it before the Parliament.
(ix) Whether for any reason its form or purport calls for any elucidation.

The committees submit their respective reports to the House. These committees have been doing an exemplary job. They are not only scrutinising the legislations submitted, but also framing norms and standards for the administration to follow in the future. The Parliamentary control over legislation becomes a reality through these committees. But these committees cannot question the policy basis on which such delegation is made.

3. **Judicial control:** The judiciary keeps control over such delegation through two tests:

(a) Substantive *ultra vires*
(b) Procedural *ultra vires.*

(a) **Substantive *Ultra vires*:** Substantive *Ultra vires* is when the contents of the delegated legislation goes beyond the purview of the delegation spirit. Such contention can be invoked under the following circumstances:

(i) Where the parent act itself is unconstitutional
(ii) Where it is unreasonable and malafide
(iii) Where the delegation is in conflict with the Constitution and the Parent Act
(iv) Where it involves sub-delegation
(v) Where it has a retrospective effect
(vi) Where it is excluded from judicial review

In the Indian Express Newspapers v. Union of India, Justice Venkataramiah stated as follows:

'A piece of subordinate legislation does not carry the same degree of immunity which is enjoyed by a statute passed by a competent legislature. Subordinate legislation may be questioned on any of the grounds on which plenary legislation is questioned. In addition, it may also be questioned on the ground that it does not conform to the statute under which it is made. It may also be questioned on the ground that it is unreasonable, not in the sense of not being reasonable, but in the sense that it is manifestly arbitrary'.

(b) **Procedural *Ultra-vires*:** Procedural *ultra vires* is when the substantive legislation fails to comply with the accepted provisions of the Parent Act. The two important requirements for these are

(i) **Publication:** With the publication of the records, it is impossible to keep record of the delegated legislation. In the United Kingdom, there is a Statutory Instruments Act, 1946, which makes compulsory the publication of the delegated legislation. Likewise in the United States, the Federal Register Act, 1935, provides for publication of all federal rules, orders, regulations etc. In India there is no such legislation. In 1960, the government enacted and codified 'Statutory Rules and Order' which initiated the publication of various rules. These were not implemented properly. Hence, there is need to make the publication of such rules mandatory so that it is useful to all the concerned parties, such as the government, judiciary and finally the people. A yearly 'consolidation index' can be drawn to keep track of such delegated legislations.

(ii) **Consultation with affected interests:** Consultation will help to devise an effective and efficient legislation. It will also help promote positive relationship between the government and the affected interests as it would make the facts and consequences of the rules clear. The United States has a system of prepublication of the rules under Section 553 of the Administrative Procedure Act, which enables the system of consultation. In the United Kingdom, pre and post publication are normal feature which is carried on without any rules or legislations supporting it. To quote Lord Chancellor, '*We no longer promulgate the regulations or rules in the Gazette and wait for representations to be made. We go to the trade or interest concerned and deal with it by getting them round the table, hearing what they have to say, and then drafting the rules after obtaining their views*'.

Hence, the government of India and the State governments should take effective measures to publish rules before and after they are made, for effective consultation with the concerned parties. And sufficient time should be given to these interested parties to respond to these rules.

3.2.3 Private Members Bill – An Appraisal

The power to make law is the most important power of the Parliament. This predominant function of law making is carried out through government legislative procedures. Either the government or member of a parliament can initiate legislation for making law.

Private Member Bill is defined as a bill that is initiated by a member of the Parliament who is not part of the government, that is, such a member is only the member of the legislature and not that of the Executive.

Any MP who is not a minister is a private member and he/she can therefore submit a legislative proposal for enacting it as a law. This mechanism provides an opportunity to private members to initiate legislative proposals concerning issues of public interest.

The procedure of Government bills and the Private Members Bill share a lot in common, but vast differences do exist between them.

The commonality between the two is that both follow a similar legislative process and the outcome of such a process is the same.

The difference in procedure between the two bills relate to the following:

- During the process of pre-legislative consultation and drafting
- In aspects relating to initiation, consideration and approval of legislative proposals

The designation 'Private Members Bill' is used in most Westminster system jurisdictions in which a private member is a legislator who is not acting on behalf of executive branch (Britain, Scotland, New Zealand).

3.2.3.1 Procedure of Private Members Bill in the Parliament

a. **Introduction**

The following section deals with the procedure of introducing the Private members bill in the Parliament; this will be helpful in analysing the bill effectively.

In Lok Sabha, the last two and half hours of sitting on every Friday are generally allotted for transaction of Private Members Business, that is, private member's bills and resolutions. If there is no sitting of the house on a Friday the speaker may direct that two and half hours on any other day in a week may be allotted to such bills. Business relating to Bills and Resolutions is transacted on alternate Fridays starting with bills on the first Friday of the session and resolutions on the next Friday and so on. In Rajya Sabha, the whole day after the Question Hour on each Friday is allocated for the transaction of private members business.

The procedure for notice is as follows:

(a) A member who wants to introduce a bill has to give prior notice thereof. The period notice for introduction of a Bill is one month unless the speaker allows introduction at shorter notice.

(b) President's recommendation if necessary should also be applied for by the member. The President's recommendation is necessary for introduction and consideration of this Bill if it involves.
- Formation of new states, alteration of areas and boundaries of exiting states under (Article 3)
- Matters affecting taxation in which states are interested under [Article 271(1)]
- Expenditure from consolidated fund of India.

If President withholds his recommendation for introduction, the Bill cannot be introduced.

The primary responsibility for drafting of private members bill is that of members concerned. The Lok Sabha secretariat nevertheless renders necessary assistance in putting the bill in proper form.

Motions for introduction of all the bills due for introduction on a particular day allotted to private members bills are included in the list of business for that day.

After the bills have been introduced and before these are taken up for consideration in the House, the committee on private members bills and resolutions classifies the bills according to their nature, urgency, importance, and allots precedence accordingly for the purpose of consideration of the house. The time for their discussion is also allocated by the committee. And such relative precedence of Bills in a particular category is determined through a ballot.

b. **General Discussion – Motions after Introduction of Bills**

The member concerned may move any of the following motions:

1. The bill be taken into consideration.
2. The bill be referred to a select committee or to a joint committee thereon.

3. The bill be circulated for the purpose of eliciting opinion thereon.

 When all the clauses and schedules of the bill have been considered and adopted by the house, the member in charge of the bill can move that the bill be passed. If the motion is adopted, the bill is deemed to have been passed.

c. **Committee on Private Members Bills and Resolutions**

 The Committee consists of 15 members nominated by the speaker. The functions of committee is to examine the bill, allot time to such bills and perform other functions related to the bills as may be assigned to it by speaker from time to time.

 Once the bills are taken up for consideration, the government is left with the following three options.

 (a) To reject it, in which case government ensures that motion for the consideration of the bill is negative.
 (b) To support it, in which government answers that the bill is passed.
 (c) To give assurance that it will incorporate the points raised in a comprehensive legislation.

3.2.3.2 *Analysis of Private Members Bill*

a. **Private Members Bill – Golden Age**

 The golden age in the context of Private Members Bill coincides with the Prime-Ministership of Nehru, which is often referred as the golden age of India's parliamentary democracy. Nehru's government encouraged such Bill's and ensured their passage in both the houses. Nehru took personal interest in strengthening the system and attended discussions and debates. The government respected the knowledge and commitment of MPs sponsoring the Private Members Bills, enlarging the scope of their engagement with the proceedings of both the houses.

 With the active support of the government, individual parliamentarians could enact a new bill, and achieve praise for their legislative initiatives. Both the houses took active interest in Private Members Bills in terms of conducting informed debates by holding multiple sittings and meticulously scrutinizing the bills in the select/joint committees.

 During 1952 and 1970, out of 14 Private Member Bills passed, 5 of them originated in Rajya Sabha and 9 in Lok Sabha. In terms of members, barring 2 independent members the rest were from the Congress party.

 Apart from enacted Private Members Bills, there were also occasions when a number of such Private bills were taken up for consideration, giving opportunities for MPs and government to engage in a constructive debate.

 This period also epitomized a healthy tradition of parliamentary debates during the consideration of these bills. Members of the Congress party enjoyed so much freedom that they could pilot Bills on subjects which ran counter to the stated ideals of the party. It was a vibrant phase during which governments approach towards Private Members Bill remained positive.

b. **Private Members Bill – An Oppositional Era**

 During the Prime Minister ship of Indira Gandhi especially during 1971–1977 and 1980–1984, the attitude towards such Bills got changed. During this period, not a single Private Members Bill received government support. It largely remained a routine and banal exercise. Because of the non-existent intra-party democracy members of the Congress party did not enjoy the freedom to express themselves independently and Private Members Bill was mainly seen as an opposition activity as majority of Bills were moved by members of opposition.

Even during Janata Government 1979, members of opposition parties still had higher stakes in Private members Bill procedure during post-Indira Gandhi period.

Only 14 private members bills passed since. They are listed in the following list as compiled by *PRS India*:

1. **The Muslim Wakfs Bill, 1952:** The bill was for providing better governance and administration of Muslim Wakfs and the supervision of Mutawallis' management of them in India. The bill was introduced by Syed Mohammed Ahmed Kasmi in the Lok Sabha and passed in 1954.
2. **The Code of Criminal Procedure (Amendment) Bill, 1953:** It was introduced by Raghunath Singh in the Lok Sabha, the bill was passed in 1956. The bill aimed to empower the revisional court to stay or suspend the final orders of lower courts.
3. **The Indian Registration (Amendment) Bill, 1955:** This bill was moved by S.C. Samanta in the Lok Sabha and was passed in 1956. The bill aimed at removing the anomaly of recording castes and sub-castes of parties in a deed for registration, as India is a secular state.
4. **The Proceedings of Legislature (Protection of Publication) Bill, 1956:** This bill was brought by Feroze Gandhi in the Lok Sabha, it was passed in 1956. It aimed to protect journalists reporting on parliament proceedings and to define by law the privilege available to publications made in good faith of reports of proceedings of legislatures.
5. **The Women's and Children's Institutions (Licensing) Bill, 1954:** It was introduced by Rajmata Kamlendu Mati Shah in the Lok Sabha and passed in 1956, the bill was to regulate and license orphanages and other institutions caring for women and children under 18 years of age and to provide for the proper custody, care and training of their inmates.
6. **The Ancient and Historical Monuments and Archaeological Sites and Remains (Declaration of National Importance) Bill, 1954:** The bill was introduced in the Rajya Sabha by Raghubir Singh aimed to get certain monuments included in the list of Monuments of National Importance declared in the principal Act of 1951.
7. **The Hindu Marriage (Amendment) Bill, 1956:** It was introduced in the Rajya Sabha by Seeta Parmanand and passed in 1956, this bill says that when both the parties belong to the Hindu religion and are marrying under the Special Marriage Act, they will be governed by the Hindu Succession Act, 1956.
8. **The Code of Criminal Procedure (Amendment) Bill, 1957:** It was introduced by Subhadra Joshi in the Lok Sabha and passed in 1960. To remove the hardship caused to a woman in spending money on litigation when her husband commits the offence of bigamy.
9. **The Orphanages and Other Charitable Homes (Supervision and Control) Bill, 1960:** It was introduced in the Rajya Sabha by Kailash Bihari Lall and passed in 1960, the bill was to provide for the supervision and control of orphanages and other charitable institutions for their better management.

10. **The Marine Insurance Bill, 1959:** The bill was introduced by M.P. Bhargava in the Rajya Sabha and was passed in 1963, this bill modified the law relating to marine insurance.
11. **The Hindu Marriage (Amendment) Bill, 1962:** It was Introduced in the Lok Sabha by Diwan Chand Sharma, the bill was passed in 1964 to make the right to apply for divorce available to both the parties in case of a decree for judicial separation or restitution of conjugal rights instead of the right being available only to the party who obtained the decree.
12. **The Salaries and Allowances of Members of Parliament (Amendment) Bill, 1964:** It was introduced by Raghunath Singh in the Lok Sabha and was passed in 1964. It was aimed to raise the salaries and allowances of members of the Parliament in order to meet the high cost of living. Also to provide air travel facilities.
13. **The Indian Penal Code (Amendment) Bill, 1967:** It was introduced by Diwan Chaman Lall in the Rajya Sabha and passed in 1969 it was to enable works of art to be exempted from the penal clauses in the principal Act relating to punishment for obscenity.
14. **The Supreme Court (Enlargement of Criminal Appellate Jurisdiction) Bill, 1968:** It was introduced in the Lok Sabha by Anand Narian Mullah and passed in 1970 aimed to enlarge the appellate jurisdiction of the Supreme Court in regard to criminal matters.

The rights of Transgender person Bill 2014 passed by Rajya Sabha is the first private members bill to get Upper House approval in the past 45 years.

3.2.3.3 Impact and Value of Private Members Bill

Significance of these bills cannot be measured merely in terms of numbers passed. Even unsuccessful proposals of the bills, had made members engaging in a meaningful debate on the subject of the bills and mobilizing support from different sections of the house.

Another prime determinant of success of such bills is its passage into law. Given the challenges they face, it is not their primary objective in introducing bills, a number of different motivation exists, which includes, addressing a gap in the law, seeking to change an existing area of government policy and raising the issue for further discussion and publicity.

The impact and value of these bills may be considered under following heads. Various Private Member Bills enacted for the following reasons:

1. **Legislation on contentious issues:** Private Member Bills are preferred methods for introducing legislation on contentious issues of social reform on which public and parliamentary opinion may be too sharply divided for the government to take initiative.
2. **Introduction of new ideas:** Private Member Bills are useful instrument in introducing new ideas into legislative process and ensure that they are discussed and enacted.
3. **Benefit the government:** Government gets the knowledge and expertise, vigilance and attention of the private members especially of the opposition on issues of public interest.
4. **Publicity and public opinion building:** If this Bill reflects an issue of abiding public interest to which government has not accorded any priority such a bill is likely to attract much public attention. Proactive media reporting and an informed public debate can force government to consider the Private members bill.

5. **Enhancement of the stature and profile of private members:** It seeks to enhance the unique 'Parliamentarian as legislator' role of MPs. It enables MPs to articulate various shades of public opinion for common good. It sharpens their legislative acumen and empowers private members.

3.2.3.4 *Obstacles to the Success of Private Members Bill*

1. The procedure is distinct from the government bills procedure. The procedural hurdles which hampers the such Bills are
   a. One month notice for introduction.
   b. Ceiling to number of bills that can be introduced by a member during a session.
   c. The relative precedence of these Bills to be held through Ballot process, which is irrational and some deserving bill to be discussed wait for long time.
   d. Prior presidential recommendation for introduction of certain Bills which includes matters concerning Article 3, Article 274 (1) & Article 117(3). If President withholds his recommendation, then the Bills cannot be introduced. This provision is derided as 'Paternalistic relic of limited democracy'. Since recommendation of the President is withheld on many occasions based on the advice of executive.
   e. **Paucity of time and Friday schedule** – Two and half hours earmarked on alternate Fridays is a limiting provision. Lack of adequate attendance of MPs on Fridays struggles to a mars sufficient support in the plenary due to member's weakly constituency commitments. MPs are often not seen as lawmakers and seldom judged on policy accomplishments. Also there is no regulation on the time taken by members while participating in the debate on these bills, which therefore leads to consuming vital time.
   f. **Absence of drafting support** – Legislative drafting requires legal knowledge, specialist competence, and adequate human and material resources. The expertise in law making and financial support are not made available to private members. Often government holds back its support to these bills on grounds of flawed drafting.

3.2.3.5 *Government Influence and Control*

Government attitude is the most important factor in determining the success of such Bills.

Government looks for an opportunity to arrogate time available for these Bills under one pretext or other since government does not want to be seen lacking legislative ideas, it lack enthusiasm in supporting the Private Members Bill. It is evident from the fact that

a. Around 56% of Private Members Bills in Lok Sabha and 65% of Private Members Bills in Rajya Sabha are withdrawn, since in Lok Sabha, members are not able to mobilize requisite support and government assurance that it will be bringing out comprehensive legislation, the Private members withdraw their bill. But government is seldom serious in bringing out legislation. Since this assurance is not monitored from the perspective of securing executive accountability.
b. Since Independence, 28% of these bills have been rejected when the government disagrees with the legislative intent of the bill.

3.2.3.6 Conclusion

Overall it is important to note that as many as 712 Private Members Bills were taken up for consideration by both the hours during first 14 Lok Sabhas, but only 14 of those bills got enacted. This calls for serious analysis of the procedure and other aspects that impedes its success. The Private Member Bill procedure should form a part of parliamentary reform agenda in India.

3.2.4 Criminalization of Politics and Politicization of Criminals

A budding criminal generally begins his activity at the local level by starting with petty crimes. And in big cities, it moves on to selling country liquor, gambling, betting and prostitution etc. The politicians use such criminals for their own selfish ends and the criminals and their cartels seek patronage and protection to carry on their illegal activities. Napoleon may be quoted here, he stated that because of great complexity with politics, that there could be no established ethics associated with it. He noted that politics and ethics seldom went together. And it at all they did, it was because of an omission, or such an ethical principle itself was distorted to suit the political ends and goals. The administration and the Police are the first causalities of the criminalization of politics, as it results in a situation of law which is neither fair nor impartial.

What is could be constituted as crime at very outset? As per *Oxford dictionary*, an action or omission which constitutes an offence and is punishable by law. And as per dictionary.com, an action or an instance of negligence that is deemed injurious to the public welfare or morals or to the interests of the state and that is legally prohibited can be defined as a crime.

The political setup seems to be suffering from multi-organ failure; and every organ seems to have stopped functioning in so far as the life of a common man. There is clear evidence of degradation of political order everywhere. The state which is both omnipresent and weak, has vacillated, and its responses vary over a wide range: indifference, intermittent concessions and repression.

The method of repression has been ineffective and this in turn has showed the breakdown of civil machinery used for protection creating a much worse law and order situation, this thus has led some section of citizens to take up protection themselves by organising private army.

The saddest situation was when the Home Minister expressed his inability to do anything regarding the prevailing lawlessness and the Prime Minister himself being helpless in the face of corruption charges faced by his ministers, who refused to tender resignation despite his advice, as was seen in the previous UPA government, where despite averments of Prime Minister Dr. Manmonhan Singh to the presence of corrupt politicians in his cabinet, who were named in various scams such as the Commonwealth games scam, 2G scam etc. was unable to remove them because of the coalition compulsion and electoral politics.

The present Prime Minister Narendra Modi, in his maiden speech in the 16th Lok Sabha, made an appeal to all the Members to raise above the petty political considerations and made a joint appeal on behalf of the members to the Chief Justice of India to ensure speedy trial of the law makers who were facing various charges under the law. But no headway has been made in this regard.

As per the analysis made by the *Association of Democratic Reforms* (ADR), the candidates charged with crime have a 2:1 chance of winning elections compared with those who have a clean record. Hence, those who have criminal record have a better chance of winning that those who are clean.

The Supreme Court in the recent case of *Manoj Narula v. Union of India*, noted that '*A democratic polity, as understood in its quintessential purity, is conceptually abhorrent to corruption and, especially corruption at high places, and repulsive to the idea of criminalization of politics as it corrodes the legitimacy of the collective ethos, frustrates the hopes and aspirations of the citizens and has the potentiality to obstruct, if not derail, the rule of law.' And it also stated that, 'Criminalisation of politics is an anathema to the sacredness of democracy' and 'Criminalisation of politics, it can be said with certitude, creates a dent in the marrows of the nation'.*

Despite such observations, the Supreme Court held that, '*While it may be necessary, due to the criminalization of our polity and consequently of our politics, to ensure that certain persons do not become Ministers,* ***this is not possible through guidelines issued by this Court****. It is for the* ***electorate to ensure that suitable*** *(not merely eligible) persons are elected to the Legislature and it is for the Legislature to enact or not enact a more restrictive law. It is not for this Court to lay down any guidelines relating to who should or should not be entitled to become a legislator or who should or should not be appointed a Minister in the Central Government. This being the position, the* ***burden of appointing a suitable person as a Minister in the Central Government lies entirely on the shoulders of the Prime Minister*** *and may eminently be left to his or her good sense. In this respect, the Prime Minister is, of course, answerable to Parliament and is under the gaze of the watchful eye of the people of the country*'.

Thus, the Supreme Court refused to interfere with the matters of appointment of tainted members as Ministers, as it was considered to be the prerogative of the Prime Minister and it would be encroaching upon the powers of the legislature if it does so.

The political leaders are maintaining double standards and double faces, acting in public and revealing real intention in private. The entire election process has been taken over by the money power and the criminal elements surrounding it.

Nani A. Palkhivala, the eminent constitutional expert observes in '*Squandered legacy*' Published in Hindustan Times in 1997, that '*I do not think India, in its entire history of five thousand years, has ever reached a lower level of degradation than it has reached now.... The picture that emerges is that of a great nation in a state of moral decay, of which crime, chaos and corruption are three of the several facets. India at fifty is sick and sad*'.

Despite this observation it would be wise to recall the memorable words of Dr. Rajendra Prasad on 26th November, 1949. He had this to say:

> '*Whatever the Constitution may or may not provide, the welfare of the country will depend upon the way in which the country is administered. That will depend upon the men who administer it. It is a trite saying that a country can have only the Government it deserves. Our Constitution has provision in it which appear to some to be objectionable from one point or another. We must admit that the defects are inherent in the situation in the country and the people at large.* ***If the people who are elected are capable and men of character and integrity, they would be able to make the best even of a defective Constitution****. If they are lacking in these, the Constitution cannot help the country. After all, a Constitution like a machine is a lifeless thing.* ***It acquires life because of the men who control it and operate it, and India needs today nothing more than a set of honest men who will have the interest of the country before them***'.

3.2.4.1 Vohra Panel Report

The Government constituted a committee with Union Home Secretary N.N. Vohra as Chairman, and Secretary R&W, Director I.B., Director C.B.I. Special Secretary Home as members to look into the matters related to crime in politics and administration.

The report categorically pointed out that the crime syndicates and the criminal mafia organisations have developed enough clout, money power, and has established associations with the administrators, political leaders and others. The report observes the following:

'An organized crime syndicate/Mafia generally commences its activities by indulging in petty crime at the local level, mostly relating to illicit distillation/gambling/organized satta and prostitution in the larger towns... In the biggest cities, the main source of income relates to real estate forcibly occupying lands/buildings. Procuring such properties at cheap rates by forcing out the existing occupants/tenants etc., Over time, the money power thus acquired is used building up contacts with bureaucrats and politicians... The money power is used to develop a network of muscle power which is also used by the politicians during elections'.

The Director of Central Bureau of Investigation has reported that '*the nexus between the criminal gangs, police bureaucracy and politicians has come out clearly in various parts of the country*'.

The Director of Intelligence Bureau in the report has also stated that

'there has been a rapid spread and growth of criminal gangs, armed senas, drug mafias, smuggling gangs, drug peddlers and economic lobbies in the country which have, over the years, developed an extensive network of contacts with the bureaucrats/government functionaries at the local levels, politicians, media persons and strategically located individuals in the non-state sector'.

In this context, the Director of Intelligence Bureau in the report has given the following examples:

1. In certain states like Bihar, Haryana and UP, these gangs enjoy the patronage of local-level politicians, cutting across party lines and the protection of Government functionaries. Some political leaders become the leaders of these gangs/armed senas and, over the years, get themselves elected to local bodies, State Assemblies and national Parliament. Resultantly, such elements have acquired considerable political clout seriously jeopardizing the smooth functioning of the administration.
2. The big smuggling syndicates having international linkages, have spread into and infected the various economic and financial activities, they indulge in various illegal activities including hawala transactions, circulation of black money and operations of vicious parallel economy causing serious damage to the economic fibre of the country. These syndicates have acquired substantial investigating and prosecuting agencies extremely difficult; even the members of the judicial system have not escaped the embrace of the Mafia.

   Director of Intelligence Bureau in the report has stated that '*the network of Mafia is virtually running a parallel Government pushing that State apparatus into irrelevance. Criminalization of politics has been responsible for the problems related to law and order in our nation*'.

   Thus, the essence of the Vohra Committee report is that '*Crime Syndicates flourish under political patronage*' and '*the politician-criminal nexus was running a parallel government pushing the State to insignificance*'.

3.2.4.2 Criminalization of Politics

L.S. Rathore in his Presidential Address in XII-Rajasthan Political Science Conference on the topic 'Political Culture of India's Ruling Class' observed that, '*Another feature in the political culture of ruling class is the politicization of crime and the criminalization of politics. Politicization of crime involves the competitive use of anti-social forces for the mobilization of party funds, for management of elections, for organizing meetings and conferences and even for recruiting workers at lower levels from among anti-social elements. It also means the misuse of criminal intelligence as a political tool for blackmailing political opponents*'.

'*Criminalization of politics means direct entry of criminals into the political parties and legislatures, including parliament, it also means the use of criminal methods and tactics to influence political processes and procedures*'.

No other vocation yields better and quicker results than politics, hence there is increase in taking over of the politics by crooks, rogues, criminals and other anti-social elements.

And today politics is no longer decent; the public life is encroached by hooligans and hoodlums. Notorious criminals, gangsters, smugglers and murderers are gaining control over the political system. Till recently these elements were only at the periphery of the political system, and now they have got considerable clout and power to manipulate the system itself.

The former Chief Minister of Bihar, Mr. Lalu Prasad Yadav once made a statement in the assembly that, some members came to the assembly carrying arms and that very soon there would be firing inside the house if such practice is not curbed. Thus, such an incident shows how criminalisation has grown in politics.

Kuldip Nayar, a renowned journalist, wrote in the Indian Express of August 7, 1995 that, '*according to the Chief Election Commissioner, 180 out of the 425 members of UP legislative Assembly had criminal records and the last general elections in Bihar were contested by as many as 243 candidates against whom charges were pending. In 1977, the Bihar Assembly had 10 MLAs who were history sheeters; by 1990, there were 40. Kalyan Singh, the Chief Minister of Uttar Pradesh, expanded his ministry in the last week of October 1997 to include every defector and criminal who supported him in the Assembly*'.

According to the leading magazine *India today*, '*of the 424 members of the Vidhan Sabha, 132 are suspected criminals, 16 of them now actually sit cabinet in the meetings presided over by Kalyan*'.

Former Election Commissioner *G.V.G. Krishnamurty*, while addressing press persons on 20th August,1997, said '*as per records, 40 members of parliament have criminal cases pending against them while nearly 700 members of state assemblies out of 4072, are named in criminal cases*'. According to him it was an internationally established norm that 'Law breakers cannot be allowed to be lawmakers', and which India must also follow.

Harinder Baweja, in his 'Changing face of Indian Parliament' report published in *India today, 1996* observes, that the teak panelled walls of the 11th Lok Sabha will shelter a host of elected representatives charged with the most brutal of crimes....Name the crime, and chances are you'll find an MP charged with it. Uttar Pradesh leads the way. A record 435 candidates with criminal backgrounds stood for election; 27 of these actually made it to Parliament. Leading the list is the BJP with 14 MPs, though they are charged mostly with petty cases. The SP has 7 MPs with criminal records, of whom 4 are history-sheeters. The BSP has 3 MPs named in criminal cases and the Congress, one.

As per the report published in Hindustan Times in 1998, at the eve of 12th Lok Sabha elections, there were 150 out of 4708 candidates all over the country, against whom charges of murder, rape, robbery and extortion had been made at one point of time or the other. In spite of the initiative taken by the Election Commission (EC) to debar historysheeters from seeking election to legislatures, at least 15 persons with criminal antecedents have made it to the Lok Sabha.

As per the Report published in *Outlook* magazine in 2004, 128 MPs in the 14th Lok Sabha had criminal charges against them. Of these, five MPs across the political spectrum score roughly the one-third of the crimes committed. A dozen had murder charges against them, another 10 had been charged with attempted murder. Around 11 of these were in public perception, known as 'dons'.

India Today magazine published in 2004, that 'the NDA has 37 MPs with criminal charges. Of 138 BJP MPs, the EC lists 26, about 20 per cent, with criminal charges. Out of 145 congress MPs, 15 close to 10 per cent, have criminal charges against them. The RJD has 40 per cent MPs with criminal charges while the BSP has over one-third 'tainted' MPs.

A preliminary analysis of the candidate **data compiled by the Association for Democratic Reforms (ADR)** for the Lok Sabha and Assembly elections gives an idea of the degree to which criminalisation has seeped into Indian politics.

This report examines the self-sworn affidavits submitted to the Election Commission of India by over 10,700 candidates who contested the Lok Sabha 2004 and 2009 elections and also takes a preliminary look at the number of criminal candidates who contested for the current Lok Sabha election. The analysis done by ADR from these affidavits has been further used and analysed to understand the patterns of criminalisation in our political system.

From ADR's compilation of data on 5380 candidates who contested the Lok Sabha election 2014, 17% have declared criminal charges in the affidavits submitted to the Election Commission; 10% have declared serious criminal charges such as murder and rape charges. Aam Aadmi Party (AAP) candidate S.P. Udayakumar, Kanyakumari constituency, Tamil Nadu, faces the highest number of criminal cases – 382 including 19 charges related to Attempt to Murder (IPC section 307) and 16 charges related to sedition (IPC section 124A). He is closely followed by M. Pushparayan, also an AAP candidate, Thoothukudi constituency, Tamil Nadu, with 380 criminal cases.

Figure 3.1 shows the proportion of candidates with criminal charges fielded by some major parties. Among the six national parties (the Indian National Congress [INC], the Bharatiya Janata Party [BJP], the Nationalist Congress Party [NCP], the Bahujan Samaj Party [BSP], the Communist Party of India [CPI], and the Communist Party of India (Marxist) [CPI-M]), the NCP has the highest percentage of candidates with criminal candidates (57%) followed by the CPI (M) (40%). The NCP also has the highest percentage of candidates with serious criminal charges (39%) followed by the BJP (18%).

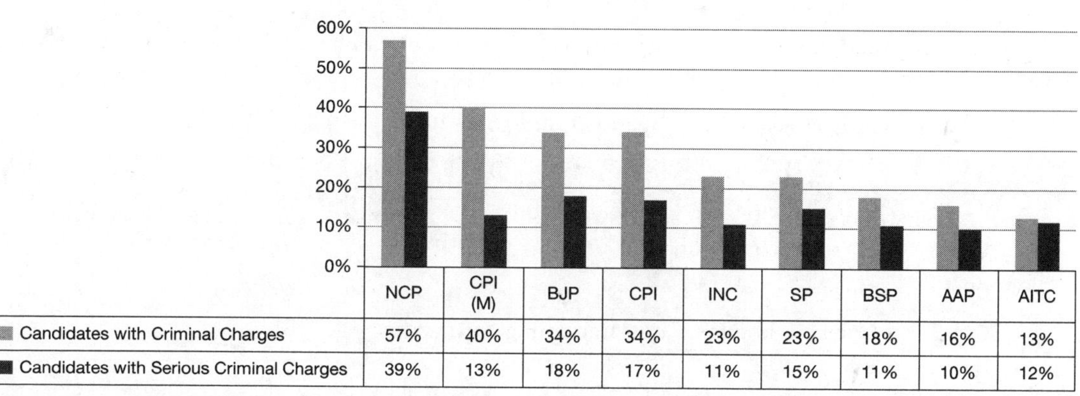

	NCP	CPI (M)	BJP	CPI	INC	SP	BSP	AAP	AITC
Candidates with Criminal Charges	57%	40%	34%	34%	23%	23%	18%	16%	13%
Candidates with Serious Criminal Charges	39%	13%	18%	17%	11%	15%	11%	10%	12%

FIGURE 3.1 Party-wise Candidates with Criminal Charges, Phase 1-Phase 5, Lok Sabha Elections 2014 *Source:* Association for Democratic Reforms.

States that top the list with the highest percentage of candidates facing criminal cases are Goa (32%), Kerala (29%), Bihar (26%) and Jharkhand (26%). On the lower end lie Rajasthan (6% candidates face criminal charges), Haryana (7% candidates face criminal charges) and Assam (7% candidates face criminal charges)

Among the 232 constituencies analysed 94 (41%) have at least three candidates with criminal cases.

The proportion of MPs in the 15th Lok Sabha facing criminal charges is not only high but actually increased between the 2004 and 2009 Lok Sabhas (see Figure 3.2). The proportion of MPs facing serious criminal charges (like murder, kidnapping and extortion) also showed an increase from 12% in 2004 to 14% in 2009.

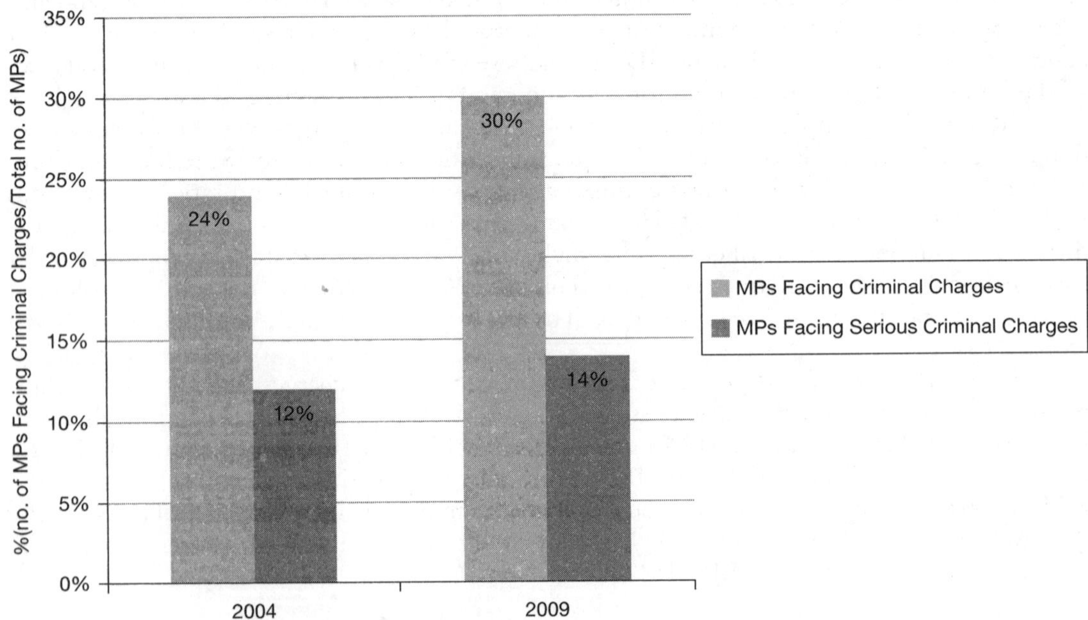

FIGURE 3.2 Proportion of MPs Facing Criminal Charges Lok Sabha 2009 *Source:* Association for Democratic Reforms.

TABLE 3.1 Serious IPC charges faced by MPs Lok Sabha 2009

IPC Section*	Offence	No of MPs Accused	No. of Women MPs Accused
307	Attempt to Murder	26	1
302	Murder	17	
304	Culpable homicide not amounting to murder	3	
384	Extortion	2	
364	Kidnapping or abducting in order to murder	7	
124	Assaulting President, Governor, etc., with intent to compel or restrain the exercise of any lawful power	7	
395	Dacoity	6	
471	Using as genuine a forged document or electronic record	6	

IPC Section*	Offence	No of MPs Accused	No. of Women MPs Accused
332 & 333	Voluntarily causing hurt or grievous hurt to deter public servant from his duty	22	1
353	Assault or criminal force to deter public servant from discharge of his duty	32	2

*Note: List is not exhaustive
Source: Association for Democratic Reforms

The current Lok Sabha has 76 MPs accused of multiple serious crimes with an average of three cases each (see Table 3.1). Out of the 37 political parties represented in the Lok Sabha, MPs from 22 parties face serious criminal charges.

In 25 constituencies, the number of candidates with criminal charges was higher than the number of candidates without any criminal charges (without taking independent candidates into account). For the recent Lok Sabha elections, out of the 1566 candidates analysed by ADR, 18% have declared criminal charges and 10% have declared serious criminal charges in their affidavits.

Figure 3.3 shows the levels of criminalisation among the candidates contesting elections and among winners, for both the 2004 and the 2009 Lok Sabha elections.

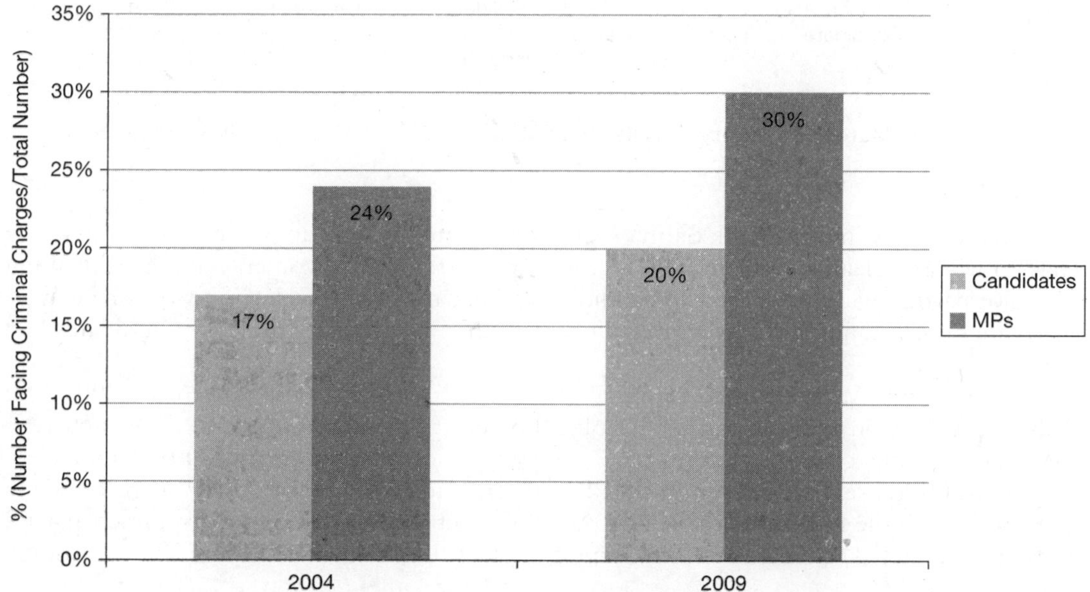

FIGURE 3.3 Percentage of Candidates and MPs Facing Criminal Charges for Lok Sabha 2004 and Lok Sabha 2009 *Source:* Association for Democratic Reforms.

3.2.4.3 Criminality and Winnability

The evident link between criminality and the probability of winning is further reinforced when we look at the winnability of a candidate. While any random candidate has one in

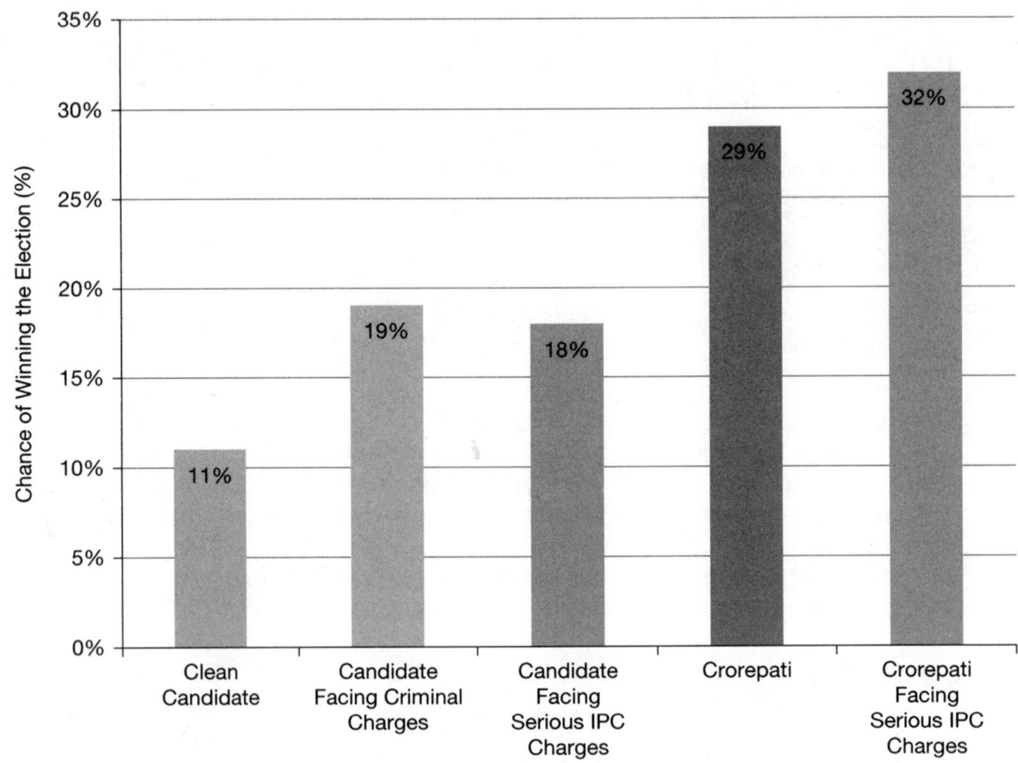

FIGURE 3.4 Candidate Winnability in 2009 Lok Sabha Election *Source:* Association for Democratic Reforms.

eight chances of winning a Lok Sabha seat, a candidate facing criminal charges is twice as likely to win as a clean candidate. The picture is no different for women candidates. Among the major parties (with more than 10 candidates), those that lost the election were on an average cleaner (14% candidates had criminal charges) than those that won (26% candidates had criminal charges).

Twenty-four MPs who had criminal charges against them and won in the 2004 Lok Sabha election, won again in the 2009 Lok Sabha election (see Figure 3.4). Eleven current MPs facing serious criminal charges have been given tickets to contest the Lok Sabha election, 2014. Of these, Ganesh Singh (BJP), Naveen Jindal (INC) and Avtar Singh Bhadana (INC) won both the Lok Sabha 2004 and the 2009 elections. This shows that political parties continue to give tickets to candidates despite the fact that they have criminal cases pending against them.

Another notable pattern is the vital link between money power and muscle power. There are more candidates as well as MPs with criminal backgrounds in the top 25% of declared asset value than in the bottom 25%. While a clean crorepati had a 29% chance of winning the Lok Sabha 2009 elections, a crorepati facing criminal charges had a 29% chance of winning. The chances increased further to 32% for a crorepati facing serious criminal charges.

For major parties, Figure 3.5 shows that the value of assets increases from candidates to winners and to winners with criminal charges (NCP is an exception).

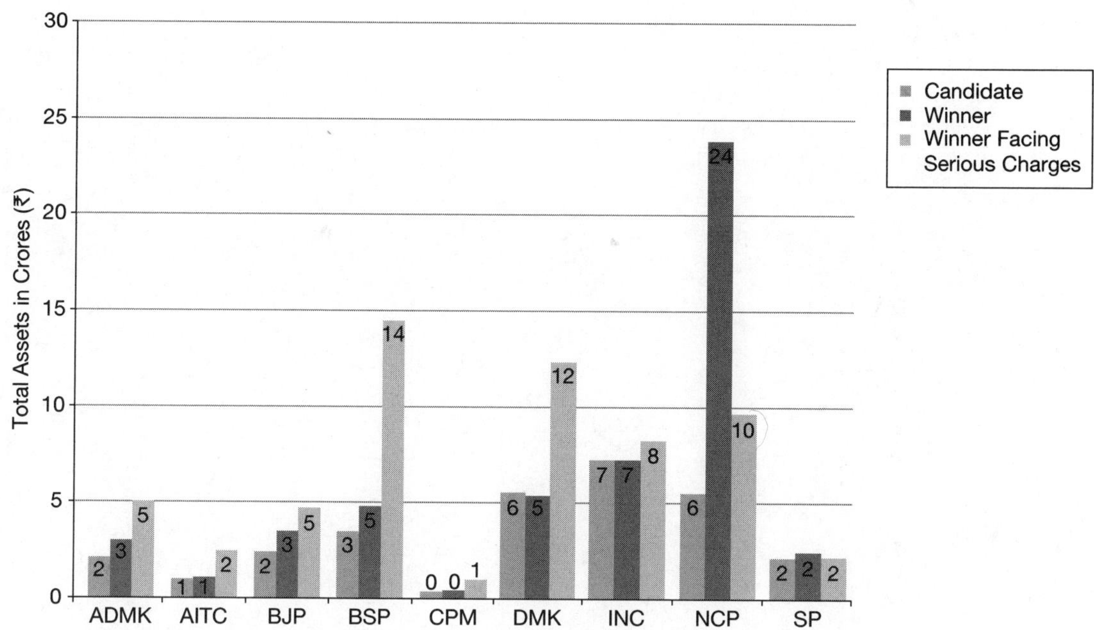

FIGURE 3.5 Party-wise Average Asset Value *Source:* Association for Democratic Reforms.

Figure 3.6 shows party-wise winning chances for candidates for the Lok Sabha election 2009.

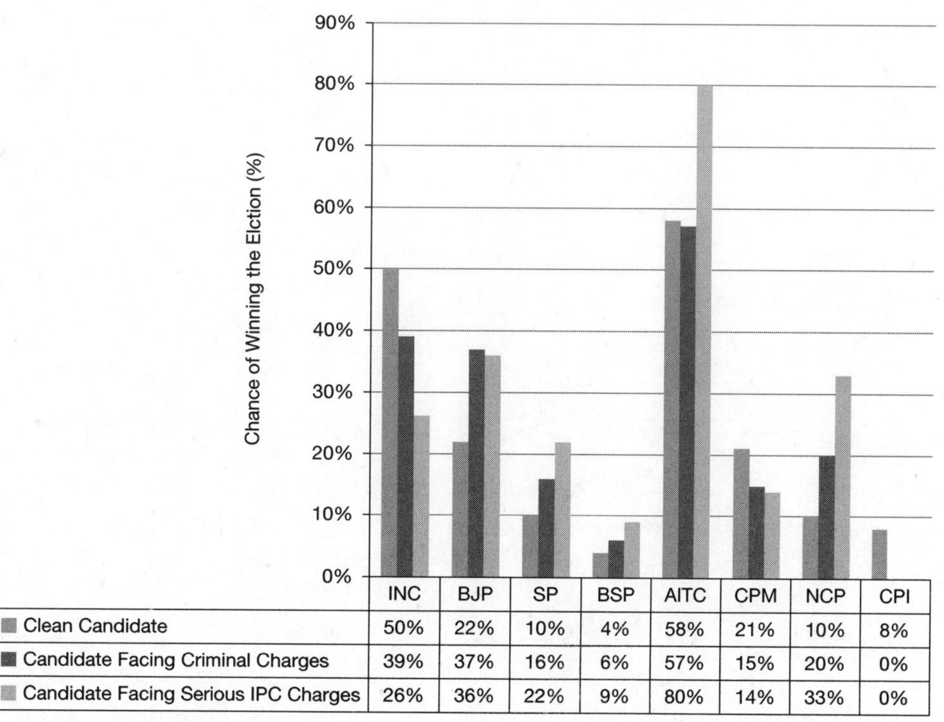

	INC	BJP	SP	BSP	AITC	CPM	NCP	CPI
Clean Candidate	50%	22%	10%	4%	58%	21%	10%	8%
Candidate Facing Criminal Charges	39%	37%	16%	6%	57%	15%	20%	0%
Candidate Facing Serious IPC Charges	26%	36%	22%	9%	80%	14%	33%	0%

FIGURE 3.6 Party-wise Winning Chances for Candidates, Lok Sabha Election 2009 *Source:* Association for Democratic Reforms.

Uttar Pradesh (UP), Gujarat and Maharashtra top the list with the highest percentage of MPs accused of criminal and serious criminal offences. UP elected 31 MPs with criminal charges, (contributing 54% of criminal MPs from UP) 23 of which are accused of serious crimes. Fifteen of these twenty-three are *crorepatis*. Similarly, in Maharashtra 10 of the 11 MPs facing criminal charges are crorepatis; in Gujarat five of the seven MPs facing criminal charges are *crorepatis*.

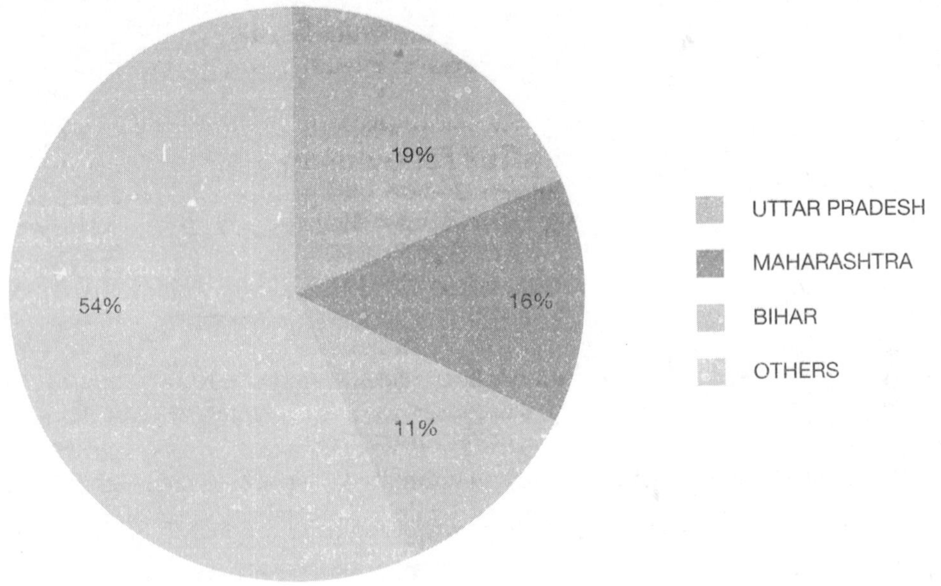

FIGURE 3.7 State-wise Percentage Share of MPs Facing Criminal Charges *Source:* Association for Democratic Reforms.

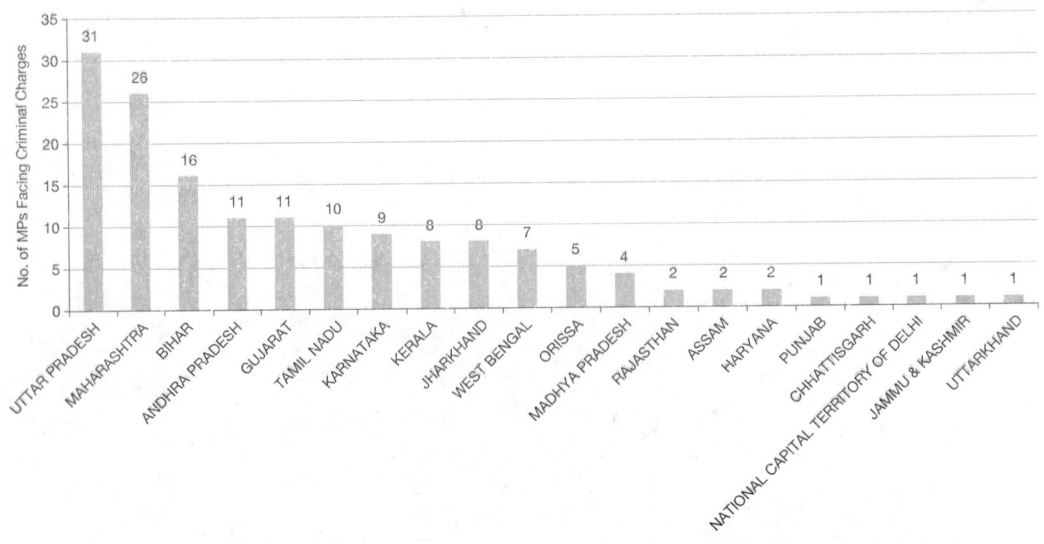

FIGURE 3.8 State-wise Number of MPs Facing Criminal Charges, Lok Sabha 2009 *Source:* Association for Democratic Reforms.

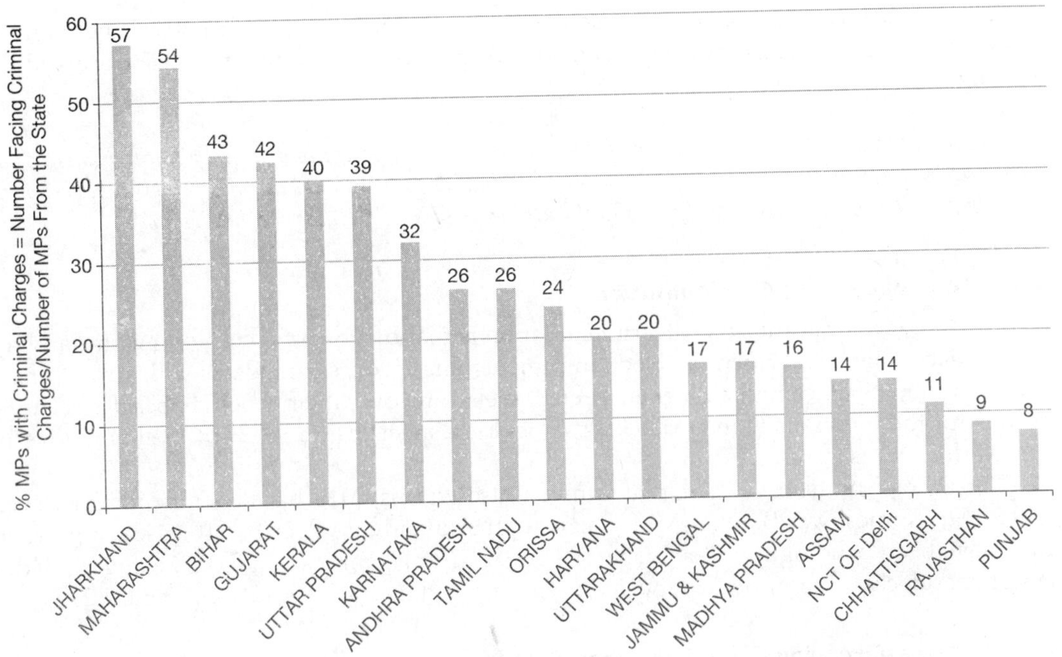

FIGURE 3.9 **State-wise Proportion of MPs Facing Criminal Charges, Lok Sabha 2009** *Source:* Association for Democratic Reforms.

The public perception that has been built over years is that politics and criminals have come to join hands together. The politics has been criminalised and the criminals have been politicised. The important reason for this is the reduction in quality of people entering politics. The days are gone when the MP or an MLA was considered to be a 'gapcloser' between the government and the public, acting as a catalyst between the masses and the government, and instead today he is considered to be a 'potential blackmailer' or 'freewheel dealer'.

The days are gone when stalwarts like Nehru, Kamaraj, Sardar Patel, Lal Bahadur Shastri, the people who wore their integrity and honesty on their sleeves. They had strong pro-people behaviour, and commitment and dedication towards public cause.

When the violence, booth capture, election rigging became order of the day, the advantage was with those who could either themselves resort to doing such acts or get others do it for them. Many of such gangsters realised that rather than helping other people win election through such acts, they themselves could, through such illegal and anti-social acts, get elected, and become ministers and legislators. And from that pedestal they could not only mock the state police but also plunder the wealth of the state. Former Bihar Director General of Police, says that, 'Until 1967, criminals were helping their political masters. Then they began to seek power themselves'. And the result therefore was entry of criminals into the legislature.

L.S. Rathore in his Presidential Address observed that, '*So brutalized has become politics today that we are handing over the country to underworld. The day is not too far when India shall have a new generation of ruling class led by these buccaneers and criminals: and that day is too near when the gangsters are going to take "giant strides" in politics*'.

The Lok Sabha passed a historic resolution at the special session of the Parliament on the occasion of the golden jubilee of independence, August 26 to September, 11997 observed the following:

'the meaningful electoral reforms be carried out so that our parliament and other legislative bodies be balanced and, effective instruments of democracy and further that political life and processes be free of the adverse impact , on governance of undesirable extraneous factors including criminalization'.

3.2.4.4 Consequences of Criminalisation

The primary sacrifice at the altar of criminalisation is that of governance, along with transparency and accountability. Expensive election campaigning favours candidates with strong financial background. Such candidates, when elected, seek to recover their expenses besides securing a corpus for the future election as quickly as possible, especially in the era of coalition governments with tenuous stability.

The average number of years that criminal cases against MPs have been pending is seven (until 2009). Kameshwar Baitha, JMM, Palamau, Jharkhand, has declared 10 cases of murder, which have been pending for an average of 12 years. Ramakant Yadav, BJP, Azamgarh, Uttar Pradesh, has declared a murder case which has been pending for 25 years (see Table 3.2).

TABLE 3.2 Years of Pending Cases, Lok Sabha 2009

S. No	MP/Party/Constituency/State	Details of Offences	No. of Years for Which the Cases have been Pending (as per Affidavits Filed in 2009 Elections)
1	Adhikari Sisir Kumar, AITC, Kanthi, West Bengal	Rioting and theft	28 years
2	Ramakant Yadav, BJP, Azamgarh, Uttar Pradesh	Murder	25 years
3	Ramkishun, SP, Chandauli, Uttar Pradesh	Attempt to commit robbery	24 years
4	Gandhi Dilipkumar Mansukhlal, BJP, Ahmednagar, Maharashtra	Concealing with intent to facilitate design to wage war	24 years
5	Venugopala Reddy Modugula, TDP, Narasaraopet, Andhra Pradesh	Attempt to murder	23 years
6	Kameshwar Baitha, JMM, Palamau, Jharkhand	Murder	20 years
7	Abdul Mannan Hossain, INC, Murshidabad, West Bengal	Attempt to Murder	20 years

Not all is lost though. A comparison of top 10 MPs with criminal charges in 2004 and 2009 Lok Sabha elections reveals that the number of MPs with serious criminal backgrounds has declined. For the top 10 MPs with serious criminal charges, the total number of cases decreased by 42%, count of serious IPC charges reduced by 32% and murder charges were reduced by 55%.

3.2.4.5 Efforts to Prevent Entry of Criminals into Politics

CPI's Indrajit Gupta says that, *'Criminalization of politics is worrying because Parliament is losing its credibility'*. Jai Pal Reddy, a leader of JD says, *'All parties have a nexus with criminals. The links just differ in degrees from party to party …. And in nature from State to state'*. As far as India is concerned, the criminal politics nexus goes beyond politics, it is not just the scramble for power. This runs so deep and wide that it virtually occupies every space in the state.

As Justice V.R. Krishna Iyer stated, corruption in public life begins with money in elections. Our system of elections is loaded with muscle power and money power, and these are abundantly available with the underworld. Section 77 of the Representation of People's Act puts an upper limit on the expenses incurred by a candidate. Other such election laws also recognise the danger of illegitimate money entering the political system through the election process.

But there are no regulations to control the money entering as donations to the political parties. These remain unaccounted for and are used in the election process. During the initial period, big businessmen and the industries sponsored and supported the political parties and its candidates. This practice continued and continues, and is supplemented by the kickbacks and the commissions received from foreign transactions. Experts are of the opinion that the political parties do not have enough legitimate money to fight elections, and hence are dependent on other sources for funding their campaign. And if the state starts to fund elections, may be such practices can be controlled and avoided. Such a state funding of elections is followed in Germany and United States of America.

Justice M.B. Shah's judgement in Electoral Reforms case on 2nd May, 2002, struck a blow to the Indian democracy by giving the voters right to know the full details about the person they are voting for.

And the Election Commission immediately on 28th June, 2002, implemented the Supreme Court's order within the specified time of two months. The Election Commission also sent recommendation to the government to amend the Forms 2A to 2E of the Conduct of Election Rules, 1961 which deals with the nomination process. The Commission also ordered the candidates to file the following information to the returning office:

1. Past criminal convictions
2. Pending criminal cases carrying a conviction of more than two years
3. Assets
4. Liabilities
5. Educational qualifications

The Supreme Court's judgement is based on two important principles:

(i) The citizen's right to know and informed, under Article 21.
(ii) The power and duty bestowed upon the Election Commission by virtue of Article 324 to conduct elections.

Every citizen has the right to know about the background of the person whom he is electing, and such information should not be hidden from the electorate.

The candidates have no reason to hide their background from the people whom they are going to represent, and if they do, they have no business in public life. The Supreme Court has not invented anything new, it has worked out the provisions within the framework of the

Constitution. There is sufficient precedent in both relating to right to know as well as the powers of the Election Commission.

3.2.4.6 Recent Decision by the Supreme Court

In a landmark judgement, the Supreme Court in 2013 ruled that the elected representatives cannot remain and continue in their office even if they had appealed to the higher court. The Court ruled that the representatives will be immediately disqualified from such date, if they are convicted.

The bench presided over by Justice A.K. Patnaik struck down Section 8(4) of Representation of People's Act as unconstitutional, this provision protected the membership of an MLA or an MP if he/she files an appeal within three months of date of conviction.

But this judgement did not act in retrospect, and thus sitting MLAs and MPs who were convicted before this verdict were not disqualified. Henceforth, an MLA or an MP will immediately be disqualified under Section 8 (1), (2) and (3), if he is convicted. Their membership will be protected if their conviction is stayed by the appellate Court.

This ruling jolted the political class, as henceforth if convicted they had no protection and will immediately be disqualified. The political parties then have to be very careful in selecting the candidates for election, as candidates having pending cases against them have their fate hanging in balance as the conviction will result in disqualification and therefore a new election to that particular constituency. No party would want to spend time, money and energy fighting for another election, and people too will become apathetic and the party will lose their support. Hence, the parties will be very careful in selecting their members to be fielded in the election.

The Supreme Court rejected the review petition filed by the government in the abovementioned case and upheld its verdict. It was an embarrassment for the entire political class. The review bench termed the judgement as 'well considered', and stated that it was 'not inclined' to grant review of the judgement which struck down the Section 8 (4) of the Representation of the People's Act.

The government immediately reacted by enacting an ordinance which was withdrawn subsequently due to public pressure.

3.2.4.7 Time-Bound Trials for Legislators

The Supreme Court has once again intervened to cleanse the political system, in trials involving MPs and MLAs, it has fixed a deadline of one year from the date of framing of charges. The Court now wants to ensure the tainted persons do not continue office, hence methods such as repeated adjournments, dilatory tactics etc. which delay the conviction and subsequent disqualification has been sought to be removed.

The Apex Court has asked the trial courts to expedite trials and finish them within a year; and if they are unable to do so, they should explain the reason for such delay to the Chief Justice of the concerned High Court. The delay in criminal justice system has worked to the advantage of the political class who are facing various charges in offences relating from corruption to attempt murder.

Many political leaders have managed to prolong their trial for years and they in the meantime stand in elections and get elected repeatedly and raise even to become Chief Ministers. Many such leaders stall the trial process by getting stay order or interlocutory orders from the higher court. The Criminal Procedure Code does not mention any time limit for completion of trials, but Section 309 says that once the examination of witness begins, then the trial has to be proceeded on a day-to-day basis until examination of all witness is over. This provision is rarely followed because of various reasons. It is impossible for a trial court to conduct the proceedings as the MLAs and MPs are influential and they engage lawyers who act to delay, and thwart the legal process. And thus the present judgement addresses this issue and empowers the trial court to refuse to grant routine repeated adjournments.

3.2.4.8 Conclusion

India Today magazine in 2004 published that, '*It is unfortunate that no countervailing force to check criminalization of politics is emerging. In recent court orders ranging from Supreme Court to High Courts to lower courts the Judiciary has been busy stumping the criminal politician, quashing his bail applications, ordering his arrest warrants and sending him to jail from hospitals. Unlike the campaign against tainted ministers in Parliament, this battle is neither partisan nor for each-finger-accusing the rival three-points towards you*'.

The **Association for Democratic Reforms (ADR)** in its report, suggests the following, The Supreme Court and the Election Commission of India (ECI) have undertaken some commendable steps for reforming the electoral process. But these two constitutional bodies are also bound by the laws enacted by the elected legislative body.

The ECI has achieved considerable success in containing the role of muscle power through measures such as the effective implementation of the model code of conduct and the setting up of the expense monitoring cell. Mandatory declaration of assets and existing criminal charges in self-sworn affidavits to the ECI prior to elections has brought in some transparency

Supreme Court judgments disqualifying convicted MPs and MLAs (*Lily Thomas v. Union of India, 2013*), barring those in jail from contesting (*Chief Election Commissioner vs. Jan Chowkidar, 2013*), directing the EC to bring the issue of election related freebies under the ambit of the Code of Conduct, the Allahabad High Court banning caste and religion based political rallies are all attempts to change the system. However, implementation of these judgements has faced unequivocal opposition from all the political parties. When the Supreme Court in its recent intervention (*Lily Thomas v. Union of India, 2013*) sought to prevent convicted MPs from continuing in office, the legislators promptly geared up to nullify the judgment through an ordinance. While the Supreme Court should be commended for taking long strides, judicial reforms targeting speedy disposal of cases could go a longer way in decriminalising the Parliament. The Supreme Court's recent order setting a deadline for the lower courts to complete trial in cases involving lawmakers within a year of framing of charges is a welcome step in this direction.

There is a widely anticipated participation of first time voters who are likely to constitute 10% of the electorate. This expected increase in voter turnout and recent civil society activism over issues, such as corruption, have stirred some awareness among voters in the 2014 Lok Sabha election. Whether this will make a difference to the criminal composition of the Parliament remains to be seen.

Levelling the electoral field by addressing the role of money power in elections is a pressing imperative. Deeper research into state-funding of elections and devising a metric to quantitatively measure the performance of individual MPs are areas of far-reaching consequences to the criminalisation of politics.

3.2.5 Rival Representative Claims of Parliament and Civil Society

3.2.5.1 Representative Claim of Parliament

Parliamentary government presumes that legislature holds the delegated sovereignty of the people (popular sovereignty). The locus of popular sovereignty remains unspecified in the Constitution due to the multiplicity of views within the constituent assembly on this question. Some argued that the Parliament is repository of sovereignty of people and some were of the view that sovereignty of people rest with head of the state since the government cannot by definition be representing the whole people. It was assumed that popular sovereignty needed a fixed locus.

K.T Shah's self-styled innovation of a referendum can be cited for sovereignty of people.

> *'Now this constitution does not provide for reference to the people, notwithstanding the fact that we talk again and again of the peoples sovereignty of the people being ultimate sovereign of this country. Our reference to the people, or consultation with people is expressed if at all only in a quinquennial election, a general election to the parliament. In a general election, however, so many issues are mixed up; so many cross-currents take place; so many moves and countermoves happen that the consultation with the people, or the verdict of the people on such variety of issues is only nominal, if I may say so without any disrespect. If you sovereign, if you want that the people be consulted in emergency when your two organs of power , viz., the legislature and the executive, are unable to agree , then the test will lie in your readiness to consult people'.*
>
> —(CAD, vol.VII, 10 December 1948:980)

3.2.5.2 Claim of Parliament

Recent time's power of the representative claim of the Parliament has been indeed derived from the **delegated power of electorate**. In various conflicts with judiciary this principle has been deployed repetitively to contrast the **unrepresentative character of judiciary**. This is quite evident in Shah Bano judgement.

The Supreme Court in Mohd. Ahmad Khan v. Shah Bano Begam and others held that if a divorced woman is able to maintain herself, the husband's liability ceases with the expiry of the period of iddat (three menstrual courses after the date of divorce, that is, roughly three months), but if she is unable to maintain herself after the period, she is entitled to have recourse to Section 125 CrPC. In the general election, 1984, Indian National Congress won absolute majority in the Indian parliament.

After the Shah Bano judgment, there was uproar in the Muslim community, fearing that the Congress will face decimation in the polls, Congress headed by the then prime minister Rajiv Gandhi enacted an act titled The Muslim Women (Protection of Rights on Divorce) Act 1986 that nullified the Supreme Court's judgment in the Shah Bano judgment. Diluting the Supreme Court judgment, the act allowed maintenance to a divorced woman only during the period of iddat, or till 90 days after the divorce, according to the provisions of Islamic law. This was in stark contrast to Section 125 of the Code. The 'liability' of husband to pay the maintenance was thus restricted to the period of the iddat only.

3.2.5.3 Microscopic Representation

In India, important shift occurred in principle of representation moving towards greater descriptive representation which mandates MPs to mirror the composition of diverse society. There is an increase in representation of backward castes due to mobilization by political party representing these groups. In case of Muslim minority or women, both of which remain hugely under-represented, compared to their proportion in the population. The idea that members of a particular group can comprehend and represent interest of these groups remains the basis for parliamentary system of government.

It's being argued that despite becoming more representative parliament has become less mindful of its representational role as an assembly of people as a whole. The civil society activists want the representative democracy to

1. Properly represent the preference and aspirations of the citizen
2. Be accountable to those who have elected them

3.2.5.4. Executives Undermining the Legislature

a. **India–United States Civil Nuclear Agreement**
   The United States of America and the Republic of India signed an agreement of nuclear cooperation, it is known as the US–India Civil Nuclear Agreement or Indo-US nuclear deal. The joint statement was made by then Indian Prime Minister Manmohan Singh and then U.S. President George W. Bush on 18th July, 2005, under which India agreed to separate its civil and military nuclear facilities and to place all its civil nuclear facilities under International Atomic Energy Agency (IAEA) safeguards and, in exchange, the United States agreed to work toward full civil nuclear cooperation with India.

   As details were revealed about serious inconsistencies between what the Indian Parliament was told about the deal, and the facts about the agreement that were presented by the Bush administration to the US Congress, opposition grew in India against the deal. Left Front, whose support was crucial for the ruling United Progressive Alliance (UPA) to prove its majority in the Indian parliament, continued to oppose the nuclear deal. The left front had been a staunch advocate of not proceeding with this deal citing national interests. UPA faced confidence vote in the Lok Sabha after the Communist Party of India (Marxist) led Left Front withdrew support over India approaching the IAEA for Indo-US nuclear deal. The UPA won the confidence vote with 275 votes to the opposition's 256, (10 members abstained from the vote) to record a 19-vote victory. This is a very clear indication of executive's dominance in the Parliament and the representatives opposing voices are ill-considered.

b. **Representative Claim of Civil Society**
   One among the pillars of democracy, Judiciary, which has been the principal antagonist of the Parliament is being replaced by civil society in recent times. This recent phenomenon of confrontation between civil society and the Parliament can be interpreted as contest of two principles: the **republican** and **liberal** citizenship.

   Judiciary, a premier institution in India has been challenging the Parliament on of what sort of departures from the constitutional principle of equality are consistent with the constitutional commitment to social, economic and cultural differences.

   The judiciary appears to be the conservative protector of individual rights and freedom and executives-in-legislature as the progressive socialist force for social justice.

   Today role of judiciary in relation to the Parliament has been replaced by the popular mobilization of civil society.

   Theorists of democracy have also paid attention to questions of **participatory** democracy, **strong** democracy and **deliberative** democracy. These express the profound dissatisfaction with the quality of democracy trapped inside representative institutions. There has been greater ineffectiveness of representative institutions in achieving the **core ideals of democracy** which includes

   (i) Active political engagement of citizens
   (ii) Creation of political consensus through dialogue means
   (iii) Design and implementation of public policies

In the context of India's democracy, its representative institutions seem to define its democracy. The apprehension of more popular mobilization of civil society seems to be sign of vulnerability and fragility of its democratic institutions to substantiate their representative claim in responsive legislation and policy.

Though the idea of popular sovereignty and popular rule that ultimately authorizes representative institutions, it is the very same principle of popular sovereignty that questions the legitimacy of these institutions. The contest is much over the questions of who really represent the people **(Parliament or civil society)** and not much about the institutional arena in which democracy is expressed.

Parliament	Civil Society
Authorized by constitution and representatives elected by legitimate procedure.	Represented by popular leaders outside political institutions backed by visible support of society.

c. **Nirbaya case**

In December 2012, a 23-year-old student was brutally gang-raped and tortured in Delhi and later succumbed to her injuries. Uproar followed the incident in the capital and the Parliament was compelled to introduce stricter laws to deal with sex crimes against women. A judicial committee headed by J. S. Verma, a former Chief Justice of India and one of India's most highly regarded Chief Justices and eminent jurists, was appointed by the Central government to submit a report within 30 days to suggest amendments to criminal law to sternly deal with sexual assault cases. The committee urged the public in general and particularly eminent jurists, legal professionals, NGOs, women's groups and civil society to share 'their views, knowledge and experience suggesting possible amendments in the criminal and other relevant laws to provide for quicker investigation, prosecution and trial, and also enhanced punishment for criminals accused of committing sexual assault of an extreme nature against women'.

The report indicated that failures on the part of the government and police were the root cause behind crimes against women. On 3rd February, 2013, the Criminal Law (Amendment) Ordinance, 2013 was promulgated by President Pranab Mukherjee. It provides for amendment of the Indian Penal Code, Indian Evidence Act, and Code of Criminal Procedure, 1973, on laws related to sexual offences. The ordinance provides for the death penalty in cases of rape. On 22 December 2015, Rajya Sabha passed the Juvenile Justice Bill, which proposed that the accused who are above 16 years of age will be treated as an adult in the court of law.

d. **Neduvasal Hydrocarbon Project Agitation**

On February 15, 2017, India's central government announced the award of contract for development and extraction of hydrocarbons from 44 contract areas nationwide, including 28 on-land fields and 16 offshore. Within a day of the announcement, protests broke out in Neduvasal, a village in Pudukottai district in southern Tamil Nadu. People from all walks of life participated in the protest garnering support for villagers' claim of damage to agricultural land and environmental degradation, if the project is furthered. The agitation halted the project and union and state ministers ensured the agitators that their demands will be met and the central government has assured the protesters that further permission will not be granted to the project till the people are consulted and operators are required to follow strict environmental norms for the use of operational land.

e. **India Against Corruption (IAC): The Civil Society Attack on Parliament**
A people's protest was organized in over 50 cities across India, to demand the passage of **a strong Lokpal (ombudsman) bill**, in the wake of revelations about misconduct in Commonwealth games and corruption in allocation of 2G spectrum. A draft of such bill was prepared by Team Anna with Anna Hazare being iconic leader of the team comprising Kiran Bedi, Santhosh Hedge, Prashant Bhushan and Aravind Kejriwal.

Over few months team Anna was consulting with different political parties with a view to build consensus on their proposed draft of Lokpal legislation. Anna went to fast at Jantar Mantar in Delhi to press this demand. There was a popular anger against the deluge of scams and the government capitulated to demand for a joint drafting committee that would include government nominees and members of civil society in equal proportion.

The committee couldn't meet consensus due to disagreement on details of the bill's provisions. When this exercise failed to yield results Anna again went to fast and found enthusiastic support from across the country.

Parliament passed a 'Sense of House' resolution accepting three principles which was put forward by Anna Hazare as non-negotiable

- A citizens' charter
- The lower-level bureaucracy to be brought within the ambit of the Lokpal
- The establishment of Lokayuktas in the states

Issues of giving Lokpal a constitutional status remained a point of contention and there was inadequate support for constitutional amendment.

When there was a lag in passing of Lokpal bill in the Parliament, Aravind Kejriwal decided to start a political party, Aam Aadmi Party (AAP) , which reiterates the commitment to the passage of a strong anti-corruption law applicable to both politicians and bureaucrats, but now seeks to achieve through participating in electoral system and also achieved stunning success in Delhi legislative assembly though it couldn't sustain a government.

A mobilization has been split into a movement and a party each representing one pole of the debate about representation.

In the recent confrontation by the civil society and parliamentarians, political party's arguments have been more in nature of ring fencing the Parliament and asserting rather than justifying or defending its supremacy. Civil society argues by dismissing parliamentary supremacy as they reiterate the original principle of popular authorization while also denying that popular authorization lies at the root of constitutional parliamentary supremacy.

Kejriwal solution to this problem is that people be given direct control over lawmaking process to a certain degree. And he proposes **two** ways in which this can be accomplished. The **first** is to **give people the initiative to propose laws via gramsabhas** and his **second** proposal is to ascertain the people's opinion on all laws in the Parliament and state legislatures.

Even in countries which have referendum provided in their constitution, this is a mechanism only of the last resort on particular contentious issues. It is not a routine method of decision making and making every citizen participate in every single legislation will elongate the time to pass any law, and also the more fundamental question is the envisioning of state legislatures and parliament as simple post office, processing the aggregate wisdom of gramsabhas.

The second claim by IAC that of authentically representing the wishes and aspirations of Indian people by citing the number of people who gathered in Anna Hazare's fast. This has become unfortunate because the validity of the claim became a simple function of numbers instead of strength of arguments offered in public reason and persuasion. There is also a further rick that other groups which claiming large supporters may make other claims that are less acceptable. On what basis can we arbitrate the representational claim of one segment of civil society as legitimate and other is not? For instance both corporates and civil society can call to speak in national interest: first in the name of prosperity of nation, and the second for welfare of citizens. As both claim to represent in name of collective good--- how, and by whom, might such representational claims be arbitrated?

f. **Conversation of rival claims**

In modern democracies both legislatures and civil societies make legitimate representational claim and these forms of representation be viewed as complementary, rather than adversarial. In Indian context, civil society has three intertwined fallacies of **Concept, Precept and Practice.**

First, civil society overstepped its role of demanding accountability and sought to blur the boundaries by dictating the exact content of legislation by insisting on particular draft of the law.

Second, civil society paid no attention to the fact that power shifted from the Parliament to be centralized to executive. Under conditions of increasing concentration and centralization of power to executive, neither the civil society nor parliamentarians' take adequate cognizance of this reality of shifting of power.

Finally it is arguable that the democratic deficit that the IAC pointed to is substantively a problem of the party system and unaccountability of political parties that have domesticated the Parliament rather than performance of the Parliament itself.

The Parliament has become more representative in descriptive terms simultaneously become unresponsive in legislation and governance and avoid accountability. There is no evidence in constitutional debates that MP's argued for parliamentary sovereignty, which asserts that they have been more inclined in increasing their sphere of operations.

In the debate on Lokpal bill, MP's defended Parliaments' prerogative and exclusive mandate to legislate. They asserted the principle of constitutional supremacy, checks and balances in the constitution, exclusive power of lawmaking by the Parliament. In spite of these assertions of parliamentary supremacy, thirty-four of the forty amendments proposed by the non-governmental members were accepted by the joint drafting committee.

Parliamentarian's position on this matter was summed up by T.K.S Elangovan in a simple straightforward way.

'The parliament has certain powers. It has its own supremacy and its own inherent powers. We are here to enact laws in the country. There may be demands but it is for the parliament to decide whether these demands are right or otherwise. It is because after two and half years from now on, the members if this house has to go to people to seek their votes; tell them what we have done; tell them how we have acted; and tell then what steps we have taken against corruption. We have to go to the people. It is the responsibility of not only the ruling party but also of the opposition parties. The people will judge us. Then it is left to civil society to go to the people and say that this government has not acted against corruption. So you need not to vote for them. This is democracy.'

This establishes quite clearly the absence of any principled justification for parliamentary sovereignty, and its relationship of sovereignty to people. Parliamentarians also do not acknowledge the constitutional ambivalence on this question

Parliament is having a legitimate right to represent since they derive legitimacy from election covering entire adult population of the country. Also the constitution gives it legitimate functional competence as the pre-eminent forum for lawmaking.

Civil society has been described as domain of action of bourgeois citizen and also been considered as undermining the democratic governance, at least until such time as they can prepare themselves to become mass organisations, internally democratic, and can generate the ability to connect citizens across the spectrum with the institutions of state. These raise questions that whether the claims of anti-corruption campaign less deserving of attention since it was made by civil society and not by political society.

A section of IAC entering politics suggests that it accept superior legitimacy of elected bodies and centrality of elections on universal adult suffrage to the principle of representation is established even when the locus of popular sovereignty remain unresolved.

3.2.5.5 Conclusion

Returning to introduction, the representational claim of the Parliament bespeak the liberal conception of citizenship which is challenged by republican conception of citizenship articulated by civil society mobilization against corruption. The liberal concept permits us to have elected institutions that may not adequately reflect views of every citizen but provide an institutional framework within which rival claims can be articulated. The republican conception is more appealing for active citizens who are willing to participate in public affairs and holds the key to a polity marked by civic engagement. The conversation between these two distinct principles is today at stake in India.

3.2.6 Measuring the Effectiveness of the Indian Parliament

The questions of how effective the particular session of a Parliament is? Or how effective is this Lok Sabha from the previous one? are hard to answer in an objective manner.

At a macro level, it can be said that the objective of the party elected to power is to improve the well-being of the citizens. This may be carried out by enacting appropriate laws, keeping effective control over the executive for implementation of such laws, and allocating such finance as required. The overall effectiveness on improving the quality of life of the citizens by such policies can be measured with help of indicators such as the Human Development Index, and measuring changes associated with it.

At a more detailed level, the effectiveness can be seen by focusing on the specific functions of the Parliament which are prescribed by the Constitution. In this chapter, to help measure the effectiveness of the Parliament and its various functions, a list of metrics has been given which is based on the research done by PRS India.

There is a limited scope of subject and content of evaluating the effectiveness of the legislative bodies. A few international assessments in this subject have been listed as follows:

1. The Commonwealth Parliamentary Association has recommended benchmarks for the Democratic Legislature. They have set standards for the procedural and institutional structures of the legislature.
2. The World Bank Institute has published a study, Legislative oversight and Budgeting-A World perspective (Stapenhurst, Pelizzo R, Olson D, von Trapp L, World Bank Institute, 2008), this includes a metric to assess the effectiveness of the legislature. For example, they list out a number of oversight tools such as committee hearings and questions, and they measure the number of times these tools have been used.
3. The Inter-Parliamentary Union has developed a toolkit to measure performance of the legislatures (Evaluating Parliament – A self-assessment toolkit for parliaments, Inter-Parliamentary Union, 2008). In this they have asked the Parliamentarians to grade a number of parameters on a scale of five. For example, they ask how effective is the Parliament in scrutinising the appointments to executive posts and holding their occupants accountable, and the Parliamentarians have to list the choice based on the scale.

The criteria to judge the effectiveness of the Parliament can be either qualitative or quantitative. The qualitative criterion though is very difficult to assess and measure in an objective manner. For example, we can easily count the number of bills passed, but it is difficult to judge the quality of such legislations. Even while measuring quantitatively, it would be difficult to say whether higher number is positive or negative indicator. For example, a large number of government bills passed in a particular session might indicate the effective functioning of the legislature, but on the other hand this may mean that, very less time is dedicated for the discussion of the bills and that legislature is not able to effectively scrutinise the proposals of the demands made by the executives.

With these constraints, the following framework for measuring the effectiveness of the Parliament has been devised. The following are the main functions of the Parliament based on which a number of parameters have been suggested to measure the effectiveness. They are

- Legislation
- Oversight
- Representation
- Budgeting

The main challenge is to identify which of these parameters can be used effectively to measure the performance and another is whether an aggregate index could be made by combining all these parameters.

The following are some of the metrics used to evaluate the effectiveness of the Parliament.

3.2.6.1 Legislation

Metric	Remarks
Type of Legislation:	
– Total number of original bills and legislations introduced by the government and private members, respectively. – The ratio of Government Bills to that of Private members bills. – Total time spent in discussion of the Private Members bills – The number of times the government has given assurance to take up a private member bill.	The number of Private members bill reflects the initiative taken by the MPs in formulating new laws. Government assurance to take up these bills by private members demonstrates the impact it has on initiatives made by private members on the legislative process.
Keeping track of legislation:	
– Monitoring whether the legislation is effectively implemented (also checking whether adequate finance has been allocated for effective implementation of the legislation.)	While determining the financial provision allocated, it should be borne in mind that such finance allocated to achieve the bill's stated objective is often quoted less.
Work of Standing Committee and Ad Hoc Committees on bills:	
– Number of recommendations of committees that have been accepted and adopted by the government as amendments to bills – Average number of sittings per bill	This measures the effectiveness a standing committee has on the law making. And the quality aspect of such recommendation is difficult to measure.
Quantity of law:	
– Total amount of time the MPs spent on debating the bills in the Parliament. – Percentage of time spent on legislative activities in the Parliament – Average time spent in discussing the bills – The time taken to discuss each bills shows the effective time spent in scrutinising the bill.	– The number of new laws and the time spent on discussing them are easily measurable and describes the priority of the Parliament to legislate.
Quality of law:	
– Quality of speeches made during a debate – Quality of the laws enacted 1. Percentage of enacted laws struck down by the Courts on grounds of constitutional invalidity 2. Percentage of enacted laws amended subsequently by the Parliament, within a. 3 years b. 3-5 years	It is almost impossible to devise an effective measure to judge the quality of legislative debates. When laws are struck down by the Courts as unconstitutional, shows inadequate and ineffective scrutiny by the legislature, and if the law is amended within a short period of time, this also shows that it was not well drafted in the first place.

Metric	Remarks
Monitoring of delegated legislation:	
– Number of times objection has been raised by MPs to the enactment of delegated legislation under relevant statute and such has been discussed in the Parliament – Work of Parliamentary Standing Committee on Subordinate Legislation 1. Number of sittings of the committee 2. Number of reports issued by the committee	Many laws delegate the implementation to the executives subject to the approval by the Parliament. MPs perform this duty both on the floor of the house and in the standing committee on subordinate legislation. The quantity of work carried out by this committee is measurable, but its quality is not.

3.2.6.2 *Oversight*

Metric	Remarks
Oversight through the committee system: – Number of issues taken up for discussion – Average number of sittings of the committee for issuing report	This measures the effective use of the committee system and the extent to which the committee examine issues in their keeping check on the executive.
Oversight through Parliamentary questions and interpretations: – Quality of the questions asked – Number of starred questions actually discussed during the question hour – Time lost due to interruptions	Considerable amount of time is lost because of the interruptions made, hence this metric is used to determine the actual time spent for questioning the executive activity. While determining the quality of the questions asked is critical to determine the effectiveness of the Parliament.

3.2.6.3 *Representation*

Metric	Remarks
Total number of issues raised by the Lok Sabha MPs under rule 377 which have an impact on their constituencies.	This metric enables quantitative ascertainment of amount of time spent by the MPs in monitoring government activities that have an impact on their constituencies.
Total number of questions asked by the Lok Sabha MPs during the Question Hour which will have an impact on their constituencies.	

3.2.6.4 Budgeting

Metric	Remarks
Ex ante consideration and approval of the budget of the government: – Quantity of time devoted to discussion of budget in the Parliament	The proposal of the government is first examined by the standing committee and then it is discussed on the floor of the house. Several other parameters may be used to measure the effectiveness of this scrutiny at these levels.
1. Number of meetings of parliamentary standing committee to discuss on budget 2. Ratio of amount of money spent to that of number of pages of the report of the committee. It is used to ascertain the time spent on discussing the big-ticket spending 3. Ration to the number of pages in the report to that of number of line items in the budget	
Number of recommendation of standing committee accepted and incorporated into the budget	
Monitoring government expenditure after the approval to ensure that it has conformed to the terms approved by the Parliament: – Number of issues raised in the debates based on the reports of Comptroller and Auditor General of India – Time spent on questioning the financial improprieties based on reports of the media – Number of issues raised by the Public Accounts Committee. Number of their recommendations accepted by the government – The Public Accounts Committee holds the executive accountable to the findings made by the CAG. It also enquires whether the government funds were used for the purpose for which it was allocated.	– Time spent in discussion of CAG reports and debates over financial improprieties indicates the parliamentary vigilance over expenditure of public finances.

4

Issues Concerning the Judiciary

LEARNING OBJECTIVES

In this Chapter, you will learn about:

- Judiciary Under Indian Constitution and Supreme Court
- Position of Supreme Court Under the Constitution
- Independence of Judiciary
- Issues in Judicial Appointments
- Conceptualizing Relevant Terms and Expressions
- Meaning of Judicial Review
- Judicial Activism in India
- Judicial Reforms
- Bangalore Declaration

"*Justice is a virtue which transcends all barriers and the rules or procedures or technicalities of law cannot stand in the way of justice*"

—R.P.Sethi, J. in Lily Thomas vs. Union of India, (2000) 6 SCC 224.

4.1 JUDICIARY UNDER INDIAN CONSTITUTION AND SUPREME COURT

The Constitution of India which came into force on 26th January 1950 contains a number of provisions concerning the structure, function and powers of the judiciary. It envisaged a unified judicial system both in Centre and States, Union Territories. It brought in a three-tier judicial system viz. Supreme Court at the Apex, High Court as the highest courts in the States and Union territories, and finally subordinate judiciary in every state and union territory arranged in a hierarchy. However, the Constitution contains only the provisions relating to Supreme Court and the High Courts and leaves the subordinate judiciary to the respective states.

The position and role of the Supreme Court came up before the Constituent Assembly for consideration. A special committee was then setup to consider and give report on the Constitution and powers of the Supreme Court. This committee comprised of *Alladi Krishna Swami Ayyar,*

K.M. Munshi, S. Varadachari, B.N. Rau, and B.L. Mitter. The report of this committee was mostly based on the provisions of the Act 1935. These recommendations are summarised as follows:

- Supreme Court has to be regarded as a necessary instrument in any federal setup.
- The Supreme Court should have final and appellate jurisdiction on questions concerning constitutional validity of the laws.
- Supreme Court should be the effective forum for the adjudication of all disputes concerning Union and constituent states or between two states and the Court should have exclusive and original jurisdiction in such matters.
- Apart from this, the Supreme Court should be vested with advisory jurisdiction.

And hence, based on this fundamental idea, the framers of the Constitution provided for a Supreme Court, the position of which with reference to its powers is considered to be an Appellate Court, as a federal court and as the guardian of the Constitution.

4.2 POSITION OF SUPREME COURT UNDER THE CONSTITUTION

Under the Constitution which was adopted by the people, the Supreme Court was bestowed with wide powers which were essential to the concept of constitutionalism. In a federal setup, the written Constitution, is considered to be the supreme. Protection of the values enshrined in the Constitution, which is the supreme lex of the land, lies with the judiciary. This is the fundamental duty given to the Court by the makers of the Constitution. Though the parliamentary form of government was adopted from the British, the setup of judiciary was taken from that which was prevailing under the U.S. Constitution. Unlike in Britain, the judiciary has been given a prominent position under the Indian Constitution.

- The constitutional expert Granville Austin points out that, during the British period, even though there were number of Indians in the government, they were not involved or responsible for the laws made.
- Neither the law nor the courts were for the Indians, they were established only to promote the colonial interest.
- Such position of courts under the Constitution was considered to be as one the most significant evidences of independence.
- Though after independence the country inherited a well-constructed and a smooth functioning judicial system from the British, which could have been directly adopted, the constitutional makers sought to make the judicial system reflect the needs and aspirations of an independent nation.

Hence, at the time of framing the Constitution, the Members raised the following queries, which provisions should be retained, and if, indeed they were retained, how they should be changed and how the jurisdiction and the powers of the courts be increased to meet the changing needs. With regard to establishment of the Supreme Court – an ad hoc committee comprising of five members – *Alladi Krishna Swami Ayyar, B.N. Rau, S. Varadachari, K.M. Munshi and B.L. Mitter* took upon the work. The very first recommendation by this committee bestowed upon the Court the power of judicial review. The court should be empowered with jurisdiction to decide upon the validity of the laws and acts as it is essential in a federal setup.

The important reason for preferring the American system of judiciary to that of system in Britain, is because of the fact that the Constitution provided for a federal system of government and hence if the judiciary is weak or insignificant as the one prevailing in Britain, it would not be able to uphold the federal principles. Moreover, there was no separate provision on the fundamental rights in Britain, whereas India like in the United States has a separate section within the Constitution providing certain inalienable and inherent fundamental rights. Since the Constitution has set up a federal state, the judiciary should therefore uphold the supremacy of the Constitution besides that of the federal principle. Hence, without the power of judicial review, the judiciary could not have accomplished such tasks such as that of limiting the power of the government. Thus, it was for the fitness of things that the framers of the Constitution opted for a stronger judiciary than that of the one prevailing in the United Kingdom.

The position of Supreme Court of India can be seen with reference to its power as an Appellate Court, guardian of the Constitution and as a federal court.

4.2.1 As a Federal Court

It is understood that a federal court is an essential element in a federal Constitution. It is the final interpreter and guardian of the Constitution, and it also determines the disputes between the constituent elements in the federal setup. It is understood that every federal Constitution aims to distribute power between the Union and the constituent state governments which are the units in the federal setup. While in a Unitary Constitution, there arises no such problem, as the local or legislative bodies are mere subordinates of the central authority. Hence, there is no need for the judiciary to determine disputes between the centre and the states.

- In a federal State, which is having a written Constitution, the powers are divided between the centre and the state governments, and it is therefore essential for some authority to determine and decide upon the disputes between them, and to maintain the distribution of the powers guaranteed by the Constitution.
- In a federal setup, the judiciary is given additional burden, apart from its role of guarding the Constitution from the transgressions by the other organs of the state, to effectively maintain the distribution of powers as recommended by the Constitution as to prevent encroachments by the Union and the State governments.
- In short the Supreme Court is considered to be the '*umpire in federal system*'.

There is no explicit agreement or treaty to distribute powers in the federal setup, but there is nevertheless, division of legislative as well as administrative powers between the Centre and the States. It is important to mention here that the Schedule VII to the Constitution contains three lists namely the Union, the State and the Concurrent lists, clearly separating, the domain of power of legislature of the Centre and the States. Administrative powers are dealt by the **Articles 256 to 263** of the Constitution which lay down the respective jurisdiction of the Union and the States. The **Articles 264 to 293** deal with the financial relation between the Centre and the States. Apart from this other disputes may occur in other areas such as demarcation of the boundaries, usage of water, power and other natural resources.

Hence, the **Article 131** of the Constitution vets the Supreme Court with original and exclusive jurisdiction to determine and decide upon the disputes between the Centre and the States and the States *inter se*. The article is read as under:

Article 131–Original Jurisdiction of the Supreme Court

Subject to the provisions of this Constitution, the Supreme Court shall, to the exclusion of any other court, have original jurisdiction in any dispute

a. *between the Government of India and one or more States; or*
b. *between the Government of India and any State or States on one side and one or more other States on the other; or*

c. *between two or more States, if and in so far as the dispute involves any question (whether of law or fact) on which the existence or extent of a legal right depends: Provided that the said jurisdiction shall not extend to a dispute arising out of any treaty, agreement, covenant, engagements, and or other similar instrument which, having been entered into or executed before the commencement of this Constitution, continues in operation after such commencement, or which provides that the said jurisdiction shall not extend to such a dispute.*

It is the interpretation made by the Supreme Court in particular cases that will hold all the forces in balance and save the original distribution of powers between the centre and states from encroachment by the Union. In this context we can observe from the words of *Sir Alladi Krishna Swami Ayyar* to quote:

> *...(the Supreme Court) has to keep the poise between the seemingly contradictory forces. In the process of the interpretation of the Constitution, on certain occasions it may appear to strengthen the Union at the expense of the Units at another time it may appear to champion the cause of provincial autonomy and regionalism.*

Thus, it is essential that the Supreme Court maintains the fine balance between the power of the Union and the rights of the States, while exercising its original power under the Article 131 of the Constitution.

4.2.2 As a Court of Appeal

The Supreme Court of India is considered to be the final appellate authority of the land, and most of the functions performed by the Apex court are in relation to its appellate jurisdiction. The Supreme Court thus exercises jurisdiction in relation to civil, criminal and constitutional matters. **Articles 132 to 136** deal with that of the appellate jurisdiction of the Supreme Court.

According to **Article 132** of the Constitution, an appeal to the Supreme Court lies to the Apex Court from any judgement, decree or final order of any High Court, in the territory of India in any civil, criminal or other proceedings, provided it involves a substantial question of law as to the interpretation of the Constitution, and the concerned High Court certifies to that effect.

Thus, this **Article 132**, ensures that though the High Court may decide upon the validity of an act or any other question involving interpretation of the Constitution, in all such cases the decision of such High Court shall not be the final and that the authority of interpreting the Constitution must rest with only the Supreme Court.

a. **Civil Appellate Jurisdiction**

Under **Article 133** of the Constitution, the Supreme Court, exercises appellate jurisdiction in civil matters as decided by the High Courts.

According to this Article, an appeal lies to the Supreme Court from the High Court from any decree, judgement or final order in a civil proceeding of a High Court in the territory of India, and if the High Court itself certifies under Article **134-A** that the matter involves substantial question of law of general importance and that in the opinion the High Court has to be addressed by the Supreme Court.

Before the 30th Constitutional Amendment, there were three alternative grounds for appeal to the Court from the High Courts in a civil proceeding, which were similar to the provisions under Sections 109, 110 of the Code of Civil Procedure, 1908. These grounds were:

1. Value of the appeal being ₹20,000 and above.
2. The matter on appeal indirectly involving some value.
3. The case being otherwise fit for appeal.

And as per aforementioned amendment, all these grounds were replaced by practically one ground viz., that the case involved substantial question of law and in the opinion of the High Court, it needs to be decided by the Supreme Court. Hence, no appeal shall lie to the Supreme Court after the date of Amendment (27-2-1973) on the grounds of pecuniary value.

The most important aspect in relation of the civil appellate jurisdiction of the Supreme Court is that because of the 30th amendment, in civil cases there is no category as a matter of right of appeal to the Supreme Court.

b. **Criminal Appellate Jurisdiction**

Prior to the enactment of the Constitution of India, there was no court of criminal appeal over and above the High Courts. Only the *Privy Council* had the power to entertain appeals in matters relating to criminal cases, though only within a limited range. The Privy Council was vested with the discretionary power and was the sole judge to grant special leave to adjudge the appeal worthiness of a criminal appeal, and these were granted only in exceptional cases.

The Constitution, by **Article 134**, set up a criminal court of appeal above the High Courts, although with limited jurisdiction. This **Article 134** empowers the Supreme Court to hear appeals from any sentence, judgement or final order in criminal proceedings of High Courts, in three cases:

1. If the High Court, on appeal, reverses the decision of acquittal of an accused person and sentences him to death. This will be the case of second appeal in a criminal case.
2. If the High Court has withdrawn for trial, to itself any case before a subordinate court and, after trial sentences him to death.
3. Besides the above two grounds, if the High Court under Article 134-A certifies that the case is a fit one for appeal to the Supreme Court.

Thus, it can be clearly seen that the criminal appellate jurisdiction of the Supreme Court is limited and is only sparingly invoked.

c. **Constitutional Appellate Jurisdiction**

The Supreme Court is empowered under **Articles 132(1), 133(1) and 134(1)** of the Constitution to hear appeals in matters related to civil, criminal or other proceedings, if the case involves a substantial question of law as to the interpretation of the Constitution itself.

The High Court under **Article 134-A** has the power to certify, if it is satisfied, that a particular matter in reference to civil, criminal or other proceedings involves a substantial question as to the interpretation of the Constitution. This power can be invoked either *suo motu* by the High Court itself, or by application made by the aggrieved party to it. This certificate can be granted only when such application is made immediately after passing of such decree, judgement, final order or sentence.

List of instances which can be said to be instances of question involving Constitutional interpretation are as follows:

1. Cases involving direct interpretation of some particular provision of the Constitution.
2. The question of application of a particular act to the facts of a case.
3. A conviction under a law which is challenged as '*ultra vires*'.
4. A suit or proceeding challenging particular statute as '*ultra vires*' or '*inconsistent*' with some mandatory provision of the Constitution.

Once such certificate is granted under **Article 134-A** by the High Court, the jurisdiction to hear such appeals is then vested with the Supreme Court and the aggrieved party can then file an appeal before the apex court by virtue of it and as a matter right, provided other provisions under the Article 134-A is complied with.

d. **Special Leave Appeal to the Supreme Court**

Apart from the provisions of regular appeals from the proceedings of the High Court given under **Articles 132 to 134-A**, there still may be some cases, where justice might require the interference of the Supreme Court. The Supreme Court thus can not only intervene in matters coming from High Court, but also from matters arising in any other court or tribunals. The framers have given the power to decide about the appeal worthiness of a case to the Supreme Court and not to the lower courts.

Hence, **Article 136** of the Constitution grants discretionary power to the Supreme Court to allow special leave appeals from any judgement, decree, determination, order or any sentence in any cause or matter passed or made by any court or tribunal in the territory of India.

Thus, this article vests an extraordinary power upon the Supreme Court in the matters of entertaining and hearing of appeals from any courts or tribunals by grant of special leave of appeal. In this context, any court includes the High Courts also, but does not include those of the army court or tribunal.

The Supreme Court opined that this power was rather a duty vested with it, to interfere in matters of serious miscarriage of justice and it is not curtailed by any limitation as to who may invoke this discretionary jurisdiction. As far as matters related to High Courts are concerned, **Article 136** can only be invoked in cases where the Court refuses to grant certificate under **Article 134-A** of the Constitution.

This provision of granting special leave under **Article 136** is sparingly used by the Supreme Court. Hence, it is clear that unlike the Court in United States which deals with only the federal and constitutional law issues, the Apex Court here is the final court of appeal on not just such issues, but also on any other matters of the ordinary law, civil, criminal or revenue. This gives wide scope for the Supreme Court to assert itself whenever the need is felt and found necessary based on the facts and circumstances of the case.

4.2.3 As a Guardian of the Constitution

The Supreme Court of India has the duty and the obligation to guard and protect the Constitution by upholding the Constitutionalism. This obligation overshadows its other roles as a federal court and as the court of final appeal in non-constitutional matters.

- The Constitution is regarded as the supreme law of the land by various constitutional systems around the world.

- Many of the written Constitutions which follow the theory of constitutional supremacy, have expressly declared in the Constitution itself that – *the Constitution is the Supreme law of the land.*

The question whether the Courts shall be guardian and interpreter of the Constitution is not based on the written or un-written nature of the Constitution, but is rather based on the theory of constitutional supremacy and the parliamentary sovereignty whereby the powers of the legislature are restricted. The British concept of parliamentary sovereignty can be cited as an example in this context.

As far as India is considered, the Constitution sets up a federal system, and also guarantees certain fundamental rights. There is no express provision in the Constitution itself, declaring it to be the supreme law of the land. Such declaration was considered to be superfluous by the framers of the Constitution, as all the organs derived power from the Constitution, and the Constitution cannot be easily altered save in the manner laid down in the Constitution itself.

It has also to be stated that there is no specific provision in the Constitution empowering the courts to invalidate the laws, but the Constitution has imposed certain limitations upon each of the organ and any transgression of such limitations will make those acts void. And the power is vested with the courts to decide whether any of the constitutional limitations has been transgressed or not.

The following Constitutional provisions substantiate the abovementioned statement:

1. **Article 13** of the Constitution declares that any law which contravenes any of the provision of Part III of the Constitution dealing with the fundamental rights, shall be declared void.
2. **Articles 251 and 254**, in case there is inconsistency between Union and States law, the state laws are declared as void.
3. **Article 246** expressly provides that the Centre and State legislatures have legislative powers over a specified list of subjects (list I, II and III).
4. **Article 245** makes the powers of both Parliament and State legislature, 'subject to the provisions of the Constitution'.

Thus, the Constitution has imposed certain limitations upon the legislative powers in the form of

1. Fundamental rights guaranteed under Part III of the Constitution.
2. Legislative competence.
3. Territorial limitation of the State legislatures.

So the courts have the power to pronounce upon the validity of any law on the above said grounds. The transgression of its powers by any legislature can be effectively checked by the higher judiciary in general and the Supreme Court in particular, with the powers of judicial review bestowed upon them under various provisions in the Constitution.

The court is also vested with the powers to check upon the excesses committed by the executive. Apart from its jurisdiction to hear cases from alleged illegal acts, the Supreme Court has been given extraordinary revisional powers through the judicial writs of *Quo-Warranto, Certiorari, Habeas Corpus, Prohibition and Mandamus* under **Article 32**. The Supreme Court is thus vested with power to issue appropriate writ when the fundamental right is infringed by any administrative or quasi-judicial body.

Sir Alladi Krishna Swami Ayyar, the illustrious member of the Constituent Assembly summed up the position and powers of the Supreme Court as follows:

With the expansion of the sphere of governmental activity, inevitable, under modern conditions in spite of the strong criticism of the late Lord Chief Justice of England, the institution of Administrative Tribunals and agencies invested with judicial or Quasi-judicial functions will continue to be a feature of modern government and has almost become unavoidable. The only safeguard against the abuse of powers vested in such tribunals and bodies is in the ultimate or revisory jurisdiction being vested in the higher courts of the realm and in the Supreme Court.

Thus, it can be clearly seen that the Supreme Court of India is the supreme and the fundamental guardian of the Constitution of India and also the supreme protector of fundamental rights of the people.

4.2.4 As a Protector of Fundamental Rights

The Constitution in its Part III contains **Articles 12 to 35**, which guarantees and protects the fundamental rights of the people. The unique feature of these fundamental rights is that these are not only considered to be fundamental but also their implementation is considered to be a fundamental right in itself. The last fundamental right in the Part III namely the right to constitutional remedies makes the Supreme Court the protector of the fundamental rights of the citizens. **Articles 32 to 35** deal with this most important fundamental right.

Article 32 is reads as follows:
32. Remedies for enforcement of rights conferred by this Part

1. *The right to move the Supreme Court by appropriate proceedings for the enforcement of the rights conferred by this Part is guaranteed*
2. *The Supreme Court shall have power to issue directions or orders or writs, including writs in the nature of habeas corpus, mandamus, prohibition, quo warranto and certiorari, whichever may be appropriate, for the enforcement of any of the rights conferred by this Part*
3. *Without prejudice to the powers conferred on the Supreme Court by clause (1) and (2), Parliament may by law empower any other court to exercise within the local limits of its jurisdiction all or any of the powers exercisable by the Supreme Court under clause (2)*
4. *The right guaranteed by this article shall not be suspended except as otherwise provided for by this Constitution*

The mere declaration of fundamental rights is not sufficient unless there are proper judicial remedies for their enforcement. **Article 32** provides such remedy and bestows upon the Supreme Court the status of champion of fundamental right, as the right to move to court in case of violation of fundamental right is itself a fundamental right.

The Supreme Court is hence considered to be the protector and guarantor of fundamental rights, and under **Article 32**, it is the duty of the courts to grant relief, where the existence of fundamental rights and its violation is clearly established. The Supreme Court considers the jurisdiction conferred to be by the **Article 32** as *'an integral and important part of the basic structure of the Constitution'*. Because it is meaningless to give fundamental rights without providing effective remedy for their enforcement if and when the rights are violated. A right without a remedy is a legal conundrum of most grotesque kind and that **Article 32** confers one of the 'highly cherished' rights.

4.2.5 As an Advisory Body

Under Article 143, the Supreme Court has been designated as an advisory body to the President of India. Thus, apart from playing the role as an appellate court, federal court, guardian of the Constitution and guarantor of the fundamental rights, the Supreme Court has also been called upon to play the role of an advisory court. It is important to note that this feature is unique to Indian Constitution and even the American federal court or the House of Lords do not exercise such powers.

Article 143 of the Constitution which vests the Supreme Court with advisory jurisdiction is as follows:

143. Power of President to consult Supreme Court

1. *If at any time it appears to the President that a question of law or fact has arisen, or is likely to arise, which is of such a nature and of such public importance that it is expedient to obtain the opinion of the Supreme Court upon it, he may refer the question to that Court for consideration and the Court may, after such hearing as it thinks fit, report to the President its opinion thereon*
2. *The President may, notwithstanding anything in the proviso to Article 131, refer a dispute of the kind mentioned in the said proviso to the Supreme Court for opinion and the Supreme Court shall, after such hearing as it thinks fit, report to the President its opinion thereon*

A clear analysis of this Article makes it clear that it vests a consultative function upon the Supreme Court. Such kind of power is not vested with any other democratic constitutions in the world. As far as India is concerned, this **Article 143** is not the first provision to vest such power, Under the Government of India Act, 1935 similar kind of power was given to the then highest court of India namely the Federal Court of India. In fact, the Clause (1) of the Article 143 is similar to the Clause (1) of Section 213(1) of the Government of India Act, 1935.

This power conferred upon the Supreme Court is not a formal power, rather it is a discretionary power given to the Court to give its opinion on any question of public importance that may be referred to it by the President. This can be justified from the fact that such advisory opinion rendered by the Supreme Court is not binding on the government.

4.3 INDEPENDENCE OF JUDICIARY

A post-colonial democracy has survived more than half a century due to the presence of a strong and independent judiciary. Its independence is safeguarded by the Constitution. The Constitutional framers envisaged a judiciary which was both independent and powerful.

Sir Krishna Swamy Ayyar, one of the eminent members of the Constituent Assembly has summarized the need to maintain the independence of Judiciary in the following words in one the Constituent Assembly debates:

> *While there can be no two opinions on the need for maintenance of judicial independence, both for the safeguarding of individual liberty and the proper working of the Constitution, it is also necessary to keep in view one important principle. The doctrine of Independence is not to be raised to the level of a dogma so as to*

enable the judiciary to function as a kind of super-Legislature or super-Executive. The judiciary is there to interpret the Constitution or adjudicate upon the rights between the parties concerned.

However, the eminent scholar warned that the judiciary as much as the legislature and executive depends for its effective functioning upon the cooperation of the other two pillars.

A closer scrutiny of the Constitutional Assembly Debates concerning the judicial provisions make it clear that the discussions were mainly concerned with the administrative aspects of the judicial system such as the tenure, salaries, allowances and retirement age of the judges and the mechanism of choosing the judges. But an in-depth analysis of these debates points us to the fact that the members were actually concerned with a desire to insulate the judiciary from forces within and outside of the government.

The following section will deal with the provision and features of the Constitution which explain the extent of independence of judiciary.

1. **Special mode of appointment of judges:** The previous section dealt elaborately with the appointment procedure and process of the judges. We are thus able to understand that why appointment process was kept free from interference by the Legislature and the Executive. It was carried out in order to maintain the independence of the Judiciary. We will now deal briefly with the landmark judgements that brought about the present system of collegium.
   - There has been a controversy as to the meaning of the expression 'Consultation' occurring in the Articles 124 and 217. Prior to 1993 there was a consensus that 'consultation' did not amount to 'concurrence'.
   - In the first *Judges Transfer case* that is in *S.P. Gupta vs. Union of India* (AIR 1982 SC 149), a seven-judge bench held that the ultimate power to appoint judges was vested with the Executive. The court held that 'consultation' meant full and *effective consultation.*
   - This principle was over-ruled subsequently in the *Supreme Court Advocates on Record Association vs. Union of India* ((1993) 4 SC 441) by a nine-judge bench with a majority 7-2 ruling. It held that in matter of appointment of judges of Supreme Court and High Courts, the President is bound to act in accordance with the opinion of the Chief Justice of India. The Chief Justice would tender his opinion after consulting with his senior most colleagues. The court further held that the appointment of Chief Justice of India was made on basis of seniority. Justice J.S. Verma who delivered the majority judgement along with Justices A.N. Ray, A.S. Anand and S.P. Bharucha made the following observation:

> *… the executive element in the appointment process has been reduced to minimum and political influence is eliminated. It is for this reason that the word 'consultation' instead of 'concurrence' was used in the constitution, but that was done merely to indicate the absolute discretion was not given to any one, not even to Chief Justice of India as an individual, much less to the executive.*

Thus, Supreme Court had effectively declared that 'consultation' means 'concurrence'.

- In Re: Presidential Reference (AIR 1999 SC 1), a nine-judge bench held that the majority view in the AIR 1994 SC 268 case in that in the matter of appointments to the Supreme Court and the High Courts, the opinion of the Chief Justice has primacy.

The opinion of the Chief Justice of India which has primacy in the matter of recommendations for appointment to the Supreme Court has to be formed in consultation with a **'collegium of judges'** and it observed that it is desirable that the collegium should consist of the Chief Justice of India and four senior most puisne judges of the Supreme Court.

2. **Security of tenure:** The judges of both higher and lower judiciary in India have a security of tenure. A judge of Supreme Court of India retires at the age of 65 while a judge of High Court retires at 62 years. They can only be removed by the way of impeachment. And the only two grounds on which they can be impeached are '*proved misbehaviour*' and '*incapacity*'. The process of impeachment is a complex one, the President can remove a judge only when an address is presented against the Judge by each house of the Parliament.

   For record it might be stated that no Judge of either High Court or Supreme Court has been impeached. An attempt was made and aborted when a sitting Judge of the Supreme Court was sought to be impeached, V. Ramaswamy on the grounds of 'proved misbehaviour' namely certain financial irregularities and excesses. But the impeachment motion was defeated in the Lok Sabha when the Congress party decided walk out. Another attempt was made in 2011 when Justice Soumitra Sen was sought to be impeached, but it fell through when the incumbent Judge tendered his resignation. Another possible impeachment failed against Justice P.D. Dinakaran who resigned as the Chief Justice of Sikkim High Court.
3. **Immunity in respect of Salaries and allowances of judges:** Under Articles 125 and 218 of the Constitution, the Supreme Court and the High Court Judges respectively are entitled to be paid salaries as determined by the Parliament. They cannot be changed by the Legislature except in case of emergency. Once appointed, every Judge is entitled to privileges and allowances and the same cannot be altered to their disadvantage. It is important to note that the salaries of the Judges are on higher scale than that of those of the members of the legislature and the executive.
4. **Administrative power of the Supreme Court and High Courts:** As per Articles 146 and 229, the Supreme Courts and the High Courts have been given authority to recruit their staff and frame other rules regarding their conditions of service. Hence, they enjoy administrative autonomy as regards to selection and appointment of non-judicial staff.
5. **Salaries drawn from consolidated fund:** The expenditure relating to the salaries and other allowances given to the judges are charged from consolidated fund of India and they cannot be subjected to vote by the legislature.
6. **Bar as to practice after retirement:** The Constitution itself debars the Judges of the Supreme Court after their retirement from pleading or appearing before any court or judicial authority in India. A similar but slightly different provision is imposed in respect to the Judges of High Court who can appear only before the Supreme Court or any other High Courts in which they did not serve as Judges.
7. **Bar as to discussion of conduct of judges:** No discussion shall take place either in the State assembly or in the Parliament regarding the conduct of any Judge of Supreme Court or of a High Court while discharging his duties. The only exception for this is given during the impeachment proceedings.

8. **Power to punish for contempt:** Under the Articles 149 and 215 the Constitution vests the Supreme Court and the High Court with the power to punish for contempt. Moreover, the Supreme Court is considered to be a Court of Record.

   This is one of the most important features which uphold the independence of the judiciary. Contempt of Court essentially constitutes anything which tends to bring the administration of justice to disrespect or interfere with the process of administration of Justice. Such acts include scandalising the judge himself and obstructing the due course of justice. The power of contempt is so important that even legislature has no power to abridge it.

   In *Delhi Judicial Service Association vs. State of Gujarat* ((1991) 4 SCC 406), the Supreme Court held that the Court has the power to punish a person for contempt of itself as well as the subordinate courts. Recently in *Re Vinay Chandra Misra* ((1995) 2 SCC 584) the Supreme Court held that the power under Article 129 and 142 cannot be curtailed by any statute and the purpose of such power is to uphold the majesty of law, the rule of law and the special function of the judiciary is to see whether the other two organs of the state function within the constitutional limitations.

   From the above discussion it can be clearly seen that the framers of the Constitution envisaged a free and independent judiciary. They have also provided enough safe guards to enable the judiciary to work in an impartial atmosphere. This is one the reasons why the judiciary is bold and never hesitates to take action against the erring executive or the legislature.

   In *C.RaviChandranIyer vs. Justice A.M. Bhattacharjee*((1995) 5 SCC 457) while dealing with the nature, role and meaning of independence of judiciary, Justice K. Ramaswamy speaking for the bench, held

> *........in this ongoing complex adjudicatory process the role of judge is not merely to interpret the law but also to lay down new norms of law and to mould the law to suit the changing social economic scenario to make the ideals enshrined in the Constitution meaningful and reality. The society demands active judicial roles. Writs formerly were considered exceptional but now a routine. The Judge must act independently if he is to perform the function as expected of him and he must feel sure that such action of his will not lead to his downfall.*

This concept of independence of judiciary is now considered to be one of the basic features of the Constitution. The Constitution provides wide powers and enough grants to make the judiciary a completely independent entity. Almost every Constitution around the world strives to create an independent and impartial judiciary, and they include such provisions to ensure that the same is continued and practiced. Eminent Jurist Nani A Palkhivala declared that independence of judiciary is the very heart of a republic. The foundation of the democracy, the source of its continued existence, the condition for its growth and the hope for its welfare – everything lie in that great institution, an independent judiciary.

4.4 ISSUES IN JUDICIAL APPOINTMENTS

The method of appointment of judges of the Chief Justice of Supreme Courts, High Courts have been laid down in the Constitution. This has been provided in Articles 124(2) and 217(1) of the Constitution.

Art. 124(2) reads:

'Every Judge of the Supreme Court shall be appointed by the President by warrant under his hand and seal after consultation with such of the Judges of the Supreme Court and of the High Courts in the States as the President may deem necessary for the purpose and shall hold office until he attains the age of sixty five years: Provided that in the case of appointment of a Judge other than the Chief Justice, the Chief Justice of India shall always be consulted...' and

Art. 217(1) reads:

'Every Judge of a High Court shall be appointed by the President by warrant under his hand and seal after consultation with the Chief Justice of India, the Governor of the State, and, in the case of appointment of a Judge other than the Chief Justice, the Chief Justice of the High Court...'

These constitutional provisions were incorporated after several meaningful debates on the basic issue of judicial independence. After a long debate the assembly adopted the system by which the President would appoint the judges with mandatory consultation with the Chief Justice of India. This consultation with the Chief Justice was done in order to check the politically motivated selections in the appointment process.

There has been two different but crucial phases in relation to the judicial appointments

1. First: the phase of appointments by the Executive – 1950–1993.
2. Second: the phase of appointments by the collegium – 1993–present.

First Phase

This was considered to be true intention of the constitutional makers that the executive be involved in the appointment process of the judges. Independence of Judiciary was ensured by securing their tenure and creating a tough impeachment process of removal of the judges. The judges as per the Constitution were not given free-hand or an exclusive privilege to make their own appointments. This phase carried on smoothly until the period of emergency. This emergency period saw several turn-arounds in various sections, and one area which got severely affected was the judiciary.

- The seniority of appointment was by-passed and a judge because of his political connections got appointed as the Chief Justice of Supreme Court.
- Several other subsequent judgements were taken in favour of the government. This severely dented the concept of independence of judiciary. Judiciary thus became a handmaiden of the government.
- Such a practice was resented and voice rose from several quarters, especially from the judiciary to rectify such a practice.
- In light of these developments, in order to maintain independence and to create an appointment which was free from political motivations the Supreme Court between the years 1982–1999, the issue of appointment was examined and reinterpreted (*S.P. Gupta* vs. *Union of India*, AIR 1982, SC 149; S.C. Advocates on Record Association *vs.* Union of India, AIR 1994 SC 268; *In re*: Special Reference, AIR 1999 SC 1.).

Since then, a system of collegium, consisting of Chief Justice of India and other senior most judges of the Supreme Court, gave recommendations for appointment of judges to Supreme Court and High Court, to the President.

Second Phase

At present after the striking down of the National Judicial Appointments Commission Act, the Collegium system of appointment is followed. Nowhere in the world there is a system of appointment of judges by the judges themselves. In this system the executive acts as a mere conduit as rest of the consultation, approval, and acceptance is taken by the judiciary and executives are not involved in any of such process.

The below is the appointment process carried out in various countries, and from this we can clearly understand that the system of appointments by collegium is unique to our country.

Appointment of judges to the highest court in different jurisdictions

Country	Method of Appointment to the Highest Court	Who is Involved in Making the Appointments
UK	Supreme Court judges are appointed by a five-person selection commission.	It consists of the Supreme Court President, his deputy, and one member each appointed by the JACs of England, Scotland and Northern Ireland. (The JACs comprise lay persons, members of the judiciary and the Bar and make appointments of judges of lower courts.)
Canada	Appointments are made by the Governor in Council.	A selection panel comprising five MPs (from the government and the opposition) reviews list of nominees and submits 3 names to the Prime Minister.
USA	Appointments are made by the President.	Supreme Court Justices are nominated by the President and confirmed by the United States Senate.
Germany	Appointments are made by election.	Half the members of the Federal Constitutional Court are elected by the executive and half by the legislature.
France	Appointments are made by the President.	President receives proposals for appointments from ConseilSuperieur de la Magistrature.

Appointments by the Collegium

The memorandum of procedure for appointing the Judges of Supreme Court of India is given in the following list. And from this procedure we can understand how the system of collegium operates.

1. Whenever a vacancy is expected to arise in the office of a Judge of the Supreme Court, the Chief Justice of India will initiate proposal and forward his recommendation to the Union Minister of Law, Justice and Company Affairs to fill up the vacancy.
2. The opinion of the Chief Justice of India for appointment of a Judge of the Supreme Court should be formed in consultation with a **collegium of the four senior-most puisne Judges** of the Supreme Court. If the successor Chief Justice of India is not one of the four senior-most puisne Judges, he would be made part of the collegium as he should have a hand in selection of Judges who will function during his term as Chief Justice of India.
3. The Chief Justice of India would **ascertain the views** of the senior-most Judge in the Supreme Court, who hails from the High Court from where the person recommended

comes, but if he does not have any knowledge of his merits and demerits, the next senior most Judge in the Supreme Court from that High Court should be consulted.

4. The **opinion of members of the collegium in respect of each of the recommendations** as well as the senior-most judge in the Supreme Court from the High Court, from which a prospective candidate comes, **would be made in writing** and the Chief Justice of India, in all cases, must transmit his opinion as also the opinion of all concerned to the Government of India as part of record. If the Chief Justice of India or the other members of the Collegium elicit views, particularly those from the non-Judges, the consultation need not be in writing but he, who elicits the opinion, should make a memorandum thereof and its substance in general terms which should be conveyed to the Government of India.
5. After receipt of the final recommendation of the Chief Justice of India, the Union Minister of Law, Justice and Company Affairs will put up the **recommendations to the Prime Minister who will advise the President in the matter of appointment.**

The following is the memorandum of procedure for appointment of Chief Justice of High Court and of other Judges of High Court. And it is carried out on similar line of appointment of the judges of the Supreme Court.

1. Initiation of the proposal for the appointment of Chief Justice of a High Court would be by the Chief Justice of India.
2. The Chief Justice of India would send his recommendation for the appointment of a puisne Judge of the High Court as Chief Justice of that High Court or of another High Court, in **consultation with the two senior-most Judges of the Supreme Court.**
3. After receipt of the recommendation of the Chief Justice of India, the Union Minister of Law, Justice and Company Affairs would obtain **the views of the concerned State Government**. After receipt of the views of the State Government, the Union Minister of Law, Justice and Company Affairs, **will submit proposals to the Prime Minister, who will then advise the President as to the selection.**
4. The proposal for appointment of a Judge of a High Court shall be **initiated by the Chief Justice of the High Court**. However, if the Chief Minister desires to **recommend the name of any person he should forward the same to the Chief Justice for his consideration.**
5. The Union Minister of Law, Justice and Company Affairs would consider the recommendations in the light of such other reports as may be available to the Government in respect of the names under consideration. The complete material would then be forwarded to **the Chief Justice of India for his advice**. The Chief Justice of India would, in **consultation with the two senior-most judges of the Supreme Court, form his opinion in regard to a person to be recommended for appointment** to the High Court. The Chief Justice of India and the **collegium of two Judges** of the Supreme Court would take into account the views of the Chief Justice of the High Court and of those Judges of the High Court who have been consulted by the Chief Justice as well as views of those Judges in the Supreme Court who are conversant with the affairs of that High Court.
6. After their consultations, the Chief Justice of India **will in course of 4 weeks send his recommendation** to the Union Minister of Law, Justice and Company Affairs.

Consultation by the Chief Justice of India with his colleagues **should be in writing** and all such exchange of correspondence with his colleagues would be sent by the Chief Justice of India to the Union Minister of Law, Justice and Company Affairs. Once the names have been considered and recommended by the Chief Justice of India, they should not be referred back to the State Constitutional authorities even if a change takes place in the incumbency of any post.

7. The Union Minister of Law, Justice and Company Affairs would then put up as early as possible, preferably, within 3 weeks, the recommendation or the Chief Justice of India to the Prime Minister who will advise the President in the matter of appointment.

Drawbacks in Collegium System

As seen from the above memorandum of procedure, the appointments are devoid of any consultation with the executive and all decisions are solely taken up by the higher echelons of the judiciary. Some of the major drawbacks of this system are as follows:

1. There prevails secrecy in the Collegiums meetings as the minutes of collegium are not being recorded which undermines the plurality opinion of the judges in the collegium. It brings out **manufactured consensus** on the list of names of appointees and transfers brought in by the Chief Justice of India.
2. The Chief Justice of India is having more say in the collegium there by this big brother attitude is reflected in not disclosing the Intelligence Bureau (IB) report of candidates to the fellow members of the collegium claiming that it is his discretion in revealing the reports.
3. The candidates rejected by the collegium on the basis of adverse report by the IB for the post of Supreme Court Judge continue to serve their present position as Judge of High Court or as advocates of High Courts. It is due to the non-disclosure of the adverse report to fellow judges (or) even to the public.
4. Those who opt for public must be prepared for certain degree of public scrutiny. Reasons for elevation and non-elevation as a judge therefore can be disclosed.
5. The dissent within the collegium is being supposed on many instances which violates the judgement provided by the **Third Judges case** which says the recommendation must be based on the decision of Chief Justice of India along with the senior-most judges.
6. The Collegium system lacks performance audit of the candidates to be elevated as the judges of Supreme Court.
7. Absence of separate secretariat for judicial appointment which is being done by the Judges themselves consumes the time of judicial activity which is also a prime reason for piling up of cases in the judicial backyard.
8. The provision of All India Judicial Service is included in the 42nd Amendment Act of 1976, but no such law has been made so far due to the opposition from High Court Chief Justices who label it as an infringement of their rights.
9. Other defects in collegium are as follows
    - Chief Justice of India acts as initiator as well as appointer
    - Increasing influence of Bar Council
    - Competence of judges is not measured only seniority prevails

- Increasing workload
- Utmost secrecy. The answers for why someone is appointed and why one is rejected are not given out.

Requirement of Independent Judicial Appointments Commission

There is presently a need for an independent judicial appointments commission because of the following reasons:

- It reduces the work burden of the judges in appointment.
- To bring transparent, fair and merit based selection.
- To bring public confidence and promote diversity.
- Reduce politicisation in appointments.
- Timely filling of vacancy as and when it arises.
- Criteria-based selection.
- It is been constantly recommended by various law commissions, National Commission on Review of Working of Constitution.

The recommendations made by various commissions and bodies in line to appointment to the Judiciary can be seen from the below table. It gives proper description of the composition of the body which is to make recommendation of the appointment.

Recommendatory Body	Suggested Composition
2nd Administrative Reforms Commission (2007)	**Judiciary**: Chief Justice of India; [For High Court judges: Chief Justice of the relevant High Court of that state] **Executive**: Vice-President (Chairperson), Prime Minister, Law Minister, [For High Court judges: Includes Chief Minister of the state] **Legislature**: Speaker of Lok Sabha, Leaders of Opposition from both Houses of Parliament.
National Advisory Council (2005)	**Judiciary**: Chief Justice of India; [For High Court judges: Chief Justice of the relevant High Court of that state] **Executive**: Vice-President (Chairman), Prime Minister (or nominee), Law Minister, [For High Court judges: Includes Chief Minister of the state] **Legislature**: Speaker of Lok Sabha, Leader of Opposition from both Houses of Parliament.
National Commission on Review of Working of Constitution (2002)	**Judiciary**: Chief Justice of India (Chairman), two senior most Supreme Court judges **Executive**: Union Law Minister **Legislature**: No representative **Other**: one eminent person

Law Commission (1987)	**Judiciary**: Chief Justice of India (Chairman), three senior-most SC judges, immediate predecessor of the Chief Justice, three senior most Chief Justices of High Courts, [For High Court judges: Chief Justice of the relevant High Court of that state] **Executive**: Law Minister, Attorney General of India, [For High Court judges: Includes Chief Minister of the state] **Legislature**: No representative **Other**: One Law academic

National Judicial Appointments Commission

This was the recently proposed body which would have been responsible for both appointments and transfer of judges in higher judiciary. This commission was setup by amending the Constitution through 99th constitution amendment passed by the Lok Sabha as the Constitution (Ninety-Ninth Amendment) Act, 2014. This commission would have replaced the collegium system of appointment as propounded by the Supreme Court. But this constitutional amendment which was also ratified by 16 states was struck down by the Supreme Court bench by a 4:1 majority as unconstitutional.

This was struck down as unconstitutional because of the following reasons:

1. This commission was considered as an executive inroad in judicial appointment which violated the Article 50, which favours separation of Judiciary and Executive.
2. Section 6(6) of NJAC says, if any two members object, the recommendation is nullified by which a veto power provided to the executive.
3. The role of eminent person is questioned as no specific qualification is provided and a greater say for executive in his appointment. Section 124 (D) in the NJAC Act, talks about such eminent person.
4. Section 5(1) of NJAC Act says that the recommendation for senior most judge of the Supreme Court as the Chief Justice if he was considered fit to hold the office. The bench noted that the Act carried no definition of 'fitness'.
5. The inclusion of law minister in the composition of NJAC militated against judicial independence.

The ongoing tussle between the judiciary and the executive for their involvement in the judicial appointment becomes baseless when a completely apolitical and autonomous body like in England's Judicial Appointments Commission is given importance.

Judicial Appointments Commission of United Kingdom has a set of reliable criteria for appointment of Judges which includes candidate's intellectual capacity, his ability to understand, communication skill, leadership and efficiency. These qualities are identified by the Judicial Appointments Commission where more than half members are selected on the basis of merit and open competition.

In similar way, National Judicial Appointments Commission could also include members based on merit and open competition rather than giving importance to the seniority of their positions in the Judiciary and Executive.

Indian Judiciary lacks a constitutional code of conduct as like in United States of America which is used to measure the performance of judge where by appointment to the higher office by promotion is justified.

Transparency can be pushed further by requesting the minutes of meeting to be submitted to Parliamentary Standing Committee by which reasons for appointment and rejection is conveyed to the people's representatives.

4.5 CONCEPTUALISING RELEVANT TERMS AND EXPRESSIONS

The following are some of the important terms which are relevant to understand judiciary and constitutional laws. These terms are discussed in brief hereunder.

4.5.1 Judicial Review

It denotes the power given to higher judiciary to test the validity of any legislation or any other executive action taken by the government. This power is inherent and given by the Constitution. Hence, judiciary can strike down any legislation which goes beyond or violates the provisions of the Constitution. This is the biggest check and all laws and legislations, rules which are covered under Article 12 must satisfy the test of constitutionality, else it is liable to be struck down by judiciary through the process of review. This power is given both to the Supreme Courts and the High Courts.

4.5.2 Judicial Power

It is an expression having widest meaning, it denotes the power exercised by the judiciary as an organ of the State. And this power varies according to the type of system in which it is present, that is adversarial or inquisitorial system of Justice. As far as India is concerned, the Judiciary is given power under the Constitution. It is made independent and it is one of the fundamental pillars of democracy. It keeps check on the other organs of the state thereby upholding the principles of the Constitution.

4.5.3 Judicial Policy Making

This is associated with the related terms such as Judicial Activism, Judicial Creativity and Judicial Legislation. These all terms mean that Judiciary is not simply an organ to interpret law and read the rules and make the other organs of state abide the principles of the Constitution. This means that they are also law makers. Thus, Judiciary do not merely declare the law, they also create the law.

- As far as India is concerned, the courts have interpreted the laws giving prominence to the rights of the individual and considering the state to be a welfare state and the courts to be the guardians of the Constitution.
- This concept of judicial legislation by the Supreme Courts and the High Courts has remained a controversial issue even today.
- Only in certain exceptional cases, the Higher Judiciary has resorted to the judicial legislation by framing rules and regulations which in normal course had to be carried out by the legislature.
- These include guidelines in the case of sexual harassment of woman at work place (*Visakha vs. State of Rajasthan*, (1997) 6 SCC 241), guidelines for adoption of minor children by foreign parents *in Lakshmi Kant Pandey vs. Union of India* ((1984) 2 SCC 244),

guidelines in *University of Kerala vs. Council of Principals of Colleges*((2009) 16 SCC 712) where steps to be taken by the educational institutions to contain the menace of ragging was suggested.

In *Raj Deo Sharma vs. State of Bihar* ((1998) 7 SCC 507) and *Raj Deo Sharma (II) vs. State of Bihar* ((1999) 7 SCC 704), the Supreme Court laid down guidelines for speedy disposal of criminal cases.

These abovementioned measures were not norms and courts in certain instances has frowned upon legislation by the Judiciary. In *Common Cause vs. Union of India* ((2008) 5 SCC 511), the Supreme Court refused to provide guidelines to regulate traffic as this would fall under the domain of the legislature. Similarly in *P. Rama Chandra Rao vs. State of Karnataka* ((2002) 4 SCC 578) the courts held that giving directions of a legislative nature is not function of the judiciary.

- The people opposing this concept say that judicial legislation is in violation of the principle of separation of powers and that it does not represent the will of the people and also that courts are not fully equipped to legislate.
- These arguments cannot simply be brushed aside.
- The problem is the legislature is taking time and there is delay in the political process in taking decisions and actions, hence there is no option but the judiciary to intervene and make legislation.
- The legislature was functioning effectively then all these issues would have been dealt earlier through legislations and laws, since there is lacunae, the judiciary through its own inherent power of legislation is filling up these gaps.

This can be seen from the fact that even after several years after framing on sexual harassment the legislature has not taken steps to legislate the same, hence it has to be agreed that such judicial legislation was a step in the right direction.

4.5.4 Judicial Activism

This term describes the assertive nature of use of judicial power. The extreme model of judicial activism is when the court begins to be intrusive and dominates all the institutions of the government. It is otherwise been termed as judicial supremacy, judicial absolutism, judicial legislation and judicial policy making. Some of the judges and advocates think that judicial activism is only the extension of the powers under judicial review and not an extraordinary power. However, for others this term means encroachment of the court in the powers of legislative and executive field.

4.5.5 Judicial Restraint

It is anti-thesis to judicial activism. And thus it denotes the self-control exhibited by the judiciary. The Encyclopaedia of American Constitution describes the judicial restraint as follows, the judicial restraint of a court is that it decides virtually nothing at all; it strains to find reason why it lacks jurisdiction, it avows deference to the superiority of other departments or agencies in construing the law; it finds endless reasons why the constitutionality of laws cannot be examined. It is a model where the government cannot take recourse to courts to enforce principles of constitution. And courts also do not involve themselves in such acts.

4.5.6 Constitutionalism

It has both descriptive and prescriptive connotations. Descriptively, it refers mainly to the historical struggle for the constitutional recognition of the rights, freedom and privileges of the people. Prescriptively it incorporates those features of the government which are seen as important elements of the constitution. Simply put, constitutionalism is the spirit of the Constitution which commands respect from both the ruler and the ruled.

4.5.7 Separation of Powers

This principle was propounded and popularised by the French political analyst, Montesquieu. It represents assigning of the three namely legislative, executive and the judicial powers in three separate organs of the government that is in the Executive, the Legislature and the Judiciary. It provides that each of these organs is separate and distinct functionally and structurally and there is no overlapping between them.

But in the present times, this concept has been substituted by the more flexible theory of Checks and Balances. This concept also means that one organ of the government should not perform or exercise the function of the other. The effective and strict implementation of this doctrine is not possible in the present era because of the growth of delegated legislation and administrative tribunals.

4.5.8 Public Interest Litigation

It is a new concept which denotes a new use of judicial power. To provide common man, the socially and economically disadvantaged section of the society, easy access to justice. It also denotes a type of representative litigation which is called the 'Social action litigation'. This concept has been induced and led by the Supreme Court of India since the early 1980s. This Public interest litigation had opened the doors of Supreme Court to the ordinary citizen. Any matter of public importance could now be taken up to the Supreme Court. And by way of this process the Court had delivered several landmark verdicts which had paved way for development of social consciousness of the people.

4.6 MEANING OF JUDICIAL REVIEW

As per the Encyclopaedia of American Constitution, the Judicial Review is defined as the power of courts to consider the constitutionality of acts of other organs of government when the issue of constitutionality is germane to the disposition of law suits properly pending before the court. This power to consider constitutionality in appropriate cases included the courts authority to refuse to enforce, and in effect invalidate, governmental acts they find to be unconstitutional.

The term acquired different meanings in various countries. And its origin can be traced to United Kingdom which has no written Constitution. But this concept has been firmly established in United States of America having a written Constitution and a federal polity.

4.6.1 Judicial Review in United Kingdom

The foundation of the concept of judicial review can be traced to the basis of natural law, and the understanding that the human conduct is guided by fundamental laws which have natural or divine origin and sanction. In the famous *Dr. Bonham's* case (1610) Chief Justice Coke stated that *'when an act of Parliament is against common right or reason, or repugnant, or impossible to be performed, the common law will control it and adjudge such Act to be void'*.

The meaning of judicial as it is understood now to strike down the unconstitutional legislations failed to establish in England because of its historical conflict between the royal prerogative on one hand and the Parliament and the people on the other. Finally the people stood victorious. It also meant that the Parliament was also victorious as it was the representative of the people. This strengthened and firmed the concept of parliamentary sovereignty as propounded by A.V. Dicey. The Parliament thus became supreme.

Hence, Dicey states that '*English judges do not claim or exercise any power to repeal any statue*'. Moreover, Dicey proceeds to state that judicial law making is '*in short, subordinate legislation*' because '*acts of Parliament may override and constantly do override the law of the judges*'.

Hence, the courts in England have exercised only a limited power of judicial review in the sense that they strike down the 'subordinate legislation' or executive action if they are 'ultra vires' of the parent Acts under which they are made. But the English Courts and the House of Lords do not have the power to declare any act of the Parliament to be null and void on any ground. The absence of a written constitution and the legal recognition of doctrine of Parliamentary Sovereignty have restricted the development of a full-fledged concept of judicial review in England.

4.6.2 Judicial Review in United States of America

Unlike in United Kingdom the United States had a written Constitution and a federal polity. And this provided the fertile ground of development of judicial review. Alexander Hamilton one of the founding fathers of the American Constitution argued that '*the limited constitution can be preserved in practice no other way than through the medium of courts of justice, whose duty it must be to declare all acts contrary to the manifest tenor of the Constitution, void*'.

But it was Chief Justice John Marshall who propounded the modern doctrine of judicial review in the *Marbury vs. Madison* in 1803. Marshall demonstrated in this classic case that the court must have power to invalidate the Acts of the Congress when it is in violation of the provisions of the Constitution. Marshall started from the understanding that the government of United States created by the Constitution is a limited government and that a '*legislative act, contrary to the Constitution, is not law*'. Marshall declared:

> *It is emphatically, the province and duty of the judicial department, to say what the law is. Those who apply the rule to particular cases, must of necessity expound and interpret that rule. If two laws conflict with each other, the courts must decide on the operation of each. So, if a law be in opposition to the Constitution; if both the law and the constitution apply to a particular case, so that the court must either decide that case, conformable to the law, disregarding the constitution; or conformable to the constitution, disregarding the law; the court must determine which of these conflicting rules govern the case; this is of the very essence of judicial duty.*

He also declared that as per all written constitutions, a law repugnant to the Constitution is void and the courts are bound by such an understanding.

The analysis of this landmark judgement given by Marshall makes it clear that the learned Chief Justice had founded doctrine of judicial review on the following basic principles:

1. The Constitution is the Supreme law of the land, it is '*fundamental and paramount law of the nation*'.

2. In the cases of written Constitution especially of federal character, the Courts have to play the role of an arbiter to maintain the balance between various constituent elements of the federating units with respect to the distribution of legislative powers.
3. The power of judicial review is inherent in a federal constitution though it is not explicitly mentioned.
4. It is emphatically the province and duty of the judicial department to say what the law is.
5. The President of the country and the Judges of the Supreme Court have taken oath to uphold the Constitution.

Over a period of time this concept of Judicial review has become the corner stone of the American Constitution. Now this power of judicial review is now come to be exercised by federal as well as by the Supreme Court to test the validity of the legislations made.

Judicial review in the interest of federalism has played a vital role in United States. This is viewed as one of the important functions of judicial review. It is importantly judicially enforcing the principles of the Constitution and recognising that Constitution is a law rather than a policy document. From the beginning made in the *Marbury vs. Madison* the Courts have now come a long way, and at present they exert a dominant role while interpreting the Constitution. This also does not mean that Supreme Court is above of all and immune from criticism.

The courts are still subject to political restraints emanating from the Constitution. The Congress can still impeach the judges, can able to restrict the jurisdiction of the federal courts, and can even amend the Constitution in order to overrun a ruling by the court. Despite these checks the role of Supreme Court has out grown them and has become the ultimate power in the country. It can be said that scarcely any question arises in United States which does not become, sooner or later, a subject matter of judicial debate.

4.6.3 Judicial Review in India

The power of judicial review is not explicitly mentioned in the Indian Constitution. But this power of judicial review of Supreme Court can be traceable to Article 13 (1) and (2) and Article 32 (1) and of High Courts to Article 226. In *State of Madras vs. V.G.Row* (AIR 1952 SC 196) Chief Justice Patanjali Shastri observed: '*our Constitution contains express provisions for judicial review of legislation as to its conformity with the Constitution. This is specially true as regards the fundamental rights as to which the court has been assigned the role of sentinel on the Qui Vive*'.

In *Kesavananda Bharati vs. State of Kerala* (AIR 1973 SC 1899), Khanna. J observed: '*If the provisions of the statute are found to be violative of any Article of the Constitution which is touchstone of the validity of all laws, Supreme Court and the High Courts are competent to strike down the said provisions*'.

Article 13 which is under Part III of the Constitution dealing with the fundamental rights provides two clauses (1) and (2) which reads as follows:

1. *All laws in force in the territory of India immediately before the commencement of this Constitution in so far as they are inconsistent with the provision of this part, shall, to the extent of such inconsistency, be void.*
2. *The State shall not make any law which takes away or abridges the rights conferred by this part and any law made in contravention of this clause, to the extent of the contravention, be void.*

Article 32 (1) provides

The right to move the Supreme Court by appropriate proceedings for the enforcement of the rights conferred by this part is guaranteed.

Article 226 (1) confers powers on different High Courts the power to enforce

Any of the rights conferred by part III and for any other purpose.

Thus, it can be clearly seen that powers have been conferred with the courts to declare any law made by the legislature as null and void if they are found to be violative of the provisions in Part III that is the fundamental rights. But there are no provisions in the Constitution to provide for when laws or rules are in violation of other Articles and Parts of the Constitution. But reading of Article 226, we can clearly come to understand that the High Courts have been granted power to strike down laws contravening laws not just in violation of provisions of Part III but also for 'any other purpose'. Hence, power of High Court extends to other provisions of the Constitution as well. Thus, from the above the Supreme Court's power of judicial review while exercising its original jurisdiction under the Article 32 is confined to only the Part III whereas in its appellate jurisdiction, the Supreme Court can exercise this power over the entire Constitution.

This power of Supreme Court can be traced to the written Constitution in a federal polity. The unconstitutionality of a law is same whether it violates Part III which are specially protected by Articles 13,32 and 226 or whether it violates rest of the Constitution which are not specially protected with regard to the Supreme Court. Hence, tracing the power of judicial review to Articles 13 and 32 will be an incomplete effort.

In *A.K. Gopalan vs. State of Madras* (AIR 1950 SC 27), Kania C.J. stated that the Article 13 was inserted in Part-III *ex abundantecautela* and that '*in India it is the constitution that is Supreme and that a statute law to be valid, must be in all conformity with the constitutional requirements and it is for the judiciary to decide whether any enactment is constitutional or not*'.

As far as India is concerned, the judicial review comprises of the following three aspects:

1. Judicial review of legislative action
2. Judicial review of judicial decision
3. Judicial review of administrative action

The Supreme Court has always held that the power of Judicial review under Article 32 and 226 to scrutinise the legislative action, even the constitutional provisions and amendments to be subjected to verification by the judiciary, to be integral to our Constitutional scheme.

In a landmark judgement having far reaching consequence, a seven-judge Bench of Supreme Court has held that even the administrative Tribunals established under Articles 323-A or 323-B of the Constitution can exercise the power of judicial review like that of Supreme Court or High Court, even though their role in this regard is supplementary. Thus, sweeping powers are vested with the Supreme Courts, High Courts and the Tribunals due to the provisions of the Constitution and also because of the judicial innovations.

4.7 JUDICIAL ACTIVISM IN INDIA

It is difficult to trace the origin of judicial activism in India. Since its establishment the Judiciary has come to be regarded as independent and separate entity of the government. The activism can be traced back even prior to the Government of India Act 1935. Some of the judges of the High Courts established under the Indian High Courts Act, 1861 exhibited flashes of activism. Back in 1893, Justice Mahmood of Allahabad High Court delivered a dissenting judgement which sowed the seed of activism in India.

The Judicial activism can be seen from the decisions and directions given by the Supreme Court. This trend can be seen in the following list:

1. The concept of 'basic structure' was introduced in 1973, whereby even the Constitutional amendment is liable to be struck down if it changes any of the basic structure of the Constitution. This kind of judicial control over the Constitution has been seen only in India (*Kesavananda Bharati vs. State of Kerala*, AIR 1973 SC 1463).
2. Even the privileges of the legislators are not absolute and they have now been brought under the purview of the courts (*Re Keshav Singh*, AIR 1965 SC 745).
3. The power of judicial review exercised by the Supreme Courts and the High Courts has not been recognised to be unchangeable 'basic structure of the constitution' (*Indira Nehru Gandhi vs. Raj Narain*, (1975) SCC Supp. 1).
4. The entire governmental administration is corrected by the Supreme Court at the apex and the other 21 High Courts under it.
5. The concept of 'state' has not been given wider meaning to include all public and quasi-public authorities. This was made possible so by various successive judgements by the Supreme Court.
6. The concept of *locus Standi* has been widened by the Courts in case of public interest litigations.
7. The Supreme Court has often resorted to make Judicial Legislation by virtue of the power given under Article 141 of the Constitution to fill the legislative lacunae (*Vishaka vs. State of Rajasthan*, (1997) 6 SCC 241).

Hence, it is clear that a clear origin of judicial activism cannot be found after the independence. Analysing the various judgements and directions given by the Supreme Court, we can come to understand that there have been flashes of activism since 1950s till 1980s and since 1980s there has been consistency in such decisions by the court. Another important aspect is that there is no uniformity in areas where such decisions have been taken. The decisions were taken in varied areas such as interpreting the Constitution, guarding the fundamental rights of the citizens, strengthening of the concept of judicial review, expanding the scope of *locus standi* in cases of public interest litigation, expanding the meaning of Article 21 and restructuring certain directive principles as fundamental rights.

4.7.1 Judicial Activism Definition

There is no precise definition of judicial activism which is accepted by all. But the widely accepted view is that it is related to problems and processes of political development in the country. Hence, judicial activism deals with the political role played by the judiciary, like its counterparts in other branches of the government, that is, the legislature and the executive.

- Judicial activism is the exercise of the judicial power in order to fundamentally alter the power relations in the state which is governed by the ruling elites.
- It is also the use to such power to infuse and enforce counter-ideologies which enable to recodify the power relations among the institutions of governance.
- The justification of such activism stems from the near collapse of the responsible government and the mounting pressure on the judiciary to step in to aid which forced it to react by venturing and making political and policy-making judgements.

- The terms 'judicial activism' and 'judicial restraint' are used to describe the assertive nature of the courts. They are two extremes in the spectrum of judicial power.
- The most extreme form of activism would be when the courts are so intrusive that it virtually dominates all spheres of the government. These above mentioned terms are generally used as descriptive approach to understand whether the court is exhibiting activism or restraint in particular cases.
- The definitions to these terms come from personal or professional view of the 'right' role of the court.
- Hence, the courts are either condemned or commended for their 'right' role in such cases.
- As far as United States is considered, individual judges have interpreted the Constitution which is highly ambiguous and based on their personal understandings. Hence, individual judges have had different understanding of what is 'proper' or 'right' judicial role.
- The term judicial activism can be equated with, judicial supremacy, judicial absolutism, judicial imperialism and judicial anarchy. This is opposed to the term 'restraint' which is popularly called 'judicial conservatism'.

The understanding of an activist or a restraintivist judges are based on definitions of groups of people who define them. Some of the major groups of people who participate in such process are mainly the 'managerial' class of bureaucrats, the set of advocates, the 'victims' which include the police and other government machinery and finally the 'beneficiaries' the common man, students, disadvantaged sections who benefit from such actions of the Court.

Thus, the definition is based on the understanding of each group of people, hence we cannot come to a concrete definition of what is judicial activism. And it is impossible for the Judge to satisfy all the groups therefore there is no uniformity in calling what activism is. It thus means different things to different people. It can be understood to be the dynamism of the judges, some consider it to be the creativity of the judiciary and some other as bringing 'social or cultural' revolution through judiciary. Though such concept of revolution seems farfetched, it does aim in bringing change in the society.

4.7.2 Reasons for Judicial Activism

The following are some of the important reasons which make the courts to be active while discharging their function as per the Constitution.

1. **Near Collapse of Responsible Government:** When the two branches of the government that is the legislature and executive fail to perform there will be a near collapse of the responsible government. Responsible government is said to be the hallmark and basis of a successful democracy and constitutionalism. And its collapse necessitates immediate and drastic action. When the legislature fails to enact legislations to suit the changing scenarios, when the administration fails to function sincerely and with integrity and honesty, all this would lead to collapse of confidence of people on the Constitution and the government. In such extraordinary circumstances, the judiciary may step in the shoes of legislature and executive and take upon the functions which usually come under their purview. Thus, the result is judicial legislation and the government by the judiciary.

2. **Pressure on judiciary to step in aid:** Presently it has been clearly established that the courts cannot be a silent spectator when the fundamental rights of the citizens are being violated either by the government or by any other third party. The judges being the members of the society feel that they too have a role to play in ameliorating the worsening conditions of the people in the country. Moreover, people in our country are infatuated with salvation by the judiciary. Thus, it has become natural for the citizens to look up to the judiciary to step in for their aid and help. Thus, this creates tremendous pressure on the judiciary to do something for the suffering masses. And therefore this may lead the judiciary to take up an activist role.
3. **Judicial enthusiasm to participate in social reform and change:** The judges who are from the society cannot be silent spectators when the times and things around them are changing. As persons who are involved in interpreting and applying law which is a dynamic concept, the judges themselves would like to involve in the social reforms process happening due to changing times. Judiciary has thus become an active participant in the social reform process. It has thus encouraged and also initiated various instruments such as the Public Interest Litigation (PIL), also called the Social Action Litigation. It such cases the courts have disregarded the usual and necessary procedures and forms and therefore have assumed the functions of investigator, counsellor and monitor of the functions of the administration.

   This has thus led to relaxation of procedural and customary rules. And it invokes the jurisdiction of the courts in a far and wide manner. And thus when the courts themselves initiate action to correct the social ills, such acts become indistinguishable from that of commissioners of grievances.
4. **Legislative vacuum left open:** In administrative law there is a saying that even when the Parliament and the state legislature work every day for 365 days and enact legislations on every such day they will not be enough to address the changing needs of the society. Even though there exists wide plethora of legislations, there are still large areas which are still left uncovered by the legislations. This may be because of inadvertence, lack of coverage of the issues, absence or indifference of the legislature.

   Thus, when the competent legislature fails to act or perform their legitimate role to meet the changing needs of the society, the court thus indulges in judicial legislation. It has to be understood in terms of statutory interpretation. The courts have thus acted to fill the void created by relinquishment of legislative responsibility.
5. **The Constitutional Scheme:** The India Constitution contains a number of provisions which provide wide scope for judiciary to assert itself. Under Article 13, the judiciary is empowered to declare any law or legislation as void if it is in violation of Part III of the Constitution. Under Article 32, any aggrieved citizen may approach the Supreme Court for enforcement of the fundamental rights. The right under this Article has been made a fundamental right under the title 'right to constitutional remedies'. Thus, the Supreme Court is designated as the guardian of the fundamental rights of the citizens and while fulfilling that role it indulges in judicial legislation making and judicial government.

   Under Article 131, the Supreme Court is vested with the power to uphold the federal principle. The Supreme Court is also the highest appellate court and it hears appeals in all matters relating to Civil, Criminal and Constitution. The Supreme Court is also given advisory powers to advice the President under Article 143 on any question of law or fact, referred to it. The Supreme Court also has the rule making power under Articles 142 and 145. It has the power to punish for contempt under Article 129.

Thus, it is clear that judiciary in India especially the Supreme Court in particular has been given vast powers under the Constitution and therefore it has enough scope to be active and uphold the fundamental principle of constitutionalism.

6. **Authority to make final declaration as to validity of a law:** Supreme Court is the final arbiter of validity of the laws. Under Article 141 the Supreme Court has the power to declare any law and such declaration is binding on all courts in India except the Supreme Court itself.

   In *Indira Sawney vs. Union of India* (AIR 2000 SC 498) a three-judge Bench encountered a peculiar situation where one of its directions in the *Mandal Commission Judgement* (AIR 1993 SC 477) to identify the creamy layer in order to exclude them from the reservation process, in the case the Kerala government enacted a legislation to give retrospective effect that there are no creamy layer in Kerala. The Court found this unconstitutional and took a serious note of action of the Kerala government and initiated contempt proceedings against it.

   The Supreme Court being the final authority to decide the validity of a law gives it wide discretionary powers without any accountability thereby creating ground for activism by the judiciary.

7. **Role of Judiciary as guardian of fundamental rights:** The Constitution has designated the higher judiciary as the guardian of fundamental rights of the citizens.

   As per Articles 13, 32 and 226 of the Constitution, it is the duty of the courts to uphold the fundamental rights of the citizens of the country.

   a. As per Article 13, it empowers the Supreme Court and High Courts to declare any law as void if it is in violation of any fundamental right.
   b. Under Article 32, the Supreme Court can issue writ, order or direction to any person or authority violating the fundamental rights of the citizens.
   c. This approach to Supreme Court has been made a fundamental right under the Constitution as per Articles 32 to 35.
   d. Under Article 226 the High Courts have been given far and wider power to enforce the fundamental or other rights of the citizens.
   e. All these powers have been vested with the courts which enable them to exercise vast powers of judicial review with respect of any legislative, quasi-legislative, executive, quasi-judicial or other actions of the government concerned.

   This is the role which has been effectively carried on by the courts. The result therefore is the growth and development of judicial activism.

8. **Public confidence on the Judiciary:** The most important and potent weapon in hands of the judiciary is the confidence and respect it commands from the people. It also inspires faith in the mind of the people. It tries to keep the scales in balance in any dispute. Even in a recent survey it was revealed that nearly 85% of the people trust the Supreme Court than the Parliament. The concept of Public Interest Litigation and Judicial activism by the Supreme Court is said to be the reason behind such popularity. The study also revealed that there is an extraordinary support for the institutions and in no other country can such support be seen for the Constitutional courts by the

ordinary public. This therefore clearly shows the public confidence and trust reposed by the masses of the country on the Supreme Court which is the ultimate guardian of their fundamental rights. The Supreme Court has withstood the test of times with the help of the weapon of Judicial Activism.

9. **Enthusiasm of individual players:** The application and development of the judicial activism can be attributed to many individual players. Some of them are civil rights activists, consumer rights groups, women rights advocates, groups for environmental action, bonded-labour groups, assorted-lawyer based groups etc. This is just a segment and not the complete list of the participants. This may seem than judicial activism is because of such collective measures, but it has also to be understood that individual role played by the judges too have contributed immensely to the growth of such activism. Without the role played by Krishna Iyer, P.N. Bhagwati, O. Chinappa Reddy and D.A. Desai, during the formative years of Public Interest Litigation there would not be the present case of wide activism by the judges in the areas of social action litigation.

   The following are the types of judicial actor classified based on the concept of judicial activism:

   (i) **The first judicial actors who laid foundation of judicial activism:** Personalities such as Desai, Chinnappa Reddy, JJ, extended the sphere of judicial activism for the protection of the bonded labours. Other actors such as Kuldip Singh J. in case of environmental jurisprudence, Justice K. Ramaswamy in case of rights of depressed class, Justice J.S. Verma in area of corruption in high places have contributed significantly for the growth of activism in these areas.
   (ii) **Restraintivist judicial actors:** Justice R.S. Pathak and Justice Venkatramaiah
   (iii) **Eclectic judicial actors:** Neither favourable nor hostile to the concept of judicial activism.
   (iv) **Gatekeeper judicial actors**
   (v) **Anti-activism judicial actors**
   (vi) **Revisionist judicial actors**

   There is yet another category of Superannuated Judicial Actors who are primarily the retired judges who have come to occupy important positions in various commissions such as the Law Commission, National Human Rights Commission, Press Council of India and Minorities Commission etc. These visible individuals play a vital role as conscience keepers. And one name if to be mentioned as the embodiment of all these roles and processes, Justice V.R. Krishna Iyer depicts a shining example of activist superannuated judicial actor.

The abovementioned reasons are the basis that compel the judiciary to play an active role or a conservative role based on the prevailing circumstances in the given society, government and in the world at large.

4.7.3 Judicial Activism and its Parameters (p-84)

There has been accepted there is a concrete relation between judicial power and judicial activism. The judiciary under any Constitution can play an active role when it carries out the following functions:

a. Interpreting the meaning and scope of the legislation made up by a competent authority.
b. Maintaining the balance between various constituent elements of the federation and between the union and the individual units.
c. Upholding the supremacy of the Constitution when such question is posed before it.
d. Protecting and upholding the fundamental rights of the people when such is guaranteed under the Constitution.
e. Dealing with the matters of institutional conflicts between legislature, executive and the judiciary.
f. Interpreting the Constitution as per the intention of its framers etc.

Thus, in all the above cases the judiciary in an active democracy can play a vital role through means of judicial review. The judiciary also on the other hand can refuse to entertain any matter posed before it. Such refusal is based on the grounds such as lack of jurisdiction or *doctrine of political questions.* The way, degree, and the amount of activism vary depending on the limitations as imposed by the Constitution and other factors like strength of other organs of the state and the willingness of the judiciary to play a political role in a changing society.

The criticism against such activist role of the courts is that it has usurped the legitimate powers of the other two organs of the state. Considering the role played by the American Supreme Court, it has never tried to block any legitimate major policy initiative taken by the Congress and the President. It did certainly strike down any law which was in contravention of the Bill of Rights, and it also struck down the means adopted by the Congress to bring about such legislations.

The abovementioned position is also applicable in case with India. Though the Supreme Court started to play activist role occasionally from *Golaknath vs. Punjab* (AIR 1967 SC 1643), and consistently from *Kesavananda Bharathi vs. State of Kerala* (AIR 1973 SC 1461), it never came in the way of Parliament to pursue the objectives as desired by the government. The traditional role of Courts to keep in check whether the other organs are functioning within the constitutional boundaries has always been carried out. The purpose of an independent court was to ensure that supremacy of the Constitution continued without any interference.

The real foe of absolutism is considered to be the law. It is the judicial realism and reasoned technique which resulted in emergence of judicial activism although its parameters differ in different constitutions around the world.

4.7.4 Typical Examples of Judicial Activism in India

Judicial activism in India is far wider, and more varied compared with its American counterpart. This is because of the fundamental ideals present in the Constitution. Apart from adhering to the principles of judicial review the Supreme Court has also upheld the idea of Constitutionalism, thereby giving itself even more and wider powers.

- As under Article 142(1) of the Constitution, the court exercises the power to do anything or give any direction to render complete justice.
- The court has also now assumed power aftermath of *Kesavananda Bharathi case* to test the validity of even the Constitutional amendment under the Article 368. And no court anywhere in the world exercises such power. This provision itself can be cited as the best example of judicial activism in India.

- Another instance which can be considered as Activism by the Judiciary was when the court exercised its mandate to give directions to some political leaders and bureaucrats, to compensate the State, for abusing the discretionary powers vested with them.
- This kind of direction to political leaders and bureaucrats is unheard of anywhere in the world. Such kind of power is exercised by the Court itself and it does not exist anywhere in the Constitution or in any statute.

The Supreme Court also refused to exercise its advisory jurisdiction under Article 143 in the matter of 'Ayodhya dispute' (*Ismail Farrouqui vs. Union of India*, (1994) 6 SCC 360). Such a kind of refusal itself is an act of judicial activism. And the Supreme Court has also resorted several times to Article 129 to punish for contempt against judiciary. In a case the Supreme Court initiated contempt proceedings against the person who had committed against a High Court and not the Supreme Court itself (*Re VinayChanraMisra* (1995) 2 SCC 584), but this was subsequently overruled and the question has been kept open.

- The Supreme Court has also broadened the scope of '*locus standi*' in cases involving violation of fundamental rights of the citizens, by initiating the concept of *Public Interest Litigation*.
- The credit for bringing in such change can be attributed to individual judges of the Supreme Court like Justice P.N. Bhagwati, Justice V.R. Krishna Iyer and Justice Kuldip Singh etc.
- The courts have also assumed the role of supervisors in certain criminal cases involving political bigwigs. In the popular scandal called the *fodder scam*, the Patna High Court asked the CBI (a central agency) to report its findings directly to the Court.
- Further the Supreme Court has assumed primacy in appointment and transfer of the judges of Supreme Courts and of the High Courts.
- The Supreme Court has held that the Chief Justice of India alone has the primacy in recommending the names of the judges.
- The Supreme Court has widened the scope of 'consultation' under Article 124 by interpreting that the Chief Justice should consult two senior most, and four senior judges before submitting such recommendation. Thus, the Supreme Court has the upper hand in the appointments of judges.

The other area where the Supreme Court exhibited such activism is while interpreting the Directive Principles of the State contained in Part IV of the Constitution. It made some of its provisions to be justiciable while interpreting the fundamental rights. The Court even directed the Parliament to enact a uniform civil code within a time bound period (*Sarala Mudgal vs. Union of India*, (1995) 3 SCC 635).

4.7.5 Judicial Activism in India before 1980s

It is indeed difficult to draw a clear pattern of behaviour of the courts before 1980s. The Courts seemed to be mechanical in its approach of interpreting the laws and approaching the problem presented before it. The Supreme Court rarely exhibited any activist behaviour before the 80s, more precisely before the emergency of 1975.

There has been an overwhelming opinion that the Courts in India during the 1940s and 1950s served the elite of the society who used it to further their interests, but within the framework of the law. The law then generally favoured the landed-class and the agrarian reforms did not happen. Thus, the circumstances forced the judges to side with the landlords and hence the judiciary took a 'not-so-progressive' outlook.

During 1950s the government lost an opportunity to establish a people friendly judiciary. One important fact to be noted in this context is that the legal machinery of lawyers, judges, prosecutors all came from the same stock as before that is of same caste, class, attitude and orientation. Hence, this is one of the major reasons why the judiciary did not adopt a very progressive approach. Even some of the experts went on to call the Supreme Court before the 80s as a 'rich man's Court'. This is because alleged turning of the Supreme Court to an 'economic activist' to protect the '*status quo*' that led to judicial passivism.

Some of the important decisions of the court are as follows:

1. In *Vajravelu vs. Special Deputy Collector* (AIR 1965 SC 2017) the Supreme Court held that a differentiation or rates of compensation awarded for compulsory acquisition of private property between one for public purpose and another has no relation to the object of the Act, disputed in the case.
2. *L.C. Golak Nath vs. State of Punjab* (AIR 1967 SC 1643) is a landmark case. A special 11-judge bench was constituted to determine the validity of constitution (seventeenth amendment) Act, 1964. The court speaking through Subba Rao C.J. declared that:
   a. Constitutional amendment is a legislative process.
   b. Amendment is 'law' within the meaning of Article 13 of the constitution.
   c. Parliament has no power from the date of the decision to amend any provision of part III of the Constitution so as to take away or abridge the fundamental rights enshrined therein etc.

   This judgment had secured the '*paramountcy of fundamental rights*' and established that even the constitutional amendment was subject to judicial review on the ground of violation of the fundamental rights. This has also laid down the doctrine of '*prospective overruling*' for the first time.
3. *Kesavananda Bharathi vs. State of Kerala (*AIR 1973 SC 1461) also called the Fundamental right's case, a 13-judge bench of the Supreme Court dealt with the validity of the Constitutional 24th Amendment, 25th Amendment and the 29th Amendment Acts. The summary of the verdict delivered by the majority nine out of the thirteen is as follows:
   a. Golak Nath's case was over ruled.
   b. Article 368 does not grant power to amend the basic structure or framework of the Constitution.
   c. The first part of Section 3 of the Constitutional (25th amendment) Act, 1971 is valid. And the second part wherein 'no law containing a declaration that it is for giving effect to such policy shall be called in question in any court on the ground that it does not give effect to such policy' is invalid etc.

Basic Structure: The Court did not define what constitutes the basic structure, rather they chose to provide the various features as basic features of the Constitution. They include

(i) Constitution is Supreme
(ii) Republican and democratic form of the government
(iii) Secular nature of the Constitution
(iv) Separation of the powers between legislature, executive and the judiciary

(v) Federal character of the Constitution
(vi) Fundamental rights and freedom
(vii) Sovereignty of India
(viii) Mandate to build a welfare state and an egalitarian society
(ix) Any of the fundamental rights

The above list is only illustrative and not exhaustive. Thus, the Court has now given to itself unprecedented power which has unparallel anywhere in the world to test the validity of a Constitutional amendment.

4.7.6 Judicial Activism in India – Post 1980's

The following are the trends that emerged after the 1980s and are presently continuing.

1. **Expanding the scope of Article 21:** In the *Maneka Gandhi vs. Union of India* (AIR 1978 SC 597) the Supreme Court delivered an epoch-making judgement. Justice Bhagwati expanded the scope 'personal liberty' under Article 21. He declared that:

   the expression personal liberty in Article 21 is of the widest amplitude and it covers a variety of rights which go to constitute the personal liberty of man and some to them have been raised to the status of distinct fundamental rights and given additional protection under Article 19.

   Another important aspect of this judgement is that it established the requirement of reasonableness of procedure in Article 21 through Article 14. This led to the conversion of 'procedure established by law' to 'due process of law' as given in the American Constitution. Since this judgement the Supreme Court has rendered a number of judgements expanding the Scope of Article 21 to include social rights, economic rights, human rights and legal rights which enable a man to lead his life with basic human dignity. Right to privacy, right to education, right-to-fair trial, right to health, right to gender equality, right against torture, right to livelihood, right to medical treatment are some of the various rights which are now included under the scope of Article 21– right to life.
2. **Curative petition:** The Supreme Court has invented a new tool for rendering complete justice called the *curative petition* in the case of *Rupa Ashok Hurra vs. Ashok Hurra* ((2002) 4 SCC 388). Justice Shah Mohammed Quadri in this case observed:

   The petitioners in these writ petitions seek reconsideration of the final judgements of this Court after they have been unsuccessful in review petitions and in that these cases are different from the cases referred above. The provision of the order XL Rule 5 of the Supreme Court Rule bars further application of review in the same matter. The concern of the court is now whether any relief can be given to the petitioners who challenge the final Judgement of this Court, though after disposal of review petitions complaining of the gross abuse of the process of the court and irremedialinjustice. In a State like India governed by Rule of Law, certainity of law declared and final decision rendered on merits in a list between the parties by the highest court in the court is of paramount importance. The principle of finality is insisted upon not on the ground that a judgement given by the Apex court is impeccable but on the maxim interest reipublicaeut sit finis litium.

   ...The upshot of the discussion in our view is that this Court, to prevent abuse of its process and to cur a gross miscarriage of justice, may reconsider its judgement in exercise of its inherent power.

3. **Fake encounter killing by police:** The Supreme Court in *Praskash Kadam vs. Ram Prasad Vishwanath Gupta* ((2011) 6 SCC 189) observed that

   ...this is a very serious case and this cannot be treated like an ordinary case. The accused who are policemen are supposed to uphold the law, but the allegation against them is that they functioned as killers.

   ... that in cases where a fake encounter is proved against policemen in a trial, they must be given death sentence, treating it as the rarest of rare cases. Fake 'encounter' are nothing but cold-blooded, brutal murders by persons who are supposed to uphold the law. In our opinion if crimes are committed by ordinary people, ordinary punishment should be given, but if the offence is committed by policemen much harsher punishment should be given to them because they do an act totally contrary to their duties.

4. **Honour killing:** In *Bhagwandas vs. State (NCT of Delhi)* ((2011) 6 SCC 396), the Supreme Court speaking through Justice Markanday Katju strongly disapproved the honour killings and advocated death penalty for those who are responsible for such killings. The court observed as follows:

   Before parting with this case we would like to state that "honour" killings have become common place in many parts of the country, particularly in Haryana, western Uttar Pradesh and Rajasthan. Often young couples who fall in love have to seek shelter in the police lines or protection homes, to avoid the wrath of kangaroo courts. We have held in Lata Singh Case that there is nothing "honourable" in "honour" killings, and they are nothing but barbaric and brutal murders by bigoted persons with feudal minds. In our opinion honour killings, for whatever reason, come within the category of rarest of the rare cases deserving death punishment. It is time to stamp out these barbaric, feudal practices which are a slur on our nation. This is necessary as a deterrent for such outrageous, uncivilized behaviour. All persons who are planning to perpetrate "honour" killings should know that the gallow await them.

5. **Caste system:** In *ArumugamServai vs. State of Tamil Nadu* ((2011) SCC 405) the court called the caste system as a curse on the nation and observed as follows:

   In the modern age nobody's feelings should be hurt. In particular in a country like India with so much diversity we must take care not to insult anyone's feelings on account of his caste, religion, tribe, language, etc. Only then we can keep our country united and strong.

6. **Election duty and education:** In the *Election Commission of India vs. St.Mary's School* ((2008) 3 SCC 390) the Supreme Court held that the legal requirement to provide staff to the election commission should be read with restricted meaning to use teachers for this purpose. Because holding of election should not result in neglect of education of children due to absence of teachers from the schools.
7. **Privileges of the Parliament:** In *Raja Ram Pal vs. Hon'ble Speaker, Lok Sabha* ((2007) 3 SCC 184) based on a sting operation which showed the MPs demanding money for asking questions and an MP asking for money for letting a NGO work under the

MPLADs scheme. A five-judge Constitutional Bench held that the Court has jurisdiction to deal with such cases even though they may relate to legislative privileges.

8. **Role of judicial activism in unearthing black money:** The Supreme Court has exhibited extraordinary spirit of judicial activism in the absence of little or no action by the government in order to unearth the black money. In *Ram Jethmalani vs. Union of India* ((2011) 8 SCC 1) the court speaking through Justice B. Sudarshan Reddy directed the government to appoint a Special Investigation Team (SIT) to probe the issue of black money.

4.8 JUDICIAL REFORMS

4.8.1 Rural Courts

- One of the most important practical reform would be to constitute rural courts. The rural courts function within the territorial limits of the panchayats.
- If we see our structure of the Judiciary, we can clearly see that there are too many judges to decide the constitutional matters both in Supreme Court and High Courts, but there is a dearth of local judges administering judges in the districts. Thus, there is an imbalance.
- Not all people can approach the High Court and their first resort is the local court and thus local justice delivering mechanisms should be strengthened and a new kind of Courts called as Rural Courts should be set up in the villages to address the local issues and thus enabling people and bringing them closer to justice.
- The procedures of this kind of court should be simple and uncomplicated so that rendering of justice is made flexible.
- These courts moreover should operate in the local language and they should be empowered to visit villages and hear cases and record such evidence locally.
- Specific timeframe should also be fixed for delivering the verdicts.
- The Law Commission in its 114th report advocated setting up of 'Gram Nyayalaya' which had the following set up:
  - The rural courts should be appointed with Special Magistrates having jurisdiction over a town, or a part of a city or a group of villages.
  - These Special Magistrates should be appointed by District Judges for a term of three years.
  - They should have exclusive civil and criminal jurisdiction. In civil cases disputes up to one lakh should be taken and for criminal cases up to an imprisonment of one year.
  - Apart from these other matters related to certain civil disputes arising out while implementing the agrarian reforms, certain property and family disputes and other disputes as entrusted by the Law Commission should also be covered by the Courts.
  - In civil cases the revision of judgement can only be made by a District Judge and that too on the grounds of improper application of law and nothing else.
  - In criminal cases where imprisonment is awarded the appeal lies with the Sessions Judge.
  - The procedures are to be made simple and the verdict should be delivered within 90 days from receiving the complaint.

4.8.2 Indian Judicial Service

The subordinate courts are functioning with inordinate delays and lower efficiency. It is high time that Indian Judicial Service is set up as an All India Service under Article 312 of the Constitution.

- All the offices of the District and the Sessions Judges should be held by persons recruited under such service after such adequate training and exposure.
- It should be a meritocratic service with competitive recruitment, having high quality and given uniform training.
- It will make sure that there are high standards of probity and efficiency which will ensure speedy and impartial justice delivery.
- A good number of Judges for the High Court can also be drawn from this service.

4.8.3 Judicial Procedure

- The Criminal Procedure Code, the Civil Procedure Code and the Evidence Act have to be revised in order to address the present day judicial problems.
- In practice these laws have become burdensome, tardy and counter-productive.
- The right to get justice for criminal case within a year and for civil cases within two years should be guaranteed by the Constitution.
- All the laws should be amended to reflect such constitutional right.
- The appeals should also be strictly limited and only one appeal should be allowed for civil cases. Such appeals should be heard and verdict delivered within 3 months for a criminal cases and 6 months for a civil case.
- All the stays should be prohibited except in exceptional circumstances and also reason for such stay should be given in writing. And no stay should exceed 15 days.
- The time limits specified for adjudication should be strictly adhered to, even in cases involving stay orders.

4.8.4 Higher Courts

- The number of judges both in the Supreme Court and the High Courts should be substantially reduced and their appellate jurisdiction severely restricted.
- The jurisdiction of the Supreme Court should only cover matters related to interpretation of the Constitution and other matters of dispute arising between centre and the States or between two states. Thus, the Supreme Court has to function like a Constitutional Court and a Federal Court.
- The High Courts should only interpret the Constitution to matters relating to the State legislature.
- The appellate powers of the High Court should also be restricted in order to reduce its case load and for ensuring the sanctity and authority of the High Courts.
- Matter relating to service, taxation, disciplinary action against employees and other labour disputes should be dealt with special tribunals constituted for the same. Appeals

should lie to the High Courts only on grounds of interpretation of the Constitution and thus the verdict of the tribunals should be final is such cases.

- The writ jurisdiction which has now become all-encompassing should be restricted and focussed on right to life, liberty and equality before law. And the courts should have unfettered powers in such cases to enforce their directions.

4.8.5 Judicial Commission

- The mechanism of appointment of judges has become very problematic and ineffective.
- The Supreme Court taking upon itself the complete power of appointment has made the remedy worse than the disease.
- Nowhere in the world has the judiciary taken such role undermining the institutions and functions of both the legislature and the executive.
- This practice of judiciary appointing itself is both self-serving and counter-productive.
- Thus, a Judicial Commission of high standards has to be appointed from members drawn the executive, legislature and the judiciary.
- Such recommendation should be made binding on the President.
- The removal of Judges has become non-functional as under Article 124(4) the impeachment process is complicated and cumbersome, and hence no judge has ever been impeached. Such a situation whereby inefficient and corrupt judges functioning with impunity will lead only to judicial terrorism causing disaster to governance process and people in the society.
- Hence, such Judicial Commission should be empowered to try such errant judges and upon its recommendation the President should remove judges guilty of high crimes and transgressions.

4.8.6 Crime Investigation

- All the functions including crime investigation, intelligence gathering, law and order control, security of State and various other functions are all carried out by a single entity – the Police.
- Hence, they are over-burdened with numerous functions and not be able to do justice to any of them.
- Thus, the criminal justice system which is wholly dependent on the Police department is very ineffective and inefficient.
- Hence, there is need to revamp the criminal justice system completely. The courts should hold the police force accountable for their overall functioning.
- The police force should be insulated from the politics by placing the investigation process under direct control of the prosecutors who should be appointed as independent constitutional functionaries.
- By making the police force accountable to the Judiciary, various inhuman practices of torture, third degree and extra-judicial and fake encounters can be curbed.

4.8.7 Reinstatement of Values: Judicial Code of Conduct

- In the conference for the Chief Justice of all High Courts held in 1999, the following code for 'Restatement of Values for Judicial Life' was adopted. These would serve as guiding principles essential for functioning of an independent, strong, respected and impartial judiciary.
- These are not exhaustive but only illustrative of what is expected of the judges.
- These codes have been described as 'restatement of the pre-existing and universally accepted norms, guidelines and conventions' observed by Judges.
- There are complete code canons of judicial ethics. It is given as follows:
  - Justice must not merely be done but it must also be seen to be done. The behaviour and conduct of members of the higher judiciary must reaffirm the people's faith in the impartiality of the judiciary. Accordingly, any act of a Judge of the Supreme Court or a High Court, whether in official or personal capacity, which erodes the credibility of this perception has to be avoided.
  - A Judge should not contest the election to any office of a Club, society or other association; further he shall not hold such elective office except in a society or association connected with the law.
  - Close association with individual members of the Bar, particularly those who practice in the same court, shall be eschewed.
  - A Judge should not permit any member of his immediate family, such as spouse, son, daughter, son-in-law or daughter-in-law or any other close relative, if a member of the Bar, to appear before him or even be associated in any manner with a cause to be dealt with by him.
  - No member of his family, who is a member of the Bar, shall be permitted to use the residence in which the Judge actually resides or other facilities for professional work.
  - A Judge should practice a degree of aloofness consistent with the dignity of his office.
  - A Judge shall not hear and decide a matter in which a member of his family, a close relation or a friend is concerned.
  - A Judge shall not enter into public debate or express his views in public on political matters or on matters that are pending or are likely to arise for judicial determination.
  - A Judge is expected to let his judgments speak for themselves. He shall not give interviews to the media.
  - A Judge shall not accept gifts or hospitality except from his family, close relations and friends.
  - A Judge shall not hear and decide a matter in which a company in which he holds shares is concerned unless he has disclosed his interest and no objection to his hearing and deciding the matter is raised.
  - A Judge shall not speculate in shares, stocks or the like.
  - A Judge should not engage directly or indirectly in trade or business, either by himself or in association with any other person. (Publication of a legal treatise or any activity in the nature of a hobby shall not be construed as trade or business).
  - A Judge should not ask for, accept contributions or otherwise actively associate himself with the raising of any fund for any purpose.

- ○ A Judge should not seek any financial benefit in the form of a perquisite or privilege attached to his office unless it is clearly available. Any doubt in this behalf must be got resolved and clarified through the Chief Justice.
- ○ Every Judge must at all times be conscious that he is under the public gaze and there should be no act or omission by him which is unbecoming of the high office he occupies and the public esteem in which that office is held.

4.8.8 Judicial Standards and Accountability Bill

- This bill will replace the Judges Inquiry Act.
- This will be headed by former Chief Justice of India, and complaints of erring judges including the Chief Justices of High Courts and Supreme Court can be lodged by the public themselves.
- The five-member committee will be appointed by the President on recommendation of three-member panel consisting of the Prime Minister, any minister and the Leader of Opposition Lok Sabha.
- On receiving, the complaints are forwarded to the scrutiny committee which has the powers of a civil court.
- If the charges are proved the committee can request the concerned Judge to resign. If the Judge does not resign, the committee can forward such recommendation to the President for taking appropriate action.
- The bill also mandates that the Judges should not have any close association with the members of the Bar.
- All the details concerning the investigation of the Judges should be put up on the websites of the respective courts.

4.8.9 Judicial Restraint against the Activism

- The activism is not validated as the Courts should be concerned with the legality of law only.
- This also raises the question of accountability as the Judges are not elected representatives of the people and they are also not answerable to the executive or the legislature.
- The decision taken by the Bench too is not predictable.
- The role of activism by the judges encroaches upon the powers of other institutions of democracy and it is in violation of separation of powers.
- There should be a clear-cut procedure for acceptance of the cases filed under Public Interest Litigation. Frivolous cases should be rejected and only cases of substantial public importance should be taken up. It will reduce the burden on the judiciary.
- Hence, there is need for restraint by the judiciary which will help in maintaining the balance of the democratic and constitutional system.

4.8.10 Amendment of Contempt of Courts Act

The Contempt of Courts Act needs to be amended. It should reflect the present condition of the society and curb the unwielded power granted to the courts to punish anyone. Some of the few recommendations in this connection are as follows:

- Every accused punished under the Contempt of Court should be given a reasonable opportunity to be heard.
- The courts themselves should not try such contempt cases. The cases should be handed over to independent commission of the district concerned.
- The words in the act defining criminal contempt as 'scandalizing the court or lowering the authority of the court' should be amended.

4.8.11 Alert Civil Society

- The civil society has become the guardian of the democracy and it acts as the check against the transgressions by the state.
- The civil society thus has an active and vigilant role to play in the times of growing power of the judiciary.
- Literally there is no check against the Judiciary, none of the other democratic institutions could be able to check its growth. Hence, only public and the real people working and reflecting the wishes of the people manage to curtail its unbridled rise.
- The civil society can educate the public and raise in public opinion will have a great impact on the Courts as the judges themselves are first members of the society.
- Thus, the civil society can act as a check against active judiciary and it can be able to protect the rights of the people and gives voice to the populace.

4.8.12 Role of Media

- The media being the fourth pillar of the democracy has a very active role to play in reforming the judiciary.
- The opinion of the masses can be taken to the ivory towers of the courts only with help of the media.
- Earlier the media was silent because of the threat of contempt of court, but since it has now been amended the freedom of expression will not be infringed upon.
- Honest and credible media can indeed bring massive change in the democratic system. It not only reflects the opinion but also can shape-up opinions.
- In the present era of governance, the media has immense role to play. The people depend more on the words of the media. The focus of the media can indeed bring about change.
- This can be seen from the focus the media gave to the Nirbhaya rape case, whereby the trial was expedited and the accused were convicted to be hanged within a shorter period. The role of media should also be appreciated for focusing on various other cases also such as the Jessica Lal murder case, BMW accident case, Arushi Talwar murder case and numerous other corruption-related cases of high-profile ministers.

4.9 BANGALORE PRINCIPLES OF JUDICIAL CONDUCT

The following principles are intended to establish standards for ethical conduct of judges. They are designed to provide guidance to judges and to afford the judiciary a framework for regulating judicial conduct. They are also intended to assist members of the executive and the legislature, and lawyers and the public in general, to better understand and support the judiciary.

These principles presuppose that judges are accountable for their conduct to appropriate institutions established to maintain judicial standards, which are themselves independent and impartial, and are intended to supplement and not to derogate from existing rules of law and conduct that bind the judge.

VALUE 1

Independence

Principle

Judicial independence is a prerequisite to the rule of law and a fundamental guarantee of a fair trial. A judge shall therefore uphold and exemplify judicial independence in both its individual and institutional aspects.

Application

1.1 A judge shall exercise the judicial function independently on the basis of the judge's assessment of the facts and in accordance with a conscientious understanding of the law, free of any extraneous influences, inducements, pressures, threats or interference, direct or indirect, from any quarter or for any reason.
1.2 A judge shall be independent in relation to society in general and in relation to the particular parties to a dispute that the judge has to adjudicate.
1.3 A judge shall not only be free from inappropriate connections with, and influence by, the executive and legislative branches of government, but must also appear to a reasonable observer to be free there from.
1.4 In performing judicial duties, a judge shall be independent of judicial colleagues in respect of decisions that the judge is obliged to make independently.
1.5 A judge shall encourage and uphold safeguards for the discharge of judicial duties in order to maintain and enhance the institutional and operational independence of the judiciary.
1.6 A judge shall exhibit and promote high standards of judicial conduct in order to reinforce public confidence in the judiciary, which is fundamental to the maintenance of judicial independence.

VALUE 2

Impartiality

Principle

Impartiality is essential to the proper discharge of the judicial office. It applies not only to the decision itself but also to the process by which the decision is made.

Application

2.1 A judge shall perform his or her judicial duties without favour, bias or prejudice.
2.2 A judge shall ensure that his or her conduct, both in and out of court, maintains and enhances the confidence of the public, the legal profession and litigants in the impartiality of the judge and of the judiciary.

2.3 A judge shall, as far as is reasonable, so conduct himself or herself as to minimize the occasions on which it will be necessary for the judge to be disqualified from hearing or deciding cases.

2.4 A judge shall not knowingly, while a proceeding is before, or could come before, the judge, make any comment that might reasonably be expected to affect the outcome of such proceeding or impair the manifest fairness of the process, nor shall the judge make any comment in public or otherwise that might affect the fair trial of any person or issue.

2.5 A judge shall disqualify himself or herself from participating in any proceedings in which the judge is unable to decide the matter impartially or in which it may appear to a reasonable observer that the judge is unable to decide the matter impartially. Such proceedings include, but are not limited to, instances where:

a. The judge has actual bias or prejudice concerning a party or personal knowledge of disputed evidentiary facts concerning the proceedings;

b. The judge previously served as a lawyer or was a material witness in the matter in controversy; or

c. The judge, or a member of the judge's family, has an economic interest in the outcome of the matter in controversy; provided that disqualification of a judge shall not be required if no other tribunal can be constituted to deal with the case or, because of urgent circumstances, failure to act could lead to a serious miscarriage of justice.

VALUE 3

Integrity

Principle

Integrity is essential to the proper discharge of the judicial office.

Application

3.1 A judge shall ensure that his or her conduct is above reproach in the view of a reasonable observer.

3.2 The behaviour and conduct of a judge must reaffirm the people's faith in the integrity of the judiciary. Justice must not merely be done but must also be seen to be done.

VALUE 4

Propriety

Principle

Propriety, and the appearance of propriety, are essential to the performance of all of the activities of a judge.

Application

4.1 A judge shall avoid impropriety and the appearance of impropriety in all of the judge's activities.

4.2 As a subject of constant public scrutiny, a judge must accept personal restrictions that might be viewed as burdensome by the ordinary citizen and should do so freely and willingly. In particular, a judge shall conduct himself or herself in a way that is consistent with the dignity of the judicial office.

4.3 A judge shall, in his or her personal relations with individual members of the legal profession who practise regularly in the judge's court, avoid situations that might reasonably give rise to the suspicion or appearance of favouritism or partiality.

4.4 A judge shall not participate in the determination of a case in which any member of the judge's family represents a litigant or is associated in any manner with the case.

4.5 A judge shall not allow the use of the judge's residence by a member of the legal profession to receive clients or other members of the legal profession.

4.6 A judge, like any other citizen, is entitled to freedom of expression, belief, association and assembly, but, in exercising such rights, a judge shall always conduct himself or herself in such a manner as to preserve the dignity of the judicial office and the impartiality and independence of the judiciary.

4.7 A judge shall inform himself or herself about the judge's personal and fiduciary financial interests and shall make reasonable efforts to be informed about the financial interests of members of the judge's family.

4.8 A judge shall not allow the judge's family, social or other relationships improperly to influence the judge's judicial conduct and judgement as a judge.

4.9 A judge shall not use or lend the prestige of the judicial office to advance the private interests of the judge, a member of the judge's family or of anyone else, nor shall a judge convey or permit others to convey the impression that anyone is in a special position improperly to influence the judge in the performance of judicial duties.

4.10 Confidential information acquired by a judge in the judge's judicial capacity shall not be used or disclosed by the judge for any other purpose not related to the judge's judicial duties.

4.11 Subject to the proper performance of judicial duties, a judge may:

a. Write, lecture, teach and participate in activities concerning the law, the legal system, the administration of justice or related matters;
b. Appear at a public hearing before an official body concerned with matters relating to the law, the legal system, the administration of justice or related matters;
c. Serve as a member of an official body, or other government commission, committee or advisory body, if such membership is not inconsistent with the perceived impartiality and political neutrality of a judge; or
d. Engage in other activities if such activities do not detract from the dignity of the judicial office or otherwise interfere with the performance of judicial duties.

4.12 A judge shall not practise law while the holding the judicial office.

4.13 A judge may form or join associations of judges or participate in other organizations representing the interests of judges.

4.14 A judge and members of the judge's family shall neither ask for, nor accept, any gift, bequest, loan or favour in relation to anything done or to be done or omitted to be done by the judge in connection with the performance of judicial duties.

4.15 A judge shall not knowingly permit court staff or others subject to the judge's influence, direction or authority to ask for, or accept, any gift, bequest, loan or favour in relation to anything done or to be done or omitted to be done in connection with his or her duties or functions.

4.16 Subject to law and to any legal requirements of public disclosure, a judge may receive a token gift, award or benefit as appropriate to the occasion on which it is made provided that such gift, award or benefit might not reasonably be perceived as intended to influence the judge in the performance of judicial duties or otherwise give rise to an appearance of partiality.

VALUE 5

Equality

Principle

Ensuring equality of treatment to all before the courts is essential to the due performance of the judicial office.

Application

5.1 A judge shall be aware of, and understand, diversity in society and differences arising from various sources, including but not limited to race, colour, sex, religion, national origin, caste, disability, age, marital status, sexual orientation, social and economic status and other like causes ('irrelevant grounds').

5.2 A judge shall not, in the performance of judicial duties, by words or conduct, manifest bias or prejudice towards any person or group on irrelevant grounds.

5.3 A judge shall carry out judicial duties with appropriate consideration for all persons, such as the parties, witnesses, lawyers, court staff and judicial colleagues, without differentiation on any irrelevant ground, immaterial to the proper performance of such duties.

5.4 A judge shall not knowingly permit court staff or others subject to the judge's influence, direction or control to differentiate between persons concerned, in a matter before the judge, on any irrelevant ground.

5.5 A judge shall require lawyers in proceedings before the court to refrain from manifesting, by words or conduct, bias or prejudice based on irrelevant grounds, except such as are legally relevant to an issue in proceedings and may be the subject of legitimate advocacy.

VALUE 6

Competence and Diligence

Principle

Competence and diligence are prerequisites to the due performance of judicial office.

Application

6.1 The judicial duties of a judge take precedence over all other activities.

6.2 A judge shall devote the judge's professional activity to judicial duties, which include not only the performance of judicial functions and responsibilities in court and the making of decisions, but also other tasks relevant to the judicial office or the court's operations.

6.3 A judge shall take reasonable steps to maintain and enhance the judge's knowledge, skills and personal qualities necessary for the proper performance of judicial duties, taking advantage for that purpose of the training and other facilities that should be made available, under judicial control, to judges.

6.4 A judge shall keep himself or herself informed about relevant developments of international law, including international conventions and other instruments establishing human rights norms.

6.5 A judge shall perform all judicial duties, including the delivery of reserved decisions, efficiently, fairly and with reasonable promptness.

6.6 A judge shall maintain order and decorum in all proceedings before the court and be patient, dignified and courteous in relation to litigants, jurors, witnesses, lawyers and others with whom the judge deals in an official capacity. The judge shall require similar conduct of legal representatives, court staff and others subject to the judge's influence, direction or control.

6.7 A judge shall not engage in conduct incompatible with the diligent discharge of judicial duties.

IMPLEMENTATION

By reason of the nature of judicial office, effective measures shall be adopted by national judiciaries to provide mechanisms to implement these principles if such mechanisms are not already in existence in their jurisdictions.

5

Issues and Challenges Pertaining to the Federal Structure

LEARNING OBJECTIVES

In this Chapter, you will learn about:

- Federalism
- Emerging Pattern of Centre-State Relations
- Impact of New Economic and Developmental Policies on Federalism
- Governor as Factor in Federal Relations Introduction
- Impact of Emergency on Federal Relations
- Coalition Politics and its Impact on Federal Relations
- Judiciary as a Factor in Federal Relations
- National Security and its Impact on Federal Structure
- Re-invention of Self-Governing Institutions and Decentralization
- Federal Fiscal Relations
- Conclusion

5.1 FEDERALISM

5.1.1 Federalism Introduction

Federalism is a harmonious system of government, in which the powers are distributed between a union government at the national level and several provincial governments at the sub-national level.

It requires a minimum of two levels of government to create a federal state: (i) The Union government, which takes the responsibility for subjects of law that have a common national interest and (ii) the provincial or state governments that look after subjects of regional or provincial interest.

In a true spirit, these governments act independent of each other, when it comes to federalism. This is guaranteed by the proportionate division of subjects and their ratification through a written constitution. It is done so as to ensure a constitutional sharing of sovereignty that prevents the accumulation of unbridled power with the Union government or vice-versa. Notable examples of federal countries include the United States of America, Canada, Australia, Germany, Switzerland and India.

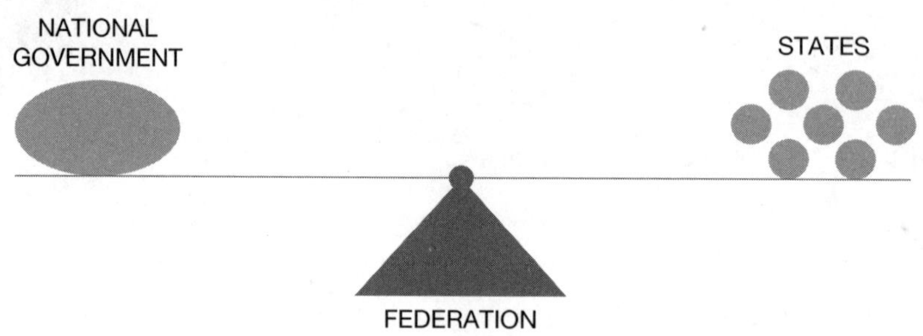

5.1.2 Types of Federalism

(a) **Classification Based on Nature of Federalism**

The concept of federalism has evolved since its inception and has developed into different models. These models can be decoded as the following types:

(i) Dual/Layer-cake federalism
(ii) Cooperative/Marble cake federalism
(iii) Competitive federalism
(iv) Permissive federalism
(v) The "New" federalism

(i) Dual/Layer-Cake Federalism

In this model, the Union government takes control of crucial subjects such as foreign policy, defence, communication, etc., leaving the rest to the provincial units. The domains of both governments are usually exclusive in nature. This characteristic feature gives it the name "layer-cake federalism". An important point to note here is that the Union government hardly interferes into the domain of the state governments. The best example of dual federalism existed in the United States prior to the civil war years

(ii) Cooperative Federalism

This form of federalism insists on the two levels working together as a team. The intergovernmental relations are mostly cooperative in nature, while the autonomy of the states in their spheres is not infringed by the Union government. There is a confluence of powers, resources, and programs between and among the Union, provincial and local governments. There are, however, possibilities of influencing the policies and decision making of the state governments. The process of cooperation is ensured through several means. Usually it is done by creating vision documents in planning, dialogues in several centre-state fora, etc. For instance, the 15-year vision document being prepared by the NITI Aayog in consultation with the states is a notable example. Similarly, the Goods and Services Tax council includes representatives of both the Government of India and the state governments.

As there is no water-tight separation of domains between the union and the states, this form of federalism is also called '*marble-cake federalism*'.

(iii) Competitive Federalism

It is a type of federalism in which the Union government, states and local bodies compete with each other. This competitive spirit is held in order to provide a better delivery of services and inclusive growth to their citizens. The competition is visible in spheres such as investment opportunities, social welfare schemes and infrastructure development. It is to be noted that competition is not the opposite of cooperation. While through cooperation the units try to seamlessly operate and find solutions, through competition, they try to effectively implement these solutions as against their peers.

(iv) Permissive Federalism

It is a quasi-unitary concept. As part of a federal setup, the states are provided with certain powers through the constitution. However, they depend on permissions from the Union government to administer and take decisions with those powers. This form of federalism is found in instances where the states derive their existence and authority from the Union government.

(v) The New Federalism

The concept of New federalism was a result of the advocacy that anything that falls outside the division of powers in the constitution shall be entrusted to the state governments. The primary objective of this model is to reduce the disproportionate accumulation of power with the Union government. An example of this is the call for restoration of autonomy and power that the states had lost to the federal government of the United States of America following the New Deal of President Franklin Roosevelt. Through New federalism, the state governments receive block grants for non-specific purposes or in general policy areas.

(b) Classification Based on Nature of Formation

Federations can also be divided based on the nature of formation. The two common forms are:

(i) Coming Together Model

Here, a number of independent states unite to form a larger unit so that they can increase their security while maintaining sovereignty. The constituent states hold equal power and are stronger in comparison to the Union government.

(ii) Holding Together Model

In this case, a Union government creates a second-tier of government for the purpose of administrative convenience, especially when a larger scale of diversity in the population is involved. The model follows the principle of "indestructible union with destructible states".

5.1.3 Importance of Federalism

- **Protection of rights and liberties:** The fundamental aspects of the constitution cannot be amended arbitrarily by one level of government alone. Such changes require the acceptance of both levels of government.
- **Judicial oversight:** Courts have the responsibility to interpret the constitution and codify powers of different levels of government, from time to time. Where there is a dispute among them, the apex court takes the role of a neutral arbitrator.
- **Financial autonomy:** Sources and proportion of revenue allocation for each level is clearly specified to ensure the financial autonomy of the units.
- **Dual objectives:** The federalism offers a grand design of living together, it two important objectives are to safeguard and promote unity of the country, while accommodating the regional diversity.
- **Opportunities for decentralisation:** These opportunities are based on the concept of self-rule and shared rule. It strives to make the governance efficient, swift and ensures grassroots involvement in the political process.

5.1.4 Why India Opted for Federalism?

Although the Indian Constitution nowhere uses the term 'federal", it has provided for a governance model, which is essentially federal in spirit. Federalism in India should be studied in the context of its pluralities of culture and its socio-economic conditions on the eve of independence.

With a large population spread across a large pluralistic framework in terms of ethnic, linguistic, religious and other diversities, it was necessary to implement a system of polity that would accommodate these pluralities. This was to be done without compromising on building a unified nation. In order to serve the objective, the constitution makers decided on a democratic structure based on federal system of government with a unitary bias. While democracy ensures freedom to the citizens, a federation would ensure the protection of pluralities. This when managed by a strong Union government, ensures the principle of 'unity amidst diversity' in order to march ahead to progress.

The perils of colonial rule made India a land of severe economic disparities and chronic under-development. As the immediate goal for the newly born nation was to turn around the economic conditions, it was necessary to bring in an administrative system that would combine regional management and centralised supervision. It was thus decided that a federal polity with an empowered Union government will best fit these requirements to achieve the goal.

5.1.5 Features of Indian Federalism

There are certain unique features in Indian federalism. They are as follows:

1. **Supreme and single constitution:** Constitution is the most supreme law of the land in India. It contains several components that together act as a rule of thumb in framing policies of the government. It guarantees a set of fundamental rights to the citizens. Similarly it demarcates the domains of power of executive, legislative and financial powers of both the government of India and the states.
2. **Dual government:** The constitution has distributed powers between the Union and the States. Through this distribution, it seeks to accommodate the diversity of India. By

providing certain powers to the state governments, the constitution allows the states to take decision with flexibility and according to local needs.

3. **Authority of the courts:** Legal supremacy of the constitution is an essential feature in the federal system. It helps in maintaining the division of powers between the union and centre. Courts have the final power to interpret the constitution and nullify actions on the part of the federal and state governments or their different units, which violate the provisions of the constitution.
4. **Mode of formation:** Unlike the United States, which was formed as a result of coming together of a group of states, Indian federalism was born out of the need for administrative convenience.
5. **Position of the states in the federation:** In the United States, since the states had existed much before the formation of federation, they held their own sovereignty vis-a-vis the federal government. Therefore, their constitution had several safeguards for the protection of state's sovereignty. Whereas in India, there was no such history of states holding a higher sovereignty. Thus, our states do not enjoy a higher authority in comparison to the Union government.

5.1.6 Criticism of Indian Federalism

Though the founding fathers of the Indian Constitution have done their best to imbibe a federal character into our polity, there are a number of criticisms against it.

1. **Not a truly rigid constitution:** The amendment process to the constitution of India follows a blend of rigidity and flexibility. Some of its provisions can be easily amended by the parliament and some require ratification from the states. While it is challenging to pass amendments that affect the federal provisions, it is not as difficult as the amendment process in the United States. **Powerful Union government:** The union holds more power as against the states. This can be understood by the number and importance of subjects under the Union list under Schedule 7 of the constitution. Even regarding the concurrent list, the constitution empowers the parliament to override any law made by the state legislature in case of a conflict with a union law on the same subject. Additionally, all residuary powers are also vested with the parliament. Besides this, it empowers the parliament to legislate in certain cases to legislate on subjects in the state list.
2. **Unequal representation of states in the upper house:** In bicameral legislatures of federal countries, it is a basic feature to have equal representation for states in the upper house. India has deviated from this principle and has opted for proportional representation based on the population of the respective states.
3. **Executive is a part of legislature:** Separation of powers is yet another essential part of a federal polity. In India though, the political executive is an integral part of the legislature.
4. **Lower house enjoys greater power than upper house:** The role of the upper house in a federation is quite significant as it features representatives from the states. In the Indian parliament however, the lower house enjoys greater powers compared to the upper house. For instance, money bills can only be introduced in a lower house; a no confidence motion against the government can only be initiated in the lower house. Interestingly, the upper house as well enjoys the unique

power such as to initiate a bill for the creation of an All-India service. Such unequal distribution of powers among the houses of parliament is contrary to the principle of federalism.

6. **Emergency powers with the Union:** The constitution has vested all the emergency powers with the Union government. By enforcing an emergency, the Union government virtually takes complete control of the country, superseding the autonomy of the state governments.
7. Integrated judiciary: Though independent, the judiciary is integrated. This means, India does not have a separate judiciary at the union and at the state level.
8. **Single citizenship:** Indian citizens hold only one citizenship that is issued by the Union government whereas in United States of America, concept of dual citizenship exists.
9. **Appointment process of Governor:** The power of appointing a governor lies with the President, who executes this power based on the advice of the council of ministers. As a result, the governor acts as an agent of the Union government.
10. **All India Services:** The Union government through the All India Services such as the Indian Administrative Service (IAS), Indian Police Service (IPS) and Indian Forest Service (IFS), veers into the governance of states and controls the executive functions. Though the immediate authority of these services lie with the state, the ultimate powers lie with the Government of India. These services provide efficiency and uniformity in administration throughout the country.
11. **Destructible states:** A state's name, territory, or its very existence can be changed by the Parliament by passing a law to that effect. All of this can be done following the procedure of an ordinary bill.
12. **Veto over states' bills:** The Governor of a state has the power to reserve certain bills for the President's consideration. The President on the other hand is provided with absolute veto on these bills. At times, he also holds the power to reject bills, when they come after reconsideration and are still found wanting. As the President follows the advice of the council of ministers in this respect, this power can be misused to keep the state legislatures under the hold of the Union government.
13. **Integrated election machinery:** Elections in India, at both the centre and states are conducted by the Election Commission of India. Though the body is independent of political intervention or influence, the Chairman and the members of the commission are appointed by the President.
14. **Integrated auditing:** Similar to the conduct of elections in India, auditing of accounts of the states and the union are done by the Comptroller and Auditor General of India. The **holder of this office** is also appointed by the President.
15. **Removal of key functionaries:** The state government is hardly empowered to remove government functionaries, even at the state level. This includes judges of the high court, state election commissioners, etc.

5.1.7 Stages of Federalism in India

Towards the end of the British Raj, the founding fathers of India were facing questions on the type of polity that the new nation will take up. Considering the diversity of the country, they decided to go for federalism, as it would ensure the protection of regional, minority and community interests. However, as the security at both external and internal spheres was threatened by various forces, they were left with no choice but to compromise on the level of federalism that was chosen for the country. It was decided to make India a strong, cohesive state, by giving more power to the national government at the centre as against limited spheres for the state governments. Moreover, it was felt that resolving the problem of economic development was comparatively easier when planning can be made in a centralized manner.

Evolution of Indian form of federalism can be classified into four waves:

- Wave of single party dominance (pre 1967)
- Wave of confrontational federalism (1967–1990)
- Wave of cooperative federalism (1990–2013)
- Wave of cooperative and competitive federalism (since 2013)

(a) The First Phase: Single Party Dominance

The initial years since independence saw the formidable power of the Indian National Congress ministry as they ruled at both the centre and state levels. Jawaharlal Nehru, the then Prime Minister was very much involved in promoting the federal relationship with the state governments. He maintained regular written communication in order to keep them informed of the developments at the national level and to take in suggestions from them in order to build a better nation. The roots for this federal organization were laid back in 1920, when the INC organized itself on the basis of provincial Congress committees.

(b) The Second Phase: Confrontational Federalism

The era of dominant rule by the INC began fading away with the fourth general elections (1967). This election witnessed routing of the INC by regional parties in nearly half of the states. They had little choice other than coexisting with opposition parties. This was once again lost with the split of 1969 and slowly the style of governance was moving towards a centralized leadership of the country by Indira Gandhi, the then Prime Minister. As a result, the federal principles of organization were set aside. And the regional accommodation, which was nurtured since the early years of the 20th century was subsequently eroded.

With the Congress obtaining near two-thirds majority in the 1972 parliamentary elections, reaping on the success of the Bangladesh liberation war, the federal government started arguing the case for a 'strong centre' not only to serve the interests of balanced development but also to safeguard the unity and integrity of the country.

This was to hit a nadir with the imposition of national emergency in 1975-77. The draconian regime was an era in which the state was almost reduced to a unitary dictatorship. The Union government was more than happy to intervene into the states' administration and Article 356 was arbitrarily applied to ward-off governments that weren't in its good books. A remarkable event of this era is the passing of the 42nd amendment to the constitution, which placed the already power-heavy Union government on higher ground compared to the states. This led to several non-Congress parties in unison demanding for state autonomy.

(c) The Third Phase: Cooperative Federalism

This wave of federalism had its advent towards the end of the 1980s. The system of coalition governments at the national level led to the strengthening of regional parties such as the *Dravida Munnetra kazhagam (DMK) in Tamil Nadu, Rashtriya Janata Dal (RJD) in Bihar, etc.* With this new-found importance, they have been able to assert their interests more vocally since this era. Thanks to this development, even when a centre-right party such as the *Bharatiya Janata Party (BJP)* came to power in the centre as part of the National Democratic Alliance (NDA) for the first time, they tread cautiously, hardly ruffling feathers with their coalition partners and counterparts at the state level. The Union government had little choice but to listen to the requirements of the states and make policy formulations accordingly.

(d) The Fourth Phase: Cooperative and Competitive Federalism

On returning to power for the second time in 2014, the NDA has been rooting for a judicious mix between cooperative and competitive federalism. The foundation stone for this was laid by replacing the decades-old Nehruvian brainchild, the Planning Commission with the National Institution for Transforming India (NITI). According to the government, while cooperative federalism will ensure an inclusive strategy towards achieving development, competitive federalism will help in realizing the same with maximum potential.

5.1.8 Cooperative Federalism to Competitive Federalism

- **Cooperative federalism** implies that the Union and states share a **horizontal relationship**, where they "**cooperate" in the larger public interest**. It's visualised as an important tool to enable states' participation in the formulation and implementation of national policies.
- **Sharing of powers and responsibilities** between the three levels of government is a key element of the concept, which involves participative policymaking. This is particularly important in areas of concurrent responsibility, where the Centre has had a tendency to ride roughshod over the states by occupying the common legislative space.
- A reform of the seventh schedule lists in the direction of greater empowerment of states would be consistent with the logic of increased financial transfers and cooperative federalism. Locating the right level for making and implementing policy is a central feature of the cooperative responsibility matrix.
- A key element in fostering cooperative federalism is the **respect for the mandate of elected governments, even those run by opposition parties**. In an era where the party system is fragmented along federal lines, the need is still felt to include state parties in federal coalitions, even when technically not necessary.
- **Competitive federalism** can refer to the relationship between the Central and state governments (vertical) or between state governments (horizontal). Post the 1990s economic reforms, this idea of federalism gained prominence.
- In a free-market economy, the spirit of competition is developed through the provision of endowments to states, their available resource base and their comparative advantages. States not only need to compete with the Centre but also among themselves for gaining these benefits. Increasing globalisation, however, has made the already existing inequalities and imbalances between states much wider. Hence, there is concern about the states' freedom to formulate their own growth policies.
- With the onset of **globalisation**, there have been new economic roles for the government. There has been complex power sharing and multi-level relationship.

- There is raise of Identity-related issues (e.g. Telangana) and resource-based issues (like Cauvery and Narmada), hence in a multi-party system it is important to forge effective federal coalitions.
- Fiscal constraints of the states have led to the proliferation of central schemes and national missions.
- Because of responsive and participative democracy, we get **asymmetric federalism** (the acceptance of inequality of states) leading to decline in inequality, tensions and dissatisfactions.

5.1.9 Steps to Achieve Cooperative Federalism

(a) Institutions

1. Inter-state council: Article 263 provides that the President may by order appoint an Inter State Council if he/she is of the opinion that public interest would be served by its establishment. This council shall be used to promote a cohesive relationship among the federal units of the Union. The organization, procedure and duties of the council shall be defined by the President.
2. Zonal councils: They were created as a result of the States Reorganization Act, 1956. These councils function as forums that would bring the states of a particular region in close conformity with each other. Currently these are five in number. They act as instruments of intergovernmental consultation and cooperation primarily in socio-economic fields and also to curb the growth of particularist tendencies among various states.

(b) Policies

1. Recommendations of the 14**th Finance Commission:** The 14th Finance Commission report is a landmark report in terms of fiscal allocation. Besides several important recommendations, the commission recommended a statutory increase in the share of divisible tax-pool from 32% to 42%. As the Union government has also raised the non-statutory share from 21% to 26%, about 68% of the division pool is to be transferred to the states.
   These imply that nearly half of the total receipts of the Union government will be transferred to the states. The larger allocations are accompanied by significant reduction in the central schemes and rationalization of remaining schemes to give greater flexibility and control to the individual states.
2. **The establishment of the NITI Aayog:** The NITI Aayog was established as the replacement to the Planning Commission. Unlike its predecessor, NITI Aayog aims to include the state governments into the planning process and give them a better say at decision making. The forum has a good potential to facilitate coordination between the states and the centre.
3. **Goods and Services Tax and the GST Council:** By creating a uniform regime of taxation, the devolution of revenue receipts to the states would get much easier and efficient. As the introduction of this new tax regime replaces several existing revenue resources for the states, a council for better managing the process and allocation of revenue has been setup as the GST council.

5.1.10 Steps to be Taken to Improve Cooperation

- **Reforms in the seventh schedule:** As India is consciously promoting cooperative federalism, it needs to focus on greater empowerment of states by shifting more subjects into the state list or at least into the concurrent list.
- On issues that have a global effect, such as treaties and multi-lateral conventions, the Union should setup a mechanism to implement these agreements with minimal or no infringement into the sovereignty of the states. These include WTO obligations, INDC recommendations, etc.

5.1.11 Indian Federalism in the Age of Globalisation

As India is constitutionally referred to as a 'Union of States', the states have a large significant role in implementing the agenda of globalization. However, the effect of globalization on our federal polity has produced a paradoxical outcome.

The economic reforms of the 1990s gave state governments lot more freedom to make policies independently. For instance, while the national government still decides on investment policies and trade tariffs, state governments are free to provide incentives to investors of foreign capital to enter their jurisdictions.

By opening their markets to globalization, states have been regularly engaging in a fierce competition among themselves in order to attract more and more foreign direct investments. As a result the political autonomy of states has been greatly reduced in favour of investments and markets. This has exposed local governance to direct or indirect influence by global and multi-national corporate entities. As a few of the states cannot compete at a major level, it leads to an unequal development and therefore paving the way for the categorization of states as 'developed' and 'special category' states.

From the point of view of an Indian state, capital from another country or from another state can be seen through the same lens, and must be treated equally on par in typical policy environments. The final impacts of the entry of capital will therefore depend also on the internal mobility of capital and labour within the sub-national government.

Hence, attention must be paid to internal mobility of goods and other factors, in addition to external liberalization in the federal system. The tax and regulatory policies of the sub-nation can assume greater importance in a scenario of economic reform under globalization. Another federal aspect of India's reform is that the decade of the 1990s has seen an increase in regional inequality in some dimensions.

While inequalities may have widened within states as well (for example, the coastal and urban areas of Maharashtra and Gujarat versus their interior rural regions), the main focus has been and will be on widening disparities across the states themselves.

This is natural, given the size and political importance of the states, and the fact that the states are the direct and indirect channels for significant financial transfers from the central government.

We also consider whether aspects of economic reform, larger global economic forces, and state-level initial conditions and policy responses are increasing regional inequalities within the country, and whether the mechanisms that exist within India's federal structures for managing regional inequalities are adequate.

The growing literature on globalization and Indian federalism, mostly written though from the standpoint of political economy, suggests that Indian federalism has been drastically changed so that it needs to be redefined.

5.1.12 Federalism in the Fiscal Sphere

The fiscal relations between the Centre and the States have been defined under the Constitutional provisions of distribution of revenues between the Union and the States. Based on this scheme, the Union gets its revenue from the following sources such as taxes on income other than agricultural income; customs duties including export duties; excise duties on goods manufactured in India except alcohol and liquors for human consumption; taxes on capital value of the assets, exclusive of agriculture land, of individuals and companies; taxes on the capital of companies; estate duty and succession duty in respect of property other than agricultural land; etc.

The revenue sources allocated to the States, on the other hand are: land revenue; taxes on agricultural income; succession duty in respect of agricultural land; estate duty in respect of agriculture land; taxes on land and buildings; taxes on mineral rights; excise duties on alcoholic liquors for human consumption; sales tax; professional taxes; taxes on the consumption of electricity; taxes on advertisements; etc.

Though the allocation of resources is limited, the states hold greater responsibilities for social, educational and economic development of citizens. It is for this reason that the Constitution provides for inter-governmental transfers through the establishment of Finance Commission, once in every five years. This body recommends the proportion at which transfer of central revenue has to be made to the states. Besides this, central plan transfers and funding for central sector and centrally sponsored schemes are also made to the states. While the proportion of funding has been climbing at a fast rate over the past few years, the states find them inadequate to meet their responsibilities.

5.1.13 Green Federalism

In the context of environmental and climate change issues, it is becoming increasingly important for governments to formulate policies and guidelines to effectively address hazards and ensure sustainable growth. As a federal country, India needs to work out a plan among its different levels of government to come up with a comprehensive strategy to tackle these challenges.

The federal provisions of the constitution of India gave generally remained silent on the environmental issues. At present there is no dedicated subject for the purpose of environmental legislation. Originally, in the seventh schedule of the constitution, all the natural resources – land, water, forests and minerals – were assigned to the states, while the central government was given the responsibilities to regulate the development of mines and mineral resources. Later this was amended to push forests and wildlife protection to the concurrent list.

But the process of green federalism doesn't end with just specifying the jurisdictional ambit of legislation alone. There are larger challenges in terms of research, governance, resources and capacity building to deal with the complex issues of environment. When the states and the union come together to play specific roles in relation to these areas, it is then that the objectives of green federalism can be effectively realized.

5.1.14 Issues in Indian Federalism

Union's influence over concurrent list: One of the main accusations on Indian federalism is the problem of pseudo-centralisation. A number of states have accused the Union government of extending a dominance over the concurrent list.

Article 200: It relates to the State bills which are reserved for the assent of the President. This provision has been abused numerous times with impunity. Anandpur Sahib Resolution by Punjab in 1973, West Bengal Memorandum in 1978 has demanded centre to restrict itself to defence, external affairs, currency and general communication.

Arbitrary Imposition of President's Rule: Article 356 is one of the most misused provisions by the Union government to restrict the proper functioning of states under the control of opposition parties. However, following the S.R. Bommai case, the Supreme Court has largely reduced the scope for the imposition of President's rule.

Removal of Governor: As the governors are appointed by the Union government, a change of ruling party will lead to the removal of governors appointed by the preceding regime. Though the governor doesn't hold a security of tenure, the practice of removing governors for political reasons does not act as a healthy indicator of cooperative federalism.

All India Services: State governments have time and again called for the abolition of the All India Services. Though the officers under these services come under the immediate supervision of the states, their service conditions are primarily managed by the Government of India.

DELHI CASE STUDY

Delhi is a peculiar case, neither being a State, nor a Union Territory. So, Article 239, which deals with Union Territories, does not apply to Delhi. Instead, **Delhi is governed by Articles 239AA and 239AB, introduced by a constitutional amendment in 1991**. The problem with the Home Ministry notification is that while it conflates Delhi as a Union Territory to suit its own interests, at other times, it treats it as a State.

Partial statehood, Delhi's peculiar constitutional situation, has posed challenges before every government that has ruled the national capital since 1993, the year an elected Vidhan Sabha was reinstated in Delhi. Central to this is the prickly issue of an elected government being forced to share powers with a non-elected Lieutenant Governor.

Article 239 (AA and AB) of the Constitution appears to grant the LG more discretionary powers than Governors in other States. Clause 4 of this Article says that there shall be a Council of Ministers in Delhi to aid and advise the LG "except in so far as he is, by or under any law, required to act in his discretion".

Such a situation created many conflict situations between the elected government of Delhi and Lt. Governor.

5.1.15 Recommendations of Various Commissions

The constitutional arrangements of Centre-State and inter-State coordination and cooperation functioned smoothly during the first twenty-five years of the working of the Constitution of India due largely to single party rule at the Centre and in almost all the States and presence of stalwart national leaders like Pandit Jawaharlal Nehru who played prominent role in the drafting the Constitution. The end of the era of single party rule since the late sixties and emergence of regional parties and coalition governments with diverse ideologies, priorities and programmes brought sharp focus into various issues of coordination in Centre-State relations and constitutional governance.

In order to study these issues and recommend measures for improving the system, a few Commissions/Committees have been set up since mid-sixties. These are:

(a) First Administrative Reforms Commission

The first Administrative Reforms Commission was constituted by the Government of India on 5 January 1966 for reviewing the public administration system of India and recommending measures for making administration fit for carrying out the social and economic policies of the government and being responsive to the people. The Commission was Chaired initially by Morarji R Desai, MP, and later on by K. Hanumanthaiah, MP when Morarji R Desai became the Deputy Prime Minister of India.

The Commission submitted its reports in 20 parts containing 537 major recommendations till the mid-seventies. The 13th report of the Commission covered the issues of Centre-State relations. With regard to Inter-State Council the Commission made the following recommendations:

(i) Establishment of an Inter-State Council under Article 263 (b) and (c) of the Constitution which would discuss all issues of national importance in which the states are interested.

(ii) Saddling the Council with functions under article 263 (a) to inquire into and advise upon disputes between the States would prevent it from giving full attention to the various problems of national concern which it ought to consider.

(iii) This body should replace the National Development Council, the Chief Minister' Conference, the Finance Minister' Conference, the Food Ministers' Conference and the National Integration Council.

(iv) The Council will be wide-embracing and will provide a standing machinery for effecting consultations between the centre and the states. Only issues of real and national importance need to be taken up there. Others should be settled by conferences convened by the ministries concerned, at a lower, preferably official level.

(v) The Council should have an appropriate secretariat. The Secretary of the Council should be an officer having the knowledge, experience and status that will enable him to work effectively.

(b) Rajamannar Committee

The Centre-State Relations Inquiry Committee was set up by the Government of Tamil Nadu on 2 September, 1969 under the Chairmanship of Dr. P. V. Rajamanar to consider the entire question regarding relationship that should subsist in a federal setup between the Centre and the States. The other two members of the Committee were Dr. A. Lakshmanaswami Mudaliar and Mr. P. Chandra Reddy.

With regard to the Inter-state Council, the Committee made the following recommendations:

a. The Inter-State Council should be constituted immediately. The proposed Council may consist of the Chief Ministers or their nominees, all the states having equal representation, with the Prime Minister as the Chairman. No other minister of the union cabinet should be a member of the Council.
b. Every bill of national importance or which is likely to affect the interests of one or more states should, before its introduction in Parliament, be referred to the Inter-State Council and its views thereon should be submitted to Parliament at the time of introduction of the Bill.
c. No decision of national importance or which may affect one or more states should be taken by the Union Government except after consultation with the Inter-State Council. Exception may be made to subjects like defence and foreign relations. But even on such matters the decision of the Central Government should be placed before the Inter-State Council subsequently without any avoidable delay.
d. If the Inter-State Council is to be really effective, its recommendations should be made ordinarily binding on both the Centre and the States. If for any reason, any recommendation of the Inter-State Council is rejected by the Central Government, such recommendation together with reasons for its rejection should be laid before the Parliament and state legislature.

(c) R S Sarkaria Commission

In the wake of the increasing strain in the Centre-State relations, the Parliament, in June 1983, appointed a Commission under the Chairmanship of Justice R S Sarkaria to go into details of the Centre-State relations and to recommend measures to make the relation efficient and cooperative.

The Commission submitted its report in January 1988. The Commission did not call for any structural change, but preferred to continue the existing arrangement because the disintegrative forces are active in the country.

However, the Commission recommended the need for restructuring the provisions of the Centre-State relations.

To begin with it suggested the Centre, to relax its financial hold over the states and to provide them more autonomy. This would make the regional powers more responsible and accountable.

Major Recommendations of the Sarkaria Commission:

1. A permanent Inter-State Council called the Inter-Governmental Council should be set up under Article 263.
2. Article 356 (President's Rule) should be used very sparingly, in extreme cases as a last resort when all the available alternatives fail.
3. The institution of All-India Services should be further strengthened and some more such services should be created.
4. The residuary powers of taxation should continue to remain with the Parliament, while the other residuary powers should be placed in the Concurrent List.

5. When the president withholds his assent to the state bills, the reasons should be communicated to the state government.
6. The zonal councils should be constituted afresh and reactivated to promote the spirit of federalism.
7. The centre should have powers to deploy its armed forces, even without the consent of states. However, it is desirable that the states should be consulted.
8. The Centre should consult the states before making a law on a subject of the Concurrent List.
9. The procedure of consulting the chief minister in the appointment of the state governor should be prescribed in the Constitution itself.
10. The net proceeds of the corporation tax may be made permissibly shareable with the states.
11. The governor cannot dismiss the council of ministers as long as it commands a majority in the assembly.
12. No change in the role of Rajya Sabha and Centre's power to reorganise the states.

(d) Second Administrative Reforms Commission

The Second ARC was setup by the Government of India on 31 August 2005 under the Chairmanship of Shri M. Veerappa Moily with the directive to suggest various measures to achieve a proactive, responsive, accountable, sustainable and efficient administration for the country at all levels of the government.

The Commission submitted its report in 15 parts during June 2006 to May 2009. Part-7 of the report titled 'Capacity Building for Conflict Resolution: Friction to Fusion' made the following two recommendations regarding the Inter-State Council:

(i) The Inter-State Council must be given the complete role provided to it under the Constitution, that is both conflict resolution and better coordination of policy and action in matters of interest to the Union and States. For resolution of conflicts, whether interstate or Union-State, the mechanism of enquiring and advising, even without having the power to adjudicate, envisaged by clause (a) of Article 263 can be an effective method to resolve disputes.

(ii) The Inter-State Council should be constituted as and when the need arises and that the Council need not exist in perpetuity. The Council could best serve its purpose as a pro-tem body with a flexible composition suited to its term of reference. The present omnibus Council may be dissolved. There should not be any bar or impediment for constituting more than one Council at a given time with different composition for each to consider different disputes or other matters of concern to different states and the Union. This approach would also facilitate meaningful, result-oriented discussions by parties directly interested in an item and facilitate time-bound solutions.

(e) Justice M M Punchhi Commission

The Commission for Centre-State Relations headed by Justice Madan Mohan Punchhi has submitted its report to the Central government without much fanfare. This is a contradiction to the Liberhan Commission Report which was "full of sound and fury, signifying nothing" and which wasted 15 years.

A comprehensive review of Centre-State Relations was undertaken by the Sarkaria Commission in the mid-eighties. In the two decades that have gone by both the polity and economy have undergone profound changes, posing new challenges for government at all levels and calling for a fresh look at the relative roles and responsibilities of each level and their interrelations. The present Commission has been entrusted with this task and asked to make recommendations that would help to address the emerging challenges.

Major recommendations may be enumerated as follows:

1. There should be an amendment in Articles 355 and 356 to enable the Centre to bring specific trouble-torn areas under its rule for a limited period.
2. The commission has proposed "localising emergency provisions" under Articles 355 and 356, contending that localised areas — either a district or parts of a district — be brought under Governor's rule instead of the whole state. Such an emergency provision should however not be of duration of more than three months.
3. The commission however supports their right to give sanction for the prosecution of ministers against the advice of the state government.
4. To make an amendment in the communal violence Bill to allow deployment of Central forces without the state's consent for a short period. It has proposed that state consent should not become a hurdle in deployment of central forces in a communal conflagration. However, such deployment should only be for a week and post-facto consent should be taken from the state.
5. Among the significant suggestions made by the Commission is, laying down of clear guidelines for the appointment of chief ministers. Upholding the view that a pre-poll alliance should be treated as one political party, it lays down the order of precedence that ought to be followed by the governor in case of a hung house:
   a. Call the group with the largest pre-poll alliance commanding the largest number;
   b. The single largest party with support of others;
   c. The post-electoral coalition with all parties joining the government; and last
   d. The post-electoral alliance with some parties joining the government and remaining including independents supporting from outside.
6. The panel also feels that governors should have the right to sanction prosecution of a minister against the advice of the council of ministers. However, it wants the convention of making them chancellors of universities done away with.
7. As for qualifications for a governor, the Punchhi commission suggests that the nominee not have participated in active politics at even local level for at least a couple of years before his appointment. It also agrees with the Sarkaria recommendation that a governor be an eminent person and not belongs to the state where he is to be posted.
8. The commission also criticises arbitrary dismissal of governors, saying, "the practice of treating governors as political football must stop". There should be critical changes in the role of the governor — including fixed five-year tenure as well as their removal only through impeachment by the state Assembly. It has also recommended that the state chief minister have a say in the appointment of governor.
9. Underlining that removal of a governor be for a reason related to his discharge of functions, it has proposed provisions for impeachment by the state legislature along

the same lines as that of President by Parliament. This, significantly, goes against the doctrine of pleasure upheld by the recent Supreme Court judgment.

10. Endorsing an NCRWC recommendation, it says appointment of governor should be entrusted to a committee comprising the Prime Minister, Home Minister, Speaker of the Lok Sabha and Chief Minister of the concerned state. The Vice President can also be involved in the process.
11. Unlike the Sarkaria report, the Punchhi report is categorical that a governor be given fixed five-year tenure. The Punchhi Commission report also recommends that a constitutional amendment be brought out to limit the scope of discretionary powers of the governor under Article 163 (2). Governors should not sit on decisions and must decide matters within a four-month period.
12. The creation of an overriding structure to maintain internal security along the lines of the US Homeland Security department, giving more teeth to the National Integration Council.
13. For the National Integration Council (NIC), the commission has proposed that it should meet at least once a year. In case of any communal incident, it has said that a delegation of five members of the Council, who would be eminent persons, should visit the affected area within two days and submit a fact-finding report.
14. The commission, however, rejects a suggestion from some stakeholders as well as the Liberhan Commission that the NIC be accorded constitutional status.
15. The commission has also studied new set-ups like the National Investigation Agency, and recommended procedures to ensure smooth cooperation of the states in terror investigations entrusted to NIA. One can say that the extreme politicization of the post of Governor must be decried and certain specific norms for the appointment and removal have to be evolved.

(f) Fourteenth Finance Commission

The Finance Commission is a Constitutional body created under provisions of Article 280; one of its important functions is to make recommendations regarding the devolution of taxes between the Centre and the states.

Fiscal federalism deals with the division of governmental functions and financial relations among various levels of government at the central, state and local levels.

Implications of the Fourteenth Finance Commission (FFC) [2015-16 to 2020-21] recommendations for fiscal federalism:

1. The total increase in FFC transfers in FY2015-16 from FY2014-15 is estimated to be about 2 lakh crores, with all states standing to gain in absolute terms.
2. The FFC transfers have more favourable impact on the states (among the General Category States) which are relatively less developed which is an indication that the FFC transfers are progressive, that is states with lower per capita net state domestic product receive relatively larger transfers per capita.
3. Also, due to a change in the horizontal devolution formula which now gives greater weight to a state's forest cover, some states are to gain more than others.
4. There would be more fiscal autonomy for states by increasing their share from 32% to 42% of divisible pool.

5. But, there could be commensurate reductions in the Central Assistance to States (CAS) to secure Centre's fiscal space.
6. However, CAS being discretionary and only mildly progressive, implementing FFC recommendations would entail even more progressivity.

In sum, the far-reaching recommendations of the FFC will further the Government's vision of cooperative and competitive federalism.

However, all the recommendations will only prove fruitful only if following measure are given priority:

- Administrative reforms particularly the bureaucracy at the state level
- Strengthening the centre-state coordination networks.
- Technical capabilities of states must be augmented
- Monitoring and audit must be given renewed thrust – CAG may be engaged.

5.1.16 Important Supreme Court Decisions

State of West Bengal vs Union of India (1962):

The case involved the question of sovereignty of individual states in India.

The Supreme Court held that

(i) The Indian Constitution does not provide for absolute federalism. It provides to decentralize the authority, so that the large territory of India can be governed efficiently.
(ii) The individual state has no power to amend the constitution which is vested only in the parliament.
(iii) The Constitution has divided powers between the centre and the states in such a way that the national policies and local governance could be executed by the centre and the individual states, respectively.
(iv) The Constitution provides supreme power to the judiciary to invalidate any law made by legislature if it violates the constitution.

S. R. Bommai vs. Union of India (1994):

In this case, the Supreme Court discussed about the provisions of **Article 356** (President's Rule). It laid down the conditions under which it can be imposed, so that the misuse of **Article 356** can be checked. The Supreme court laid down certain principles regarding **Article 356:**

(i) President has power to impose **Article 356**, but the decision is not immune from judicial review. The judiciary can examine whether the proclamation was justified or it was imposed with malafide intention.
(ii) The Supreme Court or the High Court can strike down the proclamation if it is found to be malafide or based on irrelevant grounds.
(iii) It was held that the President has conditional power and not absolute power in regards to imposition of **Article 356**.
(iv) It was held that the **Article 356** is an extreme power and is to be used as a last resort in cases where it is manifest that there is an impasse and the constitutional machinery in a state has collapsed.

5.1.17 Conclusion

The constitution of India is neither purely federal nor purely unitary but is a combination of both. It enshrines the principle that "in spite of federalism, the national interest ought to be paramount".

It is emphasized that the Centre wants to empower the states with finances, with technology and knowledge so that they are able to plan better and execute even better. For federalism to work well, states must also fulfill their role in promoting the shared national objectives. The critical element for cooperative federalism to flourish is that states commit to the path they choose within the context of the shared national objectives and then deliver on that commitment.

To conclude, the adoption of innovations involves altering human behavior, and the acceptance of change. There is requirement to promote the spirit of cooperation and harmony between all the level of governments in India to usher in a powerful and inclusive India.

5.2 EMERGING PATTERN OF CENTRE-STATE RELATIONS

5.2.1 Introduction

The most important aspect of any federation is the power sharing arrangement made between the Centre and the States. The modern conditions have created scenario whereby all federal systems are ultimately biased towards the Centre. The Constitution has deliberately granted extraordinary powers to the Centre, and since independence these powers have been freely exercised in a state adopted to planned economy. It is understood that any consideration to be given to Indian federal system should first acknowledge the fact it is centre-centered. But enormous changes have indeed taken place in the federal setup since the adoption of the Constitution. The Constitution itself was tilted in favour of the Centre, during the initial decades after independence, the Union dominated the federal setup. The government under the leadership of Nehru and with active support from the Congress party, defended the adoption of strong centre-stance in order to maintain national integrity and unity. The dominance of Congress party during the initial years paved way for centralization of all major activities concerned with politics, economics and including government.

5.2.2 Era of Nehru

Nehru gave constitutional legitimacy to the centralized planning by bringing such matters under the purview of Entry 20 of the 'Concurrent List' in the Seventh schedule, which deals with distribution of powers between Centre and the States, and thus came to de facto control the whole economy.

1. Nehru's ideological leaning towards democratic socialistic pattern of the society made him to adopt the centralized planning for the whole country.
2. From the initial stages, the Planning Commission – an extra constitutional body – took care of the disbursal of the funds and approval of the development plans of the States.
3. Hence the states were pushed to the margin and their economic consideration became secondary, they were now largely dependent on the centre for the funds.
4. The Centre also took control over all industries by enacting the Industries Development and Regulation Act 1956.

5. The states powers were also curbed by forming of all-India and specific boards for individual industries such as coffee, tea, rubber, etc.
6. During the period of Nehru and Indira, some of the important subject matters in the 'State list' of the seventh schedule was amended and encroached upon by the centre.
7. The centralization of the economy had several consequences, most importantly the identification of key industries and their location within the territory of the states.
8. It also involved nationalization of the insurance and aviation industries, culminating in nationalization of the major commercial banks in 1969 by Indira Gandhi.

(a) Nature of Federalism-Nehru Era

Nehru's phase had a strong centralizing tendency, but the centre took no effort to politically destabilise the state governments. The emergency was minimally used, and Nehru consulted with powerful state leaders before taking major policy decisions.

1. The centre-state relation during this period was relatively peaceful as the governments in the Centre and in the states were of one-single party and Nehru was its unquestioned leader.
2. It is understood that, the initial phase of Indian politics after Independence was based on elite consensus, it went uncontested because of its nearness to the national freedom movement, and the people had implicit trust on the leaders.
3. The federal structure functioned within the federal setup of the Congress party itself and not through constitutional channels.
4. During the time of Nehru and Shastri, the demands of the state were generally confined to federal fiscal matters and to other operational aspects of federalism; and centre-states disputes hovered around sharing of national revenue and states discontent was over the overarching power of the Planning Commission vis-à-vis the Finance Commission.

(b) Language Movement

During this initial phase, the language movement became more prominent. As per the provision of the Constitution, English was allowed to continue as official language of the Union for a temporary period of fifteen years. Accordingly, after the end of the period a review had to be made for further continuation of English language as the official language. But by mid 1950s debates around adopting Hindi as the official language and the link language between Union and the States started coming to the fore. Nehru in fact constituted the Official Language Commission under B.G. Kher in 1955. This commission submitted its report in 1956, and since then the language divide started to grow between the Hindi and non-Hindi speaking states, especially in south India and West Bengal.

1. The Kher commission recommended various steps for eventual replacement of English with Hindi.
2. The members of the commission from Tamil Nadu and West Bengal had submitted their dissenting notes against the recommendations.

3. A parliamentary committee was constituted under Pandit Govindh Ballabh Pant to study the Kher commission report, in order to address the growing dissent for compulsory use of Hindi by many state leaders and academic institutions.
4. Committee under Pant came out with its recommendation in 1959, it recommended that Hindi be used as the primary language of communication while English be made subsidiary one.
5. However, the anti-Hindi agitations did not subsidise and it in fact became stronger, and in south India, strong movements were launched against any possible move to make compulsory use of Hindi.
6. The movement was so strong in Tamil Nadu that, despite the assurances given by Nehru and Shastri, the Dravidian parties continued with their agitations which led to eventual fall of the Congress government in the state.
7. Despite having a strong pro-Hindi lobby, the Parliament adopted the Official Language Act of 1963 and subsequently the Official Language (Amendment) Act of 1967, which allowed for continuation of English as the official language and as a link language between the Union and the states.
8. There was no option before Nehru, but to continue make use of English as the official language.
9. He was also interested in maintaining the federal balance in order to accommodate the demands made by the non-Hindi speaking states. Nehru's comment on the introduction of Official Language Bill 1963 in the Parliament is as follows,

   This is a bill, continuation of what had happened in the past, to remove a restriction which has been placed by the Constitution on the use of English after a certain date i.e. 1965. It is just to remove that restriction that this is placed.

   As per the Official Language Rules 1976, framed under the Official Language Act, 1963,

   - Communications from a central government office to state/union territories or to any person in region "A" comprising the states of Uttar Pradesh, Uttarkhand, Himachal Pradesh, Madhya Pradesh, Chhattisgarh, Bihar, Jharkhand, Rajasthan, Haryana and UTs of Andaman and Nicobar Islands and Delhi shall be in Hindi;
   - Communications from a central government office to state/UTs in region "B" comprising of States of Punjab, Gujarat, Maharashtra and the UT of Chandigarh, shall ordinarily be in Hindi; but communication to any person in region "B" may be either in English or Hindi;
   - Communications from a central government office to state government office in region "C" comprising of all other states and UTs not included in regions "A" and "B" or to any office (not being a central government office) in region "C" to a state or a UT of "A" and "B" or to any office (not being a central government office) or persons in such state may be either in Hindi or English.

10. Though the Official Language Act and the official language rules allow continued use of English, there are still provisions in the Constitution which give importance to the promotion of Hindi language.
11. For example, the *Article 343(1)* still contains provision that says the official language of the Union is Hindi.

12. In respect to the language used in the Parliament, *Article 120(1)* says notwithstanding anything in Part XVII, but subject to provisions of *Article 348*, the business in the Parliament be transacted either in English or Hindi. Provided that the Chairman of the council of states or Speaker of the House of people, or the one who is acting in that capacity, as the case may be, may permit any member to address the House in his mother-tongue, who cannot adequately express himself in Hindi or English.
13. Article 351 states, it shall be the duty of the Union to promote the Hindi language, to develop it so that it may serve as a medium of expression for all elements of the composite culture of Indian and to secure its enrichment by assimilating without interfering with its genus, forms, style and expression used in Hindustani and other languages of India specified in Eighth schedule, and by drawing, whatever, necessary or desirable, for its vocabulary, primarily on Sanskrit and secondarily other languages.

5.2.3 First Wave of Coalition Politics

The very tendency that initially created a desire for a stronger central authority, created this counter current by the states demanding greater autonomy. During the initial two decades after independence, Nehru and his government had to concede to create several states based on the linguistic re-organisation basis. By end of 1960s and early 1970s regional political parties started to emerge successfully challenging the domination by the Congress party.

1. The first wave of coalition politics-government radically altered the centre-state relations. In fact, several coalition governments were formed during the election of 1967.
2. Leftist parties formed coalition government in West Bengal and Kerala. Coalition governments with non-Congress parties formed government in Uttar Pradesh, Bihar, Punjab, Haryana, Madhya Pradesh and Orissa.
3. In Tamil Nadu, DMK got elected, which was a state party government, predominantly based on strong Tamil identity.
4. As a result of these developments, state leaders started to question the dominance of the centre.
5. The left-led government of Kerala, DMK-led Tamil Nadu, Swatantra-led Orissa emphasised right from the beginning that the authority of the centre should be curtailed.
6. Some of the states even asked for more taxation powers. C.N. Annadurai, Chief Minister of Tamil Nadu, expressed his views on the central planning as follows:

> *The powers which the Central government has assumed in regard to mobilization, allocation and pattern of utilization of resources for the plan have reduced the States to a status of supplication from the Centre. Though the Constitution of India is described as a federal one, the balance is tilted towards the central and hence the states are not able to function freely in the administrative and financial spheres. Only such powers are necessary for the Centre to preserve the strength of India should be assigned to the Centre and all other powers should be left to the States without impairing the ideal of a strong India.*

5.2.4 Interregnum Period of Shastri

Nehru's death in 1964 brought into prominence the state party leaders of the Congress party. These State leaders took the important decision of placing Lal Bahadur Shashtri as the successor Prime Minister after Nehru.

1. By the time Nehru fell ill, and question about his successor was raised, the State units of the Congress party had become more powerful.
2. The selection of successor of Nehru had no parallel anywhere in the world.
3. The President of the Congress party consulted with the senior cabinet ministers with political backing, the Chief Ministers of states, members of Congress parliamentary party and all of them along with the Congress working committee constituted the electoral college, which included the so called 'cadre of state leadership', which was a first in Indian federation.
4. And again when question of succession came after death of Prime Minister Lal Bahadur Shashtri in Tashkent, the Congress Chief Ministers issued a joint statement to the Congress president Kamaraj to sponsor Mrs. Indira Gandhi as Shashtri's successor.

(a) Period after the 1967 Elections- Strengthening of Regional Parties

The states in India gradually started to challenge the Centre by the mid-1960s. After the 1967 elections, some of the strategically and politically important states came under the rule of non-Congress government which strengthened the regional voice.

1. The Congress power had been curtailed and many states saw formation of coalition governments either with a central party or together with support of other regional parties.
2. This signalled the weakness of the Centre and increasing strength of the states. This phase has been described as the adulthood of the Indian federation.
3. The states under the control of the non-Congress governments by the end of 1960s started demanding structural changes in the Indian federal structure.

(i) Initiatives by Government of Tamil Nadu- The Rajamannar Commission

The Government of Tamil Nadu constituted a committee under P.V. Rajamannar in 1969, to examine the working of the Constitution of India and recommend changes for reallocation of powers between centre and the states.

1. The terms of reference of the committee was clear and it wanted to examine the question "regarding the relationship that should subsist between the Centre and the States in the federal set up, with reference to the provisions of the Constitution of India; and to suggest suitable amendments to the Constitution so as to secure to the States the utmost autonomy".
2. The committee under Rajamannar favoured autonomy to the states and suggested abolition of several Articles of the Constitution, such as 344(6), 356, 249, 357, 360, etc. of the Constitution.
3. It recommended for immediate constitution of the inter-state council, it also sought to remove the directions given by the centre to the States under the Article 256, 257 and 339(2), and instead these directions have come from the inter-state council.

4. It also suggested that any bill of national importance should be placed before the council and its views should be submitted to the Parliament when the bill is introduced to be passed.
5. The committee under Rajamannar recommended that some entries in the Union list such as power to levy some excise taxes (entry 84 in Union list), non-vital industries (entry 52 in Union list), etc. should be transferred to the State list.
6. While making further recommendations about this issue, the Committee recommended that a High Power Commission should be setup to effectively redistribute entries in List-I and List-III in the Seventh Schedule of the Constitution.
7. It also gave suggestion for increasing the revenue base for the states, constitution of Planning Commission without any members from Government of India in it, appointment of Governor in consultation with the State Cabinet.
8. Regarding *Article 3*, the Committee was of the view that the territorial integrity of the states should not be interfered without the consent of the states. Another suggestion was equal representation of the states in the committee based on their population.
9. In addition to these, the committee suggested to amend *Article 297* of the Constitution, so as to make the state the sole controller of all lands, minerals and other valuable things underlying in the ocean falling within the territorial extent of the state concerned.
10. The important point to highlight here is that the state of Tamil Nadu has been, for a long time arguing for autonomy of the state.
11. The DMK party in Tamil Nadu has in fact, consistently and repeatedly raised the question of federal autonomy and greater powers to the states.
12. Even in its 2009 election manifesto, the DMK had included a section of 'federalism' which is read as follows:

> *It is DMK's consistent stand that the Constitution should be amended for the creation of a wholesome and genuine Federalism with fuller autonomy for the states. A resolution.... (on).... State Autonomy was passed in the Tamil Nadu Legislative Assembly way back in 1974 itself by DMK. DMK will continue to insist on the abolition of Article 356 which empowers the dismissal of state governments. It will continue to strive for the suitable constitutional amendments that will empower the States to States to function freely and effectively.*

(ii) Initiatives by the Government of West Bengal

The leftist government in West Bengal since mid-1960s had also started to call for revision of the Centre-State relations. The West Bengal government in December 1977 came out with a report on Centre-State relations which made the following suggestions:

1. Replacement of the word 'Union' by 'Federal' in the Constitution.
2. Repealing of Articles 356,357 and 360.
3. Mandatory consent of the state government for formation of new states and alteration of area, boundaries or names of existing states.

This memorandum was submitted to the then Prime Minister Morarji Desai by the West Bengal Chief Minister Jyothi Basu to review the Centre-State relations.

5.2.5 Emergence of New Regional Elites

The green revolution of 1960s created a new crop of elite farmers who became a powerful lobby, these farmers from some of the progressive state started to play an important role in the centre-state dynamics. From the states of Punjab, Haryana, Uttar Pradesh an interest group of rich and middle-class peasants emerged, and they started to have great impact on the regional and national politics.

1. New demands were raised by the emergent elites from the rural areas with respect to federalism and economic development.
2. Apart from lobbying for farmers issues, they started to lay out regional demands and advocated state autonomy.
3. They started to influence the policy of the centre in areas such as food procurement and agriculture marketing.
4. However, they represented the rural local dominant castes, also referred as peasant castes and now officially known as the Other Backward Classes (OBCs).
5. Thus, the rich and landholding farmers turned the table in their favour, the rural landless poor peasantry were marginalized further.

5.2.6 Era of Indira Gandhi

The centre-state relation reached to its climax during the tenure of Prime Ministers Indira Gandhi. Imposition of emergency in 1975, the move towards over centralization went unchallenged till the second wave of coalition era started to emerge in 1989.

1. The offices and institutions of the state governments were used as platforms to implement the ideas and policies of the Central government leadership.
2. Indira Gandhi deviated from the leadership style of her father Nehru.
3. The central leadership became irrational and authoritarian, and it became intolerant to any kind of dissent from the opposition and even from within its own party.
4. Coercive techniques were used by the central government to tame and control the state governments.
5. The 42nd amendment enacted during the emergency further tried to enhance the power of the Centre.
6. Education which was previously on the State list was transferred to the Concurrent list.
7. Other nationalizing measures carried out by Ms. Gandhi before and after emergency are:
   (i) Nationalization of the banks
   (ii) The political role played by the state leaders were curtailed
   (iii) The Chief Ministers of the Congress ruled states were selected by Ms. Gandhi in consultation with her kitchen cabinet.
   (iv) Unilateral deployment of CRPF and BSF to any part of the country
   (v) Unreasonable imposition of President's Rule in several states

(a) Janata Interregnum

Even the Sarkaria Commission constituted in 1988 on Centre-State relations mentioned the underlying theme was over Centralization. Even the subsequent Janata Party government which made a promise in election manifesto to revert the centralizing tendency did not reverse the trend.

a. It removed several state governments with the use of President's Rule.
b. In fact, in no time after it assumed power after the 1977 general elections, the Janata government dismissed/dissolved state governments and legislative assemblies of nine Congress ruled states namely, Haryana, Madhya Pradesh, Punjab, Uttar Pradesh, Bihar, Orissa, West Bengal, Himachal Pradesh and Rajasthan.
c. The Janata government at the Centre was a weak coalition with partners having divergent political backgrounds.
d. The following joined together, Bharatiya Jana Sangh, Socialist party, Swatantra Party, Congress (Rebels), Congress (O), Congress for Democracy and Bharathiya Lok Dal, as Janata party under one symbol.
e. This coalition could not survive for long and again the Congress led by Indira came back to power in 1980 with an overwhelming majority.
f. Still non-Congress governments in the states had a re-election. All such non-Congress governed states started to put up a united front, demanding more administrative and fiscal autonomy for them.
g. Non-Congress governments in the states of Punjab, Tamil Nadu, Andhra Pradesh, West Bengal and other States in North East have been demanding to review the overall scheme of the centre-state relations.

(b) Second Phase of Indira Gandhi – 1980s

During Indira's reign in 1980s, Chief Ministers of the non-Congress ruled states held several conclaves at various places questioning the centre's negligence of state's development programme and eroding of the autonomy of the states. They also urged to review the Centre-State relation.

1. In 1982, the Chief Ministers of the four southern states met and agreed to form a council for southern region to restructure and negotiate the centre-state relation to ensure a more equitable distribution of the resources.
2. The second phase of Indira's rule was also authoritarian, like the previous regimes President's Rule was misused through improper use of the office of the Governor and state governments got dismissed, this continued until her death in 1984.
3. Once again the Chief Ministers of the states were handpicked on her will and wishes.
4. She still thought that the policy of centralization would work in her favour. But this centralization tendency faced a strong counter from the states during the second phase unlike the first.
5. This resulted not only in regionalization of the state politics but also the party system.
6. The demand for structural change to federalism received a sudden boost after the elections of 1983 whereby a number of non-Congress state governments came into existence, especially in south.
7. They mobilised support for bringing in changes in constitutional provisions affecting the powers of the state.
8. The political leaders of the state and the elites demanded greater powers and autonomy to the states.
9. As mentioned earlier, the DMK government in Tamil Nadu and notably the government of West Bengal always protested against the 'over-centralized' federal structure.
10. The Telugu Desam Party in Andhra Pradesh also revolted against the centralization policy of Mrs. Gandhi. This party was formed in 1980s to counter the hegemony

of the Congress in the state, as many Chief Ministers were replaced continuously by Mrs. Gandhi and the party became a laughing stock in the state. The rise of regional sentiments in Assam can be seen from the sprout of Assom Gana Parishad party in the state.

11. Indira's authoritarian and dictatorial rule was one the major reasons for the rise of Khalistan movement in the state of Punjab.
12. In 1973, Anandpur Sahib resolution of the Akali leaders asserted that the Sikhs are a separate nation and demanded that the political structure has to be changed by devolving more powers to the state from the centre in all areas except defence, foreign affairs, currency and communications.
13. This resolution was used by both the extremists of the Congress and the Sikh to sabotage the attempt made by the moderate Akalis to reach a settlement on the issues of Punjab with the centre.
14. The government of West Bengal too passed a resolution suggesting that Centre play only a limited role except that pertaining to defence, foreign affairs including foreign trade, communication, currency and economic coordination, moreover all these have to get approved by the National Development Council.
15. Chief Ministers of several non-Congress ruled state walked out in the session of National Development Council opposing Centre's dissolution of democratically elected government in Jammu and Kashmir.

5.2.7 Sarkaria Commission – Recommendations

In the wake of severe criticisms faced by Indira Gandhi on her centralization moves, she announced in the Parliament a proposal to appoint a commission on Centre-State relations to be headed by R.S. Sarkaria a retired Judge of the Supreme Court. Subsequently the commission was constituted vide notification IV/11017/1/83 CSR dated June 9, 1983. Further two more members were included in the commission namely B. Sivaraman and S.R. Sen. In order to resolve the Centre-State rivalry, the Commission recommended several measures, including role and selection process of the Governor and a strict procedure to be followed for imposition of emergency. The Sarkaria Commission made the following recommendations:

1. Setting up of inter-governmental council under Article 263, comprising the Prime Minister, Chief Ministers of all states and Union Cabinet members to discuss all major problems, other economic and development issues between the Union, State and Local governments. Though the council was set up, it could not do much to change the Centre-State relation.
2. It also recommended decentralisation of powers and Centre should restrain itself from occupying subjects in the Concurrent list.
3. An informal convention should be established whereby, whenever Centre decides to legislate of matters pertaining to the Concurrent list, it has to consult the state governments concerned, except in cases of extreme emergency of urgency. The consultation should not only be done with the individual states but also with the collective of all states in the inter-governmental council.

5.2.8 Role of Governor

The controversial role played by the Governor came into prominence during the blatant use of the President's rule during the regime of Indira Gandhi and Rajiv Gandhi.

1. The states raised voice against the role played by the Governor.
2. The appointment process too was questioned as it was largely political and had no rationale, but it had a significant impact on the Centre-State relations.
3. In the era of coalition regimes also, the office of Governor was misused to bring about the President's rule.
4. The intervention by the Judiciary reversed this trend. The Sarkaria Commission recommended certain measures to be taken before the imposition of President's rule in the State, but the Supreme Court in 1994 in the landmark S.R. Bommai case brought in the proclamation of emergency within the purview of the judicial review.
5. It also laid down certain guidelines for imposition of the President's rule in the states.
6. This unhealthy trend of imposition of President's rule came under fire from the Supreme Court in its Constitution Bench decision in Bihar Assembly Dissolution case (2006), which put a stop to misuse of Article 356. In this judgement the Court quashed the imposition of President's Rule in Bihar by the Centre.
7. Even in other several occasions too, the Judiciary has played a vital role in dissolving the Centre-State conflicts.

5.2.9 Federalism in Era of Coalition Politics

In the second wave of coalition era beginning in 1989, the coalition governments have become more prominent in Centre than in the States, it has thus changed the federal dynamics of the Centre-State relations.

1. The federalism debate became more vibrant and exciting. In the elections of 1989, the National Front in its manifesto talked about "true-federalism", it promised to reverse the 'centralising tendency of the ruling government'.
2. State level parties in the present times have played prominent role in dictating the agenda of the national government. In addition to the role played by the Judiciary in restraining the imposition of President's rule under its judicial review, the rise of regional parties in the national politics has also led to the review and reassessment of use of President's Rule (Article 356) by the Centre.

5.2.10 Effect on Policies of State

The economic liberalisation policies in the 1990s had their own impact on the centre-state relations. The centre's role has undergone a radical change after a new industrial policy was formulated in the 1990s.

1. Many of the leaders of the state started to play a progressive role in external trade, commerce and investment opportunities.

2. The state governments now also play important role in shaping foreign and diplomatic relations.
3. The structural adjustment programme of the WTO could not be carried out without the cooperation of the states, hence they were to be brought on board.
4. The Central government's legislative initiatives in areas such as agriculture, rural employment, education, social welfare, health care etc. in the recent times have also changed the federal dynamics.
5. In order to implement the progressive social welfare schemes, the central government is now resorting to the concerned ministries/departments to sign Memorandum of Understanding (MOU) with the concerned state governments.
6. This is important as Centre is dependent on the resources of the state government in order to implement major decisions and policies. Thus, real decentralization of power and authority presently taking place instead of mere transfer of administrative and functional powers, is now setting the outline for centre-state dealings.

5.2.11 Views of Dr. Ambedkar

The emergence of coalition governments at the Centre has strengthened the role of regional political parties and elites, but it has created an atmosphere where the governance of the country is suffering. At present there is a competitive blackmail type bargaining between the centre and the states and this is making the governance system more inefficient and corrupt. At this juncture, it is worth quoting the visionary leader Dr. Ambedkar's argument for a strong and unified India, way back in 1939,

> *The existence in the country of one government which can speak and act in the name of and with the unified will of the whole nation is no doubt the strongest government that can be had only a strong government can be depended upon to act in an emergency. The efficiency of governmental system must be very weak where there exists within a country a number of governments into which different parts of the nation's strength flows and whose resistance to the will of the Central government is likely to be more effective than could be the resistance of individuals, because such bodies are each of them endowed with a government, a revenue, a militia, a local patriotism to unite them.*

5.2.12 Three Phases of Coalition Era

(a) Phase I

Looking into the Centre-State relations in the post independent India, we can see that it can be separated into three distinct phases. First, during the first two decades, most particularly under Nehru-Shastri, the centre-state relations can be termed as cooperative with leaning towards centralization. The centre-state relations were centralized in the areas of economic planning and national development, otherwise Nehru maintained politically balanced and cooperative federal relations.

(b) Phase II

In the second phase, after Nehru, especially after the 1967 general elections, Indira Gandhi turned the cooperative federalism of Nehru-Shastri into coercive federalism. The Centre-State relations became unidirectional initially, and later became reactionary. This kind of coercive federalism was marked by over centralization of both political and economic power. The states were virtually ruled over by the Centre. Even the Janata government elected to power on basis of discontent against the policies of Indira, did nothing to reverse the centralization trend. In the second phase of Indira after the 1980s election, many of the state governments started to react sharply against the authoritarian and over centralization measures of Indira. Rajiv Gandhi while trying to become cooperative with the states initially, took upon his mother's over centralization and authoritarian measures to take political decisions. Again the states leaders reacted sharply to such measures. This coercive and over centralized decision-making process in centre-state relations continued unabated till 1989, when a new era of coalition regime started to emerge.

(c) **Phase III**

The third phase of the Centre-State federal dynamics started after the emergence of the coalition regimes was marked simultaneously with confrontation and cooperation between the Centre and the State governments. If the bargain worked in favour of cooperation, then centre and state cooperated, otherwise the confrontation between them became obvious. A continuous phase of coalition politics has given enormous power to some of the state political parties and their leaders to work the federal bargain in favour of their respective states. Political bargain was also carried out by the central government for its own sustenance. This bargaining has led to uneven development because of trying to 'accommodate' the interests of states, valid demands have been marginalized. And centre has become weak to carry forward any strong reform, including much talked about economic liberalization measures and national security concerns.

5.2.13 Punchhi Commission

The UPA government in 2007, constituted a Commission on Centre-State relations under the Chairmanship of M.M. Punchhi in order to address the emerging concern of centre-state federal dynamics. In a lengthy report in April 2010, in volume I, the Commission commented as follows:

> .....with ever growing aspiration of the states and in some cases the concerns of the Central government, it was felt by the Government of India that time had come to have another comprehensive look at the entire gamut of Centre State relations so that a further positive headway can be made on this important subject.

It is clear that the Centre's concern about the emerging federal dynamics in centre-state relations was the main reason in constitution of the Commission under Punchhi on Centre-State relations. In fact constitution of previous Sarkaria Commission and the present Punchhi commission was based on two different considerations. In the case of Sarkaria Commission, it was constituted under the pressure from the state governments, while Punchhi Commission was constituted by Government of India on its own initiative.

5.2.14 Conclusion

Analysis of federal dynamics influencing the centre-state relations in post-Independent era may lead us to concur with the argument of J.A. Corry, that if Centralization pushed too far in any federation, it will break down in its own weight. This is particularly so because the states in a federation have territories of their own, if the territories in a federation are not well defined, then it does not constitute a true federation. In a federal structure, the Centre has to be accommodative of the states. Constitutionally powers might be granted to the Centre to discipline the states, but in a democratic federal polity, the Centre cannot unilaterally use its constitutional power to impose its dictates. The Centre is dependent on the states, particularly in present time, where the state political leaders play an important role in forming of coalition government in the Centre. In the era of coalition governments, it will be difficult for the Centre to resort to any kind of centralization of power and authority. But in coalition regime, if the states are allowed to follow its own way, without recognising the need for inter-dependence, it will destroy the unity and integrity of the federation. There is a constant need for reappraisal of centre-state relations due to changing dynamics, hence a Parliamentary Committee on Centre-State relation may be constituted for this purpose.

5.3 IMPACT OF NEW ECONOMIC AND DEVELOPMENTAL POLICIES ON FEDERALISM

5.3.1 Introduction

In 1991, India brought in some significant economic reforms in order to overcome a severe crisis and to align itself to the neo-liberal conditions as suggested by the World Bank and the WTO allegedly on behest of the developed nations. India thus liberalized and opened its economy to the world by removing strict government barriers – rules and regulations – and easing the norms for foreign investment in the country. This reform led to substantial decentralization of powers and functions with larger decision-making power to the state governments in bringing in the investments to their respective states. This was a major boost of investments to the states, and some of the states exploited the opportunity to the maximum and brought in investments to their own states. However, things changed, the economic reforms did not spill over and it could not bring in the changes for which it was intended. Down the line, major economic reforms could not be brought in because of the reluctance of many state governments. It seems that there is an organic linkage between federalism and growth of modern-market economy. According to some scholars, in 1990's India experienced de facto, not de jure, decentralization of its policy management. This decentralization was not carried out in planned or systematic manner. Another impact of this neo-liberal policy combined with the coalition politics of 1990s is that the federal relations among states became more intense and competitive.

5.3.2 Impact of the Enron Deal

Direct negotiations were carried out with the State Governments immediately once the economy was liberalized, by the multinational foreign companies and other global financial institutions like the World Bank. It was perceived that states had become important centres of economic decision making, including that of the foreign entities. One such example of this is when a historic agreement was signed for power purchase between the Maharashtra government and the Texas-based energy giant, the Enron, in 1993. Sovereign counter guarantee was given by the Centre due to the pressure given by the Maharashtra State, in order to enter into the said agreement with Enron. However, the project could not see light of day as it was flawed and had to scrapped after strong lobbying and protests against it. Though the project was scrapped, it had left denting revelations that the new economic reforms had on the Centre-State federal fiscal matters.

1. This episode with the Enron did not prevent Centre and State from carrying out other externally funded projects.
2. In fact, the sovereign guarantee given by the Centre to Enron became the basis for giving guarantees to several other external loans and funding to the state including the ones granted by the World Bank, Asian Development Bank and other agencies.
3. The World Bank has been funding development projects in some states under its structural adjustment programmes, this has caused some tension because as per *Article 292* of the Constitution, the states can borrow only within the territory of India.
4. The states were enthusiastic in getting funds from outside, hence the Central government thought over the issue because the fiscal deficits were also on the rise.
5. The Central government therefore directed the lending agencies and other international finance institutions to make sure that the funds they allocated to the states were not misused to meet revenue deficits and utilised only for the purpose it meant.
6. It also gave freedom to these institutions to discontinue funding if the state is not performing up to the standards.

5.3.3 The Deal with WTO

One of the most significant aspects of the post 1991 reforms is the negotiation carried out by the Government with the WTO and how this impacted the Centre-State relations. Under *Article 253* of Constitution of India, the Central government has a sovereign and exclusive right to enter into international bilateral and multi-lateral treaties/ agreements/ convention. But when the Centre was making such negotiations with the WTO they had to face stiff challenges from the states. As the usual practice, the Government of India without consulting the states signed the agreement with the WTO in 1994. And when the treaty had to be operated in the country from January 1995, various voices were raised by the state governments against the contentious issues of the WTO provisions already signed.

1. As per the Constitution Seventh Schedule, the subject matter of agriculture belong to the State list, hence falls under the legislative purview of the State government, but the Central Government taking advantage of powers under *Article 253*, had already made several negotiations with the WTO with various matters pertaining to the subject matter of agriculture – including agriculture production, marketing and pricing and distribution of agricultural products.
2. The WTO treaty had a far reaching consequence on the Indian federalism. Though a broad reading to the Constitution may seem to confer all the powers to the Central government to enter into such negotiations, but in reality this move went directly against the spirit of federalism.
3. Very recently, the Centre's move to introduce foreign direct investment in multi-brand retail was stiffly opposed by the states on the fact that it would impact small retailers and farmers, and thus they were able to force the Centre to revisit its policy in the same.
4. The states were given option to decide whether to allow retail investments in their states or not.

5.3.4 Impact of State Government on Centre's Policy

There are also other instances where the states have played de facto role in determining the decision of the Centre on foreign policy of Government of India. For instance, the state of Tamil Nadu has very often been directing the Central government on how it should maintain relations with the neighbouring country of Sri Lanka. The legislative assembly of the State of Tamil Nadu has even passed resolutions dictating on its own terms for the Indo-Sri Lanka relations. Recently because of the stand taken by the Government and political parties of Tamil Nadu, the Prime Minister of India had to cancel his participation in an important meeting of the Commonwealth Heads of Governments Meeting (CHOGM) in Sri Lanka. As far as the river water sharing agreement with Bangladesh is concerned, the government of West Bengal has its own stand. In the issue of sharing the water of Teesta River, the action of West Bengal government embarrassed the Government of India recently. There are various other instances where the states have played a role in influencing the foreign policy matters. States with international borders have always had a say in foreign policy matter either directly or indirectly.

5.3.5 Impact of Neo-liberal Economic Policies

Coming back to the impact of the neo-liberal economic policies on the Centre-State relations, it is important to highlight that such policies have created growth and development of numerous new central agencies and regulatory bodies in order to boost the liberalized market economy. Some of the pan-India central agencies like the Competition Commission of India, the Securities and Exchange Board of India, the Telecom Regulatory Authority of India, the Insurance Regulatory and Development Authority of India, the Central Electricity Regulatory Commission, etc. have started to play important roles and all these have far reaching federal implications. In addition to this, the National Commission to Review the Working of the Constitution (NCRWC) has recommended, that for the purpose of carrying out the objectives set out in Articles 301,302,303 and 304 of the Constitution, and for other purposes relating to needs and requirements of inter-State trade and commerce and to eliminate barriers preventing them, the Parliament should by law constitute an authority called as the 'Interstate Trade and Commerce Commission' (ITCC) under the ministry of Industry and Commerce.

1. While the neo-liberal economic policies have had made significant impact on the Centre-State relations, developmental issues are also increasingly tend to impact this relationship.
2. These development issues broadly cover a wide range of issues pertaining to governance and service delivery of some of the major areas of public concern – including agriculture, social welfare, education, health, family planning, rural development etc., most of these are under either the state jurisdiction or under Concurrent list as per the Constitution.
3. However, due to lack of sufficient funds and expertise, the states are not taking much initiative in these major areas of concern.
4. Though it is in the hands of the state governments to take initiative, they tend to look at the centre for directions in these matters. Taking Education, for example, it was initially under State list and then brought to the Concurrent list by the 42nd Amendment of the Constitution in 1976.

5. And since then all major legislative and policy decisions involving the field of Education has been made by the Central Government. Even in the case of subject of Agriculture, all major policy initiatives have been taken by the Centre.
6. The Centre is thus playing a dominant role in the areas of state concern.
7. It has brought in several major policies and legislations in the field of agriculture, social welfare, health care, family planning, education, housing, rural development, etc.
8. All these areas have been covered by the central planning, and under one or the other centrally sponsored schemes, all these factors have soured the Centre-State relationship.
9. All these acts by the Centre have eroded the responsibility and initiative of the states, even their constitutional accountability has been diminished.
10. The more the centre forms policies on the state subjects, the more damaging effect it has on the centre-state federal structure.
11. This is so because majority of these schemes were formed without the consultation of the state governments, and their views were not sought while framing the guidelines for their implementation.
12. Sarkaria Commission on Centre-State recommended that the Central schemes should be kept to a minimum and there should be maximum decentralization of plan formulation.
13. Rather than decreasing, the Centre continued to increase the centrally sponsored schemes with clear disregard to the federal system.

5.3.6 Inequality Between the States

According to scholars, India is a federation of states but its regional developmental process was relegated to the background in the clamour for fulfilling national growth objectives. This led to significant inequality gap between the states based on infrastructure and development. Though the liberalization and the reforms after 1991 put India on the fast track of growth, inequality is prevailing among the states. Hence, the several states have started demanding flexibility in their planning and growth strategies. The issue of regional disparity and inequality prevailing among the states were put forth by the backward states long before the reforms of 1991 got initiated in the country. The third five year plan in 1961, explicitly stated that the location of new enterprises, whether government or private, due consideration has to be given to create a balanced economy in different parts of the country. The Central government addressed this issue of states by issuing 'special category status' to some states based on their backwardness, presence of hilly region. Even some of the bigger states like Bihar, Orissa and Bengal are now demanding the special category status.

1. In short, the neo-liberal policies and reforms of the 1991 have radically transformed the Indian economy to a market economy and presently corporates and industries now play a dominant role in restructuring the political economy of the country.
2. Despite this, the autonomy of the state still remains an important factor for consideration.
3. It would be difficult to carry forward the growth and development agenda, without addressing the concern of the states and their autonomies in their own sphere and jurisdiction.

5.3.7 Impact of Corruption

Another major cause of concern for the Centre-State relations is the fight against corruption and criminalization of politics which has now become a predominant feature of the Indian political system. The criminal law enforcement system is heavily tilted in favour of the Centre, organizations like Central Bureau of Investigation which is responsible and accountable to the office of the Prime Minister, is the principal agency in combating high political and bureaucratic corruption not only at the centre but also in the states. Rather than combating the menace of corruption this agency has been used discriminately against the states.

5.3.8 Subject of Education

As far as sphere of education is concerned, it seems that the Centre is taking overall responsibility. Since the time of emergency, when the subject of Education was moved from the 'State list' to the 'Concurrent list', the Central government has started to bring in major legislations in that subject. Moreover the states also follow the guidelines set by the Centre in this regard. This centralized control of education by the Centre can be traced back to the British era. The Central Advisory Board of Education (CABE) established in 1920 by the colonial government marked the beginning of the centralized coordination of education in the country. Despite education being subject matter of the State list, the matters of higher education always came under the purview of the Central government. Apart from creation of University Grants Commission (UGC), the central government created several other bodies to regulate and implement its policies in the sphere of education. The All India Council for Technical Education Act, 1987 and the National Council for Teacher Education Act, 1993 have both given the control of technical and professional education to the Centre.

1. The Central government has in fact completely intruded into the sphere of education and have recently enacted many legislations pertaining to it, and the most important of those legislations is the Right to Free and Compulsory Education Act, 2009.
2. States are presently trying to attract more central institutions, such as IIT and AIIMS to their states. In order to maintain the federal balance, the Central government has created Central universities in almost all states.
3. Federal consideration is now becoming an important factor in determining the strategic location of various other central government institutions of higher and professional education.
4. *Views of Members of Constituent Assembly*
   Members of the Constituent Assembly understood the significance and hence supported the central control of the education. Some scholars such as Frank Antony proposed that the education throughout the country has to be under the control of the Centre after getting approval and endorsement of people of eminent domain associated with the sphere of education. Others such as Renuka Ray stated that in the nation-building services the unifying force has to be strong, hence the Centre should be given power to regulate and coordinate services especially education and health. Basanta Kumar Das stated that Centre should have enough power to carry out a uniform policy of education and to give financial assistance to the states so that such uniform standards

be reached. Phool Singh was also in favour of uniform education policy as elaborated by the Centre and states receiving adequate financial assistance from the Centre.

5. The above-mentioned debates in the Constituent Assembly was reflected in the contemporary educational policies in India.
6. The Sarkaria Commission on Centre-State relations was of the opinion that the best way forward in the sphere of education is that, actual norms and standards of performance are set by the Union and bodies such as UGC set up under central legislations but the actual implementation should be left to the States.
7. The Commission was also of the opinion that a system of monitoring has to be established by the Union, further it suggested that states and their universities/institutions have to be taken into confidence through close collaboration and cooperation between the Centre and the states.
8. From an overall perspective, it is clear that the States do not have adequate infrastructure and resources to carry forward the burgeoning educational requirements.

Thus, the states have to rely on the Centre which has taken de facto responsibility to control and regulate the sphere of education in almost every aspect. In establishing Central universities and institutions within the jurisdiction of the states it should follow certain minimum/uniform standards and regulations. However, modification and changes might be required so that specific and peculiar problems of each state is addressed in effective manner.

5.3.9 Conclusion

The beginning of independent India was with a unitary federal state under a highly centralized Constitution, which defined India as 'Union of States'. This term obviously meant federation, though the term was deliberately avoided in the Constitution. The federalism was an inevitable necessity. Though the Constitution was in favour of the Centre, it did make provisions for maintaining the federal characteristics. In due course of time, the federalization had strengthened as recognition was accorded to federal diversity if ethnic, regional, linguistic and other cultural communities. The process of federalization had happened through unionization and regionalization, which are expected to provide for the stability of the nation as a whole. The Constitution grants enough power to states to give representation and protect the identities and interests of the minority communities including territorial and non-territorial communities.

India though a multi-national state, is increasingly tending towards a nation-state system. The states are looking toward one government that is at the Centre, which is playing a dominant role in almost all aspects. Centralized political authority is considered to be the most suitable for any effective governance system in the country. This effectively curbs the mischief of the regional leaders and parties. Perhaps time has come now to recognise districts as constituent units of governance. The Constitution might delegate specific power and responsibility at the district level, including the criteria to create new districts. The Central government should stop its dependency on the states for implementation of its policies, instead it should deploy its own officers and set up the effectiveness of the districts so that they become the centre of implementation. The Centre can also promote the local elites. There should be no other state than that of the Nation-State with governance structure based in the districts. This may essentially solve many of the problems faced by various smaller minority and unrepresented communities.

5.4 GOVERNOR AS FACTOR IN FEDERAL RELATIONS

5.4.1 Introduction

Long before independence the office of Governor has been functioning as the head of the provinces. The office is still playing a pivotal role in the Centre-State federal relations. *Article 153* of the Constitution provides that there shall be Governor for each state and *Article 154* says that he shall be the executive head of the state. The Constitution also provides that the same person can be the Governor of two or more states. The important provision given in the Constitution has been highlighted by the Sarkaria Commission, three important facets of the Governor's role is as follows:

a. The constitutional head of state operating normally under a system of Parliamentary democracy.
b. A vital link between the Union government and the State government.
c. An agent of the Union Government in a few specific areas during normal times (e.g. *Article 239(2)*) and in a number of areas during abnormal situations (e.g. *Article 356(1)*).

Though the position of Governor in post-independent era is considered to be symbolic, he has often played a very controversial role in the relations between the Centre and the State. As per the Constitution, the post of Governor is not an elected one, rather it is appointed by the Union Government. Though he/she plays a very vital role in relations between the Centre and the State, the state has no role in the appointment process. Governor is appointed on recommendation of the Central government by the President, he can continue for a term up to 5 years and holds office at the pleasure of the President. This shows that the Governor is an agent of the Centre, but Constitution nevertheless bestows up on his office important and vital powers which is central to the functioning to the state government.

5.4.2 Origins – Office of Governor

As mentioned earlier the post of Governor is not a new one, it had its origins long before the independence of the country, under the auspices of the British Empire the office of Governor was created. In fact, the Governor had a very important role to play under the Government of India Act, 1935. But these powers granted to the Governor of the province under the 1935 Act were significantly reduced in the Constitution after the independence.

1. Serious debate took place when the powers to be granted to the Governor came up before the Constituent assembly, which was given the responsibility to frame the constitution of the country.
2. Various arguments for and against were made regarding the election/nomination of the Governor and his/her role, authority and power.
3. The Provincial Constitutional Committee had formed and submitted a model provincial Constitution, and based on this in July 1947 the Constituent Assembly had accepted the principle for the election of the Governor for all the provinces based on universal adult suffrage.
4. There were some difficulties in proceeding with direct election of the Governor with limited responsibilities.
5. Hence, the Constituent Assembly later in the discussion of the draft Constitution decided to do away with the system direct election of the office of Governor.

5.4.3 Views of Leaders on Governor's Office – Constitutional Debates

(a) Alladi Krishnaswami Ayyar

Alladi Krishnaswami Ayyar made arguments rejecting an elected Governor. He supported the concept of Presidential appointment on consultation with the cabinet. According to him, the expenses involved in process of election was disproportional to the powers vested to the office by the Constitution. Like other leaders, he saw that there would be a danger of clash when both Governor and the Chief Minister are elected by the people. Most of members of the Constituent assembly at the time of debate thought that the post of Governor will be just a mere figurehead as he/she will not be interfering with the day to day administration of the provinces.

(b) P.S. Deshmukh

According to P.S. Deshmukh, if the position of Governor is going to like that what were provided under the 1935 Act, and similar provisions were adopted in the draft constitution also, then the post of Governor has to be appointed by the President and no election process is to be involved. Like many other leaders like Ayyar, Deshmukh too had his own apprehensions about the office of elected Governor coming in conflict with the provincial government. As the debate went on further many of the members of the Constituent assembly were against the direct election based on universal adult suffrage.

(c) B.G. Kher

According to B.G. Kher, the direct election was not advocated by anyone not just because it incurred huge expenses, but also to the fact that there is already a post elected- chosen by all the people of the state and the whole power was bestowed upon this office of the Chief Minister, if another person is chosen directly by the people, there would be confusion in allocation of the responsibility and authority of the State which would further lead to conflict, and this conflict has to be avoided for smooth functioning of the administration. However, Kher disagreed with the argument that Governor is just a mere figurehead. To quote Kher,

> *So far as the Governor is concerned, we have given him very few powers. But, I do not agree with the comment that he is mere a figurehead; a figurehead is capable neither of good nor of bad. I wasn't to submit to the House, Sir, that a Governor can do a great deal of good if he is a good Governor and can do a great deal of mischief, if he is a bad Governor, is spite of the very little power given to him under the Constitution we are now framing. The powers that we purpose to give him, and the functions that we assign to him are very few such as summoning and dissolving the Assembly, to give assent to the bills passed by the State Assembly, to act as representative of the State, to nominate the Premier after the general election of the resignation of the Ministry, to represent the province on ceremonial occasions and such power as given to act in the emergency. He is the symbol of the State and we have found in actual practice that if he is an active Governor, a good man, he can, by all means of getting into touch with opponents of the party which is in power, reconcile them to good number of measures, and generally, by tours and other means make the administration run smoothly. Similarly he can do a great deal of mischief. I believe, therefore, to have as a Governor a person who is elected on a wider franchise to have at the head of the province a person who is supposed to be more representative that the Premier would be a mistake....the only insurance for smooth government in the provinces is to allow the President of the country to nominate a person who enjoys his confidence, which clearly means, the confidence of his Cabinet as also the cabinet of the Province, to be the Governor or the province any other mode, whether by election on adult suffrage or by election by the representatives of the people in the House will give rise to considerable friction.*

B.R.Ambedkar made it clear about the powers of the Governor, he stated in the Constituent assembly as follows, "*....the real issue before the house is really not the nomination or election because as I said this functionary is going to be purely ornamental functionary; how he comes into being, whether by nomination or by some other machinery is purely a psychological question*".

(d) H.N. Kunzru

According to H.N. Kunzru, the ultimate power with regard to any serious problem in the province will rest with the President, but he will not act without consulting the Governor of such province. Constituent assembly at the time of discussion about the general principles of the Constitution agreed that there has to be some provision for its breakdown, something similar to the Section 93 of the Government of India Act, 1935. It was proposed that if the Governor feels that the setup provided by the Constitution for administration of the province breaks down, then the Governor should have the power by proclamation to take over the administration of the province for a fortnight and communicate the same with the President that since constitutional machinery had failed in the state, he the Governor had proclaimed and taken over the administration to himself. This shows the dominant role played by the Governor in the provinces, there were also other voices calling for increased power to Governor and his direct election by the people.

(e) Jawaharlal Nehru

At the time of final discussion of the draft Constitution, the Constituent assembly accepted the provision to have a nominated Governor. On 31st May 1949, Jawaharlal Nehru stated as follows:

> *...... I feel that if we have an elected Governor that would to some extent encourage separatist provincial tendency. There will be far fewer common links with the Centre.... Apart from the tremendous burden of these elections for the provincial and the central legislatures, to add another election on this major scale would mean not only spending a tremendous deal of energy and time of the nation but also money of the nation and divert it from far more worthwhile projects. Apart from this it would undoubtedly mean, I think, encouraging that narrow provincial way of thinking and functioning in each province... I think it would be infinitely better if he was not so intimately concerned with the local politics of the province, with the factions in the provinces. He must be acceptable to the province, he should be acceptable to the government of the province and yet he must not be known to be a part of the party machine of that province. He may be sometimes, possible a man from that province itself. We do not rule it out. But on the whole it probably would be desirable to have people a part in politics. There may be an eminent educationist or persons eminent in other walks of life, who would naturally, while cooperating fully with the government and carrying out the policy of the government.... I think that an elective Governor is almost invariably not only likely to be that province, but is likely hardly ever to represent any of the numerous minority groups that exist in the country.*

5.4.4 Role of Governor – Constitutional Debates

Majority of the members in the Constituent assembly felt that the Governor has to play the important role of the agent of the Centre.

1. They wanted the Governor to help the Central government in implementing its policies and agenda throughout the country.
2. Many of the senior most leaders were unconcerned about the autonomy of the provinces. Their main agenda was to unite and integrate the country, and they felt that it can

be achieved by nominating the Governor by the Union, rather than having him elected directly by the people.

3. This nomination will enable the Central government to effectively control its policies and agendas.
4. They wanted the provincial government to be subordinate of the Central government.

The Chairman of the drafting committee of the Constitution, B.R. Ambedkar clarified this position in the Constituent assembly on 1st June 1949, he stated as follows:

> *Because the provincial governments are required to work in subordination to the central government, and therefore in order to see that they do act in subordination to the central government the governor will reserve certain things in order to give the President the opportunity to see that the rules under which the provincial government are supposed to act according to the constitution or in subordination to central government are observed.*

Towards the end of the constituent assembly debates, B.R. Ambedkar further highlighted the constitutional role of the governor as follows:

> *The Governor under the Constitution has no function which he can discharge by himself; no function at all. While he has no function, he has certain duties to perform, and I think the House will do well to bear in mind this distinction… a distinction has been made between the functions of the Governor and the duties which the governor has to perform. My submissions is that although the Governor has no functions still, even the Constitutional Governor, that he is, has certain duties to perform. His duties according to me, may be classified in two parts. One is, that he has to retain the Ministry in office. Because the Ministry is to hold office during his pleasure, he has to see whether and when he should exercise his pleasure against the Ministry. The second duty which the Governor has, and must have, is to advice the Ministry, to warn the Ministry, to suggest to the Ministry an alternative and to ask for reconsideration. I do not think that anybody in this House will question the fact that the Governor should have this duty case upon him; otherwise, he would be an absolutely unnecessary functionary; no good at all. He is the representative not of a party; he is the representative of the people as whole of the state. It is in the name of the people that he carries on the administration. He must see that the administration is carried on at level which may be regarded as good, efficient, honest administration. I submit that he cannot discharge the constitutional functions of a governor which I have just referred to unless he is in a position to obtain the information…. It is to enable the Governor to discharge his functions in respect of a good and pure administration that we propose to give the Governor the power to call for any information.*

5.4.5 Role of Governor – After Independence

The Constitution of independent India has vested some very important powers, roles and responsibilities on the office of the Governor.

1. The Governor plays an important role in the legislative sphere of the state concerned.
2. He may or may not give consent to the bill passed in the Assembly. In this regard, *Article 200* states that when a bill is passed in the legislative assembly of the state or, in case of states having legislative council, by both the Houses of the legislatures, it shall

be presented to the Governor, then he either gives assent, or withholds it, or he sends the bill again to the legislature for its reconsideration, or he withholds his consent and reserves the bill for the consideration of the President.

3. Further *Article 200* provides that when the reconsidered bill is again submitted before the Governor with or without amendments, he has to give his assent and cannot further delay its passage.
4. Also under *Article 201*, the Governor is given power to reserve the bill for the consideration of the President.
5. *Article 161* of the Constitution bestows power to the Governor to grant pardons, reprieves, respite and remission of punishment or to suspend, remit or commute sentence of any person convicted of any offence to which the executive power of the state extends.

5.4.6 Controversial Role of Governor

The most controversial role of the Governor which has serious repercussions on the Centre-State relations is when he submits reports to the Central government recommending the President's Rule in the state.

1. Emergency under *Article 356* can be proclaimed even without the report of the Governor by the President if he is satisfied that such situation exists, however most of the President's Rule in states have been proclaimed on basis of the reports of Governors.
2. The Central government in order to avoid controversy for taking unilateral decision on imposing Emergency, relies on the report of the Governor to impose it.
3. Since the Governor being an appointee of the Centre, generally complies and cooperates with the Centre and provides with reports as required by the Centre, in this case-recommendation report for imposition of President's Rule.
4. There are also few instances where the Governor refused to comply with the directions to the Centre and the Union government had to unilaterally impose the President's Rule.

5.4.7 Examples – Excesses by Governors

The report of the Governor based on which the President's Rule was imposed was unchallenged until the landmark Supreme Court's judgement in S.R. Bommai's case. There was no one single way or guideline based on which the report has to be submitted for recommending President's Rule.

(a) Kerala

For example, the imposition of the President's Rule in the state of Kerala in 1959 was based on the recommendation of the report of the Governor, who had felt that the ruling party had "lost support of the majority of the people". This doctrine can become a dangerous weapon in hands of the Governor and the Central government who can dismiss constitutionally elected government in the state. Even personal conviction of the Governor became grounds for dismissal of the state government and for imposing the President's Rule in the state. In the above case, the Governor did not bother to realistically analyse whether the communist government enjoyed majority or not in the assembly.

(b) Andhra Pradesh

In another incident of imposition of President's Rule, the Governor of Andhra Pradesh, in 1984, dismissed the non-Congress Chief Minister allegedly based on some information that he had lost majority in the assembly. A minority government was then installed and was given an unusual long time of a month to prove majority on the floor of the house, which it failed to do. Rather the previous dismissed Chief Minister N.T. Rama Rao of the Telugu Desam Party successfully proved his majority. This shows that how Governors arbitrarily dismiss, without any genuine reasons, a constitutionally elected government based only on political considerations. In the case of Andhra Pradesh, the Governor and the Central government came under intense public pressure, and were compelled to set aside their earlier order and had to replace the Governor; also there were raising calls for abolition of office of Governor itself.

5.4.8 Governor – An Agent of Centre

The discretionary powers granted to the Governor were in reality used by the Central government using the Governor as the proxy.

1. The office of Governor was used frequently by the Centre to install government of its choice in the State.
2. The controversy starts right at the beginning, with the appointment of Governor. The office of Governor has to be neutral as envisaged by the Constitutional makers, but in reality defeated and active politicians were appointed to the office, thereby politicising the post of the Governor, who then took active part in the politics.
3. Non-political persons such as retired Bureaucrats too were appointed as Governors, even they were loyal to the government that had appointed them.
4. The frequent use of President's rule and the role played by the Governor in it, particularly in coalition situation, created a unique practice of 'parading' the supporters before the Governor of state to convince him of the majority for forming the government.
5. The political role of the Governors can be clearly seen from the fact that they never stick to a fixed time for proving the majority. Some selected leaders and parties were given extraordinarily long time to prove majority while some others were denied the same.

The Governor's office was so politicized that when the National front government led by V.P. Singh took over the Central government, the President, in January, 1990 called for resignation of eighteen Governors "to facilitate the reshuffle by the Union". The National Front Government could not trust the impartiality of the Governors appointed by the previous Rajiv Gandhi-led Congress regime.

5.4.9 Recommendations – Sarkaria Commission

Several representations regarding the role of the Governor was made before the Sarkaria Commission on Centre-State relations by the State governments, many calling for the reduction in powers and role of the Governor. Representations were even made for the abolition of the office of Governor itself. The Sarkaria commission suggested the following four criteria for being appointed as a Governor,

1. He should be eminent in some walk of life.
2. He should be a person from outside the state.
3. He should be a detached figure and not too intimately connected with the local politics of the state.
4. He should be a person who has not taken too great a part in politics generally and particularly in the recent past.

In selecting a Governor in accordance with the above criteria, persons belonging to the minority groups should continue to be given a chance hitherto.

The Sarkaria Commission recommended that the selection should be based on consultation with the following authorities, the Vice-President of India, Speaker of Lok Sabha and the Chief Minister of the State concerned. The Commission also recommended that it is "desirable that a politician from the ruling party at the Centre is not appointed a Governor of a State which is being run by some other party or a combination of parties". The Commission observed that different Governors had adopted different methods for similar situations for the dissolution of the State assembly; and, accordingly, it was suggested by the Commission that Article 356 be amended so that "the State Legislative Assembly should not be dissolved either by the Governor or the President before the proclamation issued under Article 356(1) has been laid before Parliament and it has had an opportunity to consider it".

5.4.10 Recommendations – National Commission to Review the Working of the Constitution

The NCRWC has also made certain recommendations with regard to what role the Governor should or should not play. It recommended that the question of whether a government has lost majority in the assembly has to be decided only on the floor of the assembly and nowhere else. NCRWC also recommended that the government in the state should not be dismissed as long as it enjoys confidence of the House and the majority in the Assembly. The Governor can only dismiss the government when the Chief Minister refuses to resign even after his party had failed to prove majority on the floor of the House and on losing a no-confidence motion in the Assembly. In a situation of political breakdown, the NCRWC recommended that

> *The Governor should explore all possibilities of having a Government enjoying majority support in the Assembly. If it is not possible for such a Government to be installed and if fresh elections can be held without avoidable delay, he should ask the outgoing Ministry, (if there is one), to continue as a caretaker government, provided the Ministry was defeated solely on an issue, unconnected with any allegations of maladministration or corruption and is agreeable to continue. The Governor should then dissolve the Legislative Assembly, leaving the resolution of the constitutional crisis to the electorate.*

Regarding the imposition of the President's Rule based on the Report of the Governor, the NCRWC recommended that the report has to be a 'speaking document' containing a precise and clear statement of all material facts and grounds on the basis of which the President may satisfy himself as to the existence or otherwise of the situation contemplated in Article 356, and the governor's report based on which the President Rule is imposed should be given wide publicity in media and in full.

5.4.11 Conclusion

Even in present condition the office of Governor continues to play a major factor in the Central-State federal dynamics. Despite numerous recommendations made by various commissions on Centre-State relations the office of Governor is continued to be misused by the Central governments. It has become a ritual to reshuffle or change the Governors of the states when there is a change in the government at Centre.

5.5 IMPACT OF EMERGENCY ON FEDERAL RELATIONS

5.5.1 Introduction

There are some very unique features present only in the Constitution of India and found nowhere else. One such provision is the Emergency powers vested with the Central government. Central government has the power to turn the federation into a unitary system during this period, and in case of President's rule it has the power to suspend the state government, and during Financial emergency it controls the finances of the state. Under the *Articles 352/356*, the Central government virtually takes control over the entire legislative, administrative and executive functions of the state instead of restoring back the constitutional machinery in the state which had failed.

5.5.2 Emergency Provisions in Constitution

Except on few occasions, most of the application of President's rule was for political considerations. As per the Sarkaria commission's report, nearly 75 instances of application of President's rule was to prevent a party from forming a government or dismiss a legitimately elected government. Political controversy followed most of the President's rule and widespread protests and agitation were carried out by the people in many instances and hence leading to the removal of the Governors who have proposed the President's Rule in the State. *The Articles 352, 356* were envisaged as a last resort and as a salvage operation for the sick state, but it has been brazenly and wantonly violated by every government who has assumed power at the Centre. The word 'otherwise' given in *Article 356* has been interpreted in various ways to dismiss the state governments by the Centre without the reports of the Governors. Hence, it is clear that the emergency provisions have significantly impacted the Centre-State federal dynamics. But it is also clear that all these interregnums were temporary none were permanent, the Constitution also made it clear that these emergency provisions operated for a limited time only.

5.5.3 Emergency: The Beginning

The first controversial use of the *Article 356* was made by the first Prime Minister Jawaharlal Nehru when he imposed the President's Rule in Punjab in 1951. He forced the Congress Parliamentary board to compel the then Chief Minister of Punjab Gopichand Bhargava to resign even though he enjoyed the majority support of the Nehru's cabinet. He informed the President that after the Chief Minister resigns no new ministry would be formed, rather the Governor will submit a report that it was not possible to run the government as per the Constitution and hence the President then should invoke the President's Rule in the state and take over its administration. Nehru was careful in imposing the President's Rule then onwards, but Indira Gandhi, Rajiv Gandhi, including the Janata Government of 1977's use of this provision severely damaged the relation between the Centre and the State until the emergence of the Coalition government in 1989. For now the National Emergency has been imposed thrice, first during the Chinese aggression in 1962 and it continued and no new emergency was imposed in 1965 during the war with Pakistan, the next was in 1971 during the liberation of Bangladesh and finally the most controversial imposition of Emergency in 1975 by Indira Gandhi. The President's Rule has been imposed across States for more than 120 occasions and the financial emergency as provided in Article 360 has not been imposed so far.

5.5.4 Emergency: Indira's Time

In order to understand the increased use of President's rule during Indira's time it is important to look into the political ramifications which forced her to retort to such draconian measures of imposing President's Rule in the States and National Emergency of 1975.

1. After Nehru, Indira succeeded in his place, and Indira faced a very tough scenario. The economy was in dire state, especially the crisis was acute after the 1962 war with China and the economic scenario turned from bad to worse in subsequent years of 1960s leading to severe payment crisis and devaluation of Indian rupee.
2. There was short fall in agriculture production in mid 1960s due to two continuous drought spells. The public investments and the manufacturing saw a sharp decline. Apart from these, high inflation was prevailing and all these had a significant impact on the political scenario when Indira became the Prime Minister in 1966.
3. The political setup started to become antagonistic to the Congress system. In the south the anti-Hindi agitations often ended up being ugly and violent. Naxalite and leftist movements became more prominent in West Bengal and Kerala.
4. The dominance of Congress as a single party across the country suffered a severe setback in the general elections of 1967 as well as the mid-term election of 1969. Moreover, there were internal cracks within the Congress party itself.

(a) Changes in the Congress

Thus, Indira's tenure was engulfed with several political and structural complexities. In order to overcome them, Indira had no option but to be assertive and dictatorial. She had to resort to some tough decisions and had also to nullify criticisms against her both within and outside the party.

1. Kamaraj-led Congress syndicate which supported her succession after Shashtri gradually became hostile and started to challenge her authority. Indira too responded and retorted against the actions of the syndicate.
2. As a result Indira was expelled from the party in 1969 leading to the split in the Congress into Congress 'Organisation' wing (Congress O) which was dented by the Congress syndicate.
3. Indira then created numerous populist policies towards pleasing the people. The economic scenario too had become somewhat better by the time of emergency. If there were no violent protests against her and if her election as Member of Parliament was not embarrassing, Indira might not have resorted to imposition of emergency.

4. Indira centralized the decision making in the Congress party as all decision of the state and central organization came together under her.
5. Using emergency she was able to dictate the functioning of the state governments itself.
6. Apart from these the emergency was used as a tool to improve the economic condition and progressive economic policies were then implemented. A new twenty-point program to improve the economic condition was introduced within days of imposition of emergency, it addressed various issues like bonded labour, agriculture workers, harijans, etc.
7. Because of the imposition of emergency most of the measures to contain the inflation were implemented and also other measures to bring stabilisation were taken up such as crack down on the offenders – black marketers, hoarders and smugglers – unaccounted funds were restricted, traders were prevented from hoarding and were made to display the weights and prices properly.

(b) As Congress, as Country

Centralization were carried out not just around the country but it also happened within the Congress party itself. Using the powers under Maintenance of Infernal Security Act 1971 and various other draconian provisions, prominent opposition leaders who were spearheading campaign against Indira were arrested and detained. The press was also censored and strictly restricted.

1. The centralization in the government and party were essential for the survival of Indira and the Congress party which had suffered a great setback and got its dominance shattered during the elections of 1960s.
2. Indira was firm in her resolve to centralize the powers in the party and the government even though she suffered from several violent and disruptive protests from the opposition leaders. She had imposed strict restrictions and discipline within the party.
3. No criticism against the government was tolerated and action was immediately taken against such persons. The Congress party local level committees were all restructured, the Centre took over the command and control. In the Congress-ruled states, the Chief Ministers were frequently changed and were replaced with loyal and active supporters of Indira Gandhi.

(c) Control Over Cabinet

Indira controlled the whole cabinet, even the senior-most ministers had to fall under her dictate. She implemented the concept called as the 'kitchen' cabinet, whereby small band of very loyal followers of Indira were surrounding her to aid and advise her, hence all the decisions were taken within the 'kitchen' cabinet itself. Indira frequently changed the portfolios of the ministers so that no one can have personal hold over any ministry, and also that it will tame the senior ministers. The Prime Minister's Office created in 1964 during the tenure of Lal Bahadur Shashtri became all powerful. It bypassed the Home Ministry, the Cabinet Secretariat etc. to make appointments and promotions to high posts and positions. The Prime Minister's Office also controlled important departments like the Research and Analysis Wing, the Central Bureau of Investigation and Central Security Forces.

5.5.5 Excess During Emergency 1975–76

The emergency period was fraught with excess and several other illegal measures. The following are some of the drastic and draconian steps taken during the emergency period between 1975–76:

(i) 1,10,806 persons were arrested, detained and tortured without trial under the laws made by the then government

(ii) Press was severely repressed and journalists were harassed and detained if found to be against the government.

(iii) Nearly 25,962 government employees were prematurely retired unjustly using provisions created during the emergency.

(iv) Temporary shelters and slums of urban poor numbering 1,50,105 in Delhi was bulldozed without providing them any alternative homes.

(v) The pet project of Sanjay Gandhi the son of Indira, the compulsory sterilisation was indiscriminately carried out. Nearly 81,32,209 sterilisations were carried out in 1976-77 as against 2,64,755 carried out under the family planning programme in 1975–76.

5.5.6 The 44th Amendment

The original emergency provisions made easier for Indira to impose such measures. But this was changed by the subsequent Janata Government by bringing the 44th amendment to the Constitution.

1. The provisions given under *the Articles 352 and 356* were amended. The most controversial expression of Internal Disturbance was deleted and replaced with Armed Rebellion.
2. The recommendation to be made by the President should now be in writing from the Cabinet. Also as under *Article 74*, the President can resend such recommendation to the Cabinet for reconsideration but had to act in accordance with the reconsidered advice of the Cabinet.
3. Previously there were no such provisions and thus Indira without consulting her Cabinet colleagues proposed and impose the Emergency by recommending it to the President.
4. Previously only a simple majority of both the houses was enough to approve the emergency, but the forty fourth amendment made Special majority mandatory for approval that is it has to be approved by a majority of total members of the house and by a majority of not less than 2/3rd of the house present and voting.
5. Before the 44th amendment there was no provision to approve the Emergency provision periodically, and Emergency under *352* once approved, continued for any length of time without further approval by the Parliament.
6. The Amendment proposes that once approved by both the houses the Emergency continued for six months and after that fresh approval is needed from the Parliament for its continuation and Emergency continued for another six months unless it is revoked beforehand.
7. By the 38th amendment, Proclamation of emergency was made non-justiciable, but the 44th amendment changed that, and hence now emergency can be challenged before the courts.

5.5.7 Emergency in Present Era

The misuse of emergency provisions under *Article 356* has now been greatly reduced. The last two decades have seen a significant change in the scenario. There are several factors including the rise of coalition governments at the Centre. The Sarkaria commission on Centre-State relation suggested that to quote "*Article 356* should be used only as a last resort, a warning should be issued to the errant state, the material facts and grounds on which the Article is invoked should be made an integral part of the proclamation and the state legislature should not be dissolved until Parliament has approved it". The Supreme Court also asserted in the S.R. Bommai judgement that provisions under *Article 356(1)* were not immune and courts can look into them and strike down in case it is malafide and based on extraneous or irrelevant grounds. The NCRWC in its report recommended that the proclamation of emergency under *Article 356(1)* should be based on the report of the Governor. Moreover, it suggested that such report should be a speaking document, whereby it should state all relevant facts and grounds, based on which the President can take decision whether to or not to recommend the President's Rule in the state. The NCRWC also recommended that the State assembly should not be prematurely dissolved by the President, first the emergency has to be placed before and get approved by the Parliament. The second commission on Centre-State relations, the Punchhi commission also recommended that the government should incorporate the guidelines given by the Apex court in the landmark S.R. Bommai judgement.

5.6 COALITION POLITICS AND ITS IMPACT ON FEDERAL RELATIONS

5.6.1 Introduction

The upper middle class elite played a dominant role in running the country after its Independence, and such scenario continued for a long time both in Centre and the States. This coordination and consensus was possible between Centre and State because of the one-party dominance of the system, which is ruled in both by the Congress party. The consensual elite accommodation was possible because of the dominance of the political class by the powerful upper caste political elites, and hence similar view and line of thought was possible.

5.6.2 Initial Phase: Times after Independence

The scenario started to change after the 1960s. There were some noteworthy changes in the political system such as rearrangement of the political forces, increasing role of rural elites in the system, rise of a particolored and complex elite structure. The year 1967 marked the coming of change, the Congress party lost elections in several prominent states and first phase of coalition governments with support from regional parties started to arise in the system. This could not be sustained for a long time because of the lack of initial experience, differences and contradictions among the parties. Indira Gandhi too played a significant role in curtailing the rise of coalition politics by centralising political and economic powers. But some states did challenge such unilateral and centralising tendencies of the Union government, they also questioned the veracity of the planning by the Centre. Though the initial phase of coalition politics was temporary and short lived, it did indeed create some strong regional movement and state-specific parties in states like Tamil Nadu, Kerala, Orissa, West Bengal, Punjab, etc.

Before the beginning of the first phase of coalition politics era there was spurt of rural elites and regional interest groups in the form of farmers lobby and agriculture interest groups. The green revolution had not only economically enhanced the lives of the agriculturists but it also had a significant political impact. Their participation in regional and national politics started to rise and within a short span of time they had become a force to reckon with. This could be seen when Prime Minister Lal Bahadur Shastri tried to formulate an Integrated National food policy when the country was under a severe food crisis during the period of 1964–65, he was unsuccessful in doing so. The peasant castes have now been designated as the Other Backward Castes (OBC) and they play a substantial role in the coalition government at the centre.

5.6.3 The First Phase: The Late 1960

The Congress party underwent noteworthy changes during the 1960s. It had lost its dominant status after the 1967 elections. By the end of 1960s, the Congress had polarized into two camps and split – one led by Kamaraj called as the Syndicate-Congress (Organisation) and another under Indira called as the Congress (Ruling). Indira Gandhi faced stiff opposition within her own party, she increasingly started to reject principle of consensus and ignore long standing and established leaders of the party. She dismantled the party's decentralized structure and restricted its functioning without concern for regional and local sentiments. She practically took over the party operations completely. All senior members of the party had to fall in line with her dictates. This had not only changed working of the Congress party but it inadvertently also had significant impact on the Indian political federal system. This had led to growth of strong regional sentiment in the states. Strong case was made demanding decentralisation by sharing power of sovereignty by the states, especially Punjab and Assam during the second term of Indira Gandhi. Several prominent state-level parties came to power during Indira's second term in early 1980s- such as Assom Gana Parishad (AGP) in Assam, AIADMK in Tamil Nadu, Akali Dal in Punjab, Telugu Desam Party (TDP) in Andhra Pradesh, etc. The state governments of West Bengal and Kerala led by the United Front of the Left parties, Swatantra party in Orissa, DMK-led government in Tamil Nadu had emphasised the need to restrain the authority of Centre. In 1980s Jyothi Basu, N.T. Rama Rao and other opposition Chief Ministers came together to build a coalition of 'Non-Congress CMs' challenging the hegemony of the dominant Congress party and the so called 'centralized state'. Several conferences and conclaves were held to discuss these issues.

5.6.4 The Janata Interregnum

The Janata Party was an amalgamation of diverse interests, four opposition parties namely Bharathiya Lok Dal, the Socialist Party, Jan Sangh and the Congress (O) came together. It formed the first coalition government at the Centre. It also had support from the local dominant groups. It was expected that there would be greater decentralisation of powers, but it was not so. The Janata Government too acted like the previous Indira government and dislodged several Congress-led governments in the states using the Presidents Rule under *Article 356*.

5.6.5 The Second Phase: Late 1980's

The other major period of coalition era – the second phase started in 1989 – two years before the Economic Reform program. There was a transition from the dominant party system to a multi-party system and from a majoritarian government to a coalition government. Several unstable governments were formed in quick succession. The coalition politics got boost from the implementation of the Mandal commission reforms for reservation to OBCs by the V.P. Singh government and communalisation of the polity by the demolition of the Babri Masjid in Ayodhya. BJP emerged as a major force in the Centre, while in the states, caste-based, class-based politics of the SCs and OBCs took centre stage. Hence, now the so called national parties had to align themselves with these state-level forces in order to win the elections as national parties powers had waned.

5.6.6 Present Era of Coalition Politics

In successive years, the coalition government had become the norm in the Centre with support from the regional-state parties. Some of the dominant parties emerged in 1990s, such as Samajwadi Party (SP), Janata Dal (United) (JDU), Biju Janata Dal (BJD), Trinamool Congress, Samata Party, Nationalist Congress Party (NCP), etc.

1. It is impossible now to form a government at the centre without the support of these regional parties.
2. This had significant impact on the Federal system as states now played a dominant and decisive role in the coalition governments.
3. Though in 2014 elections BJP had won majority on its own, it still chose to form government with coalition of other parties.
4. Thus, states are now becoming increasingly assertive in Centre-State federal bargaining as their dominance has increased in the national-level politics.
5. The coalition government and its effect is not restricted to national politics alone, it has a significant impact on the neo-liberal economic policies of the centre.
6. Due to the opposition of the State governments, the centre could not carry forward many decisive economic reforms. The states now have a say in directing and modifying the economic policies.
7. The national parties too are now exploiting the coalition politics and thus the system has become more corrupt.
8. During the pre-liberalisation phase, there was a vertical competition between the national states, now it has become horizontal, that is competition is now between the regional state governments themselves.
9. Hence the policies of the Centre are now diffused across the states and it works on political considerations. Thus, the disintegration of the party system and unstable coalition has adversely affected the governance of the country.
10. There is now increased prominence of the state and regional parties because of the stability of the coalition government at the Centre.
11. The states hence now enjoy a greater degree of autonomy and they try to establish their own influence at the centre which is adversely impacting the polity.
12. The state-level parties are also in talks to create a United Federal Front to resist any centralization moves.

13. Such 'centralization' measures invite condemnation not just from the regional and state parties but also from the National Parties themselves in order to preserve the federal spirit and structure. Even the BJP-led government elected in 2014 has given greater emphasis on improving the dynamics of Centre-State relations at least on paper.

5.6.7 Conclusion

The emergence of coalition politics thus has significant impact on the Centre-State relations. The Central government's intervention in the affairs of the state has now been reduced significantly. The use of Presidents rule under Article 356 has also seen decline. The state governments are now not disbanded at the whims and fancies of the Centre, and also the legislative intervention by using the power of Governor to reserve the bill for the assent of the President too has now changed (under Article 200,201). Hence, according to scholars, the participation of the regional state parties in the coalition governments has led to 'refederalisation' of Indian democracy. Present era is moving towards increased decentralisation, refederalisation and regionalization of politics, and hence the institutions should also keep up with such changes in the political scenario for effective sharing of powers.

5.7 JUDICIARY AS A FACTOR IN FEDERAL RELATIONS

5.7.1 Introduction

The erstwhile 1935 government of India act set in motion the Constitutional federal structure of India. It established the legal basis for the present federal system. The Constitution of India, taking que from the 1935 act created a unified and independent judiciary which plays a crucial role in maintaining the centre-state federal balance. Unlike other federations where there is a dual judicial system for centre and states, Indian Constitution provides for a 'single and integrated judiciary'. Article 124 of the Constitution of India says that there shall be a Supreme Court for India, while Article 131 says that that Supreme Court shall have original jurisdiction in any dispute: (a) between the government of India and one or more states, or (b) between the government of India and any state or states on one side and one or more other states on the other, or (c) between two or more states.

5.7.2 Basic Structure and Federalism

The system of federal structure has been upheld by the judiciary a number of times in various judgements. It has treated the constitution to have established a federation in the country. It has also reiterated that the federal form of government forms the 'basic structure' of the constitution. This 'basic structure' doctrine is undefined and the court has the power to define and block any changes to the basic structure of the constitution. In the following judgements of *Minerva Mills v. Union of India (1980)* and *S.R. Bommai v. Union of India (1994)* the courts have established parliamentary federal democracy and federalism to be the basic structure of the Constitution of India. Though the courts were the defenders of the concept of federalism and its structure, in the initial 30 years after independence most of the judgements were biased in favour of the Centre.

5.7.3 Judiciary During Emergency

After the impact of national emergency imposed by Indira Gandhi, the Courts started to defend the states to some extent. By enacting the 38th amendment, Indira Gandhi tried to curtail the important aspect of judicial power – the Judicial Review. The amendment stated that the "satisfaction" of President based on the report of the Governor is not subject to the judicial review that is President's satisfaction cannot be questioned by the courts. Thus, the 38th amendment enacted in 1975 sought to block out the powers of the court. But this was short lived as the Janata government formed after the emergency enacted the 44th amendment in 1978 which restored the power of judicial review back to the courts. After this period, the judiciary started to act on its own to deliver verdicts questioning the authority of the Central government over the states. By 1980s, it started to question the rationale of using Article 356 – the President's rule to dislodge state governments by the Centre.

5.7.4 Centre-State Relation and Judiciary

1. The first major judicial intervention came in the issue of Centre-State relation when the Communist- controlled State of Kerala tried to take over the management of the private schools in the state. The Communist party had formed the government in Kerala in the year 1957. The governor had reserved this Education bill for the assent of the President. In order to avoid controversy, this was referred to the Supreme Court under the Presidential reference of *Article 143* of the Constitution. It was held by majority of seven judges that the bill violated the fundamental rights guaranteed under *Article 30(1)* and thus was unconstitutional. State governments complained that they found in difficult to regulate the educational standards in the state after such a verdict.
2. In another landmark case of *Babulal Parate v. State of Maharashtra (1960)* which had significant and far reaching impact on the federal structure. The Court held that the power to change, diminish, alter boundary, form new state and change its name given as proviso to *Article 3* does not require the consent of the state concerned. It can be altered, changed unilaterally by the will of the centre. The proviso to *Article 3* states that no Bill for the purpose shall be introduced in either house of parliament except on the recommendation of the President and unless, where the proposal contained in the bill affects the area, boundaries or name of any of the states, the bill has been referred by the President to the legislature of that state for expressing its views therein within such period as may be specified in the reference or within such further period as the President may allow and the period so specified or allowed has expired.
   The power under Article 3, the reference to the state government is not the discretionary power of the President, it is the power of the Council of Ministers and under their advice (*Article 74*). Thus, in the judgement it was held that even if the states opposed, its boundaries, area, name etc. can be changed lawfully by the Centre.
3. The Supreme Court in the *Purshothaman v. State of Kerala* held that there was no time limit for the President to give assent to a bill reserved to him by the governor. It was also held that the Bill pending before the Governor or the President does not lapse on dissolution of the assembly and on proroguing the bill pending in the legislature (either house) does not lapse.

4. In the case of *West Bengal v. Union of India* majority of the six judges upheld the Parliament's right to enact law to compulsorily acquire properties in the state by the Union. It was held that this measure would not amount to infringement of the state's sovereignty. Under the Coal Baring Areas (Acquisition and Development) Act 1957 the authority of the Union government was challenged by the state of West Bengal. It was held by the court that the Parliament's power to legislate in such matters of acquisition is unrestricted and unparalleled. B.P. Sinha J. Speaking for himself and four other Justices stated that

   > *It would be difficult to hold that parliament which is competent to destroy a state, is on account of some assumption as to sovereignty of the State, incompetent effectively to acquire by legislation property owned by the State for governmental purposes.*

   In his dissenting judgement over the other five judges Subba Rao J. held as follows:

   > *The impugned Act in so far as it conferred a power on the Union to acquire lands owned by the states, including coal mines and coal bearing lands in ultra vires. Under the constitution of India the political sovereignty is divided between the constitutional entities, that is, the Union and the States, who are juristic personalities possessing properties and functioning through the instrumentalities created by the Constitution. The Indian Constitution accepts the federal concept and distributes the sovereign powers between the coordinate constitutional entities, namely, the Union and the States. This concept implies that one cannot encroach upon the governmental functions or instrumentalities of the other unless constitution provides for such interference. The legislative fields allotted to the units cover subjects for legislation and they do not deal with the relationship between the coordinate units functioning in their allotted fields. This is regulated by other provisions of the Constitution and there is no provision which enable one unit to take away the property of another except by agreement. The power to acquire the property of a citizen for a public purpose is one of the implied powers of the sovereign. Under the Indian Constitution that sovereign power is divided between the Union and the States. It is implicit in the power of acquisition by a sovereign that it must relate only to property of the governed for a sovereign cannot acquire its own property.*

5.7.5 Judiciary on Education and Federal Issues

Education as a matter of law has impact on any federal system. Education has its own intrinsic values and universality which cannot be confined within any boundary. Every unit in the federation play an important role in the field of education. But in the Indian context, the state government – the federal units are in requirement of funds and resources from the Centre. Thus, the concept of federal autonomy has become more complex. The constitutionally guaranteed place to education has undergone major changes because of the changing federal dynamics. The role and responsibilities of the centre have increased because of the resource crunch and regional imbalances between the states.

1. Legislative process involving education had brought numerous federal questions before the Supreme Court. For example, the Gujarat government made Gujarati to be the exclusive medium of instruction in all the universities in the state, when the subject

matter of education was under their control in the State list of the seventh schedule. But the Supreme Court had struck it down as it was beyond the legislative competence of the state.

2. There was another item in the seventh schedule, under the Union list entry 66 – coordination and determination of standards in institutions of higher learning, this item was exclusively under the purview of the Centre, and Courts decided that the State cannot override the powers of the Union, and therefore they had no competence to enact such a legislation.
3. After this Gujarat University constituted the Centre set up committee consisting of members of parliament, called as the *Sapru Committee*, to suggest steps to take greater responsibility in the field of education. The committee suggested an amendment to the Constitution, to include the University education in the concurrent list of the seventh schedule, so that Centre can take greater responsibilities in that sector. But this was heavily opposed by the states and hence the proposal could not get materialized into an amendment.
4. During the emergency the situation was different and the subject of education was taken from the State list and was added to the Concurrent list. The 42nd amendment enacted in 1976 made these changes to the Constitution. Hence, today we can see the sector of education being highly centralized and the Centre assuming greater legislative and policy making competence in this sector.
5. Therefore, today the role played by the states in the field of education has greatly reduced. And the courts too have retrained the states power to legislate in many matters concerning education. Especially the states power does not extend beyond its territory, hence they cannot go beyond their territorial jurisdiction. In the landmark case of *Prof. Yashpal and Anr v. State of Chattisgarh and others* the Supreme Court specifically considered the issue of extra territorial jurisdiction of the states and their power to grant affiliation to any institution outside its jurisdiction.
6. University Grants Commission (UGC) is the central regulatory authority on higher education. It controls, regulates makes rules and regulations of the Universities, including the state-run universities on various matters. Based on the *Yashpal case*, the UGC had asked all the state governments to bring amendment so as to conform to the Supreme Court observations, also directed the private universities not to operate beyond the territorial jurisdiction of the state. UGC clarified that any university incorporated under the State act can operate only within the territory of that particular state and in no case go beyond it.
7. The judiciary based on the concept of single all-India citizenship held that admission to colleges based on the domicile of the state is highly detrimental. There is only one domicile, domicile-in territory of India, as stated in Article 5 of the Constitution of India.

5.7.6 Judiciary on Emergency Provisions of Constitution

Supreme Court as mentioned above in the Judgement of *Minerva Mills v. Union of India* established parliamentary federal democracy as one of the 'basic structure' to the Constitution of India. And since then the courts have tilted towards the Centre in support of taking over the state government under *Article 356*. The Constitutional Courts, that is the Supreme and the High Courts, made significant contribution in upholding the autonomy and status of the responsible state governments.

1. In 1977, the ruling Congress(R) dissolved the Lok Sabha, despite having another year to run as per the 42nd amendment. The elections were held and the Congress(R) faced its worst first ever defeat since Independence.
2. The coalition, Janata Party, formed the government with overwhelming majority, this is despite the fact that regionally there were a number of states ruled by the Congress party including states such as Himachal Pradesh, Haryana, Bihar, Uttar Pradesh, Orissa, Madhya Pradesh, Punjab, Rajasthan, and West Bengal.
3. The Union Home Minister addressed a letter to the Chief Ministers of these states on 18th April 1977 to 'earnestly commending' for their consideration that they may advice their Governor to dissolve their respective state assemblies under *Article 174(2)* and seek a new, fresh mandate from the people.
4. Shanti Bhusan, the Minister of Law, Justice and Company Affairs on 22nd April 1977, said that "a clear case has been made out for the dissolution of the Assemblies in the nine Congress-ruled states and holding of fresh elections since a serious doubt has been caste on their enjoying the people's confidence, their party having been rejected in the recent Lok Sabha elections".
5. The aggrieved state governments knocked the doors of the Supreme Court seeking directions against imposition of President's rule under *Article 356*. The Supreme Court refused to intervene and question the dissolution of the governments in the Congress-ruled states.
6. In fact, it seemed that the court were supportive of such moves by the Centre. The Central government of Janata party relied on the 'non-justiciable' provision under *Article 356*, which was made so in the 42nd amendment by the Indira government (it was later made justiciable by the Janata party in the 44th amendment).
7. The Judgement of Supreme Court in the case of *State of Rajasthan and Ors v. Union of India* made a serious dent in the federal consciousness of the nation. It went against the autonomous functioning of the state and legitimized the intervention of the Centre into the affairs of the state. This judgement thus had far reaching implications which changed the view of federal setup in the country. But subsequent to this judgement, the Courts started to take lenient view and supported the legitimate rights of the states.

5.7.7 Judiciary and Article 356

In *S.R.Bommai v. Union of India*, the Supreme Court made a significant shift and upheld the federal rights of the State, and questioned the indiscriminate application of *Article 356*. It stated that *Article 356* is not immune from the purview of the judicial review and the courts can strike it down when found to be malafide or based on extraneous grounds. In the *S.R. Bommai case*, the Apex Court laid down the following conditions:

(i) *The power by Article 356 upon the President is a conditional power. It is not an absolute power. The existence of material which may comprise of or include the report(s) of the Governor is a pre-condition. The satisfaction must be formed on relevant material. The recommendations of the Sarkaria Commission with respect to the exercise of power under Article 356 do merit serious consideration at the hands of all concerned.*

(ii) *The Proclamation under Article 356(1) is not immune from judicial review. The Supreme Court or the High Court can strike down the Proclamation if it is found to be mala fide or based on wholly irrelevant or extraneous grounds.*

(iii) *Burden lies on the Government of India to prove that relevant material exist (to justify the issue of Proclamation). When called upon, the Union of India has to produce material on the basis of which action was taken. It cannot refuse to do so, if it seeks to defend the action. The Court will not go into the correctness of the material or its adequacy. Its enquiry is limited to see whether the material was relevant to the action.*

(iv) *If the Court strikes down the Proclamation, it has the power to restore the dismissed Government to office and revive and reactivate the Legislative assemble wherever it may have been dissolved or kept under suspension. In such a case, the court has the power to declare that act done, orders passed and laws made during the period of Proclamation was in frce shall remain unaffected and be treated as valid.*

(v) *The Constitution of India has created a federation but with a bias in favour of the Centre. Within the sphere allotted to the States, they are supreme.*

(vi) *Any State government which pursues unsecular policies or unsecular course of actions acts contrary to the constitutional mandate and renders itself amenable to action under Article 356.*

5.7.8 Judiciary on Role of Governor

Even before the Judgement in the Minerva case, the Supreme Court in the Raghukul Tilak case in 1979 observed that,

> *...the appointment of the Governor and his tenure at the pleasure of the President "does not make the Government of India an employer of the Governor. The Governor is the head of the State and holds a high constitutional office which carries with it important constitutional functions and duties and he cannot, therefore, even by stretching the language to a breaking point, be regarded as an employer or servant of the Government of India"*

The Supreme Court further added

> *It is impossible to hold that the Governor is under the control of the Government of India. He is not amenable to the directions of the Government of India, nor is he accountable to them from the manner in which he carries out his functions and duties. His is an independent constitutional office which is not subject to the control of the Government of India.*

The Constitutional bench of the Supreme Court in the Bihar Assembly Dissolution case (2006) held that immunity granted to the Governor under *Article 356* does not stop the court from scrutinizing the proclamation made for malafide or being ultra vires. Thus, the Court's mandate put a full stop to end the unhealthy trend of unwarranted President's rule in the states. Further the *Punchhi Commission* on Centre-State relations recommended the government to adopt the directions issued in *S.R. Bommai case* with respect to the use of *Article 356*.

5.7.9 Judiciary on Minority Status

The intervention of the Supreme Court on the minority status has also affected the Centre-State relations. In the TMA Pai judgement and other similar pronouncements the courts have complicated the question of right of minorities and their relevance within the federal structure. Till then the court had asked to consider only the minorities based on religion state wise, but after the TMA Pai case, both religious and linguistic minorities were have to be considered state wise. This did have impact in identifying and notifying minorities at the state level.

5.7.10 Conclusion

It can be seen that initially the judiciary kept itself restrained and interpreted the provisions of the law literally. Moreover, due to the conditions prevailing at the time immediately after independence it is logical to derive that the courts were tilted in favour of the Union to carry forward the spirit of nation building. And decades after independence it was found that the Union was not functioning as efficiently and it is better to leave certain powers with the states themselves, moreover it was seen that Union was encroaching the powers given to the states under the Constitution and Courts carried forward a liberal interpretation of the constitutional provisions. In numerous judgements we can see this tilt towards the right of people over the national unity and integration as put forth by the Union. In the present era there is a phenomenon called as the 'Judicial activism' which makes the courts intervene into a wide range of issues. At present the Supreme Court and other courts have become the Champion of the rights of the people rather than government.

5.8 NATIONAL SECURITY AND ITS IMPACT ON FEDERAL STRUCTURE

As per the Constitution of India, law and order is the responsibility of the state. But in reality, the Central government intervenes in maintaining the law and order in the state, moreover such problems are not limited to the boundary of such state, it goes beyond it. There are a number of internal and external causes for such issues. Thus, in these conditions the question of national security is becoming a major concern for maintaining the balance of federal dynamics between the centre and the states. Presently the traditional and autonomous areas of functioning by the states are being eroded by emerging national security laws and various other security related aspects. It is clear that national security laws are being increasingly centralized, also it is naturally inclined to think that national security is predominantly, if not absolutely, the responsibility of the centre in a federation. Major national security resources and institutions are increasingly aligned towards the centre. National security intelligence activities are also penetrating into the jurisdiction of the local federal units, which however are resisting such unilateral moves by the centre.

5.8.1 Internal and External Dimensions to National Security

There is both an internal and external dimensions to national security scenario in our country. Internally, movements such as the sons of soil movement, naxalism, and other communal and sectarian violence are posing grave threat to the unity of the nation. As per the reports of the government 203 of 600 districts in 18 states in India is under the influence of left wing radical forces. In the annual report of the Union Home Ministry 2011–12, says there were nearly 1755 incidents of left wing extremist violence extending to almost nine states. And there is also a resurgence of such extremism in the southern states.

Terrorism is also a major issue having both internal and external dimensions. The government has been employing several law enforcement measures together with various national security laws (such as National Security Act-NSA, Maintenance of Internal Security Act-MISA, Terrorist and Disruptive Activities (Prevention) Act-TADA, Armed Forces Special Powers Act-AFSPA etc.). Most of these laws have direct impact on the law and order problems in the state and thus has ramifications in the centre-state relations. The state government has very little say in execution and implementation of these acts, hence the state cannot challenge any violations or misuse made by the forces under them. For example, acts of omission or commission under the AFSPA cannot be challenged in a civilian court, unless and otherwise it has had prior approval by the centre. The AFSPA is thus a draconian act, which permits the armed forces to kill with impunity without having to answer to the courts of law. AFSPA has a long chequered history, it has been used even before independence and it is now continued to be used in some of the North-Eastern states and in Jammu and Kashmir. This act has been vehemently opposed in these states and there is a grassroot movement of people against it. It has been termed as discriminatory and is having a major effect on the relation between centre and the states.

Since independence a number of security forces has been created by the Centre, there is a huge Central Police and Armed forces, Intelligence Bureau, Central Bureau of Investigation, National Investigation Agency and a host of other forensic and training institutions to train, sustain, gather intelligence, to investigate special crimes and to maintain law and order in the states. The following Central Police and Armed forces play a significant role in maintaining law and order in the states, Central Reserve Police Force (CRPF), Rapid Action Force (RAF), Central Industrial Security Force (CISF), Indo-Tibetan Border Police (ITBP), Border Security Force (BSF), Assam Rifles, National Security Guard (NSG), Sashastra Seema Bal (SSB) etc.

Most of these forces operate at the state level, but their ultimate control lies with the centre. Though the federal concept of the Constitution envisages the law and order to be maintained by the state government, stationing of such huge armed police force who function under the direction of the Centre has unduly influenced the functioning of the states. This is the most unusual feature of the Indian Federation, where a separate, parallel police force is being maintained by the centre. The First Administrative Reform Commission, has made the following observation,

> *The Central Reserve Police and the Border Security Force are armed forces raised by the Union to meet the needs of the security if the country, both external and internal. In the circumstances, the use of the armed forces of the Union in aid of the civil power of a state is perfectly constitutional. It is also clear that such aid can be provide at the request of the state government or suo moto. The question whether such aid is needed must obviously be a matter of judgement by the centre.*

It is understood by eminent scholars that such unilateral deployment of the central forces in the states based on its own judgement violates the federal autonomy guaranteed by the Constitution. A new entry 2A – empowering Union to deploy armed forces in the State 'in aid of civil power' was added to the Union list of the Constitution by the 42nd amendment, apart from Union list, it also amended the State list entry 2, where police power of the state is now subject to entry 2A of the Union list. The states presently have come to have accepted the fact that some circumstances do warrant such deployment of the central forces, and they do need their help in maintaining the law and order situation in such cases. Moreover, the Centre and State have now devised a mechanism to effectively deploy the forces when the need arises. The states are in short of revenue, therefore maintaining a huge armed police forces has become a burden. Lack of equipment and training also adversely affect the maintenance of law and order situation in the states.

5.8.2 Anti-terror Laws in India

A number of anti-terror laws has been enacted by the Centre over the years in order to cope up with the increasing menace of terrorism. But these laws have been opposed by most of the state governments. The Terrorist and Disruptive Activities (Prevention) Act (TADA), 1985 was enacted to manage the raising anti-national activities in the states, especially in Assam and Punjab. Initially it was introduced as a temporary measure to curtail the violence and disruptions caused by the secessionist Khalistani movement. But the Union government continued the use of the act in other states also. TADA was seen as continued interference of the Union into the affairs of the state. It also enormously increased the power of the state police forces which is controlled by the state government. As per the provisions of the TADA Act, the Central government is the final authority to decide how the act is to be implemented.

5.8.3 National Investigation Agency

The Central government had set up the National Investigation Agency created by passing the National Investigation Agency Act 2009, after the horrifying Mumbai terror attacks in order to take up cases having international and inter-state implications with serious impact on the national security. The government had also thought of setting up the National Counter Terrorism Centre as recommended under the Punchhi Commission on Centre and State relations, but this has been resisted by the state governments as this NCTC encroached on the law and order, which is essentially a state subject. States have raised their voices against setting up of such commission as such unilateral on the pretext of national security erodes the power of state over maintaining the law and order in the state, which essentially comes under the ambit of duty of the state governments, moreover such action by the centre lacks accountability. The centre has taken up to set this up under the Article 355 of the Constitution which entails the Centre to protect the states against external aggression and internal disturbance. It also ensures that the states function as per the constitutional provisions. But this justification of using Article 355 does not hold water as it can only be used during the Emergency and not for everyday law and order functioning of the state governments.

National security is indeed the concern of the Union government, but it cannot act unilaterally. Any measure taken by the Centre has impact and influence on the law and order of the state. Such measures also involve stationing of the central security forces within the territory of the state, these measures cause friction between the centre and the state and this tension cannot be simply overlooked.

5.9 RE-INVENTION OF SELF-GOVERNING INSTITUTIONS AND DECENTRALIZATION

5.9.1 Introduction

The concept of local self-government has a very long history in India. Any system of governance within the country would be incomplete without the mention of the independent small village republics. During the Vedic period, the Sabhas and Samitis played a key role in the administration of the village republic. Even under the Gupta rulers the villages were important administrative units and panchayats were important local self-governing institutions. Charles Metcalfe in his famous minute of 1830, has best described the autonomous village as follows:

> *The village communities are little republics, having nearly everything they can want within themselves... They seem to last where nothing else lasts. Dynasty after dynasty tumbles down, revolution succeeds revolution... but the village community remains the same.... This union of the village communities, each one forming a separate little state in itself, has... contributed more than any other cause to the preservation of the peoples of India... and the enjoyment of .... Freedom and independence.*

5.9.2 British Era

The British started to develop the modern local self-governing institutions in India towards the end of seventeenth century, in the form urban municipal bodies. Likewise, municipal corporations were set up in the presidency town of Madras in 1688 and in Bombay and Calcutta in 1726.

1. Lord Mayo turned bodies into elected representative bodies in the 1870 resolution.
2. Lord Ripon carried forward this to the panchayat and rural localities, he created district board at district level and rural board at taluka/tehsil level under the resolution of 1882.
3. However, it was the passing of the Bengal Local Self Government Act 1885 that led to the spreading of modern self-governing institutions beyond the cities to the rural areas.
4. It led to establishment of district boards across the province of Bengal. To quote the Second Administrative Reforms Commission,

> *Within a span of five years, a large number of district boards came into existence in other parts of the country, notably Bihar, Assam and North West Province. The Minto-Morley Reforms, 1909 and the Montague Chelmsford Reforms, 1919, when Local Self Government became a transferred subject, widened the participation of the people in the governing process and, by 1924-25, district boards had a preponderance of elected representatives and a non-official Chairman.*

5. The origin of the statutory panchayats is attributed to the 1907 Royal Commission on decentralization, which in its report had suggested setting up of village panchayats for cutting down the financial burden on the provincial government and to extend the concept of local self-government to the villages. And based on this recommendation, various provincial governments enacted the Village Panchayats Act to extend the governance to the villages.

5.9.3 Panchayats – Post Independence Debate

Though this system of village panchayat has long historic tradition, it is disappointing to find that the Constitution of India made no representation for the self-governing bodies. The Constitution makers sought to project India as a giant nation, forgetting the consequences of being a giant.

1. While several attempts were made before and after independence to create and develop local self-governing political institutions, the same could not take a formal constitutional shape until the early 1990s.
2. Even before the independence Gandhi was in favour of decentralization and handing over political powers to the villages and districts.
3. Gandhiji wanted lesser power to be wielded by the Centre, and villages be granted autonomous power to govern themselves through sarpanchs and panchas, village chief and councillors. Though this idea of Gandhiji's self-governing village republics came up for debate in the Constituent Assembly, but they did not find a mention in the final draft of the Constitution.
4. Though this concept of village level self-governing institutions found support among few of the members of the Constituent Assembly, the drafting committee of the constitution deliberately avoided making any provision for local self-governing institutions.

5.9.4 Ambedkar's View on Panchayats

Dr. Ambedkar, the Chairman of the drafting committee did not find any merit in such system of governance. While moving the draft constitution for approval in the Constituent Assembly on fourth November 1948, Dr. Ambedkar spoke at length against the concept of village self-governing institutions as follows:

> *The love of the intellectual Indians for the village community is of course infinite if not pathetic.... It is largely due to the fulsome praise bestowed upon it by Metcalfe who described them as little republics having nealy everything that they want within themselves, and almost independent of any foreign relations. The existence of these village communities each one forming a separate little State in itself has according to Metcalfe contributed more than any other cause to the preservation of the people of India, through all the revolutions and changes which they have suffered, and is in a high degree conducive to their happiness and to the enjoyment of a great portion of the freedom and independence. No doubt the village communities do not care to consider what little part they have played in the affairs and the destiny of the country; and why? Their part in the destiny of the country has been well described by Metcalfe himself who says: "Dynasty after dynasty tumbles down. Revolution succeeds turn but the village communities remain the same. In times of trouble they arm and fortify themselves. A hostile army passes though the country. The village communities college their little cattle within their walls and let the army go unprovoked." .... Such is the part the village communities have played in the history of their country. Knowing this, what pride can one feel in them? That they have survive through all vicissitudes may be a fact. But mere survival has no value. The question is on what plane they have survived. Surely on a low, on a selfish level. I hold that these village republics have been the ruination of India. I am therefore surprised that those who condemn Provincialism and communalism should come forward as champions of the village. What is the village but a sink of localism, a den of ignorance, narrow-mindedness and communalism? I am glad that the Draft Constitution has disregarded the village and adopted the individual as its limit.*

1. Ambedkar was fundamentally opposed to the idea of independent village republics because he thought that it would be detrimental to the interests of the minorities and particularly to the interests of the untouchables, the Dalit community.

2. Ambedkar argued that villages were the cause of ruination of the country, empowering such villages will perpetuate the dominance of the upper castes, who would continue to dominate the downtrodden people. Autonomy to the village panchayats was also against his centralization project.
3. Ambedkar even wanted limited powers to be given to the provincial governments as he believed that such localized governments would not sincerely protect and safeguard the rights and interests of the minorities and the Dalit communities.

5.9.5 Countering Ambedkar's Views

This idea of Ambedkar drew comments from various quarters of the Constituent Assembly.

1. K. Hanumanthaiya argued that in such a vast country, it is impossible for any human or government to effectively control all the administration. Even as late as 1949, Hanumanthaiya was arguing for the effective decentralization, he also reminded the Constituent Assembly that this decentralization was the principle based on which Gandhi had wanted the Constitution to be constructed.
2. In order to defuse the situation created by Ambedkar's comment, and to air their resentment against the omission of the village panchayats, some of the members of the Constituent Assembly, including Alladi Krishnaswami Ayyar had to clarify that, although the Draft Constitution had not provided for establishment of such panchayats, the provinces had power to create such autonomous units in their states, providing them with administrative powers.
3. Subsequently, consensus emerged within the Constituent Assembly, thereby the decentralization of power and provision of village panchayat was made into the Constitution in the form of Directive Principles of State Policy.
4. Thus, panchayats only found a peripheral place in the original Constitution, among the Part IV, the Directive Principle of State Policy, and *Article 40* provides that the state shall take steps to organize village panchayats and endow them with such powers and authority as may be necessary to enable them to function as self-governing institutions.
5. The *Article 40* does not provide steps of constituting the village panchayat. Under it, the creation of panchayat as statutory institutions was left with the state legislatures. Under the seventh schedule Entry 5 list II, the State List, empowers the state legislatures to make laws with respect to local self-government or village administration.

5.9.6 Local Governance – Community Development Programmes

Only two tiers of government – Centre and State was recognised by the original Constitution post-Independence. However, the idea of local self-government was raised from time to time.

1. In compliance with the Directive Principle to establish villages as independent self-governing institutions, the Central government launched ambitious Community Development Programme in 1952 with the intention to bring socio-economic transformation of village life through people's own democratic and cooperative organisations, with the government providing technical services, supply and credit to the village bodies.
2. Participation of whole community was the key element of this experiment, and under this, 100 to 150 villages formed a community development block, to strengthen the foundation of the grass roots democracy.

3. Scientific and technical knowledge of agriculture, animal husbandry and rural craft sectors was transferred to the people by establishment of National Extension Service in 1953.
4. The second five year plan in 1956, recommended that the village panchayats should be linked with other organisations at the higher level, and in stages the democratic body should take over all the functions of general administration and development of the district excluding the functions such as law and order, administration of justice and a few functions of revenue administration. In view of this, the government of India set up a committee under the Chairmanship of Balwantrai Mehta in 1957.

5.9.7 Balwantrai Mehta Committee Recommendations

The Balwantrai Mehta committee suggested that for effective implementation of the development programmes, there should be administrative decentralization. And the local bodies should control the implementation of development programmes and also other administrative functions.

1. It recommended for further extension of the Community Development Programme and National Extension Service throughout the country, in all developmental blocks. It should be placed under an elected panchayat samiti for effective functioning.
2. The Balwantrai Mehta report recommended popular participation in the decision-making process at the local level, for that to happen, there has to be democratic decentralization of power to the sub-district level.
3. Based on this report, a three-tier panchayati-raj system was introduced in various states consisting of gram-village panchayats at the base, mandal or taluka panchayat in the middle and zila panchayat at the district level.
4. The panchayati raj was also promoted by the Union government as a matter of policy from 1957 to 1963, where the state governments were pressurized to adopt democratic decentralization and to directly involve the people at the village level in the planning process. Based on this, states of Andhra Pradesh, Rajasthan, Maharashtra, and Gujarat took legislative and administrative initiatives to set up the panchayati raj institutions.

5.9.8 Santhanam Committee Recommendations

Santhanam Committee was appointed in 1963 to solely look into the issue of the finances of the panchayati raj institutions (PRIs). It gave the following recommendations:

(i) The panchayats should have special powers to levy special tax on land revenues, home tax, etc.
(ii) A Panchayat Raj Finance Corporation should be set up which would look into the financial resources of PRIs at all three levels, provide loans and financial assistance to these grass root level government and also provide support for non-financial support of the villages.

5.9.9 Ashok Mehta Committee Recommendations

The momentum started to decrease and by mid-1960s, the support for panchayati raj system started declining as the most of the political leadership in the states were reluctant to devolve powers to the district level, they feared that if powers were devolved, these local institutions would become alternative sources of political influence and patronage, which would threaten the leadership at the top, and degrade their ability to influence and control at the grassroot level. Hence by 1970s, only the skeleton existed, the panchayats were there but without any powers or functions. And simultaneously during this period, the centralization carried out by Indira Gandhi made the panchayats completely redundant. After the controversial tenure of Indira Gandhi, the subsequent Janata government in 1977 setup a new committee on panchayati raj, under the Chairmanship of Ashok Mehta.

1. It assessed the problems faced by the panchayat system and recommended establishment of a two tier system, one at mandal and other at district level.
2. The committee chose the district to be the first point of decentralization below the State level.
3. Under its recommendation, the zilaparishad – the district boards were to be given full control over all the development activities to be carried out.
4. The law and order would remain under the control of the existing administrative apparatus.
5. The most important aspect of this committee was that it introduced taxation powers by the local bodies.
6. While submitting its report in 1978, the committee was of opinion that the rhetoric over panchayat empowerment was not of much use unless it received a Constitutional standing.

5.9.10 Other Committees

1. In 1985, the GVK Rao committee recommended that PRIs at district level and below be assigned responsibility to implement, monitor and plan the rural development programmes and the block development office should be the spinal cord of the rural development.
2. In line with the Ashok Mehta committee recommendation, the L.M. Singhvi committee in 1986 recommended that the local self-government be constitutionally recognised, protected and preserved by including a new chapter in the Constitution.
3. As per the report of the second Administrative Reform Commission,

   By end of 1982, except Meghalaya, Nagaland, Mizoram and Union territory of Lakshadweep, all other States and UTs had enacted legislation for the creation of PRIs. In 14 States/UTs there was a three-tier system, in 4 States/UTs it was a two-tier structure and in 9 States/UTs only one tier functioned.

4. Strong arguments were continued to be made for the re-organization of the Indian federation with smaller political units. The requirement for this re-organization was for greater political participation and effective democratic governance at all levels of governance.
5. Demands were also made to setup second State Reorganisation Commission. It was argued that there was much room for the states to devolve their power to the lower, district, panchayati level. It was said that failure of panchayati raj institutions can be attributed to the ineffective devolution of the powers.

6. The Sarkaria Commission set up in 1988 in its report recommended that the local self-governing bodies have to be significantly strengthened both functionally and financially. It also recommended that a Parliamentary law be enacted so that it is uniformly applicable throughout the country.

5.9.11 Constitutional Amendments

The landmark move in the process of decentralized governance came in 1989, when 64th and 65th constitutional amendment bills were introduced in the Parliament by Rajiv Gandhi, making it mandatory for all states to set up elected panchayats and urban local bodies, providing more powers and functions to the local bodies, even authorizing the panchayats to levy and collect taxes/ tolls and fees, etc. These bills were finally passed in 1993 under the stewardship of Prime Minister Narasimha Rao as 73rd and 74th Constitutional amendment, resulting in insertion of new parts Part IX and IXA, and new Articles 243 to 243ZG.

1. The 73rd and the 74th amendments created the panchayats and the urban local bodies.
2. They brought back the three-tier system of governance back, which was initially proposed by the Balwantrai Mehta committee.

5.9.12 The 73rd Amendment

The important aspect of the 73rd amendment is that it brought in Constitutional legitimacy to the panchayat raj institutions.

a. It has provided panchayats at village, intermediate and district levels, with an exception that states having population less than 20 lakh need not constitute the panchayat at the intermediate level.
b. A new Part IX has been inserted to the Constitution for legitimising the panchayats.
c. In pursuit of this, the states have to devolve administrative and financial responsibilities to the panchayats in respect to the 29 matters listed in the new inserted eleventh schedule.

5.9.13 The 74th Amendment

The urban local bodies too received constitutional recognition, as the Parliament enacted the seventy-fourth amendment in 1992, known as the Nagarpalika Act, which received the assent of the President in April 1993 and came into force in June 1993.

1. This new amendment has added a new Part IXA to the Constitution. It mentions the subject matters pertaining to the municipalities.
2. The act has provided for three kinds of municipal bodies – Municipal Corporations for larger urban areas, Municipal Councils for smaller urban areas and Nagar Panchayats for rural-urban transitional areas.
3. These amendments have special provision with respect to participation of SCs/STs and especially women in the Panchayats and Urban local bodies. Another important aspect is that it has given power to the local bodies to impose tax.

4. Apart from the three-tier structure, some new provisions have been made for the establishment of district and metropolitan committees under Articles 243 ZD and 243 ZE.
5. The job of the district planning committee is to consolidate the plans prepared by the panchayats and the urban local bodies in the district and prepare a draft plan for the district as a whole, while the metropolitan planning committee is "to prepare a draft development plan for the metropolitan area as a whole".
6. The composition of these committees is left to the state legislature.
7. Though the panchayats and the urban local bodies are directly elected by the people, they are subjected to the political control of the state through its legislative assembly.
8. Most of the panchayats continue to be treated as an agency of the state for implementation of its schemes, though it is accepted that the essential services for providing drinking water, rural sanitation, preventive health and primary education come under the panchayats legitimate core functions.

5.9.14 Devolution of Finance

In order to effectively devolve finance to the third tier, the Constitution has given additional task to Finance Commission, which is now burdened with to recommend measures to supplement resources of the third tier, including grants, which are supplementary to the devolutions by the State Finance Commission. Although the 11th and 12th Finance Commission has provided for united grants to these institutions, there is a doubt regarding their financial capacity. Hence, we can see that the PRIs exist as over-structured but under-empowered organizations, they boast to have constitutional status, but suffer from lack of effective devolution of powers, functions and finance from the state governments.

5.9.15 Other Recommendations

The National Commission for Review the Working of the Constitution, in order to address the gap between state governments and the local self-governing institutions, had recommended that a provision be made for creation of State panchayat council, with Chief Minister at its head, in line of inter-state council, created under the provision made under Article 263 of the Constitution. It further recommended that the leader of opposition be made the de facto Vice-Chairman of the council, to provide for a consensus-based approach for the development of panchayats as fully democratic, effective and responsible institutions.

5.9.16 Extension of Panchayats to Scheduled Areas

The 73rd amendment excluded the adivasi and the scheduled areas from its purview. But it was always open for the Parliament to extend to same to these areas, as per the provisions of the Article 243M(4). Bhuria committee was constituted in 1994 to formulate law for extending the provisions of the Part IX to the Scheduled areas and to suggest modifications in other acts relevant to the fifth schedule in order to further strengthen the local self-governing areas. The recommendation of this committee culminated in the enactment of the Panchayats (Extension to the Scheduled Areas) (PESA) Act 1996, which came into effect on 24th December 1996. The PESA Act has led to the extension of the panchayats act to the tribal areas of Andhra

Pradesh, Orissa, Gujarat, Chhattisgarh, Himachal Pradesh, Jharkhand, Maharashtra, Madhya Pradesh, and Rajasthan. This enables the tribal society to effectively take control of their traditional rights over natural resources.

5.9.17 Conclusion

It has been proposed for some time now that all the functions of the district be devolved to the district government, including the police, land administration and other economic and social functions associated with the district. The Ashok Mehta committee report in 1978 had considered district to be an important governing unit. In carrying forward its recommendation, the Second Administrative Reform (ARC) Commission in its report on the local governance has also recommended setting up of the District Government, with each district constituting a district council having elected representatives both from the panchayats and the urban local bodies. The ARC also recommended that the post of District Collector should be eventually abolished. In the interim period the Collector will play a dual role as head of the administration and the secretary to the DG. The observation of the ARC is as follows:

> *... there must be a single elected District Council with representatives from all rural and urban areas, that will function as a true local government for the entire district. In such a scheme, the District Council will be responsible for all the local functions, including those listed for them in the Eleventh and Twelfth Schedules. The DPC in its present form will be redundant, once a District Council comes into existence as envisaged by the Commission. Planning for the whole district- urban and rural- will become an integral part of the District Council's responsibility. The role of District Collector/DM also needs to be reviewed in the context of the District Council and the District Government.... The institution of District Collector must remain in the current form for some more time. Eventually, the District Council should have its own Chief Officer. Meanwhile, as an interim mechanism, there is a merit in utilizing the strength of the Collector's institution to empower local governments. The commission is of the considered view that a golden mean between these two positions is desirable and the District government must be empowered while fully utilizing the institutional strength of the District Collector. The Commission believes that these two objectives can be realized, by making the District Collector function as the Chief Officer of the District Council. In such a case, the Collector's appointment should be in consultation with the District Council. The District Collector-cum-the Chief Officer would have dual responsibility and would be fully accountable to the elected District Government on all local matters, and to the State government on all regulatory matters not delegated to the District government.*

5.10 FEDERAL FISCAL RELATIONS

5.10.1 Introduction

Centre state fiscal relation forms important aspect in any federation. Imbalances and disparities exist between the constituent states and this can only be removed by redistribution and reallocation of the economic and fiscal resources. Imbalance exists not just between different states but also between different tiers of government in a federation and thus the fiscal federalism helps in distribution of goods and resources to the sub-national governments so that they can be allocated as per the public consumption entailing responsibility between different levels of government. Thus, redistribution and reallocation of financial resources become important aspect of fiscal federalism. Various ways and means such as revenue sharing, specific purpose grants, general purpose grants, conditional grants, matching grants, central policies/ rules and centrally administered prices, local incidence of central expenditures, such as, central government investment, etc., help in redistribution of the resources in a federal state.

5.10.2 Role of the Centre

As far as India is concerned, the Central government play an important role, it retains the control over the economy and frames most of the fiscal rules and regulations. The Centre has more resources than it needs while the sub-national state governments have less than needed. There is always fiscal imbalance between Centre and the States and also more between the States themselves. In the Indian federal system, the states governments have very little choice in revenue raising and spending.

In the fiscal federalism the intergovernmental fiscal transfers constitute an important policy mechanism. It helps in removing the inequalities between various federating states and also to remove the fiscal mismatch between the revenue sources and expenditure needs of the constituent states. But this sharing of the fiscal resources has always been controversial in the federal system. The method of fiscal transfer to the states has always been politicized, especially the controversial use of Planning Commission in distribution of fiscal resources. The various centrally sponsored schemes and uneven distribution of centrally controlled public resources has made the matters more politicized and contentious.

5.10.3 The Finance Commission

The framers of the Constitution had anticipated the mismatch and the problems that could arise due to the presence of gap between the fiscal capacities and the needs of the states. And thus they had constituted an impartial transfer the revenue to the states from the Centre through the Finance Commission (*Article 280*).

1. The Finance Commission is an independent constitutional body. It is constituted every five years and submits its report to the President. Its basic terms of functioning are set under *Article 280* of the Constitution, which are as follows:
    - (i) Distribution between the Union and the States of the net proceeds of the taxes which are to be, or may be, divided between them under Chapter 1 Part XII of the Constitution and the allocation between the states of the respective shares of such proceeds.
    - (ii) The principles which should govern the grants in aid of the revenues of the states out of the consolidated fund of India and the sums to be paid to the states which are in need of assistance by way of grants in aid of their revenues under Article 275 of Constitution for purposes other than those specified in the provisions to clause(I) of that article.
    - (iii) The measures needed to augment the consolidated fund of the state to supplement the resources of the panchayats and municipalities in the state on the basis of the recommendations made by the Finance Commission of the state.
2. This transfer of fiscal resources from Centre to State through the Finance Commission is called as the statutory transfer.
3. It has been fixed based on a formula and cannot be deviated from it.

4. Apart from this, the Finance Commission has also to recommend the distribution of grant in aid to the states under the *Article 275*. The *Article 275* specifies special grant given to the states based on its backwardness or whether it is a hill state, and thus some states were categorized and given special status.
5. Through *Article 275* the Finance Commission gives specific grants to the individual states based on the problems faced by them, and thus the Commission meets the requirement of the special category state through these grants. The Special Category States receive relatively favourable treatment in case of federal fiscal transfer. Eleven states were categorized as special Category State by the Planning Commission. The share of such grants under Article 275 in the total Finance Commission's transfers has been between 15%–18%.
6. The twelfth Finance Commission brought in new provisions based on maintenance of forest to provide grant-in-aid to the states.
7. In this regard, the state of Uttarkhand submitted a memorandum before the thirteenth Finance Commission to review and properly evaluate its Ecosystem services (ESS) and asked for special compensatory grant based on ESS to the state.
8. The Punchhi Commission of centre-state relation also gave recommendation that an expert body has to be constituted with representatives from Centre and States on a periodic basis to determine the amount of compensation to be granted to the forest-rich states.

5.10.4 The Planning Commission

The role of Finance Commission has been undermined and reduced by providing grants under *Article 282* by the non-statutory, permanent Planning Commission and by giving loans to the states by the Centre under *Article 293* of the Constitution. Right from its inception the Planning Commission, which was not envisaged initially by the Constitution makers, started to play a dominant role in economic policies and in distribution of central resources to the States.

1. The Planning Commission had distributed larger share of the Central resources compared to the statutory transfers made by the Finance Commission up until the annual plans of 1966–69.
2. This influence of non-statutory Planning Commission created a dilemma because before the fourth plan period there was no objective criteria used by them to transfer the central funds. Apart from these, other discretionary transfers such as the budgetary transfers and the transfers by the ministries were also quite high during this period.
3. The inherent nature and functions of the Planning Commission were not federal but unitary in nature. And in the name of development the successive Planning Commissions too tended to expand and extend the authority of the Union government with total disregard to the spirit of federalism emulated in the Constitution.

5.10.5 Planning Commission and Finance Commission – A Comparison

Till recently, the Planning Commission has been controlling major share of the transfers to the states. Though the transfers were made based on the Gadgil formula, revised from time to time, the inherent objective of the Planning Commission and the Finance Commission were entirely different.

1. The statutory transfers made by the Finance Commission were largely fixed and predetermined based on distribution of net proceeds from the central taxes.
2. In 1960s, a clear-cut distinction was made between the roles and jurisdiction of Finance Commission and the Planning Commission with regard to transfer of central funds to the states.
3. All planned expenditure came under the purview of the Planning Commission, while the non-plan expenditure was disbursed by the Finance Commission to the states.
4. Apart from these, a major chunk of the federal fiscal transfers is through the ministries under their welfare schemes and programmes, the transfers are made to the states directly from the Centre.
5. After 1984, the federal fiscal transfer made by the Finance Commission year-on-year basis to the states were between 35% and 40%. The remaining share of the transfers were carried out either under the plan or discretionary powers of the centre.

5.10.6 Centralization of Economy

(a) **Under Nehru**

The Centralization of the economic policy making was carried out by Nehru through regulation and development of large scale industries, including their distribution and location. The majority of the investments were from the Centre and the most basic industries were reserved for the public sector.

1. Several constitutional amendments were carried out by Nehru to centralize the economic planning. For example, the third amendment in 1954 amended the Entry 33 of the concurrent list by adding "production of and trade in certain food stuffs and cattle fodder and raw cotton and raw jute" to the industrial products which were under the legislative jurisdiction of the states so that they could be brought under the Union's by a parliamentary enactment in 'Public Interest'.
2. The Sixth amendment in 1956 amended Article 286 to give power to the Union in order to determine the principles governing inter-state trade and commerce and also to implement the intention of the constitution makers not to allow the States to tax goods passing through its territory meant for sale or purchase in some other state or outside the country.
3. Further economic and political centralization was made by further amending the Seventh Schedule by bringing in the Seventh amendment in 1956.

(b) **Under Indira**

Indira furthered the Economic Centralization tendency of the Union by drastically nationalizing the major commercial Banks in 1969. The states virtually became satellites of the centre because of the centralized economic planning, increasing role of Planning Commission in the federal fiscal transfers and through other discretionary transfers to the states by way of centrally sponsored social and welfare schemes and policies. The states thus were totally dependent on the Centre for the funds. Apart from these, there were also other indirect transfers such as the food and fuel subsidy, schemes involving tax expenditure, etc.

5.10.7 Role of Discretionary Grants

Plan and discretionary transfer is influenced by the political consideration and bargain made by the states. Hence, when there is political consideration, it is impossible to expect the central ministers to take unbiased decisions to effectively allocate their budgetary funds to develop all regions equally. The most astounding fact is that the discretionary grant has continued to play a substantial part in the federal fiscal fund transfer. Majority of the resources needed to implement important development plans of the state's concern, such as education, health, agriculture, rural development, etc., come from the means of various central government schemes and programmes. Majority of the activities under the education and social welfare have now become central subjects. The central ministries thus play an important role in allocation of its discretionary funds to the states. The Planning Commission also play a role in allocation of the discretionary funds as it approves the plans proposed by the States. Key role in development and design of some of the centrally sponsored schemes was carried out by the Planning Commission.

5.10.8 From Planning to NITI

1. The role of Planning Commission as a decision-making body went unchallenged during the first two decades after independence as there was a single party rule across the country, thus the Planning Commission's failure to include representatives from the states went unquestioned.
2. This scenario changed when other party governments were formed in the states and when era of coalition governments started to rise in the Centre. These challenged the powers and functions of the Planning Commission, and questioned the contradicting federal aspect of the Commission.
3. The Commission was seen as a stumbling block when the government initiated the liberalising measures after the 1990's crisis.
4. Then Prime Minister Manmohan Singh tried to alter the nature and infuse new dynamism to the Commission by appointing pro-market specialists to manage the Commission.
5. The states started creating their own federal space whereby they could dictate the path of national development. This increasing role of the states pushed forth the requirement of cooperative federalism among the centre and the states and also among the states themselves.
6. In order to foster this new need, the present NDA government under Narendra Modi established a new body – NITI Aayog (National Institution of Transforming India).
7. NITI Aayog came into existence through an executive order replacing the Planning Commission. The present organisation too is under the command of the Central government and it is feared that this body too will follow the path taken by the erstwhile Planning Commission. But the performance and outcome of the NITI Aayog is not over yet to be judged.

Nevertheless the abolition of Planning Commission and establishment of NITI Aayog are expected to infuse energy towards a beginning of a new kind of fiscal federalism. There is already a recommendation made by the 14th Finance Commission to increase the state's share in the centre's new divisible tax pool to 42% from current 32%. It has also recommended to remove the distinction between plan and non-plan expenditures. Even this measure might have political implications as there is still inequality existing between various states. The centrally sponsored schemes are sought to be cut down and states duties and responsibilities are to be increased in these spheres. The NITI Aayog is set to prioritize the plan and development needs of the states individually.

5.10.9 Role of Centrally Sponsored Schemes

The States and Centre have always mulled with the idea and functioning of the centrally sponsored schemes. Time and again, the states have expressed their genuine concerns about the design and implementation of these schemes. Most of the time, these schemes are unilaterally, without getting inputs from the states, constructed and no room is given for local and regional specifities. Several committees were formed to examine various centrally sponsored schemes in view of the dissent raised by number of state leaders. Some of the leaders consider these schemes to be encroachment of their constitutionally guaranteed powers and functions. Opposing the central government's recent implementation of the Direct Benefit Transfer (DBT) scheme, which was implemented by bypassing the state governments, former Chief Minister of Tamil Nadu, Late. J. Jayalalithaa stated as follows:

> *"They insidiously seek to secure for the Government of India unnecessary influence and authority over the finances of the States".... "We are equally opposed to the direct transfer of cash to the Bank accounts of the beneficiaries by the Government of India by passing the State Governments altogether"..... "This was neither an administratively sound practice nor in keeping with the spirit of federalism..... Planning Commission had issues a series of instructions and guidelines on number of conceptual and operational issues relating to DBT with virtually no consultation with the State Governments. Once decisions were taken and the scheme was finalized unilaterally by the Centre, the States were required only to place their field machinery at the disposal of the Central Government to implement the mechanism......." Are the State Governments expected to look on as mere bystanders, far removed from the process of administering the scheme, after having placed their entire field machinery at the disposal of the Government India? This is clearly an infringement of the authority of the State Governments and totally violative of the federal polity of the country and the spirit of democratic decentralisation".*

1. The centrally sponsored schemes (CSS) have been undermining the autonomy and the fiscal powers of the state.
2. Larger expenses by the centre on the CSSs has its impact on the resources to be transferred to the states, as their availability becomes less, and hence the states suffer.
3. The smaller states are faced with other problems due to these schemes, these states are forced to allocate resources in the form of monetary and human resource. As they are already backward, these states struggle even more to implement the schemes of the centre.
4. A sub-committee appointed by the National Development Council (NDC) in 1966 recommended abolition of several centrally sponsored schemes.
5. The First Administrative Reform Commission too recommended minimizing these schemes. In, 1968 the NDC took decision so as to keep the transfers to the states outside the fixed Gadgil formula to be one-sixth of the total central assistance to the states.

6. In 1985, committee headed by K. Ramamuti recommended that the number of CSSs has to be reduced and its primary aim should be to initiate the process of change. Another high level committee in the year 1985 recommended to transfer some of the CSSs to the states. But in reality, against all these said recommendations the number of CSSs has only risen with bigger budget allocation and outlays, and in name of CSS these schemes intervened into the subject matter of the State list.
7. Accordingly, decision was taken at the Chief Ministers Conference (headed by the Prime Minister) in 1996 to transfer the funds of those CSSs which fall under the State list.
8. The CSSs have other implications too, such as when the Centre coerces the state to take part and share cost in some of the major CSSs like Sarva Siksha Abhiyan (SSA) scheme.
9. The Union government being in the dominant position and as the major funder of these schemes, dictates terms to be followed by the state governments even on matters pertaining and falling within the constitutional jurisdiction of the states.

(a) Views of Puncchi Commission – Centrally Sponsored Schemes

a. The Punchhi Commission on Centre-State relations was of the view that these CSSs tended to erode the state powers and created an unbalanced fiscal relation between the centre and the states.
b. In line with various other recommendations made by other committees, Punchhi commission recommended a comprehensive review of all fiscal transfers made to the states with a view of reducing the discretionary transfers through the centrally sponsored schemes.
c. It has also suggested that some of these schemes should be completely transferred to the states while some others in-built flexibility be incorporated so that states can individually design and implement the schemes based on their need.
d. The Commission also suggested that the additional expenditure liabilities on the states for implementing the central legislation should be borne by the central government and it should not burden the already overburdened state governments.

5.10.10 Taxation Powers

The Constitution itself provides a favourable position to the Centre with regards to the revenue and financial resource generation. The taxation powers of the centre are vast compared to that of the state. The most productive part of the taxes, the Income and Corporate tax, duties of customs and excises are assigned to the Union. The Eighty-eighth Constitutional amendment in 2003 inserted a new entry No. 92C to the Union list, giving exclusive jurisdiction to the Union government to levy taxes on services, which has now become a major source of revenue in the Economy.

The proceeds of the states taken together are less compared to that of the Union. Though the Constitution allows the Centre to retain and control major resources, it does provide for transfer and assignment of these resources to the states, some of such provisions are:

1. *Article 268*: Levied by Centre but collected and appropriated by the States.
2. *Article 269*: Levied and collected by the Centre but assigned to the States.

3. *Article 270*: taxes levied and collected by the Union, but assigned to both Union and States. Mandatory sharing through the Finance Commission.
4. *Article 275*: Statutory Grants-in-aid, based on the recommendation of the Finance Commission.
5. *Article 282*: Grants for any public purpose
6. *Article 293*: loans granted for any purpose

5.10.11 Borrowing Powers

Under *Article 292* of the Constitution the Union government has unrestricted power to borrow subject to the limits imposed by the parliament. But borrowing powers of the states are restricted under *Article 293*. This article says that the executive power of the state extends to borrowing within the territory of India and not outside. It also says that the state cannot raise a loan without the consent of the Government of India or its guarantee. Even after the economic liberalisation the Constitutional structure and nature of Centre-State fiscal federalism has not changed. Foreign funding to the state government and its projects are routed through the central ministries or through central financial institutions. Major industrial and investment policies are still under the control of the Central government, or under boards or agencies appointed by it. As per Article 301 of the Constitution, trade, commerce and intercourse throughout the territory of India shall be free, but restrictions can be imposed for 'public Interest' both by Centre and the States. Movement of commodities which play a vital role in life of common people though cannot be restricted even for such 'public interest'. Article 285 says that the property of the Union shall be exempt from all taxes imposed by the states or any other authority within the state and similarly Article 289 provided that the property and income shall be exempt from the taxation by the Union.

5.10.12 Conclusion

There are multiplicity of sub-national structures and political institutions in a federation, which undesirably affect the implementation capacity of the National governments which tries to formulate macro-economic reforms. The Indian federation is no different in this regard. As seen in the beginning, India is a giant multi-national system and many states within the system are now demanding reform in the Centre-State fiscal dynamics. The third tier – the Panchayats, which are still under the control of the state governments, have been already covered under the federal fiscal transfers. The states are now claiming their share from the National resources which till now were under the exclusive jurisdiction of the Union government. The states still look to the Centre for most of the things, but this dynamics is now changing in the era of coalition politics, the states are not just expecting but are bargaining and demanding from the Centre. And such dependence of states on the Centre eliminates the fundamental federal principles. To quote the State Reorganization Commission,

> *It is no doubt true that all the States of the Indian Union are now dependent in varying degrees on central aid for development expenditure. However, we must not lose sight of the fact that excessive dependence on the Centre detracts from the federal principle, since a real division of the political power is not possible without an adequate separation of financial powers and resources. The balance of a federal union is bound to be disturbed, if there are among its constituent unit's poor relations or mendicants, particularly if they are inclined to be extravagant.*

Thus in such scenario, shift towards Centralization is inevitable if a nation and its macro-economic status has to progress. Effective federal fiscal and macro-economic management can be carried out by a unitary federal system. It can also generate several prospects for de-centralization also.

5.11 CONCLUSION

5.11.1 What is a Federation?

It is important to highlight the fact that Constitution of India does not define what 'federalism' is. During the Constituent Assembly debates, the terms 'federal' and 'federation' were very much discussed but they did not find favour to be included in the final draft of the Constitution of India. Instead, the Constitution declares India to be a Union. During the final stage of the Constituent Assembly debates, the drafting committee deliberately tried to avoid the usage of the words 'federal' or 'federation' in the Constitution.

5.11.2 Need for a Strong Centre

A strong centralized government has gathered forces and has brought a sense of unity and created a feeling of nationality among the people. Support has been there for a strong Centre in the federation, which can be seen from the debates and discussions in support of strong centre in the constituent assembly. G.N. Joshi, in 1937 much before the constituent assembly started its debates, he argued as follows:

> *Having regard to the political problems of India, the composition of her population, her economic requirements, and the danger of provincial patriotism intensified by communal feeling running amok, effective solutions of her vital problems are only possible if they are attempted on an all India scale.*

Such a feeling is even present now among some of the contemporary political scientists in India. Only at a political level, the political parties, and state political leaders are demanding for better federalized structure and are raising voice against the centralization moves by the Union government. These pressures have resulted in gradual move towards decentralization.

5.11.3 Federalism in the Constitution

The Constitution of India tried to project India as a unified whole. Even though it contains several unfederal features, India is still considered to be a federal country. Several federal features have been incorporated into the Constitution, such as devolution of powers. Unlike the standard federal setup, the Indian constituent federal setup did not willingly join the continental structure. Forceful arguments were made for federalism during the initial years as there was difference in culture, social conditions and even history among the constituent states. But today 'federalism' is being held as one of the basic features of the Constitution.

1. The Constitution of India has recognised and acknowledged asymmetries existing between various states in the federation.
2. The representation of the states in the central legislature, that is the Parliament is highly asymmetrical in nature.

3. The seats reserved for the MPs from each states varies according to its size and population of the states.
4. It is not understood why asymmetrical pattern of representation based on population which was followed in the Lower house – Lok Sabha of the Parliament got replicated in the Upper house – Rajya Sabha also.
5. Considering the Centre-State federal fiscal relation, there exists a wide gap between the constituent states.
6. There is also a preference for more centralized or unionized fiscal system as the tax structure is largely controlled by the Central government.
7. There is mismatch in the pattern, growth and development of different units of the federation.
8. The developments of the constituent units are now increasingly tied to the central government.
9. Apart from these, the Constitution itself has provided explicit asymmetric federal provisions for the state of Jammu and Kashmir, North Eastern States and some other tribal states and regions. These provisions have been laid down in the Articles 370 and 371 and fifth and Sixth schedules of the Constitution. Also Article 275 has laid the foundation for categorization of some of the states as 'special category' states.

5.11.4 Constitutional Powers to the Centre

The Constitution has empowered the Centre to create new constituent states, change areas and nomenclature of existing states. Thus, territorial integrity is not protected by the Constitution. This is a major deviation from the fundamental federal principles. The constituent states are trying and re-trying to define the powers and functions on their own, including demand for more autonomy. Since independence, the Indian federation has undergone number of reorganisation and changes in its boundaries. There are still more demands for reorganisation and creation of more states. Intellectually demands are also being made for smaller constituent states for better administration of Indian federation.

5.11.5 Theory of Federalism

Coming to the theoretical aspect of the Indian federalism, it is presumed that the main issue involved is distribution of powers and functions between different organs of the government and distribution of functions and powers between different constituent state governments. While talking about federalism, we generally tend to link federalism with functional and territorial aspects. We tend to ignore other non-territorial aspects and other socio-cultural norms, including community participation and representation which tend to govern these relationships. Territorial federalism and power distribution had resolved the initial conflict facing the Indian federation-issues based on ethnicity and language. Of late contemporary issues including issues of non-territorial communities, such that of religious, caste and other cultural issues, have become important to maintain the political stability.

5.11.6 Indian Model of Federalism

1. In many academic discussions, it is argued that India has its own model of federalism-with its own unique features.

2. Federalism in India is significantly different from other existing models practiced elsewhere.
3. They are marked by certain distinct features. Unlike any other federations, there exists a centralized power setup which determines the powers and functions of the territorial and non-territorial units within its ambit.
4. The centre-state relation and the political power distribution are centrally controlled.
5. This is against the basic tenet of concept of federalism. In recent times when the constituent states are demanding more power and autonomy, we can see the growth of power of the centralized power structure, which is becoming more dominant.
6. However, when the central government is trying to take some of the important roles and functions of the state governments, the emergence of the coalition governments has bulldozed some of the constitutionally guaranteed powers of the central government over the states.
7. The distressing fact of emergence of the coalition politics is that it has led to development of some blackmail-type bargaining in centre-state federal relations.
8. As far as India is concerned, federalism means a dynamic process of maintaining vertical relations between the constitutionally powerful federal government and the constituent state governments.
9. Federalism has a long historic tradition in India and it has also undergone numerous changes.
10. In the post-independent era the political leaders have played a decisive role in shaping and re-shaping of Indian federalism.
11. Apart from them, the State Governors and the Constitutional Courts have played important role in shaping and re-shaping of the federalism.
12. Effort was made in 1990s to constitutionally recognise the third tire of the Indian federalism, this reinvention of Indian federalism did not alter much of the basic centralized structure and these institutions are yet to become effective governing bodies on their own.

5.11.7 Features of Federalism

It should be understood that federalism is a dynamic process in its relations and power sharing among arrangements among the constituent states. It has been argued that the success and the stability of the federation is based on how it is allowed to work.

1. The political leaders play a key role in maintaining this dynamic federal relationship between the constituent units.
2. In a federation it is important to maintain the balance between relations of centre and the constituent state units.
3. Any move towards over-centralization will break down the federation.
4. A strong and united India is always welcome, but for that to happen the constituent states have to be strong and resilient, which then can create a strong and united India.
5. Power sharing among the federal constituent units is very essential for sustaining and maintaining the democracy in deeply divided societies such as India.

5.11.8 Reorganisation of States

As already stated before, since independence the reorganisation of the state boundaries and territories are regular features. Time-to-time, new states have been created through the process of reorganisation, and hence there are now demands for more states based on regional tribal identities. Intellectually arguments have been put forth that smaller states would be easier to manage in Indian context. In fact, in reality some of the states are too large to manage or govern effectively. It is perhaps now the right time to constitute a second state reorganisation commission to look into the rationale behind demands of such states and consider the importance of size, population and cultural settings of the people. There is now also the need to devolve the power to the districts in order to strengthen the grassroots level governance.

5.11.9 Role Played by the Regional Parties

The centre-state relation dynamics has undergone change because of the growing role of regional parties and their participation in the coalition governments. This growth has led to informal re-federalization of the Indian political system.

1. This kind of federalism is tending to undermine the national development perspective.
2. On the other hand, as the country in fast developing in terms of industry and capital the concept of federalism is losing its significance.
3. Nonetheless, the constituent federal units are trying to re-enforce the concept of dynamic federalism in order to protect their power, authority and functional autonomy.
4. The role and power of the Central government were enhanced by extra constitutional bodies such as the Planning Commission (now reconstituted as NITI Aayog), but presently extra-constitutional features such as the coalition regimes are undermining the power of the Centre and the states are trying to enforce their will.

5.11.10 Steps to be Taken by the Centre

It is perhaps time that centre relieves its responsibility for each and every aspect concerning the country.

1. It must restrict its responsibility to limited subjects concerning national importance.
2. It must stop relying on the states to implement its policies and programmes. It must implement them using its own resources, infrastructures and offices.
3. It can even liaison with the district governments directly for implementation of such programmes.
4. For subjects under the purview of the state governments, the centre should ask the people to seek out to the state government they have elected for their implementation.
5. If the state governments could not guarantee and fulfil its public duty obligation to its citizens, the centre may coerce it to act and in extreme circumstances may take over the administration of the states for a temporary period.
6. In brief it can be stated that federation is anti-thesis to the concept of nation-state; but nonetheless it plays a key role in nation development.

7. Though Union of India is the basis of our national identity, it must be accepted that the strength and stability of the Union depends on the strength and capacity of the constituent states to develop and grow on their own.
8. The central government must not distraught the powers and functions given to the constituent state units.

5.11.11 Contemporary Status of Federalism

It is a known fact that India has voluntarily federalized itself to accommodate both territorial and non-territorial interests within the framework of broader power sharing arrangements and through recognition of linguistic and cultural autonomies of the constituent state concerned.

1. The independent India is undergoing a federalizing process and through this the federal diversity is also increasing.
2. In order to govern the vast diversified people divided historically, culturally, ethnically, etc. led to establishment of the federal structure in order to help them govern themselves.
3. The republic of India is thus a federation; but it has many distinctive features which essentially modifies these federal features.
4. In India the federation was created paradoxically to contain the divisive forces. Since independence several states have been added by modifying and rearranging the boundaries of the existing states.
5. There is growing demand for further creation of smaller states and their reorganisation.
6. Number of communities based on caste, religious and other cultural identities are demanding legitimate space of their own within the federal system in form of cultural autonomy.
7. In such a scenario, the nature of federal dynamics is changing rapidly.
8. The raise of coalition politics has also given boost to new dynamics in the federal debate in India. Today, every policy and programme of the central government, including development and welfare measures in some of the most important sectors such as- education, agriculture, rural development, health, etc. are directly linked to the emerging federal relations.
9. Apart from these, emerging security concerns in areas such as terrorism and naxalism have also given a new push to the federal dynamics in the country.
10. Additionally, in order to address diverse demands made by the constituent states, the Indian State has resorted to numerous asymmetrical and special federal arrangements, including that of asymmetric fiscal federal measures.
11. In short, the Independent India started with a unitary federal state with strong unifying tendency.
12. The Constitution was also highly centralized. Though the Constitution was in favour of a strong central government, it did have several provisions for maintaining the federal character of the state.
13. As time passed, the independent India underwent federalizing process, it recognised the regional federal diversity, ethnic diversity, linguistic and other cultural diversities.

14. This federalization process contained both unionizing and regionalizing features, which were expected to provide stability to the federal union and thus consolidate India as a federal state.
15. The Constitution guarantees enough powers to the state governments to protect interests and identities of various territorial and non-territorial minority communities.
16. It may be still be argued that India is still a multi-national state; but it is strongly moving towards a nation-state system.
17. People and the states are looking towards the one government that is the National government.
18. And even Centre government is playing a dominant role in every aspect possible. But as the states are demanding the centre should recuse itself from all activities and provide enough autonomy and powers to the states to take decisions on their own.
19. The Centre should also stop relying on the states for implementation of its policies and programmes.
20. It should intervene directly and reach people at the ground level through its own officers or with help of the district administration.
21. This will help in doing away with the negative role played by some of the state leaders and parties.
22. Perhaps time has now come to realize that districts are the constituent units of governance.
23. Constitution may itself delegate powers and functions at district level and create a mechanism to elect a representative, democratic, responsible government at district level.

Finally, it is important to understand that any demand for strong federalizing features will not in turn create a stable political governance system. Political leadership has a crucial role to play in the changing federal dynamics. What needed is not just a federal political leadership to understand the dynamic underlying federal relations. Thus, the federalism in India is a dynamic process based on needs and aspirations of a diversified population.

Following findings and observations can be derived from the above study:

1. Since ancient times, federalism has reminded an important instrument for political organisation in the country. Centralized states have been formed by alliances and counter-alliances of the kings and emperors during the medieval and ancient period. There existed several autonomous and semi-autonomous provinces having a limited sovereignty. In fact, some of the masterful personalities of ancient India controlled vast empires consisting of several smaller feudatory kingdoms. The emperor who had captured the kingdoms always treated them to be as subordinate alliance by the local ruler and king; but he respected the local laws and customs and never tried to introduce his principles in those territories ruled by him. In course of this, we have to acknowledge that the kingdoms in ancient India never joined together or united under one single ruler or system to form a strong unitary state nor was there any effective federal structure.
2. The local self-governing institutions and the village republics played a crucial role in the political organisation of people in ancient India.
3. While kingdoms in ancient India never came together to form a strong military state or a pure federal system, it has been established that all successful empires in that

time was highly centralized. This centralization became distinct during the medieval period. It has to be noted that strong centralizing tendencies of the ancient empires was followed by simultaneous devolution of powers that is by providing regional and provincial autonomy. Though the personality of the emperor held together the empire together, he had to give some kind of recognition to the regional kingdoms and autonomous states from time to time. There did exist a number of such autonomous provinces within the centralized structure and the rulers of these states did enjoy varying degree of power and autonomy.

4. The British tried to rule the country as a unitary system; but even they introduced several measures for administrative decentralisation and paved way for formal decentralisation of the federal system by enacting the Government of India Act 1935. Thus credit has to be given to the British for the emergence and growth of federal idea in modern India. The role played by the British brought in several territorial and non-territorial units of the Indian federation. In order to suit their vested interests the British even recognised and accommodated the princes, the minorities, the depressed classes and various other functional communities. They made systemic efforts for representation of these communities in the legislative and the public bodies.
5. The federal structure underwent a change by the enacting of the Government of India Act 1919, popularly known as the Montagu Chelmsford reforms. It marked the beginning of emergence of federalism in the country as it had clear cut provisions of separation of revenue heads between the centre and the provinces. It introduced the concept of 'diarchy' for sharing the sovereignty at the provincial level; it transferred many subjects to the Indian ministers answerable to the provincial government and rest other subjects were under the consideration of the provincial Governor's discretionary power. These reforms also provided for a representative bicameral legislature at the centre, a council of state and central legislative assembly; and a consulting and advisory body of chamber of Princes. For the first time ever the Provincial legislatures were given legal and financial authority over important subject 'heads' like health, education, irrigation, public works, agriculture etc.
6. In the history of development of federalism in the country, the Government of India Act 1935 remains a landmark instrument. The Government of India Act 1935 not only served as the governing instrument till the Independence, it also served as a reference for the members of the constituent assembly. If this Act had not been enacted, it would have been difficult for the members of the constituent assembly to frame the Constitution of India within the time they had taken to do it. Almost every provision present in the Constitution of India finds a mention in the Government of India Act, 1935 either directly or indirectly. The Constituent Assembly simply modified or changed the most of the existing provisions present in the 1935 act and adopted what suited them. They were thus not required to introduce any major fresh subjects.
7. The existence and presence of large number of princely states was a unique problem faced by the Indian federation which had no parallel anywhere. Their merger and integration with the Union of India within a short span after the independence was a unique exceptional achievement.

8. Initially the Constituent Assembly started with a very positive spirit to draft a federal constitution for India and also envisioned that India is a federation of states. However, right after the independence and the scenario that existed during the partition made the Constituent Assembly to think in the other extreme and it in fact decided to create a strong centralized structure. In the end, the Constituent Assembly even avoided the use of words 'federal' or 'federation' in the Constitution and supported for a strong Union. The Constitution of Independent India was biased towards the centre. The consociational provisions as provided in the Government of India Act, 1935 for the minorities, depressed classes were taken away by the Constituent Assembly. But certain special concessions to the SCs and STs (to some extent the Anglo Indians) were allowed to continue.
9. The territorial integrity and unity of the constituent states have not been recognized by the Constitution of India. Since the time of independence several state reorganisations have taken place. As per the Article 3 of the Constitution, the Centre has not only created several new states, but have also altered boundaries, changed names etc. of the existing states. The reorganisation of the states is still a burning issue as still now there are demands for autonomy.
10. The constituent states in the federation vary in terms of size and population. Apart from this there is significant difference in terms of economic growth and levels of economic development between the constituent states. In the Indian political setup the larger states enjoy much more dominant power and status. All these asymmetries existing between the states will impact on inter-state concord and discord and it fill further reinforce state wise son of the soil movement. Asymmetrical features present in the Constitution for representation of the states in the Parliament have led to major imbalances in the power structure of larger and smaller states. In order to mitigate this imbalance in power and socio-economic backwardness of the smaller states, some asymmetric provisions have also been incorporated into the Constitution. It has had a negative effect as some of these provisions have further reinforced the asymmetry and thus making it difficult to manage the political process.
11. In the future the reorganisation of the states is going to be still a major concern for the Indian federation. The delimitation of the electoral constituencies (which was freezed till 2016 by the eighty-fourth Constitutional Amendment) is likely to open new problems as this will have a significant impact on the representation of the states in the Parliament. Based on population proportionality the northern states having larger population will walk away with more seats in the parliament compared to other states which have effectively implemented population control measures. This is likely to create problem among the states which might lead to further reorganisation.
12. In order to deal with several asymmetrical aspects and to provide effective governance, it is perhaps time to realize the need to make further reorganisation of the states and create new smaller states. It is indeed time to fix the minimum and maximum size of the states in terms of its population and size. The bigger states may be divided so as to fit the maximum size provided. This may not be as easy, thus there is now a requirement for a new state reorganization commission for effectively dealing with the issue. This reorganisation has to happen with the involvement of several experts and other representative members to be present in the commission.

13. In the Parliament of India, the Lok Sabha has a differential representation of members based on population of each state, hence there is no logic behind using the same formula for the representation of the upper house that is Rajya Sabha also. Such kind of similar proportionate representation for the both houses for the constituent state was in fact questioned in the constituent assembly, and thus the composition of the states in the Parliament especially Rajya Sabha is a subject matter of debate for a long time. The smaller states did have concerns regarding such composition in the Rajya Sabha as it was favouring the larger states having larger population, thus these larger states can impose a legislation on large number of the smaller states even without their consent or support. The Rajya Sabha being the house of states and accordingly the Rajamannar Committee in 1971 recommended for equal representation of states in it. This issue of equal representation was raised before the Sarkaria Commission on centre-state relations. The Punchhi commission on centre-state relations went a step further are recommended that relevant provisions should be amended so as to provide equal representation of states irrespective of their population size. It also suggested that the Section 3 of the Representation of the People's Act be placed back to its original position before its amendment in 2003 and thus representatives of the state in RajyaSabha should again be linked to the territory of the concerned states.
14. The centre-state as well as the interstate conflict resolution mechanism is not very well developed. The Rajamannar Commission, the Sarkaria Commission, the National Commission on Review of Working of the Constitution, the Punchhi Commission etc. all suggested for a stronger role for the inter-state council. In fact, inter-state council was established by the V.P. Singh government, but it was kept in deep freeze. No proper role and function has been allocated to the inter-state council. As far as inter-state river waters are concerned, the inter-state river water tribunals have failed to resolve such issues within reasonable time. Such disputes have continued for a long time and the procedure behind the Water Disputes Act has remained a lengthy one. Even the interference of the Courts in such matters have not made any significant changes to resolve these issues. Hence there is pertaining need to bring proper and effective legislation concerning the inter-state sharing of river water and restructuring of the role of the tribunals in such matters.
15. There is now urgent need for a balanced and equal growth and development among different zones of the country such measures will strengthen the 'Union' on India against any fissiparous tendency.
16. The extra-constitutional role played by the political parties and their leaders have significantly changed the dynamics of federalism in the post-independent India. A perusal of federalism in the post-independent India shows that Indian federalism has experienced three different phases of centre-state federal setup. First, during the first two decades after independence, most particularly under Nehru and Shashtri, the federal relation was marked by centralized but cooperative federalism between the centre and the states. The relations were centralized from the perspective of the economic planning and national development. As far as the political relations were concerned Nehru maintained a balanced and coordinated federal relationship. Nehru with strong support from the Congress party defended the strong centre in order to maintain the national unity and integrity. The single party dominance by the Congress party during

the first two decades played an important role in centralizing all the important economic and government activities.

17. The second phase starts after Nehru, significantly after the 4th general elections in 1967. Indira Gandhi changed the cooperative federalism of the Nehru-Shashtri era to coercive federalism. The centre state relation was highly reactionary to each other. The coercive federalism of Indira was seen by over centralization of both political and economic spheres. The centre virtually ruled over all the states. Even the Janata government formed after over throwing the Indira government did nothing to reverse this trend. Rajiv Gandhi though initially tried to be cooperative with the states ultimately tried to revive his mother's centralized and authoritarian mode of taking decisions. The coercive and over centralized phase of the centre-state federal relations continued till 1989 when the emergence of coalition politics virtually changed the federal dynamics.
18. The second phase of the centre-state federal relation started after the strong role played by Kamaraj-led Congress syndicate's influence of the state leaders of the Congress party. This syndicate later turned out to be a spoiler for Indira and was in fact responsible for her over centralization measures and the subsequent proclamation of emergency. The states by mid-1960s started to challenge the centre, and after the 1967 elections the domination of the Congress party in strategically important states got eliminated and non-Congress took up the power in these states, thus strengthening the regional voice. The Congress party got trounced in several state and coalition of regional parties or national party with regional parties support formed the government. This signalled the weakening of the centre and the strengthening of the clout of the states. This is described as the adulthood of the Indian states within the Indian federal structure. Apart from challenging the dominance of the Congress party these non-Congress ruled states started demanding structural changes be made to the Indian federalism. Indira's centralization move virtually defeated the adulthood of the Indian federalism.
19. The third phase marked with cooperation and confrontation between the centre and the states due the emergence of coalition politics. The centre-state relations became a kind of federal bargain between the centre and the states, if the bargain resulted in favour of cooperation both the centre and state cooperated, in case otherwise they confronted each other. A perennial kind of era in coalition politics has given power to some of the leaders of the states who have become powerful and have influenced the bargain in favour of their own state and party. Even the central government started to bargain in order to have its own political sustenance. Unfortunately, the federal structure has served as the breeding ground for uneven development as the regional political groups have started to exert pressure on the central government to work on their interests, thus marginalizing the reforms to be carried forward by the centre. These kinds of bargain has weakened the ability of the central government to carry forth strong economic and political reforms.
20. The emergence of coalition politics and the role played by the judiciary has reduced the misuse of the office of the Governor and the controversial use of President's Rule in the states. In the present political scenario it can be easily inferred that constitutionally Indian federalism still remains centralized in nature but practically it has

turned out to be decentralized one. Within Indian federalism there is shift in balance of centre-state relation in favour of the states.

21. As far as the fiscal federalism is considered the centre still plays a dominant role. The extra constitutional role played by the Planning Commission in discretionary allocation of the funds and other discretionary fiscal transfers in the form of centrally sponsored schemes and welfare policies and other budgetary support undermined the growth of true federal spirit.
22. There are plethora of centrally sponsored schemes (CSSs) and in particular the manner in which such schemes are designed and implemented has greatly undermined the authority of the states concerned. Almost all the CSSs are designed by the central government without the consultation with the state governments and it does not give due recognition to the regional and local specificities for such schemes. Importantly, in some on the major centrally sponsored scheme involving huge funds, the states have been coerced to share the financial burden. Many state political leaders consider the same to be an encroachment upon their federally allocated jurisdiction.
23. Time has indeed come for the need to review and reframe the various centrally sponsored schemes and policies of the central government. If the subject matter they deal with fall under the purview of the State list, then such schemes have to be transferred to the states for its administration and implementation. Even if the schemes of the centre has to be administered by the states, they have be consulted and involved in the design and development of such schemes and policies. Any such centrally sponsored schemes has to be fully funded by the centre without financially burdening the state government. States may also be provided with scope of additional revenue generation by implementing various welfare schemes of their own.
24. In order to avoid controversy with regard to implementation of various CSSs and other direct benefit transfer schemes, the central government may use its own resources and offices, administrative infrastructure, and thus directly deal with the concerned people and avoid using the resources and machineries of the states.
25. Districts have traditionally remained the units of administration and governance. It is perhaps time to realize its importance, effectiveness and recognize the elected district governments. The idea of elected district government can be enhanced and implemented as part of already existing constitutionally provision giving power to local self-governance.

6

Citizen's Participation in Governance

LEARNING OBJECTIVES

In this Chapter, you will learn about:

- Civil Society
- People's Participation
- Why Citizen's Participation Has to Be Strengthened
- Theories of Management Related to Good Governance Linking Public Participation
- Contextualizing People's Participation
- Use of Tools for People's Participation
- Relationship Between People's Participation and Good Governance
- Models of Good Governance on the Basis of Participation Levels
- Effective Participation for Good Governance
- Citizen and Administration: An Accountability Perspective

"*Success of democracy is impossible without participation of the people*".

—Hon'ble Prime Minister Shri Narendra Modi

As per the UN World Public Sector Report (2008), citizen participation implies the involvement of citizens in a wide range of policymaking activities, which includes the determination of levels of service, budget priorities and the acceptability of physical construction projects in order to orient government programs towards community needs, build public support and encourage a sense of cohesiveness within neighbourhoods.

The working definition for citizen engagement as per the United Nations Public Administration Country Studies (UNPACS) is:

> *Citizen engagement in public administration implies the involvement of citizens in decision-making process of the State—through measures and/or institutional arrangements—so as to increase their influence of public policies and programmes ensuring a more positive impact on their social and economic lives.*

6.1 CIVIL SOCIETY

The World Bank in its report defines civil society as follows:

> *Civil society refers to the wide array of non-governmental and not-for-profit organizations that have a presence in public life, expressing the interests and values of their members or others, based on ethical, cultural, political, scientific, religious or philanthropic considerations. Civil Society Organizations (CSOs) therefore refer to a wide of array of organizations: community groups, non-governmental organizations (NGOs), labour unions, indigenous groups, charitable organizations, faith-based organizations, professional associations, and foundations.*

The term *civil society* has come to enjoy political, intellectual and administrative importance in the recent years. But the concept has been in existence for a long time. Traditionally the terms civil society and state have been used interchangeably, and treated as synonyms.

Hegel was the first philosopher to separate civil society and the State, and this was followed by a number of other scholars.

6.1.1 Definitions of Civil Society

The following are the various definitions given to the civil society; from this we can come to understand the concept and principle behind establishment and existence of the civil society.

The *Concise Oxford Dictionary of Politics* defined civil society as *the set of intermediate associations which are neither the state nor the (extended) family; civil society therefore includes voluntary associations and firms and other corporate bodies.*

The definition for civil society as given by various scholars is as follows:

> *The realm of spontaneously created social structures separate from the state that underlie democratic political institutions.*
>
> —Fukuyama (1995:8)

> *[c]ivil society is broadly regarded as the domain of relationships which falls between the private realm of the family on the one hand and the state on the other*
>
> (Dunn 1996:27).

> Charles Taylor defined civil society as *a web of autonomous associations independent of the state, which bind citizens together in matters of common concern, and by their existence or actions could have an effect on public policy*
>
> (Kligman 1990:420).

> Schmitter defined civil society as [*a*] *set or system of self-organized intermediary groups*
>
> (Schmitter 1995:1).

> Civil society is *the social relationships which involve the voluntary association and participation of individuals acting in their private capacities. In a simple and simplistic formula, civil society can be said to equal the milieu of private contractual relationships*
>
> (Tester 1992:8).

According to Andrew Heywood, civil society refers to *a realm of associations, business, interest groups, classes, families and so on.*

According to Jan Aart Scholte, *civil society can be understood to be a political space where voluntary associations deliberately seek to shape the rules that govern aspects of social life.*

6.1.2 Features of Civil Society

The following are the features of Civil Society:

1. It refers to an organised form of society.
2. It covers a large space in the society.
3. Even though it is an autonomous entity, it is still subject to control by the state.
4. It is in pursuit of common good of the people.
5. It helps in the formulation of public opinion and sets up demand which are general in nature.
6. It is an advocate of pluralism in order to reduce the domination of the state.
7. It serves as a moral compass in the community value system.
8. It is a non-state institution.
9. Its existence implies that there is freedom of expression, freedom of thought and other fundamental rights of the people.
10. It is in opposition to authoritarianism and totalitarianism.
11. By educating the people, it promotes citizenship.
12. It covers all the intermediary groups which is present between the state and the family.
13. It facilitates participation of the citizens in administrative matters.
14. It does not coerce, rather it encourages voluntarism.

The current positive thinking is civil society is an arena of freedom which correctly identifies its basic value as a condition for democracy; there can be no effective citizens where there is no democracy, the capacity of the citizens to choose their identities, duties, entitlements within the legal-politico framework is not possible without the development and role played by the civil society in a democracy.

Public organisation is a necessary requirement in a liberal democracy, and for developing such values and norms, the role played by civil society is essential. Larger interests of the population, common civic ends can only be achieved through existence of a vibrant civil society.

6.1.3 Components

The following organisations and groups are included under the ambit of civil society:

- Community- based organisations
- Cooperative societies
- Youth groups
- Farmers organisations
- Religious associations
- Trade unions
- Non-governmental organisations

- Indigenous people's organisations
- Women's groups
- Other similar organised groups in the society

In countries like the United States, civil societies are well established, while in developing countries like India, it is still under-developed. It can be understood by the case in India that, here the civil society groups in opposition to the government are well developed, but civil society as an associational group representing interests of wide segments of the society is not fully functional yet.

In India, the civil society groups are apart from voluntary associations, seen as fluid associations of social groupings based on caste, kinship, religious ties, etc.

The civil society organisation in India can be classified into the following five categories:

1. Religious associations such as Deobandi movement, Sikh Khalsa groups, Ramakrishna mission, other Church missionaries, etc.
2. Membership associations of various types, such as,
   - Professional associations (viz., lawyers, doctors, etc.).
   - Self-help groups (viz., ward committees, women's organised self-help groups and community-based organisations in the villages, etc.).
   - Representational institutions (viz., farmers organisation, trade unions, etc.)
   - Sociocultural groups based on sports, other recreational activities, etc.
3. Social movements of different kinds, such as,
   - Movements to reform particular social evils (e.g., dowry, alcoholism, etc.).
   - Movements focussing on process of governance (e.g., anti-corruption campaign, civil liberties movement etc.).
   - Movements focusing on need of particular vulnerable groups (viz., women, tribal groups etc.)
   - Movements of protest against disruptions and displacement due to developmental activities.
4. Intermediary associations of various kinds, such as:
   - Philanthropic groups (e.g., Child Relief and You [CRY], GATE foundation, and other associations, etc.
   - Mobilisation-based groups which help to fight for and mobilise the marginalised groups in the society.
   - Service delivery groups (viz., schools, old age homes, etc.).
   - Advocacy groups which give voice for particular cause.
   - Other networks, which extend the collective voice of the people.
   - Supportive groups, which provide support to the community-based groups in the society.
5. Traditional associations formed based on caste, tribe and ethnicity.

6.1.4 Role

The civil society organisations play a very important role in the welfare and development of people in the society. The various dimensions of their role are as follows:

1. They help in the facilitation of people's participation in governance.
2. They help the administration by identifying the target groups.

3. They help create political consciousness among the people by discussing various political issues with them.
4. They help strengthen the principle of self-help.
5. They act as the watchdog of public interest.
6. They make the administrative machinery more responsible and responsive to the needs and aspirations of the people.
7. They mobilise and organise the poor for the purpose of socioeconomic development.
8. They help in identifying and using the local resources for the purpose of development and thereby make the communities self-reliant.
9. They disseminate information and help make people aware of the various schemes, programs, and activities, developed by the government for their welfare.
10. They try to reduce the scope of corruption, by imposing a community system of accountability on the administration at lower levels.

It must be said here that the role of voluntary agencies is not to compete with the government, rather complement its activities.

Apart from this, the advantages of involving voluntary agencies in the development process is as follows:

- It creates a sense of solidarity among the people;
- It gives opportunity for the governing agencies to interact with the people directly for implementation of the development goals and
- It strives for participation in decision-making process.

The voluntary agencies also have other advantages over the governmental bodies. They are as follows:

1. They can have better rapport with the local people than that by the government officials;
2. They can be very flexible and act in such a manner as they are not bound by rigid bureaucratic rules, regulations and procedures;
3. The volunteers involved are more sincere and dedicated to the task of reducing the sufferings of the poor than the governmental staffs;
4. They can motivate the public to participate more effectively than the governmental agencies; and
5. The efforts carried out by such agencies are more economical than that of the governmental bodies.

6.1.5 Limitations

Though there are numerous advantages of the civil society, they do suffer from a number are limitations as follows:

1. Interference and involvement of the political parties.
2. Lack of qualified and trained professionals.
3. Presence of diverse socioeconomic environment in the country, such as casteism, poverty, communalism, etc.
4. Noncooperation and even resistance by the bureaucrats.
5. No holistic perspective, rather they have a limited narrow perspective.

6. They do not have sufficient financial resources.
7. They lack adequate and proper information base.
8. The resistance offered by local landlords, moneylenders, etc.

Assessing both the merits and other disadvantages of the voluntary sector, the World Development Report in 1997 gave the following observation: *The voluntary sector not only brings its own strengths to the table, but also its own weakness. It does a lot of good work in increasing public awareness, voicing citizens' concerns, and delivering services. Local self-help organisations are sometimes the preferred providers of local public goods and services, because of their closeness to local concerns. But their concern is often for certain religious or ethnic groups and not the society as a whole. Their accountability is limited and their resources are often constrained.*

6.2 PEOPLE'S PARTICIPATION

People's participation implies the participation of people in the administrative process. It means that citizens' control over the administration or the influence of the public on the machinery of administration. This is essential for smooth and effective functioning of the administration. It makes the administration more responsive to the needs of the people. The support of the people is secured, thereby making the policies and programs of the government a success. It is an important mean to secure and enforce the administrative accountability.

The basis of democratic government is the 'doctrine of popular sovereignty', which essentially means that the people are supreme in a democracy, or the final authority in a democracy is vested with its people. Hence, the administration functioning in a democracy is ultimately responsible to its people. And hence in this context, the participation of people in administration assumes significance. It transforms the representative democracy into a participatory democracy. It lays stress on the concept of 'bottom-up approach'.

The participation of people in administration can be studied under two heads as follows:

1. Participation in General Administration and
2. Participation in Development Administration.

6.2.1 Participation in General Administration

The people do not have knowledge about the administrative process, and they are unorganised; hence, they cannot have a definite and effective influence on the administration. Therefore the public influence on the administrative process is generally informal and indirect. However there are certain formal modes of participation of the people in administration. They are as follows:

1. **Election**

   The representative form of democracy is classified into two kinds: one is the presidential form and the other parliamentary form. The Presidential form of government is carried out in the United States, where the President is directly elected by the people. He is the Chief Executive and enjoys all the powers of the executive under the government. He is not responsible to the Congress—the legislature but, to the people ultimately. Thus there is direct control by the people over the administration in such systems.

   In the Parliamentary form, which is prevalent in India and Britain, the real executive—the Cabinet, is drawn from the legislature, and hence they remain responsible to it for its actions and functions. And the legislature in turn is responsible to the people. Thus there is indirect popular control over the administration by the people, in Parliamentary from of democracy.

In any form of democratic governmental systems, whether Presidential or Parliamentary, when the government becomes corrupt, inefficient, unresponsive and irresponsible, it can be removed from the government by way of periodic elections. The elections are means and medium of expression of people's confidence over the elected popular government.

2. **Recall**
   It is a device used in direct democracy. It is seen used in Switzerland and 13 states of the United States where the administrative officials are directly elected by the people. This system of recall helps the people to remove the elected officials before the end of their tenure, when they fail to represent the popular will of the people. In other words, the official has to vacate his/her office before end of his/her term if he/she is defeated in a recall poll.

   This device is used when the people are dissatisfied with the performance of the elected official while in office, and this process does not require any charges of illegal actions against them. The important aspect of this device is that it enables the people to hold the public administrators continuously responsible for their official acts and duties.

3. **Pressure Groups**
   This term originated in the United States. It is a group of people who are voluntarily actively organised for the purpose of promoting interest common to them. Some examples of such groups are: trade unions, voluntary organisations, professional associations, student unions, etc.

   These groups are also known as interest groups or vested groups. They exert pressure on the administration through legitimate and legal methods, such as petitioning, propagandising, publicity, public debating and maintaining contact with the legislators and the administrators, etc.

   They act as the bridge between the administration and its members. However, these groups resort to some illegal or illegitimate methods, such as violent acts, corruption and strikes which damages the integrity of the administration and cause public disruption.

4. **Advisory Committees**
   These are otherwise known as Advisory Councils or Boards. They are attached to the administrative system all the way from the bottom to the top. They consist of expert members, citizens and other representatives of special interest. They act as the link between the administration and the public. They provide advice to the agencies on how to formulate acts, policies, etc., and on how to implement them effectively.

   But these recommendations made by these agencies are only advisory in nature and not binding on the administration. However, they act as effective instrument identifying defects in the department and make the administration more democratic in character.

5. **Public Opinion**
   This is an informal mode of public participation in administration. This is the opinion of the public regarding the policies of the government. It is expressed through various agencies, such as the public platform, radio, political parties, press, cinema, pressure groups,

educational institutions and television, etc. And among these, independent press is the most effective agency, which acts as a mirror of public opinion. Therefore it is known as the 'fourth estate' of democracy.

The importance of public opinion, as a mode of participation by the people, is highlighted in the following points:

- It keeps the administration responsive and acts as a watchdog over it.
- It safeguards the liberty of the individual, by keeping check on the unpopular and undemocratic acts and functions of the government.
- It also acts as a source of law, and it facilitates implementation of the governmental policies.
- It mainly influences the policies and programmes of the government.

6.2.2 Participation in Development Administration

People's participation in development administration means that the people are directly involved in the process of administering development programmes meant for bringing socioeconomic changes in the society. It has the following dimensions:

(i) Participation in decision-making process.
(ii) Participation in implementation process.
(iii) Participation in the evaluation and monitoring of the program.
(iv) Participation in sharing of the developmental benefits.

People participate in development administration through various agencies, such as the Panchayati raj institutions, farmers associations, mahila mandals, cooperative institutions, yuva kendras and other voluntary/nonvoluntary organisations.

The benefits of people's participation in administration are as follows:

1. It helps in selection of project, which is directly relevant to the people.
2. It reduces the financial burden on the government by making the program function even after the removal of its support, with help of local resources provided by the beneficiary people themselves.
3. It acts as a safeguard against the abuse of authority of administration and thus reduces the scope of corruption.
4. It makes the local people bear and accept the developmental change and other issues associated with such change.
5. It promotes the concept of *esprit de corps* among the people in the community and thus strengthens the democracy at the grass root level.
6. A wealth of information is provided to the administration regarding the local economic, sociocultural, ecological and technical conditions. This information is highly useful in the process of programming, planning and implementation of the development programmes.
7. It increases the capability and competence of the people to take up responsibility and solve the problems on their own. It develops the spirit of self-reliance, leadership and initiative among the people.

8. It helps in the facilitation of mobilisation of local resources in the form of labour, cash, and materials, etc., which are essential for the successful implementation of the program.
9. It helps in prevention of hijacking of the projects by the richer and powerful sections of the society, as there is involvement of all section, especially the poor and weaker section in the development process. Thus it leads to equitable sharing and distribution of the benefits in the society.

However, there are number of factors which act as impediment for effective participation of the people in the administration. These are as follows:

(i) Negative political involvement and interference
(ii) Improper administrative procedure
(iii) Lack of culture of participation
(iv) Aristocratic and mechanical bureaucracy
(v) Role played by the middle men
(vi) Time constraints, that is, time-bound nature of the activities
(vii) Unfavourable socioeconomic environment like presence of communalism, casteism, regionalism, illiteracy and poverty, etc.
(viii) Presence of corruption and low standards of conduct in administration.

6.3 WHY CITIZENS' PARTICIPATION HAS TO BE STRENGTHENED

Citizen participation in local governance means involvement of the common man in assessing their own needs and also participating in local project planning and budget monitoring. This is important as it improves the public resource management and reduces corruption, by making the public administrators and the politicians accountable to the people.

In order for the citizens' participation to work, transparency in providing the government information is needed. Those people whose needs are assessed and for whom the policies are formulated should be involved in the decision-making process. Exclusion of such weak and powerless from this process is one of the cause of poverty as it denies them rights and creates unequal power relationships in the system.

The human rights include civil and political rights, including access to information and freedom of expression. These also form basis for political participation of the people. The citizen participation requires the following:

- Trust: Trust in their co-participants and others.
- Belief: Belief that such participation can make some difference.
- Wholeness: To feel the social inclusiveness.

In order to make a strong impact and better participation of the citizens in local governance, they need to understand and involve themselves and participate in local political issues. They should be confident and should have information on where and how to participate. And the local institutions should also be prepared to facilitate such engagement of citizens.

Engaging and involving the citizens in local governance can:

- Improve accountability.
- Improve ability of the local authority to solve problems.
- Create more inclusive and cohesive communities.

There is growth in number and quality of initiatives made by the communities.

One of the means to improve such participation and empowerment of citizen is through increasing their access to technology and in particular the social media. Number of grassroots-level application has shown the potential of social media in improving and widening the participation of citizens in governance.

6.4 THEORIES OF MANAGEMENT RELATED TO GOOD GOVERNANCE

A number of theories have been suggested linking management and economics with that of good governance centring on people's participation. Some of the most important theories suggesting this are as follows:

- New Public Management (NPM)
- Total Quality Management (TQM)
- Public Choice theory (PCT)
- Public value theory (PVT)

All these theories have had impact on the introduction and implementation of the good governance strategies. These theories are explained in brief in the succeeding paragraphs.

6.4.1 Theory of New Public Management

The theory of New Public Management (NPM) emerged around late 1970s and 1980s as the key reform agenda in the OECD countries. The initial aim was to improve the efficiency and effectiveness of the public sector institutions. The philosophical foundation of NPM laid emphasis on local's participation through the private sector. This las led to emergence of new organisational economics and managerialism, which is sponsoring new professional management and self-motivation in the centre to improved institutional performance. This is regarded as a paradigm shift as the old rules-driven and highly processed management style is replaced by a new strategy 'which attempts to combine modern management practices with the logic of economics, while retaining the core public values'. Researchers generally recognise eight core elements of NPM, which are as follows:

- Cost effectiveness
- Greater transparency in service delivery resource allocation
- Traditional institutions are to be decentralised
- Management efficiency within public sector agencies
- Disaggregating public service functions from their purchase
- Introducing stakeholder approaches
- Performance-based management system
- Contractual services and performance-based appraisal
- Increasing the emphasis on service quality, standard setting and public responsiveness

Thus all these elements have transformed the role of the local government into a more active, independent and economic organisation. It has also been said that the present traditional public administration will, in the future, inevitably be managerial, both in theory and in practice.

Thus all these aspects of NPM drive the public management to the doors of the local stakeholder and use their local knowledge and expertise to make more effective and sustainable development. In the traditional bureaucratic system, the people were considered to be *clients*. And now NPM has changed this view by considering them to be *customers*, and thus use their knowledge to bring about effective development. The client was considered to a passive recipient who obtained services without any exchange, while the customer is understood be an active recipient who obtains services by exchanging local knowledge. Therefore the customer poses more rights than the client. Hence NPM creates an environment that is more transparent, accountable and predictable, and this in consequence leads to promote and develop good governance at local levels. Other important and essential foundations for NPM in practice as identified by the researchers are as follows:

- Establishing democratic political governance frameworks
- Bottom-up accountability
- Local stakeholders acceptable performance

And today the public value is the principle of NPM which is in forefront of political agendas of many developed countries. There is also an alternate view that NPM is a threat to participatory work and it obstructs good governance. This is because this approach in improving performance creates a silo mentality which works against networking and partnership. On the other hand, there are other scholars who argue that NPM helps in good governance.

- In developing countries, the international development agencies (IDAs) included this NPM as on the vital preconditions for obtaining the foreign assistance.
- These IDAs have argued that NPM-based reforms in the country will increase the accountability and efficiency in public service delivery, which will therefore result in reaping maximum benefits out of the aid assistance.
- Several other scholars have also argued that traditional bureaucratic system has to be replaced by people-oriented NPM to make such reforms effective.
- Some scholars view good governance and NPM as mutually supportive, since both reinforce each other to enhance accountability and efficiency in public institutions.
- In order for establishment of good governance, the mentality and attitude of the government officials and the people's representatives should be changed, and NPM can help change the management style to foster good governance.

Some of the other scholars indicated that the scope of application of NPM in the developing countries is less encouraging because of inadequate economic, technical and sociopolitical institutions. But indeed, NPM has brought quite some changes and reforms in the Western countries. The reforms which were carried out under NPM can be broadly classified into the following heads: marketization, accountability, decentralisation and efficiency. By contrasting the main features of good governance and NPM, a shared dimension between them can be drawn. This can be seen from the following diagram:

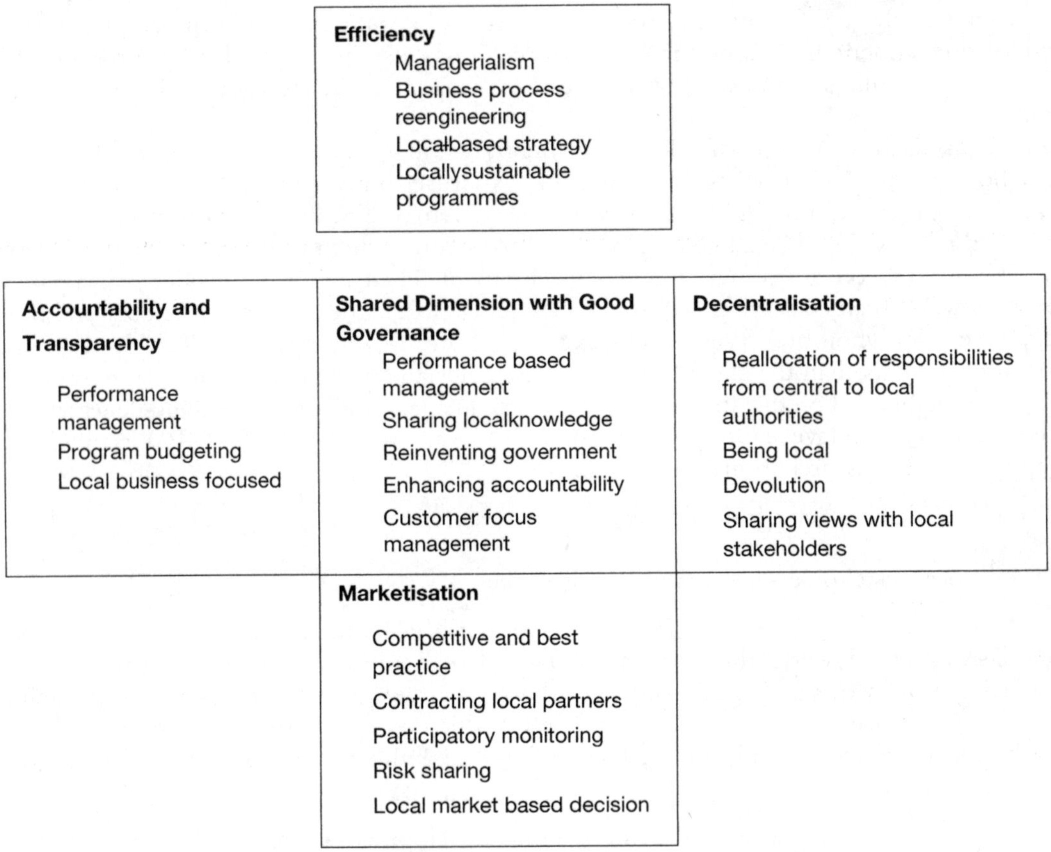

	Efficiency Managerialism Business process reengineering Localbased strategy Locallysustainable programmes	
Accountability and Transparency Performance management Program budgeting Local business focused	**Shared Dimension with Good Governance** Performance based management Sharing localknowledge Reinventing government Enhancing accountability Customer focus management	**Decentralisation** Reallocation of responsibilities from central to local authorities Being local Devolution Sharing views with local stakeholders
	Marketisation Competitive and best practice Contracting local partners Participatory monitoring Risk sharing Local market based decision	

- Some scholars do call for training of the sustainable development managers to effectively survey and engage local people, collect data and translate those findings into meaningful statements which can be used to support informed discussion which is possible by introducing NPM.
- World Bank calls for the government and the elected officials to be transformed as 'change agent' for the implementation of good governance.
- The World Bank also viewed the public managers as 'agents of development'.
- They must be resourced and equipped for such role. When governments move beyond NPM, new avenues involving community and local knowledge enter the public administration with consequences of changes in skills needed for the administrators.

From the above analysis, it can be seen that NPM envisions rule *for* the people while good governance calls for rule *with* the people. While NPM helps bring the officers themselves to open the door, good governance equips and empowers the local communities to open the door for the officials. This means that NPM teaches the officials to treat people as customers and open the door to invite them in, in contrast, good governance is for empowering the people as citizens of the society to open the door. Hence both these acts are required at the same time for creating a congenial and non-conflicting situation for establishing good governance.

NPM has indeed brought in potential for changing the traditional governing process. Through implementation of NPM, the governing process has become multifunctional opposed to the traditional uni-factorial state that runs services to the people. This might open up new avenues for the local people to envision governance process at local levels.

6.4.2 Total Quality Management

The fundamental philosophy of Total Quality Management (TQM) is to—in all activities concerned in an institution—maintain professionalism and perfection in them. It gained prominence among the scholars and practitioners during the 1990s. Since then, this theory has got established itself as a system for improving the performance of the institutions and raising the satisfaction of the customers. TQM is said to have both internal and external focus on an institution's business management. The core values of TQM identified by the scholars are as follows:

- Management commitment
- Local-based decision
- Customer focus
- Process focus
- Continuous improvement in delivering of services

Though the concept of TQM is generally exercised within the enterprises, it can also be used in public sector as well. The important suggestion of the TQM experts is knowing and understanding the local people first for improving quality of services in the public sector. According to the external customers, the management activities related to the delivering of the public services should be improved. And today, the aim of a good public management is to effectively design the services that makes sense to citizens, business and international clients.

TQM has internal focus too; as in, it is focused on improving the internal management to effectively deliver customer service. Today both customers and employees are central to the governance phenomena. And hence any strategy to improve the service delivery should read the society and local places. The TQM is focused on its internal employees, as it believes that if the quality of employees is improved, then customers automatically receive quality service. And hence when performance of employees are improved, the performance of service delivery is also simultaneously improved.

Hence the common element of TQM and good governance are to recognise the importance of the local people for the development of the institution. The important elements are as follows:

- Overcome barriers in networking with the external customers, that is, local people;
- Improve relationship between the institution and its beneficiaries;
- Restructuring of the administrative functions and process and
- Motoring the performance of the officials, making them accountable to the beneficiaries.

Thus, idea underlying the concept of TQM influence is good governance.

6.4.3 Public Choice Theory

This theory originated within the economics arena. It basically focused on people's choice in selecting the public service. This theory considers the public as buyer of the best product and hence conceptualises market-like competition in public service delivery. The public choice theorists argue that monopolistic production of goods by both private and public sector leads to inefficiency in service delivery management.

The application of strategies elaborated by the Public Choice Theory (PCT) makes the institutions provide innovative, cost effective, and locally sustainable products. In order to follow this strategy, the public institutions have undergone more decentralisation and the public service delivery has been outsourced. It is suggested based on evidence that better efficiency comes from competition rather than public or private nature of the organisation. Implementation of this theory thus is advantageous to the local people and other beneficiaries over that delivered by the public officials. PCT has also introduced participatory implementation and monitoring of the local public service delivery mechanisms. Thus the core concept of good governance matches with the central element of participation in PCT.

Therefore it can be seen clearly that PCT matches with the concept of good governance because of having the following characteristics:

- Management functions has to be decentralised to local levels, and it has to be shared with the local stakeholders to provide services according to choice of the local people.
- The role of central government in providing public service has to be reduced and local people should be influenced to create best innovative local institution.
- The traditional management has to be re-engineered to make it more people focussed.
- Civil, private and the NGOs should be increasingly involved to make the service delivery locally sustainable and more efficient.
- Local knowledge and resources should be used to get cost effective and best alternative choices for service deliberation.

6.4.4 Public Value Theory

The basic and fundamental assumption of the Public Value Theory (PVT) is to provide services according to the interest of the public. Public interest is defined as what people would choose 'if they thought sensibly, saw clearly and acted generously and disinterestedly'. Thus this theory calls for desired outcomes of public programs and participation of the expected beneficiaries to see the outcome of the public services when delivered by the government bodies. The concept of PVT operates at the highest levels, such as in the philosophical discourses about the public interest, or at the operational levels, whereby focus is on the desired outcomes. Thus this theory persuades the public institutions to recognise the public value of goods, resources and services and to effectuate the procedure under what 'is the public best served'.

- The concept of public interest was seen a few decades ago as too vague, too value loaded, too conflicting and too ambitious with the policies of group accommodation; but today, even in the developing countries, the public programs and policies are levelled as 'for the public interest'.
- This idea of embracing the people and their interests makes the government to introduce good governance, which is transparent and conceivable by the people especially when such program is introduced by the development agencies.
- Recently researchers have suggested to move beyond the NPM's framework towards new and alternative paradigms, such as Public Value Management—'a way of thinking which is both post-competitive and post-bureaucratic'.

'Theory of public value' states that public sector can stay alive and effective by creating public value through proper and successful practice of public management. It is also said that this concept turned the old bureaucratic practice of service delivery towards a new way of thinking, by incorporating people's interest and choice for the services rendered. PVT envisages a more proactive and political role for the public sector managers. The role of public sector managers included managing up to authorising level and also managing to the citizen level.

Thus this theory included that public officials and other representatives should include people at the centre of making decisions for service delivery. And, thus, it also pursues the ideal of good governance as it both focuses on the people.

6.5 CONTEXTUALISING PEOPLE'S PARTICIPATION

Traditionally, people in a democracy use their right to elect their representatives who then hold the public administrators accountable for implementing any decisions that affect the people. This is the common practice followed in any representative democracy or representative local governance, where the people elect those who rule them. This means that people should participate in the governing process through their representatives to get services from the government. This scenario is changing as people do want themselves to be considered as clients in the representative form of democracy. Today, especially in developed societies, the citizens want to put forth their opinion regarding any decision that has effect over them in the future.

- It is identified by many scholars that representative democracy is not working as expected to meet the needs and aspirations of the people.
- They call for direct democracy, where the people will be directly consulted to recognize and implement their desired programs.
- This form of direct democracy is in consonance with the concept of good governance, which supports the view that involved citizens become more informed and eager to dedicate their time in pursuit of finding a solution.

Hence today, many academicians, politicians, civil societies and donor agencies call for direct participation of the people in the governing process. It is believed that people are entitled to participate in all such public affairs which have effect on their lives, and such participation will remain at the heart of today's governance. Presently there is also increasing awareness among the people in matters of public affairs which, therefore, has forced the government to share their authority with the people. Hence the best outcome of this process has forced all concerned institutions to place the people at the centre of governance. Thus the term governance has been defined as not only working with the people but also

- being accountable to the people;
- being transparent to the people and
- following laws of the local people.

The attributes of good governance, as pointed out by the international development agencies, indicate a growing emphasis on economic development through effective people-oriented government process, that is, governance. The governance indicators, such as the *accountability, efficiency, transparency, participation, effectiveness*, etc., need to meet the public belief of good governance.

Even though all the four elements of good governance are mutually supportive of each other, we can find that people's participation is central element among these. That is a people-participatory government ensures more transparency is more accountable and ensures predictability governance to its people. Therefore good governance is considered to be 'not just pro-people of people-centred; it has to be owned by the people themselves'.

Good governance is also otherwise described as 'government for the people, transparent to the people, accountable to the people, stand by rule of people and for the betterment of the people'. This is similar to the Gettysburg address by Abraham Lincoln where he called the democratic government as, *government of the people, by the people and for the people*. This means that the people are at the heart of true democracy. Thus a true democracy should ensure the participation of its citizens not just at the central level, but also at the local level.

- In 1989, the Organisation for Economic Cooperation and Development (OECD) released a 'Policy Statement on Development Cooperation in the 1990s', which stated that the participatory development is the most important issue on development aid agenda for the years to come.
- Governance means that involvement of number of actors in the decision-making process brings together multiple actors, for example, state, corporate, private sector and the civil society.
- In process of governance, the State is only one of the actor, and the others being the civil society, which is the people, the beneficiaries of the decisions.
- This is understood that, people become inseparable part of the decision-making process and in the implementation of the decided programs.

Through proper and effective policies and regulations, government can open the door to let people in to take part in the decision-making process that has an effect on them. And this does not mean that people will come forward immediately to take part in such processes. What needs to be done is that the people have to be empowered enough to make them come forward and take active control to make decisions for themselves. And when people are empowered, even if the government is unwilling to let the people in, they themselves will force it to open the doors for them.

Empowered people will come forward and participate and protest against any anti-people decisions. Hence, particularly in developing societies, where people are illiterate, not united and not aware about their rights, they need to be empowered more with more participation. In fact, in developing countries, good governance would not be attained unless participation of the people is ensured at the local level. It is argued that 'it is logical that development should start with people as development is about improving the lives of the people'.

- World Bank defines participation as a process through which people share and effect control over the development initiatives and the decisions and resources which affect them.
- It is also defined as the process by which the members of the society share power with the public officials in taking important decisions and actions related to the community.
- Most scholars consider participation as central to sustainable development programmes, even though it might cause some delay, or increase in cost or raise some conflicts.
- Participation is considered to be a social transformation mechanism, where the power is transferred from the implementing agency to the civil society.

The following is the World Bank report, which described four categories of people's participation for different kinds of programs. There four categories are follows:

1. **Information sharing:** Service providers like the project designers and managers inform the local people in order to facilitate action by them. Information helps the locals to understand and perform their tasks better. In family planning and nutritional programs, such information sharing works better.
2. **Consultation:** The local people are consulted at every or key stage in a project cycle. There is opportunity for the people here to interact and provide feedback to the service providers which could be included in the design and implementation stages. If the farmers are consulted during the extension programs and arrangements, the project outcomes are likely to be better than that when they were merely informed.
3. **Decision-making:** This happens when the beneficiaries have a decision-making role in matters of program design and implementation. Decisions can be made jointly with the service providers on certain issues related to the project. Thus slum dwellers may be involved in the process of upgrading their house together with the project staff on the design.
4. **Initiating action:** In this category, the beneficiaries are able to take initiative in terms of actions/decisions pertaining to the project. This implies a proactive capacity and confidence to get the services on their own. The beneficiary group identifies a new need and decides to respond on its own; they are thus taking initiative for their own development.

However other researchers argue that people's participation is a continuous process, and it passes through a number of stages. Accordingly, people are first informed, and then they reach control position of a decision through continuous participation process. People therefore should participate from or before the beginning of a project so that they can take effective control over the project for the sustainable use of the outcomes.

The following are the various stages of people's participation as identified by number of studies and scholars:

1. As per the International Association of People's Participation:
   a. Inform: One-way communication
   b. Consult: Two-way communication
   c. Involve: Participatory process
   d. Collaborate: Partnership
   e. Empower: Implementing what public decides
2. A metaphoric eight-rung ladder of participation as developed by Arnstein:
   a. Manipulation
   b. Therapy
   c. Informing
   d. Consultation
   e. Placation
   f. Partnership
   g. Delegated power
   h. Citizen control

3. A study carried out by Wilcox identified the following five stages:
    a. Informing
    b. Consulting
    c. Deciding together
    d. Acting together
    e. Supporting independent community interests

6.6 USE OF TOOLS FOR PEOPLE'S PARTICIPATION

Governments use different type of instruments to create awareness for different levels of engagement to develop awareness in the local community. Here the term *instrument* means the devise used by the organisations to sustain and organise people's participation. In the World Bank report in 1987, Samuel Paul described the following three instruments used for people's participation:

1. **Field workers of the project agency:** A project may use its field staff to mobilize and interact with beneficiary groups. They operate at the grassroots level and yet are part of the project agency. In agricultural and irrigation projects, field workers are often used to organize and interact with farmer groups. Field workers' orientation and commitment to Citizen Participation are key determinants of their effectiveness as instruments of Citizen Participation. Training can be used to influence their community mobilization skills and attitudes. If they see themselves primarily as agents of the government or donor, their ability to promote and sustain Citizen Participation is likely to suffer. If this perception is also shared by beneficiaries, the chances are that field workers will not be able to facilitate Citizen Participation except at a relatively low level of intensity.
2. **Community workers/committees:** A project agency may draw upon workers or volunteers from among beneficiaries to act as community mobilizers. Such persons may or may not be paid by the agency. However, in all cases, the community may have had a say in their selection and the roles they play. If they are selected through a community consensus or a consultative process, they are likely to identify better with the community's problems and feelings and facilitate Citizen Participation more effectively. Instead of community workers, committees which represent beneficiaries may be organized as an instrument of Citizen Participation. Where large numbers of people are involved, committees are a useful device for beneficiaries to reach higher levels of Citizen Participation intensity, provided they truly represent the community's interests. Committees have acted as a Citizen Participation instrument in several primary healthcare projects.
3. **User groups:** Where the number of beneficiaries is manageable either because of the local nature of a project or the specialized nature of the group (farmers, mothers with small children, etc.), it is possible to organize viable groups of users as an instrument of Citizen Participation. This instrument has the potential to reach the highest level of Citizen Participation though its creation and sustenance are the most complex. User groups may operate at any level of intensity and, over time, may rise from one level to another. Of all the instruments, user groups are likely to involve the maximum number of relevant beneficiaries in a given project context. The use of one instrument, however, does not preclude the use of others. User groups may coexist with community volunteers or committees.

Unlike field workers, who by definition can be organized only through external intervention (e.g., by the project agency), it is conceivable that user groups could be created through the medium of internal leadership or external intervention. Where user groups are energized by local leadership, the intensity of Citizen Participation is likely to be high. Intermediary organizations, such as NGOs can also be a medium for the use of any of these instruments. Needless to say, it will take a highly committed NGO to create and sustain user groups at a high level of Citizen Participation intensity.

6.7 RELATIONSHIP BETWEEN PEOPLE'S PARTICIPATION AND GOOD GOVERNANCE

The level of good governance increase through effective participation by the people in development programs. The Japan International Cooperation Agency in 1995 reported that good governance is the foundation for the participatory development inasmuch as it provides the government methods needed to encourage the people's participation and create environment where they can participate effectively. Such effective participation by the people can enhance the transparency of the developmental works, increase the accountability of the implementing authority, compliance with the local law and which therefore consequently establishes good governance. Thus, this indicates that people's participation and good governance are inseparable from each other.

The Japan International Cooperation Agency (JICA) in 1995 developed a diagram showing the link between the participatory development and good governance, which thereby can enhance democracy in the country. This is presented as in Fig. 6.1:

There are various other models of governance developed by number of scholars, on the basis of interaction between the citizen and the government. They can be seen as follows:

1. **Managerial Model**
   The people here are seen as passive recipients of information. The governing bodies unilaterally deliver message to the people. This is a top-down approach of implementation.
2. **Consultative Model**
   This model is direct contrast to the managerial model. In this, the governing body uses information to inform people, which therefore facilitates communication between the government and the people. This model is also called as the 'pull' model as it reduces the gap between the citizens and the government.
3. **Participatory Model**
   In this model, the proper information is provided to the people, which facilitates their involvement in the government programs. There are no practical barriers to the involvement of the people. The power of this information helps people to form civil society. Almost all section of the society are involved in the decision-making process. Mutual understanding and assistance helps to achieve the goal.
4. **Disciplinary Model**
   In this model, people—when they are fully empowered—may initiate collective social programs. This model imposes responsibility the local governing bodies to provide for better policy to the people.

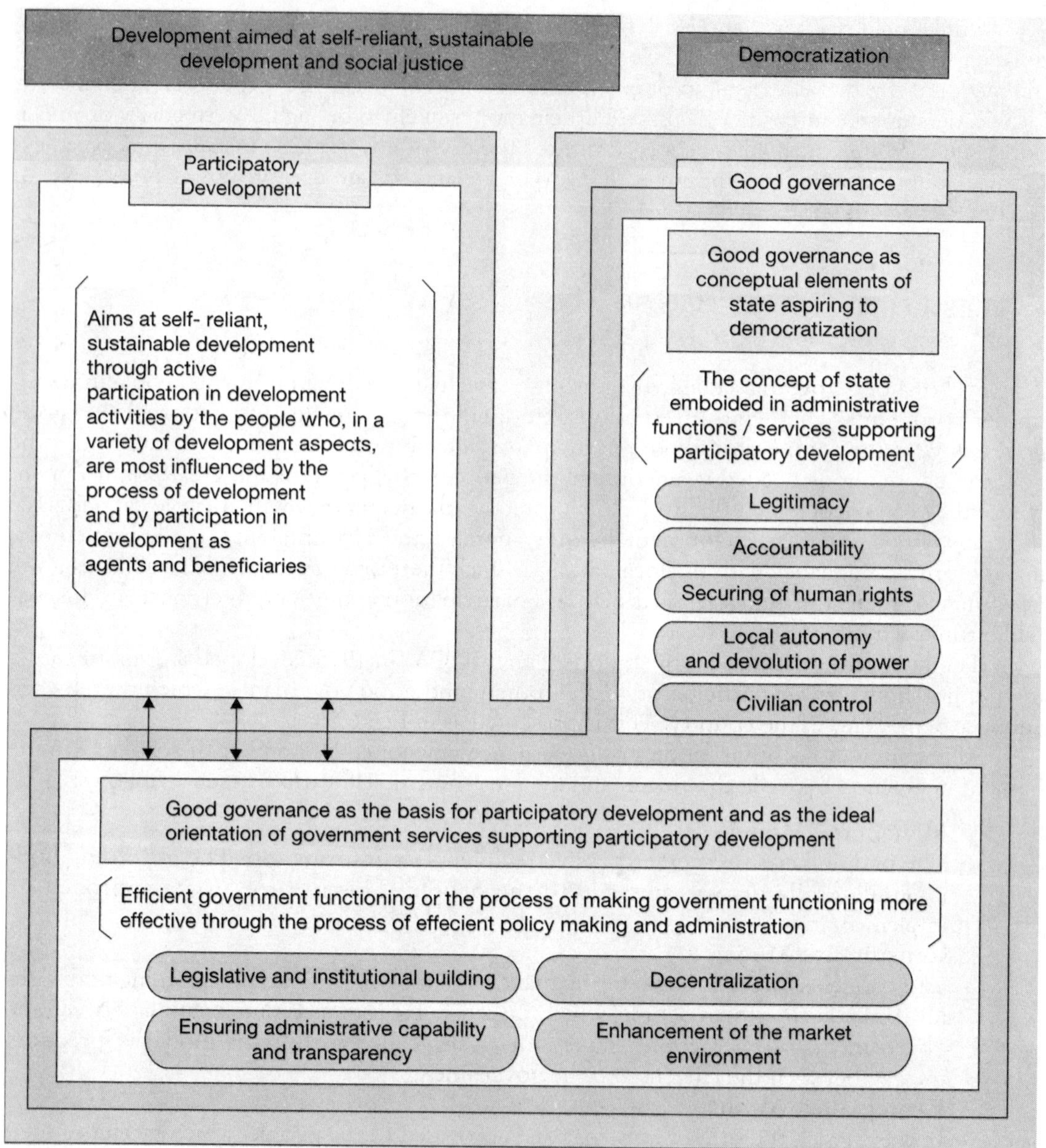

FIGURE 6.1 Relationship Between Participatory Development and Good Governance

5. **Network Model**
   In this model, the reciprocal communication between the parties develop trust in each other. The collaboration and networking between the service providers and the receivers evolve in a friendly environment.
6. **Community Empowerment Model**
   It is a bottom-up approach. It happens because of extensive participation from the community.

From the above we can draw the correlation between the various stages of participation and the model of governance associated with it. This is depicted in the table below:

Stage of Participation	Model of Governance
Stage 1: Inform**:** It is a one-way process, where the governing agency tells the people the decision it takes before or during the implementation of programs.	**Authoritarian Model:** In this model, the decision is taken from the top and it trickles down. It is mostly implemented by the bureaucrats. This program process in not transparent, predictable or accountable.
State 2: Consult**:** It is a two-way communication; but, here the engagement of the people is limited in the decision-making process. The feedback is got from the people, but the governing agency unilaterally makes decisions and implements them.	**Bureaucratic Model:** In this model, people's participation is not enough to transfer of the power. The program process is less transparent and less predictable. The implementing agency is accountable not to the people but to its superiors.
State 3: Involve**:** In this model, the view of the participants are not only listened, but they are also engaged during the implementation stage. They are also engaged during the budget discussion and program implementation. But the entire community is not involved in this process.	**Political Model:** In this model, the people's participation is sought and they are engaged. But here the participation is carried out only by certain segment in the society, which leads to raise in tension and conflicts between different interest groups. The governing body is transparent and accountable not to the whole community, but rather to a section of the populace.
Stage 4: Empower**:** At this stage, the governing body allows the people themselves to directly get involved in the decision-making process. They are encouraged to come up with their own decisions and resources to implement the development programs together. Here the governing body works as a facilitator.	**Democratic Model:** This model allows for developing partnerships between people and the governing body. The authority is delegated to the people to take decisions and to implement program by sharing of local knowledge. The entire process is completely transparent, predictable and accountable.

6.8 MODELS OF GOOD GOVERNANCE ON THE BASIS OF PARTICIPATION LEVELS

The following are the models of good governance based on the basis of people's participation:

1. **Authoritarian Model**
   This model evolves when the people's participation is at the information level. Here the decisions and the resources come from the top. The implementation of the project is carried out by the bureaucrats of the local agency, by following traditional, rigid processes and where the people are treated as passive recipients of the services. Authorities use local representatives or some display board or snail mail to inform the people regarding the development programs. The entire process is not transparent or accountable. It therefore has:

   - Low accountability
   - Low transparency
   - Low predictability
   - Low participation

2. **Bureaucratic Model**
   This is the model which develops when the people's participation is at consultation level. In this model, the governing agencies consult with the people and use resources of the people. But they do not share power with them in making decisions or policy. The participation is not complete/full enough to allow people have knowledge about the resources; hence, this leave scope for corruption. A public meeting is usually conducted for consultation. The authorities treat the people here as either customer or clients as they do not share the whole process of project implementation. Despite the governing body remaining accountable to the people, it is still less transparent and less predictable. Therefore this has,

   - Accountability
   - Less transparency
   - Less predictable
   - Participation

3. **Political Model**
   This model evolves when the participation is at the stage of involvement. Here the governing agency shares knowledge, authority and resources with the local people in order to take decision to implement the project. Moreover, the important aspect of this model is that the people and the governing body jointly form a kind of coalition where both these parties share histories, values, rituals and other common interests, and thereby establish a more cooperative network to develop any program. And the problem arises when only a particular faction of people are engaged in such consultation process. The people here are treated as partners, players, but the trust between the governing body and the locals remain weak as the only a segment of population is involved in consultation process. Thus predictability, transparency and accountability are high in this model, albeit only for a section of the society. Therefore this has:

   - High accountability
   - High transparency
   - High predictability
   - Segmented participation

4. **Democratic Model**
   This model evolves gradually as people attain empowerment. This model calls for developing partnership with people, implementing programs, delegating authority to make decision, by sharing the local knowledge, resources and values. Participatory planning and strategic decision-making, which enable the development of a common vision, effective, efficient and transparent management which create a positive joint-working environment. Predictability, transparency and accountability are relatively high. This is the most rational model, as the people here are considered as stewards or navigators. But the authorities here should be open, flexible and encourage the development of such a model. Therefore this has:

   - High accountability
   - High transparency
   - High predictability
   - High participation

Hence democratic good governance can be achieved by proper cooperation between governing agencies and the local people. On the one hand, the governing agencies should come closer to the local people by extending and smoothening the pro-people systems and approaches. On the other hand, to make effective joint decisions, the local people have to be empowered enough. Only through such reciprocal activities, people's participation can be made effective enough to achieve good governance.

6.9 EFFECTIVE PARTICIPATION FOR GOOD GOVERNANCE

World Bank defines, 'Effective Participation', as a process through which people influence and share control over the development initiatives. Thus the word 'effective' means situations where the participation of the people makes a difference within the decision-making process or the policy outcome of the government. Thus it means more empowerment of the local people, and when people are more empowered, there is more accountable, more predictable and transparent government. And this makes the people's participation in the local development more effective. But empowering people alone will not be enough to achieve good governance. The governing agents at the local level, the officials have to change their attitudes to welcome people to the decision-making process.

As the term good governance means, creating a bridge between the governed and the government, hence both officials and the local people need to cooperate with each other to uphold the value of direct people's participation. On the one hand, an effective, robust participatory system and laws complementing them should be made to build the capacity of the local governing agencies. And on the other hand, high social capital and strong civil society groups are required for the empowerment of the local people. Thus the effective network between the governed and the governing bodies depend on fulfilment of some normative elements in the society, such as the equity, empowerment and power-balance and social capital.

- The two major aspects of developing social capital are social norms and trust, which help people in networking with each other.
- People share values, concerns with help of such networks, and this consequently transforms into group energy.
- This group energy then helps to hold the local authority accountable for delivering of services and development.
- In this way, social capital can be used to achieve good governance.
- Both the people and the governing agencies should act mutually to develop trust and norms, that is, social capital.
- Effective participation in a society is not possible if its normative values are not adhered to.
- Local stakeholders, those who are in networks with the social capital, have to be included in consultations for the development of policies of the government that can ensure effective participation of the people.

For a long time, governments in various countries have been following 'technocratic policy analyses' for making the public management systems more effective. This meant that the governmental agencies did not include the local people, or did not use the knowledge of the local people, for making decision that would have effect on the local people. In contrast to this approach, scholars have suggested that local elements and knowledge have to be considered in making a public system sustainable. The 'Participatory policy analysis' helps to find out the actual problem and identifies ways to overcome them. Therefore local knowledge and normative elements should be considered when planning on how to make local government more sustainable by warranting effective people's participation.

6.10 CITIZEN AND ADMINISTRATION

Welfare orientation is the characteristic of a modern democratic state. Hence the government has come to play a significant role in socioeconomic development of the nation. This has resulted in the expansion and growth of the bureaucracy and multiplication of the administrative process, which has resulted in increased administrative discretion and power enjoyed by the civil servants at various levels of government. Such discretionary power might result in harassment, malpractices, maladministration and corruption.

Hence such a situation gives rise to citizens' grievances against the administration. The success of a democracy and realisation of socioeconomic development lies in the fact that grievances of the citizens are effectively addressed. Hence the following institutions have been created across the world in order to effectively address the citizens' grievances:

- The Ombudsman System
- The Administrative Courts System
- The Procurator System

The Scandinavian Ombudsman is the earliest of the institution in the world, which was created to address the grievance of the citizens. Ombudsman is called to be a unique institution which is appropriate for dealing with the complaints of ordinary citizens about the unfair actions taken by the administration.

6.10.1 Ombudsman System

The first institution of ombudsman was created in Sweden in 1809. The term 'Ombud' is of Swedish origin, which refer to a person who acts as a representative of another person. The Ombudsman also refers to an officer who is appointed by the legislature to handle complaints against the administrators and the judiciary.

The following matters are dealt by the Swedish Ombudsman:

- Maladministration, that is, inefficiency in achieving the targets;
- Nepotism, supporting one's own kith and kin for employment and various other purposes;
- Administrative discretion is abused, official power and authority is misused;
- Discourtesy, use of abusive language and misbehaving with the people and
- Corruption in administration, asking for bribe for doing official work.

The Ombudsman is appointed for a term of 4 years by the Parliament. He/she can only be removed by the Parliament on the grounds of loss of confidence in him/her. The annual report is submitted to the Parliament; hence he/she is also termed as 'Parliamentary Ombudsman'. But he/she is independent of all the three institutions: legislature, executive and the judiciary.

It is a constitutional authority, which enjoys power to supervise the compliance of rules and regulations, by the administrators, and verify whether they are performing their job properly. Hence, in other words, we can say that the Ombudsman keeps a watch over the civil, judicial, military officials so that they function objectively, impartially and legally in accordance with the law of the land. But he/she does not have the power to reverse or quash a decision and he/she has no direct control over the administration and the judiciary.

The Ombudsman acts either on the complaints received from the citizen or on his/her own, that is, suo moto. He/she has the power to persecute any official, including the judges. But he/she has no power to impose any punishment. He/she can report to the higher authorities to take necessary action against the erring officials. The following are the characteristics of the Swedish Ombudsman:

- Impartial and unbiased inquiry into the complaints received;
- Unlimited and uninterrupted to all files related to administration;
- A very wide publicity is given for its functioning in the media;
- It has suo moto power to initiate investigation;
- It is a very direct, cheap, informal and speedy method of handling the complaints;
- It's action is independent from the executive and
- The report is submitted to the Parliament and not the executive. The institution of Ombudsman is based on doctrine of administrative accountability to the legislature.

From Sweden, this institution spread to other Scandinavian Countries, such as Finland (1919), Denmark (1955) and finally Norway (1962). The country of New Zealand was the first from the Commonwealth nations to adopt this system in the form of appointment of a Parliamentary Commissioner for Administration in 1967. And nearly 40 countries have adopted this system of ombudsman in one form or the other with different nomenclature and functions. In India, this system is called as Lokpal and Lokayukta.

The system of Ombudsman is the bulwark against the official tyranny by the democratic government. It is considered to be institutionalized form of public conscience.

The administrative court which was first developed in France, also acts as an important instrument for redressal of grievances of the citizens. Because of its successful functioning in France, this system has been adopted in a number of countries around the world, such as in European countries like Belgium, Greece, etc., and other African countries.

The procurator system operated in socialist countries like former USSR, Hungary, Poland, China, Czechoslovakia and Romania, etc. This was the system used to address the grievances of the citizens. The office or Procurator General is still operational in Russia. He/she is appointed to office for a tenure of 7 years.

6.10.2 Institutions in India

The following are the existing legal and institutional framework to address the grievances of citizens in India:

- Special Police Establishment, 1941
- Delhi Police Establishment Act, 1946
- Central Bureau of Investigation, 1963
- State Vigilance Commission, 1964
- Lokayukta in States
- Divisional Vigilance Boards
- National Consumer Disputes Redressal Commission
- Commission for SCs and STs

- Directorate of Public Grievances in the Cabinet Secretariat, 1988
- Anti-Corruption Bureau in States
- Public Servants (Enquiries) Act, 1850
- All-India Services (Conduct) Rules, 1954
- Prevention of Corruption Act, 1947
- Supreme Court and High Courts in States
- Central Civil Services (Conduct) Rules, 1954
- Administrative Tribunals
- Parliament and its committees
- Vigilance organisations in the ministries/departments, attached, subordinate offices and public undertakings
- Indian Penal Code, 1860
- Railway Services Conduct Rules, 1956
- 'File to Field' innovative programs operate in some States (e.g., Kerala), where administration goes to the village and hears the grievances of the people directly in the field, and take immediate action.

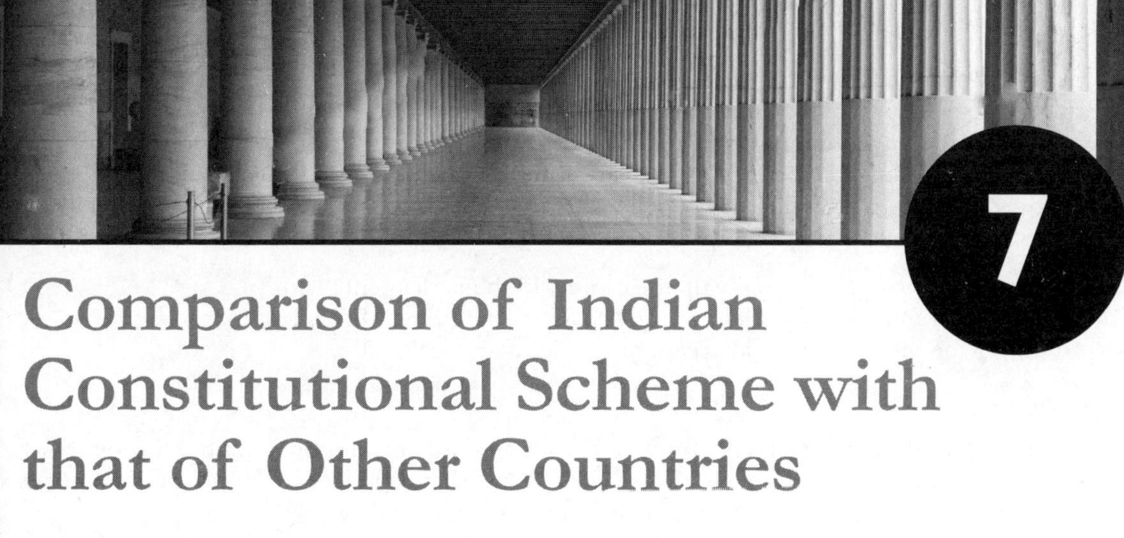

7

Comparison of Indian Constitutional Scheme with that of Other Countries

LEARNING OBJECTIVES

In this Chapter, you will learn about:

- British Constitution
- American Constitution
- Chinese Constitution
- Swiss Constitution
- Japanese Constitution
- French Constitution

7.1 BRITISH CONSTITUTION

7.1.1 Introduction

The Constitution of present United Kingdom has evolved from the past which contained smaller states and has been continuing till the present. The defining feature of the British Constitution is its unwritten form. Absence of a Constitution does not mean Britain does not have one, it does but it is unwritten and other elements, such as statues, judicial precedents, conventions, treaties, etc., collectively form together the essence of constitution. Hence it is termed as uncodified Constitution rather than unwritten constitution.

> *According to Munro "the British Constitution is a complex amalgam of institutions, principles and practices. It is a composite of charters and statutes, of judicial decisions, of common law, of precedence, usages and traditions. It is not one document but hundreds of them. It is not derived from one source but from several.... It is a child of wisdom and chance."*

7.1.2 Sources of the British Constitution

(a) *Conventions*

British Constitution is based generally on the traditions and conventions of the English society. Without these conventions, it is difficult work with it and they are considered to be sacred. Most of the fundamental features of the Constitution is based on the conventions only. Therefore, the conventions are called as the living soul of the British Constitution. Let us now look at some of the important conventions.

(i) Collective responsibility of the cabinet to the Parliament
(ii) Appointment of leader of largest party as the Prime Minister
(iii) King or Queen should accept the advice of the cabinet

(b) *Charters*

The great charters and agreements provide the source for Constitution defining the powers of the crown, rights of the citizen, etc. These charters have gained historic importance and hence act as guide to the constitution. Some of the important charters are as follows:

(i) Magna Carta, 1215
(ii) Bill of Rights, 1689
(iii) Act of Union with Scotland, 1707

(c) *Statues*

The statues or laws are passed by the parliament from time to time and hence act as important source for the constitution. The British Parliament has full power to amend and/or remove these statues any time it wishes. Some of the important statues are as follows:

(i) Parliament Act, 1911
(ii) Representation of People's Act, 1918
(iii) Indian Independence Act, 1947

(d) *Judicial decisions*

Judgements and interpretations of British courts act as another important source of constitution. These judgements, interpretations, etc., define the validity, scope of the statues, charters and the common law. These judiciary act as vanguard on upholding the constitutional values, hence Dicey termed the British Constitution to be a judge-made constitution.

(e) *Eminent works*

Eminent works of great scholars too serve as basis for constitution. *Dicey's Law and constitution, Blackstone's Commentaries of English constitution, etc.*, are some of them.

(f) *Common law*

The common law exists apart from the statues and the charters. These are generally not in written form but have evolved from historical growth of the British society, these are important rules and regulation which are based upon the customs and traditions of the English society and which are later validated by the courts. The right of trial by jury, right of freedom of speech and assembly, etc., are some of the important common laws.

7.1.3 Salient Features of the British Constitution

Let us now look at some of the fundamental aspects of the British Constitution.

(a) ***Partially written and partially unwritten constitution***

The British Constitution is mostly in unwritten form. The written form consists of important parts like the Magna Carta, Bill of Rights, etc., but the unwritten form is more remarkable and noticeable. What unwritten here means is that unwritten part of the Constitution is larger than the written part, the written part of the Constitution was not created at a single instance, whenever statues, laws were enacted it was not for improving the constitution, they indirectly helped in identifying the values of the constitution. Thus the British Constitution is largely based on traditions and conventions of the English society.

(b) ***Evolutionary***

The British Constitution is the oldest of the written constitutions. It has been in continuous usage without any change for the past few centuries. British society also has not faced any drastic revolutions like the French or the Russian. The basic idea of the Constitution has grown like an organism from period to period. It has been evolutionary and gradually the constitutional values and ideals were incorporated in various statues, laws, conventions and traditions.

(c) ***Difference in theory and reality***

Many features which exists as constitutional features are not practiced in actual practice. In theory, all power of Government rests with the crown. All laws should receive consent of the Crown, King is the commander-in-chief of all forces and only he can declare war and conclude peace treaties. Thus in theory, British Government is an absolute monarchy and in actual reality it is democratic republic. The King presently is just a figurehead and no real power is vested in him. The people via the parliament are more powerful than the crown.

(d) ***Parliamentary sovereignty***

Legally, the British Parliament can do anything, save just make man a woman or woman a man. There is no law which the parliament can make. Everything comes under the purview of the parliament and changes can be brought by simple act. It can abolish monarchy, abolish House of Lords, prevent someone from attaining the throne and deprive all powers of the crown and many more. The important aspect is that no court can question the legality of such acts. Acts, laws cannot be struck down like in India or America for being ultra vires of the constitution. The British Parliament is both the law making and the constituent authority, and there is no legal difference between them.

(e) ***Unitary constitution***

In India and America some of the powers are vested with the regional governments, and it is shared between the centre and the states. But Britain is not a federation or union of states, and hence it has a unified constitution. Powers, thus, are completely appropriated by the government with its head at London. Though local governments exists, they derive power from the union, which can give greater or deprive of the present powers of the local governments. Thus, British Constitution is unitary in essence and practice.

(f) *Flexible constitution*

There is no separate procedure for amendment of constitutional provisions, it is passed like any other bill requiring simple majority. Constitutional law is thus treated like any other law, making it flexible. Thus British Constitution can adapt itself to new conditions easily.

(g) *Rule of law*

Though it is not explicitly stated, rule of law is inherently present in the British Constitution. We may see that British Constitution does not contain defined provisions for protection of its citizens unlike in America or India, but the British citizens are well protected and their rights are derived from the presence of Rule of Law. All institutions the King, Parliament, courts, even the citizens are subject to it. Tradition and public opinion upholds the ideal from any infringement by the parliament.

(h) *Parliamentary form of government*

Unlike America's Presidential style, England follows a Parliamentary form of government. The King-Crown is the nominal head of the state and the Prime Minister acts as the head of the government. The King listens and adheres to the advice of the ministers. And the ministers are collectively responsible to the Parliament. Being themselves the member of the parliament, there is less conflict between the executive and the legislature leading to smooth functioning of the government.

(i) *Separation of powers combined with concentration of responsibility*

There is strict separation of power between the executive, legislature and the judiciary. Each institution performs its function separately without encroaching on another. But the cabinet In England has come to play very prominent role. It controls the agenda of the parliament and to an extent even influences the judiciary, thus cabinet is called as the steering wheel, which steers the ship called the government.

(j) *Blend of Monarchy, aristocracy and democracy*

The British Constitution is a balance between monarchy, aristocracy and democracy. The Crown-King represents the monarchy, the House of Lords (the Upper House) represents the aristocracy and the House of Commons represents the Lower House giving representation to the common man, thus upholding the ideals of democracy. Though the powers of Monarch and Aristocrats have been drastically reduced they have not been scrapped. These institutions serve as remnants of the bygone era serving little purpose in the present.

(k) *Bicameral legislature*

British has a bicameral parliament. The House of Lords having hereditary membership is the Upper House and the House of Common is the Lower House. House of Commons is more powerful than the Upper House. It is elected by people having universal adult franchise.

7.1.4 Executive

Cabinet is the real executive. The crown obeys the advice of the cabinet. Thus, the cabinet is central to the functioning of the government. However there is difference between the ministry and the cabinet. The ministry has larger composition and they do not meet as a body and hence do not have collective function. Whereas cabinet consists of members of the ministry, it the circle within the circle of the ministry. The Prime Minister appoints his inner circle consisting of most important members to advise him, to formulate policies and to implement them.

The important feature of the cabinet is the exclusion of the King from the cabinet. The King does not preside over it. Since the cabinet members come from the parliament, and Prime Minister is the leader of a majority party, there is complete cooperation and harmony between the parliament and the cabinet. Ministerial responsibility is the inherent feature of the cabinet system. There are two kinds of responsibilities: legal and political. Legal responsibility comes from the fact that every law that is passed is first signed by the King and the minister responsible for it countersigns it. Hence in case of illegality, the minister is held responsible and not the crown. Political responsibility comes with the collective responsibility of the cabinet to the parliament. They either sail or sink together. Prime Minister is the leader of the cabinet, and the ministers work under him. Being from same party gives the cabinet political homogeneity, which helps its smooth functioning.

The Cabinet has both individual and collective functions. As individuals, the ministers are in charge of departments and carry out its functions. Collectively, the cabinet is responsible for final determination of policy which is to be submitted to the parliament, it exercises complete control over the national executives and cabinet also helps in cooperation and coordination between various departments, thus helping in effective functioning of the government.

Prime Minister is the leader of the largest party of the parliament. He is called upon by the King to form the government. Prime Minister recommends the names of the members to be appointed as ministers and as the cabinet. He is free to choose whom to be included in the cabinet. He allocates each minister his/her portfolio. He can also reshuffle/remove any minister as it comes under his discretion as he is the head of the government. He coordinates the work between the cabinet members. As chairman of the cabinet, he summons and prepares agenda of the meeting. Prime Minister is thus called as the keystone of the cabinet without whom the structure would cease to exist.

Apart from his important role in the cabinet, the Prime Minister acts as the leader of the House of Commons. He acts as the representative of the cabinet in the house and presents the parliament the agenda of the government. Another most important power of the Prime Minister is his power to dissolve the government. Only he can recommend the crown to dissolve the house and propose a date for election. Prime Minister also acts as the important channel of communication between the cabinet and the crown. In his capacity as head of the government, he is the chief adviser to the crown. In the international stage, the Prime Minister represents the nation. He formulates the foreign policy.

The most important part of the executive is the crown. It has the supreme executive authority. It can declare war or peace, appoints all the executives, supreme command over the armed forces, conducts the foreign relations. But in reality, the cabinet exercises all these powers. The crown acts per the advice of the Prime Minister and the cabinet. Apart from this, crown also forms part of the legislature. The King summons, prorogues sessions of the parliament, he also dissolves the house. The King gives final assent to any bill passed by the parliament. Even in such legislative functions, the King adheres to the voice of the cabinet and acts accordingly. In no place does the King have discretion to act on his own except is case where there is no party having majority, King decides on whom to call to form the government.

Though it may seem the King is mere ceremonial head, but he does have some inherent rights, right to be consulted, right to warn and right to encourage. Prime Minister has to keep the King informed and should consult him in important cases of public interest. The King also renders warning and advice whenever such situation arises, and the cabinet cannot ignore such messages.

7.1.5 Legislature

The parliament is the ultimate sovereign institution, and it has very wide powers. It has the right to make or unmake any law, and there is no authority which can question or declare it is ultra vires of the constitution. Also there is no distinction between common law and the constitutional law. It reality, there are other factors which play important role limiting the extreme sovereign powers of the parliament. The parliament is bound by moral limitations, rule of law is fundamental feature governing the land, public opinion too play an important role is limiting the sovereign powers of the parliament, judicial precedents and judge made laws also become important conventions. The parliament is at present overburdened with work, hence it cannot take up all the matters on its own, delegated legislation has thus come to play an important role, this also limits the sovereign powers of the parliament.

The House of Commons or the Lower House is the elected body. When the King dissolves the parliament, it is the house of commons which is dissolved hence we can say parliament is nothing but the House of Commons. It enjoys highest power in law making, control of the executive and financial administration.

Being the popular chamber, the House of Commons takes up the law making and has been given enormous power. Though House of Lords, the Upper House, is present, its powers has been curtailed and been made subordinate to the House of Commons. It has the final say in all the legislative actions. Decision regarding all non-monetary bills now rests with the commons. Thus House of Commons supremacy is well established and functional.

All money bill should originate in the House of Commons. House of Lords have very limited power regarding the money bill, at most it can delay it only for a month. House of Commons can get the ascent of the King without support from the Lords, thus it control over money bills is complete and decisive. It also controls the purse of the nation. Budget making is an important instrument to keep check over the executive. Raising taxes or expenditure needs its seal of approval.

In the parliamentary setup, the council of ministers are responsible to the popular chamber. The council has a collective responsibility towards the commons. So long as the council of ministers enjoy confidence of the house, they can continue to run the government and when they lose it they have to render their resignation. The House of Commons keep check over the executive by seeking information about the functions and actions of the government and by criticising it. Ministers are obliged to reply to questions asking in the house. 'Question hour' helps the house to scrutinize the working of the government. Apart from law-making, the house debates the policies and actions of the government.

The house of Lords is the oldest functioning second chamber in the world. Unlike the House of Commons, it consists of hereditary members, Lords, Nobles. Since 1911, its powers have been very much curtailed. A bill can originate in any house, and it has to be approved by both the houses for it to be passed. Being a historical institution, the House of Lords maintains the tradition and custom of English way of life. It helps prevent drastic deviation in laws made by the commons. Private member bill arising from the house helps in saving time of the commons. The second chamber upholds the ideals of bicameralism, and it helps in detailed scrutiny of the bills, creates an atmosphere for free and fair discussion. It acts as the revisory chamber for bills originating from the House of Commons. The house of Lords is also bestowed with important judicial functions.

7.1.6 Judiciary

There is no single judicial system followed throughout entire United Kingdom. England and Wales follow a system, Scotland follows a different system and Northern Ireland follows yet another system. Hence there is no uniform judicial courts throughout the country. Rule of law is supreme in England, and hence there are no separate administrative courts. Everyone is treated equally before the law. But there is no concept of judicial review. No law can be declared to be ultra vires of the constitution. Parliament is thus supreme, and no authority can question the validity of a law. Unlike courts of America, where a law has to pass the judicial scrutiny, English courts do not scrutinize the laws. Important aspect of the British judiciary is its quality and quickness. The procedures are simple, and hence cases move faster unlike courts in India. Fairness and speed are the essential features English courts. English judges enjoy high degree of independence.

The judges are appointed for life and can be removed only by elaborate procedure in the parliament. The trial is open to all, and anyone can attend it. The judges are impartial and people trust the system to deliver justice. Trial by jury is an essential feature which can be demanded by the accused. The courts uphold the human rights, helping in upholding civil rights, freedom of speech, movement, freedom of press, etc. Free legal aid is provided to those who cannot afford it from a financial point of view.

7.2 AMERICAN CONSTITUTION

7.2.1 Introduction

Philadelphia Convention held in 1787 forms the basis for the American Constitution. It came into force in 1789 after ratification of required number of states. It is one of the briefest Constitution in the world consisting of originally seven articles. Around 26 amendments have been carried out exposing the rigid character of the constitution. The concept of Montesquieu's separation of power has found ideal application in the American system, all the institutions are separate and it has checks and balances to prevent overreach. Though constitutionally the federal government is weak, judicial interpretation by the Supreme Court has strengthened its position.

7.2.2 Salient Features of the American Constitution

The following are the salient features of the American Constitution:

(a) **Written form**

Like any other federal constitution, it is in written character. It is simple and elegant consisting of only seven articles. It was created as a skeleton Constitution where the framers created just the important broad outlines where rest of the details will be filled by the acts of the Congress. Thus, Constitution is just the starting point. Other than the written character, there are elements like conventions, customs, legislative measures and judicial decisions which form the unwritten part forming a vital part of the constitutional provisions. Though election of President as per the Constitution is indirect in character, present convention is that it is a direct contest between the individuals.

(b) **Rigidity**

It is the most rigid Constitution in the world. Though amendment is possible, it is very lengthy and cumbersome, and it requires ratification of three-fourth of the states. Hence any proposed amendment takes years before it is implemented. The rigidity can be seen from the fact that only 26 amendments have been carried out in all these years of existence of the constitution. Though it seems rigid, the Constitution has adapted well to changing circumstances, from the Industrial Revolution to the present technological revolution.

(c) Federal nature

Originally it was a federation of 13 states, which is now expanded into 50 states. There is constitutional division of powers between union and the states. The Constitution has elaborated the powers of the centre and has left all the residual powers to the states. Thus Constitution has created a weak centre and strong federal states. But in practice, this is not followed, the powers of centre has increased manifold due to the concept of 'implied powers' as propounded by the Supreme Court of America.

(d) Supremacy of the constitution

The Constitution is supreme law of the land. Neither the centre nor the states can override the constitution. Any law passed by state or centre can be declared ultra vires of the Constitution if it is in violation by the Supreme Court.

(e) Separation of powers

Though there is no direct statement in Constitution regarding separation of powers, the concept is implied and seen from the fact that the constitutional makers have attempted to keep separate executive, legislature and judiciary as much as possible. The President is the head of the executive, he is indirectly elected and he has nothing to do with the Congress. The Congress is thus only the legislative body. President is not responsible to the Congress and thus cannot be removed by vote of no-confidence. He also does not participate in its debates. Both the organs are independent of each other. Supreme Court enjoys enormous freedom and independence of function. In actual practice, there is no complete separation of powers between the institutions. Today the President controls the legislative policy of the Congress. There is coordination between the executive and the legislature. Thus in practice, there is overlap and sharing of powers between different institutions.

(f) Checks and balances

Power of each institution is checked by another, and thus balance of power is maintained. President can veto the bills of the Congress. International treaty needs approval from the senate. Internal appointments too need ratification from the senate, thus senate checks the power of the President. Organisation of judiciary is determined by the Congress, and the President has the power to appoint the judges of the Supreme Court, subject to the approval by the senate. The Supreme Court has powers to strive down bills of both centre and states if is in violation of the constitutional provisions.

(g) Bill of rights

The basic fundamental rights of life, property and liberty was not incorporated into the original constitution. By subsequent first 10 amendments, these rights got approval and made as part of the constitution. The citizens can take a recourse to courts if their fundamental rights are violated. These rights can only be modified or suspended by another constitutional amendment. Thus citizens of America enjoy freedom of speech, habeas corpus, freedom of worship, freedom from unreasonable seizure, etc., as they have been made as fundamental feature of the constitution.

(h) Judicial review

The judicial review is sometimes called as the judicial veto as this keeps in check the powers of the legislature and the executive. The courts thus act as custodian and guardian of the constitutional rights, any bill which violates it will be struck down. Judiciary has also expanded the power of the centre with its doctrine of 'implied powers', hence Constitution is what judiciary interprets. The judiciary interprets the Constitution according to the changing circumstances of the society. This has made the Constitution relevant to any period in the time scale.

(i) Republican form of government

Unlike monarchical form followed in the United Kingdom, the United States has adopted a republican form. The head of the state, the President is elected. The people drive the Constitution. The Constitution makes it binding to adopt republican form of government.

(j) Presidential government

President is head of the state and government. He is vested with all the executive powers. Unlike parliamentary form followed in the United Kingdom and India, the President is not responsible to the Congress. He does not attend any session, not directly introduce any legislation nor participates in the debates. The Congress too cannot remove the President by no-confidence motion. He enjoys problem-free 4-year tenure. Also, the President cannot dissolve the Congress. The cabinet of the President consists of members of his own selection, and they need not be from the Congress.

(k) Dual citizenship

The Constitution provides for dual citizenship. The individual is thus citizen of both the state and the country.

(l) Popular sovereignty

The people are the ultimate sovereign. The preamble of the Constitution establishes this idea. Rest of the government and its institutions are subjected to sovereignty of the people.

(m) Spoils system

The Spoils System is an important part of the constitution. The Pendleton Act (1883) has curtailed and made only 20% of the offices subject to patronage of the President. Previously, all the offices were considered to be the spoils of victory of election of the President. He appointed his followers and supporters in the key posts. They worked not for the government but for the President and to help in his re-election. And when a new President is elected, the previous members resign and he appoints his own supporters to the posts. This system created numerous problems and inefficiency. This was rectified by the Pendleton Act though not completely removing the Spoils System.

(n) Bicameral legislature

Like United Kingdom and India, the United States, too, follows a bicameral system. Its lower house is called as the House of Representatives and upper house the Senate. Its upper house is the most powerful upper house in the world. Senate, thus, has more powers than the House of Representatives. It has executive, legislative and judicial powers. It has compact membership of hundred having a tenure of 6 years, whereas the lower house has 2-year tenure consisting of 435 members.

7.2.3 Executive

United States follow the Presidential form of government, hence the President here is not mere head of the state, and he is also the head of the government. He appoints the cabinet, carries out functioning of the government independent of the Congress, he is neither responsible nor is controlled by the Congress, and Congress too cannot remove him. The President is supported by a Vice President who succeeds him in case the chair falls vacant for any reason. The President of America is considered to be the most powerful office in the world comparable to none. But the powers is limited by the constitutional checks and balances by giving powers to the legislature and judiciary.

The Presidential powers and functions can be studied under his executive, legislative, financial, judicial and emergency powers.

As the chief executive the President is responsible for implementation and overseeing of the policies. He is responsible for the execution of constitutional provisions, laws made by the Congress and decrees given by the Supreme Court. He is given power to make appointments and also removal of the high executives like the ambassador, ministers and federal judges. President is the brain behind the formulation of the national policy which bears his stamp. He also negotiates and concludes agreement with foreign countries. 'Executive agreements' skirt the approval from the senate, thus helping the President securely uphold the treaties.

Though the President is not the part of the legislature, he still has been given powers to legislate. The President can send messages to the Congress or even personally read them. Though it is not compulsory to adopt such messages, it carries weight of the office of the President which cannot be ignored. He can also call upon extraordinary session of the Congress to legislate on some important issue. He can also give ordinances which has to be later taken up by the Congress. The other important role played by the President is in exercising his veto powers. He can either give ascent or send back the bill to the Congress with some recommendations. He has to approve the bill within 10 days. And if the Congress is adjourned within the 10 days, the bill dies. Thus the President is given pocket veto in this case, where he can delay unwanted bills without giving ascent and waiting for the Congress to adjourn. Any bill sent again for review if passed by two-third majority of the Congress, the President has to approve it. Thus, the President has absolute, qualified and pocket veto powers.

The President has been given powers to grant reprieve, pardon or amnesty. His power to do so is confined to federal matters and does not apply in case of state laws. Budget making and giving annual financial statement to the Congress is the prerogative of the President. Thus maintaining healthy financial environment is one of the responsibilities of the President.

Though he cannot directly declare war, only the Congress can do so, he can create situation where it is inevitable for the Congress but to declare war. The President makes appointment of the heads of armed forces. During emergency situations, the powers of President increase enormously.

The cabinet is called as the extension of the shadow of the President. Unlike cabinets in the United Kingdom and India, which leads an independent existence with respect to its leader and is responsible to their parliaments, the American cabinet is neither independent of and nor responsible to the Congress. All the appointments of the cabinet is the personal wish of the President. Hence it is also called as the 'kitchen cabinet'.

7.2.4 Legislature

The federal legislature consists of two bodies: the upper senate and the lower house of representatives. The senate consists of 100 members where each state sends two members each. The lower house is composed of 435 members elected based on territorial representation on demographic basis. There is also significant difference in life of each house, lower house is shorter having 2- year tenure and upper house having a 6-year time period. The houses of American legislature is not a sovereign body like the British Parliament, hence it has to act according to the boundaries prescribed by the constitution. Also the President has veto power over the bills, and if he sends the bill again for reconsideration it has to be passed by two-third majority in the house. The judiciary also strikes down any law which is ultra vires of the Constitution that is law which violates the constitutional provisions. There is also the underlying concept of separation of powers, where each institution is independent of each other.

The Constitution has granted set of powers on which Congress can make laws. Rest of the residual powers fall under the purview of the states. But the power of the Congress has expanded under the doctrine of 'implied powers' as given by the Supreme Court. Under this, the powers of the Congress has been widened to cover areas where state is responsible. The Constitution also provide for the concurrent powers shared by Congress and the state, but the Congress can override the state in case of conflict.

Apart from the legislative powers, the Congress has other powers which comes under electoral, constituent, executive, financial, judicial, inquisitorial, directing and supervisory.

The constitutional amendment bill can be passed by the Congress with two-third majority. It can also call for constitutional convention if two-third of the state requests it. The electoral powers of the Congress is important. If the Presidential candidates fail to secure majority in the Electoral College, it the duty of the lower house to select the President from the top three securing the majority and senate chooses the Vice President. Apart from this, the lower house elects its speaker and senate it President pro tempore.

Senate confirms all the appointments and the foreign treaties. Congress approves the resolution of war and peace. The house can set up investigative committee to check into complaints regarding alleged misappropriation of funds or a scandal. The lower house has power of initiating impeachment proceedings against the President, Vice President and other high-ranking public servants and the senate. Impeachment is passed if two-third of the house vote for it. The Constitution grants the financial supremacy of the constitution. The Congress thus controls the purse of the nation. No amount of money can be appropriated without its approval. Though budget is prepared and presented by the President, it is Congress that approves it. Thus Congress plays decisive role in functioning of the government.

7.2.5 Judiciary

Federal judiciary was considered to be the important organ of the state. Its key role was to maintain the checks and balances on the legislature and executive. It was considered to be the guardian and protector of the constitutional principles. Any law which is in violation of the Constitution is struck down. Constitution does not provide for the qualification and the appointment process of the judges of the court, hence the President is free to appoint anyone. The judges are appointed for life. It is their prerogative to retire at either 65 after completing 15 years of service or at 70 after completing 10 years of service. With 'good behaviour', the judge can continue his service. The lower house can initiate impeachment proceeding based on allegation of treason, bribery or other high crime of misdemeanour, and it goes to the senate where a resolution is passed by two-third majority supporting the removal.

The Supreme Court has both original and appellate jurisdiction. The original jurisdiction covers action by the centre against a state, action by one state against another, in cases involving high-ranking public servants and ambassadors, and in cases where state act against citizen belonging to another state or alien. Appeals lie to the Supreme Court from the lower district courts, and from state courts where federal question is involved. The important aspect of American Supreme Court is that it does not exercise advisory jurisdiction.

Two important aspects of the judiciary is the concept of judicial review which has made the courts the guardian of the Constitution and the concept of 'due process of law' which is the safe guard against the arbitrary executive action.

7.3 CHINESE CONSTITUTION

7.3.1 Introduction

The first Constitution of People's Republic of China was promulgated in 1954. Its main objective was to build socialism step by step. It did not follow the socialism of Soviet but rather developed its own version under the influence of Mao Tsetung came to be known as 'Maoism'. This Constitution was in force till 1975 when it subjected to revision. The new Constitution was a brief document, and it enumerated the achievements of the previous constitution. There was no major deviation and it followed the path laid by the Chairman Mao. Once again this Constitution was subjected to revision soon in 1978. This Constitution was fairly liberal than the earlier ones, but it did not affect any major changes to the old setup. This was old wine in new bottle.

Under the leadership of Deng Xiao-ping, the Constitution was again revised in the year 1982, and it has been continuing till the present. The preamble elaborates the achievements of the communist state till then. It took major deviation in Mao's views. Economy was given precedence.

7.3.2 Salient Features of Chinese Constitution

The important aspects of the 1982 Constitution are as follows:

(a) Written character

Like the previous other constitutions, it is also a written document. It presently consists of 138 articles. Hence it is not so brief like the 1975 Constitution and even bigger than the 1954 Constitution, which contained 116 articles.

(b) Flexible

It is fairly easier to amend the constitution. The amendment can be moved either by the standing committee or by one fifth of the members of the Congress. Once approved, it is deemed passed if two-third of the members of the Congress give approval. Since it is a one party, communist-dominated Congress, it is easy for the amendment to be approved and passed.

(c) Unitary state

The Constitution provides for a strong unitary state where people of all nationality come under single state. There is no provision of creation of autonomous provinces or states in the style of India or Canada, though limited powers to provinces has been envisaged. There are 21 provinces, 5 autonomous regions and 2 cities, but all these are mere names as the central government has complete control over them. The government in the provinces act as agents of the centre.

(d) Power to the people

Constitution is based on the power of the people. All power belongs to them. The national People's Congress and the local People's Congress are elected directly by the people. All organs of the state maintain close contact with the people to fulfil their wishes and heed to their opinions.

The feudal lords and the capitalists have been stripped of all political rights. And thus ordinary people are considered to be the foundation of the Chinese communist state.

(e) Planned economy

Like its Russian counterpart, China, too, adopted the planned growth of the economy. It is vital and important aspect for a socialist state. Revolutionary changes have been brought about in agriculture and in industries. Most of the industries were brought under the control of the state. The planning is carried out to provide better living condition for the people, thus it is both social and economic planning which is carried out.

(f) People's democratic dictatorship

China cannot be categorised either as a parliamentary form or a Presidential form even though it has some of the features of both. It is a republic state headed by the President who is just a nominal head performing ceremonial functions. The real executive power lies with the Prime Minister who heads the state council which is responsible to the National people's Congress which is an elected body. The democratic character comes from the fact that the Prime Minister cannot become a dictator as he is given only two terms of totally 10 years. But the dictatorship character arises because the state council is ultimately controlled by the communist party of China. The chairman of the party holds all the power.

(g) Democratic centralism

All organs of the state follow this principle of democratic centralism. National people's Congress is an elected body, some organs of the state too is elected hence they are responsible and accountable to the people. This reflects the democratic character of the state. All policy making is centralised. It is controlled by the state committee of National People's Congress and state council. The communist party is the highest decision-making authority. This policy of democratic centralism was adopted from the erstwhile Soviet Union.

(h) Fundamental rights

The citizens are guaranteed economic, social, political, cultural, civil and personal rights and liberties. They also enjoy equality before law and equal protection from it. Right to education, right to get elected, freedom of speech and expression, association, freedom of religion, etc., are guaranteed to the people. There is also no discrimination based on sex. But all these rights are curtailed by one Article 51, which says all these rights should not violate principles of the state, community and of other citizens. This article thus gives blanket power to the state to control the fundamental freedom of the citizens. Apart from rights, there is also set of important duties like joining the militia, pay tax, practice family planning, etc., which has to be carried out by every single person.

(i) Socialist state

Article 1 declares that China is a socialist state. This is interpreted ideology of Marx, Engels and Lenin by Mao. The Chinese society is led by working class which is comprised of alliance of both workers and peasants. This alliance is against the enemies—the feudalists, the imperialists and the bureau-capitalists. All power is given to the people which is exercised under the guidance of the communist party of China.

(j) Unicameral legislature

The National People's Congress forms the legislature of the Chinese state. NPC along with the standing committee carries out the legislative functions of the state. It is elected for a period of 5 years, and it is the sole law-making body in the country. It has power to appoint all important positions from Prime Minister, President and to judicial officers, etc., it has also been given power to remove these persons. Though it may sound impressive, all these are only formal power. In practice, the NPC acts according to the direction of the communist party.

(k) **Provision of standing committee**

This standing committee is elected by the members of the NPC. It is the executive body of the Congress. It has life till the Congress is functioning. The power of the standing committee has been very much curtailed at the present.

(l) **Judiciary**

The judiciary is completely different from the western systems. The Supreme People's court is the apex court which guarantees the socialist legality. It has both appellate and original jurisdiction. The judicial structure is basically pyramidal, where the local people's court forms the base and the Supreme Court sits at the Apex. These courts too come under the democratic dictatorship system and is controlled by the dictates of the communist party of China.

7.3.3 Executive

The President is elected for a 5-year term by the National people's Congress. The President can continue for another term, thus he has maximum period of 10 years. The office is for ceremonial reasons and his functions are formal.

The Prime Minister, here called as the Premier, is appointed by the President. Other officers too are appointed by him based on the recommendation from the NPC of the standing committee. Those appointed by him are also removed by him on basis of recommendation from the NPC or the standing committee. State of war and martial law are declared by him. He is also given special pardoning powers. He receives the foreign Ambassadors and other dignitaries on behalf of the state. He also ratifies the foreign treaties and other agreements signed by the government.

All these functions are carried out on the recommendation and guidance of the standing committee of the NPC. Thus, the President is a ceremonial figure having no power on his own.

The state council is the real government. It is equivalent to the cabinet system in other countries. Premier is the head of the council and NPC selects other members based on his recommendation. The office runs till the term of the NPC that is for 5 years. The President has the power to remove the members based on the recommendation from the NPC.

The important power of the state council are it is the central government, thus it forms all the policies and implements them, it carries out the administration of the country, it sends various legislative proposals for the consideration of the NPC, it lays down responsibilities and functions of each ministry, it also supervises the functioning of the provinces, autonomous regions and other areas, they all fall under the direct control of the central government, it ensures the country is defended effectively, it recruits, trains and appoints the civil servants to various administrative posts and it prepares the budget document to get approved from the NPC.

Though the position of the Premier is not as equivalent to that of British or Indian Prime Minister, he does enjoy enough powers. The premier does not create or destroy the state council. He can only select those members he want to get appointed to the council and the NPC makes such recommendation to the President who finally appoints them. He is just the head of the state council, hence the government. He plays the role of coordinating between the various ministries and controlling their functions.

7.3.4 Legislature

The national people's Congress is the unicameral legislature. Since China follows a unitary form of government, secondary chamber to represent the interests of the states were not needed. Thus, NPC forms the highest instrument of state to form the laws and the sole authority to approve and pass them. The time period is of 5 years and the periodic elections are conducted by the state council.

The functions of the NPC are, they can ask questions to the state council or the ministers. All the members have to abide by the Constitution and protect its secrets. NPC is the one and only law-making body. Standing committee does this function when the NPC is in recess. The other important function of the NPC is to supervise the working of the constitution. Apart from these, the NPC elects all major important institutions, the President, Vice President, the Prime Minister and his council of ministers, the auditor and secretary general of the state council, the chairman of the central military commission. It also elects the President of Supreme people's court, and the Procurator General of the Supreme People's procuratorate. The NPC has the power to amend the constitution, the proposal for amendment is submitted by the standing committee or one-fifth of the deputies of the NPC.

It takes care of the development and the social planning of the country. It first examines such plans, approves them and finally submit report of their implementation. The budget of the government is approved by the NPC. It has power to alter the boundaries of the provinces, autonomous regions, etc. Apart from electing people it has power to remove or recall them.

It has power to take decisions on matters which are not specified in the constitution. Thus, NPC has been given enormous powers. But all these exist in paper and the real power lies with the communist party of China. NPC cannot take all decisions on its own. Thus in reality, the communist party of China is the power centre and all other institutions function in relation to it.

The standing committee of NPC is the smaller version of the Congress. The whole NPC is very large and meets only once a year, thus the standing committee only takes care of the day to day functions and working of the government. It is headed by a chairman, followed by a vice chairman, the secretary general and members. It has the life time of the NPC, and when new NPC is constituted a new standing committee is elected.

The legislative function of the standing committee are: it can summon the NPC, it enacts the legislation when NPC is not in session, it supervises the working of all major state organs like the State council, Central military commission, etc., it has been delegated the power to legislate on behalf of the NPC.

Its elective functions are: when NPC is not in session, it decides on the choice of ministers, the auditor general and the secretary general. It has the power to appoint and remove the Vice Presidents and judges of Supreme People's court, the deputy procurators general and Procurator of the Supreme people's procuratorate.

The following are its executive functions: though the ambassadors and diplomatic personals are appointed by the President, they are removed by the standing committee; ratification of treaties are also decided by the committee; the decision to pardon criminals though approved by the President, he is advised to do so by the standing committee; it has also been given power to declare war when NPC is not in session.

The standing council interprets the law which is generally the function of the Supreme courts (United States and India). It also interprets the Constitution and helps in its implementation. It supervises the function of the state council and can even rejects its decisions.

The standing committees play a minor role in proposing amendment to the constitution. But the power to amend rests with the NPC.

7.3.5 Judiciary

The structure of judiciary is simple and is in form of a pyramid. The local people's court constitute the base and the supreme people's court is at the apex. Every provinces too has its set of courts which has entire jurisdiction over it.

The Constitution does not provide the functions of the supreme people's court. But some of its important functions are: to supervise the courts below it, the NPC has the power to widen the powers of this court, it has original jurisdiction over cases of national importance, it also hears appeals against the decisions of the high courts in the provinces.

China also has a unique procuratorate system. Starting from the local procuratorates it goes till the apex, the supreme people's procuratorate. Each procuratorate is managed by the one above it. These bodies are elected by the local organ of the state authority and hence are responsible only to it. The main function of these procuratorates are: to prosecute people who violate the socialist principles of the state, it also advices the government on legal matters, the supreme people's procuratorate acts as the chief public prosecutor of the government, apart from citizens it can also take action against the government and its officials, and finally they act as the protector of the socialist legacy of China.

Some of the important features of the Chinese judiciary are: it has a single well-integrated judicial system unlike in the United States where state and federal courts are separated, the judiciary is not completely independent as at all levels the judicial officials are elected by the government, the Constitution moreover does not specify the tenure and qualification of the judges, thus everything falls under the discretion of the NPC and other government bodies, generally trials are conducted in open and only few exceptions are there for closed trials, unlike in major democracies the supreme court of China has no power to declare any law made by the legislature as ultra vires of the constitution, even the judiciary has no power to question the action of the executives, since all actions of either legislature or the executive comes only after the blessing from the communist party, they can never be violation of the constitution. Thus the Chinese judiciary is a committed judiciary, the one which is committed to the communist ideology, the communist party, and to the communist government.

7.4 SWISS CONSTITUTION

7.4.1 Introduction

The Swiss Constitution was first adopted in the year 1848. Loose organisations of small states called cantons came together to create this constitution. The most important feature of this Constitution is the tilt towards strong and unified government based on federalism. It terminated the system of cantons and created 'confederation' of states. This Constitution of 1848 underwent two revisions one in 1874 and another in 1999 and the present Swiss system is governed by this constitution. It gave more powers to the federal government in controlling the military.

The new Constitution was ratified by the people and came into force on 1 January, 2000. It consists of 197 articles. The structure has more or less remained the same. It makes Switzerland a social welfare, democratic and a republican state.

7.4.2 Salient Features of the Swiss Constitution

The following are the salient features of the Swiss constitution:

(a) Written and enacted document

Like American Constitution, it is also a written document consisting of 197 articles. The Constitution is the supreme law of the land. It creates a balance between federal government and the cantons. It seeks to prevent friction and internal strife. It is also voluminous.

(b) Rigid

It is difficult of carry out amendments to the Constitution, but it is not so rigid like the American constitution. Any amendment has to be passed by the parliament, and it has to be ratified by majority of the cantonal governments and also by majority of people in the referendum. It is flexible in the sense that people have more powers through instruments of 'initiative' and 'referendum'. Thus it widens the democratic powers of the people. And in each instance, it is passed by a simple majority.

(c) Plural executive

Switzerland has unique system of plural executive also known as collegial or plural presidency. Seven members or ministers are all designated as the Presidents. Usual practice is power is vested with one individual either Prime Ministers or President and he controls the government. Here all the seven members have equal powers. To carry out ceremonial functions, the senior member is elected as the President of the federation and another the Vice President for a year. Each canton gets its representation in the presidency and no two President should belong to the same political party. Hence there is wide diversity and is always a coalition government.

(d) Federal system

The Constitution declares Switzerland to be a confederation. The powers are shared between the centre and the cantons. Certain subjects which are of national importance like foreign affairs, military affairs, declaration of war, etc., comes under the centre, there are some concurrent powers shared both by centre and the cantons such as control of press, regulation of industries, etc., and rest of the residuary power lies with the canton. The federal court has been set up to interpret the provisions of the Constitution and help settle legal disputes arising between centre and the cantons. Like United States, the federal states have been given enough autonomy and hence can be considered as a true federation.

(e) Direct democracy

Modern democracy is called as representative government because people do not rule themselves directly, they select-elect their representatives to rule on their behalf. Though Switzerland has such kind of representative structure, it also has three important concepts which widens the power of democracy, they are Initiative, referendum and landsgemeinde. *Initiative* refers to initiative of at least one lakh voters to send proposal to the parliament to adopt it as a bill or send it back to the people as referendum. Constitutional amendment bills and some 'urgent' bill of public importance should be placed before the people after passed by the parliament. Eight cantonal governments or at least 50,000 voters can demand referendum on any other bill. Thus, referendum places the final veto power in the hands of the people. The system of town parliament in the five small cantons is called as the landsgemeinde. Each adult member is the member of the town assemble and hence cantonal elections do not take place here.

(f) Social welfare state

Each person is ensured social security and health care by the government. It is the responsibility of the centre and cantonal government to ensure everyone are economically protected, shielded against illness, old age issues, and maternity and against widowhood, etc. The Constitution thus has created a social welfare state which strives to protect its members.

(g) Fundamental rights

It is so expansive that it covers social, economic and political sphere. And it is much wider than the provisions contained in the universal declaration of human rights adopted by the general assembly of the United Nations in 1948. Economic rights include right to free choice of vocation, formation of union, people have right over their property and they have to be fully compensated if such property is acquired by the state. Political freedom ensures free press: print and electronic, editorial secrecy is guaranteed, freedom to form opinion and express it, arbitrary arrest and detention are prevented. But all these political rights are tied to citizenship that is only a Swiss national enjoys all these freedoms.

(h) Republican constitution

Republicanism is not just at the centre but every canton also follows it. Swiss equality is for everyone in the society, hence it had abolished the aristocratic and oligarchic privileges. All political institutions are elective in character. The principle of republicanism is the fortification of Swiss democracy.

(i) Secondary position of judiciary

The apex judicial body has no power to review the laws made by the centre. The Constitution has made it secondary to the legislative body unlike in countries like the United States or India. The judiciary can only review laws made by the cantons and declare it unconstitutional if it is in violation. The judges too are elected by the federal assembly. Thus the Swiss federal tribunal has only limited judicial review powers.

(j) Bicameral system

It has upper house known as the council of states representing the cantons on equal basis like American senate. It is a small body consisting of 46 members. The lower body is larger having 200 members elected by the people. The lower body is called the National Council. Both the bodies have equal power and one does not dominate over the other.

(k) Dynamic constitution

The Swiss Constitution is very dynamic. It has adapted well according to changing situations. Growing aspirations of the people have been addressed by widening their rights. The state too intervenes whenever rights of the citizens are threatened and laws have been made subsequently to protect it.

7.4.3 Executive

The Swiss executive is headed by a ceremonial office of the President. Senior most member of the seven ministers is elected President for 1- year tenure. He is neither *primus inter pares* or does he enjoy precedence over his colleagues. Since some jobs cannot be performed as a group, an individual is appointed to the role of the President. He receives envoys, appoints ambassadors and represents the country at international fora. Thus, the Swiss executive is plural or a collegial system. No single individual enjoys the power. And after expiration of 1 year, he returns back to his membership and other persons are elected based on rotation of seniority. The Swiss executive is also very stable and cannot be easily dismissed before its end of tenure.

As per the Constitution, the executive is subordinate to the legislature. The executive cannot act independently of the assembly. The Swiss executive is not like the cabinet system of the British. The members here are from different political parties, and hence bring unity in diversity. They are not the members of the legislature but are elected by the national assembly. They are also neither individually nor collectively responsible to the legislature. But ministers take part in deliberations of the legislature to get approval. Hence it is not like the American system where the executive is completely separated from the legislature.

The function of the executive is to oversee the working of the cantons. It checks whether canton is functioning on basis of the constitution. It also helps in resolving dispute between two cantons. It carries out foreign relations, signs treaties and protects independence and sovereignty of the nation. It also looks after the law and order situation, and if any cantonal government fails to uphold it, it can intervene on behalf of the legislature. It controls the federal army and has power to deploy troops in case of emergency when parliament is not in session.

The executive submits the draft of the bill to the legislature for deliberation. Thus the government initiates debate in the parliament, and the parliament can pass the bill with or without amendments. It periodically submits report to the parliament on functioning of the cantons, internal condition of the country and its foreign relation. It also submits set of recommendations to promote welfare of the citizens to be adopted by the parliament. Though they are not members of the legislature, they are allowed to participate, debate, deliberate and answer question. They also attend meetings of the parliament committees discussing the bills and influence it with their knowledge and experience.

The executive submits the budget and it collects revenue and supervises the expenditure. It has some powers of judicial nature. It hears appeals of private individuals against decisions of various departments and federal railway authority. It also has appellate jurisdiction over decisions of cantonal government in some discrimination cases.

Thus the Swiss system is neither parliamentary nor Presidential. It is unique by itself. It is non-partisan and has high integration and cooperation among its members.

7.4.4 Legislature

The federal parliament is of bicameral nature. It represents the federal nature of Indian and American system. The similarity ends there, the Swiss Constitution provides equal power to both the houses, and thus no house is subordinate to the other. It is also one of the other unique feature of the Swiss system.

The senate is similar to American senate, each full canton has two members and each half canton one member. Thus all cantons receive equal representation. These members are elected by the cantons themselves based on their own system; thus each canton can have their own system of electing, determining the tenure, salary, etc., the cantons have also the power to recall or replace their representatives.

The members of House of Representatives are elected by the people directly based on proportional representation with list system and secret ballot. Population and size of the canton determine the number of representatives sent by it. The President acts as the chairman of the house. He regulates the business, protect the privilege and dignity of the house.

The legislative powers include passing of federal laws, approval of treaties, passing of constitutional amendment and approval of budgets, etc. It can demand information from the executive and question it. It elects the seven members of the government and appoints one of them as the President. It also elects members of the federal judiciary, appoint commander-in-chief of the armed forces, etc. It has the power to declare war or peace. It has judicial power to grant amnesty and pardon. It also hears appeal against the government in administrative cases.

The constitutional amendment power is subject to people's verdict. Any such amendment has to be ratified by the parliament first and then approved in a referendum by the people and the cantons.

7.4.5 Judiciary

It is the youngest institution in the Swiss system. It consists of 26 judges elected by the parliament. One of them is appointed as its President and another vice-President. The judges represent all the linguistic background.

It covers both civil and criminal cases and also other issues of public law. Its civil jurisdiction covers all suits between federation and the cantons and also between cantons themselves. It also takes up cases between individual and the federation. It decides cases relating to loss of nationality or citizenship dispute between communes of different cantons. The final appeal from the cantonal courts lie to the federal court.

7.5 JAPANESE CONSTITUTION

7.5.1 Introduction

The present Constitution also known as 'Mac Arthur' Constitution is mostly continuation of the older Meiji Constitution. It differs from the older in some crucial important aspects. The Japanese Constitution is the only document to be called the 'peace document' of the world. Though it was a post-war gift by the Americans, it makes Japan a demilitarized state and a democracy.

7.5.2 Salient Features of the Japanese Constitution

The following are the salient features of the Japanese constitution:

(a) **Document of peace**

It openly renounces war. It also says japan will not maintain any standing armed forces. The preamble declares that Japan is a peace-loving country and strives for peace in the world. Though there is no armed forces, the Constitution provides for setting up self-defence forces to protect national interest.

(b) **Sovereignty of people**

The older Constitution vested the power on the monarch. It held imperial sovereignty and people had no power. The present Constitution restores democracy and gives back power to the people. The people are thus made sovereign and they elect their representatives to the diet to voice their concerns. The emperor is made symbolic and has no power. The government derives power from the people as stated in the preamble.

(c) **Unitary system**

Unlike the United States, it is not a federal state. All powers are held by the central government and there is no distribution of powers between the centre and the provinces. Though there are separate local, provincial assemblies they all derive power from the laws passed by the parliament and not from the constitution.

(d) Rigid

Like the United States, it is difficult to amend the constitution. Apart from two-third majority in the parliament, it has also to be ratified by the people in a special referendum. Japanese Constitution has not been amended even once.

(e) Limited judicial review

The Supreme Court is the last resort to validate the law against the violation of the constitution. The Constitution thus has specifically provided for judicial review. But the Supreme Court has not used this power like its counterpart in the United States, it is due to the fact that the conduct of the judges is subject to review after 10 years by the people. The rights and liberties of the people are thus protected by the Constitution by keeping judicial review as a check on the executive and legislature.

(f) Parliamentary form of government

Japan follows British type of system, where the monarch is simply a figurehead and the actual power is vested in the Prime Minister and his cabinet. The parliament can pass a no-confidence motion to remove the government. The Prime Minister and his cabinet are responsible to the diet.

(g) Fundamental rights and duties

A detailed bill of fundamental rights and duties are important feature of the new constitution. It is a comprehensive document covering all areas of social, economic and political rights of the citizens. Apart from rights to citizens, it also speaks about duties by the citizens. Some of the fundamental rights are equality and equal protection before the law, freedom of religion is guaranteed to all, bonded labour is abolished, right to life has been guaranteed to all, etc. These rights are also protected by the courts.

(h) Separation of powers and checks and balances

Previous Meiji Constitution had given enormous power to the monarch and relegated the institutions of parliament and judiciary to a secondary position. Thus the new Constitution explicitly separates and protects the independence of each institutions. The people are made the new sovereign from whom the power is derived. The judiciary is independent and powerful to keep check on the other democratic institutions.

7.5.3 Executive

In the Meiji Constitution, the emperor was accorded the status of divine. He ran the government and all the powers were bestowed upon him, the diet was merely there to approve the wishes of the emperor. After the World War II, the scenario changed and the powers of the emperor was stripped down and was made a nominal head of the state. He now acts on the advice of the Prime Minister and his cabinet.

The emperor has been given power to appoint the Prime Minister as designated by the diet. He attests the final ratification of law, international treaties and appointment of ambassadors. All laws, amendments, etc., are promulgated by the President. He convenes and dissolves the diet. The emperor has also the power the grant amnesty, reprieve, commutation of punishment, etc. He appoints the chief judge of Supreme Court on the advice of the cabinet. Thus all powers of the emperor are merely formal, and he acts as the figurehead of the state. He cannot veto or send back any bills back to the diet unlike his counterpart, the British Monarch.

The cabinet headed by the Prime Minister takes care of the functioning of the government. It takes all important political and administrative decisions. It submits law to be promulgated by the diet. It prepares the budget and get financial approval from the diet. It designates who will be the chief justice of the Supreme Court and makes appointments of the other judges. The cabinet controls and administers the civil service. It submits to the emperor who can be granted amnesty, reprieve and commutation of sentence. The cabinet is made responsible to the diet by the constitution.

The Prime Ministers is considered to be the keystone and performs some important functions. He selects members of his cabinet and forms the government. He can also remove, reshuffle the cabinet whenever he wants. Being chairman of the cabinet, he supervises its function or chairs any committee. He is also the leader of diet in general and the lower house of representatives in particular. He makes appointments of all important positions in the government. He also selects the date of election for the diet which is then approved by the emperor.

The Prime Minister and his cabinet continue as long as they enjoy confidence of the diet. The lower house can pass a motion of no confidence.

7.5.4 Legislature

The parliament is called as diet in Japan. It consist of two houses: the Upper House of Councillors and the Lower House of Representatives. This type of system existed even in the Meiji constitution, but the parliament has no power then.

The House of Representatives play a crucial role and considered to be more powerful than the upper chamber. The house enjoys wide powers in matter of legislature. Bills rejected or amended by the upper house can be passed by the lower house as it was earlier with a two-third majority. And it can pass the bill if the upper house fails to take action on any bill for more than 60 days. Though the House of Councillors can delay the bill, the power to pass the bill lies with the lower house.

The lower House of representative controls the executive. The Prime Minister and his cabinet are made responsible to it by the constitution. If the house passes the no-confidence motion, the government has to resign. The executive has to submit periodic reports to the house. The house can also set up committees to investigate in any wrong doings. And without the approval from the diet, no treaty can be implemented. The parliamentary control of the executive is also carried out by asking questions, debating, etc. The Prime Minister is generally the choice of the lower house, even the minister mostly belong to the Lower House of Representatives.

The purse of the nation is controlled by the lower house. The budget has to be introduced before it. No tax can be added or increased without the approval from the house. The upper house can only delay passing of the financial bill; thus even in financial matters, the lower house overrides the upper chamber.

The diet acts as the final court of impeachment of the judges of Supreme Court. Both the chambers have equal number of members in the court of impeachment. The Constitution provides the lower house to amend the electoral law of the country. Thus there should be no discrimination between race, sex, creed, family origin, education, income, property or social status. Both houses participate to elect the Prime Minister. But in such elections, the lower house has upper hand.

Both the houses can initiate amendments to the Constitution and it has to be passed by two-third majority by each. After it is passed, it is sent to people for ratification in a special referendum. Once majority of people approve it, it is considered to have amended the Constitution and thus becomes a part of it.

The upper house, though comparatively weaker than the lower house of representative, carries out the important function of giving stability and continuity to the diet as it is a permanent house which cannot be dissolved. It also moderates and restraints extreme views of the lower house. Thus it is not so powerful like the second chambers of England or the United States.

7.5.5 Judiciary

The doctrine of separation of powers is followed. Thus the judiciary is separated from the executive and the legislature. The Supreme Court controls all the lower courts. The Constitution has also provided for the power of judicial review—to strike down any law which is ultra vires of the constitution.

The judges can only be removed by the process of impeachment, thus maintaining the independence and integrity of the judiciary. Every 10 years, people review the appointment and working of the judges. If the people disapprove any judge, he is then dismissed. Constitution thus provides review of appointment of the judges for every 10 years.

There is no separate administrative tribunal appointed by the executive as everything is taken up by the courts themselves. Open trials are conducted, only the judges can issue warrants for arresting a person. Every lawyer, judge or a public prosecutor has to pass from the legal research and training institute which is under the control of the Supreme Court. Thus, those practising law in japan are very few as compared with other countries.

7.6 FRENCH CONSTITUTION

7.6.1 Introduction

French Constitution is different from various others in the world. From the French revolution in 1789, it has undergone numerous changes, from becoming a republic to directorate under Napoleon and once again ruled by Bourbons, and now finally a democratic republic. In these years, France has seen 12 regime changes and 13 Constitutions. Thus extreme political changes has given France a new Constitution.

The first republic was inaugurated in 1792. It was comparable to the traditional American or the British system of government having a cabinet system. The powers were separated between the institutions. The powers of monarchy was also severely cut down. A new Constitution was adopted in 1793 giving more powers to the assembly which was to be elected directly by the people. This Constitution was once again replaced in 1799 with Constitution of the Consulate giving powers to Napoleon Bonaparte. He once again issued another Constitutional Charter of 1814 restoring divine rights of the Monarch. Napoleon's regime was replaced by monarchy of Louis-Phillipe, and new Constitutional Charter of 1830 was adopted. This gave limited powers to the Monarch.

People were not satisfied and rose against this regime and overthrew it. The National Assembly adopted a new Constitution in 1848 making France a republic once again. This period from 1848 till fall of the regime in 1870 is called as the Second Republic.

Once again, effort was taken to form a new constitution. This Constitution was very rigid, it created a republic, and made sure that this form of government could not be changed even by constitutional amendment. This 'Third Republic' which lasted till 1940 is considered to be the longest in the French republican government history.

President Petain assumed despotic powers bring the third republic to an end. The new Constitution called the 'Fourth Republic' was adopted in 1946 and did not last more than 12 years. This gave enormous powers to the parliament and made the President weaker and subject to control by the parliament.

The final and present Fifth Republic was created under the leadership of Charles de Gaulle. The National Cabinet was assembled and the new Constitution was drafted by Debre. It was presented to the people who gave acceptance to the Constitution in the referendum.

7.6.2 Salient Features of the French Constitution

The following are the salient features of the Fifth Republic constitution:

(a) Written and endorsed Constitution

It is a brief, written document presently having 92 articles. It was written by a constituent committee headed by de Gaulle. It was first endorsed by the cabinet, then by the parliament. Finally, people overwhelmingly adopted the Constitution in the referendum. The Constitution has given immense power to the President who is elected by the people. He is vested with the powers of the state and can deal with any crisis within the country or abroad. Thus President is the actual head of the government as well as the formal head of the state.

(b) Rigid

Unlike Indian Constitution, which has provision to amend the Constitution easily, amending French Constitution is quite a task. It does have provision to amend the Constitution, but certain conditions have to be met. The bill will be proposed by the President to the premier and to the members of the parliament. Both houses of the parliament should pass the bill identically, and the bill becomes definitive after the approval from a referendum. The President if so wishes can cancel the referendum and instead submit the bill to the joint session of the parliament in which it has to be passed. And no amendment is possible when integrity of the territory is in question. Also the republican nature of the Constitution cannot be amended.

(c) Unitary system

French Constitution creates a unitary system. This is rooted in the French constitutional history where power is biased towards the centre. The centre is more powerful than the British union. There does exist local governments at various levels in France. The territory is divided into 'departments' and these are further divided into cantons, arrondissements and communes. They have restricted powers, and this comes from acts of parliaments and not from the constitution. These local governments are nothing but the agents of the centre and are subjected to its control. Thus French system is more rigid and centralised than its British counterpart.

(d) Separation of powers

The most important aspect of the Fifth Republic is that it has separated the executive and legislative institutions, but has made the executive accountable to the legislature through the concept of ministerial responsibility. The cabinet functions under the Prime Minister, but the President has the overall control. The cabinet members cannot be members of the legislature, and if so they are, they should resign to enter into the government. Though the cabinet is not from the parliament, it is accountable to it. Though the President has overall control, he is not directly accountable to the parliament, only the cabinet headed by the Prime Minister is accountable to it. The legislature may pass a vote of no-confidence in the government, and in such case the government has to resign.

(e) Quasi-Presidential government

Against the quasi-parliamentary form, French system is more of a quasi-Presidential type since authority of the President is far wider than of the Prime Minister. He is not a titular head like his British counterpart, rather he is more like the American President. The French President appoints the Prime Minister and other ministers on recommendation of the Prime Minister. He chairs the cabinet meetings and thus makes his wishes get adopted by the government. But he is not responsible, only the Prime Minister and his cabinet are accountable to the parliament. The President has also been given wide veto powers. His position is strengthened by his 5-year-long tenure and his election by the people. His removal too is a difficult process to be followed.

(f) Syncretisme

The Fifth Republic has introduced some set of principles which are together called as syncretisme by the French people. Some of the principles are: President has been given vast powers in determining and promulgating emergency, the parliament is bi-cameral system where both upper senate and lower national assembly has coordinate powers, though the Prime Minister and the cabinet are not from the parliament they are responsible to it, in theory the President is the head of the state and Prime Minister head of the government, in practice the President assumes both the role when he wills and the Prime Minister is subordinate to powers of the President, the President can refer bills of public importance for referendum by the people. Thus these basic principles guide and form basis of the French constitution.

(g) Constitutional council

It is a unique institution having 9 members (3 nominated by the President, 3 nominated by the President of the national assembly, and 3 nominated by the President of the senate). The members enjoy 9-year tenure and are not eligible for reappointment. The former Presidents are ex-officio members of the council. This institution is neither a cabinet, nor a judicial body and neither a legislative organ, but it is a fusion of all three. It has controlling, adjudicatory and consultative powers. Its important functions are, to oversee the Presidential and parliamentary elections, it also declares the result of the referendum. It verifies the constitutional validity of act made by the executive or by the parliament. The President has to consult the body before declaring the state of emergency. Though it was not envisaged such kind of powers, it has come to play dominant and restraining role on the executive and the legislature.

(h) Economic and social council

The Constitution provides for creation of such body. It renders advice and opinion of the bills submitted before it. Generally it is consulted on economic and social issues by the government.

(i) Recognition of political parties

In India and the United States, the Constitution does not recognise the political parties. The important feature of the French Constitution is its recognition of political parties and the role played by them. Political parties which is not loyal to France and respect democracy can be banned.

(j) Administrative law

Though all citizens are equal before law, France provides separate courts for trying of public servants. Citizens have ordinary courts and the civil servants have specially constituted administrative courts following administrative law.

(k) Popular sovereignty

The people are the ultimate sovereign. The Constitution provides of 'equality, liberty and fraternity'. The Constitution also declares France to be an indivisible secular, democratic and social republic. The people exercise their sovereignty through their representatives and by the referendum process. The Constitution provide for universal adult suffrage, anyone who is a major is allowed to exercise their right to vote.

7.6.3 Executive

French President is different from his counterparts in Britain and the United States. He is head of the state like the British monarch and he also heads the government like the American President. The tilt is more towards the American system even though he has some symbolic powers. This is an important feature of the Fifth Republic which sought to make the position of the President stronger compared to the previous Constitution (the Fourth Republic).

The President has the following executive powers: he appoints the Prime Minister and on his recommendation appoints other members and removes them, he presides over the meeting of the council of ministers, he negotiates and ratifies the treaties with foreign nations, he is the commander in chief of the armed forces and makes appoints to all civil and military posts, he also appoints three members of the constitutional council, he also does the symbolic job of receiving and accrediting foreign ambassadors and envoys.

His legislative powers includes: he is given power to send back any bill for reconsideration to the parliament if certain conditions are met, he can summon extraordinary sessions of the parliament when he wishes, he signs the ordinance and orders decided by the council of ministers, he can dissolve the national assembly in consultation with the Prime Minister and the President of the assemblies, the President can also submit bills of enormous public importance for referendum and thus ratifies it, if it is accepted by majority of the people.

The following are his judicial powers: he has the power to grant pardon, he also presides over the high council of judges to which he nominates some members, and upon President is the responsibility to guarantee the independence of the judiciary.

President has also been given unlimited powers during the emergency. Thus the President can declare emergency and take necessary action to defend the independence and integrity of France. Also only the President can decide when to withdraw the emergency, he can prolong it for any period. President has thus been given sweeping powers in this case.

The President is the arbiter of the constitution, he has the right to interpret the constitution. He should oversee the effective observation of the constitution.

The Prime Minister is appointed by the President. The Prime Minister then selects his ministers who are also appointed by the President. He cannot shuffle the cabinet as he wishes. The Prime Minister is responsible for the conduct of the government affairs. He should ensure the legislations are implemented properly. The Prime Minister is the important link between the executive and the legislation. Though he is not a member of the legislature, he is responsible for that. Legislature too has the power to remove the Prime Minister by passing a no-confidence motion. Unlike other democracies, the Prime Minister cannot claim to be the head of the council of ministers; it is the President who presides over them.

The council of ministers have the power to enact ordinances. This is one form of delegated legislative powers given to the council of ministers by the legislature. The council of ministers can also declare martial law. The council though not from the parliament is responsible to it. The council with President as its head determine and conduct the policy of the nation. The council of ministers can also promulgate finance bill as an ordinance if the parliament fails to ratify it within the given time frame. Like the Prime Minister, the council too is responsible to the national assembly. Its powers are limited due to the presence of President and their responsibility to the Prime Minister who appoints and removes them to the constitutional responsibility to the national assembly.

7.6.4 Legislature

The French parliament has two houses: the upper senate and the lower national assembly. Unlike the British system, the President is not part of the legislature. The parliament is bound to meet twice a year. The lower house is elected by direct universal adult suffrage and the upper house by indirect election.

The parliament is basically a legislative body, and its important function lie in passing laws and approving bills. The parliament is given wide powers to make law in various areas like civil rights and fundamental guarantees given to the citizens, national defence, criminal procedure, amnesty, creation of new jurisdiction, tax rates, etc.

The Prime Minister and his council of ministers are responsible to the national assembly. The national assembly can pass a censure motion to challenge the responsibility of the ministers. The other ways of controlling the executives is through commissions, oral or written questions, resolutions, debates and not passing the budget. The parliament has the power to impeach the President for high treason, but it will be investigated by the high court of justice.

The parliament controls the purse of the nation. Both national assembly and the senate enjoy co-equal power in approving the finance bill. The parliament can only delay passing of the budget, and it cannot be more than 70 days after which the government can pass the ordinance. It cannot outrightly reject the budget but can propose amendments.

The President of national assembly and the senate nominate three members each to the constitutional council. Equal members are elected from both national assembly and the senate to the high court of justice from amongst its members.

Some of the other powers are: wars can be declared only after the approval by the parliament, martial law can be extended beyond 7 days after the approval by the parliament, any constitutional amendment bill has to be passed by the parliament, any international treaty need approval of the parliament, and it can also set up commissions to carry out inquiry. Except in few instances, the senate acts subordinate to the national assembly, which has been given more powers in the Fifth Republic.

7.6.5 Judiciary

The French judiciary is unique and different from the British system. It has codified law for both criminal and civil cases. The judge does not depend upon precedents and is free to give his own judgement, unlike England and USA where precedents play important French system assigns insignificant role to it. The important features are Unity, Symmetry and authority.

The judges are not elected but are appointed by high council of judges and by other bodies like the President.

The French system follows dual hierarchy, it has a separate ordinary courts to try civil and criminal cases. Its appeal lies to the court of cassation. The other entity is the administrative courts which take up issues concerning the administrative authorities and also public grievances against them. The top most court is the *Council d' Etat* (the council of state). There is separate court of conflict to deal with disputes between these two separate courts.

French court unlike in the United States derive powers from the parliament and not the constitution. Thus they do not have power to declare any law passed by the parliament as unconstitutional. They, thus, do not possess the power of judicial review. The constitutional council determines the validity of a law on request by either President or Prime Minister or the Presidents of both houses of the parliament.

The office of Parquet is similar to the public prosecutor. They are agents of state who cannot be removed. Both criminal and some civil cases are handled by them. They also monitor the execution of the judgements and decrees.

The French system guarantees independence of judiciary by keeping the executive out from the appointment process. The President is the guarantor for this independence to the judiciary. At lower level, judges are appointed through competitive exams. They are also given training, making the French judges competent and of high calibre.

The Constitution guarantees protection against arbitrary arrest and detention. Judiciary thus acts to protect individual liberty. Unlike in the United States, which adopts the fundamental feature of separation of powers, the French system has made judiciary subversive to executive and the legislature. The judges are made to work under a minister of the judicial department. All judgements are delivered by collegiality of judges, this is to ensure judgements are not corrupted. Only at higher level, there is a separate court to hear appeals of criminal and civil side; in lower levels, there are no separate courts. Thus a court can preside over both civil and criminal cases. There is also provision to create separate courts for issues like industrial disputes, commercial tribunals, etc.

Apart from these, the French Constitution provides for three new courts. They are the Supreme council of judges, High court of justice and the constitutional council. The supreme council of judges is headed by the President of the republic, apart from him there are other members appointed by him. The function of this body is to make appointments to the higher courts like court of cassation, etc. it also acts as the disciplinary council for the judges.

The high court of justice consists of equal number of members appointed by the national assembly and the senate. The President is tried by this body if he is indicted for high treason, other government officials are tried for conspiracy against the security of the state.

The constitutional council decides the constitutionality and validity of an act or law before even passed by the parliament. Unlike the United States, India where judicial review is a fundamental feature, French courts have not been given the power to declare any law to be unconstitutional. Apart from this, they also ensure that election of President is held regularly, examine complaints regarding the election to the President and declare the results of the Presidential election and of the referendums. Though the President is not bound by the advice of council, it is important for him to seek its advice as the council is considered to be the pulse of the French people.

8

Statutory, Regulatory and Quasi-Judicial Bodies

LEARNING OBJECTIVES

In this Chapter, you will learn about:

- Statutory Bodies
- Regulatory Bodies
- Quasi-Judicial Bodies
- Some Important Bodies

8.1 STATUTORY BODIES

Statutory bodies are those entities that are created by an Act of Parliament or State Legislatures. They are set up by the respective governments to consider the evidence and make judgments in some field of activity. They are usually established to carry out specific functions which a government considers may be more effectively performed outside a traditional departmental executive structure. They fulfil the need for some operational independence from the government funding arrangements that are not reliant on the annual appropriations processes or to establish a separate legal entity. They are typically found in countries which are governed under Parliamentary Democracy form of political setup.

By law, statutory bodies function as organisations with the authority to keep an eye on the legal and official compliances of a business or an organisation. For instance, the Medical Council of India is a statutory body which regulates the quality of medical education and medical practitioners in India. Statutory bodies, however, may be established to allow a certain level of independence from the government, the government is still responsible to ensure that taxpayers funds expended in the operations of statutory bodies are spent in the most efficient, effective and economic manner.

These bodies may be subject to varying degrees of ministerial control, depending on the acts that give rise to their existence. In turn, ministers are responsible to the Parliament and state legislatures for the operation of all government boards and agencies within their portfolios and are required to table their annual reports before the respective houses.

The definition of a 'statutory body' may differ depending upon the legislation. For example, a local council is not a statutory body for the purposes of the Financial Accountability Act, but it is for the purposes of the Statutory Bodies Financial Arrangements Act.

Examples of statutory bodies are Reserve Bank of India under the Reserve Bank of India Act, State Bank of India under a similar act, etc. They differ from constitutional bodies, which take root from specific provisions and objectives of the constitution. Examples are Supreme and High Courts, Election Commission of India, Pay Commissions etc.

Statutory bodies operate under the provisions of their own enabling legislation, which set out the purpose and powers of the agency. The enabling legislation may also include provisions, examples are:

- The levels of fees to be charged for services/products provided by the statutory body.
- The power of the statutory body to borrow or invest funds.
- Whether the board can delegate powers to officers of the statutory body.
- Whether the body represents the state.
- Whether it comes under the Reserve Bank of India Act or State Bank of India under a similar Act, etc.
- For the sake of distinction, the constitutional bodies are formed to continue the objectives of the Constitution. Examples are Supreme and High Courts, Election Commission of India, Pay Commissions etc.

8.2 REGULATORY BODY

A Regulatory body or Regulatory agency is a public authority or a Government agency, responsible for exercising autonomous authority over some area of human activity in a regulatory or supervisory capacity, established by Legislative act in order to set standards in a specific field of activity, or operations, in the private sector of the economy and to then enforce those standards.

Regulatory agencies function outside executive supervision. Because the regulations that they adopt have the force of law, part of these agencies' functions is essentially legislative. But because they may also conduct hearings and pass judgments concerning adherence to their regulations, they also exercise a judicial function – often carried out before a quasi-judicial official called an administrative law judge, who is not part of the Court system.

In almost all other countries outside the USA, including India, the role of regulatory agencies is taken by the regular administrative departments of government and in the case of utilities and public transportation, often by means of state ownership.

Regulatory agencies are usually a part of the executive branch of the government, or they have statutory authority to perform their functions with oversight from the legislative branch. Their actions are generally open to legal review. Regulatory authorities are commonly set up to enforce standards and safety, or to oversee use of public goods and regulate commerce. Examples of regulatory agencies in India are IRDA, SEBI, TRAI, AERB, DGCA, PESO, etc.

8.3 QUASI-JUDICIAL BODIES

Quasi-judicial bodies are organisations or bodies which have powers similar to that of the law imposing bodies but they are not courts. They mainly govern the administrative areas. The courts (judiciary) have the power to preside over all kinds of disputes but the quasi-judicial bodies are the ones with the powers of imposing laws on administrative agencies.

These bodies help in reducing the burden of court. Quasi-judicial activity is limited to the issues that concern the particular administrative agency. These actions may be appealed in a court of law.

Such bodies usually have powers of adjudication in matters such as breach of discipline, conduct rules and trust in the matters of money or otherwise. Their powers are usually limited to a particular area of expertise, such as financial markets, employment laws, public standards, immigration, or regulation.

Awards and verdicts of quasi-judicial bodies often depend on a pre-determined set of guidelines or punishments depending on the nature and gravity of the offence committed. Such punishments may be legally enforceable under the law of a country. However, they can also be challenged in a court of law, which is the final decisive authority. Some examples of quasi-judicial bodies in India are – National Human Rights Commission, State Human Rights Commission, Central Information Commission, State Information Commission, National Consumer Disputes Redressal Commission, State Consumer Disputes Redressal Commission, Competition Commission of India, Appellate Tribunal for Electricity, Railway Claims Tribunal, Income Tax Appellate Tribunal and Intellectual Property Appellate Tribunal.

8.4 SOME IMPORTANT BODIES

8.4.1 Central Vigilance Commission (CVC)

8.4.1.1 History

- The Central Vigilance Commission was set up by the Government in February, 1964 on the recommendations of the Committee on Prevention of Corruption, headed by Shri K. Santhanam, to advise and guide Central Government agencies in the field of vigilance.
- CVC is conceived to be the apex vigilance institution, free of control from any executive authority, monitoring all vigilance activity under the Central Government and advising various authorities in Central Government organisations in planning, executing, reviewing and reforming their vigilance work.
- The CVC Bill was passed by both the houses of Parliament in 2003 and the President gave his assent on September 11, 2003. Thus, the Central Vigilance Commission Act 2003 came into effect from that date.

8.4.1.2 Organisational Structure

The Central Vigilance Commissioner and the Vigilance Commissioners are appointed by the President after obtaining the recommendation of a Committee consisting of:

- The Prime Minister—Chairperson
- The Home Minister—Member
- The Leader of the Opposition in the Lok Sabha—Member
    - The Central Vigilance Commissioner and a Vigilance Commissioner, before he enters upon his office, is required to make and subscribe to oath or affirmation.
    - The Central Vigilance Commissioner or any Vigilance Commissioner can be removed from his office only by order of the President on the ground of proved misbehaviour or incapacity after the Supreme Court, on a reference made to it by the President, has, on inquiry, reported that the Central Vigilance Commissioner or any Vigilance Commissioner, as the case may be, ought to be removed.
    - The President may suspend him from the office, and if deem necessary prohibit him also from attending the office during inquiry, the Central Vigilance

Commissioner or any Vigilance Commissioner in respect of whom a reference has been made to the Supreme Court until the President has passed orders on receipt of the report of the Supreme Court on such reference.

- The President may, by order, remove from office the Central Vigilance Commissioner or any Vigilance Commissioner if the Central Vigilance Commissioner or such Vigilance Commissioner, as the case may be is adjudged an insolvent; or has been convicted of an offence, which, in the opinion of the Central Government, involves moral turpitude; or any engagement during his term of office in any paid employment outside the duties of his office; or in the opinion of the President, is unfit to continue in office by reason of infirmity of mind or body; or has acquired such financial or other interest as is likely to affect prejudicially his functions as a Central Vigilance Commissioner or a Vigilance Commissioner.
- The CVC is headed by a Central Vigilance Commissioner who is assisted by two Vigilance Commissioners.
- The Central Vigilance Commission has its own Secretariat, Chief Technical Examiners' Wing (CTE) and a wing of Commissioners for Departmental Inquiries (CDI).

Secretariat

- The Secretariat consists of a Secretary of the rank of Additional Secretary to the Government of India, one officer of the rank of Joint Secretary to the Government of India, ten officers of the rank of Director/Deputy Secretary, four Under Secretaries and office staff.
- Chief Technical Examiners' Wing (CTE) – The Chief Technical Examiner's Organisation constitutes the technical wing of the Central Vigilance Commission and has two Engineers of the rank of Chief Engineers (designated as Chief Technical Examiners) with supporting engineering staff.

8.4.1.3 Functions

- Technical audit of construction works of Governmental organisations from a vigilance angle.
- Investigating specific cases of complaints relating to construction works.
- Assisting the CBI in their investigations involving technical matters and for evaluation of properties in Delhi.
- Assisting the Commission and Chief Vigilance Officers in vigilance cases involving technical matters.

Commissioners for Departmental Inquiries (CDI): There are fifteen posts of CDI in the Commission, 14 in the rank of Deputy Secretaries/Directors and one in the rank of Joint Secretary to Government of India.

The CDIs function as Inquiry Officers is to conduct inquiries in departmental proceedings initiated against public servants.

The Directorate General of Vigilance: The Directorate General of Vigilance, Income Tax is the apex body under the Central Board of Direct Taxes for the vigilance matters.

The Directorate General interfaces with the Central Vigilance Commission, the Central Bureau of Investigation, field formations of CBDT who are also having

their vigilance wings and others in all the matters relating to vigilance, preliminary investigation of complaints, obtaining CVC/CVO's first stage advice.
Wherever required, assistance to Ministry in issuance of charge sheets, monitoring the charge sheet issued by the disciplinary authorities in the field, monitoring the progress in inquiry proceedings, processing of enquiry reports, obtaining CVC/ CVO's second-stage advice, wherever required and communication thereof to disciplinary authorities and monitoring compliance/implementation of the advice.

8.4.1.4 Functions and Powers

Under the Central Vigilance Commission Act, 2003 it has various powers and functions. Some of them are discussed as follows;

- Superintendence over the functioning of the Delhi Special Police Establishment (CBI) insofar as it relates to the investigation of offences under the Prevention of Corruption Act, 1988; or an offence under the CrPC for certain categories of public servants.
- Power to give directions to the DSPE in Special Police Establishment (CBI) for superintendence insofar as it relates to the investigation of offences under the Prevention of Corruption Act, 1988.
- Inquire or cause an inquiry or investigation to be made on a reference by the Central Government.
- Inquire or cause an inquiry or investigation to be made into any complaint received against any official belonging to such category of officials specified in the CVC Act, 2003.
- Review the progress of investigations conducted by the DSPE into offences alleged to have been committed under the Prevention of Corruption Act, 1988 or an offence under the CrPC.
- Review the progress of the applications pending with the competent authorities for sanction of prosecution under the Prevention of Corruption Act, 1988.
- Tender advice to the Central Government and its organisations on such matters as may be referred to it by them.
- Exercise superintendence over the vigilance administrations of the various Central Government Ministries, Departments and organisations of the Central Government.
- Commission has all the powers of a Civil Court while conducting any inquiry.
- Respond to Central Government on mandatory consultation with the Commission before making any rules or regulations governing the vigilance or disciplinary matters relating to the persons appointed
- To the public services and posts in connection with the affairs of the Union or to members of the All India Services.

Limitations of CVC

- CVC is only an advisory body. Central Government Departments are free to either accept or reject CVC's advice in corruption cases.
- CVC does not have adequate resources compared with number of complaints that it receives. It is a very small set up with sanctioned staff strength of 299; whereas it is supposed to check corruption in more than 1500 Central Government departments and ministries.

- CVC cannot direct CBI to initiate inquiries against any officer of the level of Joint Secretary and above on its own. Such permission has to be obtained from the concerned department.
- CVC does not have powers to register criminal case. It deals only with vigilance or disciplinary cases.
- CVC has supervisory powers over CBI. However, CVC does not have the power to call for any file from CBI or to direct CBI to investigate any case in a particular manner. CBI is under administrative control of Department of Personnel and Training (DoPT) which means that, the powers to appoint, transfer, suspend CBI officers lie with DoPT.
- Appointments to CVC are indirectly under the control of Goverment of India, though the leader of the Opposition (in Lok Sabha) is a member of the Committee to select CVC and VCs. But the Committee considers candidates put up before it. These candidates are decided by the Government.
- As a result, although CVC is relatively independent in its functioning, it has neither resources nor powers to inquire and take action on complaints of corruption that may act as an effective deterrence against corruption.

8.4.1.5 Recent Initiatives

Preventive vigilance measures declared by CVC can broadly be categorised as

1. **Simplification and standardisation of rules:** Simplification and standardisation of rules and procedures results in reducing of discretion and arbitrariness. Identifying areas of discretion which are not governed by guidelines along with a review of existing rules and regulations will help to bring about clarity and accountability.
2. **Leveraging technology and automation:** Technology as an enabler for fighting corruption has been effectively demonstrated. E-procurements, E-payments, use of websites for dissemination of information and creating awareness, use of CCTV in places of public dealing, use of appropriate analytical tools, computer assisted audit techniques for detecting frauds are examples of how technology strengthens the system of preventive vigilance. Automation reduces interface/interaction between public officials and common public, thus leading to reduction in corruption.
3. **Process re-engineering (BPR):** BPR is very important as it helps the organisations rethink how they do their work and in the process encourages a full-scale recreation of processes in order to meet the objectives of the organisation. Existing processes may be re-engineered to even prevent leakage of revenue.
4. **Transparency:** Transparency removes the information gap between the public and officials which in turn reduces corruption. The website of the department/organisation should contain rules and regulations, contact details of officials and all other information useful for common public/customers.
5. **Accountability:** A system with clear accountability and assigned responsibility at each level is necessary not only for smooth functioning but also for increased transparency, efficiency and for ensuring effective punitive action in case of misconduct.
6. **Control and supervision:** Regular and routine inspections, surprise inspections, audit and reviews help to keep a check on aberrant and corrupt behaviour. A structured interaction between vigilance and internal audit will enable better monitoring and also help identify potential problem areas.

7. **Time-bound and effective punitive action:** Punitive action within short period of occurrence of misconduct and finalisation of such cases in a time-bound manner resulting in award of exemplary and adequate punishment deters others from committing such misconduct.
8. **Conducive work environment:** Conducive work environment for preventive vigilance may include drawing up a list of sensitive posts, rotation policy for sensitive posts, Annual Report 2016 129 identification of persons of doubtful integrity and keeping them away from sensitive posts/public dealing. It would be necessary also to create an environment that promotes ethical behaviour. Protection to Whistle Blowers must also be ensured in order to bring to light cases of corruption.
9. **Training and Awareness:** Capacity building and sensitisation at all levels and across all functional areas is important. Public officials should be made aware of their duties and responsibilities, code of conduct, rules and regulations through regular training and awareness programmes. A list of Dos and Don'ts for employees/officials is a simple yet effective tool. Likewise, familiarisation with Standard Operating Procedures relating to different spheres of activity will enhance awareness and reduce procedural violations/inadvertent errors arising out of a lack of awareness. Knowledge sharing initiatives such as publishing/circulating information relating to areas where fraud/misconduct has been detected and sharing information on best practices are other effective awareness generation methods for more effective preventive vigilance.
10. **Awareness among public:** If public is made aware of their rights, and also of the rules and regulations, then they will be able to resist unfair treatment and arbitrary behaviour by public officials. Public should be encouraged to demand the services due to them and to raise their voice when their rights are denied or powers are misused by public officers. Organisations should prominently display information relevant/useful to the common public on their office notice board/website.
11. **Inculcating moral values:** Inculcating ethical behaviour among public, particularly the younger generation is an important tool of preventive vigilance. Vigilance Awareness Week (VAW), celebrated every year during the last week of October is aimed at creating such awareness. This opportunity needs to be utilised by all CVOs/Organisations to create awareness among public as well as among its own officials regarding need for imbibing right values.

8.4.2 Central Information Commission

8.4.2.1 History

- The Right to Information (RTI) Act, 2005, which came into force on 12 October 2005, marked a new and higher level of evolution of India's parliamentary democracy.
- The Supreme Court has, in various judgments, held that the right to information is a part of the fundamental right to freedom of speech and expression under Article 19(1) of the Constitution, since the right cannot be properly exercised if the people did not have the right to information.

The clearest enunciation of the fundamental right to information was seen in the Supreme Court ruling in the State of U.P v. Raj Narain in which Justice K.K. Mathew said:

- The people of this country have a right to know every public act, everything that is done in a public way, by their public functionaries.

- They are entitled to know the particulars of every public transaction in all its bearing.
- The right to know, which is derived from the concept of freedom of speech, though not absolute, is a factor which should make one wary, when secrecy is claimed for transactions which can, at any rate, have no repercussion on public security…
- Thus, the Right to Information (RTI) Act, 2005 is designed to set up a practical regime for citizens to access information available with public authorities, in order to promote transparency and accountability in their working.

8.4.2.2 *Organization Structure*

- This Act provides for the Constitution of the Central Information Commission (CIC) to be responsible for the implementation of the Act.
- Central Information Commission was constituted by the Central Government through a Gazette Notification in October 2005.
- The Commission includes 1 Chief Information Commissioner (CIC) and not more than 10 Information Commissioners (IC) who are appointed by the President of India.
- Oath of Office is administered by the President of India according to the form set out in the First Schedule.
- CIC defines 'information' as any material in any form including records, documents, memos, e-mails, opinions, advices, press releases, circulars, orders, logbooks, contracts, reports, papers, samples, models, data material held in any electronic form and information relating to any private body which can be accessed by a public authority under any other law for the time being in force.

8.4.2.3 *Powers and Functions*

- The CIC is empowered to receive and inquire into complaints from any person relating to access to information under the control of public authorities and to decide appeals against the decisions of designated appellate officers.
- The Commission shall impose penalties on erring Central Public Information Officers and recommend disciplinary action against those who have, without any reasonable cause, denied access to information under the provisions of the Act.
- The quantum of penalty liable to be imposed is ₹250 each day till the application is received or information is furnished subject to the total amount not exceeding ₹25,000.
- The decision of the Commission on an appeal is binding and is not subject to further appeal in a Court of law.
- The Commission may make recommendations to public authorities not conforming to the provisions or the spirit of the Act, specifying the steps which, in its opinion, they ought to take for promoting such conformity.
- The Commission may, during the inquiry into any complaint, examine any record under the control of the public authority, and no such record may be withheld from it on any grounds.
- The Commission shall recommend to the Government every year, reforms on any 'matter relevant for operationalising the right to access information'.

Some cases in which RTI Act with the help of CIC disclosed the corrupt practices in the nation:

a. RTI exposes employment generation scheme
    - Rajani, an RTI activist trainer by Sakshi was concerned about the poor implementation of the National Rural Employment Guarantee Act (NREGA).

- The NREGA is designed to provide work to the poor rural Indians by providing them 100 days of work every year to build productive assets like roads, schools and irrigation projects in their villages.
- As is often the norm, the money is misappropriated by the contractor-babu-politician nexus.
- Rajani asked for the details of the projects implemented under NREGA in Santhpur Village in Bidar District of Karnataka.
- She received reports of four projects for Santhpur village but three of the project report did not have any details of the project making inspection impossible.
- Further the people employed in all four projects were the same (member of a local politician's family who have never stepped out ever for any hard labour).
- None of the projects and labour rolls contained signatures or thumb impressions of the recipients.
- In a hearing on a complaint filed by the Rajani at the Karnataka Information Commission, the Commissioner pulled up the CEO of the District and asked him to investigate the matter immediately and report back to the Commission.
- The CEO's report is awaited. In the meanwhile Rajani has held a press conference in Bidar to highlight the issue and 15 more RTI applications were filed.
- The villagers of Santhpur who accompanied Rajani to the hearing were delighted. Whenever they went to meet the CEO he would refuse to even meet them.
- They really feel empowered to see the CEO being forced to come to Bangalore and being pulled for not doing his work properly that too in front of them.

b. Greenpeace and RTI Together Receive Victory

- In the beginning of last year, environmental watchdog Green Peace approached Sakshi for RTI training for their campaigners.
- From that training their two campaigners Jaikrishna and Divya got on to the case of the Department of Biotechnology which is the approving body for testing and release of genetically modified crops in India.
- After a long drawn-out battle, this April, the CIC directed the Department of Biotechnology to make the information on the toxicity of GM crops public.
- This information has been a secret despite the risks it has for every Indian. With the information in the public domain, it is now possible to analyse the feasibility of the products in view of the environmental effects and human consumption.
- The issue of Genetic Engineering is being widely debated across the world on account of its detrimental impacts.
- It is evident the RCGM has not used the right kind of protocols for bio-safety testing. It is a giant leap for activists as it opens doors to the secretive realm of biotechnology.
- Ultimately the Right to Know of citizens regarding the industry and its impacts has been assured.
- Governance improves with heightened trust between people and the Government. Trust improves with transparency.
- A transparent and open Government increases the faith and trust of the public in its functioning, while at the same time reducing suspicion.
- This creates space for the free flow of information, which allows citizens to participate in decisions taken in their interest.
- Thus, CIC has helped in increasing the transparency and faith of common man in the government procedures and activities.

8.4.3 National Human Rights Commission

8.4.3.1 History

- The National Human Rights Commission (NHRC) of India is an autonomous public body constituted on 12 October 1993 under the Protection of Human Rights Ordinance of 28 September 1993.
- It was given a statutory basis by the Protection of Human Rights Act, 1993 (TPHRA).
- The NHRC is a national human rights institution, responsible for the protection and promotion of human rights, defined by the Act as 'rights relating to life, liberty, equality and dignity of the individual guaranteed by the Constitution or embodied in the International Covenants'.
- 'Human Rights' means the rights relating to life, liberty, equality and dignity of the individual guaranteed by the constitution or embodied in the International covenants and enforceable by courts in India.
- 'Commission' means the National Human Rights Commission constituted under Section 3 of Protection of Human Rights Act, 1993. All human beings are born free and equal in dignity and rights known as Human rights, these are commonly understood as the rights that every human being is entitled to enjoy freely irrespective of his religion, race, caste, sex and nationality. The Declaration of Independence acknowledged the fundamental human rights.
- Human right means different thing to different people. Human Rights are not static. New rights are recognised and enforced from time to time.
- Only persons fully conversant with the latest development about the expanding horizons of human rights can promote their awareness better than others.

8.4.3.2 Organisational Structure

The NHRC consists of:

- A Chairperson
- One Member who is, or has been, a Judge of the Supreme Court of India
- One Member who is, or has been, the Chief Justice of a High Court
- Two Members to be appointed from among persons having knowledge of, or practical experience in, matters relating to human rights
- In addition, the Chairpersons of four National Commissions of (1. Minorities 2. SC, 3. ST 4. Women) serve as ex-officio members.

The Chairperson and members of the NHRC are appointed by the President of India, on the recommendation of a committee consisting of:

- The Prime Minister (chairperson)
- The Home Minister
- The Leader of the Opposition in the Lok Sabha (House of the People)
- The Leader of the Opposition in the Rajya Sabha (Council of States)
- The Speaker of the Lok Sabha (House of the People)
- The Deputy Chairman of the Rajya Sabha (Council of States)

8.4.3.3 Powers and Functions

TPHRA mandates the NHRC to perform the following functions:

- Proactively or reactively inquire into violations of human rights or negligence in the prevention of such violation by a public servant.

- With the permission of court, to intervene in court proceeding relating to human rights
- Visit any jail or other institution under the control of the State Government, where persons are detained or lodged for purposes of treatment, reformation or protection, for the study of the living conditions of the inmates and make recommendations.
- Review the safeguards provided by or under the Constitution or any law for the time being in force for the protection of human rights and recommend measures for their effective implementation.
- Review the factors, including acts of terrorism that inhibit the enjoyment of human rights and recommend appropriate remedial measures.
- Study treaties and other international instruments on human rights and make recommendations for their effective implementation.
- Undertake and promote research in the field of human rights.
- Engage in human rights education among various sections of society and promote awareness of the safeguards available for the protection of these rights through publications, media, seminars and other available means.
- Encourage the efforts of NGOs and institutions working in the field of human rights.
- Such other functions as it may consider it necessary for the protection of human rights.

8.4.3.4 Recent Initiatives

Amend PHR Act to make Human Rights Commissions more effective, says Mr. Justice P. Sathasivam, Governor of Kerala and former Chief Justice of India, on Human Rights Day

Mr. Justice P. Sathasivam, Governor of Kerala and former Chief Justice of India, said excesses of laws, lack of awareness about them, inadequacies of the legal system and the lack of sufficient support from the legal services authorities need to be focused on to ensure protection of human rights in the country He was addressing the Human Rights Day function of the NHRC as a Chief Guest.

Mr. Justice P. Sathasivam lauded the role of the NHRC towards Promotion and Protection of Human Rights. However, he said that the Commission should consider approaching Parliament through the Government to seek an amendment in the Protection of Human Rights (PHR) Act to make its recommendation effective. It should be able to execute its recommendations.

Addressing the gathering, Mr. Bezwada Wilson, National Convener of the Safai Karamchari Andolan and recipient of Magsaysay award, said, despite several efforts a lot needs yet to be done to build awareness about the necessity to recognise the rights and dignity of people working in sanitation area.

Earlier, addressing the gathering Mr. Justice H.L. Dattu, Chairperson, NHRC, said the Commission represents the work, dedication, and relentless spirit that are vital to the realisation of the vision we have for our country – a vision of freedom, justice and equity. He expressed confidence that by incorporating human rights as a way of life, a fundamental change can be brought about in our efforts to eradicate the scourge of poverty, ignorance, prejudices and discrimination based on sex, caste, religion, disability and other forms, from our society.

Highlighting the significance of Human Rights Day, Justice Dattu said, 'let us pledge to rededicate ourselves to achieve a just and equitable society through upholding the principles and ideals enshrined in our Constitution and the Universal Declaration of Human Rights for the protection and promotion of human dignity and the inviolable rights of all citizens of the country'.

The UN Secretary General, Mr. Ban Ki Moon, in his message on Human Rights Day, read by Mr. Rajiv Chandran, the representative of United Nations Information Centre in Delhi, said that 'Upholding Human Rights is in the interest of all. Respect for Human Rights advances well-being for every individual, stability for every society, and harmony for our international world'. At a time of multiplying conflicts, the Universal Declaration of Human Rights reminds us of the importance of the freedom, justice and peace in the life of human beings. He said that people must stand up for others' rights – is the theme of this year's Human Rights Day.

Marking the Human Rights Day celebrations, prizes were given to the winners of NHRC's Short Films on Human Rights Award Scheme 2016. These included 'Black & White' by Anuj S.R. from Kerala, first prize of ₹One lakh, 'Tumling Street' by Rimbik Das, second prize of ₹75,000 and 'Ambrosia' by Somnath Chakraborty, third prize of ₹50,000. They were also given a certificate and a trophy each. The Commission received a huge response to its Short Film Award Scheme this year.

Justice Sathasivam also released four NHRC publications, including two journals in Hindi and English carrying articles on important aspects of Human Rights issues by eminent persons. He also opened NHRC's photo and children's paintings exhibition marking the Human Rights Day.

Several prominent dignitaries, including Judges of Supreme Court, High Courts, former Judges of Supreme Court and High Courts, UN representatives, diplomats, senior Government functionaries, civil society representatives, senior officers of Paramilitary Forces, and NHRC attended the function.

8.4.4 National Commission for Women

8.4.4.1 History

- The National Commission for Women (NCW) is a statutory body for women established in 1992 by Government of India under the provisions of the Indian Constitution, as defined in the 1990 National Commission for Women Act. The first head of the commission was Ms. Jayanti Patnaik.
- It is often said that the status and position of women in society is the best way to understand a civilisation, its progress and its shortcomings.
- In the case of India, women have come a long way from women sages and scholars in the Vedic period to women in the armed forces, IT sector, politics, industry and other significant areas while balancing their role as a daughter, wife and mother.
- This journey towards modernisation has not been easy. Women have had to fight the traditional Indian male-dominated society to emerge as stronger and independent entities.
- While all these are positive developments, cases of rape, harassment at workplace and dowry deaths are rampant. Illiteracy and ignorance about their rights are still prevalent among a majority of the women.
- It was in this background that the Committee on the Status of Women in India (CSWI) recommended nearly two decades ago, the setting up of a National Commission for Women to fulfil the surveillance functions to facilitate redressal of grievances and to accelerate the socio-economic development of women.
- In January 1992, the National Commission for Women (NCW), was set up as a statutory body under the National Commission for Women Act, 1990 (Act No. 20 of 1990

of Government of India) to review the constitutional and legal safeguards for women; recommend remedial legislative measures, facilitate redressal of grievances and advise the Government on all policy matters affecting women.

8.4.4.2 *Functions*

- The Commission has initiated generation of legal awareness among women, thus equipping them with the knowledge of their legal rights and with a capacity to use these rights. It assists women in redressal of their grievances through pre-litigation services.
- To facilitate speedy delivery of justice to women, Parivarik Mahila Lok Adalats are organised in different parts of the country to review the existing provisions of the Constitution and other laws affecting women and recommending amendments thereto, any lacunae, inadequacies or shortcomings in such legislations.
- It organises promotional activities to mobilise women and get information about their status and recommend paradigm shift in the empowerment of women. The Complaints and Counseling Cell of the commission processes the complaints received oral, written or suo moto under Section 20 of the NCW Act.
- The complaints received are generally related to domestic violence, harassment, dowry, torture, desertion, bigamy, rape, refusal to register FIR, cruelty by husband, deprivation, gender discrimination and sexual harassment at work place.
- NCW tackles the problems by ensuring that investigations by the police are expedited and monitored. Family disputes are resolved or compromised through counseling.
- As per the 1997 Supreme Court Judgment on Sexual Harassment at Workplace, (Vishakha v. State of Rajasthan) every employer is required to provide for effective complaints procedures and remedies including awarding of compensation to women victims.
- In sexual harassment complaints, the concerned organisations are urged to expedite cases and the disposal is monitored. For serious crimes, the Commission constitutes an Inquiry Committee which makes spot enquiries, examines various witnesses, collects evidence and submits the report with recommendations. The implementation of the report is monitored by the NCW.
- The complaints received by the NCW show the trend of crimes against women and suggest systemic changes needed for reducing them.
- The complaints are analysed to understand the gaps in the routine functioning of government in tackling violence against women and to suggest correctional measures.
- The complaints are also used as case studies for sensitisation programmes for the police, judiciary, prosecutors, forensic scientists, defence lawyers and other administrative functionaries.

Activities

The objective of the NCW is to represent the rights of women in India and to provide a voice for their issues and concerns.

- The subjects of their campaigns include dowry, politics, religion, equal representation for women in jobs and the exploitation of women for labour.
- The Commission also discusses police abuses against women.
- The Commission regularly publishes a monthly newsletter, Rashtra Mahila, in both Hindi and English

- As the problem of violence against women is multifaceted, the NCW has adopted a multi-pronged strategy to tackle the problem.
- From time to time the Commission conducts seminars, workshops and conferences and sponsors such events by providing financial assistance to research organisations and NGOs.
- The important areas so far covered include women in detention; violence against women; sexual harassment at work place; educational, health and employment aspects; women in agriculture and panchayati raj sector; and custodial justice and mental health institutions.
- The NCW holds public hearings on issues affecting large sections of women such as crime against women, women in unorganised labour sector, women in agriculture and women of minority groups.
- The deposition at these enquiries helps in appreciating the problems and initiating remedial action.
- As a measure of arousing public awareness and breaking bureaucratic apathy, public hearings under vigilant activists like Justice V.R. Krishna Iyer and Swami Agnivesh were held to understand problems and expedite solutions in the case of Kol women of Bundelhekhand; deserted women of hill districts in UP, rape case of girl children of Tamil Nadu, unorganised women labour and minority communities of Tamil Nadu; creche workers' enquiry and tribal women of Dindigul, Tamil Nadu.
- Special studies are conducted by the NCW on social mobilisation, maintenance and divorced women, panchayat raj in action, women labour under contract, gender bias in judicial decisions, family courts, gender-component in various Commissions' reports on women, violence against women, women's access to health and education in slums to help in formulation of NCW's policies for recommendations.
- Special studies of NCW focus on development of health facilities among women belonging to the scheduled tribe communities; women of weaker sections – socio-economic development of scheduled caste women; mentally disabled women; credit needs of women – the Gramin Banks, and the widows of Vrindavan.
- The NCW also constitutes Expert Committees for dealing with such special issues as may be taken up by the Commission from time to time. Some important issues taken up by the NCW include sexual harassment at workplace, women in detention, anti-arrack movement, issues concerning prostitution and political and technological empowerment of women in agriculture.
- To meet the information needs of the Commission and various interested individuals and organisations, the NCW started its own library in 1994. It has now evolved as a de facto Resource Centre for research scholars/activists with a collection of nearly 2300 books covering different issues relating to women's advancement.
- Besides, the library collection includes important reference books, like encyclopedia, Directories of NGO's as well as the complete set of Halsbury's Laws of England (4th Edition).
- Besides publishing its own books from time to time, the NCW also sponsors research studies on various aspects concerning women issues and helps in getting them published. Nearly a hundred publications, both in English and Hindi, have so far been published.

- The Commission undertakes visits to evaluate the progress of development of women in various states. It has so far covered Tamil Nadu, Andhra Pradesh, Rajasthan, Uttar Pradesh, Orissa, Sikkim, Madhya Pradesh, Assam, Tripura and Manipur.
- Women's movement in the country was brought to the forefront by the efforts of NGOs. The Commission interacts and networks with NGOs and the State Commissions for ensuring gender equality and empowerment of women.
- The Commission also interacts with the media, social activists and academics to suggest ways of ensuring due representation of women in all spheres.

8.4.4.3 Recent Initiatives

WCD Minister Smt. Maneka Gandhi releases Draft National Policy for Women, 2016 for consultation . The salient features of the policy are as follows:

Background: Nearly a decade and half has passed since the National Policy for Empowerment of Women, 2001 was formulated. Since then significant strides in global technology and information systems have placed the Indian economy on a trajectory of higher growth impacting the general populace and women in particular in unique and different ways. The discourse on women's empowerment has been gradually evolving over the last few decades, wherein paradigm shifts have occurred – from seeing women as mere recipients of welfare benefits to mainstreaming gender concerns and engaging them in the development process of the country. These changes have brought forth fresh opportunities and possibilities for women's empowerment while at the same time presenting new and emerging challenges which along with persisting socio-economic problems continue to hinder gender equality and holistic empowerment of women. The policy aims to create sustainable socio-economic, political empowerment of women to claim their rights and entitlements, control over resources and formulation of strategic choices in realisation of the principles of gender equality and justice.

The policy envisions a society in which women attain their full potential and are able to participate as equal partners in all spheres of life. It also emphasises the role of an effective framework to enable the process of developing policies, programmes and practices which will ensure equal rights and opportunities for women.

The broad objective of the policy is to create a conducive socio-cultural, economic and political environment to enable women enjoy de jure and de facto fundamental rights and realise their full potential.

Priority Areas

1. **Health including food security and nutrition:** Focus on recognising women's reproductive rights, shift of family planning focus also to males, addressing health issues in a life cycle continuum such as psychological and general well-being, healthcare challenges related to nutrition/hygiene of adolescents, geriatric health care, expansion of health insurance schemes and addressing the intergenerational cycle of under-nutrition
2. **Education:** Improve access to pre-primary education, enrolment and retention of adolescent girls, implement innovative transportation models for better schooling outcomes, advocate gender champions and address disparities with regard to ICTs.
3. **Economy:** Raising visibility, engendering macro-economic policies and trade agreements, generate gender-disaggregated land ownership database, skill development and training for women, entrepreneurial development, review of labour laws and policies,

equal employment opportunities with appropriate benefits related to maternity and child care services, address technological needs of women.

4. **Governance and decision making:** Increasing women's participation in the political arena, administration, civil services and corporate boardrooms,
5. **Violence against women:** Address all forms of violence against women through a lifecycle approach, Legislations affecting/relating to women will be reviewed/harmonised to enhance effectiveness, improve child sex ratio (CSR), strict implementation of advisories, guidelines, standard operating procedures (SoPs) and protocols, prevention of trafficking at source, transit and destination areas for effective monitoring of the networks.
6. **Enabling environment:** Gender perspective in housing and infrastructure, ensuring safe drinking water and sanitation, gender parity in the mass media and sports, concerted efforts towards strengthening social security and support services for all women especially the vulnerable, marginalised, migrant and single women.
7. **Environment and climate change:** Addressing gender concerns during distress migration and displacement in times of natural calamities due to climate change and environmental degradation. Promotion of environmental friendly, renewable, non-conventional energy, green energy sources for women in rural households.

The policy also describes emerging issues such as making cyber spaces safe place for women, redistribution of gender roles, reducing unpaid care work, review of personal and customary laws in accordance with the constitutional provisions, review of criminalisation of marital rape within the framework of women's human rights etc. relevant in the developmental paradigms.

Operational strategies laid down in the policy provide a framework for implementation of legislations and strengthening of existing institutional mechanisms through action plan, effective gender institutional architecture. Advocacy and stakeholder partnerships, inter-sectoral convergence, gender budgeting and generation of gender disaggregated data have also been given due focus.

Operational strategies

- **Enabling safety and security of women** with initiatives such as One-Stop Centres, Women Helpline, Mahila Police volunteers, Reservation of women in police force, creating immediate response mechanism through panic buttons in mobiles, public and private transport, and surveillance mechanisms in public places.
- **Creating eco-systems to encourage entrepreneurship amongst women** through platforms like Mahila E-Haat, dedicated theme-based exhibitions, focussed skill training, mentoring through Women Entrepreneurship Council, availability of easy and affordable credit and financial inclusion.
- **Training and capacity building of all stakeholders** including youth through Gender Champion initiative, frontline workers, women sarpanches and all officials dealing with policy and delivery systems impacting women.
- **Facilitating women in workplace** through gender friendly work place, flexi timings, increased maternity leave, provision of child care/creches at workplace, life cycle health care facilities.

8.4.5 National Commission for Minorities

8.4.5.1 History

- The term 'Minority' represent a group numerically inferior to the rest of the population of a state, and in a non-dominant position whose members being nationals of the state poses ethnic, religious or linguistic characteristics differing from those of the rest of the dominant population and show, if only implicitly, a sense of solidarity, directed towards preserving their culture, traditions, religions and language.'
- Though the Constitution of India uses the term 'Minorities' at two places under Article 29 and 30, it does not define the word 'Minority' anywhere and left it for the wisdom of future generation deliberately as the country had just come over the traumatic shock of communal violence and partition, and a growing tendency was visualised where different group, sect, religion were claiming special rights under different notion of 'minority' concept, endangering national unity.
- India represent an unparalleled diversity where six major religions Hinduism, Islam, Sikhism, Christianity, Buddhism and Zoroastrianism; two major language families, Aryan and Dravidian, with 22 official languages and innumerable dialects and tribal tongues; three racial strains, Aryan, Dravidian, and proto-Australoid; and over two thousand castes, hierarchically ranked, endogamous and occupational are found. Thus, in a pluralistic society as of ours any monolithic definition of nationalism is bound to create a situation of conflict between the majority and the minorities. Visualising it the Constitution has mooted the concept of Secularism on one hand and on the other hand imposed on the state under different general and special laws, positive and negative duties to ensure the effective realisation of several rights conferred to different minorities.
- In order to strengthen the cause of the minorities, the United Nations promulgated the 'Declaration on the Rights of Persons belonging to National or Ethnic, Religious and Linguistic Minorities' on 18th December 1992 proclaiming that 'States shall protect the existence of the National or Ethnic, Cultural, Religious and Linguistic identity of minorities within their respective territories and encourage conditions for the promotion of that identity'.
- To ensure the rights of Minorities in India, the National Commission for Minorities Act was enacted in 1992 The National Commission for Minorities, a statutory body was constituted by the Central Government with a view to preserve secular traditions, promote national integration exercise the powers conferred on, and perform the functions assigned to it under this Act.
- For the purposes of this Act, 'Minority', means a community notified as such by the Central Government vide a Gazette notification issued on 23rd October 1993. The Ministry of Welfare, Government of India has notified five religious communities viz; the Muslims, Christians, Sikhs, Buddhists and Zoroastrians (Parsis) as minority communities.

8.4.5.2 Functions

The Commission shall perform all or any of the following functions:

- Evaluate the progress of the development of minorities under the Union and States.

- Monitor the working of the safeguards provided in the Constitution and in laws enacted by Parliament and the State Legislatures.
- Make recommendations for the effective implementation of safeguards for the protection of the interests of Minorities by the Central Governments or the State Governments.
- Look into specific complaints regarding deprivation of rights and safeguards of the minorities and take up such matters with the appropriate authorities.
- Promote studies to be undertaken into problems arising out of any discrimination against minorities and recommend measures for their removal.
- Conduct studies, research and analysis on the issues relating to socio-economic and educational development of minorities.
- Suggest appropriate measures in respect of any minority to be undertaken by the Central Government or the State Governments.
- Make periodical or special reports to the Central Government on any matter pertaining to minorities and in particular the difficulties confronted by them.
- Any other matter which may be referred to it by the Central Government.

  Andhra Pradesh, Assam, Bihar, Chattisgarh, Delhi, Jharkhand, Karnataka, Maharashtra, Madhya Pradesh, Manipur, Rajasthan, Tamil Nadu, Uttarakhand, Uttar Pradesh and West Bengal have also set up State Minorities Commissions in their respective States.

  Their offices are located in the State capitals. The functions of these Commissions, inter-alia, are to safeguard and protect the interests of minorities provided in the Constitution and laws enacted by Parliament and the State Legislatures.

  Aggrieved persons belonging to the minority communities may approach the concerned State Minorities Commissions for redressal of their grievances.

  They may also send their representations, to the National Commission for Minorities, after exhausting all remedies available to them.

8.4.5.3 *Recent Initiatives*

1. **Status of Conditions of Minorities**

   Six religious communities – Muslims, Christians, Buddhists, Sikhs, Zoroastrians (Parsis) and Jains – have been notified as minority communities under Section 2(c) of the National Commission for Minorities Act, 1992.

   The National Commission for Religious and Linguistic Minorities (NCRLM) constituted under the Chairmanship of Justice Ranganath Misra to recommend measures for the welfare of socially and economically backward sections among religious and linguistic minorities submitted its report in 2007 and the same was laid on the table of both the Houses of Parliament on 18 December, 2009. The findings of the NCRLM on the conditions of minorities are available in the report.

   A High-Level Committee, constituted under the Chairmanship of Justice (Retired) Rajinder Sachar to gather data/information for preparation of a comprehensive report on the social, economic and educational status of the Muslim community of India, in its report in 2006 had indicated that the Muslim community lags behind the mainstream in social, economic and educational sectors. The report had been laid on the Table of both the Houses of Parliament on 30 November, 2006.

   To improve the socio-economic and educational status of Minorities, following schemes are being implemented by the Ministry:

a. Multi-sectoral development programme: The multi-sectoral development programme (MsDP) is an area development initiative to address the development deficits by creating socio-economic infrastructure and providing basic amenities. The programme was implemented in 90 Minority Concentration Districts (MCDs) of the country during the 11th Five Year Plan (2012–2013). The Programme was restructured in 2013–2014 to make it more effective and more focused on the targeted minorities for its implementation during the 12th Five Year Plan period. In the restructured MsDP, the unit area of planning has been changed to blocks/towns/clusters of villages instead of district for sharper focus on the minority concentration areas.
b. Pre-matric scholarship scheme: Under this Scheme, scholarships are awarded to minority students up to class X, who have secured not less than 50% marks in the previous final examination and the annual income of their parents / guardian from all sources does not exceed ₹1.00 Lakh. Around 30% of the scholarships are earmarked for girl students. This is a Central Sector Scheme with 100% central assistance.
c. Post-matric scholarship scheme: Under this Scheme, scholarships are awarded to minority students from class XI onwards who have secured not less than 50% marks or equivalent grade in the previous final examination and the annual income of whose parents/guardian from all sources does not exceed ₹2.00 lakh. Around 30% of the scholarships are earmarked for girl students. This is a Central Sector Scheme with 100% central assistance.
d. Merit-cum-Means–based scholarship scheme: The Merit-cum-Means–Based Scholarship Scheme provides financial assistance to the poor and meritorious minority students pursuing professional studies at graduate and post-graduate levels. Around 30% of the scholarships are earmarked for girl students. This is a Central Sector Scheme with 100% central assistance.
e. Maulana Azad National Fellowship: The Fellowship is provided to students from minority communities, as notified by the Central Government to pursue higher studies such as M.Phil and Ph.D. The Fellowship covers all Universities/Institutions recognised by the University Grants Commission (UGC).The Fellowship is on the pattern of UGC Fellowships awarded to research students pursuing regular and full time M.Phil and Ph.D. courses. Around 30% of the scholarships are earmarked for eligible girl students.
f. Free Coaching and Allied scheme: This scheme is to assist students belonging to the minority communities by way of special coaching for qualifying examinations for admission in technical/professional courses such as engineering, medical and competitive examinations for recruitment to Group 'A', 'B' and 'C' services and other equivalent posts under the Central and State governments including public sector undertakings.
g. Padho Pardesh (interest subsidy on educational loans): This scheme is to award interest subsidy to meritorious students belonging to economically weaker sections of notified minority communities so as to provide them better opportunities for higher education abroad at Masters and Ph.D levels and enhance their employability.
h. Support to minority candidates clearing Prelims conducted by UPSC/SSC, State Public Service Commission (PSC) etc. This Scheme provides financial support to the minority candidates clearing prelims conducted by Union Public Service Commission, Staff Selection Commission and State Public Service Commissions to adequately equip them to compete for appointment to Civil Services in the Union and

the State Governments and to increase the representation of the minorities in the Civil Services.

i. Seekho aur Kamao (Learn & Earn): It is a placement linked skill development programme for minority youths, being implemented since the year 2013–2014. This scheme aims at upgrading the skills of minority youths in various modern as well as traditional skills which can earn them suitable employment or make them suitably skilled to go for self-employment. The scheme ensures placements of minimum 75% trained youths, out of which at least 50% placement is in organised sector.
j. Nai Roshni (leadership development of minority women): This is a scheme for women empowerment through sensitisation and leadership development of minority women being implemented all over the country by the ministry since 2012–2013. The objective of the scheme is to empower and instill confidence in women, by providing knowledge, tools and techniques for interacting with Government systems, banks, and intermediaries at all levels.
k. USTTAD (Upgrading the Skills and Training in Traditional Arts/Crafts for Development): The scheme was launched on 14 May, 2015 to preserve rich heritage of traditional arts/crafts of minorities, set standards of crafts practiced by minorities, build capacity of poor traditional artisans/craftsmen and link them with market.
l. National Minorities Development and Finance Corporation (NMDFC): NMDFC is a Central Public Sector Enterprise (CPSE) under administrative control of this Ministry, provides concessional loans for self-employment and income generating activities to eligible minorities. The loans are extended to individuals or Self-Help Groups through State Channelising Agencies (SCAs) nominated by the concerned State Governments/UT administrations.
m. Maulana Azad National Academy for Skills (MANAS): MANAS has been established on 11/11/2014, as Special Purpose Vehicle (SPV) for addressing all skill development needs of minority communities, to ensure provision of sustainable livelihoods to them, with emphasis on self-employment. Based on market demand, the Academy provides an All India level training framework for Entrepreneurship and Skill Development Programme (E&SDP) based on PPP model, for imparting training to minority population, with concessional credit linkages.
n. Jiyo Parsi: For containing the population decline of the Parsi community, a Central Sector Scheme 'Jiyo Parsi' was launched in 2013–2014. The objective of this scheme is to reverse the declining trend of Parsi population by adopting a scientific protocol and structured interventions to stabilise their population and balance their population in India.
o. Nai Manzil: An integrated education and livelihood initiative for the minority communities scheme has been launched on 08 August, 2015 on pilot basis for formal education of school dropouts and Madarsa students to enhance their education and skills in various trade to enable them for gainful employment.

8.4.6 National Commission for Backward Classes

8.4.6.1 History

National Commission for Backward Classes came into effect on the 2 April, 1993. The Act provides that the Commission shall consist of five Members, comprising of a Chairperson who is or has been a judge of the Supreme Court or of a High Court; a social scientist; two persons, who have special knowledge in matters relating to backward classes; and a Member-Secretary, who is or has been an officer of the Central Government in the rank of a Secretary to the Government of India.

8.4.6.2 *Functions of the Commission*

- The Commission shall examine requests for inclusion of any class of citizens as a backward class in the lists and hear complaints of over-inclusion or under-inclusion of any backward class in such lists and tender such advice to the Central Government as it deems appropriate.
- The advice of the Commission shall ordinarily be binding upon the Central Government.

8.4.6.3 *Powers of the Commission*

The Commission shall, while performing its functions have all the powers of a civil court trying a suit and in particular, in respect of the following matters:

- Summoning and enforcing the attendance of any person from any part of India and examining him on oath
- Requiring the discovery and production of any document
- Receiving evidence on affidavits
- Requisitioning any public record or copy thereof from any court or office
- Issuing commissions for the examination of witnesses and documents
- Any other matter which may be prescribed.

What is OBC?

- Backward class people are a collective term, used by the Government of India, for castes which are economically and socially disadvantaged.

What is Creamy Layer?

- The Government of India has evolved the criteria for exclusion of certain socially advanced persons/sections from the benefits of reservation available to OBCs in civil posts and services under the Government of India and this is called the 'Creamy Layer criteria'.

Mandal Commission Recommendations:

- Mandal commission set up in 1979 recommended a 27% of reservation owing to the legal constraint that the total quantum of reservation should not exceed 50%.
- Candidates belonging to OBC recruited on the basis of merit in an open competition should not be adjusted against their reservation quota of 27%.
- The above reservation should also be made applicable to promotion quota at all levels.
- Reserved quota remaining unfilled should be carried forward for a period of three years and de-reserved thereafter.
- Relaxation in the upper age limit for direct recruitment should be extended to the candidates of OBC in the same manner as done in the case of SCs and STs.
- An intensive time-bound programme for adult education should be launched in selected pockets with high concentration of OBC population.
- Residential schools should be set up in these areas for backward class students to provide a climate especially conducive to serious studies.

- All facilities in these schools including board and lodging should be provided free of cost to attract students from poor and backward class families.
- It was recommended that seats should be reserved for OBC students in all scientific, technical and professional institutions run by the Central as well as State Governments.
- The quantum of reservation should be the same as in the Government Services, that is, 27%.
- These recommendations in total are applicable to all recruitment to public sector undertakings, both under the Central and State Governments as well as to Nationalised Banks.
- All private sector undertakings which receive financial assistance from the Government in one form or other should also be obliged to recruit personnel on the aforesaid basis.
- All universities and affiliated colleges should also be covered by the above scheme of reservation. The Commission prepares its annual report, giving a full account of its activities during the previous financial year and forward a copy thereof to the Central Government. Annual report and audit report to be laid before Parliament.
- The Central Government shall cause the annual report, together with a memorandum of action taken on the advice tendered by the Commission and the reasons for the non acceptance, if any, of any such advice, and the audit report to be laid as soon as may be after they are received before each House of Parliament.

8.4.6.4 Recent Initiative

Cabinet gives approval for introduction of Constitution (i) One Hundred and Twenty-third Amendment Bill 2017 and (ii) National Commission for Backward Classes (Repeal) Bill, 2017 in the Parliament

Approval also granted for retention of posts and office premises for the proposed new National Commission for Backward Classes.

The Union Cabinet chaired by the Prime Minister Shri Narendra Modi has given (I) Ex-post facto approval for introduction of (i) Constitution (One Hundred and Twenty-third Amendment) Bill 2017 and (ii) National Commission for Backward Classes (Repeal) Bill, 2017 in the Parliament; and (II) approval for retention of posts/incumbents and office premises held by the existing National Commission for Backward Classes by the proposed new National Commission for Backward Classes

1. The approval is for the proposal to bring about a Constitutional Amendment namely the Constitution (One Hundred Twenty-third Amendment) Bill, 2017 by:

   a. Constitution of a Commission under Article 338B for socially and educationally backward classes by name of National Commission for Backward Classes; and
   b. Insertion of Clause (26C) under Article 366 with modified definition viz. 'socially and educationally backward classes' means such backward classes as are so deemed under Article 342A for the purpose, this Constitution and

2. Introduce a Bill for:

   a. Repeal of the National Commission for Backward Classes Act, 1993 along with Savings Clause for namely the National Commission for Backward Classes (Repeal) Bill, 2017; and
   b. Dissolution of the National Commission for Backward Classes with effect from such date as the Central Government may appoint in this behalf and the National

Commission for Backward Classes constituted under sub-section (1) of Section 3 of the said Act shall stand dissolved.

3. a. Appropriation of the sanctioned 52 posts, along with incumbents wherever filled of the existing National Commission for Backward Classes in the proposed National Commission for Backward Classes to be constituted under Article 338B; and
   b. Retention of the office premises of the existing National Commission for Backward Classes at Trikut-1, Bhikaiji Cama Place, New Delhi-110066, by the Natinal Commission for Backward Classes to be constituted under Article 338B.

The above decisions will lead to overall welfare of socially and educationally backward classes.

The proposed Act of repeal is necessary in view of setting up of the National Commission for Backward Classes by insertion of Article 338B of the Constitution.

The decision will also enable effecting continuity in the functioning of the National Commission for Backward Classes under Article 338B.

8.4.7 National Commission for Disabled Persons

8.4.7.1 History

- Persons with Disabilities (PWD) are defined as those suffering from four types of disabilities viz., visual, loco-motor, hearing and speech, and mental disabilities.
- In the Ninth Plan (1992–1997), the earlier paradigm shift in approach from 'welfare' to development was moved further to 'empowerment' which is more holistic by including both the welfare and development perspectives.
- The major thrust in the Tenth Plan has been to consolidate and strengthen the various programmes through coordinated efforts and innovative interventions in attending to the special problems and needs of these disadvantaged groups.
- One of the thrust areas during the Tenth Plan has been to prepare disabled-friendly policies to create a hurdle-free environment.
- According to the Census 2001, there are 2.19 crore persons with disabilities in India who constitute 2.13% of the total population.
- This includes persons with visual, hearing, speech, locomotor and mental disabilities. Around 75% of persons with disabilities live in rural areas, 49% of disabled population is literate and only 34% are employed.
- The earlier emphasis on medical rehabilitation has now been replaced by an emphasis on social rehabilitation.
- The Government constituted the National Commission for Persons with Disabilities with the former Governor, Sunder Singh Bhandari, as its chairperson.
- It recommends programmes for the elimination of inequalities in status and on facilities and opportunities for the disabled in order to give the appropriate education and vocational training.
- The Commission also recommends packages for poverty eradication, employment and other support services to achieve the goal of psycho-social acceptance of the disabled.
- It also reviews the working of the rehabilitation institutions. The members will represent people with hearing impairment, visual impairment and locomotor disability.

8.4.7.2 Recent Initiatives

Rights of Persons with Disabilities Bill – 2016 Passed by Parliament

The Lok Sabha has passed '**The Rights of Persons with Disabilities Bill - 2016**'. The Bill will replace the existing PwD Act, 1995, which was enacted 21 years back. The Rajya Sabha already passed the Bill on 14.12.2016.

The salient features of the Bill are:

(i) Disability has been defined based on an evolving and dynamic concept.

(ii) The types of disabilities have been increased from existing 7 to 21 and the Central Government will have the power to add more types of disabilities. The 21 disabilities are as follows:

1. Blindness
2. Low-vision
3. Leprosy Cured persons
4. Hearing Impairment (deaf and hard of hearing)
5. Locomotor Disability
6. Dwarfism
7. Intellectual Disability
8. Mental Illness
9. Autism Spectrum Disorder
10. Cerebral Palsy
11. Muscular Dystrophy
12. Chronic Neurological conditions
13. Specific Learning Disabilities
14. Multiple Sclerosis
15. Speech and Language disability
16. Thalassemia
17. Hemophilia
18. Sickle Cell disease
19. Multiple Disabilities including deafblindness
20. Acid Attack victim
21. Parkinson's disease

(iii) Speech and Language Disability and Specific Learning Disability have been added for the first time. Acid Attack Victims have been included. Dwarfism, muscular dystrophy have has been indicated as separate class of specified disability. The New categories of disabilities also included three blood disorders, Thalassemia, Hemophilia and Sickle Cell disease.

(iv) In addition, the Government has been authorised to notify any other category of specified disability.

(v) Responsibility has been cast upon the appropriate governments to take effective measures to ensure that the persons with disabilities enjoy their rights equally with others.

(vi) Additional benefits such as reservation in higher education, government jobs, reservation in allocation of land, poverty alleviation schemes etc. have been provided for persons with benchmark disabilities and those with high support needs.

(vii) Every child with benchmark disability between the age group of 6 and 18 years shall have the right to free education.
(viii) Government-funded educational institutions as well as the government recognised institutions will have to provide inclusive education to the children with disabilities.
(ix) For strengthening the Prime Minister's Accessible India Campaign, stress has been given to ensure accessibility in public buildings (both Government and private) in a prescribed time-frame.
(x) Reservation in vacancies in government establishments has been increased from 3% to 4% for certain persons or class of persons with benchmark disability.
(xi) The Bill provides for grant of guardianship by District Court under which there will be joint decision–making between the guardian and the persons with disabilities.
(xii) Broad-based Central & State Advisory Boards on Disability are to be set up to serve as apex policy making bodies at the Central and State level.
(xiii) Office of Chief Commissioner of Persons with Disabilities has been strengthened who will now be assisted by two Commissioners and an Advisory Committee comprising of not more than 11 members drawn from experts in various disabilities.
(xiv) Similarly, the office of State Commissioners of Disabilities has been strengthened who will be assisted by an Advisory Committee comprising of not more than 5 members drawn from experts in various disabilities.
(xv) The Chief Commissioner for Persons with Disabilities and the State Commissioners will act as regulatory bodies and Grievance Redressal agencies and also monitor implementation of the Act.
(xvi) District-level committees will be constituted by the State Governments to address local concerns of PwDs. Details of their constitution and the functions of such committees would be prescribed by the State Governments in the rules.
(xvii) Creation of National and State Fund will be created to provide financial support to the persons with disabilities. The existing National Fund for Persons with Disabilities and the Trust Fund for Empowerment of Persons with Disabilities will be subsumed with the National Fund.
(xviii) The Bill provides for penalties for offences committed against persons with disabilities and also violation of the provisions of the new law.
(xix) Special Courts will be designated in each district to handle cases concerning violation of rights of PwDs.

The New Act will bring our law in line with the United National Convention on the Rights of Persons with Disabilities (UNCRPD), to which India is a signatory. This will fulfil the obligations on the part of India in terms of UNCRPD. Further, the new law will not only enhance the Rights and Entitlements of Divyangjan but also provide effective mechanism for ensuring their empowerment and true inclusion into the Society in a satisfactory manner.

8.4.8 Central Electricity Regulatory Commission

- Electricity is an essential requirement for all facets of our life. It has been recognised as a basic human need. It is a critical infrastructure on which the socio-economic development of the country depends.

- Supply of electricity at reasonable rate to rural India is essential for its overall development.
- Equally important is availability of reliable and quality power at competitive rates to Indian industry to make it globally competitive and to enable it to exploit the tremendous potential of employment generation.
- Services sector has made significant contribution to the growth of our economy. Availability of quality supply of electricity is very crucial to sustained growth of this segment.
- Recognising that electricity is one of the key drivers for rapid economic growth and poverty alleviation Central Electricity Regulatory Commission (CERC), a key regulator of power sector in India, has been set up in 1998 as a 'statutory body functioning with quasi-judicial' status.
- The Commission intends to promote competition, efficiency and economy in bulk power markets, improve the quality of supply, promote investments and advise Government on the removal of institutional barriers to bridge the demand supply gap and thus foster the interests of consumers.
- In pursuit of these objectives, the Commission aims to improve the operations and management of the regional transmission systems through Indian Electricity Grid Code (IEGC), Availability Based Tariff (ABT), etc; formulate an efficient tariff setting mechanism, which ensures speedy and time-bound disposal of tariff petitions, promotes competition, economy and efficiency in the pricing of bulk power and transmission services and ensures least cost investments; to facilitate open access in interstate transmission; to facilitate technological and institutional changes required for the development of competitive markets in bulk power and transmission services.
- The National Electricity Policy has been evolved in consultation with and taking into account views of the State Governments, Central Electricity Authority (CEA), Central Electricity Regulatory Commission (CERC) and other stakeholders.

The National Electricity Policy aims at achieving the following objectives:

- Access to Electricity – Available for all households in next five years
- Availability of Power – Demand to be fully met by 2012. Energy and peaking shortages to be overcome and adequate spinning reserve to be available.
- Supply of reliable and quality power of specified standards in an efficient manner and at reasonable rates.
- Per capita availability of electricity to be increased to over 1000 units by 2012.
- Minimum lifeline consumption of 1 unit/ household/day as a merit good by year 2012.
- Financial turnaround and commercial viability of electricity sector.
- Protection of consumers' interests.
- Recently, CERC announced Renewable Energy Certificate (REC) system for fulfilment of its mandate to promote renewable sources of energy and development of market in electricity.
- REC mechanism is aimed at addressing the mismatch between availability of renewable energy resources in state and the requirement of the obligated entities to meet the renewable purchase obligation (RPO).
- Renewable energy generators will have two options: either to sell the renewable energy at preferential tariff or to sell electricity generation and environmental attributes associated with RE generations separately.

- The environmental attributes can be exchanged in the form of Renewable Energy Certificates (REC). The value of REC will be equivalent to 1 MWH of electricity injected into the grid from renewable energy sources.
- The REC will be exchanged only in the power exchanges approved by CERC within the band of a floor price and a forbearance (ceiling) price to be determined by CERC from time to time.
- There shall be two categories of certificates, viz., solar certificates issued to eligible entities for generation of electricity based on solar as renewable energy source, and non-solar certificates issued to eligible entities for generation of electricity based on renewable energy sources other than solar.
- Further with the objective of making easier grid connectivity to the hydro electric power stations and the other generating stations based on renewable sources of energy, CERC has liberalised Grid Access to Green Projects.
- While the threshold capacity for connecting to inter-State grid is 250 MW for thermal power stations, the threshold has been reduced to 50 MW for the hydro-electric generating stations and other generating stations using renewable sources of energy.
- Another important regulatory change has been made to permit connectivity to inter-State grid to such hydro generating stations and renewable energy source based stations which have individually installed capacity of less than 50 MW but approach the Central Transmission Utility (Power Grid) collectively with an aggregate installed capacity of 50 MW and above.
- For example, two hydro generating stations having capacity of 30 MW and 20 MW can collectively seek connectivity with inter-State grid at a single connection point if they mutually agree to undertake operational and commercial responsibilities through a lead generator which can be one of these two generating stations.

Recent Initiatives:
CERC has played a parenting role in the regulatory set up of the country- Shri Piyush Goyal

Inaugurates CERC's New Logo and Website
Shri Piyush Goyal, Union Minister of State (IC) for Power, Coal and New & Renewable Energy said that Central Electricity Regulatory Commission (CERC) has played a parenting role in the regulatory set up in the country. While speaking at the function of CERC's foundation day, Shri Goyal said that CERC has acted as benchmark regulator in the country. Complimenting CERC for completing 17 years of remarkable contribution and service to the nation, the Minister said that regulator has to act as a bridge between developers and the consumers and the regulator simultaneously balancing the interest of both parties. He expressed his satisfaction that the regulators in India have contributed immensely in this regard. He narrated five principles of proportionality, consistency, accountability, transparency and targeting for better productivity. Shri Goyal underlined the need for fast decision making and also to keep power affordable.

On the occasion , Sh. M.J. Akbar, Member of Parliament (RS), in his annual day lecture, emphasised the role of electricity in enhancing productivity of work, creation of jobs, elimination of poverty and democratisation of knowledge. Shri Gireesh Pradhan, Chairperson CERC, said that the institute has contributed to the growth and development of power sector over the years.

The Minister also inaugurated the modified website of CERC on the occasion. The website is given a new presentation in order to improve user interface and to provide better access to information to the masses. Shri Goyal also unveiled new logo of CERC along with the website. The new logo was designed by National Institute of Design, Ahmedabad to symbolise the changing face of CERC in the country from merely being a 'tariff setter' to a 'facilitator of development' of power sector and the market. The existing logo of CERC was designed in late 1990s which basically focussed on CERC role of being fair and impartial regulator balancing the interest of generators of power and the consumers.

8.4.9 National Consumer Dispute Redressal Commission

- The National Consumer Disputes Redressal Commission is a quasi-judicial commission which was set up in 1988 under the Consumer Protection Act of 1986.
- The Consumer Protection Act, 1986 is a benevolent social legislation that lays down the rights of the consumers and works for promotion and protection of the rights of the consumers.
- National Consumer Disputes Redressal Commission is headed by a sitting or retired Judge of the Supreme Court of India.
- In order to help achieve the objects of the Consumer Protection Act, the National Commission has also been conferred with the powers of administrative control over all the State Commissions by calling for periodical returns regarding the institution, disposal and pendency of cases.

The National Commission is empowered to issue instructions regarding

- Adoption of uniform procedure in the hearing of the matters,
- Prior service of copies of documents produced by one party to the opposite parties,
- Speedy grant of copies of documents.
- Generally over-seeing the functioning of the State Commissions and the District Forums to ensure that the objects and purposes of the Act are best served, without interfering with their quasi-judicial freedom.
- The Consumer Protection Act covers 'goods' as well as 'services'. The goods are those which are manufactured or produced and sold to consumers through wholesalers and retailers. The services are in the nature of transport, telephone, electricity, housing, banking, insurance, medical treatment, etc.

Recent Initiatives

48,998 calls received at National Consumer helpline in e-commerce sector during April 2016–February 2017

The number of calls for e-commerce companies, as registered in the National Consumer Helpline, over the last three years is as under:

Call Received at National Consumer Helpline in e-commerce Sector

Year	Calls
May 2014–March 2015	16,919
April 2015–March 2016	28,331
April 2016–February 2017	48,998

The redressal of the complaints are registered by a complainant with the three-tier system of quasi-judicial bodies namely the District Consumer Disputes Redressal Forum, State Consumer Disputes Redressal Commission and the National Consumer Disputes Redressal Commission established under the provisions of the Consumer Protection Act, 1986. Besides, Consumer Grievances addressed to the National Consumer Helpline (NCH) are redressed by forwarding the complaints to concerned departments and the companies and the progress is constantly monitored in their redressal. The NCH has established partnership with 225 companies under a convergence programme for speedy redressal.

The Government is aware about the functioning of e-commerce companies. The rights of the consumers involved in e-commerce are equally protected as per the provisions of the Consumer Protection Act, 1986, in a manner similar to transactions involving goods and services.

The draft amendment to the Packaged Commodities Rules, 2011 made under the provisions of Legal Metrology Act, 2009 proposes that the mandatory labeling declarations as per the rules shall be displayed on the online trading platforms.

A consumer dealing in e-commerce can file complaints in consumer courts for deficiency in service and defective products, under the provisions of the Consumer Protection Act, 1986 which has provisions regarding jurisdictional issues. The Consumer Protection Bill, 2015, introduced in August, 2015, seeks to strengthen the provisions regarding jurisdictional and also has provisions regarding Alternate Disputes Resolution.

8.4.10 Advertising Standards Council of India

A self-regulatory voluntary organisation of the advertising industry. The Advertising Standards Council of India (ASCI), established in 1985, is committed to the cause of self-regulation in advertising, ensuring the protection of the interests of consumers. ASCI was formed with the support of all four sectors connected with advertising, namely advertisers, advertising agencies, media (including broadcasters and the press) and others like PR Agencies, market research companies etc.

The Consumer Complaints Council is ASCI's heart and soul. It is the dedicated work put in by this group of highly respected people that has given tremendous impetus to the work of ASCI and the movement of self- regulation in the advertising.

Mission
To maintain and enhance the public's confidence in advertising.

Goals
ASCI seeks to ensure that advertisement confirm to its code for self-regulation.

Advertisements need to be:

- Truthful and honest
- Truthful, fair and non-derogatory to competitors. Advertisements should not be misleading and plagiarised.
- Non-offensive to public
- Within the bounds of generally accepted standards of public decency and propriety
- Against harmful products/unsafe situations
- Not used indiscriminately for the promotion of products, hazardous or harmful to society or to individuals particularly minors, to a degree unacceptable to society at large.
- Fair in competition

It also ensure that advertisements observe fairness in competition so that the consumer's need to be informed on choices in the market place and the canons of generally accepted competitive behaviour in business are both served.

Functions

1. To monitor administer and promote standards of advertising practices in India with a view to
   - ensuring the truthfulness and honesty of representations and claims made through advertising and safeguarding against misleading advertising.
   - ensuring that advertising is not offensive to generally accepted norms and standards of public decency.
   - safeguarding against the indiscriminate use of advertising for the promotion of products or services which are generally regarded as hazardous to society or to individuals or which are unacceptable to society as a whole.
   - ensuring that advertisements observe fairness in competition and the canons of generally accepted competitive behaviour.
2. To adopt and from time to time modify the code of advertising practices in India and implement, administer, promote and publicise such a code.
3. To promote, maintain and uphold fair, sound, ethical and healthy principles and practices of advertising.
4. To promote better understanding of the benefits of fair, sound and ethical advertising amongst the practitioners of advertising and in society at large.
5. To represent, protect, inform and guide the members of the company on matters related to advertising.
6. To foster and promote cooperation amongst persons or companies engaged and involved in advertising.

Is ASCI a Government Body?

ASCI is not a Government body. It is a voluntary self-regulatory organisation. However, ASCI is represented in all committees working on advertising content in every Ministry of the Government of India.

Recent Updates:

ASCI releases guidelines for celebrities in advertising

Celebrities have been deployed by marketers to add credibility to their brand offering. These celebrities however have a huge responsibility to ensure that the products they endorse or feature in, are true to the claims made in those advertising messages. Advertising Standards Council of India (ASCI) has developed a set of guidelines to protect consumers' interest while encouraging celebrities and advertisers to refrain from endorsing misleading advertisements. At a time when the Consumer Affairs Ministry is intending to review the Consumer Protection Act and may have a provision to deal with misleading advertisements featuring celebrities, these guidelines by ASCI could serve as a good reference for advertisers.

The following guidelines would help while creating advertisements featuring celebrities or involving celebrity endorsements:

- Celebrities, for the purpose of this guideline, are those people who are from the field of entertainment and sports and would also include other well-known personalities like doctors, authors, activists, educationists, etc. who get compensated for appearing in advertising.
- All advertisements featuring celebrities should ensure that it does not violate any of the ASCI code in letter and spirit. Celebrities are expected to have adequate knowledge of these codes and it is the duty of the advertiser and the agency to make sure that the celebrity they wish to engage with is made aware of them.
- Testimonials, endorsements or representations of opinions or preference of celebrities must reflect genuine, reasonably current opinion of the individual(s) making such representations, and must be based upon adequate information about or experience with the product or service being advertised.
- Celebrity should do due diligence to ensure that all description, claims and comparisons made in the advertisements they appear in or endorse are capable of being objectively ascertained and capable of substantiation and should not mislead or appear deceptive.
- Celebrities should not participate in any advertisement of a product or treatment or remedy that is prohibited for advertising under:

  (i) The Drugs & Magic Remedies (Objectionable Advertisements) Act 1954 as updated from time to time
  (ii) The Drugs & Cosmetic Act 1940 and Rules 1945: (Schedule J) as updated from time to time
  (iii) A product which by law requires a health warning '…..is injurious to health' on its packaging or advertisement.

- If the celebrity either directly or through the concerned advertiser/agency chooses to seek advertising advice from ASCI on whether the advertisement potentially violates any provisions of the ASCI code or not and if the advertisement is developed fully following the advertising advice provided by the ASCI, then the Celebrity would be considered as having completed due diligence.

However, ASCI's advertising advice will not be construed as a pre-clearance of the advertisement.

8.4.11 Animal Welfare Board of India

The Animal Welfare Board of India is a statutory advisory body on Animal Welfare Laws and promotes animal welfare in the country. Established in 1962 under Section 4 of the Prevention of Cruelty to Animals Act, 1960 (No. 59 of 1960), the Animal Welfare Board of India was started under the stewardship of Late Smt. Rukmini Devi Arundale, well known humanitarian. From ensuring that animal welfare laws in the country are diligently followed, to provide grants to Animal Welfare Organisations and advising the Government of India on animal welfare issues, the Board has been the face of the animal welfare movement in the country for the last 50 years.

The Board consists of 28 Members. The term of office of Members is for a period of three years.

Constitution of Animal Welfare Board of India

The Animal Welfare Board of India, the first of its kind to be established by any Government in the world, was set up in 1962, in accordance with Section 4 of the Prevention of Cruelty to Animals Acts 1960 (No.59 of 1960).

Shrimati Rukmini Devi Arundale pioneered the setting up of the Board, with its headquarters at Chennai. She guided the activities of the Board for nearly 20 years till her demise in 1986.

The Board consists of 28 members who are as follows:

1.	Chairman	
2.	Vice-Chairman	
3.	Inspectors General of Forests	1
4.	Animal Husbandry Commissioner	1
5.	Representative of Ministry of Home Affairs	1
6.	Representation of Ministry of HRD (Education)	1
7.	MPs – Lok Sabha*	4
8.	MPs – Rajya Sabha*	2
9.	Individuals	3
10.	Humanitarians	3
11.	SPCAs	3
12.	AWOs	3
13.	Representative of Indian Board for Wildlife	1
14.	Representative of Indian Veterinary Association	1
15.	Representative of Indian Medicine	1
16.	Representative of Allopathic Medicine	1
17.	Municipal Corporations	2
	Total	28

* To be nominated

Functions

1. To keep the law in force in India for the Prevention of Cruelty to Animals under constant study and to advise the government on the amendments to be undertaken in any such law from time to time.
2. To advise the Central Government on the making of rules under the Act with a view to preventing unnecessary pain or suffering to animals generally, and more particularly when they are being transported from one place to another or when they are used as performing animals or when they are kept in captivity or confinement.

3. To advise the Government or any local authority or other person on improvements in the design of vehicles so as to lessen the burden on draught animals.
4. To take all such steps as the board may think fit for amelioration of animals by encouraging, or providing for the construction of sheds, water troughs and the like and by providing for veterinary assistance to animals.
5. To advise the government or any local authority or other person in the design of slaughter houses or the maintenance of slaughter houses or in connection with slaughter of animals so that unnecessary pain or suffering, whether physical or mental, is eliminated in the pre-slaughter stages as far as possible, and animals are killed, wherever necessary, in as humane a manner as possible.
6. To take all such steps as the Board may think fit to ensure that unwanted animals are destroyed by local authorities, whenever it is necessary to do so, either instantaneously or after being rendered insensible to pain or suffering.
7. To encourage by the grant of financial assistance or otherwise, the formation or establishment of Pinjara poles, rescue homes, animals shelters, sanctuaries and the like, where animals and birds may find a shelter when they have become old and useless or when they need protection.
8. To cooperate with, and coordinate the work of associations or bodies established for the purpose of preventing unnecessary pain or suffering to animals or for the protection of animals and birds.
9. To give financial assistance and other assistance to Animal Welfare Organisations functioning in any local area or to encourage the formation of Animal Welfare Organisations in any local area which shall work under the general supervision and guidance of the Board.
10. To advise the Government on matters relating to the medical care and attention which may be provided in animal hospitals, and to give financial and other assistance to animal hospitals whenever the Board think it is necessary to do so.
11. To impart education in relation to the humane treatment of animals and to encourage the formation of public opinion against the infliction of unnecessary pain or suffering to animals and for the promotion of animal welfare by means of lectures books, posters, cinematographic exhibitions and the like.
12. To advise the Government on any matter connected with animal welfare or the prevention of infliction of unnecessary pain or suffering on animals.

Recognition

The Board grants recognition to the newly started Animal Welfare Organisations (AWOs). For this purpose, the Board has framed certain guidelines according to which the AWO has to submit the registration certificate under the Societies Registration Act or Trust Act, Audited Statement of Accounts and Annual Reports for the last three years, two copies of Memorandum of Association/Bye-laws and Animal Welfare Activities Report. The AWO has to agree to nominate a representative of the AWBI on its Managing/Executive Committee and also for regular inspection of its functioning. The new organisations are inspected by Board Members/authorised Inspection Agencies and if the inspection report is satisfactory, then they are considered for grant of recognition.

Financial Assistance

One of the most important functions of the Board is to provide financial assistance to the recognised Animal Welfare Organisations (AWOs). The applications in the prescribed format received from the AWOs are scrutinised and eligible applications are placed before the Board for sanction of grant. Financial assistance is released in two instalments after obtaining audited statement of accounts and utilisation certificate for the earlier grants and satisfactory Inspection reports. The Board provides financial assistance to AWOs under various schemes viz. Regular Grant, Cattle Rescue Grant, Provision of Shelter House for looking after the Animals, Animal Birth Control (ABC) Programme, Provision of Ambulance for the animals in distress and Natural Calamity grant.

Recent Initiatives (incidents involving AWBI)

Animal Welfare Board moved to SC challenging the Tamil Nadu government's new law allowing Jallikattu. The petitions were submitted in the back drop of the Tamil Nadu assembly, in a special session, passed an amendment to conduct Jallikattu in the state without any hurdles replacing an ordinance promulgated earlier.

The Animal welfare Board of India has moved to the Supreme Court challenging the new Act allowing the tranditional sport of Jallikattu in Tamil Nadu. The court has listed the matter for 30th January, 2017 along with the Centre's plea for withdrawing the 2016 notification allowing Jallikattu.

8.4.12 Bureau of Civil Aviation Security

History

The Bureau of Civil Aviation Security was initially set up as a cell in the Directorate General of Civil Aviation (DGCA) in January 1978 on the recommendation of the Pande Committee constituted in the wake of the hijacking of the Indian Airlines flight on 10th September, 1976. The role of the cell was to coordinate, monitor, inspect and train personnel in Civil Aviation Security matters.

The BCAS was reorganised into an independent department on 1st April, 1987 under the Ministry of Civil Aviation as a sequel to the Kanishka Tragedy in June 1985. The main responsibility of BCAS are to lay down standards and measures in respect of security of civil flights at International and domestic airports in India.

Organisation

BCAS is the regulatory authority for civil aviation security in India. It is headed by an officer of the rank of Director General of Police and is designated as Commissioner of Security (Civil Aviation).

Commissioner of Security (CA) is the appropriate authority for implementation of Annexure 17 to Chicago Convention of International Civil Aviation Organisation (ICAO).

Commissioner of Security (CA) is responsible for the development, implementation and maintenance of the National Civil Aviation Security Programme.

BCAS Headquarters is located at 'A' Wing, I-III floor, Janpath Bhavan, Janpath, New Delhi-110001. It has got four Regional Offices located at International airports, that is, i.e. Delhi, Mumbai, Kolkata and Chennai. The Regional Office is headed by an officer of the rank of Deputy Commissioner of Security (CA).

Functions

- Lay down Aviation Security Standards in accordance with Annex 17 to Chicago Convention of ICAO for airport operators, airlines operators, and their security agencies responsible for implementing AVSEC measures.
- Monitor the implementation of security rules and regulations and carrying out survey of security needs.
- Ensure that the persons implementing security controls are appropriately trained and possess all competencies required to perform their duties.
- Plan and coordinate aviation security matters.
- Conduct surprise/dummy checks to test professional efficiency and alertness of security staff
- Conduct mock exercise to test efficacy of contingency plans and operational preparedness of the various agencies.

AVSEC Rules and Regulations

Acts

AIRCRAFT ACT- 1934
AIRCRAFT RULES-1937
Tokyo Convention 1975 Act
Anti-Hijacking Act 1982
Anti Hijacking Act 1994 (Amendments 1994)
The Suppression of Unlawfull Acts Against Safety of Civil Aviation Act 1982
The Suppression of Unlawfull Acts Against Safety of Civil Aviation Act 1994

International Conventions

Recent Updates:

In a major exercise by the Bureau of Civil Aviation Security (BCAS), it has suspended the licence of budget carrier IndiGo's aviation security training facility for alleged lapses in the examination system conducted by it. Indigo's aviation security training centre licence has been suspended for leaking question papers. BCAS suspended the licence of IndiGo's aviation security training centre on Friday after several lapses were detected in the examination procedure it was following. If security training is being compromised, it raises serious questions

1. BCAS has made it mandatory to furnish Aadhaar card while applying for the Airport Entry Pass (AEP). The AEP is issued by the BCAS after obtaining complete details from those seeking the pass for entry into the airport and for exit. The entry pass is issued to officials and staff of Airports Authority of India (AAI), personnel of the CISF guarding the airport, officials of Customs, Immigration, airlines and other agencies working at the airport. The AEP which contains the photograph of the pass holder and their complete details is valid for a period of one year. It is sent for renewal to the BCAS on expiry. Without the AEP the CISF personnel providing round-the-clock security would not allow any person inside the airport

8.4.13 Bureau of Indian Standards (BIS)

Overview

BIS is the National Standard Body of India established under the BIS Act 1986 for the harmonious development of the activities of standardisation, marking and quality certification of goods and for matters connected therewith or incidental thereto.

BIS has been providing traceability and tangibility benefits to the national economy in a number of ways – providing safe reliable quality goods; minimising health hazards to consumers; promoting exports and imports substitute; control over proliferation of varieties etc. through standardisation, certification and testing.

Origin of BIS

In the twilight years of British rule in India, when the country was faced with the gigantic task of building up the industrial infrastructure, it was the Institution of Engineers (India), which prepared the first draft of the Constitution of an Institution which could take up the task of formulation of National Standards. This led to the Department of Industries and Supplies issuing a memorandum on 3rd September, 1946, formally announcing the setting of an organisation called the 'Indian Standards Institution'. The Indian Standards Institution (ISI) came into being on the 6th January, 1947 and in June 1947 Dr. Lal C. Verman took over as its first Director.

In the initial years, the organisation concentrated on standardisation activity. To provide the advantages of standardisation to common consumers, the Indian Standards Institution started operating the Certification Marks Scheme under the Indian Standards Institution (Certification Marks) Act, 1952. The Scheme, which was formally launched by ISI in 1955–1956, enabled it to grant licences to manufacturers producing goods in conformity with Indian Standards and to apply ISI Mark on their products. To meet the requirements of the Certification Marks Scheme, the nucleus of a laboratory was started in 1963. While the product certification was being operated under the Indian Standards Institution (Certification Marks) Act, 1952, the formulation of standards and other related work were not governed by any legislation. A Bill with this objective was therefore introduced in the Parliament on 26th November, 1986.

Bureau of Indian standards (BIS) came into existence, through an act of Parliament dated 26th November, 1986, on 1st April, 1987, with a broadened scope and more powers taking over the staff, assets, liabilities and functions of erstwhile ISI. Through this change over, the government envisaged building a climate for quality culture and consciousness and greater participation of consumers in formulation and implementation of national standards.

The Bureau is a Body Corporate consisting of 25 members representing both Central and State governments, Members of Parliament, industry, scientific and research institutions, consumer organisations and professional bodies; with Union Minister of Consumer Affairs, Food and Public Distribution as its President and with Minister of State for Consumer Affairs, Food and Public Distribution as its Vice-President.

Vision

The Bureau of Indian Standards (BIS), the National Standards Body of India, resolves to be the leader in all matters concerning Standardisation, Certification and Quality.

Mission

BIS Act 1986 provides for the establishment of a Bureau for the harmonious development of the activities of standardisation, marking and quality certification of goods and for matters connected therewith or incidental thereto.

Objectives

1. Formulate need-based standards and participate in International Standardisation
2. Satisfy the customer's need for quality and safety of goods and services through operation of Certification Schemes (Product Certification, Registration, Management System Certification, Hallmarking) of BIS.
3. Test samples generated through product certification scheme of BIS
4. Organise training programmes for Industry to enable and encourage them to produce quality goods.
5. Generate awareness on standards, standard mark, and safety and quality of products through seminars, awareness programmes and publicity campaigns.
6. Improve the quality and competitiveness of Indian industry and thereby enhance export of Indian goods and services through conformance to Indian Standards and acceptance of BIS mark by importers.
7. Improve transparency in functioning and thereby allowing greater participation of stakeholders in various activities of BIS.

Functions

The major functions of Bureau of Indian Standards are to establish, publish and promote the Indian Standard, in relation to any article or process.

1. Recognise as an Indian Standard, any standard established by any other Institution in India or elsewhere, in relation to any article or process.
2. Specify a Standard Mark to be called the Bureau of Indian Standards Certification Mark which shall be of such design and contain such particulars as may be prescribed to represent a particular Indian Standard.
3. Grant, renew, suspend or cancel a licence for the use of the Standard Mark.
4. Seek recognition of the Bureau and of the Indian Standards outside India on such terms and conditions as may be mutually agreed upon by the Bureau with any corresponding institution or organisation in any country.

BIS is involved in various activities as follows:

- Standards Formulation
- Product Certification Scheme
- Compulsory Registration Scheme
- Foreign Manufacturers Certification Scheme
- Hall Marking Scheme
- Laboratory Services
- Laboratory Recognition Scheme
- Sale of Indian Standards
- Consumer Affairs Activities

- Promotional Activities
- Training Services, National & International level
- Information Services

Foreign Manufacturers Certification Scheme

Bureau of Indian Standards (BIS) has been operating a Foreign Manufacturers Certification Scheme (FMCS) since the year 2000 under BIS Act, 1986 and Rules & Regulations framed there under.

Under FMCS, licence is granted to a Foreign Manufacturer for use of Standard Mark on a product that conforms to an Indian Standard.

The Scheme is applicable for grant of licence for all products except Electronics and IT Goods notified by DeitY .

The licence is granted by Foreign Manufacturers Certification Department (FMCD) located at BIS Headquarters, New Delhi.

Product Certification

The Bureau of Indian Standards, empowered through an Act of the Indian Parliament, known as the Bureau of Indian Standards Act, 1986, operates a product certification scheme by which it grants licences to manufacturers covering practically every industrial discipline from agriculture to textiles to electronics. The certification allows the licensees to use the popular ISI Mark, which has become synonymous with quality products for the Indian and neighbouring markets over the last more than 55 years. The Bureau's predecessor, the Indian Standards Institution began operating the product certification Scheme since 1955.

Operating Principle

The BIS Product Certification Scheme operates in an impartial, non-discriminatory and transparent manner. The documents stating the powers, functions and responsibilities of BIS are published by the Government of India as the Bureau of Indian Standards Act, 1986, BIS Rules, 1987 and BIS (Certification) Regulations, 1988. The specific procedure for operating a licence is given in another document called the Scheme of Testing and Inspection (STI), described later. Procedures provide for maintaining a very high degree of confidentiality and integrity among its personnel who perform certification-related tasks. A body called the 'Certification Advisory Committee', composed of persons from varied sectors like manufacturers, consumers, Government agencies, industries associations, reviews the performance of the scheme and advises on key policy issues.

Certification System

The BIS product certification scheme is essentially voluntary in nature, and is largely based on ISO/IEC Guide 28 which provides general rules for third party certification system of determining conformity with product standards through initial testing and assessment of a factory quality management system and its acceptance followed by surveillance that takes into account the factory Quality management system and the testing of samples from the factory and the open market. All BIS certifications are carried out in accordance with Indian Standards, which are amenable to certification. A large number of operational elements of the BIS product certification scheme correspond with the requirements of ISO/IEC 17065.

Types of Licensing

Although, the scheme itself is voluntary in nature, the Government of India, in public interest (for example: public health and safety, security, infrastructure requirements, mass consumption) has enforced mandatory certification on various products through various Quality Control Orders issued from time to time under various Acts. While BIS continues to grant licences on application, the enforcement of compulsory certification is done by the authorities notified in such quality control orders. For the list of items brought under mandatory certification, together with the corresponding Indian Standard Number, and the authorities responsible for enforcing the orders.

List of Products under Mandatory Certification

Under separate arrangements with Statutory agencies, some products have been placed under special certification schemes of lot or batch inspection carried out by BIS Inspecting officers. A majority of gas cylinders, regulators and valves are certified through such schemes.

For all other products, the manufacturer is permitted to self-certify the products after ascertaining its conformity to the standard licensed for. Through its surveillance operations, the Bureau maintains a close vigil on the quality of certified goods.

The BIS Product Certification Scheme is open to manufacturers in all countries without discrimination. Overseas applicants are also granted licence for use of ISI mark under separately designed scheme, FMCS

Resources

The finances of the Bureau are self-managed, with certification operations accounting for about 90% of the revenue. The BIS employs competent engineers and scientists to cater to all its fields of operations. They are trained into evaluation and assessment techniques to a high degree of professional competence. All preliminary and surveillance inspections are carried out by qualified personnel only. BIS has set up eight laboratories in different cities of India for testing samples of products taken during preliminary and surveillance operations. In addition, independent laboratories having demonstrated ability and a quality system complying with IS/ISO/IEC 17025 have been recognised for testing of samples.

The certification scheme operates through a network of 34 branch offices set up in state capitals or major industrial towns and five regional offices overseeing the work of the Branch offices BIS directory.

Environment Management System Certification

The Bureau is operating EMS certification scheme against IS/ISO 14000 standards under the BIS Act, 1986.

Technical Information Services

The world trade is growing bigger day by the day and with it comes the increased number of standards, technical regulations and conformity assessment procedures. The exporters and importers, user organisations and government agencies are today faced with lack of information/clarity on the above.

The Technical Information Services Department of BIS offers a range of services as enumerated in the following list:

1. WTO-TBT Enquiry Point
2. Technical Enquiries about standards and technical regulations
3. World Manufacturer Identifier (WMI) Code
4. Issuers Identification Number (IIN)
5. Registered Application Provider Identifier (RID)

Rajiv Gandhi National Quality Award

Rajiv Gandhi National Quality Award was instituted by the Bureau of Indian Standards in 1991, with a view to encouraging Indian manufacturing and service organisations to strive for excellence and giving special recognition to those who are considered to be the leaders of quality movement in India. It is one of the most prestigious awards for organisations who have excelled in the field of 'quality', either in manufacturing sector or in service sector. The recipients of this award, over the years, have excelled to become the benchmark of quality in their respective fields, for which they have even earned international recognition.

Rajiv Gandhi National Quality Award would help Indian Industry to improve quality by:

a. Encouraging Indian Industry to make significant improvements in quality for maximising consumer satisfaction and for successfully facing competition in the global market as well.
b. Recognising the achievements of those organisations which have improved the quality of their products and services and thereby set an example for others.
c. Establishing guidelines and criteria that can be used by industry in evaluating their own quality improvement efforts.

The award has been designed in line with similar awards in other developed countries, like Malcolm Baldrige National Quality Award in USA, Deming Prize in Japan and European Quality Award.

Consumer Protection

Complaint regarding BIS certified products under various schemes/services can be lodged in the following manner:

- Through Online Complaint Registration on BIS website at www.bis.org.in or mobile application or by email at complaints@bis.gov.in
- Personally contacting/writing to Public Grievance officer of the nearest Regional/Branch office of BIS or directly to the Head (Consumer Affairs Department)

BIS and Consumer Rights

1. Right to be protected against the marketing of goods which are hazardous to life and property.
2. Right to be informed about the quality, quantity, potency, purity, standard and price of goods so as to protect the consumer against unfair trade practices.
3. Right to be assured, whenever possible, access to variety of goods at competitive prices.
4. Right to be heard and to be assured that consumers interests will receive due consideration at appropriate forums.
5. Right to seek redressel against unfair trade practices or unscrupulous exploitation of consumers.
6. Right to consumer education.

Product Certification Mark

Quality Systems Certification Mark

Environment Friendly Products Mark

916
(22 Carat)

Hallmarking of Gold Jewellery

The Bureau of Indian Standards Bill, 2015

- The Bureau of Indian Standards Bill, 2015 was introduced in Lok Sabha by Mr. Ram Vilas Paswan, Minister of Consumer Affairs, Food and Public Distribution on August 7, 2015. The Bill replaces the Bureau of Indian Standards Act, 1986. The Act establishes a Bureau for the purpose of standardisation, marking and certification of articles and processes. The Bill seeks to broaden its ambit, and allow the Central Government to make it mandatory for certain notified goods, articles, processes, etc. to carry the standard mark.
- **Ambit of the Bureau of Indian Standards:** Under the 1986 Act, standardisation, marking and certification processes applied to certain articles and processes. The Bill includes goods, services and systems. A good, service, article, process and system have been defined in the Bill.

- **Establishment of the Bureau of Indian Standards:** The Bureau of Indian Standards will be a national body which will formulate, implement and certify certain standards of quality for goods, services, articles, processes and systems. The Bureau will constitute technical committees of experts for the purpose of formulating such standards. The Bill constitutes a Governing Council which would be responsible to look at the general superintendence, direction and management of the Bureau.
- **Certification of goods, services, articles, etc:** The Bureau would be a licensing authority for quality standards. A person may apply to the Bureau for a license to use a standard mark, or a certificate of conformity, depending on the good, article, process, etc. A license or certificate of conformity indicates that the item conforms to the Indian standard as set by the Bureau. The Bureau will establish and maintain testing laboratories for quality assurance and conformity assessment of goods, articles, services, etc.
- **Certification of precious metals:** A hallmark will be used to certify precious metal articles including silver, gold, platinum and palladium or their alloys. A hallmark indicates a proportionate content of the precious metal in the article, as per the Indian standard. Such articles will be sold in certified sales outlets.
- **Mandatory certification of certain goods:** The Bill allows the central government to notify certain goods, articles, etc., which will need to compulsorily carry a standard mark. Such goods or articles will be notified by the government if it thinks them to be necessary for: (i) public interest or for the protection of human, animal or plant health, (ii) safety of the environment, (iii) prevention of unfair trade practices, or (iv) national security.
- **Recall of goods, services, articles etc.:** The Bureau may recall a good or article which is already out for sale or supply. This will be done if the Bureau is convinced that the good or article does not conform to the requirement of a particular standard.
- **Penalties:** The penalty for improper use of the Indian standard mark will be a fine of up to five lakh rupees. The Bill also prescribes penalties for: (i) the improper use of the standard mark by testing and marking centres, and (ii) manufacturing or selling goods and articles which do not carry a standard mark and have been mandated to do so, among others. The Bill provides for compounding of offences punishable with fine except when a person has committed such an offence for the second time or if such an offence committed by him has been compounded earlier.
- **Offences by companies:** When a company commits an offence under the Bill, the persons responsible for or in charge of the company will be presumed to be guilty irrespective of whether the offence was committed without their knowledge, consent or connivance.
- **Appeals:** An appeal against an order regarding the granting of a license or certificate of conformity, or compounding of offences, may be made to the Director General of the Bureau. A further appeal against the order of the Director General may then be made to the Central Government.

8.4.14 Central Board of Film Certification (CBFC)

Introduction

Central Board of Film Certification (CBFC) is a statutory body under Ministry of Information and Broadcasting, regulating the public exhibition of films under the provisions of the

Cinematograph Act 1952. Films can be publicly exhibited in India only after they have been certified by the Central Board of Film Certification. The Board consists of non-official members and a Chairman (all of whom are appointed by Central Government) and functions with headquarters at Mumbai. It has nine Regional offices, one each at Mumbai, Kolkata, Chennai, Bangalore, Thiruvananthapuram, Hyderabad, New Delhi, Cuttack and Guwahati. The Regional Offices are assisted in the examination of films by Advisory Panels. The members of the panels are nominated by Central Government by drawing people from different walks of life for a period of 2 years. The Certification process is in accordance with The Cinematograph Act, 1952, The Cinematograph (certification) Rules, 1983, and the guidelines issued by the Central government u/s 5 (B)

Vision

To ensure the good and healthy entertainment in accordance with the provisions of the Cinematograph Act 1952 and the Cinematograph (Certification) Rules 1983.

Mission

1. Ensure healthy entertainment, recreation and education to the public.
2. Make the certification process transparent and responsible.
3. Create awareness among advisory panel members, media and film makers about the guidelines for certification and current trend in films through workshops and meetings.
4. Adopt modern technology for certification process through computerisation of certification process and upgradation of infrastructure.
5. Maintain transparency about Board's activities through voluntary disclosures, implementation of e-governance, prompt replies to RTI queries and publication of annual report.
6. Develop CBFC as a Centre of Excellence

Organisation

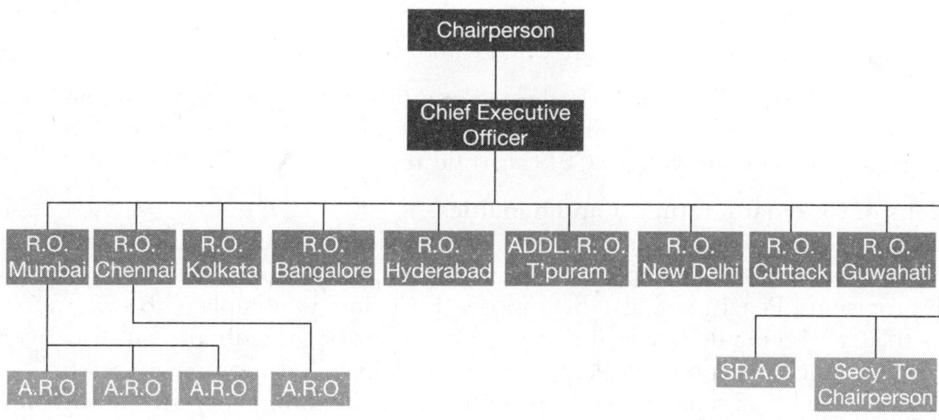

Basic Functions

1. Ensure the good and healthy entertainment in accordance with the provisions of the Cinematograph Act 1952 and the Cinematograph (Certification) Rules 1983 by certifying the films produced in and outside India for public exhibition as under

a. 'U' certificate for universal exhibition
b. 'A' certificate for public exhibition to Adults only
c. 'UA' certificate for public exhibition of films which can be viewed by children below the age of 12 years under parental guidance only
d. 'S' certificate for public exhibition of films meant for members of any profession or any class of persons

2. Refuse certificate to the film unsuitable for public exhibition if the film or any part of it is against the interests of the sovereignty and integrity of India, the security of the States, friendly relations with foreign state, public order, decency or morality or involves defamation or contempt of court or is likely to incite commission of any offence.

The Central Board of Film Certification is responsible for certifying films. The enforcement of compliance to the provisions of the Cinematograph Act, 1952 is entrusted to the State Governments/Union Territory Administrations, since exhibition of films is a state subject.

The violation of the provisions of the Act and Rule may take place in various forms which are discussed in the following section.

Violations of Cinematograph act and penalties.

The following are the major violations that agitate the minds of the public:

a. Exhibition of an A certified film to a non-adult
b. Exhibition of an S certified film to persons other than those for whom it is meant;
c. Exhibition of a film in a form other than the one in which it was certified. Such violations are known as interpolations. Interpolations can be described as follows

   (i) Re-insertion in the prints of a film, those portions which were deleted by the Board while certifying the film
   (ii) Insertion in the prints of a film, portions which were never shown to the Board for certification;
   (iii) Exhibition of 'bits' unconnected with the certified film.

d. Exhibition of a film which was refused a certificate (or banned in common parlance)
e. Exhibition of uncertified films with forged certificates of other films.
f. Exhibition of films without CBFC certificate.

Violations of Cinematograph act and penalties.

Offences with regard to violations of certification provisions are cognizable. Furthermore, they are non-bailable. Section 7 of the Cinematograph Act provides penalties for violation of censorship provisions. Penalty can also be imposed for failure to comply with section 6A which requires that any person delivering a film to an exhibitor or a distributor will also give to him details of all cuts, certification, title, length and conditions of certification.

A person guilty of violation while exhibiting celluloid films is punishable with imprisonment for a term which may extend to three years, or with fine which may extend to ₹1 lakh, or with both, and with a further fine up to ₹20,000 for each day for continuing the offence. Similarly, showing of video films which violate the rules in the manner prescribed in this section will attract imprisonment of not less than three months which may be extended to three years and a fine of not less than ₹20,000 which may extended to ₹1 lakh and a further fine up to ₹20,000 each day for a continuing the offence.

Furthermore, the trial court can direct that the offending film be forfeited to the Government. Under Section 7A, any police officer can enter a hall where an offending film is being screened, search the premises and seize the print. Films can also be seized when they are likely to be exhibited in violation of Cinematograph Act.

Guidelines

The Cinematograph Act lays down that a film shall not be certified if any part of it is against the interest of the sovereignty and integrity of India, the security of the State, friendly relations with foreign States, public order, decency or involves defamation or contempt of court or is likely to incite commission of any offence.

Under Section 5B(2) the Central Government has issued the following guidelines.

A film is judged entirely from the point of view of its overall impact and is examined in the light of the period depicted in the film and the contemporary standards of the country and the people to whom the film relates, provided that the film does not deprave the morality of the audience. Guidelines are applied to the titles of the films also.

1. **Objectives of Film Certification**
   - (i) The medium of film remains responsible and sensitive to the values and standards of society.
   - (ii) Artistic expression and creative freedom are not unduly curbed.
   - (iii) Certification is responsible to social changes.
   - (iv) The medium of film provides clean and healthy entertainment.
   - (v) As far as possible, the film is of aesthetic value and cinematically of a good standard.
2. **In pursuance of the above objectives, the CBFC shall ensure that**
   - (i) Anti-social activities such as violence are not glorified or justified.
   - (ii) The modus operandi of criminals, other visuals or words likely to incite the commission of any offence are not depicted.
   - (iii) Scenes
     - a. showing involvement of children in violence as victims or perpetrators or as forced witnesses to violence, or showing children as being subjected to any form of child abuse.
     - b. showing abuse or ridicule of physically and mentally handicapped persons; and
     - c. showing cruelty to, or abuse of animals, are not presented needlessly
   - (iv) Pointless or avoidable scenes of violence, cruelty and horror, scenes of violence primarily intended to provide entertainment and such scenes as may have the effect of de-sensitising or de-humanising people are not shown.
   - (v) Scenes which have the effect of justifying or glorifying drinking are not shown.
   - (vi) Scenes tending to encourage, justify or glamorise drug addiction are not shown.
   - (vii) Scenes tending to encourage, justify or glamorise consumption of tobacco or smoking are not shown.
   - (viii) Human sensibilities are not offended by vulgarity, obscenity or depravity.
   - (ix) Such dual meaning words as obviously cater to baser instincts are not allowed.
   - (x) Scenes degrading or denigrating women in any manner are not presented.

(xi) Scenes involving sexual violence against women like attempt to rape, rape or any form of molestation or scenes of a similar nature are avoided, and if any such incidence is germane to the theme, they shall be reduced to the minimum and no details are shown.
(xii) Scenes showing sexual perversions shall be avoided and if such matters are germane to the theme they shall be reduced to the minimum and no details are shown
(xiii) Visuals or words contemptuous of racial, religious or other groups are not presented.
(xiv) Visuals or words which promote communal, obscurantist, anti-scientific and anti-national attitude are not presented.
(xv) The sovereignty and integrity of India is not called in question.
(xvi) The security of the State is not jeopardised or endangered.
(xvii) Friendly relations with foreign states are not strained.
(xviii) Public order is not endangered.
(xix) Visuals or words involving defamation of an individual or a body of individuals, or contempt of court are not presented. Scenes that tend to create scorn, disgrace or disregard of rules or undermine the dignity of court will come under the term 'Contempt of Court'.
(xx) National symbols and emblems are not shown except in accordance with the provisions of the Emblems and Names (Prevention of Improper Use) Act, 1950 (12 of 1950).

3. **The Board of Film Certification shall also ensure that the film**
   (i) is judged in its entirety from the point of view of its overall impact.
   (ii) is examined in the light of the period depicted in the films and the contemporary standards of the country and the people to which the film relates provided that the film does not deprave the morality of the audience.

4. Films that meet the above-mentioned criteria but are considered unsuitable for exhibition to non-adults shall be certified for exhibition to adult audiences only.

5. (i) While certifying films for unrestricted public exhibition, the Board shall ensure that the film is suitable for family viewing, that is to say, the film shall be such that all the members of the family including children can view it together.
   (ii) If the Board, having regard to the nature, content and theme of the film is of the opinion that it is necessary to caution the parents/guardian to consider as to whether any child below the age of twelve years may be allowed to see such a film, the film shall be certified for unrestricted public exhibition with an endorsement to that effect.
   (iii) If the Board having regard to the nature, content and theme of the film, is of the opinion that the exhibition of the film should be restricted to members of any profession or any class of persons, the film shall be certified for public exhibition restricted to the specialised audiences to be specified by the Board in this behalf.

6. The Board shall scrutinise the titles of the films carefully and ensure that they are not provocative, vulgar, offensive or violative of any of the above-mentioned guidelines.

Recent updates related to CBFC:

Report of the Expert Committee on CBFC

An Expert Committee (Chaired by Mr. Shyam Benegal) constituted to recommend guidelines for certification of films by the Central Board of Film Certification (CBFC) submitted its report in April 2016.

- The Committee was created on January 1, 2016, by the Ministry of Information & Broadcasting. The terms of reference of the Committee included: (i) to study the procedures of certification being followed by CBFC, (ii) to recommend guiding principles with respect to certification of films, within the ambit of the Cinematograph Act, 1952 and (iii) suggest a suitable staffing structure for a more efficient service.
- Role of CBFC: The Committee observed that an owner of a film has complete rights over it. Any alteration or change in the film can only be made by the owner or with his consent. It is recommended that the current system of suggesting modifications and amendments to a film by the CBFC should be done away with and the Board must function only as a film certification body.
- **Modification to 1991 guidelines:** Guidelines were issued in 1991 under section 5B of the Cinematograph Act, 1952. Section 5B states that a film will not be certified if a part of it or the entire film is against the interest of the sovereignty and integrity of the country, decency or morality, etc. The Committee noted that some of the objectives under these guidelines, such as requiring the film to be sensitive to the values of the society, providing clean and healthy entertainment, were not within the ambit of the CBFC.
- In this regard, the Committee has drafted a new set of guidelines. The objective of the guidelines is: (i) artistic expression and creative freedom of filmmakers is protected through parameters that are objective, (ii) audiences are empowered to make informed viewing decisions, and (iii) the process of certification is responsive to social change. The guidelines also state that an applicant must mention in his application, (i) the category of certification he seeks and (ii) the target audience. Further, any cuts in a film can only be made by the applicant, depending on the certification he needs for his film.
- **Sub-division of existing categories of certification:** The Committee also suggested that **two categories of certification**, that is **UA** (films that contain certain scenes not suitable for children below the age of 12) and **A** (films suitable for adults only), should be **further sub-divided into sub-categories**. The UA category should be divided into two sub-categories: UA 12+ and UA 15+. While UA 12+ will cater to young teenagers yet to be exposed to the adult world, UA 15+ will cater to young adolescents at an age where they are being exposed to issues in the adult world, in a moderate manner. The A category should include an A-C (films suitable for adults only, with caution) sub-category, for films that may contain explicit material, such as nudity, violence, etc. This categorisation will help audiences to make distinct choices.
- **Guidelines for certification:** The Committee has proposed guidelines for certification which have been divided into three categories: (i) general, (ii) issue related, and (iii) category specific. The general guidelines define the approach to be followed while certifying a film, with respect to general factors in a film, such as context, theme, etc. The

issue-related guidelines list issues in a society that apply to all categories of certification. Category-specific guidelines lay down the approach that CBFC should take with respect to various categories of film certification.

- **Functions of CBFC:** The Committee recommended that the CBFC should confine itself to

  (i) submission of an annual report to the central government, containing an analytical study of the trends in the film industry, to be tabled in Parliament each year
  (ii) prescribing the manner in which the records and accounts of the Board will be kept.
  (iii) reviewing the work of regional officers and the Regional and Central Advisory Panels.
  (iv) periodically review guidelines laid down for certification of films, etc.

- **Staffing pattern of CBFC:** In order to reduce the human interface between applicants and officials of the CBFC, the Committee recommended that process of application, and selection of members for the Examining Committee (that will sit through the screening of a film and deliberate on it) and Revising Committee (that will function as the first point of appeal) should be done through a computerised software.

Censorship

In most countries of the world there is a mechanism/process of certifying feature films and documentaries. However, it has to be ensured that in doing so, artistic creativity and freedom do not get stifled/curtailed and the people tasked with the work of certification understand these nuances. Indian films have glorious history. A whole lot of Indian films have enriched the cultural milieu of the country besides making astonishing advances in technical aspects of film making.

The Central Board of Film Certification is there to certify films, not censor them. That's one argument that's often been voiced, especially in recent days

When did the Central Board of Film Certification (CBFC) begin working like a censor board?

As it turns out, from the time it started certifying films.

The CBFC is a body constituted under the Cinematograph Act, 1952. Indeed, when it was created it was called the Board of Film Censors. Its powers of certifying a film for public consumption was introduced by way of an amendment in 1959.

The Cinematograph Act prescribes that all movies aimed at 'public exhibition' will be first examined by the CBFC. The Board can ask for parts of the movie to be cut or removed before showcasing it in public in case it is 'against the interests of the sovereignty and integrity of India the security of the state, friendly relations with foreign states, public order, decency or morality, or involves defamation or contempt of court or is likely to incite the commission of any offence'.

This power to censor, was justified by the apex court when it said the CBFC had the right to ask for cuts while certifying a film. The question was decided by the Supreme Court, in the case of K.A. Abbas versus Union of India, in September 1970. That case involved Abbas' documentary *A Tale of Four Cities* in which the CBFC asked for certain scenes to be cut. The award-winning filmmaker approached the Supreme Court saying the cuts asked for amounted to a violation of his freedom of expression.

The court (in a judgement delivered by then chief justice Mohammad Hidayatullah) approved of censorship and noted in its judgement, 'Our standards must be so framed that we are not reduced to a level where the protection of the least capable and the most depraved amongst us determines what the morally healthy cannot view or read. The standards that we set for our censors must make a substantial allowance in favour of freedom thus leaving a vast area for creative art to interpret life and society with some of its foibles along with what is good'.

The court said films were a powerful media and had greater impact than books. It ruled that censorship, including cutting parts of movies before public release, was valid under the Constitution.

It also ruled that in the absence of any self-regulatory organisation that could suggest or ask for cuts in films, it was up to the government appointed CBFC to do so.

8.4.15 Competition Commission of India (CCI)

Competition is the best means of ensuring that the 'Common Man' or 'AamAadmi' has access to the broadest range of goods and services at the most competitive prices. With increased competition, producers will have maximum incentive to innovate and specialise. This would result in reduced costs and wider choice to consumers. A fair competition in market is essential to achieve this objective. Our goal is to create and sustain fair competition in the economy that will provide a 'level playing field' to the producers and make the markets work for the welfare of the consumers.

The Competition Act

The Competition Act, 2002 was passed by the Parliament in the year 2002, to which the President accorded assent in January, 2003. It was subsequently amended by the Competition (Amendment) Act, 2007. In accordance with the provisions of the Amendment Act, the Competition Commission of India and the Competition Appellate Tribunal have been established. The Competition Commission of India is now fully functional with a Chairperson and six members. The Act prohibits anti-competitive agreements, abuse of dominant position by enterprises and regulates combinations (acquisition, acquiring of control and M&A), which causes or likely to cause an appreciable adverse effect on competition within India.

Competition Commission of India

The objectives of the act are sought to be achieved through the Competition Commission of India (CCI), which has been established by the Central Government with effect from 14th October 2003. CCI consists of a Chairperson and six Members appointed by the Central Government. It is the duty of the Commission to eliminate practices having adverse effect on competition, promote and sustain competition, protect the interests of consumers and ensure freedom of trade in the markets of India. The Commission is also required to give opinion on competition issues on a reference received from a statutory authority established under any law and to undertake competition advocacy, create public awareness and impart training on competition issues.

The CCI is quasi-judicial statutory body established under The Competition Act, 2002. It was established in 2003 to eliminate practices that adversely affect competition in different industries and protect interests of consumers and ensure freedom of trade. Its predecessor was the MRTPC (Monopolies and Restrictive Trade Practices Commission) which was functional prior to 1991 Economic Reforms.

Vision

To promote and sustain an enabling competition culture through engagement and enforcement that would inspire businesses to be fair, competitive and innovative; enhance consumer welfare; and support economic growth.

Mission

Competition Commission of India aims to establish a robust competitive environment by

- proactive engagement with all stakeholders, including consumers, industry, government and international jurisdictions.
- being a knowledge intensive organisation with high competence level.
- professionalism, transparency, resolve and wisdom in enforcement.

Objectives of the Commission

- Prevent practices having adverse effect on competition
- Promote and sustain competition in markets
- Protect the interests of consumers
- Ensure freedom of trade

Split between Regulation and Competition

Business regulation is perhaps as old as the businesses themselves. While modern, liberalised economies have increasingly relied upon markets for allocation of resources, markets can also fail and lead to undesirable upshots. These extreme possibilities with the market has ensured that governments oscillate between the limbs of regulation and competition in order to ensure that when market fails, it does not crash land but is provided with a suitable parachute. Regulation, implemented through sector-specific regulators and competition regulation, through the competition authority, differ in their approach to regulating business in the market. Competition law seeks to promote efficient allocation and utilisation of resources, which are usually scarce in developing countries. A good competition law lowers the entry barriers in the market and makes the environment conducive to promoting entrepreneurship.

Regulations, on the other hand, are public constraints on market behaviour or structure. They usually refer to a diverse set of instruments by which governments set requirements on businesses and citizens. Regulations can be categorised as under: (i) Economic Regulations – Those which intervene in market decisions such as pricing, competition and entry/exit. (ii) Technical Regulations: Those which regulates the technical aspects which are distinct and unique to the sector (iii) Social regulations – Those which protect public interest such as health, safety, environment. (iv) Administrative regulations – administrative formalities through which government collects information and intervenes in individual economic decisions. The objective of a sectoral regulator is to provide good quality service at affordable rates, but the promotion of competition and prevention of anticompetitive behaviour may not be high on its agenda or the laws governing the regulator may be silent on this aspect. It is not uncommon for sectoral regulators to be more closely aligned with the interest of the firms being regulated, which is also known as 'regulatory capture'. Besides, a sectoral regulator may not have an overall view of the economy as a whole and may tend to apply yardsticks which are different from the ones used by the other sectoral regulators. In other words, there is a possibility of the lack of consistency across sectors. The following table summarizes the difference in their approach.

Sector-specific Regulator Competition Authority tells businesses 'what to do' and 'how to price products', also tells businesses 'what not to do', focuses upon specific sectors of the economy, focuses upon the entire economy and functioning of the market. Ex ante addresses behavioural issues before problem arises, Ex post addresses behavioural issues after problem arises. It focuses upon orderly development of a sector that would presumably trickle down in a sector ensuring consumer welfare. It also focuses upon consumer welfare and unfair transfer of wealth from consumers to firms with market power. Sectoral regulators are usually more appropriate for access and price issues such as changing the structure of the market, reducing barriers to entry and opening up the market to effective competition. Competition legislation is usually more appropriate for affecting conduct and maintaining competition Therefore, it is evident that the role of sector-specific regulators is overlapping but quite distinct. Unlike the sector-specific regulators, competition authority takes a holistic view of the economy and addresses behavioural issues after the problem arises. The competition authority also addresses the unfair transfer of wealth that may take place between the consumers and firms wielding market power.

What is bid rigging?

The explanation to sub-section (3) of Section 3, of the Act defines

'bid rigging' as 'any agreement, between enterprises or persons referred to in sub-section (3) engaged in identical or similar production or trading of goods or provision of services, which has the effect of eliminating or reducing competition for bids or adversely affecting or manipulating the process for bidding'.

Bid rigging takes place when bidders collude and keep the bid amount at a pre-determined level. Such pre-determination is by way of intentional manipulation by the members of the bidding group. Bidders could be actual or potential ones, but they collude and act in concert

What is a cartel?

Cartel is defined in section 2, clause (c) of the Act:

'Cartel' includes an association of producers, sellers, distributors, traders or service providers who, by agreement amongst themselves, limit, control or attempt to control the production, distribution, sale or price of, or, trade in goods or provision of services;'

Cartels are agreements between enterprises (including a person, a government department and association of persons / enterprises) not to compete on price, product (including goods and services) or customers. The Act gives a detailed definition of an enterprise in Section 2 (h). The objective of a cartel is to raise price above competitive levels, resulting in injury to consumers and to the economy. For the consumers, cartelisation results in higher prices, poor quality and less choice for goods or/and services.

What constitutes competition law and policy?

Competition law and policy is defined as those Government measures that affect the behaviour of enterprises and structure of the industry with a view to promote efficiency and maximise welfare.

There are two elements of such government measures:

Competition policy: Set of policies, such as liberalised trade policy, relaxed FDI policy, de-regulation, etc., that enhances competition in the markets.

Competition law: To prevent anti-competitive practices with minimal intervention.

Organisational Chart

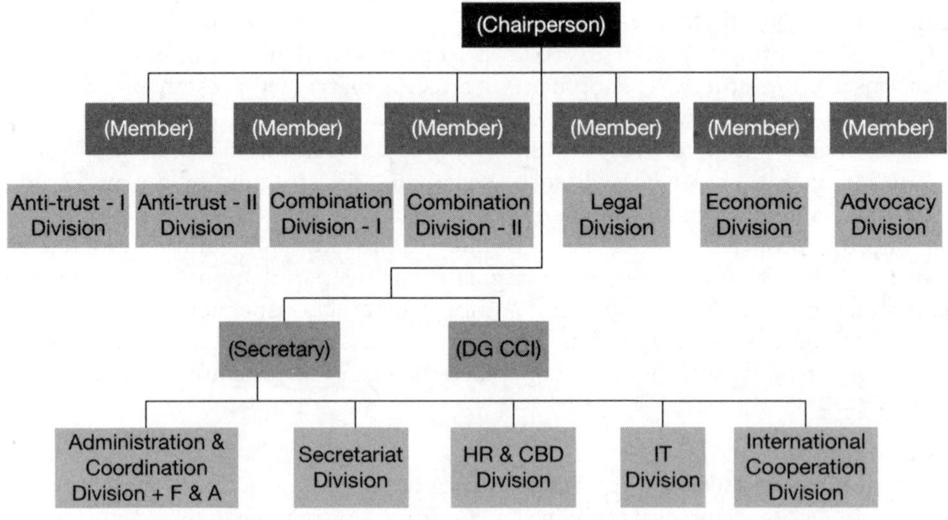

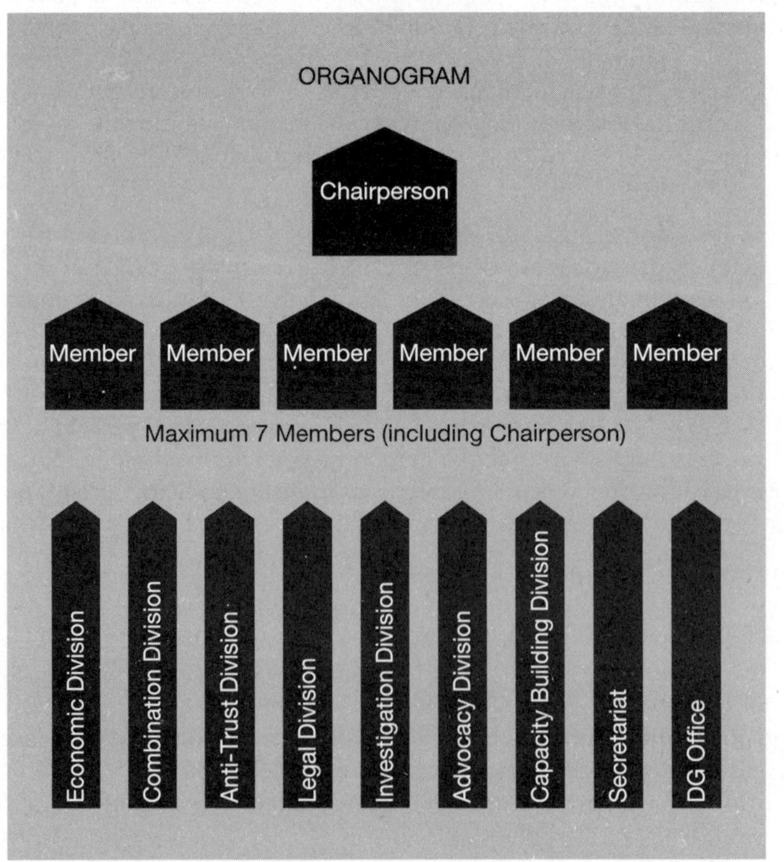

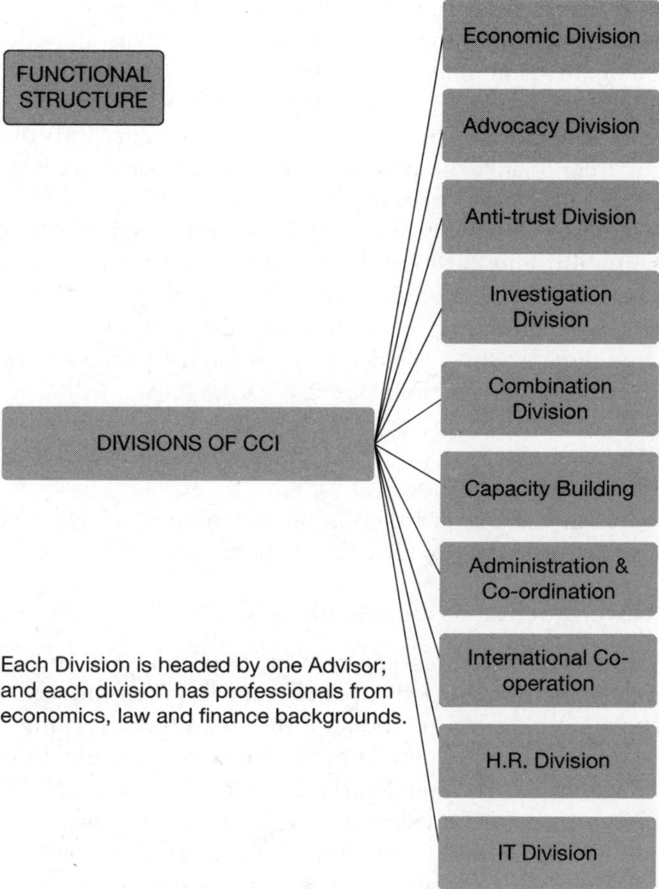

Functions of the Commissions:

- Enforcement
- Advocacy

Duties & Powers of CCI

- Sustain competition in markets, protect freedom of trade and interests of consumers in markets.
- Sustain competition in markets, CCI has power to make inquiries in case of any certain agreement, abuse of dominant position or any combination by any person or body corporate on its own or on receipt of complaint by consumer or by reference of government or any authority.
- Inquire into any of acts outside India that causes adverse impacts on competition within India.
- The Chairperson shall constitute benches to exercise powers of CCI and a bench shall consist of at least 2 members include at least 1 judicial member (qualified to be a judge of High Court). The Bench where Chairperson presides is known as Principal bench and others are known as additional benches.

- The CCI has power to make inquiry (either suo motu or on request of any person, consumer or trade association) and pass order for any certain agreement, abuse of dominant position or any combination that cause adverse effect on competition within India.
- The CCI can impose penalties on enterprises or on persons which shall not be > 10% of turnover of enterprise or person in case of any offence as provided under this act. Also CCI can order to any enterprise or person to pay compensation to person or enterprise who suffered from acts of that person or enterprise.
- The CCI can advise Central government for division of a dominant enterprise to ensure that it does not abuse its position. Consequently, government can take action either same as advised by CCI or in other form as the case may be.
- The CCI has power equivalent to a civil court while discharging its functions in matters such as summoning, producing evidences etc. Also has power to regulate its own procedure such as place of sittings, timings, etc.
- Any person or enterprise can appeal to Supreme Court against order of CCI within 60 days from the date of order. But no appeal shall be allowed if order passed by CCI involves consent of both parties.
- No Civil court can exercise jurisdiction on any matter under this act or any matter on which CCI is empowered to exercise jurisdiction.

Power of Central Government to issue directions

1. Without prejudice to the foregoing provisions of this Act, the Commission shall, in exercise of its powers or the performance of its functions under this Act, be bound by such directions on questions of policy, other than those relating to technical and administrative matters, as the Central Government may give in writing to it from time to time: Provided that the Commission shall, as far as practicable, be given an opportunity to express its views before any direction is given under this sub- section.
2. The decision of the Central Government whether a question is one of policy or not shall be final. Power of Central Government to supersede Commission 56. (1) If at any time the Central Government is of the opinion—
   a. that on account of circumstances beyond the control of the Commission, it is unable to discharge the functions or perform the duties imposed on it by or under the provisions of this Act; or
   b. that the Commission has persistently made default in complying with any direction given by the Central Government under this Act or in the discharge of the functions or performance of the duties imposed on it by or under the provisions of this Act and as a result of such default the financial position of the Commission or the administration of the Commission has suffered; or
   c. that circumstances exist which render it necessary in the public interest so to do,

The Central Government may, by notification and for reasons to be specified therein, supersede the Commission for such period not exceeding six months, as may be specified in the notification:

Provided that before issuing such notification, the Central Government shall give a reasonable opportunity to the Commission to make representations against the proposed supersession and shall consider representations, if any, of the Commission.

Amendment 2007 (Key Features)

- A Competition Appellate Tribunal (CAT) is established to hear and dispose of appeals against certain decisions made by the CCI. Some of the decisions that can be challenged include:
  1. The CCI's decision that an agreement is not causing adverse effect on competition or an enterprise is not abusing its dominant position.
  2. The CCI's order to discontinue the abuse of dominant position, modify agreements or divide an enterprise.
  3. The CCI's decision on whether a combination is having an adverse effect on competition, and if so, the steps to be taken to rectify the matter.
     - The CAT would consist of a Chairperson and a maximum of two members, appointed by the Central Goverment from the panel of names proposed by the Selection Committee. The Chairperson would have to be a Judge of the SC or the Chief Justice of the HC.
     - Any person can appeal the decision of the CAT in the SC within 60 days from the date on which the order of the CAT is communicated to the person.
     - The bill also repeals the MRTP Act, 1969 but MRTP Commission may continue work for next 2 years on subjects it was working on before this act.

Issues with the Bill

- Both the CCI and certain sectoral regulators are mandated to deal with anti-competitive practices. Such overlap could lead to turf issues between these bodies.
- Although one of the main functions of the CCI is to promote competition, it does not have the power to give its opinion on competition-related issues to the Central and State Governments on its own accord.
- The CCI can grant reduced penalty to any member of a cartel who is willing to disclose vital information. However, the Bill does not lay down the extent of the reduction in penalty or what kind of information would be considered as vital.
- Enterprises can impose reasonable conditions to protect their intellectual property rights. However, the term 'reasonable conditions' has not been defined.
- The employees of MRTPC are to be absorbed in the CCI or the CAT after two years. This differs from the Principal Act, which placed the onus of absorbing these employees on the central government.

Recent Steps Taken by CCI

1. **The Competition Commission of India (CCI) has imposed penalties on 10 cement companies**
   The Competition Commission of India (CCI) has imposed penalties on 10 cement companies and their umbrella association – Cement Manufacturers Association (CMA) for cartelisation. The CCI has levied penalties on 10 cement companies namely ACC, ACL, Binani, Century, India Cements, JK Cements, Lafarge, Ramco, UltraTech and Jaiprakash Associates. The final order has been passed by CCI pursuant to the directions issued by Competition Appellate Tribunal remanding the matter back while setting aside the original order of CCI.

While holding the cement companies and CMA in contravention of the Act, it was noted by CCI that the cement companies used the platform provided by CMA and shared details relating to prices, capacity utilisation, production and dispatch and thereby restricted production and supplies in the market, contravening the provisions of Section 3(1) read with Section 3(3)(b) of the Act. Further, CCI also found the cement companies to be acting in concert in fixing prices of cement in contravention of the provisions of Section 3(1) read with Section 3(3)(a) of the Act.

While highlighting the role played by trade associations in promoting the interests of their members and the industry they serve, CCI noted in its order that cement companies were interacting using the platform made available by the trade association (CMA). Such interactions have been found to have transgressed the limits in sharing of information and extended to discussions on cost, prices, production and capacities, thereby, facilitating the enterprises to determine prices and production in a concerted and collusive manner, than in a competitive manner. CCI cautioned that all those who participate in association activities, through meetings or otherwise, whether as a member or an executive or manager or employee, have to be sensitive to the discussions not transgressing advertently or otherwise into anti-trust behaviour or practices

2. **CCI imposes penalty on bidders for cartelisation in tenders of Indian Railways**
The Competition Commission of India 'CCI' has imposed penalties on three firms for bid rigging of tenders floated by Indian Railways for procurement of Brushless DC fans in the year 2013. A final order has been passed by CCI in a case taken up suo motu under Section 19 of the Competition Act, 2002 ('the Act') based on the information received from Central Bureau of Investigation, New Delhi.

CCI has held that the firms had shared the market by way of allocation of tenders of Indian Railways for Brushless DC fans amongst themselves under an agreement/arrangement and indulged in bid rigging/collusive bidding in contravention of the provisions of Section 3(3)(c) and3(3)(d) read with Section 3(1) of the Act. The anti-competitive conduct of the firms has been established based on exchange of rates to be quoted in upcoming tenders amongst the errant firms, numerous calls amongst the key persons of these firms before and during the period of the tenders and admission by one of the firms which confirmed and revealed the existence and modus operandi of the cartel.

Accordingly, a penalty of ₹62.37 lakhs, ₹20.01 lakhs and ₹2.09 crores was imposed on the firms M/s Pyramid Electronics, M/s R. Kanwar Electricals and M/s Western Electric and Trading Company, respectively in terms of provision to Section 27 (b) of the Act. While imposing penalty, Commission took into consideration all the relevant factors including the duration of the cartel, volume of the tender affected by the cartel and value thereof and decided to impose penalty on M/sPyramid Electronics and M/s Western Electric and Trading Company calculated at 1.0 time of their profit respectively in the year 2012–2013 and on M/s R. Kanwar Electricals at the rate of 3% of its turnover for the year 2012–2013.

Additionally, considering the totality of facts and circumstances of the case, penalty was also imposed on persons-in charge of the three firms, that is, Shri Sandeep Goyal of M/s Pyramid Electronics, Shri Ashish Jain of M/s R. Kanwar Electricals and Shri Ramesh Parchani of M/s Western Electric and Trading Company at the rate of 10% of the average of their income for the last three preceding financial years

CCI had received an application under Section 46 of the Act read with Regulation 5 of the Competition Commission of India (Lesser Penalty) Regulations, 2009 from

M/s Pyramid Electronics. This application was received when the investigation in the matter was in progress and the report from the DG was pending. Considering the cooperation extended by M/s Pyramid Electronics in conjunction with the value addition provided by it in establishing the existence of cartel and the stage at which it had approached CCI, it was granted 75% reduction in the penalty than would otherwise have been imposed, had it not cooperated with the Commission. Accordingly, the penalty imposed on M/s Pyramid Electronics was reduced to ₹15.59 lakhs and penalty imposed on Shri Sandeep Goyal was reduced to ₹11,648 only.

CCI invites comments from public in respect of proposed merger between Sun Pharma and Ranbaxy

On 6th May, 2014, the Competition Commission of India received a notice from Sun Pharmaceuticals Industries Limited (Sun Pharma) and Ranbaxy Laboratories Limited (Ranbaxy) in relation to the merger of Ranbaxy into Sun Pharma.

In terms of Section 29(2) of the Competition Act, 2002 (Act), the Commission formed a prima facie opinion that the combination is likely to have an appreciable adverse effect on competition and accordingly directed Sun Pharma and Ranbaxy (Parties) to publish details of the combination within 10 working days for bringing the combination to the knowledge or information of the public and persons affected or likely to be affected by such combination. The parties are required to publish the details of the combination in All India editions of four leading daily newspapers, including at least two business newspapers, and also host the same on their respective websites.

As per the provisions of Section 29(3) of the Act, the Commission invites comments/ objections/ suggestions in writing, from any person(s) adversely affected or likely to be affected by the combination, to be addressed to the Secretary, Competition Commission of India.

Predatory Pricing

The 'predatory price' under the Act means 'the sale of goods or provision of services, at a price which is below the cost, as may be determined by regulations, of production of goods or provision of services, with a view to reduce competition or eliminate the competitors'.

Predation is exclusionary behaviour and can be indulged in only by enterprises(s) having dominant position in the concerned relevant market.

The major elements involved in the determination of predatory behaviour are:

- Establishment of dominant position of the enterprise in the relevant market
- Pricing below cost for the relevant product in the relevant market by the dominant enterprise ['Cost', for this purpose, has been defined in the Competition Commission of India (Determination of Cost of Production) Regulations, 2009 as notified by the Commission.]
- Intention to reduce competition or eliminate competitors This is traditionally known as the predatory intent test

Abuse of Dominance

Dominance is not considered bad per se but its abuse is. Abuse is stated to occur when an enterprise or a group of enterprises uses its dominant position in the relevant market in an exclusionary or/ and an exploitative manner.

The Act gives an exhaustive list of practices that shall constitute abuse of dominant position and, therefore, are prohibited. Such practices shall constitute abuse only when adopted by an enterprise enjoying dominant position in the relevant market in India.

Abuse of dominance is judged in terms of the specified types of acts committed by a dominant enterprise. Such acts are prohibited under the law. Any abuse of the type specified in the Act 5 by a dominant firm shall stand prohibited.

Section 4 (2) of the Act specifies the following practices by a dominant enterprises or group of enterprises as abuses:

(i) Directly or indirectly imposing unfair or discriminatory condition in purchase or sale of goods or service
(ii) Directly or indirectly imposing unfair or discriminatory price in the purchase or sale (including predatory price) of goods or service
(iii) Limiting or restricting production of goods or provision of services or market
(iv) Limiting or restricting technical or scientific development relating to goods or services to the prejudice of consumers
(v) Denying market access in any manner
(vi) Making conclusion of contracts subject to acceptance by other parties of supplementary obligations which, by their nature or according to commercial usage, have no connection with the subject of such contracts.
(vii) Using its dominant position in one relevant market to enter into, or protect, other relevant market

Central Information Commission and State Information Commission

The central information commission was set up under Right to Information Act, 2005. It entertains complaints and appeals pertaining to offices, financial institutions, public sector undertaking, etc., under the central government and union territories.

It includes one chief commissioner and not more than 10 information commissioners to be appointed by the president of India. The appointment committee includes Prime minister (Chair), leader of the opposition in the Lok Sabha and Union cabinet minister to be nominated by Prime Minister. The members to be appointed as Information Commissioners should not be a Member of the Parliament and should not hold any office of profit.

State Information Commission:

- It is constituted by state government through a gazette notification.
- It will have state chief commissioners and not more than 10 state information commissions to be appointed by the governors.
- Appointment committee will be headed by chief minister, Leader of Opposition in the legislative assembly and one cabinet minister nominated by the Chief Minister.

Power and function of Information Commission

1. The Central Information Commission/State Information Commission has a duty to receive complaints from any person who has not been allowed to submit an information request because a Public Information Officer has not been appointed, refused to give information, received no response to this/his information at specified time, information given was incomplete false, thinks fees charged was unreasonable, and other matter relating to obtaining information under this law.
2. Powers to order inquiry if there are reasonable grounds.
3. CIC/SIC will have powers of civil courts such as,
   - Summoning and enforcing attendance of persons, compelling them to give oral written evidence on oath and to produce documents or things.

- Requiring the discovery and inspection of documents.
- Receiving evidence on affidavit.
- Requisitioning public records or copies from any court or office.
- Issuing summons for examination of witnesses or documents.
- Any matter which can be prescribed.

4. All records covered by this law (including those covered by exemptions) must be given to CIC/SIC during inquiry for examination.
5. The commission has power to secure compliance of its decision from the public authority and these powers include
   - Providing access to information in a particular form.
   - Directing the public authority to appoint a public information officer.
   - Publishing information or categories of information.
   - Making necessary changes to the practices relating to management, maintenance and destruction of records.
   - Enhancing training provision for officials on the right information.
   - Seeking an annual report from the public authority on compliance with this act.
   - Requiring the public authority to compensate for any loss or other determent suffered by the applicant.
   - Imposing penalties under this act.
   - Rejecting the application.
6. The Central Information Commission submits an annual report to the Central Government on the implementation of the provision of this set and state information commission to State Government and it places this report before each house of the Parliament and SIC to state legislative assembly.

8.4.16 Central Pollution Control Board (CPCB)

The **Central Pollution Control Board (CPCB)**, statutory organisation, was constituted in September, 1974 under the Water (Prevention and Control of Pollution) Act, 1974. Further, CPCB was entrusted with the powers and functions under the Air (Prevention and Control of Pollution) Act, 1981.

It serves as a field formation and also provides technical services to the Ministry of Environment and Forests of the provisions of the Environment (Protection) Act, 1986. It coordinates the activities of the State Pollution Control Boards by providing technical assistance and guidance, and also resolves disputes among them. It is the apex organisation in country in the field of pollution control, as a technical wing of MoEF. The board is led by its chairman, who is nominated by the Central Government. CPCB along with its state counterparts, the State Pollution Control Boards (SPCBs), are responsible for the implementation of legislation relating to prevention and control of environmental pollution.

Basic Functions/Objectives

Principal Functions of the CPCB, as spelt out in the Water (Prevention and Control of Pollution) Act, 1974, and the Air (Prevention and Control of Pollution) Act, 1981,

(i) Promote cleanliness of streams and wells in different areas of the states by prevention, control and abatement of water pollution.
(ii) Improve the quality of air and to prevent, control or abate air pollution in the country.

Functions of the Central Board at the National Level

1. Advise the Central Government on any matter concerning prevention and control of water and air pollution and improvement of the quality of air.
2. Plan and execute a nation-wide program for the prevention, control or abatement of water and air pollution.
3. Coordinate the activities of the State Board and resolve disputes among them.
4. Provide technical assistance and guidance to the state boards, carry out and sponsor investigation and research relating to problems of water and air pollution, and for their prevention, control or abatement.
5. Plan and organise training of persons engaged in programme on the prevention, control or abatement of water and air pollution.
6. Organise through mass media, a comprehensive mass awareness programme on the prevention, control or abatement of water and air pollution.
7. Collect, compile and publish technical and statistical data relating to water and air pollution and the measures devised for their effective prevention, control or abatement.
8. Prepare manuals, codes and guidelines relating to treatment and disposal of sewage and trade effluents as well as for stack gas cleaning devices, stacks and ducts;
9. Disseminate information in respect of matters relating to water and air pollution and their prevention and control.
10. Lay down, modify or annul, in consultation with the state governments concerned, the standards for stream or well, and lay down standards for the quality of air.
11. Perform such other functions as may be prescribed by the Government of India.

Functions of the Central Board as State Boards for the Union Territories

1. Advise the Governments of Union Territories with respect to the suitability of any premises or location for carrying on any industry which is likely to pollute a stream or well or cause air pollution.
2. Lay down standards for the treatment of sewage and trade effluents and for emissions from automobiles, industrial plants, and any other polluting source.
3. Evolve efficient methods for disposal of sewage and trade effluents on land.
4. Develop reliable and economically viable methods of treatment of sewage, trade effluent and air pollution control equipment.
5. Identify any area or areas within Union Territories as air pollution control area or areas to be notified under the Air (Prevention and Control of Pollution) Act, 1981.
6. Assess the quality of ambient water and air, and inspect wastewater treatment installations, air pollution control equipment, industrial plants or manufacturing process to evaluate their performance and to take steps for the prevention, control and abatement of air and water pollution.

As per the policy decision of the Government of India, the CPCB has delegated its powers and functions under the Water (Prevention and Control of Pollution) Act, 1974, the Water (Prevention and Control of Pollution) Cess Act, 1977 and the Air (Prevention and Control of Pollution) Act, 1981 with respect to Union Territories to respective local administrations. CPCB along with its counterparts State Pollution Control Boards (SPCBs) are responsible for implementation of legislations relating to prevention and control of environmental pollution.

Organisation

CPCB is led by its *Chairman* following by the *Member Secretary*. The CPCB performs its various functions through the following nine major project\ budget heads:

1. Pollution assessment (survey and monitoring)
2. R&D and laboratory management
3. Development of standards and guidelines for industry-specific emissions and effluents standards
4. Training
5. Information database management and library
6. Pollution control technology
7. Pollution control enforcement
8. Mass awareness and publications
9. Hazard waste management

To execute these schemes, CPCB has drawn detailed organisational structure (Figure 1) comprising of various divisions. The schemes are executed through in-house technical manpower or by outsourcing some of the components to the Government and Private Consultants. The State Pollution Control Boards/Committees are also entrusted for the execution of certain components to get State specific feedback.

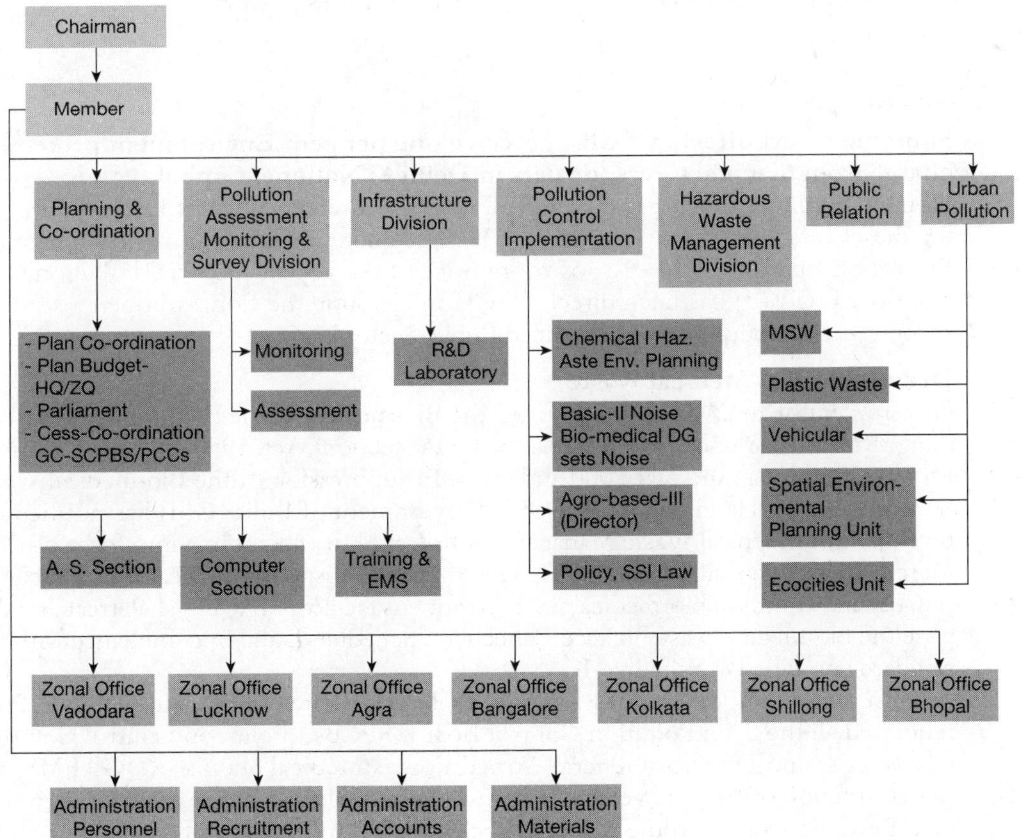

Departments

- Pollution Control Planning Division
- Pollution, Assessment, Monitoring & Survey
- Pollution Control Implementation Division –I
- Pollution Control Implementation Division –II
- Pollution Control Implementation Division –III
- Urban Pollution Control Division
- Hazardous Waste Management Division
- Environment Survillance Squad Division
- Information Technology
- Material
- Environmental Training Unit
- Legal Cell
- PR Section
- Assistant Secretary Section
- Building Section
- Library
- Hindi Section
- Administration (recruitment)
- Pollution Control Implementation (Small Scale Industries)
- Accounts

Recent updates:

1. **Supreme Court directs CPCB to receive one per cent Environment protection charge from manufacturers/dealers in Delhi & National Capital region**
   Hon'ble Supreme Court has directed all manufacturers/dealers of Delhi-NCR, selling diesel cars with engine capacity of 2000 cc and above, to pay 1% Environment Protection Charge (1% of ex-showroom price of the vehicle). Central Pollution Control Board (CPCB) has been directed by Hon'ble Supreme Court to open a separate account for this purpose in a Scheduled Public Sector bank

2. **Disposal of Bio-Medical Waste**
   Government of India (GoI) has notified the Bio-medical Waste (Management & Handling) Rules, 1998 under the Environment (Protection) Act, 1986 and these rules are further amended in the year 2000 and 2003. In suppression of the Bio-medical Waste (Management & Handling) Rules, 1998, Government of India (GoI) has notified the revamped Bio-medical Waste Management Rules, 2016 which came into force on 28th March, 2016. According to Rule 7 (i) Treatment and disposal: the health care facilities (HCFs) and common bio-medical waste treatment facility (CBWTF) shall treat and dispose the bio-medical waste in accordance with Schedule-I, and in compliance with the standards provided in Schedule-II.

   Central Pollution Control Board (CPCB), vide letter dated 25th October, 2016 requested all the State Pollution Control Board (SPCBs,) Pollution Control Committees (PCCs) and Director General Armed Forces Medical Services (DGAFMS) for (i) Constitution of 'State Level Advisory Committee (SLAC)' by the State Government or UT Administration in the respective State or UT and the activities initiated by the

SLAC; and (ii) Constitution of the 'District Level Monitoring Committee (DLMC)' by the State Government or UT Administration in the respective State/UT and the activities initiated by the State Level Advisory Committee (SLAC) and also to take necessary steps for ensuring effective implementation of the Bio-medical Waste Management Rules, 2016 notified under the Environment (P) Act, 1986.

CPCB has also prepared the following guidelines relating to management of Bio-Medical Waste:

1. Common Bio-Medical Waste Treatment Facilities (CBWTFs).
2. Design & Construction of Bio-Medical Waste incinerators.
3. Disposal of Bio-Medical Waste generated during Universal Immunisation Programme.
4. Guidelines for Environmentally Sound Management of Mercury Waste generated from the Health Care Facilities.

The above guidelines are circulated to all State Pollution Control Board/Pollution Control Committees for its implementation and the same is also uploaded at CPCB website, http://www.cpcb.nic.in/guidelines.php, for access of various stakeholders to help in complying the standards stipulated in the BMW Rules.

CPCB regularly carries out inspection of AFHCEs falling under the jurisdiction of Director General Arms Forces Medical Services as required by the rules and recommendations communicated to Director General Armed Forces Medical Services (DGAMFS) periodically for carrying out necessary improvement. During the last eight years, from February 2008 to February 2016, CPCB inspected 52 number of AFHCEs and recommendations communicated to the DGAFMS for ensuring necessary improvements.

8.4.17 Directorate General of Civil Aviation (DGCA)

The Directorate General of Civil Aviation (DGCA) is the regulatory body in the field of Civil Aviation, primarily dealing with safety issues.

It is responsible for regulation of air transport services to/from/within India and for enforcement of civil air regulations, air safety, and airworthiness standards. The DGCA also coordinates all regulatory functions with the International Civil Aviation Organisation (ICAO).

Vision

Endeavour to promote safe and efficient air transportation through regulation and proactive safety oversight system

Functions

The main function of the Directorate General of Civil Aviation is to regulate all civil aviation matter. Some of the salient functions are as follows:

- Regulation of air transport services to/from/within India in accordance with the provisions of the Aircraft Rules, 1937, including bilateral and multilateral with foreign countries and the policy pronouncements of the government.
- Registration of civil aircraft.
- Laying down airworthiness requirement for civil aircraft registered in India and grant of Certificate of Airworthiness to such aircraft.
- Licensing of pilots, aircraft maintenance engineers and monitoring of flight crew standards.

- Licensing of aerodromes and air carriers.
- Rendering advice to the Government on matters pertaining to civil aviation.
- Processing amendments to Aircraft Act, 1934 and the Aircraft Rules, 1937, and other acts relating to aviation, with a view to implementing in India the provisions of the Chicago Convention and Annexes thereto and other International Convention relating to aviation.
- Coordination of the work relating to International Civil Aviation Organisation and sending replies to state letters after consulting the concerned agencies.
- Investigation of minor air accidents and incidents and rendering technical assistance to the Courts/Committees of Inquiry.
- Supervision of training activities of flying/gliding clubs.
- Development of light aircraft, gliders and winches.
- Type certification of aircraft.

RECENT NEWS

UDAN scheme:

- The Ministry of Civil Aviation had launched the Regional Connectivity Scheme (RCS) (UDAN) on 21st October, 2016. RCS was a key component of the National Civil Aviation Policy which was released by the Ministry on 15th June, 2016. The scheme, which would be in operation for a period of 10 years, envisages providing connectivity to un-served and under-served regions of the country through revival of existing air-strips and airports. This would be achieved through a financial stimulus in the form of Central and State government concessions, as well as Viability Gap Funding to the interested airlines to kick-off operations from such airports, so that the passenger fares are kept affordable. The fare for a one-hour journey of approximately 500 km on a fixed wing aircraft or for a 30 minute journey on a helicopter would be capped at ₹2500 under the scheme, with proportionate pricing for routes of different lengths/duration. To ensure that operations on ground start with minimum time-gap after the bidding is completed, parallel action has also been initiated by the Ministry of Civil Aviation with AAI, State Governments, DGCA and Bureau of Civil Aviation Security.
- DCGA has asked domestic airlines to formulate a policy on electronic cigarettes and display warnings inside lavatories and passenger briefing cards as part of safety measures.
- In wake of an increasing number of pilots failing to report for duty or showing up late, thereby, causing last-minute flight disruptions, so India's aviation regulator has now decided to act tough against such pilots and also stated that actions of such pilots have a bearing on flight safety and public interest.
- The Directorate General of Civil Aviation has taken serious note of the incident and suspended the flying licenses of the two pilots. Putting the lives of passengers in danger, an IndiGo aircraft flew close to the road running parallel to the Jaipur Airport runway.
- The Directorate General of Civil Aviation (DGCA) has come out with the new guidelines following a review of the earlier block hours for different routes and in consultations with all stake holders including airlines and airport operators because of the domestic air passenger traffic growing by over 20% and airlines facing slot crunch.
- Aviation regulator DGCA has prohibited flight crew from taking selfies in aircraft besides asking the airlines to ensure that passengers do not 'indulge into photography' while boarding or deboarding a plane. Though earlier rules also put some restrictions on

in-flight photography, the fresh guidelines come in the wake of certain cases coming to the light about possible security risks from clicking cockpit selfies.

8.4.18 Food Safety and Standards Authority of India (FSSAI)

The Food Safety and Standards Authority of India (FSSAI) has been established under Food Safety and Standards, 2006 which consolidates various acts & orders that have hitherto handled food-related issues in various ministries and departments. FSSAI has been created for laying down science-based standards for articles of food and to regulate their manufacture, storage, distribution, sale and import to ensure availability of safe and wholesome food for human consumption.

Highlights of the Food Safety and Standard Act, 2006

Various central acts like

- Prevention of Food Adulteration Act,1954,
- Fruit Products Order , 1955,
- Meat Food Products Order,1973,
- Vegetable Oil Products (Control) Order, 1947,
- Edible Oils Packaging (Regulation)Order 1988,
- Solvent Extracted Oil, De-Oiled Meal and Edible Flour (Control) Order, 1967,
- Milk and Milk Products Order, 1992

will be repealed after commencement of FSS Act, 2006.

The Act also aims to establish a single reference point for all matters relating to food safety and standards, by moving from multi-level, multi-departmental control to a single line of command. To this effect, the Act establishes an independent statutory Authority – the Food Safety and Standards Authority of India with head office at Delhi. Food Safety and Standards Authority of India (FSSAI) and the State Food Safety Authorities shall enforce various provisions of the Act.

Establishment of the Authority

Ministry of Health & Family Welfare, Government of India is the Administrative Ministry for the implementation of FSSAI. The Chairperson and Chief Executive Officer of Food Safety and Standards Authority of India (FSSAI) are appointed by Government of India. The Chairperson is in the rank of Secretary to Government of India.

Functions

1. Frame regulations to lay down the standards and guidelines in relation to articles of food and specifying appropriate system of enforcing various standards thus notified.
2. Lay down mechanisms and guidelines for accreditation of certification bodies engaged in certification of food safety management system for food businesses.
3. Lay down procedure and guidelines for accreditation of laboratories and notification of the accredited laboratories.
4. Provide scientific advice and technical support to Central Government and State Governments in the matters of framing the policy and rules in areas which have a direct or indirect bearing of food safety and nutrition.

5. Collect and collate data regarding food consumption, incidence and prevalence of biological risk, contaminants in food, residues of various, contaminants in foods products, identification of emerging risks and introduction of rapid alert system.
6. Create an information network across the country so that the public, consumers, panchayats, etc., receive rapid, reliable and objective information about food safety and issues of concern.
7. Provide training programmes to people who are involved or intend to get involved in food businesses.
8. Contribute to the development of international technical standards for food, sanitary and phyto-sanitary standards.
9. Promote general awareness about food safety and food standards.

Initiatives taken by FSSAI

1. **Food Safety Voice**

   To secure National Food Safety, FSSAI wishes to bring each citizen on-board to share their concerns regarding food safety violations. This portal allows a consumer to share their concerns, know their rights, track Food Business Operators license/registration certificate authenticity and view related articles/videos on food safety.

   Consumer can post their concern through either of the following modes:

   - Web based
   - Mobile based

Know Your Rights

1. A purchaser of food article may, if he so desires, can have the article analysed by the Food Analyst as per the provisions of the Act.
2. The purchaser shall pay the prescribed fee to the Food Analyst carrying out the analysis which will be refunded if the food sample is sub-standard.
3. The food analyst shall send to the purchaser his report on the analysis of the article of food and if the finding of the report is to the effect that the article of food is adulterated/misbranded/contaminated or does not conform to the standards prescribed under the act or the regulations, the purchaser shall be entitled to get a refund of the fees paid by him.

2. **Labelling**

   It is mandatory that every package of food intended for sale should carry a label that bears all the information required under FSS (Packaging and Labelling) Regulation, 2011.

   Food package must carry a label with the following information:

   - Common name of the Product
   - Name and address of the product's manufacturer
   - Date of manufacture
   - Ingredient list with additives

- Nutrition facts
- Best before/Expires on date
- Net contents in terms of weight, measure or count
- Packing codes/Batch number
- Declaration regarding vegetarian or non-vegetarian
- Country of origin for imported food

SoFTeL (Strengthening of Food Testing Laboratories)
Six Initiatives of the Scheme:

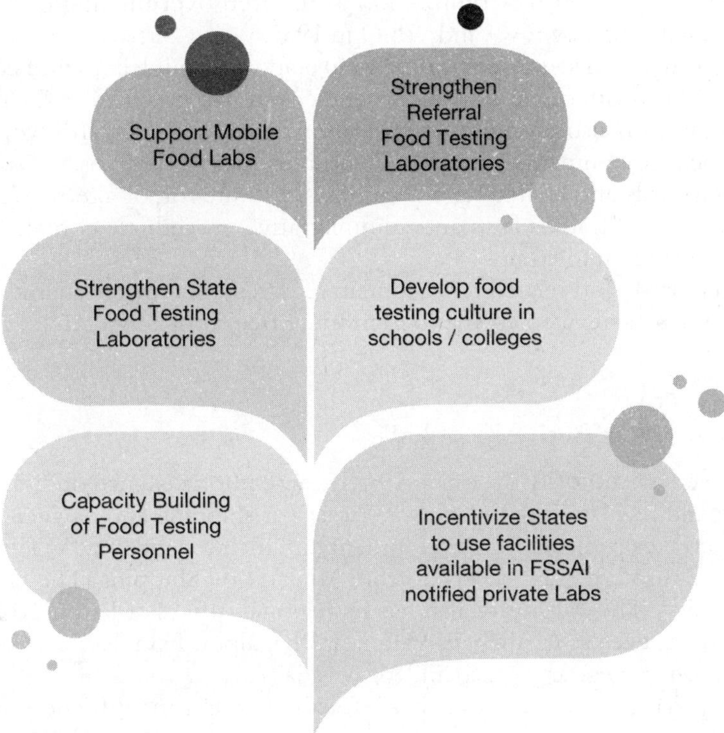

3. **National Milk Quality Survey**

   Objective

   A National Milk Quality Survey to assess the quality of milk with focus on unsafe/adulterated milk is being planned. The survey will be carried out in more than 120 cities across India which will be spread over all the states and Union Territories. Over 1700 samples will be picked up and tested for fat and SNF content and 13 common adulterants. Common sampling SOP has to be followed all over the country for picking up samples, sample transportation and delivery. Testing laboratories will follow common testing protocol provided by FSSAI for testing the samples.

- Over 1700 samples to be picked up.
- Survey to be carried out in all the States and Union territories across India.
- Active involvement of all stakeholders like State Food Safety Authorities, Dairy Co-operatives, Analytical Laboratories and Research Institutions.
- Tests to be carried out: FAT&SNF, Vegetable Oil, Detergent, Hydrogen Peroxide, Formalin, Sugar, Glucose, Urea, Starch, Boric Acid, Ammonium Sulphate, Nitrates, Cellulose Maltodextrin

19. Codex Alimentarius Commission

- The Codex Alimentarius Commission is an intergovernmental body of the United Nations, established by FAO and WHO in 1963.
- It develops harmonised international food standards, guidelines and codes of practice to protect the health of the consumers and ensure fair practices in the food trade.
- The Commission also promotes coordination of all food standards work undertaken by international governmental and non-governmental organisations.
- Codex standards and related texts are not a substitute for, or alternative to national legislation. Every country's laws and administrative procedures contain provisions with which it is essential to comply.
- Codex standards and related texts contain requirements for food aimed at ensuring for the consumer a safe, wholesome food product free from adulteration, correctly labelled and presented.

8.4.20 Inland Waterway Authority of India

The Inland Waterways Authority of India (IWAI) came into existence on 27th October, 1986 for development and regulation of inland waterways for shipping and navigation. The Authority primarily undertakes projects for development and maintenance of IWT infrastructure on national waterways through grant received from Ministry of Shipping. The head office of the Authority is at Noida. The Authority also has its regional offices at Patna, Kolkata, Guwahati and Kochi and sub-offices at Allahabad, Varanasi, Bhagalpur, Farakka, Hemnagar, Dibrugarh (Assam), Kollam, Bhubaneswar (Odisa) and Vijaywada (A.P.)

Inland water transport (IWT) offers cost effective, environment friendly and fuel-efficient mode of transport, especially for bulk goods, hazardous cargo and over-dimensional cargo.

Inland Waterways Authority of India is a statutory body duly constituted and established under Section 3 of Inland Waterways Authority of India Act, 1985, for the regulation and development of inland waterways for purposes of shipping and navigation and for matters connected therewith or incidental thereto.

India has about 14,500 km of navigable waterways which comprise of rivers, canals, backwaters, creeks, etc. About 55 million tonnes of cargo is being moved annually by Inland Water Transport (IWT), a fuel-efficient and environment-friendly mode of transport. Its operations are currently restricted to a few stretches in the Ganga-Bhagirathi-Hooghly rivers, the Brahmaputra, the Barak river, the rivers in Goa, the backwaters in Kerala, inland waters in Mumbai and the deltaic regions of the Godavari-Krishna rivers. Besides these organised operations by mechanised vessels, country boats of various capacities also operate in various rivers and canals and substantial quantum of cargo and passengers are transported in this unorganised sector as well.

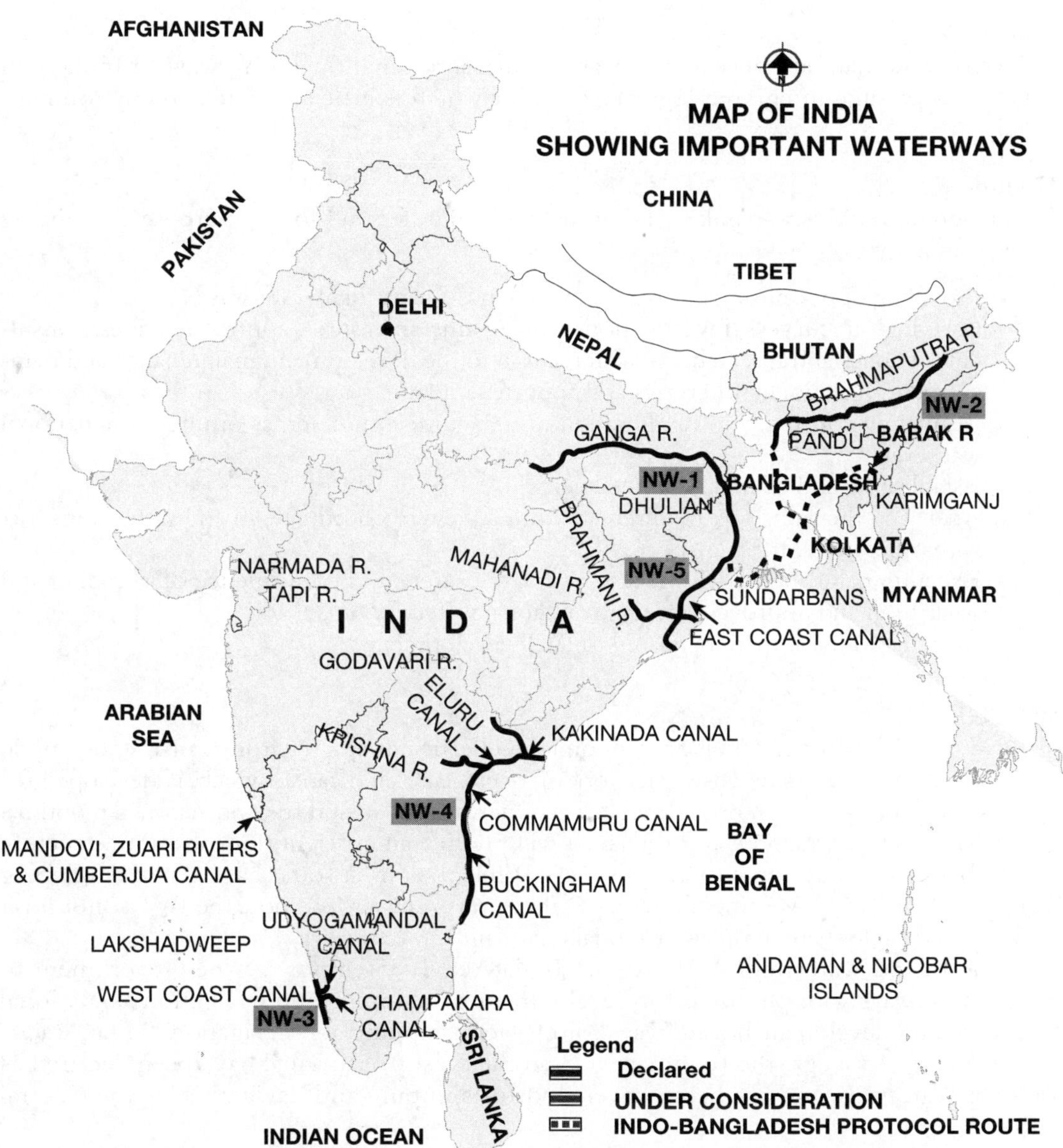

Mandate

As per section 14 of IWAI Act, 1975, IWAI is mandated with the development and regulation of waterways which are declared as national waterways. 111 waterways have so far been declared as National waterways (NW). Besides NWs, IWAI is developing and maintaining the Indian side of Sunderbans waterways under the Indo-Bangladesh Protocol for transit and trade under which the inland vessels of one country can transit through specified routes of the other country.

Vision

To develop and maintain necessary infrastructure across national waterways in India with an aim of providing integrated logistics corridor which is efficient, safe and environment friendly.

Mission

The mission of IWAI is to regulate and develop inland waterways for the purpose of shipping and navigation by:

- Providing or permitting infrastructure facilities for national waterways.
- Carrying out surveys, investigations, conservancy measures, control activities, consultancy studies and research works in relation to the development, maintenance and management of national waterways and appurtenant land.
- Regulating construction or alteration of structures on or across or under the national waterways.
- Establishing and maintaining pilotage.
- Analysing the transport requirement with a view to coordinate inland water transport with other modes of transport.
- Executing all other works necessary for the safety and convenience of shipping and navigation and improvement of the national waterways etc.
- Advising MoS on matters related to IWT development.

IWT Policy

Inland Water Transport (IWT) is an economic, fuel-efficient and environment-friendly mode of transport. India has an extensive network of rivers, lakes and canals which, if developed for shipping and navigation, can provide an efficient network of inland transportation. An optimal mix of road, rail and inland water transport will provide an efficient transport infrastructure with mobility, flexibility and cost effectiveness. While the thrust so far has been in developing road and rail sectors, Government recognises the need to actively promote the IWT sector for it to take a reasonable share in the inter-modal mix of inland transport.

The Inland Waterways Authority of India Act, 1985 empowers the Government to declare waterways with potential for development of shipping and navigation as National Waterways and develop such waterways for efficient shipping and navigation. So far, waterways namely, the Ganga, the Brahmaputra and the West Coast Canal have been declared as National Waterways and are being developed for shipping and navigation by the Central Government.

The revival plan of Inland Water Transport would include increasing the coverage of National Waterways and provision of necessary infrastructure for shipping and navigation and in augmenting the IWT fleet. While there would be a need for budgetary support for the development of the IWT sector, equally important would be a large-scale private sector participation both for creation of infrastructure and for fleet operations.

The IWT strategy aims at generating a more pro-active role by various agencies for the development of this sector. It has now been decided to enlarge the scope of the role of the Government as a provider, facilitator and regulator and, at the same time, offer various concessions to the private sector for their effective participation by way of investment for creation of enhanced IWT infrastructure and fleet operations.

Functions

National Waterways

- Survey
- Navigation, infrastructure and regulations
- Fairway development
- Pilotage
- Coordination of IWT with other modes

General

- Advise Central Government
- Carry out hydrographic surveys
- Assist state sovernments
- Develop consultancy services
- Research and development
- Classification of waterways
- Standards and safety

Act, Rules, Regulations and Notifications

- The National Waterways Act, 2016
- Notification of The National Waterways Act, 2016
- IWAI Act, Regulations, Amendments & Classifications
- IV Act 1917 & Central Act
- Rule & Regulation Under IV Act 1917
- The synopsis of the statute on Inland Vessels

Indo-Bangladesh Protocol

An Inland water transit and trade protocol exists between India and Bangladesh under which inland vessels of one country can transit through the specified routes of the other country. The existing protocol routes are (i) Kolkata-Pandu-Kolkata, (ii) Kolkata-Karimganj-Kolkata, (iii) Rajshahi-Dhulian-Rajshahi and (iv) Pandu-Karimganj-Pandu. For inter-country trade, four ports of call have been designated in each country namely: Haldia, Kolkata, Pandu and Karimganj in India and Narayanganj, Khulna, Mongla and Sirajganj in Bangladesh. Under the Protocol, 50:50 cargo sharing by Indian and Bangladeshi vessels is permitted both for transit and inter-country trade. IWAI is the Competent Authority on Indian side.

Recent Updates

Development of Inland Waterways

Under the National Waterways Act, 2016, 111 inland waterways have been declared as National Waterways (NWs) in addition to the five existing NWs, across 24 states for utilising them as an environment friendly and sustainable mode of transport.

Out of these 111 NWs, the following waterways are operational:

(i) NW-1: Ganga-Bhagirathi-Hooghly river system (Allahabad-Haldia)
(ii) NW-2: River Brahmaputra
(iii) NW-3: West Coast Canal (Kottapuram-Kollam) along with Udyogmandal and Champakara Canals

(iv) NW -68: Mandovi
(v) NW-97: Sundarbans waterways
(vi) NW -111: Zuari

The **Jal Marg Vikas** Project has been commissioned for capacity augmentation of NW–1 (river Ganga) from Haldia to Varanasi with an objective to facilitate movement of 1500–2000 tonne vessels. The project has been undertaken with the technical and financial support of the World Bank at an estimated cost of ₹4200 crore. The project is scheduled to be completed in six years. Under this project, various sub projects include fairway development and construction of multimodal terminals at Varanasi, Sahibganj and Haldia and a new navigation lock at Farakka. On NW-2 (river Brahmaputra) a Ro-Ro service has started and a ship repair facility is being constructed at Pandu (Guwahati).

Commencement of development of six more waterways is planned in this financial year. These waterways are NW-4 (Kakinada–Puducherry Canal alongwith Krishna & Godavari Rivers), NW- 5 (East Coast Canal with Brahmani–Mahanadi Delta), NW-16 (Barak), NW-37 (Gandak), NW-40 (Ghagra River) and NW-58 (Kosi).The development of NW-4 and 5 has already been initiated.

Integrated National Transportation Waterway Grid Study

1. An Integrated National Waterways Transportation Grid (INTG) Study was undertaken by IWAI through RITES with an aim to link the National Waterways [viz. River Ganga from Haldia to Allahabad (NW-1: 1620 km), River Brahmaputra from Dhubri to Sadiya (NW-2: 891 km), West Coast Canal from Kottapuram to Kollam with Udyogmandal and Champakara Canals (NW-3: 205 km), Kakinada–Puducherry stretch of canals with River Godavari and River Krishna (NW-4: 1078 km), East Coast Canal with River Brahmani and River Mahanadi's delta (NW-5: 588 km), River Barak between Lakhipur–Bhanga (proposed NW-6: 121 km)] to National/ State Highways, Railways (wherever feasible) and Sea Ports (wherever feasible) so that all these waterways become an integral part of the total transportation grid.
2. As per outcome of this study an indicative investment of ₹22,763 crore is required to develop infrastructure such as fairway, terminals, ports, road and rail connectivity. This public investment is expected to attract private investment of about ₹65,600 crore on inland ship building ship repair and cargo movement in the IWT Sector by the end of the 13th Plan, that is, 2023.
3. Based on the outcome of the study, a Cabinet Note to undertake and implement the project for setting up of Integrated National Waterways Transportation Grid at an estimated cost of ₹2631 cr. for phase- I (2015- 18) and ₹20132 cr. for phase- ii (2018- 23) totalling ₹22763 cr. was prepared. Subsequently, an EFC Note for the proposal has since been circulated among the concerned Ministries for their concurrence.

Memorandum of Understanding (MoU) signed between IWAI and IPGPL on the Kaladan Multimodal Transit Transport Project

The Kaladan Multimodal Transit Transport Project (KMTTP) in Myanmar was conceptualised and is being administered by the Ministry of External Affairs (MEA) with a view to facilitate connectivity between the mainland and the North Eastern States of the country through maritime shipping, inland waterways and roads of Myanmar. The link between North Eastern States of India and Myanmar will pave the way for enhanced trade and commerce across the border and enable cultural and social integration at the regional level. MEA had appointed Inland Waterways Authority of India (IWAI) as the Project Development Consultant (PDC) for the implementation of the Port and Inland Water Transport (IWT) component of the Kaladan Project on 19th March, 2009 and by Supplementary Agreement dated 28th April, 2016.

India Ports Global Private Limited (IPGPL) has been established as a Joint Venture between Kandla Port Trust and Jawaharlal Nehru Port Trust for the purpose of development of ports overseas. IPGPL was asked to partner IWAI in the Kaladan project as a sub-PDC. This was suggested mainly to use and develop the capabilities of IPGPL which has been created for a specialised purpose, completing the implementation of Kaladan project within the scheduled timeframe of April 2019 and to provide relief to IWAI whose responsibilities have increased manifold due to declaration of 106 new National Waterways and implementing the ambitious 'Jal Marg Vikas' project.

Accordingly, a Memorandum of Understanding (MoU) has been signed between IWAI and IPGPL on 1st June, 2016 for implementation of the following three additional works, which are independent of the ongoing works and are estimated to cost ₹476 crore.

(i) Container handling facilities at Sittwe and Paletwa
(ii) Operation and Maintenance of the completed works
(iii) Wrecks removed in Sittwe Port basin area

IWAI shall remain as the overall PDC to MEA for implementation of PORT and IWT component of Kaladan project.

8.4.21 Insurance Regulatory and Development Authority

IRDA – Insurance Regulatory Development and Authority is the statutory, independent and apex body that governs and supervises the Insurance Industry in India..

It was created upon the recommendations by the **Malhotra Committee** report of 1994. The report recommended that an independent authority to regulate the insurance industry in India should be established.

Objective

- Promote the interest and rights of policy holders.
- Promote and ensure the growth of Insurance Industry.
- Ensure speedy settlement of genuine claims and to prevent frauds and malpractices
- Bring transparency and orderly conduct of in financial markets dealing with insurance.

Composition of Authority

IRDA, a **ten-member body** consists of:

- One Chairman (For 5 years and Maximum Age – 60 years)
- Five whole-time Members (For 5 years and Maximum Age – 62 years)
- Four part-time Members (Not more than 5 years)

The chairman and members of IRDAI are appointed by the **Government of India**

Functions of Insurance Regulatory and Development Authority

The Insurance Regulatory and Development Authority (IRDA) is a national apex regulatory agency of the Government of India. It performs the following functions with respect to the insurance sector in India.

- It issues the certificate of registration or renewal to Insurance companies, insurance agents or surveyors and Insurance brokers. To function in the insurance sector, a company has to register with the IRDA.
- IRDA protects the interests of the policyholders in matters like nomination by policyholders, assigning of the policy, insurable interest, surrender values of the policy, settlement of insurance claim, and various other terms involved in the conditions of contracts of insurance.
- It specifies the requisite qualification, practical training, and code of conduct for agents, insurance brokers, and surveyors.
- IRDA is involved in promoting efficiency in insurance business conduction.
- It promotes and regulates professional organisations that connect with the insurance and re-insurance business.
- IRDA also specifies the code of conduct for surveyors and loss assessors.
- It regulates the fees and other similar charges levied by the insurance companies, brokers, agents, surveyors, etc.
- IRDA controls the rates, advantages, and terms and conditions which are offered by the insurers.
- It specifies the form and manner in which books of accounts are to be maintained by the insurers and other insurance intermediaries.
- It regulates the investment of funds made by the insurance companies and firms.
- IRDA settles disputes between insurers and intermediaries, whenever they arise.
- It also regulates the maintenance of margin of solvency (to possess sufficient funds to settle insurance claim amounts).
- It specifies the percentage of premium income of the insurer that can go to finance schemes for promotion and regulation of professional organisations.
- It also specifies the percentage of life insurance business and general insurance business that can be undertaken by the insurer in the social and rural sector.
- It supervises the working of the Tariff Advisory Committee also.
- IRDA has the power to frame regulations regarding the Insurance market.
- It promotes competition among the insurance companies and insurers in order to enhance customer satisfaction, by providing increased choice to consumers. Like it allowed Health Insurance Portability.
- IRDA is also involved in the field of consumer education and assistance.

Recent Initiatives

Pension and Life Insurance Fund Scheme for NRIs

The government has approved the Pension and Life Insurance Fund (PLIF) for overseas Indian workers having Emigration Check Required passports in January, 2012. The objective of PLIF scheme is to encourage and enable overseas Indian workers by giving co-contribution to (a) save for their return and resettlement, (b) save for their old age and (c) obtain a low-cost life insurance cover against natural death during the period of coverage.

Overseas Indian workers with emigration check required (ECR) passports and aged between 18 and 50 years who are emigrating overseas or have already emigrated overseas on an employment/contract visa are eligible to join the PLIF scheme. The scheme will benefit overseas Indian workers with ECR passports in ECR countries. These countries are Afghanistan, Bahrain, Indonesia, Iraq, Jordan, Kuwait, Saudi Arabia, Libya, Lebanon, Malaysia, Oman, Qatar, Sudan, Syria, Thailand, United Arab Emirates and Yemen.

The Lump sum return and resettlement withdrawals as well as pension benefits through NPS-Lite shall be paid into the bank account of each individual PLIF subscriber. The workers would also be given life insurance cover against natural death during the period of coverage.

Insurance Cover to Disabled Persons

As per Insurance Regulatory and Development Authority of India (IRDAI) mentally challenged people get covered under medical insurance policies sold by Public Sector General Insurance Companies (PSGICs). Presently, the PSGICs provide mental illness cover to children if covered with or both parents simultaneously in the policy. Some PSGICs also provide mental illness cover to the persons under Employer–Employee Group Health Insurance Policies. While Life Insurance Risk coverage is offered to handicapped and mentally challenged persons by the life insurance companies (both public sector and private sector) based on their board approved underwriting policy, the disclosures made in the proposal form, every life insurance company will rate the people to be insured from the point of view of risk assessment and underwriting as standard or sub-standard lives in order to determine acceptance of proposal and the premium to be charged. While there are no restrictions for providing insurance facilities to handicapped and mentally challenged persons, it is the professional decision of the insurance company based on their own risk bearing capacity and approach. There are no specific regulations/guidelines issued by the Authority in this regard.

8.4.22 National Biodiversity Authority

The National Biodiversity Authority (NBA) was established in 2003 to implement India's Biological Diversity Act (2002). The NBA is an autonomous body that performs facilitative, regulatory and advisory function for Government of India on issue of conservation, sustainable use of biological resources and fair equitable sharing of benefits of use.

The Biological Diversity Act (2002) mandates implementation of the act through decentralised system with the NBA focusing on advice of the Central Government on matters relating to the conservation of biodiversity, sustainable use of its components and equitable sharing of benefits arising out of the utilisation of biological resources; advice the State Government in the selection of areas of biodiversity importance to be notified under sub-section (1) of section 37 as heritage sites and measures for the management of such heritage sites;

The State Biodiversity Board (SBBs) focuses on advice to the State Government, subject to any guidelines issued by the Central Government, on matters relating to the conservation of biodiversity, sustainable use of its components and equitable sharing of the benefits arising out of the utilisation of biological resources;

The SSBs also regulate, by granting of approvals or otherwise requests for commercial utilization or bio-survey and bio-utilization of any biological resource by Indians. The local level Biodiversity Management Committees (BMCs) are responsible for promoting conservation, sustainable use and documentation of biological diversity including preservation of habitats, conservation of land races, folk varieties and cultivars, domesticated stocks and breeds of animals and microorganisms and chronicling of knowledge relating to biological diversity.

The NBA with its headquarters in Chennai, India delivers its mandate through a structure that comprises of the authority, secretariat, SBBs, BMCs and Expert Committees.

Since its establishment, NBA has supported creation of SBBs in 29 States, facilitated establishment of around 37,769 BMCs, advised notification.

Organisational Structure

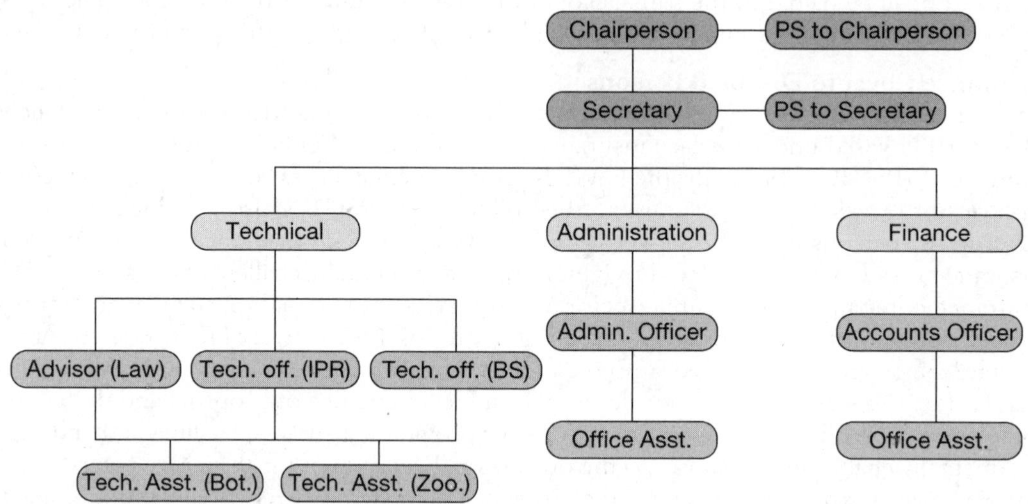

Besides the above Officers and staff, the NBA is supported by the Consultants to assist in technical and miscellaneous matters as per Rule 12(6). The role of consultant is more or less similar to 'Amicus Curiae' in the Court of Law. Besides they assist Chairman and Secretary in preparation of scientific and position papers and project reports etc.

The functions of NBA include:

1. Creating an enabling environment, as appropriate, to promote conservation and sustainable use of biodiversity.
2. Advising the Government of India on matters relating to conservation of biodiversity, sustainable use of its components and equitable sharing of benefits arising out of utilisation of biological resources.
3. Regulating activities and issue guidelines for access to biological resources and for fair and equitable benefit sharing in accordance with the Sections 3, 4 and 6 of the Biological Diversity Act, 2002. Certain individuals/nationals/organisations require prior approval of NBA for obtaining biological resources and/or associated knowledge for use.
4. Taking necessary measures to oppose the grant of intellectual property rights in any country outside India on any biological resource obtained from India or knowledge associated with such biological resource derived from India illegally.
5. Advising the State Governments in the selection of areas of biodiversity importance.

Functional Committees

1. Expert Committee on Agro Biodiversity
2. Expert Committee on Normally Traded Commodities
3. Expert Committee on Access and Benefit Sharing
4. Expert Committee on Medicinal Plants
5. Expert Committee on Red Sanders
6. Expert Committee on Invasive Alien Species

Initiatives by NBA:

Centre for Biodiversity Policy and Law

National Biodiversity Authority (NBA) has proposed to start a Centre for Biodiversity Policy and Law (CEBPOL) to deal with emerging and current biodiversity governance and policy related issues. The Government of Norway and India decided to collaborate and a letter of intent for technical and institutional cooperation was signed on 19th November, 2010 between Mr. Erik Solheim, Norwegian Minister of Environment and Development and Mr. Jairam Ramesh in New Delhi. The main objectives of the Centre include:

1. Provide professional support, advice and expertise to the Government of India and Norway on a sustained basis on matters relating to biodiversity policies and laws at the national level, as well as in international negotiations relating to biodiversity in multilateral forums.
2. Develop professional expertise in biodiversity-related policies and laws, inter alia through encouragement of research, development and training in matters relating to Convention on Biological Diversity, as well as its interface with other multilateral environment agreements and United Nations bodies.
3. Develop and implement an array of capacity building programmes through multidisciplinary research and customised training programmes for a wide range of stakeholders focusing on human resource development.
4. Facilitate interactive information sharing through web conferencing, web seminars and virtual meetings involving relevant research centres and environmental law associations within India, Norway and other countries where such expertise is available.
5. Help develop India as a regional and international resource centre for biodiversity policy and law through provision of training and human resource development.

8.4.23 Global Environmental Facility (GEF)

The objective of the UNEP-GEF MoEF project on ABS is to increase the institutional, individual and systemic capacities of stakeholders to effectively implement the Biological Diversity Act, 2002 and the Rules 2004 to achieve biodiversity conservation through implementing access and benefit sharing agreements in India.

This project is being implemented in 10 states of India namely Andhra Pradesh, Gujarat, Goa, Karnataka, Odisha, Telangana, Tripura, West Bengal, Himachal Pradesh and Sikkim. The executing organisation includes NBA in collaboration with the 10 SBBs, Botanical Survey of India (BSI), Zoological Survey of India (ZSI), United Nations Development Programme (UNDP), United Nations Environment Programme – Division of Environmental Law and Conventions (UNEP/DELC), United Nations University – Institute of Advanced studies (UNU-IAS) and Global Environment Facility (GEF).

The following are the objectives of the project:

- Develop standardised economic valuation methods for valuing biodiversity in the selected ecosystem
- Developing database on biological resources to tap ABS potential in project states
- Assessing and quantifying the economic value of biological diversity present at local, state and national levels using appropriate methodologies.

8.4.24 National Bank For Agriculture and Rural Development (NABARD) Genesis

At the instance of Government of India, Reserve Bank of India (RBI) constituted a committee to review the arrangements for institutional credit for agriculture and rural development (CRAFICARD) on 30 March 1979, under the Chairmanship of Shri B. Sivaraman, former member of Planning Commission, Government of India to review the arrangements for institutional credit for agriculture and rural development. The Committee, in its interim report, submitted on 28 November 1979, felt the need for a new organisational device for providing undivided attention, forceful direction and pointed focus to the credit problems arising out of integrated rural development and recommended the formation of National Bank for Agriculture and Rural Development (NABARD). The Parliament, through Act 61 of 1981, approved the setting up of NABARD. The bank came into existence on 12th July, 1982 by transferring the agricultural credit functions of RBI and refinance functions of the then Agricultural Refinance and Development Corporation (ARDC). NABARD was dedicated to the service of the nation by the late Prime Minister Smt. Indira Gandhi on 05th November, 1982. NABARD was set up with an initial capital of ₹100 crore.

National Bank for Agriculture and Rural Development (NABARD) is an apex development bank in India, headquartered at Mumbai with branches all over India. The Bank has been entrusted with 'matters concerning policy, planning and operations in the field of credit for agriculture and other economic activities in rural areas in India'. NABARD is active in developing financial inclusion policy and is a member of the Alliance for Financial Inclusion.

Mission

Promote sustainable and equitable agriculture and rural prosperity through effective credit support, related services, institution development and other innovative initiatives.

Organisational Structure

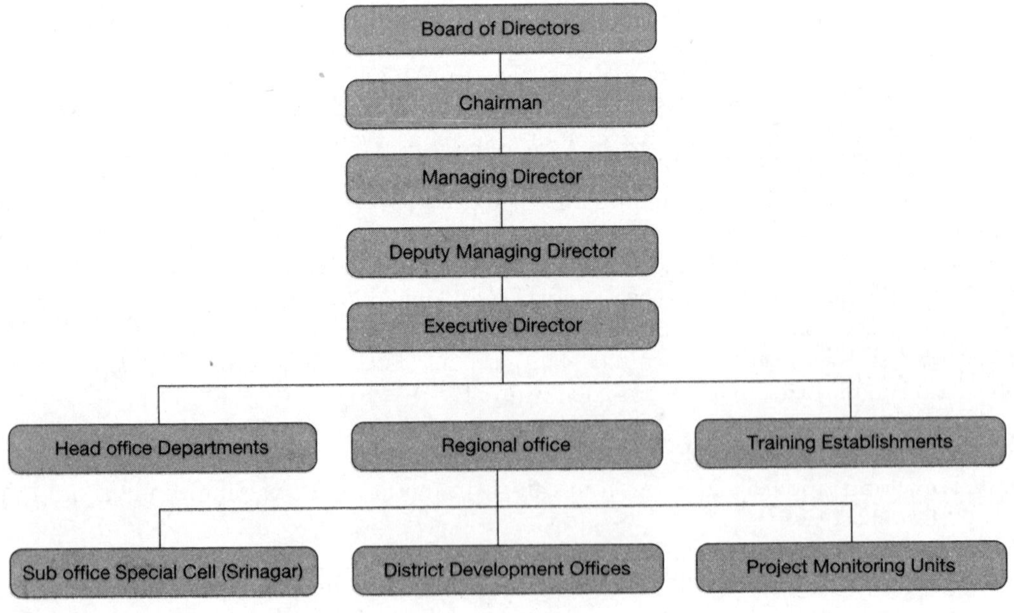

Role

NABARD has been instrumental in grounding rural, social innovations and social enterprises in the rural hinterlands. It has in the process partnered with about 4000 partner organisations in grounding many of the interventions be it SHG-Bank Linkage programme, tree-based tribal communities' livelihoods initiative, watershed approach in soil and water conservation, increasing crop productivity initiatives through lead crop initiative or dissemination of information flow to agrarian communities through Farmer clubs. Despite all this, it pays huge taxes too, to the exchequer – figuring in the top 50 tax payers consistently. NABARD virtually ploughs back all the profits for development spending, in their unending search for solutions and answers. Thus, the organisation had developed a huge amount of trust capital in its three decades of work with rural communities.

1. NABARD is the most important institution in the country which looks after the development of the cottage industry, small scale industry and village industry, and other rural industries.
2. NABARD also reaches out to allied economies and supports and promotes integrated development.
3. NABARD discharges its duty by undertaking the following roles:
    - Serves as an apex financing agency for the institutions providing investment and production credit for promoting the various developmental activities in rural areas.
    - Takes measures towards institution building for improving absorptive capacity of the credit delivery system, including monitoring, formulation of rehabilitation schemes, restructuring of credit institutions, training of personnel, etc.
    - Coordinates the rural financing activities of all institutions engaged in developmental work at the field level and maintains liaison with Government of India, state governments, Reserve Bank of India (RBI) and other national-level institutions concerned with policy formulation.
    - Undertakes monitoring and evaluation of projects refinanced by it.
    - Refinances the financial institutions which finances the rural sector.
    - Partakes in development of institutions which help the rural economy.
    - Keeps a check on its client institutes.
    - Regulates the institutions which provide financial help to the rural economy.
    - Provides training facilities to the institutions working in the field of rural upliftment.
    - Regulates the cooperative banks and the RRB's, and manages talent acquisition through IBPS CWE.

NABARD's refinance is available to state cooperative agriculture and rural development banks (SCARDBs), state cooperative banks (SCBs), regional rural banks (RRBs), commercial banks (CBs) and other financial institutions approved by the RBI. While the ultimate beneficiaries of investment credit can be individuals, partnership concerns, companies, state-owned corporations or cooperative societies, production credit is generally given to individuals

Functions

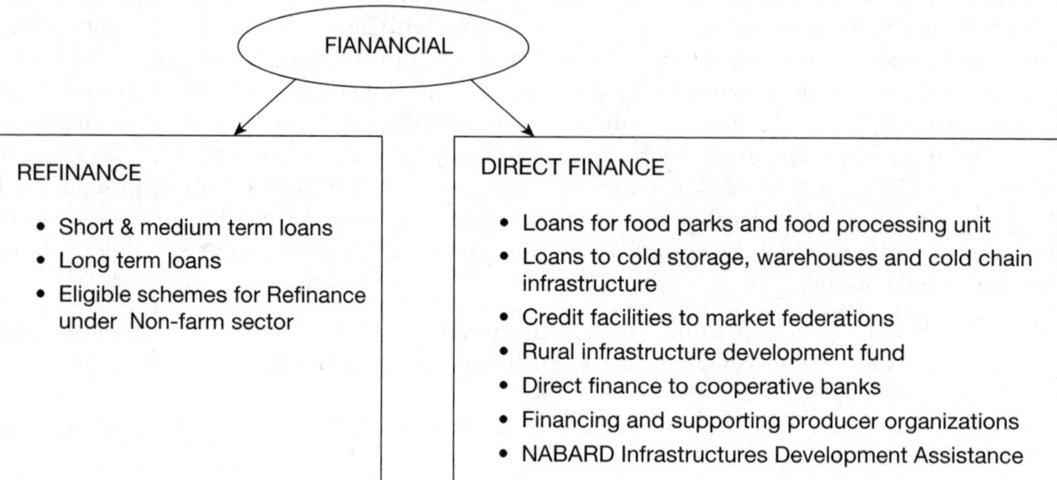

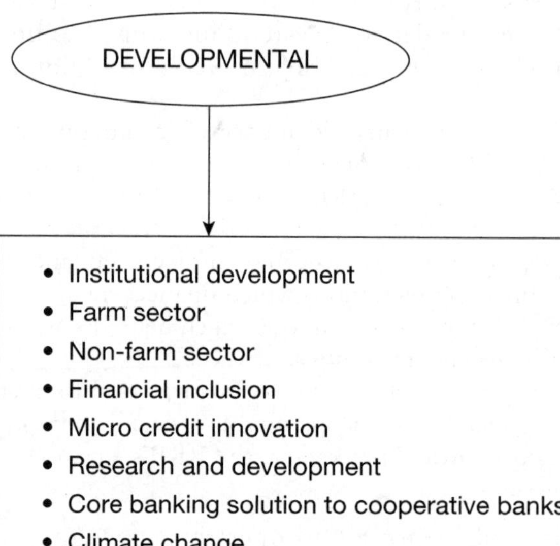

Functions of NABARD

Credit Functions

- Frame policy and guidelines for rural financial institutions.
- Provide credit facilities to issuing organisations.

- Monitor the flow of ground-level rural credit.
- Prepare credit plans annually for all districts for identification of credit potential.

Development Functions

- Help cooperative banks and regional rural banks to prepare development actions plans for themselves.
- Help regional rural banks and the sponsor banks to enter into MoUs with state governments and cooperative banks to improve the affairs of the regional rural banks.
- Monitor implementation of development action plans of banks.
- Provide financial support for the training institutes of cooperative banks, commercial banks and regional rural banks.
- Provide financial assistance to cooperative banks for building improved management information system, computerisation of operations and development of human resources.

Supervisory Functions

- Undertake inspection of regional rural banks and cooperative banks (other than urban/primary cooperative banks) under the provisions of Banking Regulation Act, 1949.
- Undertake inspection of state cooperative agriculture and rural development banks (SCARDBs) and apex non-credit cooperative societies on a voluntary basis.
- Provide recommendations to Reserve Bank of India on issues of licenses to cooperative banks, opening of new branches by state cooperative banks and regional rural banks.
- Undertakes portfolio inspections besides off-site surveillance of cooperative banks and regional rural banks.

Acts

- NABARD Act, 1981
- Banking Regulation Act
- Regional Rural Bank Act

Recent Initiatives

- NABARD has been accredited by the Green Climate Fund as an implementing entity for undertaking climate change related projects in India. NABARD has been accredited by GCF as **national implementing entity (NIE)** for undertaking climate change adaptation and mitigation projects from India. Accreditation to the NABARD, means that the national financial institution will act as a channel through which the GCF will deploy its resources in India. It also makes the bank eligible to identify communities and areas which are most vulnerable to climate change and submit proposals to the fund for financial support. The funding will support a range of activities including installation of renewable (solar, wind and bio-mass) energy, enabling farmers to grow drought-resistant crops.
- NABARD signed a Memorandum of Understanding (MoU) with **National Remote Sensing Center** (NRSC) for web-based monitoring of watershed projects. Under the MoU, Hyderabad-based NRSC, will create a separate page for NABARD on Bhuvan

web-portal develop customised software tool and mobile application for real-time monitoring, online comparison and visualisation with respect to activities implemented in the projects sanctioned by NABARD.

- NABARD started a pilot project for complete digitisation of women self-help groups (SHGs) to improve the quality of interface between members and banks for efficient and hassle free delivery of banking services with an objective to promote financial inclusion. Nabard has taken this proactive step to address issues and constraints faced by different stakeholders of the SHG bank linkage programme (SHG-BLP), such as need for improving the quality of interface between SHG members and banks, timely credit linkage of SHGs, challenges in book keeping by low literate clients and convergence with pro-poor government programmes

Digitisation will bring transparency, credibility to operations of SHGs through inbuilt grading MIS and thereby increasing the comfort of bankers in credit appraisal, disbursement and monitoring.

It will facilitate mainstreaming of SHG members with Aadhar-based financial inclusion and Pradhan Mantri Jan Dhan Yojana (PMJDY) enabling access to wide range of financial services, the process will ease transfer of social benefits and direct benefit transfer, leading to better participation of SHG members in PMJDY.

The ultimate beneficiary would be rural poor members of SHGs through easy e-book keeping of their records. The data of SHGs and their members will be fed into the input device (tablet/mobile handset) which will be uploaded in the secured and dedicated website, eshakti.nabard.org

8.4.25 National Green Tribunal

Introduction

The National Green Tribunal was established in 2010 under the act of National Green Tribunal Act, 2010.

Origin

During Rio-de-Janerio summit of United Nation Conference on Environment and Development in June 1992, India vowed to provide judicial and administrative remedies for the victims of pollutants and other environmental damage. Also India's move to Carbon Credit, so tribunal may play a vital role in ensuring the control of emission and maintain the desired levels.

India is the third country following Australia and New Zealand to have this tribunal.

Objective

It is for effective an expeditious disposal of cases related to environmental protection and conservation of forests and other natural resources including enforcement of legal right relation to environment and giving relief and compensation for damages to persons properly and for matters connected therewith or incidental hitherto.

The tribunal jurisdiction in environmental matter shall provide speedy justice and will reduce the burden of courts. It draws inspiration from the India's constitutional provision of Article 21, which assures the citizen of India the right to healthy environment.

This set is proposed to set up five sitting place of tribunal. New Delhi is the principle place of sitting of tribunal and Bhopal, Pune, Kolkata and Chennai shall be the other four sitting places of the tribunal.

Composition

Members and their Qualification

- It has a full-time chairperson. The person should have been either a judge of India's Supreme Court or Chief justice of a High Court in India.
- It has full-time judicial members at least 10 to maximum 20 members. The member should also be judge of Supreme Court, or Chief Justice or judge of High Court.
- It has a full-time expert members at least 10 to 20 in numbers. A member should have either a degree in Master of Science (in physical sciences or life sciences) with a doctorate degree or Master of Engineering or Master of Technology. and should have an experience of 15 years in the relevant field and administrative experience of 15 years in Central or a State Government or in a reputed national- or state-level institution.

Appointments

- Appointment of member is done by Central Government.
- Appointment of chairperson is done by Central Government in consultation with Chief Justice of India.
- Judicial members and expert members of the tribunal are appointed on the recommendation of such selection committee.
- Chairperson, judicial members and expert members hold office for five years.
- Maximum age of chairperson is 70 years if he has been a Supreme Court judge and 67 years if he has been a High Court judge.
- Chairperson can be removed from his office via an order made by the Central Government after an inquiry made by the Supreme Court in which the such chairperson or judicial members has been informed of the charges against him and given a reasonable opportunity of being heard in respect of those charges.

Jurisdiction

The NGT has the power to hear **all civil cases relating to environment** that are linked to the implementation of laws listed in schedule - I of the NGT act.

These includes the following:

- The Water (prevention and control of pollution) Act, 1974.
- The Water (prevention and control of pollution) Cess Act, 1977
- The Forest (conservation) Act, 1980
- The Air (prevention and control of pollution) Act, 1981
- The Environment (Protection) Act, 1986.
- The Public Liability Insurance Act, 1991
- The Biological Diversity Act, 2002

If any violation pertaining to these laws or order or decision making by the government under these laws should be challenged before the NGT and civil court cannot hear matter relating to the NGT. Importantly, NGT has not been vested with power relating to Wildlife (protection) Act, 1972, the Indian Forest Act 1927 and various laws enacted by state legislature to forest, tree preservation, etc.

Review and Appeal

Under Rule 22 of the NGT rule, there is a provision for seeking a review of a decision or order of the NGT. If this fails, an NGT order can be challenged before the Supreme Court within 90 days.

Importance of NGT

1. India is one of only few countries to have to specialised environmental court system, that is, NGT.
2. It permits direct access to environmental justice.
3. It reduces the pressure and burden on the High Courts and Supreme Courts.
4. It aims to achieve the objective of Article 21 (Protection of Life). Article 47, (Duty of state to raise the level of nutrition and the standard of living to improve public health. Article 51A-g (to protect and improve the natural environment including forest lakes, rivers and wild life and to have compassion for living creature).
5. NGT regulation towards environment paves a way to attain sustainable development, goal of UN.
6. Today, there is a fear among industry and environment regulations that some action would be taken if a case is heard by NGT.

Recent Judgments

1. In a landmark judgment, NGT banned light and heavy diesel vehicles, which are more than 10-years old in six major cities of Kerala, including state capital Thiruvananthapuram and commercial capital Kochi and other cities like Kollam, Thrissur, Kozhikodu and Kannur.
2. NGTs notice to states and union territories on effective implementation of the Biological Diversity Act is timely.
3. NGT passed the order that 'Manja' posed a threat to the environment and imposed interim ban because manja being coated with glass, metals and other sharp material and the strings act as good conductor of electricity.
4. NGT directed a Panama-based shipping company and its two Qatar-based sister concerns to pay ₹100 crore as damages for causing an oil spill when a cargo vessel sank off at Mumbai coast in 2011.
5. NGT announced a fine of ₹5000 on those using pressure horns and for removing silencers from their vehicles and causing noise pollution.
6. The Southern Bench of the National Green Tribunal suspended the Environmental Clearance (EC) granted to the India-based Neutrino Observatory (INO) that was to come up in Theni and asked the project proponent to make a fresh application.
7. NGT has imposed an environmental compensation of ₹15 crore on a charitable hospital in Dwaraka in Delhi for beginning construction without environmental clearance.
8. NGT assessed the damage caused to the Yamuna flood plain in Delhi where the World Culture Festival was held and found that the event had extensively damaged Yamuna floodplain.

Criticism

1. NGT decision can be challenged before the Supreme Court as well as High Court under Article – 226. This weakens the tribunal and penalty imposed on convict is postponed sometimes.

2. In a recent issue of Yamuna floodplain, a large number of vegetation cover was destroyed. NGT imposed only fine instead of protecting the forest before it gets destroyed.
3. Despite the high percentage of cases being disposed of, there is also an increasing backlog of cases in NGT. It reduces the trust of tribunal among the people.
4. Usually, the expert members are experts of one particular field and not of environment as a whole. This reduces the quality of judgment.
5. NGT is based only in big cities, when the problem arises in rural or tribal areas, people cannot afford to approach and pursue the case before NGT.

8.4.26 National Housing Bank

National Housing Bank (NHB), a wholly owned subsidiary of Reserve Bank of India (RBI), was set up on 9 July 1988 under the National Housing Bank Act, 1987. NHB is an apex financial institution for housing. NHB has been established with an objective to operate as a principal agency to promote housing finance institutions both at local and regional levels and to provide financial and other support incidental to such institutions and for matters connected therewith.

NHB registers, regulates and supervises Housing Finance Company (HFCs), keeps surveillance through on-site and off-site mechanisms and coordinates with other regulators.

Genesis

- The sub-group on housing finance for the Seventh Five Year Plan (1985–1990) identified the non-availability of long-term finance to individual households on any significant scale as a major lacuna impeding progress of the housing sector and recommended the setting up of a national-level institution.
- The Committee of Secretaries considered the recommendation and set up a high-level group under the Chairmanship of Dr. C. Rangarajan, the then Deputy Governor, RBI to examine the proposal and recommended the setting up of National Housing Bank as an autonomous housing finance institution. The recommendations of the high-level group were accepted by the Government of India.
- The Hon'ble Prime Minister of India, while presenting the Union Budget for 1987–1988 on 28th February, 1987 announced the decision to establish the National Housing Bank (NHB) as an apex-level institution for housing finance. Following that, the National Housing Bank Bill (91 of 1987) providing the legislative framework for the establishment of NHB was passed by the Parliament in the winter session of 1987 and with the assent of the Hon'ble President of India on 23rd December, 1987, it became an Act of Parliament.
- The National Housing Policy, 1988 envisaged the setting up of NHB as the apex-level institution for housing.
- In pursuance of the above, NHB was set up on 9th July, 1988 under the National Housing Bank Act, 1987.
- NHB is wholly owned by Reserve Bank of India, which contributed the entire paid-up capital.
- The general superintendence, direction and management of the affairs and business of NHB vest, under the Act, in a Board of Directors.
- The Head Office of NHB is at New Delhi.

Preamble

The Preamble of the National Housing Bank Act, 1987 describes the basic functions of the NHB as

'... to operate as a principal agency to promote housing finance institutions both at local and regional levels and to provide financial and other support to such institutions and for matters connected therewith or incidental thereto ...'

Vision

Promoting inclusive expansion with stability in housing finance market

Mission

To harness and promote the market potentials to serve the housing needs of all segments of the population with the focus on low and moderate income housing

Objectives

NHB has been established to achieve, inter alia, the following objectives:

- Promote a sound, healthy, viable and cost-effective housing finance system to cater to all segments of the population and to integrate the housing finance system with the overall financial system.
- Promote a network of dedicated housing finance institutions to adequately serve various regions and different income groups.
- Augment resources for the sector and channelise them for housing.
- Make housing credit more affordable.
- Regulate the activities of housing finance companies based on regulatory and supervisory authority derived under the act.
- Encourage augmentation of supply of buildable land and also building materials for housing and to upgrade the housing stock in the country.
- Encourage public agencies to emerge as facilitators and suppliers of serviced land for housing.

Regulation

- In terms of the National Housing Bank Act, 1987, National Housing Bank is expected, in the public interest, to regulate the housing finance system of the country to its advantage or to prevent the affairs of any housing finance institution being conducted in a manner detrimental to the interest of the depositors or in a manner prejudicial to the interest of the housing finance institutions. For this, National Housing Bank has been empowered to determine the policy and give directions to the housing finance institutions and their auditors.
- Besides the regulatory provisions of the National Housing Bank Act, 1987, National Housing Bank has issued the Housing Finance Companies (NHB) Directions, 2001 as also Guidelines for Asset Liability Management System in Housing Finance Companies. These are periodically updated through circulars and notifications. As part of the supervisory process, an entry-level regulation is sought to be achieved through a system of registration of housing finance companies.
- National Housing Bank supervises the sector through a system of on-site and off-site surveillance.

Schemes

Energy Efficient Housing Scheme (EEHS)

- NHB has formulated a scheme called Energy Efficient Housing Scheme (EEHS), 2011 for lending towards energy efficient housing units/buildings. The objective of the Scheme is to provide refinance assistance to Housing Finance Companies (HFCs) in respect of their direct lending up to ₹50 lakhs to individuals for purchase/construction of new energy efficient housing units in urban areas. While the broad policy framework, eligibility of HFCs for refinance, operational procedures are the same as for the other schemes of refinance there are certain changes in terms and conditions and eligibility of the end borrower. This self-contained brochure containing all necessary information is given as under. This scheme was launched in financial year 2011–2012. The disbursement made under the scheme (from 01st July, 2011 to 07th June, 2012) was ₹81.36 crore.
- HFCs are expected to utilise this refinance assistance and assist such persons to have an energy-efficient shelter of their own by extending need-based housing loans to them. HFCs are also encouraged to avail of refinance from NHB under its other scheme to enable 'leverage' of EEHS so that the principal objective of increasing housing stock in the urban areas is served.
- Refinance from NHB will be available to the extent of 100% of housing loans sanctioned and disbursed by the HFCs for acquisition/construction of new housing units, in accordance with the provisions of the scheme. The refinance assistance under this dispensation would remain valid up to 30th December, 2013 or till such further time as decided by NHB.

1. **Pradhan Mantri Awas Yojana**
   National Housing Bank, the central nodal agency for the implementation of Pradhan Mantri Awas Yojana-Credit Linked Subsidy Scheme. Credit Linked Subsidy will be available for housing loans availed for new construction and addition of rooms, kitchen, toilet etc. to existing dwelling as incremental housing. The beneficiaries are individuals from Economically Weaker Section(EWS) and Low Income Group (LIG) seeking housing loans from banks, housing finance companies and other such institutions. Housing and Urban Development Corporation (HUDCO) and National Housing Bank (NHB) have been identified as Central Nodal Agencies (CNAs) to channelise this subsidy to the lending institutions and for monitoring the progress of this component.

2. **Solar Capital Subsidy Scheme**
   The Scheme will be known as Loan-cum-Capital Subsidy Scheme for installation of solar water heating and solar lighting equipment in homes. The objective of the scheme is to channelise the capital subsidy provided by the MNRE for purchase and installation of (a) solar water heating equipment and (b) solar lighting equipment in homes. The capital subsidy routed by NHB through the implementing Primary Lending Institutions (PLIs) will be passed on by them to their borrowers together with the loan for purchase of the equipment. The subsidy will be applicable only on purchase and installation of solar water heating and/or solar lighting equipment which conform to the specifications of the MNRE as provided on MNRE's website, www.mnre.gov.in, or as specified separately.

3. **Credit Risk Guarantee Fund Trust for Low Income Housing**
   The urban affordable housing deficit is estimated to be about 26 million. The total housing loan outstanding was about ₹3.06 lakh crore of which only about 24% is for loans up to ₹5 lakhs of which only a part is estimated as flowing to the economically weaker sections and low income groups. The establishment of such a government-supported Credit Risk Guarantee Fund would facilitate credit enablement of the urban poor and the flow of institutional finance for affordable housing. The Credit Risk Guarantee Fund (CRGF) is intended to act as a risk-mitigant, thereby enhancing the confidence of the lending institutions in lending to this segment.
   The CRGF Trust will administer and operate the CRGF Scheme. The key principle of the CRFG Scheme is that the lender shall secure the housing construction/upgradation loan purely on the assets financed, without any other collateral.

8.4.27 National Pharmaceutical Pricing Authority

NPPA is an organisation of the Government of India which was established, inter alia, to fix/revise the prices of controlled bulk drugs and formulations and to enforce prices and availability of the medicines in the country, under the Drugs (Prices Control) Order, 1995. The National Pharmaceutical Pricing Authority (NPPA) was established through a Government of India Resolution on August 29, 1997. NPPA is responsible for the implementation of the National Pharmaceutical Pricing Policy, 2012 and the Drugs (Prices Control) Order (DPCO), 2013. Drug price control, which is prevalent in one form or the other throughout the world, assumes special importance, as it directly impacts the quality of public health.

Established as an independent body of experts to be called as the National Pharmaceutical Pricing Authority, consisting of a Chairperson in the status of the Secretary to the Government of India, Members having expertise in the field of pharmaceuticals, economics and cost accountancy and Member Secretary in the status of Joint Secretary/Additional Secretary to the Government of India, and the same is entrusted with the task of price fixation revision and other related matters such as updating the list of drugs under price control by inclusion and exclusion on the basis of the established criteria/guidelines. The National Pharmaceutical Pricing Authority shall be empowered to take final decisions, which shall be subject to review by the Central Government as and when considered necessary. The Authority shall also monitor the prices of decontrolled drugs and formulations and oversee the implementation of the provisions of the Drugs (Prices Control) Order

The headquarters of the authority is at New Delhi.

The organisation is also entrusted with the task of recovering amounts overcharged by manufacturers for the controlled drugs from the consumers. It also monitors the prices of decontrolled drugs in order to keep them at reasonable levels.

With a view to carrying out its functions in a holistic manner, the NPPA maintains close coordination with the concerned Ministries of the Central Government, State Governments, industry associations, consumers and other stakeholder organisations. The price fixation notifications are uploaded on website along with the calculation sheets which has ensured absolute transparency in the process. NPPA also entertains representation from industry and open to any correction if needed.

NPPA is governed by the provision of DPCO, 2013

Salient features of DPCO, 2013.

1. Drug formulations listed under the National List of Essential Medicines are under price control.
2. Ceiling price calculations are based on 'market based data' as opposed to 'cost based inputs' under DPCO, 1995.
3. It controls only drug formulation price as opposed to both bulk drugs and their formulation under DPCO, 1995.

Aim

The primary aim of the NPPA is to ensure adequate availability of essential and life-saving drugs at affordable prices and in doing so, it carefully balances the interests of both the producers and the consumers.

Parent Department

Department of Pharmaceuticals, Ministry of Chemicals and Fertilizers

Constitution of Authority

The constitution of NPPA is as under

- Chairman (in the rank of Secretary/Addotional Secretary to Govt. of India).
- Member Secretary (in the rank of Joint Secretary to Government of India).

Ex-Officio Members

- Drugs Controller General (India), Department of Health.
- Economic Adviser, Department of Economic Affairs
- Adviser (Cost), Department of Expenditure

Functions of National Pharmaceutical Pricing Authority

- Implement and enforce the provisions of the drugs (prices control) order in accordance with the powers delegated to it.
- Deal with all legal matters arising out of the decisions of the Authority.
- Monitor the availability of drugs, identify shortages, if any, and to take remedial steps.
- Collect/Maintain data on production, exports and imports, market share of individual companies, profitability of companies etc, for bulk drugs and formulations.
- Undertake and/ or sponsor relevant studies in respect of pricing of drugs/ pharmaceuticals.
- Recruit/Appoint the officers and other staff members of the Authority, as per rules and procedures laid down by the Government.
- Render advice to the Central Government on changes/ revisions in the drug policy.
- Render assistance to the Central Government in the parliamentary matters relating to the drug pricing.

Integrated Pharmaceutical Database Management System (IPDMS)

The online platform Integrated Pharmaceutical Database Management System (IPDMS) enables online submission of mandatory forms prescribed. IPDMS when fully operational will bring in better transparency and facilitate monitoring and enforcement. In spite of several earnest appeals to all the drug manufacturers to submit the required information within the stipulated period of time and several extensions of the deadline, the response from the industry so far has been unsatisfactory. NPPA has now been constrained to issue show cause notices to individual manufacturers for non-compliance.

Pharma Jan Samadhan (PJS)

The Pharma Jan Samadhan (PJS), a public grievance portal was launched last year, to facilitate the submission of grievances by the public. PJS has a web-enabled system as well as telephonic helpline. NPPA is committed to redress all the public grievances coming to its notice on priority. An internal guideline in order to streamline the process of recovery from the companies

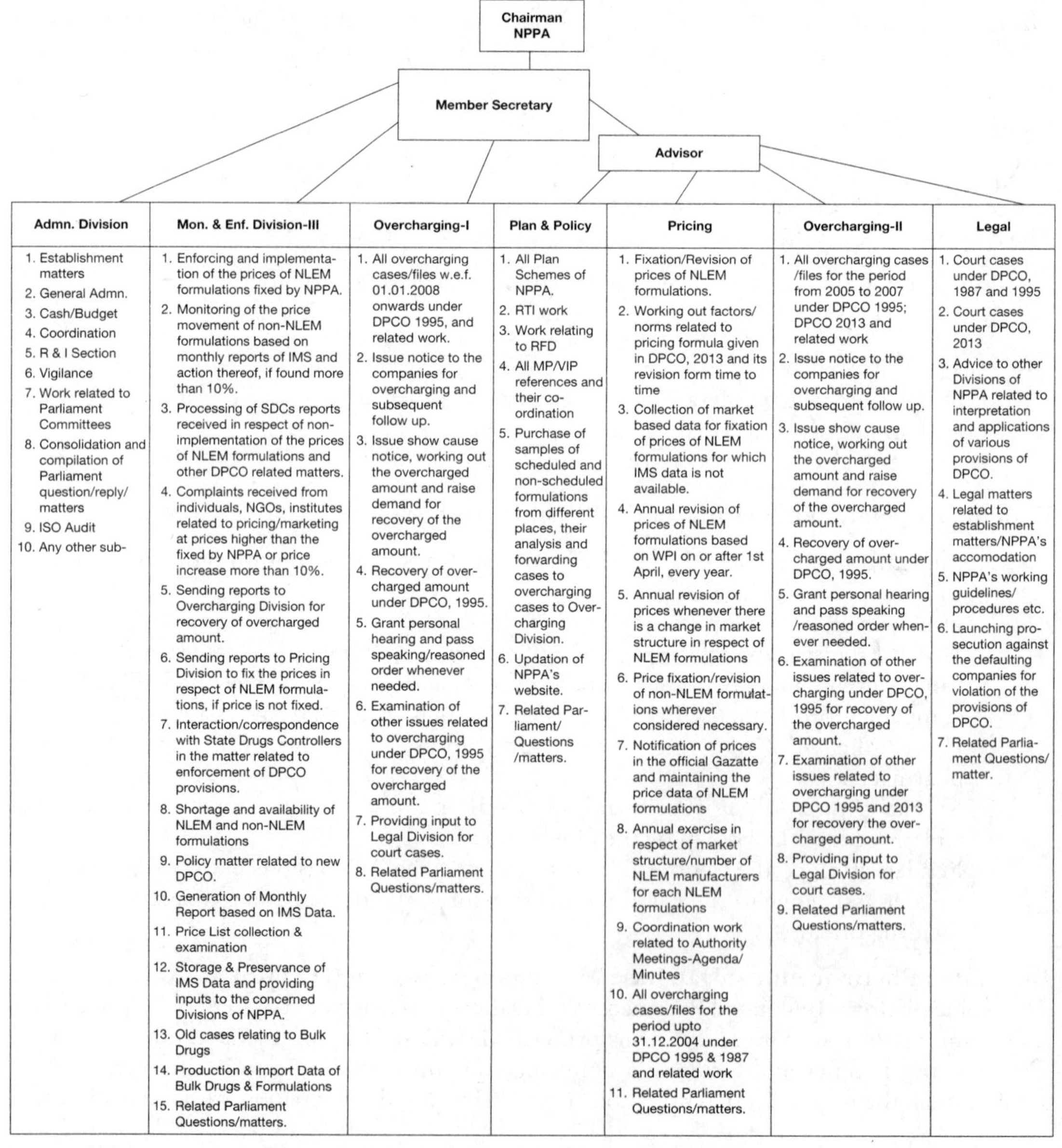

Admn. Division	Mon. & Enf. Division-III	Overcharging-I	Plan & Policy	Pricing	Overcharging-II	Legal
1. Establishment matters 2. General Admn. 3. Cash/Budget 4. Coordination 5. R & I Section 6. Vigilance 7. Work related to Parliament Committees 8. Consolidation and compilation of Parliament question/reply/ matters 9. ISO Audit 10. Any other sub-	1. Enforcing and implementation of the prices of NLEM formulations fixed by NPPA. 2. Monitoring of the price movement of non-NLEM formulations based on monthly reports of IMS and action thereof, if found more than 10%. 3. Processing of SDCs reports received in respect of non-implementation of the prices of NLEM formulations and other DPCO related matters. 4. Complaints received from individuals, NGOs, institutes related to pricing/marketing at prices higher than the fixed by NPPA or price increase more than 10%. 5. Sending reports to Overcharging Division for recovery of overcharged amount. 6. Sending reports to Pricing Division to fix the prices in respect of NLEM formulations, if price is not fixed. 7. Interaction/correspondence with State Drugs Controllers in the matter related to enforcement of DPCO provisions. 8. Shortage and availability of NLEM and non-NLEM formulations 9. Policy matter related to new DPCO. 10. Generation of Monthly Report based on IMS Data. 11. Price List collection & examination 12. Storage & Preservance of IMS Data and providing inputs to the concerned Divisions of NPPA. 13. Old cases relating to Bulk Drugs 14. Production & Import Data of Bulk Drugs & Formulations 15. Related Parliament Questions/matters.	1. All overcharging cases/files w.e.f. 01.01.2008 onwards under DPCO 1995, and related work. 2. Issue notice to the companies for overcharging and subsequent follow up. 3. Issue show cause notice, working out the overcharged amount and raise demand for recovery of the overcharged amount. 4. Recovery of over-charged amount under DPCO, 1995. 5. Grant personal hearing and pass speaking/reasoned order whenever needed. 6. Examination of other issues related to overcharging under DPCO, 1995 for recovery of the overcharged amount. 7. Providing input to Legal Division for court cases. 8. Related Parliament Questions/matters.	1. All Plan Schemes of NPPA. 2. RTI work 3. Work relating to RFD 4. All MP/VIP references and their co-ordination 5. Purchase of samples of scheduled and non-scheduled formulations from different places, their analysis and forwarding cases to overcharging cases to Over-charging Division. 6. Updation of NPPA's website. 7. Related Parliament/ Questions /matters.	1. Fixation/Revision of prices of NLEM formulations. 2. Working out factors/ norms related to pricing formula given in DPCO, 2013 and its revision form time to time 3. Collection of market based data for fixation of prices of NLEM formulations for which IMS data is not available. 4. Annual revision of prices of NLEM formulations based on WPI on or after 1st April, every year. 5. Annual revision of prices whenever there is a change in market structure in respect of NLEM formulations 6. Price fixation/revision of non-NLEM formulations wherever considered necessary. 7. Notification of prices in the official Gazette and maintaining the price data of NLEM formulations 8. Annual exercise in respect of market structure/number of NLEM manufacturers for each NLEM formulations 9. Coordination work related to Authority Meetings-Agenda/ Minutes 10. All overcharging cases/files for the period upto 31.12.2004 under DPCO 1995 & 1987 and related work 11. Related Parliament Questions/matters.	1. All overcharging cases /files for the period from 2005 to 2007 under DPCO 1995; DPCO 2013 and related work 2. Issue notice to the companies for overcharging and subsequent follow up. 3. Issue show cause notice, working out the overcharged amount and raise demand for recovery of the overcharged amount. 4. Recovery of over-charged amount under DPCO, 1995. 5. Grant personal hearing and pass speaking /reasoned order whenever needed. 6. Examination of other issues related to over-charging under DPCO, 1995 for recovery of the overcharged amount. 7. Examination of other issues related to overcharging under DPCO 1995 and 2013 for recovery the over-charged amount. 8. Providing input to Legal Division for court cases. 9. Related Parliament Questions/matters.	1. Court cases under DPCO, 1987 and 1995 2. Court cases under DPCO, 2013 3. Advice to other Divisions of NPPA related to interpretation and applications of various provisions of DPCO. 4. Legal matters related to establishment matters/NPPA's accomodation 5. NPPA's working guidelines/ procedures etc. 6. Launching prosecution against the defaulting companies for violation of the provisions of DPCO. 7. Related Parliament Questions/ matter.

indulging in overpricing the medicines and violating various provisions of DPCO, 2013 has been uploaded on the website to ensure transparency and uniformity in dealing with such cases. NPPA has further strengthened its monitoring system for ensuring price compliance and there are about 2700 cases of price violation under examination.

Drug Policies
Drug Policy 1986
National Pharmaceutical Pricing Policy 2012
Drug (Price Control) Order 2013

Methodology/Procedure for price fixation or revision of bulk drugs

As per par 3 of DPCO, 1995 prices of scheduled bulk drugs are fixed by the NPPA to make them available at a fair price from different manufacturers. These prices are fixed from time to time by notification in official gazette.

Following steps are involved in fixation/revision of bulk drug prices :

Step 1: Identification of bulk drugs

Bulk Drugs are taken up for study on the following basis:

(i) Whose validity period is due to expire.
(ii) Request from the concerned manufacturer/company.
(iii) Drug produced in the country for which no price has been notified under DPCO, 1995.

Step 2: Collection of data

Data is collected by issuing questionnaire/Form I of DPCO, 1995/cost-audit report etc. and verification by plant visits, if required.

Step 3: Preparation of actual cost statement

Actual cost for the year for which data is submitted is prepared based on data submitted / collected and verified during plant visit.

Step 4: Preparation of technical parameters

Technical parameters are prepared based on data submitted, collected and verified during plant visits. Plant capacity is assessed considering 330 working days for normal operation of plant leaving 35 days for scheduled maintenance of plant. The achievable production level is considered at 90% utilisation of assessed capacity allowing 10% production loss on account of unforeseen break down and non-scheduled maintenance.

Step 5: Preparation of estimated cost

The estimated cost for the pricing period are then prepared based on actual cost and the technical parameters. While projecting the future cost, an increment is recognised at 5% per annum in respect of salaries and wages. Wage agreement, if any, which has been finalised and signed is also recognised while preparing the estimates. In respect of other overheads of fixed/semi-variable nature, increase at 2.5% per annum is made to cover the normal incremental effects. The customs duty and other taxes as per the current budget are considered.

Step 6: Calculation of fair price of bulk drug

Fair price is calculated by providing returns as specified in sub para (2), para 3 of DPCO, 1995.

While fixing the maximum sale price of the bulk drug, a post tax return of 14% on net-worth or a return of 22% of capital employed or in respect of a new plant an internal rate of return of 12% based on long-term marginal costing is considered depending upon the option exercised by the manufacturer of the bulk drug. In case, the production is from basic stage, additional 4% return is considered on net worth/capital employed.

Step 7: Fixation of maximum sale price of the drug

When the number of manufacturers of the said drug is more than one, the maximum sale price is fixed at 2/3rd cut-off level or weighted average price, depending upon the situation.

Step 8: Notification of bulk drug price in official gazette

	Suo-motu Pricing	Pro-rata Pricing
Who Fixes?	**NPPA**	**Manufacturers**
	The NPPA also fixes/revises prices of both bulk drugs and formulations on suo-motu basis, where it is felt that manufacturers are not filing their applications as per the provisions of the DPCO, 1995 after the decrease in bulk drug prices and statutory duties, etc.	NPPA has issued notification on pro -rata pricing on 27th January, 1998. According to this notification, the manufacturers of all the scheduled formulation pack sizes different from the notified pack sizes under sub- paragraphs (1) and (2) of the paragraph 9 of the DPCO, 1995, shall have to work out the price for such pack sizes, in respect of tablets and capsules of the same strength or composition packed in different strips or blisters, on pro-rata basis of the latest ceiling price fixed
Purpose	This is done to ensure with a view to passing on the benefits of such decreases to the consumers, suo-motu price is fixed.	• This is done to ensure that manufacturers are not forced to approach frequently for price approvals for different pack sizes. • the manufacturers do not change the pack sizes in a bid to remain out of price control.

NPPA-CIFG

As part of consumer awareness for dissemination of information regarding drug pricing and availability and also to create an online facility for logging complaints with NPPA on the above issues, a scheme for setting up an Internet-based centre for information, facilitation and grievances has been started in consultation with NIC. The objective is to disseminate information on the availability and the notified price of scheduled drugs and formulations and to create consumer awareness and facilitate speedy complaint redressal on

- overcharging in [prices of] scheduled formulations.
- non-availability or shortage of any medicine.
- sale of scheduled formulations without prior price approval of NPPA.

Any individual or organisation may lodge complaint through Internet directly to NPPA. Action on any complaint received with required information has to be initiated within 30 days by NPPA.

NPPA-CIFG are being set up on pilot basis initially in five states namely, Tamil Nadu, Maharashtra, Bihar, West Bengal and Gujarat. These centres are proposed to be run by a local NGO recommended by the State Government. The NGOs are required to provide space for the NPPA-CIFG in a prominent location, easily accessible to people in the selected city. The NGOs are being given the permission to run this centre initially for a period of 3 years. They are required furnish through the State Government to NPPA an agreement in prescribed form for running and operating the centre. The NGOs have also to execute indemnity bonds in respect of the hardware and software to be provided under the scheme to them by NPPA through the State Government. Following hardware and software are being provided

- Desktop computer
- Scanner
- Laser printer
- MS Office software
- Software on online complaint submission and redressal system
- Internet connectivity

NPPA-CIFG is being funded by NPPA for hardware, software and connectivity and the project is implemented by NIC. The NPPA-CIFG will be run and operated by NGO selected by the state government.

NPPA has already extended the facility of online complaint redressal by providing connectivity with 555 CICs in North-East States and 135 CICs in Jammu and Kashmir. This scheme has also been linked to 10 centres in various government buildings in New Delhi.

8.4.28 Press Council of India (PCI)

Press Council is a mechanism for the Press to regulate itself. The raison d'être of this unique institution is rooted in the concept that in a democratic society the press needs at once to be free and responsible. If the Press is to function effectively as the watchdog of public interest, it must have a secure freedom of expression, unfettered and unhindered by any authority, organised bodies or individuals. But, this claim to press freedom has legitimacy only if it is exercised with a due sense of responsibility. The Press must, therefore, scrupulously adhere to accepted norms of journalistic ethics and maintain high standards of professional conduct.

The Press Council of India was first set up in the year 1966 by the Parliament on the recommendations of the First Press Commission with the object of preserving the freedom of the press and of maintaining and improving the standards of press in India. The present council functions under the Press Council Act 1978. It is a statutory, quasi-judicial body which acts as a watchdog of the press. It adjudicates the complaints against and by the press for violation of ethics and for violation of the freedom of the press, respectively.

The basic concept of self-regulation in which the Press Councils and similar media bodies world over are founded, was articulated by Mahatma Gandhi, who was an eminent journalist in his own right, and according to him:

'The sole aim of journalist should be service. The newspaper press is a great power, but just as unchained torrent of water submerges the whole country side and devastates crops, even so an uncontrolled pen serves but to destroy. If the control is from without, it proves more poisonous than want of control. It can be profitable only when exercised from within.

The fundamental objective of journalism is to serve the people with news, views, comments and information on matters of public interest in a fair, accurate, unbiased, sober and decent manner. To this end, the Press is expected to conduct itself in keeping with certain norms of professionalism, universally recognised.

Composition

The Council is headed by a Chairman, who has by convention, been a retired judge of the Supreme Court of India. The council consists of 28 other members of whom 20 represent the press and are nominated by the press organisations/news agencies recognised and notified by the Council as all India bodies of categories such as editors, working journalists and owners and managers of newspaper and news agencies, five members are nominated from the two Houses of Parliament and three represent cultural, literary and legal fields as nominees of the Sahitya Academy, University Grants Commission and the Bar Council of India.

Press Council Act, 1978
Objects and Functions of the Council

1. The objects of the Council shall be to preserve the freedom of the Press and to maintain and improve the standards of newspapers and news agencies in India.

   The Council may, in furtherance of its objects, perform the following functions, namely:

   a. Help newspapers and news agencies to maintain their independence.
   b. Build up a code of conduct for newspapers, news agencies, journalists in accordance with high professional standards.
   c. Ensure on the part of newspapers, news agencies and journalists, the maintenance of high standards of public taste and foster a due sense of both the rights and responsibilities of citizenship.
   d. Encourage the growth of a sense of responsibility and public service among all those engaged in the profession of journalism.
   e. Keep under review any development likely to restrict the supply and dissemination of news of public interest and importance.
   f. Keep under review cases of assistance received by any newspaper or news agency in India from any foreign source including such cases as are referred to it by the Central Government or are brought to its notice by an individual, association or persons or any other organisation. Provided that nothing in this clause shall preclude the Central Government from dealing with any case of assistance received by a newspaper or news agency in India from any foreign source in any other manner it thinks fit.
   g. Undertake studies of foreign newspapers, including those brought out by any embassy or other representative in India of a foreign State, their circulation and impact.

Functioning of the Council

The Council discharges its functions primarily through the medium of its Inquiry Committees, adjudicating on complaint cases received by it against the Press for violation of the norms of journalism or by the Press for interference with its freedom by the authorities. There is a set procedure for lodging a complaint with the Council.

A complainant is required essentially to write to the editor of the respondent newspaper, drawing his attention to what the complainant considers to be in breach of journalistic ethics or an offence against public taste. Apart from furnishing to the Council a cutting of the matter complained against, it is incumbent on the complainant to make and subscribe to a declaration that to the best of his knowledge and belief he has placed all the relevant facts before the Council and that no proceedings are pending in any court of law in respect of any matter alleged in the complaint; and that he shall inform the Council forthwith if during the pendency of the inquiry before the Council any matter alleged in the complaint becomes the subject matter of any proceedings in a court of law. The reason for this declaration is that in view of Section 14(3) of the Act, the Council cannot deal with any matter which is sub-judice.

If the Chairman finds that there are no sufficient grounds for inquiry, he may dismiss the complaint and report it to the Council; otherwise, the Editor of the newspaper or the journalist concerned is asked to show cause why action should not be taken against him. On receipt of the written statement and other relevant material from the editor or the journalist, the Secretariat of the Council places the matter before the Inquiry Committee. The Inquiry Committee screens and examines the complaint in necessary details. If necessary, it also calls for further particulars or documents from the parties. The parties are given opportunity to adduce evidence before the Inquiry Committee by appearing personally or through their authorised representative including legal practitioners. On the basis of the facts on record and affidavits or the oral evidence adduced before it, the Committee formulates its findings and recommendations and forwards them to the Council, which may or may not accept them. When the Council is satisfied that a newspaper or news agency has offended against the standards of journalistic ethics or public taste or that an editor or working journalist has committed professional misconduct, the Council may warn, admonish or censure the newspaper, the news agency, the editor or journalist, or disapprove the conduct thereof, as the case may be. In the complaints lodged by the Press against the authorities, the Council is empowered to make such observations as it may think fit in respect of the conduct of any authority including government. The decisions of the Council are final and cannot be questioned in any court of law. It will thus be seen that the Council wields a lot of moral authority although it has no legally enforceable punitive powers.

The inquiry regulations framed by the Council empower the Chairman to take suo motu action and issue notices to any party in respect of any matter falling within the scope of Press Council Act. The procedure for holding a suo motu inquiry is substantially the same as in the case of a normal inquiry except that for any normal inquiry a complaint is required to be lodged with the Council by a complainant. For the purpose of performing its functions or holding an inquiry under the Act, the Council exercises some of the powers vested in a Civil Court trying a suit under the Code of Civil Procedure, 1908, in respect of the following matters, namely:

- Summoning and enforcing the attendance of persons and examining them on oath
- Requiring the discovery and inspection of documents
- Receiving evidence on affidavits.
- Requisitioning any public record or copies thereof from any court or office
- Issuing commissions for the examination of witnesses or documents
- Any other matter, which may be prescribed

Broad Principles Evolved

Some of the broad principles evolved by the Council in course of its adjudication on various subjects both in respect of standards of journalism and the freedom of the Press are summarised as under:

A. JOURNALISTIC STANDARDS

1. **Communal Writings**
   Scurrilous and inflammatory attacks should not be made on communities and individuals. Any news on communal events based on rumours will be violative of the

journalistic ethics. Similarly, distorted reporting making important omissions will not be correct. While it is the legitimate function of the Press to draw attention to the genuine grievance of any community with a view to seeking redress in a peaceful and legal manner, there should be no invention or exaggeration of grievances, particularly those which tend to promote communal discord.

It will be highly conducive to the creation of a healthy and peaceful atmosphere if sensational, provocative and alarming headlines are avoided, and acts of violence or vandalism are reported in such a manner as may not undermine people's confidence in law and order machinery of the State and may at the same time have the effect of discouraging and condemning such activities.

Defaming a community is a serious matter and ascribing to it a vile, anti-national activity is reprehensible and amounts to journalistic impropriety.

There is no impropriety in publishing historical facts in order to warn the present generation against repetition of past mistakes even though these mistakes may not be palatable to a particular community.

There is no objection in making statements about religious communities if they are couched in temperate language and are not exaggerated or incorrect.

2. **Journalistic Impropriety**

Some of the principles evolved by the Council through its adjudications in respect of journalistic impropriety are:

a. Any matter discussed or disclosed in confidence ought not to be published without obtaining the consent of the source. If the editor finds that the publication is in the public interest, he should clarify it in an appropriate footnote that the statement or discussion in question was being published although it had been made 'off the record'.
b. An advertisement containing anything unlawful or illegal, or the one which is contrary to good taste or journalistic ethics or propriety should not be published.
c. Proper care should be taken by newspapers in maintaining accuracy in respect of quotations.

When a newspaper is charged with violation of journalistic ethics, a plea that it has ceased publication will afford the editor no defence, since it is his conduct which is subject of the complaint.

3. **Obscenity and Bad Taste**

The meaning of taste varies according to the context. For a journalist it implies that 'which on grounds of decency or propriety he should not publish'. Where a matter has 'a tendency to stimulate sex feelings' its publication in a journal meant for the lay public, young or old, undesirable. Exploitation of sex falls short good taste. Public taste is to be judged in relation to the environment, milieu as well notions of taste prevailing in contemporary society.

The basic test of obscenity is whether the matter is so gross or vulgar that it is likely to deprave or corrupt. Another test is whether depiction of the scene and language used can be regarded as filthy, repulsive, dirty or lewd.

Whether a story is obscene or not, will depend on such factors as literary or cultural nature of the magazine, and the social theme of the story. The relevancy of a picture to the subject matter of a magazine or a paper has a bearing on the question whether the matter published falls below the standards of public taste. One of the relevant factors for judging whether the picture falls below the standard of public taste will be the purpose or nature of the magazine – whether it relates to art, painting, medicine, research or reform of sex.

The Press Council expressed concern over the increasing instances of obscene advertisements in the print media. It was opposed to censorship but favoured preventive steps to check any obscene material at pre-publication stage. Since most of such advertisements are routed through advertising agencies, the Council felt that this task should not be difficult if these agencies were to exercise more caution and restrain in preparing and releasing the advertisements that may be considered objectionable to family viewing by an average citizen. It felt that the Association of Advertising Agencies of India as an Umbrella organisation of all these advertising agencies could play a very meaningful and positive role in the matter and sought its cooperation to contain advertisements that are likely to damage the socio-cultural ethos of the country in the longer run. The Council appealed to the newspapers also to carefully scrutinise the advertisements received by them either directly from the advertisers or through the advertising agencies and exercise a self-restraint by rejecting such advertisements as may be considered obscene and objectionable. It has also reiterated the following guidelines framed by it to counter against obscene publication.

'Newspapers shall not display advertisements which are vulgar or which through depiction of a woman in nude or lewd posture, provoke lecherous attention of males as if she herself was commercial commodity for sale'.

Whether a picture is obscene or not, is to be judged in relation to three tests; namely

(i) Is it vulgar and indecent?
(ii) Is it a piece of mere pornography?
(iii) Is its publication meant merely to make money by titillating the sex feeling of adolescents and among whom it is intended to circulate? In other words, does it constitute an unwholesome exploitation for commercial gain.

Other relevant considerations are whether the picture is relevant to the subject matter of the magazine. That is to say, whether its publication serves any preponderating social or public purpose, in relation to art, painting, medicine, research or reform of sex.

4. **Right of Reply**

The prime principle that emanates from the various adjudications on this subject upholds the editors discretion in publication of letters. He would, however, be expected to voluntarily rectify an incorrect statement or report on a matter of public nature; the general reader can claim a locus standi on the basis of the public right to know. Besides, any person who has been specifically referred to in a publication can claim an automatic right to reply in the columns of the paper. Though the Council does not have the power to force a newspaper to publish a rejoinder it may direct it to publish the particulars of the inquiry against it.

5. **Pre-verification of News**

Verification of news is necessary before publication, especially when the report has slanderous or libellous overtones or could lead to communal tension; nor can the publication of rumours as views of a cross-section of people be justified under any circumstances. The editor shall make necessary amends when any false or distorted publication is brought to his notice.

6. **Defamation – Scurrilous writings**
Under the second exception to Section 499 of the Indian Penal Code, it is not defamation to express in good faith any opinion whatever respecting the conduct of a public servant in the discharge of his public functions, or respecting his character, so far as his character appears in that conduct, and no further. The Council has accordingly held the opinion that fair comments on the public life cannot be held to be improper. But if any factual statements are made, they must be true and correct. In case a defamatory element is involved, more good faith will not be a defence in any civil action for damages.

7. **Right to privacy v. Public figures**
The Press Council of India formulated guidelines to achieve a balance between the right to privacy of the public persons and the right of the press to have access to information of public interest and importance. The issue under heated debate at both national and international level and the international conference of the World Association of Press Councils (WAPC) held in April 1998 in Delhi, stressed that there is a need for reconciliation between three competing constitutional values at play on this count, namely: (a) an individual's right to privacy, (b) freedom of the press, and (c) the people's right to know about public figures in public interest.

The Council has prepared a report on the issue and framed the guidelines as follows:

'Right to privacy is an inviolable human right. However, the degree of privacy differs from person to person and from situation to situation. The public person who functions under public gaze as an emissary/representative of the public cannot expect to be afforded the same degree of privacy as a private person. His acts and conduct are of public interest ('public interest' being distinct and separate from 'of interest to the public') even if conducted in private may be brought to public knowledge through the medium of the press. The press has, however, a corresponding duty to ensure that the information about such acts and conduct of public interest of the public person is obtained through fair means, is properly verified and then reported accurately. For obtaining the information in respect of acts done or conducted away from public gaze, the press is not expected to use surveillance devices. For obtaining information about private talks and discussions, while the press is expected not to badger the public persons, the public persons are also expected to bring more openness in their functioning and co-operate with the press in its duty of informing the public about the acts of their representatives'.

B. Freedom of the Press

1. **Threats to Press Freedom**
   - An attack on a paper or those connected with it editorially or in management with a view to pressurising or intimidating them for the opinion expressed in the paper, constitutes a gross interference with the freedom of the Press (case of Malayala Manorama, PCI Review, Jan 1983 p. 62).

- Tendencies to coerce newspapers to desist from publishing facts or toe a particular line are matters of concern. (Case of Malayala Manorama, PCI Annual Report 1968, p. 38)
- The local administration is expected to help the journalist to perform his duties without being under duress or pressure (case of Blitz, PCI Review April 1984, p. 30)
- Implication of an editor of a newspaper in a fabricated case by the police authorities with a view to harassing him for his treatment of the news or critical writings amounts to interference in the freedom of the Press. (Case of Mahajati, PCI Review October 1983, p. 55)
- Groups raids on newspaper offices by unruly mobs interferes with the freedom of the press. Suitable precautionary protective measures ought to be taken by the police. The same applies to the blockade of newspapers offices. (Suo motu action by the Press Council against the Government of Karnataka, PCI Review April 1982, p. 36)
- Harassment and victimisation of journalists by police is a direct attack on the freedom of the Press. (Case of Madhya Pradesh Small Newspapers' Association, PCI Annual Report 1972, p. 66)
- Seizure of camera and removal of film by police from a press photographer while covering the news would amount to preventing the journalist from performing his duties and is a matter to be viewed seriously. (Case of Searchlight, PCI Annual Report 1972, p. 65)
- Filing of motivated frivolous cases against a journalist would amount to interfering with his functions. (Case of Malayala Manorama, PCI Annual Report, 1968, p. 38 and PCI Annual Report 1967, p. 52-58)
- Any attempt by a minister to browbeat a reporter into toeing his line in the matter of reporting would be inconsistent with maintaining the proper standards of ministerial conduct towards the Press. (Case of Dainik Janambhumi, PCI Annual Report 1980, p. 56)
- Disaccreditation and withdrawal of housing facilities from a newspaper correspondent because of articles/news items written by him would amount to an attempt to pressurise the correspondent and, therefore, the press. (Case of Chandigarh Union of Journalists, PCI Annual Report, 1974, p. 68)
- The Press and Registration of Books Act, 1867, does not empower the District Magistrate to obtain 'Assurance Letters' from prospective editors before granting or refusing a declaration. (Case of U.P. Small and Medium Newspapers Editors' Council, PCI Review, Jan. 1983, p. 58)
- Declaration of newspapers under the Press and Registration of Books Act, 1867, cannot be cancelled on the ground that the newspapers concerned were indulging in yellow journalism. Any complaint in regard to yellow journalism should be filed with the Press Council (Suo Motu action by the Press Council, PCI Annual Report 1983, p. 37)
- Closeness of the date of appearance of a critical article and the date of disaccreditation would be material factors determining whether the disaccreditation was on account of that article. (Case of Sarita, Mukta etc., PCI Annual Report 1981 p. 60)

2. **Advertisement and Press Freedom**
   - The giving or withholding of advertisements, whether by individuals or by the government as a lever to influence the editorial policy constitutes a threat to and

jeopardises the liberty of the Press or the freedom of the editor. This is especially so in the case of the government since it is the trustee of public funds and, therefore, bound to utilise them without discrimination. (Case of Tribune, PCI Annual Report 1970, p. 45)

- Advertisements, from any party including the government cannot be claimed as a matter of right by a newspaper. Government can frame its policy of placing advertisements based on objective criteria. But this should be based upon publicly stated principles without taking into consideration the editorial policy of the paper. (Cases of Saptahik Mujahid, PCI Review July 1983, p. 44, and Tribune, PCI Annual Report 1970, p. 45)
- If an editor is guilty of an action or an impropriety de hors his paper, he can be proceeded against personally but this would not justify denial of advertisements to the paper of which he happens to be the editor. This applies to an employee or even the proprietor of a newspaper. (Case of Searchlight and Pradeep, PCI Annual Report 1974, p. 11)
- The outside activities of the editor or other journalists might throw light on what he wrote for the paper, and in the event of such writings being improper, action against the paper is justified. However, this is for improper publication and for the employees' activities de hors the paper. (Ibid)

3. **Impropriety and Press Freedom**

- It is improper to offer an inducement to a journalist to adopt a particular line of comment, and for the journalist to accept such an inducement. In the event of improper inducement being offered by the government the situation would be worse, since, then the media would become an arm of law enforcement. (Ibid)
- It is improper for a journalist to accept an assignment which would be incompatible with the integrity and dignity of his profession or exploitation of his status as journalist. (Ibid)
- The editor of a newspaper cannot be asked to divulge the source of information of a letter published in his paper. (Case of Arjun Baan, PCI Review, July 1983, p. 53)
- Asking a journalist to divulge his personal and confidential source of information amounts to violation of his obligation to report on events of public interest and constitutes a threat to Press freedom. (Case of Press Correspondent, Hind Samachar, PCI Annual Report 1973, p. 27)
- The editor of a newspaper cannot be directed by the police to alert his correspondent against the publication of a news item relating to the acts of the police, as it would be against the fundamental right of the Press. (Case of Vishwa Manav, PCI Review, October 1983, p. 52)
- The motivated stoppage of subscription of teleprinter service of a news agency due to the feeling that reportage of a certain situation was exaggerated and to pressurise the agency would amount a threat to the freedom of the press. (Case of ex-Member of Parliament, PCI Annual Report 1972, p. 7)
- Singling out news despatches to a newspaper and arrest of editors for activities in discharge of their professional duties and issue of warning letter from the government to newspapers to desist from publishing anything relating to certain activities of some groups, could legitimately give rise to an apprehension of threat to the

freedom of the Press. (Suo motu action by the Press Council, PCI Review April 1983, p. 52)

Recent Initiatives:

1. **Paid News**
The Press Council of India (PCI) defines paid news as any news or analysis appearing in print or electronic media for consideration in cash or kind. The PCI had sought amendment in the Press Council Act, 1978, to make its directions binding on government authorities and bring the electronic media under its purview.
The recommendations of PCI were as follows:
Representation of the People Act, 1951 should be amended to make incidence of paid news a punishable electoral malpractice.
The Press Council of India must be fully empowered to adjudicate the complaints of 'paid news' and give final judgment in the matter.
Press Council Act be amended to make its recommendations binding and electronic media be brought under its purview, and Press Council of India should be reconstituted to include representatives from electronic and other media.
2. Press Council of India has sought a status report from the Kerala High Court regarding the restrictions imposed on media in reporting court proceedings and denial of entry to media personnel to various courts in the state, including the high court. The Council's secretary issued a letter to the registrar general of the High Court and the chief secretary of the state that stated, 'Since the matter prima facie concern free functioning of the press and the statute amandates the Press Council to preserve the freedom of the Press, I have been directed by Hon'ble Chairman to seek information in this regard.
3. Press Council of India to ink alliance with South Asian media councils. The alliance would be in a bid to promote peace and fair and fearless journalism. The alliance will be headquartered in New Delhi and will soon be extended to South East Asia and other regions of the sub-continent. 'This alliance will aim to promote best and ethical journalism practice, will have shared programmes between journalists of various countries among other things. It is still at a nascent stage and we will decide on the final constitution after our meetings'.

8.4.29 Pension Fund Regulatory and Development Authority

The Pension Fund Regulatory & Development Authority (PFRDA) Act was passed on 19th September, 2013 and the same was notified on 1st February, 2014. PFRDA is regulating NPS, subscribed by employees of Govt. of India, state governments and by employees of private institutions/organisations and unorganised sectors. The PFRDA is ensuring the orderly growth and development of pension market.

The Government of India had, in the year 1999, commissioned a national project titled 'OASIS' (an acronym for old age social and income security) to examine policy related to old age income security in India. Based on the recommendations of the OASIS report, Government of India introduced a new Defined Contribution Pension System for the new entrants to Central/State Government service, except Armed Forces, replacing the existing system of Defined Benefit Pension System. On 23rd August, 2003, PFRDA was established through a resolution by the Government of India to promote, develop and regulate pension sector in India. The contributory pension system was notified by the Government of India on 22nd December, 2003, now named the National Pension System (NPS) with effect from the 1st January, 2004. The NPS was subsequently extended to all citizens of the country from 1st May, 2009 including self-employed professionals and others in the unorganised sector on a voluntary basis.

Vision Statement
To be a model Regulator for promotion and development of an organised pension system to serve the old-age income needs of people on a sustainable basis.

Act
PFRDA Act 2013

Authority
The authority consists of the following Members:

a. a Chairperson
b. three whole-time members
c. three part-time members

All these members are to be appointed by the Central Government from amongst persons of ability, integrity and standing and having knowledge and experience in economics or finance or law with at least one person from each discipline.

Powers and Functions
The powers and functions of the Authority include

- Regulating the National Pension System and the pension schemes to which this Act applies.
- Approving the schemes, the terms and conditions thereof and laying down norms for the management of the corpus of the pension funds, including investment guidelines under such schemes
- registering and regulating intermediaries
- issuing to an intermediary, on application, a certificate of registration and renewing, modifying, withdrawing, suspending or cancelling such registration
- protecting the interests of subscribers by
  a. ensuring safety of the contribution of subscribers to various schemes of pension funds to which this act applies
  b. ensuring that the intermediation and other operational costs under the National Pension System are economical and reasonable
- establishing mechanism for redressal of grievances of subscribers to be determined by regulations
- promoting professional organisations connected with the pension system
- adjudication of disputes between intermediaries and between intermediaries and subscribers
- collecting data and requiring the intermediaries to collect such data and undertaking and commissioning studies, research and projects
- the powers and functions of the authority shall include

- undertaking steps for educating subscribers and the general public on issues
- relating to pension, retirement savings and related issues and training of intermediaries
- standardising dissemination of information about performance of pension
- funds and performance benchmarks
- regulating the regulated assets
- levying fees or other charges for carrying out the purposes of this act
- specifying by regulations the form and manner in which books of account shall be maintained and statement of accounts shall be rendered by intermediaries.
- calling for information from undertaking inspection of, conducting inquiries and investigations including audit of, intermediaries and other entities or organisations connected with pension funds

National Pension Scheme

National Pension System (NPS) which is administered and regulated by Pension Fund Regulatory and Development Authority (PFRDA) was created by an Act of Parliament.

National Pension System (NPS) is a voluntary, defined contribution retirement savings scheme designed to enable the subscribers to make optimum decisions regarding their future through systematic savings during their working life. NPS seeks to inculcate the habit of saving for retirement amongst the citizens. It is an attempt towards finding a sustainable solution to the problem of providing adequate retirement income to every citizen of India.

Under the NPS, individual savings are pooled in to a pension fund which are invested by PFRDA regulated professional fund managers as per the approved investment guidelines in to the diversified portfolios comprising of government bonds, bills, corporate debentures and shares. These contributions would grow and accumulate over the years, depending on the returns earned on the investment made.

At the time of normal exit from NPS, the subscribers may use the accumulated pension wealth under the scheme to purchase a life annuity from a PFRDA empanelled life insurance company apart from withdrawing a part of the accumulated pension wealth as lump-sum, if they choose so.

The scheme is structured into two tiers:

Tier-I account: This is the non-withdrawable permanent retirement account into which the accumulations are deposited and invested as per the option of the subscriber.

Tier-II account: This is a voluntary withdrawable account which is allowed only when there is an active Tier I account in the name of the subscriber. The withdrawals are permitted from this account as per the needs of the subscriber as and when claimed.

Atal Pension Yojana

Atal Pension Yojana (APY) is open to all bank account holders. The Central Government would also co-contribute 50% of the total contribution or ₹1000 per annum, whichever is lower, to each eligible subscriber, for a period of 5 years, that is, from financial Year 2015– 2016 to 2019–2020, who join the APY before 31st December, 2015, and who are not members of any statutory social security scheme and who are not income tax payers. Therefore, APY will be focussed on all citizens in the unorganised sector.

Eligibility for joining APY: APY is open to all citizens of India who have a savings bank account. The minimum age of joining APY is 18 years and maximum age is 40 years.

Recent initiatives by PFRDA

1. **PFRDA bars third party payments in Tier II accounts of NPS**
   To check misuse of NPS, regulator PFRDA has said contribution to savings account (also called Tier-II account), which is attached to pension funds, can only be made by the subscriber and not by any third party.

   National Pension System (NPS) is structured into Tier-I (main pension account) and Tier-II (voluntary savings account).

   'Keeping in view the nature of the Tier-II account and facility of any time withdrawal, it has been decided to disallow any third party contribution in Tier-II account henceforth,' Pension Fund Regulatory and Development Authority (PFRDA) said in a circular.

   It has asked the nodal offices and Points of Presence (POPs) to ensure that NPS contribution by the subscriber to the NPS Tier-II account 'is being made from his/her own bank account' and through own legitimate source of funds.

   Further, Central Record Keeping Agency and nodal officers/POPs have been asked to take a declaration from subscriber .

2. **PFRDA smoothens the process of registration of retirement advisers; Process of submitting application transformed from physical mode to online mode.**
   In order to smoothen the process of registration of retirement advisers, Pension Fund Regulatory and Development Authority (PFRDA) has transformed the process of submitting application from physical mode to online mode.

   The applicants can now submit their application online and upload scanned images of all the required documents. This will reduce the application processing time. PFRDA is registering retirement advisers for widening the coverage of NPS by facilitating on boarding of the subscribers and also providing advisory services to them for allocating assets under NPS and choosing pension fund managers.

   'Retirement Adviser' can be any individual, registered partnership firm, body corporate, or any registered trust or society, which desires to engage in the activity of providing advice on National Pension System or other pension schemes regulated by PFRDA to prospects/existing subscribers or other persons or group of persons and is registered as such under the PFRDA (Retirement Advisers) Regulations.

   NISM and FPSB India are providing necessary certification in order to become eligible for registration as Retirement Adviser. However, Investment Advisers registered with SEBI are exempted from the requirement of such certifications and they can directly submit their application to PFRDA for registration.

8.4.30 Petroleum and Natural Gas Regulatory Board

The Petroleum and Natural Gas Regulatory Board (PNGRB) was constituted under The Petroleum and Natural Gas Regulatory Board Act, 2006 (NO. 19 OF 2006) notified via Gazette Notification dated 31st March, 2006.

The Act provide for the establishment of Petroleum and Natural Gas Regulatory Board to protect the interests of consumers and entities engaged in specified activities relating to petroleum, petroleum products and natural gas and to promote competitive markets and for matters connected therewith or incidental thereto.

Further as enshrined in the act, the board has also been mandated to regulate the refining, processing, storage, transportation, distribution, marketing and sale of petroleum, petroleum products and natural gas excluding production of crude oil and natural gas so as and to ensure uninterrupted and adequate supply of petroleum, petroleum products and natural gas in all parts of the country.

Vision of PNGRB

'To create a vibrant energy market with rapid and orderly growth through facilitation of flow of investments into the basic infrastructure for efficient transportation and distribution of petroleum, petroleum products and natural gas at minimum cost and high level of protection of consumer interests through fair trade practices and competition amongst the entities so as to ensure the enhanced competitiveness of Indian economy and customer satisfaction'.

Functions of Board

The Board shall

1. protect the interest of consumers by fostering fair trade and competition amongst the entities
2. register entities to
   - market notified petroleum and petroleum products and, subject to the contractual obligations of the Central Government, natural gas
   - establish and operate liquefied natural gas terminals
   - establish storage facilities for petroleum, petroleum products or natural gas exceeding such capacity as may be specified by regulations
3. Authorise entities to
   - lay, build, operate or expand a common carrier or contract carrier
   - lay, build, operate or expand city or local natural gas distribution network
4. declare pipelines as common carrier or contract carrier
5. regulate, by regulations,
   - access to common carrier or contract carrier so as to ensure fair trade and competition amongst entities and for that purpose specify pipeline access code
   - transportation rates for common carrier or contract carrier
   - access to city or local natural gas distribution network so as to ensure fair trade and competition amongst entities as per pipeline access code
6. in respect of notified petroleum, petroleum products and natural gas-
   - ensure adequate availability
   - ensure display of information about the maximum retail prices fixed by the entity for consumers at retail outlets
   - monitor prices and take corrective measures to prevent restrictive trade practice by the entities
   - secure equitable distribution for petroleum and petroleum products
   - provide, by regulations, and enforce, retail service obligations for retail outlets and marketing service obligations for entities
   - monitor transportation rates and take corrective action to prevent restrictive trade practice by the entities
7. levy fees and other charges as determined by regulations
8. maintain a data bank of information on activities relating to petroleum, petroleum products and natural gas

9. lay down, by regulations, the technical standards and specifications including safety standards in activities relating to petroleum, petroleum products and natural gas, including the construction and operation of pipeline and infrastructure projects related to downstream petroleum and natural gas sector
10. perform such other functions as may be entrusted to it by the Central Government to carry out the provisions of this Act.
11. determination of marketing margin letter

Powers regarding complaints and resolutions of disputes by the Board

a. The Board shall have jurisdiction to
   1. adjudicate upon and decide any dispute or matter arising amongst entities or between an entity and any other person on issues relating to refining, processing, storage, transportation, distribution, marketing and sale of petroleum, petroleum products and natural gas according to the provisions of Chapter V, unless the parties have agreed for arbitration
   2. receive any complaint from any person and conduct any inquiry and investigation connected with the activities relating to petroleum, petroleum products and natural gas on contravention of-
      - retail service obligations
      - marketing service obligations
      - display of retail price at retail outlets
      - terms and conditions subject to which a pipeline has been declared as common carrier or contract carrier or access for other entities was allowed to a city or local natural gas distribution network, or authorisation has been granted to an entity for laying, building, expanding or operating a pipeline as common carrier or contract carrier or authorisation has been granted to an entity for laying, building, expanding or operating a city or local natural gas distribution network
      - any other provision of this Act or the rules or the regulations or orders made there under

b. While deciding a complaint under sub-section (1), the Board may pass such orders and issue such directions as it deems fit or refer the matter for investigation according to the provisions of Chapter V.

Issues

1. **Ministry to revamp oil and gas regulatory board to minimise conflict**
   The government may issue directives to the Petroleum and Natural Gas Regulatory Board for minimising conflicts and also 'streamline the working' of the regulator.

   A senior official said that the functioning of the PNGRB will continue to be as per the existing PNGRB Act and that the government will restructure the regulator's working and clearly define powers.

   Another official added that the government will be 'looking at working more closely with the PNGRB to streamline its role in consonance with the government's vision'.

   PNGRB ran into trouble with the Ministry and Indraprastha Gas Ltd after the regulator had attempted to fix retail price of compressed natural gas and piped natural gas. A July 2015 Supreme Court verdict put this controversy to rest and noted that the power to fix tariff was not vested with the board.

A PNGRB official said that the government will soon come up with a notification vesting the regulator with penal powers in consonance with the Supreme Court's verdict.

Changing Stance

The regulator's change in stance is evident as it has now withdrawn its objections to the Jagdishpur-Haldia/Bokaro-Dhamra gas pipeline. In November last year, the regulator had locked horns with the government when it red-flagged a portion of GAIL (India) Ltd's pipeline.

PNGRB had opposed the Centre's order to grant GAIL the rights to develop the eastern gas grid by avoiding the competitive bidding route. PNGRB had said that such authorisation would need an amendment of Section 42 of the PNGRB Act, as it contradicted the objectives of regulation and infringed upon the regulator's autonomy.

The regulator has now accepted that the Bokaro/Dhamra section is an extension of the Jagdishpur-Haldia pipeline and would not be requiring its approval as the project was conceived before the regulator was instituted.

According to the PNGRB Act, pipeline networks conceived and approved before the regulator was instituted in 2006 are exempted from the framed rules.

There is only one board member left within the PNGRB Board, resulting in a lack of quorum hampering the working of the institution. In the absence of a Member (Legal), the Board has been unable to suitably reply to judicial queries, according to a PNGRB official.

8.4.31 Reserve Bank of India

History

The Reserve Bank of India is the central bank of the country. Central banks are a relatively recent innovation and most central banks, as we know them today, were established around the early twentieth century.

The Reserve Bank of India was set up on the basis of the recommendations of the Hilton Young Commission. The Reserve Bank of India Act, 1934 (II of 1934) provides the statutory basis of the functioning of the Bank, which commenced operations on 1st April, 1935.

The Bank was constituted to

* regulate the issue of banknotes
* maintain reserves with a view to securing monetary stability
* operate the credit and currency system of the country to its advantage

The Bank began its operations by taking over from the Government the functions so far being performed by the Controller of Currency and from the Imperial Bank of India, the management of Government accounts and public debt. The existing currency offices at Calcutta, Bombay, Madras, Rangoon, Karachi, Lahore and Cawnpore (Kanpur) became branches of the Issue Department. Offices of the Banking Department were established in Calcutta, Bombay, Madras, Delhi and Rangoon.

Burma (Myanmar) seceded from the Indian Union in 1937 but the Reserve Bank continued to act as the Central Bank for Burma till Japanese occupation of Burma and later up to April, 1947. After the partition of India, the Reserve Bank served as the central bank of Pakistan up to June 1948 when the State Bank of Pakistan commenced operations. The Bank, which was originally set up as a shareholder's bank, was nationalised in 1949.

An interesting feature of the Reserve Bank of India was that at its very inception, the Bank was seen as playing a special role in the context of development, especially agriculture. When

India commenced its plan endeavours, the development role of the Bank came into focus, especially in the 60s when the Reserve Bank, in many ways, pioneered the concept and practise of using finance to catalyse development. The Bank was also instrumental in institutional development and helped set up institutions like the Deposit Insurance and Credit Guarantee Corporation of India, the Unit Trust of India, the Industrial Development Bank of India, the National Bank of Agriculture and Rural Development, the Discount and Finance House of India etc. to build the financial infrastructure of the country.

With liberalisation, the Bank's focus shifted back to core central banking functions like Monetary Policy, Bank Supervision and Regulation, and Overseeing the Payments System and onto developing the financial markets.

Establishment

The Reserve Bank of India was established on April 1, 1935 in accordance with the provisions of the Reserve Bank of India Act, 1934.

The Central Office of the Reserve Bank was initially established in Calcutta but was permanently moved to Mumbai in 1937. The Central Office is where the Governor sits and where policies are formulated.

Though originally privately owned, since nationalisation in 1949, the Reserve Bank is fully owned by the Government of India.

Preamble

The Preamble of the Reserve Bank of India describes the basic functions of the Reserve Bank as:

'...to regulate the issue of Bank Notes and keeping of reserves with a view to securing monetary stability in India and generally to operate the currency and credit system of the country to its advantage'.

Central Board

The Reserve Bank's affairs are governed by a central board of directors. The board is appointed by the Government of India in keeping with the Reserve Bank of India Act, appointed/nominated for a period of four years

Constitution

Official Directors

Full-time : Governor and not more than four Deputy Governors

Non-Official Directors

Nominated by Government: ten Directors from various fields and two government Official

Others: four Directors: one each from four local boards

Legal Framework

1. Acts administered by Reserve Bank of India
   Reserve Bank of India Act, 1934
   Public Debt Act, 1944/Government Securities Act, 2006
   Government Securities Regulations, 2007
   Banking Regulation Act, 1949
   Foreign Exchange Management Act, 1999

Securitisation and Reconstruction of Financial Assets and Enforcement of Security Interest Act, 2002 (Chapter II)
Credit Information Companies(Regulation) Act, 2005
Payment and Settlement Systems Act, 2007
Payment and Settlement Systems Regulations, 2008 and Amended up to 2011 and BPSS Regulations, 2008
The Payment and Settlement Systems (Amendment) Act, 2015 - No. 18 of 2015
Factoring Regulation Act, 2011

2. Other relevant Acts are
Negotiable Instruments Act, 1881
Bankers' Books Evidence Act, 1891
State Bank of India Act, 1955
Companies Act, 1956/ Companies Act, 2013
Securities Contract (Regulation) Act, 1956
State Bank of India Subsidiary Banks) Act, 1959
Deposit Insurance and Credit Guarantee Corporation Act, 1961
Banking Companies (Acquisition and Transfer of Undertakings) Act, 1970
Regional Rural Banks Act, 1976
Banking Companies (Acquisition and Transfer of Undertakings) Act, 1980
National Bank for Agriculture and Rural Development Act, 1981
National Housing Bank Act, 1987
Recovery of Debts Due to Banks and Financial Institutions Act, 1993
Competition Act, 2002
Indian Coinage Act, 2011: Governs currency and coins
Banking Secrecy Act
The Industrial Development Bank (Transfer of Undertaking and Repeal) Act, 2003
The Industrial Finance Corporation (Transfer of Undertaking and Repeal) Act, 1993

Main Functions

1. **Monetary authority**
Formulates, implements and monitors the monetary policy.
Objective: maintaining price stability and ensuring adequate flow of credit to productive sectors.

2. **Regulator and supervisor of the financial system**
Prescribes broad parameters of banking operations within which the country's banking and financial system functions.
Objective: maintain public confidence in the system, protect depositors' interest and provide cost-effective banking services to the public.

3. **Manager of foreign exchange**
Manages the Foreign Exchange Management Act, 1999.
Objective: to facilitate external trade and payment and promote orderly development and maintenance of foreign exchange market in India.

4. **Issuer of currency**
Issues and exchanges or destroys currency and coins not fit for circulation.

Objective: to give the public adequate quantity of supplies of currency notes and coins and in good quality.

5. **Developmental role**
   Performs a wide range of promotional functions to support national objectives.
6. **Related Functions**
   Banker to the Government: performs merchant banking function for the central and the state governments; also acts as their banker.
   Banker to banks: maintains banking accounts of all scheduled banks.

Organisation Structure

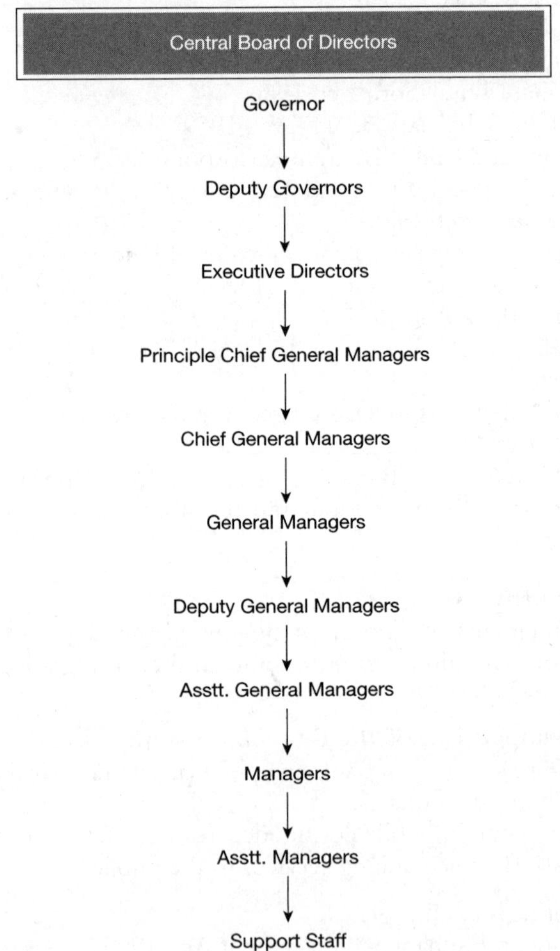

Recent RBI related updates:
Demonitisation:
The legal tender character of the bank notes in denominations of ≠ 500 and ≠ 1000 issued by the Reserve Bank of India till November 8, 2016 (hereinafter referred to as Specified Bank

Notes) stands withdrawn. In consequence thereof these Bank Notes cannot be used for transacting business and/or store of value for future usage. The Specified Bank Notes (SBNs) were allowed to be exchanged for value at RBI Offices till December 30, 2016 and till November 25, 2016 at bank branches/Post Offices and deposited at any of the bank branches of commercial banks/Regional Rural Banks/Co-operative banks (only Urban Co-operative Banks and State Co-operative Banks) or at any Head Post Office or Sub-Post Office during the period from November 10, 2016 to December 30, 2016.

Impact of demonitisation observed by RBI

The impact of demonetisation on the various segments of the financial market has varied. Overnight call money market rate remained within the policy corridor, but with a softening bias due to surplus liquidity at banks. After initial softening, G-sec yields increased significantly on two occasions, that is, after the announcement of application of incremental cash reserve ratio (ICRR) and the status quo in monetary policy in December 2016. Thereafter, yields have moved in either direction on account of both domestic and external factors, including the change in monetary policy stance in February 2017, which was largely not expected by market participants. Reflecting the expected slowdown in sales and earnings, share prices of cash intensive sectors such as automobiles, FMCG, consumer durables and real estate declined sharply in November–December 2016. Most of these sectors have more than recovered the lost ground subsequently. In fact, the consumer durable sector outperformed the overall increase in the stock market post-demonetisation. The impact on the forex market was transitory.

Demonetisation has impacted some segments of the export sector such as readymade garments, gems and jewellery. The impact, however, was transitory. Imports of gold increased sharply in November, but moderated in December. There has been a significant improvement in the use of digital modes of payments post demonetisation, although their base is still small. Overall, demonetisation has had some negative macroeconomic impact, which, however, has been transient as remonetisation has moved at an accelerated pace in last twelve weeks. More importantly, demonetisation is expected to have a positive impact over the medium to long-term. In particular, there is expected to be greater formalisation of the economy with increased use of digital payments. The reduced use of cash will also lead to 44 greater intermediation by the formal financial sector of the economy, which should, inter alia, help improve monetary transmission.

Specified Bank Notes (Cessation of Liabilities) Act 2017

On February 27, 2017 Government of India notified the Specified Banknotes (Cessation of liabilities) Act 2017. The Act repealed the Specified Banknotes (Cessation of liabilities) Ordinance 2016 providing for cessation of liabilities for the Specified Banknotes (SBNs) and for matters connected therewith and incidental thereto, with effect from 31st December, 2016. The SBNs cease to be the liabilities of the Reserve Bank under Section 34 of the RBI Act and cease to have the guarantee of the Central Government.

A grace period has been provided during which the Specified Bank Notes can be deposited at five RBI Offices (Mumbai, New Delhi, Chennai, Kolkata, and Nagpur) by Indian citizens who make a declaration that they were outside India between November 9 and December 30, 2016, subject to conditions or any class of persons for reasons that may be specified by notification by the Central Government. The Reserve Bank, if satisfied after making the necessary verifications, that the reasons for failure to deposit the notes till 30th December, 2016 are genuine, will credit the value of notes in the KYC (Know Your Customer) compliant bank account of the tenderer.

The grace period for resident Indians expired on 31st March, 2017. For non- resident Indians (Indian passport holders), the grace period is till 30th June, 2017.

Any person aggrieved by the refusal of the Reserve Bank to credit the value of notes as mentioned above may make a representation to the Central Board of the Reserve Bank within 14 days of the communication of such refusal to him/her.

In terms of Section 6 of the Act, whoever knowingly or wilfully makes any false declaration shall be punishable with a fine which may extend to ₹50,000 or five times the amount of the face value of the SBNs tendered whichever is higher.

In terms of Section 5 of the Act, with effect from 31st December, 2016 no person shall knowingly or voluntarily hold, transfer or receive any specified banknotes. **After the expiry of grace period, holding of not more than 10 notes in total, irrespective of denomination or not more than 25 notes for the purpose of study/ research/ numismatics is permitted**. Also, nothing contained in this section shall prohibit the holding of specified banknotes by any person on the direction of a court in relation to any case pending in the court.

In terms of Section 7, contravention of Section 5 shall be punishable with fine which may extend upto ₹10,000 or five times the face value of the SBNs involved in the contravention, whichever is higher.

In case the contravention/default in terms of Sections 6 and 7 is by a company, every person who was in charge of and responsible to the company at the time of contravention/ default shall deemed to be guilty and will be liable to be proceeded against and punished. If the offence is proved to be attributable to the conduct by any director/manager/secretary/officer/ employee of the company, such person shall also be deemed to be guilty of the offence and will be liable to be proceeded against and punished accordingly.

8.4.32 Security and Exchange Board of India (SEBI)

SEBI was established in 1988 to regulate the functions of securities market, initially SEBI was not able to exercise complete control over stock market transactions. Therefore, SEBI was granted a legal status under SEBI Act, 1992.

'An act to provide for the establishment of a board to protect the interest of investors in securities and to promote the development and to regulate the securities markets and for matters connected therewith'.

It shall extend to the whole country.

Composition:

- Chairman
- Two members from amongst the officials of Union Ministry of Finance
- One member from amongst the officials of Reserve Bank
- Five other members of whom at least three shall be whole time members to be appointed by the Central Government.

Functions:

- Quasi-legislative
- Quasi-judicial
- Quasi-executive

SEBI drafts regulation in its legislature capacity. It conducts investigation and enforcement action in its executive and orders in its judicial capacity.

1. Regulating stock exchanges and other securities market.
2. Registering and regulating the working of stock brokers, sub-brokers, share transfer agents and any other intermediaries who are associated with securities markets in any manner.
3. Registering and regulating the working of depositories.
4. Registering and regulating the working of venture capital funds and collective investment schemes including mutual funds.
5. Promoting and regulating self-regulatory organisations and prohibiting fraudulent and unfair trade practices relating to securities markets.
6. Prohibiting insider trading in securities (insider is any person connected with the company such as directors, promoters, etc.)

Securities Appellate Tribunal

It is a statutory body estate under the provision of section 15k to hear and dispose of appeals against the orders passed by SEBI or by an adjucated officer. A securities appellate tribunal shall consist of presiding officer and two other members to be appointed by the Central Government.

Mergers of FMC with SEBI

In 2015, Forward Market Commission was merged with SEBI. The merger was aimed to streamline the regulations and curb wild speculations in the commodities market which facilitating further growth. The merger will increase economies of scope and economies of scale for government, exchanges, financial and stakeholders.

8.4.33 The Telecom Disputes Settlement and Appellate Tribunal (TDSAT)

The Telecom Disputes Settlement and Appellate Tribunal (TDSAT) was established to adjudicate disputes and dispose of appeals with a view to protect the interests of service providers and consumers of the telecom sector and to promote and ensure orderly growth of the telecom sector.

- Telecom Disputes Settlement Appellate Tribunal (TDSAT) was established in 2000 through an amendment of the TRAI 1997 act.
- The primary objective of TDSAT's establishment was to release TRAI from adjudicatory and dispute settlement functions in order to strengthen the regulatory framework.
- Any dispute involving parties like licensor, licensee, service provider and consumers are resolved by TDSAT. Moreover, any direction, order or decision of TRAI can be challenged by appealing in TDSAT.

Composition of the Tribunal

Since its inception, the TDSAT has only had former judges of the Supreme Court of India as the Chairperson. The Members of the Tribunal are also selected from amongst senior officers who have in-depth technical, legal and regulatory expertise and have prior high-level experience in their respective fields. The composition of the Tribunal with members possessing judicial as well as technical and administrative expertise has led to a harmony of approach and a comprehensive understanding and a balanced perspective in respect to issues dealt with by the TDSAT. This has also lent greater credibility to the Tribunal and its stature within the Indian judicial/ legal system.

An integral feature which marks TDSAT in comparison to similar bodies across various international jurisdictions is that in cases where Appeals against orders of the TRAI are heard, such orders are not automatically suspended upon being appealed. Appeals against TRAI's orders are evaluated on a case-to-case basis by the TDSAT taking into account factors such as balance of probabilities, irreparable loss/ injury to parties and a *prima facie* case. The Petitioner has to establish immediate loss etc. to seek stay / suspension of TRAI's orders. This feature harmonises the role of the regulator and the appellate authority and sets a fine balance between their powers and responsibilities.

Functioning of the Tribunal

The various functions of TDSAT (Telecom Disputes Settlement & Appellate Tribunal) are that it can adjudicate any disputes that arise between a group of consumers and service providers, a licensee and a licensor, and also between two or more than the service providers. The Government of India opened the telecom sector to the private enterprise in the 1990s and this has given a major boost to this sector. A great variety of telecom services such as voice mail, audio text services, mobile services, electronic mail, and data services are now available to the consumers. As many service providers entered the telecommunication sector in the country an appellate tribunal such as TDSAT was required to settle the disputes that arise all to often due to the intense competition in the sector.

In the TDSAT, any person, local authority, state government, or central government for the adjudication of a dispute can file cases. The power and function of Telecom Disputes Settlement & Appellate Tribunal includes that it can hear the appeal and also dispose appeals that are against any order, direction, or decision of the TRAI. The person or government authority has to file an appeal with the time period of 30 days, which is counted from the date on which they have received a copy of the order that has been made by TRAI. TDSAT (Telecom Disputes Settlement & Appellate Tribunal) may hear an appeal after the lapse of the 30-day time period if it is satisfied that there are sufficient reasons for not filing an appeal within the time period.

In TDSAT (Telecom Disputes Settlement & Appellate Tribunal), an appeal can be filed by filling up the standard application form, which is available on line in the website of the Appellate Tribunal. The Miscellaneous Application or Petition or Appeal has to be duly supported by a sworn affidavit. Once the case has been filed in the TDSAT (Telecom Disputes Settlement & Appellate Tribunal), the chairperson and the members hear it. The case can be disposed off at the very 1st hearing itself or the opposition party can be ordered to file a reply within the time period that has been fixed. When the pleadings have been completed, the case is finally heard by the TDSAT and then disposed off.

TDSAT (Telecom Disputes Settlement & Appellate Tribunal) thus, has been set up so that it can settle all kinds of disputes that arise in the telecommunications sector in India. This will help the telecommunications sector in India to grow and prosper.

RECENT NEWS

- The TDSAT direction came while hearing a petition filed by Bharti Airtel, which has moved the tribunal against TRAI's decision allowing Reliance Jio to continue with its free promotional offer beyond the stipulated 90 days, alleging that the regulator acted as 'a mute spectator' to violations.

- The telecom tribunal has struck down a ₹3500-crore spectrum contiguity levy imposed by the Department of Telecom on Sistema Shyam Teleservices Ltd, said the same rules need to be followed for all telecom operators.
- Telecom tribunal TDSAT has rejected a petition filed by Loop Telecom seeking a refund of ₹2231 crore in licence fee and interest from the government for permits which it lost in 2G spectrum case in 2012.
- The Telecom Disputes Settlement and Appellate Tribunal (TDSAT) has asked the Telecom Regulatory Authority of India (Trai) to examine if agreements drawn between broadcasters and distributors of television signals are in consonance with regulations.

8.4.34 Telecom Regulatory Authority of India (TRAI)

TRAI is a statutory body and is wholly funded by grant received from the Consolidated Fund of India. The Telecom Regulatory Authority of India (TRAI) was established with effect from 20th February, 1997 by an Act of Parliament, called the Telecom Regulatory Authority of India Act, 1997, to regulate telecom services, including fixation/revision of tariffs for telecom services which were earlier vested in the Central Government. This Act, along with the notification of the Government dated 9th January, 2004, empowers TRAI to recommend conditions for entry of new telecom service providers as well as terms and conditions of license and ensure compliance of the terms and conditions of the license.

The Act also empowers TRAI to lay down the standards of quality of service and ensure compliance, specify the tariff policy and make recommendations regarding terms and conditions on which addressable systems of TV shall be provided to the customers. TRAI's scope of work also includes issues relating to ease of access for the public to different telecom services, resolution of conflicts that may arise due to market developments and diverse network structures for various telecom services. TRAI also facilitates development of forums for interaction amongst service providers and interaction of the Authority with consumer organisations to further the consumer interest.

The entry of private service providers brought with it the inevitable need for independent regulation. TRAI's mission is to create and nurture conditions for growth of telecommunications in the country in a manner and at a pace which will enable India to play a leading role in emerging global information society.

One of the main objectives of TRAI is to provide a fair and transparent policy environment which promotes a level playing field and facilitates fair competition.

In pursuance of above objective TRAI has issued from time to time a large number of regulations, orders and directives to deal with issues coming before it and provided the required direction to the evolution of Indian telecom market from a Government owned monopoly to a multi operator multi service open competitive market.

The directions, orders and regulations issued cover a wide range of subjects including tariff, interconnection and quality of service as well as governance of the Authority.

The TRAI Act was amended by an ordinance, effective from 24th January, 2000, establishing a Telecommunications Dispute Settlement and Appellate Tribunal (TDSAT) to take over the adjudicatory and disputes functions from TRAI. TDSAT was set up to adjudicate any dispute between a licensor and a licensee, between two or more service providers, between a service provider and a group of consumers, and to hear and dispose of appeals against any direction, decision or order of TRAI.

Structure

As per the Telecom Regulatory Authority of India Act, 1997 [as amended by TRAI (Amendment) Act, 2000], the Authority shall consist of a Chairperson and not more than two whole-time Members and not more than two part-time Members. The Chairperson and other members of the Authority shall hold office for a term not exceeding three years.

The authority functions with a Secretariat headed by a Secretary and assisted by various divisional heads.

The functional divisions of TRAI are as follows:

1. Administration & Personnel Division
2. Broadcasting & Cable Services Division
3. Converged Network Division
4. Economic Division
5. Financial Analysis and Internal Finance & Accounts Division
6. Fixed Network Division
7. Legal Division
8. Mobile Network Division
9. Quality of Service Division
10. Regulatory Enforcement Division

Authority

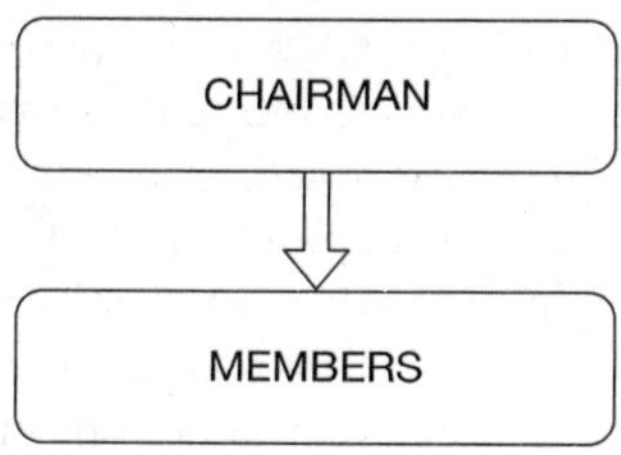

Organisational Setup

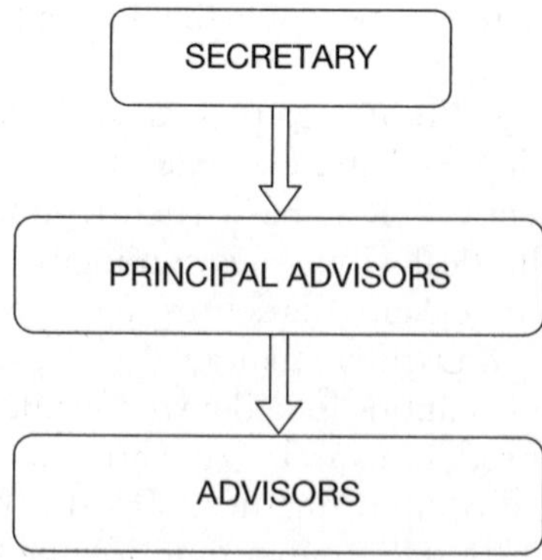

Goals and Objectives

- Transparency in decision-making by affording an opportunity to all stakeholders. Providing consumer with adequate choice, affordable tariffs and high quality of service.
- Promoting level playing field and fair competition among service providers.

- Access to world class quality telecommunications, broadcasting and cable services.
- Promoting efficiency in operations in all the tiers of the industry.
- Adoption of emerging technologies within the framework of a technology neutral policy.
- Ensuring technical compatibility and effective interconnection between service providers

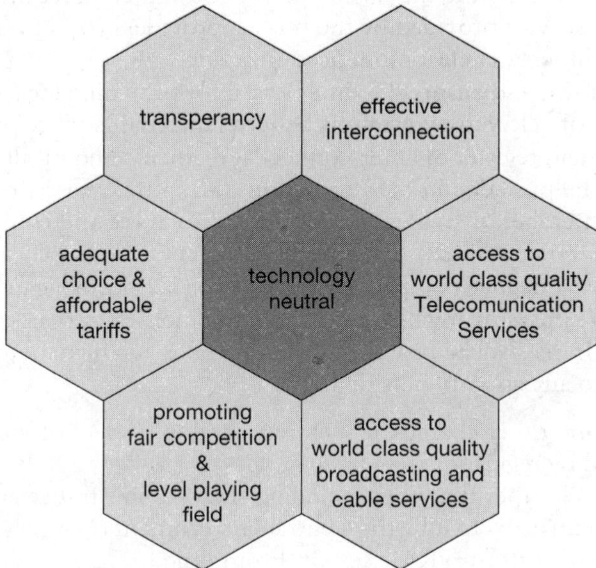

Functions

The functions of the Telecom Regulatory Authority of India are **two-fold**, one **recommendatory** and the other **mandatory** in nature. As per the provisions of the TRAI Act, 1997 the functions of the Authority shall be ----

1. a. Discharge its functions which are **recommendatory** in nature either suo motu or on request from the Government on the following matters, namely:
   (i) need and timing for introduction of new service provider.
   (ii) terms and conditions of licence to a service provider.
   (iii) revocation of license for non-compliance of terms and conditions of license.
   (iv) measures to facilitate competition and promote efficiency in the operation of telecommunication services so as to facilitate growth in such services.
   (v) technological improvement in the services provided by service providers.
   (vi) type of equipment to be used by the service provider after inspection of equipment used in the network.
   (vii) measures for the development of telecommunication technology and any other matter relatable to telecommunication industry in general.
   (viii) efficient management of available spectrum.

   b. Discharge the **mandatory** functions which include the following:
   (i) ensure compliance of terms and conditions of license.
   (ii) fix the terms and conditions of inter-connectivity between the service providers.

(iii) ensure technical compatibility and effective inter-connection between different service providers.
(iv) regulate arrangement amongst service providers for sharing of revenue from providing telecommunication services.
(v) lay-down the standards of quality of service to be provided by the service providers and ensure the quality of service and conduct the periodical survey of such service provided by the service providers so as to protect interest of the consumers of telecommunication service.
(vi) lay-down and ensure the time period for providing local and long distance circuits of telecommunications between different service providers.
(vii) maintain register of inter-connect agreements and of all such other matters as may be provided in the Regulations. Keep the register open for inspection to any member of public on payment of such fee and compliance of such other requirement as may be provided in the regulations.
(viii) ensure effective compliance of universal service obligation(USO).
(ix) notify the rates at which the telecommunication services, within India and outside India shall be provided including rates at which message shall be transmitted to any country outside India.

c. Levy fees and other charges at such rates and in respect of such services as may be determined by regulations.
d. Perform such other functions including such administrative and financial functions as may be entrusted to it by the Central Government or as may be necessary to carry out the provisions of TRAI Act. (2) From time to time, by order, notify in the Official Gazette the rates at which the telecommunication services within India and outside India shall be provided including the rates at which messages shall be transmitted to any country outside India.

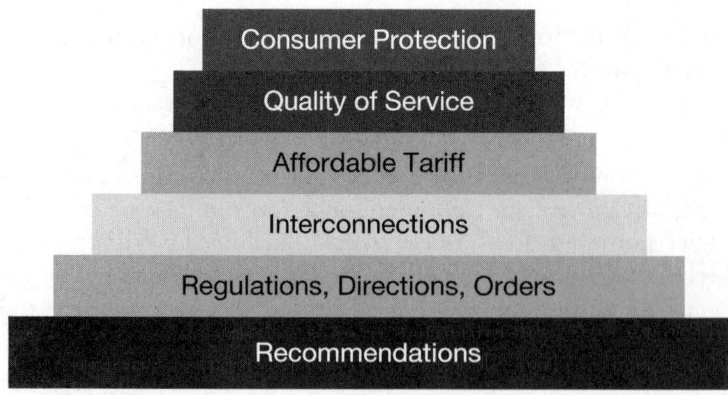

Acts & Policies
TRAI Acts & Policies

1. TRAI Act, 1997
2. The Telecom Regulatory Authority of India (Amendment) Act, 2000
3. The Telecom Regulatory Authority of India (Amendment) Act, 2014

Other Acts & Policies

Acts

1. Indian Telegraph Act,1885
2. The Indian Wireless Telegraphy Act, 1933
3. Cable Television Network Act 1995
4. Cable Television Network (Regulation) Amendment Act
5. Cable Television Network Rules 1994
6. The Cable Television Networks (Regulation) Amendment Act, 2011
7. Cable Television Networks (First Amendment) Rules, 2012
8. Cable Television Networks (Second Amendment) Rules, 2012

Policies

1. National Telecom Policy 1994
2. New Telecom Policy 1999
3. Broadband Policy 2004
4. National Telecom Policy 2012

TRAI PORTALS

TRAI Analytics Portal

It facilitates users and service providers to explore and resolve various issues in different telecom services. It has three portals for different Quality of Service parameters:

- TRAI MySpeed Portal: It facilitates users to explore the mobile data experience of customers across India. Users can submit data by downloading the app and testing their data speeds.
- TRAI Drive Test Portal: It is a portal to explore the results of independent drive tests done by TRAI.
- TRAI QoS Analysis Portal: It facilitates users to explore the call drop rate of various TSPs. Through this portal the Quality of Service performance of service providers can be identified for any specific location in India. Users can also navigate and view performance metrics from service area to district to city and finally to the BTS level.

TCCMS Portal

This portal has been developed to help the customer in processing their complaints. It facilitates customers by providing details of the complaint centre for lodging a complaint with their telecom service provider, details of the appellate authority to escalate the issue in case their complaint has not been addressed satisfactorily by the telecom service provider, view the status of a complaint already lodged, and check the status of the appeal lodged with the appellate authority.

NCCP Portal

The primary objective of the National Do Not Call Registry (NDNC Registry) is to curb Unsolicited Commercial Communication (UCC). The NDNC Registry will be a database having the list of all telephone numbers of the subscribers who do not want to receive UCC. The Telemarketer will have to verify their calling telephone numbers list with the NDNC registry before making a call.

MIS Portal

It is a web portal used to upload telco (2G, 3G, CDMA, GPRS, etc.) data by TSPs for MIS reports. Data is being uploaded by TSPs on this portal and after the verification of uploaded data by concerned division of TRAI, data is pushed to the database to generate MIS reports.

TRAI APPS

DND Services (TRAI)

DND (Do Not Disturb) Services app helps smart phone users to register their mobile number under DND to avoid Unsolicited Commercial Communication (UCC)/Telemarketing Calls/ SMS. After registration if telecom subscriber still receives any UCC via SMS or call, then this app will facilitate users to register complaint with their respective Telecom Service Provider (TSP).

MySpeed (TRAI)

This application allows you to measure your data speed experience and sends the results to TRAI. The application captures and sends coverage, data speed and other network information along with device and location of the tests. The app does not send any personal user information. All results are reported anonymously.

ISSUES

Net Neutrality

Network neutrality is a complex and controversial topic and is an important part of a free and open Internet. Enabling access, choice, and transparency of Internet offerings empowers users to benefit from full access to services, applications, and content available on the Internet. Net neutrality is the principle that individuals should be free to access all content and applications equally, regardless of the source, without Internet service providers discriminating against specific online services or websites. In other words, it is the principle that the company that connects you to the internet does not get to control what you do on the internet.

Without net neutrality rules in place, Internet service providers(ISPs) can prevent users from visiting some websites, provide slower speeds for services or even redirect users from one website to a competing website. Net neutrality rules prevent this by requiring ISPs to connect users to all lawful content on the internet equally, without giving preferential treatment to certain sites or services.

In the absence of net neutrality, companies can buy priority access to ISP customers. Larger, wealthier companies like Google or Facebook can pay ISPs to provide faster, more reliable access to their websites than to potential competitors. This could deter innovative start-up services that are unable to purchase priority access from the ISPs. Also, if ISPs can charge online services to connect to consumers, consumers would ultimately bear these additional costs

On 8th February, 2016, TRAI took a revolutionary decision, prohibiting telecom service providers from levying discriminatory rates for data, thus ruling in favour of net neutrality in India.

- No service provider can offer or charge discriminatory tariffs for data services on the basis of content.
- No service provider shall enter into any arrangement, agreement or contract, by whatever name called, with any person, natural or legal, that the effect of discriminatory tariffs for data services being offered or charged by the service provider for the purpose of evading the prohibition in this regulation.
- Reduced tariff for accessing or providing emergency services, or at times of public emergency has been permitted.
- Financial disincentives for contravention of the regulation have also been specified
- TRAI may review these regulations after a period of two years.

Call Drop

In telecommunication, the dropped-call rate (DCR) is the fraction of the telephone calls which, due to technical reasons, were cut off before the speaking parties had finished their conversational tone and before one of them had hung up (dropped calls). This fraction is usually measured as a percentage of all calls.

The main reasons for dropped calls in mobile networks are:

- Lack of radio coverage (either in the downlink or the uplink)
- Radio interference between different subscribers
- Imperfections in the functioning of the network

Telecom Regulatory Authority of India (TRAI) has sought from the government the power to levy financial penalty on operators. The TRAI wants the power to levy penalties, something which it does not have currently, as it feels it will give more teeth in terms of dealing with mobile operators.

It is not that in the past, TRAI did not collect fines from the operators for not meeting the quality of service parameters, but it was never termed as a penalty. It was called financial disincentive.

Telecom regulator launched a new portal that allows mobile users to check the level of call drops, network coverage and call quality of telecom operators across India. It is a transparency portal where consumers will get information on all parameters of quality of service (QoS) including call drops, coverage or call quality. Consumers, in a particular location, can see the number of towers around the area, see the call drop rate, and what is the performance of individual service providers on different parameters in that area.

Denying Adequate Interconnections

India's telecom regulator slapped a combined penalty of ₹3050 crore on Bharti Airtel, Vodafone India and Idea Cellular for violating licence norms by denying adequate interconnection points to Reliance Jio Infocomm and said their actions appeared to be aimed at stifling competition and were anti-consumer and against public interest. Telecom Regulatory Authority of India recommended that DoT take action against each of the three carriers, saying that violation of licence norms warranted revocation of their permits.

- TRAI recommends for 'reasonable' free mobile internet for rural areas

The telecom regulator has recommended an aggregator model and 100 MB of free data for mobile phone subscribers in rural or remote areas to help bridge the 'affordability' gap and give a thrust to the government's cashless economy agenda. The Telecom Regulatory Authority of India (TRAI) suggested that the Universal Services Obligation Fund (USOF) be used to foot the bill for providing government-incentivised free data schemes to rural subscribers.

Aadhaar-Based E-KYC Service

Communication dated 6th January, 2016 regarding adoption of Aadhaar-based e-KYC service, in order to make subscriber verification system more secure and robust, it is important that the entire process should be completely (end-to-end) technology driven, digital and paperless. Aadhaar-linked e-KYC service, provided by the Unique Identification Authority of India (UIDAI) is a fool-proof mechanism to verify the identity of the person electronically, instantaneously from the source itself. E-KYC verification will not only reduce the risk of identity fraud and document forgery but it will also make the entire process of subscriber verification paperless. Keeping in view of above, through letter dated 6th January, 2016 the Authority recommended to the DoT for acceptance and adoption of Aadhaar-based e-KYC service along with Aadhaar based e-sign as a valid alternative process to the existing process for digitally signed, biometric based verification of the new mobile subscribers.

9

Representation of People Act

LEARNING OBJECTIVES

In this Chapter, you will learn about:

- Fundamental Concepts Regarding Indian Election
- The Election Commission of India – Powers and Functions
- The Representation of People Act – An Introduction
- Background of the Representation of People's Acts
- An Overview of Representation of People's Acts 1950 and 1951
- Important Provisions of Representative of People's Acts 1950 and 1951
- Criminalisation of Politics
- Electoral Reforms
- Recent Landmark Judgments of the Supreme Court
- Q & A Regarding Elections and Process Associated with It
- Conclusion

"*The only way in which you can establish democracy by the will of the people is by the conduct of free and fair elections*"

—Former Chief Election Commissioner Shri. T.N. Seshan in his 'a heart full of burden'

9.1 FUNDAMENTAL CONCEPTS REGARDING INDIAN ELECTION

The following are the fundamental bases which are important in order to understand the electoral system in the country. The Representation of the People's Act deals with all the points mentioned in the following list, and understanding these fundamentals will better help the readers grasp its provisions.

9.1.1 Indian Election Scenario

India is a constitutional democracy with a parliamentary system of Government, and at the heart of the system is a commitment to hold regular, free and fair elections. These elections determine the composition of the Government, the membership of the two houses of Parliament, the State and Union Territory legislative assemblies, and the Presidency and Vice Presidency

Elections are conducted according to the constitutional provisions, supplemented by laws made by the Parliament. The major laws are Representation of the People Act, 1950, which mainly deals with the preparation and revision of electoral rolls; and the Representation of the People Act, 1951 which deals, in detail, with all aspects of conduct of elections and post-election disputes. The Supreme Court of India has held that where the enacted laws are silent or make insufficient provision to deal with a given situation in the conduct of elections, the Election Commission has the residuary powers under the Constitution to act in an appropriate manner.

9.1.2 Indian Elections – Scale of Operation

Elections in India are events involving political mobilisation and organisational complexity on an amazing scale. In the 2004 election to Lok Sabha there were 1351 candidates from six National parties, 801 candidates from 36 State parties, 898 candidates from officially recognised parties and 2385 independent candidates. A total number of 38,99,48,330 people voted out of total electorate size of 67,14,87,930. The Election Commission employed almost 4 million people to run the election. A vast number of civilian police and security forces were deployed to ensure that the elections were carried out peacefully.

Conduct of General elections in India for electing a new Lower House of Parliament (Lok Sabha) involves management of the largest event in the world. The electorate exceeds 670 million electors in about 7,00,000 polling stations spread across widely varying geographic and climatic zones. Polling stations are located in the snow-clad mountains in the Himalayas, the deserts of the Rajasthan and in sparsely populated islands in the Indian Ocean.

9.1.3 Constituencies and Reservation of Seats

The country has been divided into 543 parliamentary Constituencies, each of which sends one MP to the Lok Sabha, the lower house of the Parliament. The size and shape of the parliamentary constituencies are determined by an independent Delimitation Commission, which aims to create constituencies which have roughly the same population, subject to geographical considerations and the boundaries of the states and administrative areas.

9.1.4 How Constituency Boundaries are Drawn Up

Delimitation is the redrawing of the boundaries of parliamentary or assembly constituencies to make sure that there are, as near as practicable, the same number of people in each constituency. In India boundaries are meant to be examined after the ten-year census to reflect changes in population, for which Parliament by law establishes an independent Delimitation Commission, made up of the Chief Election Commissioner and two judges or ex-judges from the Supreme Court or High Court. However, under a constitutional amendment of 1976, delimitation was suspended until after the census of 2001, ostensibly so that state' family-planning programs would not affect their political representation in the Lok Sabha and Vidhan Sabhas. This has led to wide discrepancies in the size of constituencies, with the largest having over 25,00,000 electors, and the smallest less than 50,000. Delimitation exercise, with 2001 census data released on 31st December 2003, has been completed.

9.1.5 Reservation of Seats

The Constitution puts a limit on the size of the Lok Sabha of 550 elected members, apart from two members who can be nominated by the President to represent the Anglo-Indian community.

There are also provisions to ensure the representation of scheduled castes and scheduled tribes, with reserved constituencies where only candidates from these communities can stand for election.

9.1.6 System of Election

Elections to the Lok Sabha are carried out using a first-past-the-post electoral system. The country is split up into separate geographical areas, known as constituencies, and the electors can cast one vote each for a candidate (although most candidates stand as independents, most successful candidates stand as members of political parties), the winner being the candidate who gets maximum votes.

9.1.7 Parliament

The Parliament of the Union consists of the President, the Lok Sabha (House of People) and the Rajya Sabha (Council of States). The President is the head of the State, and he appoints the Prime Minister, who runs the Government, according to the political composition of the Lok Sabha. Although, the Government is headed by a Prime Minister, the Cabinet is the central decision making body of the Government. Members of more than one party can make up a Government, and although the governing parties may be a minority in the Lok Sabha, they can only govern as long as they have the confidence of a majority of MPs, the members of the Lok Sabha. As well as being the body, which determines whom, makes up the Government, the Lok Sabha is the main legislative body, along with the Rajya Sabha.

9.1.8 Rajya Sabha – The Council of the States

The members of the Rajya Sabha are elected indirectly, rather than by the citizens at large. Rajya Sabha members are elected by each State Vidhan Sabha using the single transferable vote system. Unlike most federal systems, the number of members returned by each State is roughly in proportion to their population.

At present there are 233 members of the Rajya Sabha elected by the Vidhan Sabhas, and there are also twelve members nominated by the President as representatives of literature, science, art and social services. Rajya Sabha members can serve for six years, and elections are staggered, with one third of the assembly being elected every 2 years.

9.1.9 Nominated Members

The President can nominate two members of the Lok Sabha if it is felt that the representation of the Anglo-Indian community is inadequate, and 12 members of the Rajya Sabha, to represent literature, science, art and the social services.

9.1.10 State Assemblies

India is a federal country, and the Constitution gives the States and Union Territories significant control over their own Government. The Vidhan Sabhas (legislative assemblies) are directly elected bodies set up to carry out the administration of the Government in the 28 States of India. In some States there is a bicameral organisation of legislatures, with both an Upper and Lower House. Two of the seven Union Territories viz., the National Capital Territory of Delhi and Pondicherry, also have legislative assemblies.

Elections to the Vidhan Sabhas are carried out in the same manner as for the Lok Sabha election, with the States and Union Territories divided into single-member constituencies, and the first-past-the-post electoral system used. The assemblies range in size, according to population. The largest Vidhan Sabha is for Uttar Pradesh, with 403 members; the smallest Pondicherry, with 30 members.

9.1.11 President and Vice President

The President is elected by the elected members of the Vidhan Sabha, Lok Sabha, and Rajya Sabha, and serves for a period of 5 years (although they can stand for re-election). A formula is used to allocate votes so there is a balance between the population of each State and the number of votes assembly members from a State can cast, and to give an equal balance between State Assembly members and National Parliament members. If no candidate receives a majority of votes there is a system by which losing candidates are eliminated from the contest and votes for them transferred to other candidates, until one gains a majority. The Vice President is elected by a direct vote of all members elected and nominated, of the Lok Sabha and Rajya Sabha.

9.1.12 Who Can Vote?

The democratic system in India is based on the principle of universal adult suffrage; that any citizen over the age of 18 can vote in an election (before 1989 the age limit was 21). The right to vote is irrespective of caste, creed, religion or gender. Those who are deemed unsound of mind, and people convicted of certain criminal offences are not allowed to vote.

9.1.13 The Electoral Roll

The electoral roll is a list of all people in the constituency who are registered to vote in Indian Elections. Only those people with their names on the electoral roll are allowed to vote. The electoral roll is normally revised every year to add the names of those who are to turn 18 on the 1st January of that year or have moved into a constituency and to remove the names of those who have died or moved out of a constituency.

If one is eligible to vote and is not on the electoral roll, they can apply to the Electoral Registration Officer of the constituency, who will update the register. The updation of the Electoral Roll stops only during an election campaign, after the nominations for candidates are closed.

9.1.14 Computerisation of Rolls

In 1998 the Commission took a historic decision to computerize the entire electoral rolls of 620 million voters. This work has been completed and now well-printed electoral rolls are available. The photo identity card number of the voter has also been printed in the electoral rolls, for cross linking. The printed electoral rolls as well as CDs containing these rolls are available for sale to general public. National and State parties are provided these free of cost after every revision of electoral rolls. Entire country's rolls are also available on Election Commission's website.

9.1.15 Electors' Photo Identity Cards

In an attempt to improve the accuracy of the electoral roll and prevent electoral fraud, the Election Commission ordered the making of photo identity cards for all voters in the country in August 1993. To take advantage of latest technological innovations, the Commission issues revised guidelines for EPIC Program in May 2000. More than 450 million identity cards have been distributed till now.

Electoral Photo Identity Card (EPIC) is an identity document issued by the Electoral Registration Officer. The EPIC contains details of the elector like Name, Father's/Mother's/Husband's Name, Date of Birth/Age on the qualifying date, Sex, Address and most importantly, the photograph of the elector. EPIC is a permanent document for an elector. It is to be used by the elector to establish one's identity at the time of polls. It is compulsory for an elector who has been issued an EPIC to produce the EPIC at the time of polling to enable voting.

Every EPIC is issued under a unique EPIC Number. EPIC Number is an alphanumeric string with 3 alphabetical codes followed by a seven-digit number. While the first 3 alphabetical codes, called the Functional Unique Serial Number (FUSN) code is unique for every Assembly Constituency and is provided by the Election Commission, the numeric code that follows the FUSN code is a six digit running serial number followed by one digit checksum making a total of seven digits

9.1.16 When Do Elections Take Place?

Elections for the Lok Sabha and every State Legislative Assembly have to take place every five years, unless called earlier. The President can dissolve Lok Sabha and call a general election before five years is up, if the Government can no longer command the confidence of the Lok Sabha, and if there is no alternative Government available to take over.

Governments have found it increasingly difficult to stay in power for the full term of a Lok Sabha in recent times, and so elections have often been held before the five-year limit. A constitutional amendment passed in 1975, as part of the Government declared emergency, postponed the election due to be held in 1976. This amendment was later rescinded, and regular elections resumed in 1977.

Holding of regular elections can only be stopped by means of a constitutional amendment and in consultation with the Election Commission, and it is recognised that interruptions of regular elections are acceptable only in extraordinary circumstances.

9.1.17 Scheduling the Elections

When the five-year limit is up, or the legislature has been dissolved and new elections have been called, the Election Commission puts into effect the machinery for holding an election. The constitution states that there can be no longer than 6 months between the last session of the dissolved Lok Sabha and the recalling of the new House, so elections have to be concluded before then.

In a country as huge and diverse as India, finding a period when elections can be held throughout the country is not simple.

The Election Commission, which decides the schedule for elections, has to take account of the weather – during winter constituencies may be snow-bound, and during the monsoon access to remote areas restricted, the agricultural cycle – so that the planting or harvesting crops is not disrupted, exam schedules – as schools are used as polling stations and teachers are employed as election officials, and religious festivals and public holidays. On top of this there are the logistical difficulties that go with holding an election – sending out ballot boxes or EVMs, setting up polling booths, recruiting officials to oversee the elections.

The Commission normally announces the schedule of the elections in a major press conference a few weeks before the formal process is set in motion. The Model Code of Conduct for guidance of candidates and political parties immediately comes into effect after such announcement. The formal process for the elections starts with the Notification or Notifications calling upon the electorate to elect members of a House. As soon as notifications are issued, candidates can start filling their nominations in the constituencies from where they wish to contest. These are scrutinised by the Returning Officer of the constituency concerned after the last date for the same is over after about a week. The nominated candidates can withdraw from the contest within two days from the date of scrutiny. Contesting candidates get at least two weeks for political campaign before the actual date of poll. On account of the vast magnitude of operations and the massive size of the electorate, polling is held at least on three days for the national elections. A separate date for counting is fixed and the results is declared for each constituency by the concerned Returning Officer. The Commission compiles the complete list of members elected and issues an appropriate notification for the due Constitution of the House. With this, the process of elections is complete and the President, in case of the Lok Sabha, and the Governors of the concerned States, in case of the State Legislatures, can then convene their respective Houses to hold their sessions. The entire process takes around 5 to 8 weeks for the national elections, 4 to 5 weeks for separate elections only for Legislative Assemblies.

9.1.18 Candidates in Election

Any Indian citizen who is registered as a voter and is over 25 years of age is allowed to contest elections to the Lok Sabha or State Legislative Assemblies. For the Rajya Sabha the age limit is 30 years.

Every candidate has to make a deposit of ₹10,000/- for Lok Sabha election and ₹5000 for Rajya Sabha or Vidhan Sabha elections, except for candidates from the SC and ST who pay half of these amounts. The deposit is returned if the candidate receives more than one-sixth of the total number of valid votes polled in the constituency. Nominations must be supported at least by one registered elector of the constituency, in the case of a candidate sponsored by a registered party and by ten registered electors from the constituency in the case of other candidates. Returning Officers, appointed by the Election Commission, are put in charge to receive nominations of candidates in each constituency, and oversee the formalities of the election.

9.1.19 Number of Candidates

The number of candidates contesting each election has steadily increased. In the general election of 1952 the average number of candidates in each constituency was 3.8; by 1991 it has risen to 16.3, and in 1996 stood at 25.6.

As it was far too easy for 'frivolous' candidates to stand for election, certain remedial measures were taken in August 1996, which included increasing the size of deposit and increasing the number of people who have to nominate a candidate. The impact of such measures was quite considerable at the elections which were subsequently held. As a result, in 1998 Lok Sabha elections, the number of candidates came down to an average of 8.74 per constituency. In 1999 Lok Sabha elections, it was 8.6, and in 2004 it was 10.

9.1.20 Campaign

The campaign is the period when the political parties put forward their candidates and arguments with which they hope to persuade people to vote for their candidates and parties. Candidates are given a week to put forward their nominations. These are scrutinised by the Returning Officers and if not found to be in order can be rejected after a summary hearing. Valid nominated candidates can withdraw their nominations within two days after their nominations have been scrutinised. The official campaign lasts at least two weeks from the drawing up of the list of nominated candidates, and officially ends 48 hours before polling closes.

During the election campaign, the political parties and contesting candidates are expected to abide by a Model Code of conduct evolved by the Election Commission on the basis of a consensus among political parties. The Model Code lays down broad guidelines as to how the political parties and candidates should conduct themselves during the election campaign. It is intended to maintain the election campaign on healthy lines, avoid clashes and conflicts between political parties or their supporters and ensure peace and order during the campaign period and thereafter, until the results are declared. The Model Code also prescribes guidelines for the ruling party either at the Centre or in the State to ensure that level field in maintained and that no cause is given for any complaint that the ruling party has used its officials position for the purposes of its election campaign.

Once an election has been called, parties issue manifestos detailing the programmes they wish to implement if elected to Government, the strengths of their leaders, and the failures of opposing parties and their leaders. Slogans are used to popularise and identify parties and issues, and pamphlets and posters are distributed to the electorate. Rallies and meetings where the candidates try to persuade, cajole and enthuse supporters, and denigrate opponents, are held throughout the constituencies. Personal appeals and promises of reform are made, with candidates travelling the length and breadth of the constituency to try to influence as many potential supporters as possible. Party symbols abound, are printed on posters and placards.

9.1.21 Polling Days

Polling is normally held on a number of different days in different constituencies, to enable the security forces and those monitoring the election to keep law and order and ensure that voting during the election is fair.

9.1.22 Ballot Papers and Symbols

After nomination of candidates is complete, a list of competing candidates is prepared by the Returning Officer, and ballot papers are printed. Ballot papers are printed with the names of the candidates (in languages set by the Election Commission) and the symbols allotted to each of the candidates. Candidates of recognised parties are allotted their party symbols.

9.1.23 Voting

Voting is done by secret ballot. Polling stations are usually set up in public institutions, such as schools and community halls. To enable as many electors as possible to vote, the officials of the Election Commission try to ensure that there is a polling station within 2 km of every voter, and that no polling stations should have to deal with more than 1500 voters. Each polling station is open for at least 8 hours on the day of the election.

Since 1998, the Commission has increasingly used Electronic Voting Machines instead of ballot boxes. In 2003, all State elections and byelections were held using EVMs. Encouraged by this, the Commission took a historic decision to use only EVMs for the Lok Sabha election due in 2004. More than 1 million EVMs were used in this election.

9.1.24 Political Parties and Elections

Political parties are an established part of modern mass democracy, and the conduct of elections in India is largely dependent on the behaviour of political parties. Although many candidates for Indian elections are independent, the winning candidates for Lok Sabha and Vidhan Sabha elections usually stand as members of political parties, and opinion polls suggest that people tend to vote for a party rather than a particular candidate. Parties offer candidates organisational support, and by offering a broader election campaign, looking at the record of Government and putting forward alternative proposals for government, help voters make a choice about how the Government is run.

9.1.25 Registration with Election Commission

Political parties have to be registered with the Election Commission. The commission determines whether the party is structured and committed to the principles of democracy, secularism and socialism in accordance with the Indian Constitution and would uphold the sovereignty, unity and integrity of India. Parties are expected to hold organisational elections and have a written constitution.

9.1.26 Recognition and Reservation of Symbols

According to certain criteria, set by the Election Commission regarding the length of political activity and success in elections, parties are categorised by the Commission as National or State parties, or simply declared registered – unrecognised parties. How a party is classified determines a party's right to certain privileges, such as access to electoral rolls and provision of time for political broadcasts on the state-owned television and radio stations – All India Radio and Doordarshan – and also the important question of allocation of the party symbol. Party symbols enable illiterate voters to identify the candidate of the party they wish to vote for. National parties are given a symbol that is for their use only, throughout the country. State parties have the sole use of a symbol in the State in which they are recognised as such registered-unrecognised parties can choose a symbol from a list of 'free' symbols.

9.1.27 Limit on Poll Expenses

Amendment in October 2003 has increased expenses limits. For Lok Sabha seats in bigger States, it is ₹25.,00,000. In other States and Union territories, it varies between ₹10,00,000 to ₹25,00,000. Similarly, for Assembly seats, in bigger states, it is ₹10,00,000, while in other States and Union Territories, it varies between ₹5,00,000 to ₹10,00,000.

Although supporters of a candidate can spend as much as they like to help out with a campaign, they have to get written permission of the candidate, and whilst parties are allowed to spend as much money on campaigns as they want, recent Supreme Court judgement have said that, unless a political party can specifically account for money spent during the campaign, it will consider any activities as being funded by the candidates and counting towards their election expenses. The accountability imposed on the candidates and parties has curtailed some of the more extravagant campaigning that was previously a part of Indian elections.

9.1.28 Free Campaign Time on State-Owned Electronic Media

By Election Commission, all recognised National and State parties have been allowed free access to the state-owned electronic media – AIR and Doordarshan – on an extensive scale for their campaigns during elections. The total free time allocated extends over 122 hours on the state-owned television and radio channels. This is allocated equitably by combing a base limit and additional time linked to poll performance of the party.

9.1.29 Splits and Mergers and Anti-Defection Law

Splits, mergers and alliances have frequently disrupted the compositions of political parties. This has led to a number of disputes over which section of a divided party gets to keep the party symbol, and how to classify the resulting parties in terms of national and State parties. The Election Commission has to resolve these disputes, although its decisions can be challenged in the courts.

9.1.30 Election Petitions

Any elector or candidate can file an election petition if he or she thinks there has been malpractice during the election. An election petition is not an ordinary civil suit, but treated as a contest in which the whole constituency is involved. Election petitions are tried by the High Court of the State involved, and if upheld can even lead to the restaging of the election in that constituency.

9.1.31 Election Observers

The Election Commission appoints a large number of observers to ensure that the campaign is conducted fairly, and that people are free to vote as they choose. Observers also keep a check on the amount that each candidate and party spends on the election.

9.1.32 Counting of Votes

After the polling is finished, the votes are counted under the supervision of Returning Officers and Observers appointed by the Election Commission. After the counting of votes is over, the Returning Officer declares the name of the candidate to whom the largest number of votes has been given as the winner, and as having been returned by the constituency to the concerned house.

9.1.33 Media Coverage

In order to bring as much transparency as possible to the electoral process, the media are encouraged and provided with facilities to cover the election, although subject to maintaining the secrecy of the vote. Media persons are given special passes to enter the polling stations to cover the poll process and the counting halls during the actual counting of votes.

9.1.34 Model Code of Conduct

A visible and rigorous enforcement of Model Code of Conduct enhances the credibility of the elections and gives confidence to the stakeholders/voters. It is ensured that official machinery for the electoral purposes is not misused. It is also ensured that electoral offences, malpractices and corrupt practices such as impersonation, bribing and inducement of voters, threat and intimidation to the voters, is prevented by all means. Introduction of photo electoral roll by the Election Commission is expected to play a crucial role in minimising the scope for impersonation.

9.1.35 Vulnerability Mapping

The threat and intimidation to the voters particularly, the voters from vulnerable sections of the society in some parts of the country has been a cause of concern. With a view to meet this challenge, the Commission has recently introduced the system of 'Vulnerability Mapping'. A free and fair election can be conducted only in a conducive atmosphere from the law and order point of view. Hence, it becomes imperative to keep track of the law and order situation during the run up to the election and on the poll day.

9.1.36 Electronic Voting Machines

The Electronic Voting Machine was used universally in all polling stations in the country during the Lok Sabha election 2004. However, the voter awareness about the EVM cannot be taken for granted. It is an endeavour of the Commission to spread the awareness about the EVM among all the voters particularly, in the remote areas and among the new voters. The Commission has introduced the system of randomisation of EVMs for allotment of EVMs to the polling stations and specific responsibility has been given to the Returning Officer. By the system, the first-level checking of EVMs are carried out only by BEL/ECIL Engineers, as the case may be, only at the District Headquarters. At this stage, the EVMs are randomised in the presence of representative of recognised political parties for distribution to Assembly Constituencies. The second randomisation of EVMs for allotting to specific polling stations is done in the presence of candidate or his election agent or authorised representative of the candidate and Election Commission's Observer.

9.1.36.1 Voter Verifiable Paper Audit Trail System (VVPAT)

The Election commission has introduced VVPAT system at selected polling stations and has ordered that a printer with drop box of such design, as may be approved by the Election Commission may also be attached to a voting machine for printing a paper tail of vote, in such constituency or constituencies or parts thereof as the Election commission may direct where printer for paper trial is used, the electors shall be able to view through the transparent window of the printer, the printed paper slip showing the serial number, name and the symbol of the candidate to whom he has cast his vote before such slips gets cut and drops in the drop box of the printer.

9.1.36.2 None of the Above: NOTA

The provision of NOTA option is an expression of decision not to vote for the contesting candidates. The Hon'ble Supreme Court, in its judgments dated 27th September, 2013, in a writ Petition No 161 of 2004 directed that the Commission should make necessary provision in the ballot papers/EVM for 'None of the Above (NOTA)' option so that the electors who do not wish to vote for any of the candidates can exercise their right not to vote for any candidate without violation of the secrecy of their decision. A ballot panel with the words 'None of the Above: NOTA' will be available after the panel containing the name and particulars of the last candidate on the ballot paper. The electors who do not wish to vote for any of the candidate can exercise their right not to vote for any candidate without violation of the secrecy of their decision. For example, if there are 15 candidates contesting the election, the words 'None of the Above' shall be written on the 16th panel and the ballot button against such 16th panel shall also be kept open.

9.2 THE ELECTION COMMISSION OF INDIA – POWERS AND FUNCTIONS

9.2.1 Constitutional Body

India is a socialist, secular, democratic republic and the largest democracy in the world. The modern Indian nation State came into existence on 15th August 1947. Since then free and fair elections have been held at regular intervals as per the principles enshrined in the Constitution, Electoral Laws and System.

The Constitution of India has vested in the Election Commission of India the superintendence, direction and control of the entire process for conduct of elections to Parliament and Legislature of every State and to the offices of President and Vice President of India.

Election Commission of India is a permanent Constitutional body. The Election Commission was established in accordance with the Constitution on 25th January 1950. The commission celebrated its Golden Jubilee in 2001.

Originally the commission had only a Chief Election Commissioner. It currently consists of Chief Election Commissioners and two Election Commissioners.

For the first time two additional Commissioners were appointed on 16th October, 1989 but they had a very short tenure till 1st January, 1990. Later, on 1st October, 1993 two additional Election Commissioners were appointed. The concept of multi-member Commission has been in operation since then, with decision-making power by majority vote.

9.2.2 Appointment and Tenure of Commissioners

The President appoints Chief Election Commissioner and election Commissioners. They have tenure of six years, or up to the age of 65 years, whichever is earlier. They enjoy the same status and receive salary and perks as available to Judges of the Supreme Court of India. The Chief Election Commissioner can be removed from office only through impeachment by Parliament.

9.2.3 Transaction of Business

The Commission transacts its business by holding regular meetings and also by circulation of papers. All Election Commissioners have equal say in the decision making of the Commission. The commission, from time to time, delegates some of its executive functions to its officers in its Secretariat

9.2.4 Setup

The Commission has a separate Secretariat at New Delhi, consisting about 300 officials, in a hierarchical setup.

Two or three Deputy Election Commissioners who are the senior most officers in the Secretariat assist the Commission. They are generally appointed from the National Civil Service of the country and are selected and appointed by the Commission with tenure. Directors, Principal Secretaries, and Secretaries, Under Secretaries and Deputy Directors support the Deputy Election Commissioners in turn. There is a functional and territorial distribution of work in the Commission.

The work is organised in Divisions, Branches and sections; each of the last mentioned units is in charge of a Section Officer. The main functional divisions are Planning, Judicial, Administration, information Systems, Media and Secretariat Coordination. The territorial work is distributed among separate units responsible for different zones into which the 35 constituent States and Union Territories of the country are grouped for convenient management.

At the State level, the election work is supervised, subject to overall superintendence, direction and control of the Commission, by the Chief Electoral Officer of the State, who is appointed by the Commission from amongst senior civil servants proposed by the concerned State Government. He is, in most of the States, a full-time officer and has a small team of supporting staff.

At the district and constituency levels, the district Election Officers, Electoral Registration Officers and Returning Officers, who are assisted by a large number of junior functionaries, perform election work. They all perform their functions relating to elections in addition to their other responsibilities. During election time, however, they are available to the Commission, more or less, on a full-time basis.

The gigantic task force for conducting a countrywide general election consists of nearly five million polling personnel and civil police forces. This huge election machinery is deemed to be on deputation to the Election Commission and is subject to its control, superintendence and discipline during the election period, extending over a period of one and half to two months.

9.2.5 Budget and Expenditure

The Secretariat of the Commission has an independent budget, which is finalised directly in consultation between the commission and the Finance Ministry of the Union Government. The latter generally accepts the recommendation of the Commission for its budgets. The major expenditure on actual conduct of elections is, however, reflected in the budgets of the concerned constituent units of the Union, States and Union Territories. If elections are being held only for the Parliament, the expenditure is borne entirely by the Union Government while for the elections being held only for the State Legislature, the expenditure is borne entirely by the concerned State. In case of simultaneous elections to the Parliament and State Legislature, the expenditure is shared equally between the Union and the State Governments. For capital equipment, expenditure related to preparation for electoral rolls and the scheme for Electors Identity Cards too, the expenditure is shared equally.

9.2.6 Executive Interference Barred

In the performance of its functions, Election Commission is insulated from executive interference. It is the commission which decides the election schedules for the conduct of elections, whether general elections or byelections. Again, it is the commission which decides on the location of polling stations, assignment of voters to the polling stations, location of counting centres, arrangements to be made in and around polling stations and counting centres and all allied matters.

9.2.7 Political Parties and the Commission

Political parties are registered with the Election Commission under the law. The Commission ensures inner party democracy in their functioning by insisting upon them to hold better organisational elections at periodic intervals. Political parties so registered with it are granted recognition at the State and National levels by the Election Commission on the basis of their poll performance at general elections according to criteria prescribed by it. The Commission, as a part of its quasi-judicial jurisdiction, also settles disputes between the splinter groups of such recognised parties.

Election Commission ensures a level playing field for the political parties in election fray, through strict observance by them of a Model Code of Conduct evolved with the consensus of political parties.

The commission holds periodical consultations with the political parties on matters related to the conduct of elections, compliance of Model Code of Conduct and new measures proposed to be introduced by the Commission on election-related matters.

9.2.8 Advisory Jurisdiction and Quasi-Judicial Functions

Under the Constitution, the Commission also has advisory jurisdiction in the matter of post-election disqualification of sitting members of Parliament and State Legislatures. Further, the cases of persons found guilty of corrupt practices at elections which come before the Supreme Court and High Courts are also referred to the Commission for its opinion on the question as to whether such person shall be disqualified and, if so, for what period. The opinion of the Commission in all such matters is binding on the President or, as the case may be the Governor to whom such opinion is tendered.

The Commission has the power to disqualify a candidate who has failed to lodge an account of his election expenses within the time and in the manner prescribed by law. The Commission also has the power for removing or reducing the period of such disqualification under the law.

9.2.9 Judicial Review

The decisions of the Commission can be challenged in the High Court and the Supreme Court of the India by appropriate petitions. By long standing convention and several judicial pronouncements, once the actual process of elections has started, the judiciary does not intervene in the actual conduct of the polls. Once the polls are completed and result declared, the commission cannot review any result on its own. This can only be reviewed through the process of an election petition, which can be filed before the High Court, in respect of elections to the Parliament and State Legislatures. In respect of elections for the offices of the President and Vice President, such petitions can only be filed before the Supreme Court.

9.2.10 Media Policy

The Commission has a comprehensive policy for the media. It holds regular briefings for the mass media – print and electronic – on a regular basis, at close intervals during the election period and on specific occasions as necessary on other occasions. The representatives of the media are also provided facilities to report on actual conduct of poll and counting.

They are allowed entry into polling stations and counting centres on the basis of international and national media. The Commission also publishes statistical reports and other documents which are available for research and study to members of the academic fraternity; media representatives and anybody else interested.

The Commission has, in cooperation with the State owned media – Doordarshan and All India radio – taken up a major campaign for awareness of voters. The Prasar Bharti Corporation which manages the national Radio and Television networks, has brought out several innovative and effective short clips for this purpose.

9.2.11 International Cooperation

India is a founding member of the International Institute for Democracy and Electoral Assistance (IDEA) Stockholm, Sweden. In the recent past, the Commission has expanded international contacts by way of sharing of experience and expertise in the areas of Electoral Management and Administration, Electoral Laws and Reforms. Election Officials from the national electoral bodies and other delegates from the several countries – Russia, Sri Lanka, Nepal, Indonesia, South Africa, Bangladesh, Thailand, Nigeria, Namibia, Bhutan, Australia, the United States and Afghanistan etc. – have visited the Commission for a better understanding of the Indian Electoral Process. The Commission has also provided experts and observers for elections to other countries in cooperation with the United Nations and the Commonwealth Secretariat.

9.2.12 New Initiatives

The Commission has taken several new initiatives in the recent past. Notable among these are, a scheme for use of state-owned electronic media for broadcast/telecast by political parties, checking criminalisation of politics, computerisation of electoral rolls, providing electors with Identity cards, simplifying the procedure for maintenance of accounts and filling of the same by candidates and a variety of measures for a strict compliance of Model Code of Conduct, for providing a level playing field to contestants during the elections.

9.3 THE REPRESENTATION OF PEOPLE ACT – AN INTRODUCTION

In modern times, unless otherwise indicated, the word democracy stands for representative democracy, a practice whereby the people choose their *representatives*, who conducts the government on behalf of their electorates, the people. If people choose their representatives and vest (if nor surrender) with them their power, then how to ensure that they would stay moral and represent the genuine interests of the people?

'And the people always put forward a single champion of their interests, whom they nurse to greatness. Here, plainly enough, is the root from which despotism invariably springs', Plato warned us so in his *Republic* which he wrote around 380 BC. The reader by now might have got an assumption that the modern representative democracies must have devised some mechanism to ensure that such champions of peoples interest remain great, and if they fail in their greatness, they would be deprived of their power. Undoubtedly, the world's largest democracy has its own mechanism to make certain this idea.

It comes to us in the form of Constitutional provisions, the Representation of People's Act 1950 and the Representation of People's Act 1951. The two acts stand today along with several amendments and a wide array of healthy and active judicial interpretations. Together they serve as the guardian of our representative democracy and electoral politics. What are such provisions of

Constitution and these two Acts dealing with the representatives and electorates? Whether these provisions had prevented the Plato-warned-not-so-great personalities from entering the Parliament or State Legislatures? Or even if they have entered whether they have been disqualified promptly? Had the electors played their part in keeping Indian democracy healthy? These questions, in the same order, would remain as the guiding force for both the author and the reader, the active citizens of the Indian democracy, in their respective attempts of exploring and understanding.

9.4 BACKGROUND OF THE REPRESENTATION OF PEOPLE'S ACTS

The Constitution when came into force, contained certain articles which laid down the basic fundamental details regarding peoples representatives, elections and the election machinery. As they themselves would not be sufficient, the articles empowered the Parliament to enact laws to supplement them. As the reader knows, since independence on 15th August, 1947, the Constituent Assembly functioned as the Provisional Parliament. Part XXI of the Constitution contained the translational provisions. It empowered the Provisional Parliament to make legislations. The first general election to the Indian Parliament was to be held once the Constitution gets ready. This necessitated the Provisional Parliament to make an act to govern the election. Accordingly the Provisional Parliament enacted two acts in succession, *'The Representation of the People's Act1950'and'The Representation of the People'sAct 1951'*, before the first general election which was held from October 1951 to March 1952. Governance is a dynamic process which has to keep pace with the changing aspirations and needs of the society. Accordingly the Act was amended several times (the latest one being 2010) to incorporate and repeal certain provisions.

9.5 AN OVERVIEW OF THE REPRESENTATION OF PEOPLE'S ACTS 1950 AND 1951

Representation of People's Act 1950

This Act contains 32 Sections in 8 Parts

PART I (Sec. I and 2)	• Gives the title and definitions
PART II (Sec. 3 to 13)	• Provides for allocation of seats and delimitation of Constituencies in the Lok Sabha and the State Legislative Assemblies and Councils
PART IIA (Sec.13A to 13CC)	• Details the officers connected with the preparation of Electoral Rolls
PART IIB (Sec. 13D)	• Provides for Electoral Rolls of Parliamentary Constituencies
PART III (Sec. 14 to 25A)	• Provides for Electoral Rolls for Assembly Constituencies
PART IV (Sec.27)	• Provides for Electoral Roll for Council Constituencies
PART IVA (Sec.27A to 27K)	• Provides for the manner of filling seats in the Council of States
PART V (Sec. 28 to 32)	• Gives general provisions with regard to the jurisdiction of Civil Courts; making available staff from local authorities, etc.

Along with the above Parts, the Act has got four Schedules. They are,

- The First Schedule – Allocation of seats in the House of the People.
- The Second Schedule – Total number of seats in the Legislative Assemblies.

- The Third Schedule – Allocation of seats in the Legislative Councils.
- The Fourth Schedule – Local authorities for purposes of elections to Legislative Councils.

Representation of People's Act 1951

This Act contains 171 Sections in 13 Parts

PART I (Sec. 1 and 2)	• Preliminary
PART II (Sec 3-11B)	• Qualifications and Disqualifications
PART III (Sec 12-16)	• Notification of General Elections
PART IV (Sec 19-29)	• Administrative Machinery for Conduct of Elections
PART IV A (Sec 29A-29C)	• Registration of Political Parties
PART V (Sec 30-78)	• Conduct of Elections • Free Supply of Certain Material to Candidates of Recognised
PART V A (Sec 78A-78B)	• Political Parties
Part VI (Sec 79-122)	• Disputes Regarding Elections
Part VII (Sec 123-138)	• Corrupt Practices and Electoral Offences
Part VIII (Sec 139-146C)	• Disqualifications
Part IX (Sec 147-151A)	• Byelections
Part X (Sec 152-168)	• Miscellaneous
Part XI (Sec 169-171)	• General

While the provisions of Parts II A, II B, III and IV of RP Act 1950 and Parts II, VI, VII and VIII of RP Act 1951 and the issues emerged out of them would be the subject matter of this unit, the remaining Parts would be discussed under the next unit, *'Constitutional Provisions and Representation of the People Act II– Election Machinery, Elections and Electoral Reforms'*.

9.6 IMPORTANT PROVISIONS OF REPRESENTATION OF PEOPLE'S ACTS 1950 AND 1951

The Representation of People's Acts have a number of significant provisions which deals with the election process. The Parliament framed these rules in order to effectively conduct the elections in the country. The following are some of the important provisions in the Act, and by studying this we would be able to analyse various problems and issues associated with it.

9.6.1 Qualifications of Elected Representatives of People in Parliament and Assembly (RP Act, 1951)

The Representative of People Act talks about the qualification of persons who can contest the election. Apart from the Act, the Constitution also contains provisions regarding the qualification of person contesting the elections. The qualifications are provided under the Articles 84 and 173 of the Constitution.

Constitutional Provisions: A person shall not be qualified to be chosen to fill a seat in Parliament unless

a. He is a citizen of India.
b. As per the Third Schedule, he makes and subscribes oath or affirmation before some person authorised by the Election Commission
c. He is not less than 25 years of age with regard to lower house – Lok Sabha not less than 30 years with regard to the Council of States – Rajya Sabha.
d. He is not less than 25 years of age with regard to lower house – Legislative Assembly, not less than 30 years with regard to the Legislative Council.
e. He possesses other such qualifications as prescribed under any law made by the Parliament.

Provisions for Qualifications under the Representative of People's Act 1951:

a. A person is not qualified to be chosen as representative in the State assembly or council unless he is an elector.
b. A person shall not be qualified to be chosen to fill a seat in the **House of the People** unless
   (i) In the case of a seat reserved for the Scheduled Castes in any State, he is a member of any of the Scheduled Castes and is an elector for any Parliamentary constituency in the State.
   (ii) In the case of a seat reserved for the Scheduled Tribes in any State (other than those in the autonomous districts of Assam), he is a member of any of the Scheduled Tribes, whether of that State or of any other State (excluding the tribal areas of Assam), and is an elector for any Parliamentary constituency.
   (iii) In the case of a seat reserved for the Scheduled Tribes in the autonomous districts of Assam or in the Union territory of Lakshadweep, a person has to satisfy two conditions. One, he should be a member of any of those Scheduled Tribes and two, he should be an elector for the Parliamentary constituency in that autonomous district or the Union Territory, respectively.
   (iv) In the case of the seat allotted to the State of Sikkim, he is an elector for the Parliamentary constituency for Sikkim.
   (v) In the case of any other seat, he is an elector for any Parliamentary constituency.
c. A person shall not be qualified to be chosen to fill a seat in the **Legislative Assembly of a State** unless
   (i) In the case of a seat reserved for the Scheduled Castes or for the Scheduled Tribes of that State, he is a member of any of those castes or of those tribes, and is an elector for any Assembly constituency in that State.
   (ii) In the case of a seat reserved for an autonomous district of Assam, he is a member of a Scheduled Tribe of any autonomous district and is an elector for the Assembly constituency in which such seat or any other seat is reserved for that district.
   (iii) In the case of any other seat, he is an elector for any Assembly constituency in that state.

d. A person shall not be qualified to be chosen to fill a seat in the **Legislative Council of a State** unless
   (i) He is an elector for any Assembly constituency in that state.
   (ii) He is ordinarily a resident of the State.

9.6.2 Disqualifications of an Elected Representative of People in Parliament and Assembly (RP Act 1951)

The following are the provisions regarding disqualification of a member as provided in the Constitution and the Representative of People's Act. The Articles 102 and 191 in the Constitution of India talk about these provisions of disqualification. The Constitution now also lays down an additional disqualification on the ground of 'defection', but it is relevant only for sitting members of Parliament and state legislatures for continuing as such member. Part 102(2) and 191(2) read with the Tenth Schedule to the Constitution].

Constitutional Provisions: A person shall be disqualified for being chosen as, and for being, a member of either House of Parliament or State Legislature

a. If he holds any office of profit under the Government of India or the Government of any State, other than those office declared by Parliament by law (a person shall not be deemed to hold an office of profit under the Government of India or the Government of any State by reason only that he is a Minister either for the Union or for such State).
b. If he is of unsound mind and declared so by a competent court.
c. If he is an undischarged insolvent.
d. If he is not a citizen of India, or has voluntarily acquired the citizenship of a foreign State, or has acknowledged allegiance or adherence to a foreign state.
e. If he is so disqualified by/under any law made by the Parliament.
f. A person shall be disqualified for being a member of either House of Parliament or the Legislative Assembly or Legislative Council of a State if he is so disqualified under the Tenth Schedule – Anti-defection law.

Provisions for Disqualifications under the RP Act 1951:

These disqualifications have been presently prescribed by the Parliament in chapter III of Part II of the 1951 Act, containing Sections 7 to 11 thereof. These disqualifications are:

a. Disqualification on conviction for certain offences (S 8);
b. Disqualification on ground of commission of corrupt practices (S 8A);
c. Disqualification for dismissal from government service for corruption or disloyalty (S 9);
d. Disqualification for contract with 'appropriate government' (S 9A);
e. Disqualification for holding office under government company (S 10); and
f. Disqualification for failure to lodge account of election expenses (S 10A).

'Disqualification' is defined in Section 7(b) to mean disqualification for being chosen as, and for being, a member of either House of Parliament or of the legislative assembly or legislative council of a state.

'Appropriate government' is defined in Section7(a) to mean in relation to any disqualification for membership of Parliament, the Central Government, and in relation to any disqualification for membership of a state legislature, the government of the state concerned.

(a) Disqualification on Conviction for Certain Offences

Object of the provision: Conviction for certain offences–electoral, economic or criminal–has been considered by the Parliament a sufficient ground for disqualification of the convicted person for membership of Parliament and of state legislatures (**Section 8, 1951 Act**). The Supreme Court has observed in K Prabhakaran v P Jayarajan, that the purpose of enacting disqualification under **Section 8**: '.... is to prevent criminalisation of politics. Those who break the law should not make the law'.

Classification of offences: Parliament has classified offences under Section 8 into three categories having regard to the nature and gravity of those offences.

The first category of offences is listed out in S8 (1), where the mere conviction itself, without reference to any quantum of punishment therefore, attracts disqualification. These offences are:

a. Section 153 A – (offence of promoting enmity between different groups on ground of religion, race, place of birth, residence, language, etc., and doing acts prejudicial to maintenance of harmony) or Section 171 E (offence of bribery) or Section 171 F (offence of undue influence or personation at an election) or sub-section (1) or sub-section (2) of section 376 or Sec 376A or Sec 376B or Sec 376C or Sec 376D (offences relating to rape) or section 498A (offence of cruelty towards a woman by husband or relative of a husband) or sub-Section (2) or sub-Section (3) of Section 505 (offence of making statement creating or promoting enmity, hatred or ill-will between classes or offence relating to such statement in any place of worship or in any assembly engaged in the performance of religious worship or religious ceremonies) of the Indian Penal Code 1860;
b. The protection of Civil Rights Act 1955, which provides for punishment for the preaching and practice of 'untouchability', and for the enforcement of any disability arising there from;
c. Section 11 (offence of importing or exporting prohibited goods) of the Customs Act 1962;
d. Sections 10 to 12 (offence of being a member of an association declared unlawful, offence relating to dealing with funds of an unlawful association or offence relating to contravention of an order made in respect of a notified place) of the Unlawful Activities (Prevention) Act 1967;
e. The Foreign Exchange (Regulation) Act 1973;
f. The Narcotic Drugs and Psychotropic Substances Act 1985;
g. Section 3 (offence of committing terrorist acts) or Section4 (offence of committing disrupting activities) of the Terrorist and Disruptive Activities (Prevention) Act 1987;
h. Section 7 (offence of contravention of the provisions of Sections3 to 6) of the Religious Institutions (Prevention of Misuse) Act 1988;
i. Section 125 (offence of promoting enmity between classes in connection with the election) or Section135 (offence of removal of ballot papers from polling stations) or Section135A (offence of booth capturing) or cl (a) of sub-Section(2) of Section136 (offence of fraudulently defacing or fraudulently destroying any nomination paper) of the Representation of the People Act 1951;
j. Section 6 (offence of conversion of a place of worship) of the Places of Worship (Special Provisions) Act 1991;

k. Section 2 (offence of insulting the Indian National Flag or the Constitution of India) or Section3 (offence of preventing singing of National Anthem) of the Prevention of Insults to National Honour Act 1971;
l. The Commission of Sati (Prevention) Act 1987;
m. The Prevention of Corruption Act 1988;
n. The Prevention of Terrorism Act 2002

The disqualification under this Section 8(1) is for a period of six years from the date of conviction where the convicted person is sentenced to fine only. Where, however, the convicted person is sentenced to imprisonment for any period, he shall be disqualified from the date of conviction and shall continue to be disqualified for a further period of six years since his release.

The second category of offences listed in **Section 8(2)** relate to **hoarding or adulteration of food or drugs or dowry**, where the conviction coupled with a sentence of imprisonment for not less than six months invites disqualification. The resultant disqualification runs during the period of sentence of imprisonment and for a further period of six years from the release.

The third category **in Section 8(3**) includes all other offences for which a person is convicted and sentenced to imprisonment for not less than two years. Here also, the disqualification is operative during the period of sentence of imprisonment and for a further period of six years from his release.

(b) Section 8(4) of the RP Act 1951

Other than the above-mentioned offences, **Section 8(4)** of the RP Act 1951 says that, if a person convicted of any offence and sentenced to imprisonment for not less than two years in any other case shall be disqualified from the date of such conviction and shall continue to be disqualified for a further period of six years since his release. But in this case if the convicted person makes an appeal to a higher court against the verdict given in the lower court within a period of three months of the lower court's conviction then he can continue to be a member until the appeal is disposed in the higher court. (One has to note here that on 10th July, 2013, in the Lilly Thomas v. Union of India Case, the Supreme Court has struck down this provision as unconstitutional and hence void. This would be discussed later under *'Judiciary and RP Act–A Savior for CleansingElectoralPolitics'*)

(c) Disqualification for Dismissal from Government Service for Corruption or Disloyalty

Dismissal for corruption or disloyalty – A government servant dismissed for corruption or for disloyalty to the state shall be disqualified for five years from the date of such dismissal [**Section 9(1), 1951 Act**]. The words 'corruption' and 'disloyalty to the state' have not been defined in the 1951 – Act, and these words will have to take their respective meanings from other relevant laws, like the Prevention of Corruption Act 1988 and the Indian Penal Code 1860.

If during the period of five years since dismissal, any dismissed government servant wishes to contest an election, he has to produce a certificate from the Election Commission that he has not been dismissed for corruption or disloyalty to the state and such certificate by the Election commission shall be conclusive of the fact [**Section 9(2), 1951 Act**]. Such certificate has to be annexed to the nomination paper itself and in the absence of such certificate accompanying a nomination paper, the candidate shall not be deemed to be duly nominated and his nomination shall be liable to be rejected on this ground alone [s 33(3), 1951 Act].

(d) Disqualification for Contracts with Government

Disqualification for contracts, underlying object – A contract by a person with the government may also disqualify him for membership of Parliament and of state legislatures [**Section**

9A, 1951 – Act]. The underlying intention here also is to ensure that there is no conflict between public duty and private interests.

Contracts which disqualify – But it is not every contract with the government which attracts disqualification. Only specified types of contracts entail disqualification. Under the present law, a person shall be disqualified by reason of a contract with the government if: (a) the contract has been entered into by him in the course of his trade or business; (b) the contract is for the supply of goods to, or for the execution of any works undertaken by, the government; (c) the contract is with the appropriate government; and (d) the contract is still subsisting.

(e) **Disqualification for Holding Office under Government Company**

Only specified offices to attract disqualification – While dealing with the question of disqualification on holding an office of profit, it has been mentioned that, according to the tests laid down by the Supreme Court for determining the question whether an office shall entail disqualification, the employees of government companies, corporations and undertakings shall normally not attract the disqualification for the purpose under the Constitution. However, it is provided by Parliament that if a person is holding the office of a: (i) managing agent; (ii) manager; or (iii) secretary of any company or corporation (other than a cooperative society) in the capital of which the appropriate government has not less than 25% shares, such person shall also be disqualified (s 10, 1951 Act). It, however, deserves to be noted that the disqualification shall be attracted only by the persons holding the above-mentioned offices and not by the other employees of such government companies or corporations. Further, all cooperative societies also fall outside the purview of this disqualificatory provision. No definition of managing agent, manager or secretary has been provided in the 1951 Act, and these offices may derive their meanings from the Companies Act 1956.

A clerk in the Coal India Ltd., a government company, was not held to be holding the office of Manager though he occasionally performed some supervisor function. A Khalasi or meter reader holding a non-executive post in Bokaro Steel Plant, a government company, was also held not to be disqualified within the meaning of **Section 10** of the 1951 Act or art 191 (1) (a) of the Constitution.

(f) **Disqualification for Failure to Lodge Account of Election Expenses**

Disqualification for failure without good reason or justification – Every candidate at an election to the House of the People or to a state legislative assembly has to keep and maintain a separate account of his election expenses incurred or authorised by him or by his election agent between the date on which he has been nominated as such candidate and the date of declaration of result of the election, both dates inclusive [**Section 77(1), 1951 Act**]. The law further requires that every contesting candidate shall lodge a true copy of the account of his election expenses with the district election officer of the district in which his constituency falls, within a period of 30 days from the date of declaration of result of the election (**Section 76**).

Rule 86 of the 1961 Rules prescribes that the account should be maintained from day to day and should show the particulars mentioned in that rule. In order to ensure that the candidates maintain their accounts in the manner required, the Election Commission has now devised a register in which such account is to be maintained by every candidate. It is supplied by the returning officer to each candidate as soon as he files his nomination paper. After the election, this very register is now required to be submitted by the candidate to the district election officer, along with some abstract statements showing the details of his expenditure under various heads and sub-heads. The account of expenditure may be maintained in English, Hindi or any local language in which the electoral roll is printed.

If a candidate fails to lodge the account of his election expenses within the time and in the manner required, he shall be disqualified by the Election Commission, if he has no good reason or justification for his failure (**Section 10A**). Such disqualification shall be operative for a period of three years from the date of order of the Election Commission so disqualifying him.

(g) Disqualification on Ground of Commission of Corrupt Practices

Apart from the above conditions, *a candidate contesting in an election* shall be disqualified on account of ***'corrupt practices'*** made by him during and in election. There are some corrupt practices which are provided in the IPC, but these are general in nature and relate to all elections held under any law to any elective body. The provisions under the Representative of People's Act, 1951, is applicable only to the elections held to the State legislature and the Parliament, it does not cover other elections including to that of the office of President and Vice President.

In cases of corrupt practices, whether it is committed by the candidate or any person authorised by the candidate, it has the effect of vitiating the whole election and the whole constituency suffers as it would have to face re-election. Hence, the person committing such acts suffers from criminal liability.

Any such corrupt practices can be dealt by means of an election petition, and only when the said election is over in accordance with the provisions under Article 329 of Constitution of India.

If the high court in the trial of an election petition, or the Supreme Court on appeal, finds a person guilty of commission of corrupt practice, it names him so by an order under **Section 99** of the 1951 Act. Such guilty person may invite disqualification for contesting elections in future to Parliament and state legislatures [**Section 8A (1)**, **1951 Act**], for six years from the date the order of the court, finding him guilty takes effect [proviso to **Section 8A (1)**].

The person so found guilty of commission of corrupt practice under **Section 99** may not necessarily be a candidate at the election. He can even be a third person.

The question whether such a person should be disqualified and, if so, for what period, is determined by the President. Before giving his decision in the matter, the President is required to obtain the opinion of the Election Commission and he is bound to act according to such opinion [**Section 8A (3)**].

Meaning of corrupt practice – The term 'corrupt practice' here means only the corrupt practices as defined in **Section 123** of the 1951 Act, and not any other irregularity or malpractice at an election.

According to Section123 of the Act, the following are the 'corrupt practices' done by a candidate.

a. **Bribery** – providing any gift, offer of promise or of any gratification with the object of influencing the voter to vote or to stop from voting; to a candidate to withdraw from contesting.
b. **Undue influence** – any direct or indirect interference or attempt to interfere with the free exercise of any electoral right, by threatening any candidate or any elector with physical injury and social ostracism, or ex-communication or expulsion from any caste or community.
c. The appeal to vote or refrain from voting for any person on the ground of his religion, race, caste, community or language or the use of, or appeal to religious symbols or the use of, or appeal to, national symbols, such as the national flag or the national emblem.
d. The promotion of, or attempt to promote, feelings of enmity or hatred between different classes of the citizens of India on grounds of religion, race, caste, community or language.

e. The propagation of the practice or the commission of sati or its glorification by a candidate.
f. The publication by a candidate of any statement of fact which is false in relation to the personal character or conduct of any other candidate.
g. The obtaining of any assistance (other than the giving of vote) for the furtherance of the prospects of that candidate's election, from any person in the Government service.
h. Booth capturing by a candidate or his agent or other person (inserted in 1989).

But here in this *'corrupt practices'* matter, the procedure for disqualification is different from that of others specified under para 1 to 7. Let us see what is the procedure for it? First, regarding corrupt practices done by a candidate who contests in election, it has to be challenged in the High Court under whose jurisdiction the offence takes place. It cannot be challenged through an ordinary case but only through an electoral petition. What does an electoral petition mean? The Act defines it as a petition calling in question any election presented to the High Court *by any candidate at such election or any elector* within 45 days from the date of election of the returned candidate. The High Court may reject the petition if it does not comply with the provisions of the Act. Or as soon as after an election petition has been presented to the High Court, it shall be referred to the Judge/Judges who has/have been assigned by the Chief Justice for the trial of election petitions. The Act says, *'The trial of an election petition shall, so far as is practicable consistently with the interests of justice in respect of the trial, be continued from day to day until its conclusion, unless the High Court finds the adjournment of the trial beyond the following day to be necessary for reasons to be recorded. Every election petition shall be tried as expeditiously as possible and endeavour shall be made to conclude the trial within six months from the date on which the election petition is presented to the High Court for trial'*. The High court may declare the election of all or any of the returned candidates to be void and even has the power to declare in its order that the petitioner or any other candidate to have been duly elected. But one has to note here that the order of the High Court alone cannot disqualify the person. It can only declare that particular election to be void. The person can be disqualified to stand in further elections only by the President of India. But before taking any decision on that matter, the President has to act in accordance with the advice given by the Election Commission. So in the analysis, one could see that in the ultimate, the Election Commission wields power with respect to disqualifying a representative on the grounds of 'corrupt practices'.

9.6.3 Registration of Political Parties

Part IV A, Section 29A of The Representation of the People Act, 1951 empowers the Election Commission of India to register associations and bodies as political parties. All such associations or political parties in their Memorandum of the Rules should contain a specific provision that the association or body shall bear true faith and allegiance to the Constitution of India as by law established, and to the principles of socialism, secularism and democracy, and would uphold the sovereignty, unity and integrity of India and the decision taken by the Commission shall be final.

There are many benefits of registering a party. First, the Representation of People's Act allows political parties to accept contributions voluntarily offered to it by any person or company other than a government company. Apart from this, candidates of registered parties get preference in allotment of election symbols. Other candidates are identified as independents and do not get preference in symbol allocation.

Registered political parties, in course of time, can get recognition as 'State Party' or 'National Party' subject to the **fulfilment of the conditions prescribed by the Commission in the Election Symbols (Reservation and Allotment) Order, 1968**, as amended from time to time.

If a party is recognised as a 'State Party', it is entitled for exclusive allotment of its reserved symbol to the candidates set up by it in the state in which it is so recognised, and if a party is recognised as a 'National Party' it is entitled for exclusive allotment of its reserved symbol to the candidates set up by it throughout India. Recognised 'State' and 'National' parties need only one proposer for filing the nomination and are also entitled for two sets of electoral rolls free of cost at the time of revision of rolls and their candidates get one copy of electoral roll free of cost during General Elections. Further they get broadcast/telecast facilities over Akashvani/ Doordarshan during general elections. Political parties are entitled to nominate 'Star Campaigners' during General Elections. A recognised National or State party can have a maximum of 40 'Star campaigners' and a registered un-recognised party can nominate a maximum of 20 'Star Campaigners'. The travel expenses of star campaigners are not to be accounted for in the election expense accounts of candidates of their party.

The registered Political party has to keep the commission duly informed of any change in its name, head office, office bearers, address or any other matters.

A political party shall be treated as a recognised political party in a State, if and only if the political party fulfils any of the following conditions:

- At General Elections or Legislative Assembly elections, the party has won 3% of seats in the legislative assembly of the State (subject to a minimum of 3 seats).
- At a Lok Sabha General Elections, the party has won 1 Lok Sabha seat for every 25 Lok Sabha seats allotted for the State.
- At a General Election to Lok Sabha or Legislative Assembly, the party has polled minimum of 6% of votes in a State and in addition it has won 1 Lok Sabha or 2 Legislative Assembly seats.
- At a General Election to Lok Sabha or Legislative Assembly, the party has polled 8% of votes in a State.

Similarly, a political party shall be treated as a recognised national party, if and only if the political party fulfils any of the following conditions:

- The party wins 2% of seats in the Lok Sabha (11 seats) from at least three different states.
- At a General Election to Lok Sabha or Legislative Assembly, the party polls 6% of votes in four states and in addition it wins 4 Lok Sabha seats.
- A party gets recognition as a State Party in four or more states.

Both national and state parties have to fulfil these conditions for all subsequent Lok Sabha or State elections. Else, they lose their status.

9.6.4 Election Petitions

Part VI of RPA, 1951 deals with the disputes regarding the elections and provides for the manner of presentation of election petitions, their trial and procedure. **Section 80 of RPA**, 1951 provides that, 'No election shall be called in question except by an election petition presented in accordance with the provisions of this part'. The power is given to High Court to try these matters. Thus, the High Court of the particular state has the original jurisdiction to deal with such matters related to the election.

An election petition is a procedure for inquiring into the validity of the election results of Parliamentary or local government elections. In other words, it is a means under law to challenge the election of a candidate in a Parliamentary, Assembly or local election. It can be filed by any candidate, or an elector relating to the election personally, to the authorised officer of the High Court. It shall be filed within the time period of 45 days from the date of declaration of results.

The grounds for filing the election petition are given under Section 100 of the RPA. The election of a particular candidate can be declared void under section 100 of the Representation of People Act, 1951, if the High Court is of the opinion that

a. On the date of his election a returned candidate was not qualified or was disqualified to be chosen to fill the seat.
b. Any corrupt practice has been committed by a returned candidate or his election agent or by any other person with the consent of a returned candidate or his election agent.
c. the nomination has been improperly accepted.
d. any improper reception, refusal or rejection of any vote or the reception of any vote which is void is done.
e. the candidate has not complied with the provisions of the Constitution or RPA or any rules or orders made under this act.

When many election petitions are presented to the High Court in respect of the same election, all of them shall be referred for trial to the same judge who may, in his discretion, try them separately or in one or more groups. The Representation of Peoples Act recommends that every election petition shall be tried as expeditiously as possible and as far as practicable for the interests of justice. Every endeavour, its suggests, should be made on the part of the High Court to conclude a trial for an election petition within six months from the date on which the election petition was presented to the High Court for trial. And when the election of a candidate is declared void, any of his acts or proceedings in which that candidate has participated as a Member of Parliament or State Legislature, shall not be invalidated by reason of that order, nor shall such candidate be subjected to any liability or penalty on the ground of such participation.

9.6.5 Delimitation of Constituencies

The concept of delimitation involves not only demarcation or redrawing of boundaries of the territorial constituencies, but also adjustments in the allocation of seats to various states in the Lok Sabha and in the legislative assembly of the State.

The basic objective of the delimitation is to secure an equal representation for equal segments of the population in legislative bodies.

Principles of Delimitation laid down by The Constitution of India

- Constitution mandates that Delimitation of constituencies as determined by the authority, which was entrusted with the task, should be final and there should not be any intervention by any authority. This has been provided in the **Article 329 (a)** of the Indian Constitution.

- The constitution provided that, upon the completion of each census, the representation of several territorial constituencies in the house of people and legislative assembly of each state shall be, as parliament may by law determined (Article 81 (3) and 174) but Constitution was silent on who should undertake the initial territorial divisions. This gap has been filled by Representation of People Act, 1950.
- As per the constitutional mandate, delimitation has been done after every census.
- After the 1951 census, delimitation became due in all the states, Election Commission recommended to the government that the future delimitation of constituencies should be made by an independent commission and the decisions of such commission should be made final in law.

The government accepted their suggestion of the Election Commission and accordingly provided for the constitution of an independent Delimitation commission under the Delimitation Commission Act, 1952.

It has been done successively after the decennial censuses of 1961 and 1971. The **forty second Amendment Act, 1976** freezed the number of seats allocated to various states in the house of people, the total number of seats in the various state legislative assemblies and the extent of all parliamentary and assembly constituencies until the next census taken after the year 2000.

The **Constitution (Eighty Fourth Amendment) Act 2001**, provided that the number of seats allocated to various states in the house of people and the total number of seats in the state legislative assemblies, as determined on the basis of 1971 census, would remain further frozen till the **year 2026**. But that eighty fourth constitutional amendment further provided that all parliamentary and assembly constituencies in the country would be delimited afresh on the basis of 1991 census. Subsequently delimitation without increasing the number of seats has been done.

Authority to Delimit Council Constituencies

The power to delimit council constituencies is vested with the President. The President makes the order delimiting council constituencies on the basis of recommendation of Election Commission.

The procedure laid down in **section 13 of the Representation of the People Act, 1950**, was followed in delimiting the constituencies in 1951. In actual experience it was found that the procedure did not work very smoothly or satisfactorily. In particular, sub-section (3) of that section made the Delimitation Orders issued by the President subject to amendments by the Parliament and many of them were in fact materially amended by the Parliament.

The Election Commission recommended to the Government accordingly that future delimitation of constituencies should be made by an independent body, more or less judicial in composition and that the scheme of delimitation worked out by it should be made final in law. This recommendation was accepted and the Delimitation Commission Act, 1952 (Act 81 of 1952) was enacted by the Parliament. Under this Act, a Commission is required to be constituted for readjusting the representation of the territorial constituencies of the House of the People and the Legislative Assembly of each State, other than Jammu and Kashmir, and delimiting these constituencies. The Commission is to consist of three members, two of the members being serving or retired Judges of the Supreme Court or High Courts, while the third member is to be the Chief Election Commissioner ex-officio. The Commission that was eventually set up had a retired Judge of the Supreme Court as its Chairman and a retired Chief Justice of a High Court as the second member. The law provides that in the performance of its duties, the Commission is to be assisted by two to seven associate members for each State drawn from the members of the House of the People representing the State and of the Legislative Assembly of the State. The associate members were appointed by the Speaker of the House of which they were members. In making these appointments due regard was paid by the Speaker to the composition of the House. The associate members were not given the right to vote or to sign any decision of the Commission. In the case of the three Part 'C' States — Kutch, Manipur and Tripura which had no Legislative Assemblies, the two members of the House of the People representing each of the States were appointed as the associate members for the State.

All decisions were taken by the Delimitation Commission after consultation with the associate members. In ease of any difference of opinion amongst the members of the Commission, the opinion of the majority prevailed.

The Delimitation Commission Act laid down the procedure to be followed by the Commission in readjusting the representation and in delimiting the constituencies. The Commission was first to determine on the basis of the latest census figures the number of seats to be allotted to each of the states in the House of the People and to its Legislative Assembly. The Commission was also required in respect of each state to determine on the basis of the figures of population the number of seats, if any, to be reserved for the Scheduled Castes and the Scheduled Tribes of the State in the House of the People and in its Legislative Assembly. The Commission was then to distribute the seats so reserved amongst the constituencies to be delimited for the House of the People and the Legislative Assembly.

The following were the principles, to be followed in the delimitation of constituencies:

a. Every constituency shall be either a single-member or a two-member constituency.
b. The Commission was given the discretion, however, to continue either or both of the existing three-member constituencies. (These were a-House of the People constituency in West Bengal and a Legislative Assembly constituency in Bombay). In any such three-member constituency, one seat was to be reserved for the Scheduled Castes and another for the Scheduled Tribes.
c. Wherever practicable, seats were to be reserved for the Scheduled Castes or for the Scheduled Tribes in single-member constituencies.
d. In every two-member constituency, one seat was to be reserved either for the Scheduled Castes or for the Scheduled Tribes, while the other seat would not be so reserved.
e. Constituencies in which a seat is reserved either for the Scheduled Castes or for the Scheduled Tribes were, as far as practicable, to be located in areas in which the population of the Scheduled Castes or, as the case may be, of the Scheduled Tribes is most concentrated. In regard to the Scheduled Castes, however, care was to be taken to distribute the seats reserved for them in different areas of the State.
f. All constituencies should, as far as practicable, consist of geographically compact areas, and in delimiting them, regard was to be had to physical features, the existing boundaries of administrative units, facilities of communication and public convenience.

9.6.6 Electoral Roll – Issues Concerning Qualifications and Disqualifications of an Elector

For a free and fair election, an accurate and error-free electoral roll is the most important prerequisite. Some of the electoral malpractices like bogus voting and impersonations can be attributed, to a large extent to the defective electoral rolls. For enhanced participation of electors in the electoral process and reducing the electoral malpractices, it is essential to improve the registration processes which will in turn increase the credibility of the electoral rolls. Therefore, adequate stress has to be given to the preparation and revision of the electoral rolls.

Constitutional provisions in regard to electoral roles:

1. Under Article 324(1) of the Constitution of India, the superintendence, direction and control of the preparation of the electoral rolls for all elections to Parliament and to the Legislature of every state is vested in the Election Commission.
2. Article 325 of Constitution of India provides that there shall be one general electoral roll for every territorial constituency and no person shall be ineligible for inclusion in any such roll or claim to be included on grounds only of religion, race, caste or sex.
3. Under Article 326 of Constitution of India, every person who is a citizen of India and who is not less than 18 years of age and is not disqualified under the Constitution or any law made by the appropriate legislature on the ground of non-residence, unsoundness of mind, crime or corrupt or illegal practice, shall be entitled to be registered as a voter at any election to the House of the People or to a State Legislative Assembly.
4. The Parliament has been authorised by Article 327 of the Constitution to make provisions by law with respect to all matters relating to elections to either House of Parliament or to the House or either House of the Legislature of a State including preparation of electoral rolls. In exercise of such power, the Parliament has enacted the Representation of the People Act 1950.

Provisions of Representation of People's Act 1950 with regard to electoral roles

The RP Act 1950 has conferred on the Central Government, the power to make rules, after consulting the Election Commission for carrying out the purposes of the aforesaid Act. In exercise of this power the Central Government has promulgated the Registration of Electors Rules (RER), 1960. The Election Commission has issued various directions under the RPA, 1950 and the RER, 1960 from time to time. In addition, the Commission has also issued a number of instructions and clarifications. All the above constitute the framework of law under which the preparation and revision of electoral roll has to be carried out.

The Delimitation of Parliamentary and Assembly Constituencies Order, as amended from time to time, defines the territorial extent of each Assembly Constituency and the Parliamentary Constituency. A number of Assembly Constituencies comprise a Parliamentary Constituency. All Assembly and Parliamentary Constituencies are territorial, that is, have fixed geographical boundaries. An exception is the Sangha Assembly Constituency in Sikkim which comprise of monks residing in recognised monasteries all over the State of Sikkim.

The electoral rolls are maintained Assembly Constituency (AC) wise. The electoral roll of a Parliamentary Constituency consists of the electoral rolls for all the assembly constituencies comprised within that parliamentary constituency. J&K and Union Territories (UTs) not having a Legislative Assembly are the exceptions. In them the electoral rolls are prepared separately for Parliamentary Constituencies and separately for Assembly Constituencies.

In order to maintain the credibility of roll and to keep it updated, the aforesaid Acts and Rules provide for periodic revision of rolls. It is prepared based on house to house visit by the Enumerator. The electoral rolls are prepared or revised with reference to

- First day of January of the year in which the rolls are so prepared or revised.
- Before each general election to the House of the People or to the Legislative Assembly of a State.
- Before each byelection to fill a casual vacancy in a seat allotted to the constituency.
- Further, the Election Commission may at any time, direct a special revision of the electoral roll for any constituency or part of a constituency.

Publication of the Roll

Putting the roll on the website, immediately as it is published, is a very important step in the revision process. The website shall further facilitate an elector to check whether he/she has been registered as an elector or not and what are the details registered against his/her entry in the roll.

Disqualifications for Registration in an Electoral Roll

a. According to the RP Act 1950, a person shall be disqualified for registration in an electoral roll if he/she
   (i) Is not a citizen of India; or
   (ii) Is of unsound mind and stands so declared by a competent court; or
   (iii) Is, for the time being, disqualified from voting under the provisions of any law relating to corrupt practices and other offences in connection with elections.
b. The name of any person who becomes so disqualified after registration shall forthwith be struck off from the electoral roll in which it is included.
c. No person shall be entitled to be registered in the electoral roll for more than one constituency and no person shall be entitled to be registered in the electoral roll for any constituency more than once.

Qualifications and Conditions for Registration in an Electoral Roll

a. According to the provisions of RP Act 1950, subject to the above said restrictions, every person shall be entitled to be registered in the electoral roll of the Constituency who-
   (i) Is not less than 18 years of age on the qualifying date and
   (ii) Is a permanent resident of the constituency.
b. Members of Parliament and the State Legislatures are entitled to be registered in their home constituencies notwithstanding the fact that they are away from their normal place of residence in connection with their activities as legislators.
c. Inmates of jails, other legal custody, hospitals, beggar homes, asylums etc. should not be included in the electoral rolls of the constituency in which such institutions are located.
d. Students, if otherwise eligible, living in a hostel or mess or lodge more or less continuously, can be held to be ordinarily resident in the place where the hostel or mess or lodge is situated. However, if they so wish, they have the option of retaining their enrolment at their residence with their parents instead.
e. Service voters: Normally, the serving members of the armed forces of the Union or the central paramilitary forces, State Armed Police personnel posted outside the state, and the government servants posted outside India in Indian Missions/High Commissions are enrolled in their native places and not at their places of postings. They are called 'Service Voters'.
f. Overseas electors: The RP Act 1950 was amended in 2010 and was provided that every overseas elector, that is, an Indian citizen who is absenting from his place of

ordinary residence in India owing to employment, education or otherwise, and has not acquired citizenship of any other country and who is not included in the electoral roll, is entitled to have his/her name registered in the electoral roll of the constituency in which his/her place of residence in India as mentioned in his/her passport is located. In order to facilitate the NRIs and improve their enrolment in the electoral rolls, Form 6A shall be distributed among the family members of overseas electors, residing in India, through the Booth Level Officer (BLO) in the area assigned to him/her.

g. Persons holding declared offices: The holder of a declared officers such as President, Vice President, Governors, Ministers etc., who desire to be registered as an elector in the constituency in which, but for his holding such office, he would have been ordinarily resident, can also get registered there.

Penal Provisions

1. If any person deployed to perform any official duly in connection with the preparation, revision or correction of an electoral roll, is guilty of any act or omission in breach of such official duty, he shall be punishable with imprisonment for a term which shall not be less than 3 months but may extend to 2 years and with fine.
2. The responsibility for getting the names of ineligible persons entered in the electoral roll can be placed squarely on the head of the family and if he provides false information, then he shall be punished with imprisonment for a term which may extend to one year, or with fine or with both.

9.7 CRIMINALISATION OF POLITICS

The understanding of the process of Criminilisation of politics is of special concern to an active citizen of Indian democracy because the Indian Constitution, following the British practice, envisages the principle of Parliamentary Supremacy. The Parliament is constituted out of representatives, the representatives are part and parcel of politics and the criminalisation of politics would necessarily lead to criminalisation of the representative institution, which would in turn gets reflected in the governance of this largest democracy. The problem becomes more acute when one takes into account of the structure that the real administrators, the Executive is drawn from the Parliament and they remain as an executive as long as they hold majority in the Parliament. India, with still being a home to millions of poor and ignorant population, the subject can be neglected by its active citizens only in their own and their nation's peril.

9.7.1 The Process of Criminalisation of Politics – Why and How?

9.7.1.1 Use of Muscle Power to Win Elections

As early as in 1977, the National Police Commission headed by Dharam Vira observed: '*the manner in which different political parties have functioned, particularly on the eve of periodic election, involves the free use of musclemen and 'Dadas' to influence the attitude and conduct of sizable sections of the electorate*'. When a candidate thinks that he cannot come to power since the people have no faith in him, he chooses the other way, that is, to generate fear to gather peoples vote. Moreover, having musclemen at their command would help them to capture election booths and tamper the EVM or ballot box. Since the voters are common people in most cases, they are too reluctant to take measures that would curtail the criminal activities.

This initial practice has given way to another trend presently, that is, giving tickets to the confirmed criminals and history sheeters. In a country where most of the voters are common people who are reluctant to question the criminals, and where the institutional mechanisms entrusted with the task of conducting free and fair elections are either inadequate or corrupted, then fielding a criminal directly by the party would ensure victory for sure. Moreover, it would be more beneficial for a criminal to get himself elected as this would give him a direct control over administration. In case of India, though after the introduction of EVM and through various electoral reforms, elections in the past decade seems comparatively free from violent instances, it is not completely free of such instances.

9.7.1.2 Money Power to Win Elections

Corruption and criminalisation goes hand in hand together. The expenses in elections to Parliament and State Legislatures are very high and it is a widely accepted fact that this huge election expenditure is the major root cause for corruption in India. Unless a candidate spends lakhs of rupees, he wouldn't get elected and even if he gets elected, the total salary he receives during his tenure as an MP/MLA will be very less compared to his actual election expenses. How can he bridge the gap between the income and expenses? Publicly, through donations and secretly, through illegal means. A political party has to reach millions of voters, face Union, State and Panchayat elections almost round the year. Where is this money to come from? Only criminal activity can generate such large sums of untaxed funds. This facilitates the entry of criminals in politics. They have money and muscle, so they win and help others in their party win as well.

9.7.1.3 Vote Bank Politics

The majority are the people those who do not know why they ought to vote in this country. Therefore, majority of the voters are easily manoeuvrable and purchasable. Their support is easier to gain for the crooked than the hardworking and honest persons. The muscle and money power fetches important votes. Elections are won and lost on swings of just 1% of the vote, so parties cynically woo every possible vote bank, including those headed by accused robbers and murderers. Legal delays in convicting criminals ensures that the process remain unchecked.

9.7.1.4 Corruption at the Institutional Levels

Corruption had become a serious problem in our country that almost every democratic institution, right from the lower organs to supreme organs, is not out from its ugly tentacles. Corrupted institutions of democracy would naturally facilitate the entry of criminal elements. For instance, the Transparency International's Corruption Perception Index (CPI) placed India at 94th rank out of 176 nations in its December 2012 report. India had a score of 36 out of 100 on a scale from 0 (highly corrupt) to 100 (very clean). First launched in 1995, the corruption perceptions index has been widely credited with putting the issue of corruption on the international policy agenda. The report is based on an average of 13 different surveys and assessments from 12 different institutions including World Bank's Country Performance and Institutional Assessment, the World Economic Forum, World Justice Project and Global Insight Country Risk Ratings. India was ranked 72 among 180 countries in 2007, at 87 in 2010 and the position was 95 in 2011. There are also instances of voters choosing to elect those parties which lure them with cash or kind.

This tactic of luring voters is effective in the case of gullible illiterate and passive voters who are ignorant of the consequences of their action. The political parties take undue advantage of this ignorance and the result is that the voter is left to suffer for next five years. Most of the rural masses who do not have enough access to literacy or media or news channels may not be able to judge the political parties and there is the possibility of them voting for the wrong candidate. Yet another pertinent aspect is the caste factor. The caste factor plays a crucial role during election and many a time a voter prefers to vote for a party or a candidate based on his caste and religion, without bothering about the present scenario. Criminalisation of politics can be prevented to a great extent if a voter is aware enough and chooses the best and ideal candidate.

9.7.1.5 Denial of Justice and Rule of Law

Laws that are either ridiculously in deterrent against certain offences or improperly enforced against convicted criminals further encourage the process of criminalisation. A majority of the provisions in the RP Act provides punishments which are far from ground reality. For example Section 130 of RP Act 1951 prohibits canvassing in or near polling station, soliciting the vote of any elector, persuading any elector not to vote for any particular candidate or persuading any elector not to vote at the election and are termed as as 'Electoral Offences'. Any person who contravenes these provisions is punishable with fine which may extend to ₹250, says the same section. Even if the laws are deterrent to the level of disqualifying a candidate, the problem of delayed verdicts by the judiciary ensures representative institutions a safe heaven for criminals.

9.7.1.6 Non-Transparency in the Functioning of Political Parties

The major share of funding for Political Parties comes from voluntary contribution. One knows that undeniably such monetary sources influence voting behaviour. The high cost of elections provides logic for corruption in the public arena. A heavy donor invariably becomes a benefiter, as the law of pressure group politics would suggest. As the reader know already, in the 2003 order, the Election Commission of India, in pursuance of the Supreme Court judgment dated 13th March, 2003 mandated that candidates for electoral office must submit an affidavit disclosing his assets and liabilities. This order, however, does not apply to political parties. Though all the major commissions of reforms viz., Law Commission, Administrative Reforms Commission, National commission for Review of working of Constitution and Election Commission had called for annual disclosure of accounts of political parties, this has not been enforced so far.

In 2011, an RTI query was made by the Association for Democratic Rights to the Central Information Commission since political parties had refused to share information although by all accounts they were public bodies. The appeals were upheld in an order dated 3rd June issued by the full bench of CIC, which ruled that six national political parties needed to provide information as sought by establishing the RTI apparatus as required. The logic was that they were recipients of valuable state resources in the form of land, accommodation, and tax exemptions which amounted to 'substantial funding' by the public exchequer. Accordingly, they were to be treated as public bodies and made answerable as such. But this has not been enforced adequately so far.

9.8 ELECTORAL REFORMS

India's democratic setup is a paradigm for many countries in the world due to its remarkable success over the past six decades. The heart of India's democratic system witnesses regular elections with the participation of the largest electorate in the world. In order to safeguard the core values of fair and free elections in this dynamic scenario, it is important to have a just and unbiased electoral process with a greater citizen participation. Thus, in accordance to the responsibility bestowed upon by the Constitution of India, the Election Commission of India has always remained actively involved in finding out ways through which the purity and integrity of the election process is preserved.

However, there are certain challenges and issues that electoral system has faced over the years. Trust and confidence of citizens in electoral system can be affected if these challenges remain unattended. Thus, keeping in view these difficulties the Election Commission of India after conducting extensive study and research recommends certain changes that need to be taken up expeditiously to amend certain provisions of law.

These suggested reforms will prove to be extremely useful in addressing the existing issues and challenges and would go a long way in enhancing the quality of democracy in India. The following are the reforms as suggested by the Election Commission of India.

9.8.1 Amendment Proposed to Constitution of India

(a) **Constitutional protection for all members of the Election Commission of India:** Under Clause (2) of Article 324, the Election Commission shall consist of the Chief Election Commissioner and such number of other Election Commissioners, if any, as the President may from to time specify and the appointment of the Chief Election Commissioner and Election Commissioners shall, subject to the provisions of any law made in that behalf by Parliament, be made by the President.

Article 324(5) of the Constitution was incorporated to ensure the independence of the Commission and free it from external, political interference and thus expressly provides that the removal of the Chief Election Commissioner from office shall be on 'like manner and on the like grounds as a Judge of the Supreme Court'. The Article 324(5) also specifies that any other Election Commissioner or a Regional Commissioner shall not be removed from office except on the 'recommendation of the Chief Election Commissioner'.

The Goswami Committee in its Report on Electoral Reforms in 1990 recommended that the 'protection of salary and other allied matters relating to the Chief Election Commissioner and the Election Commissioners should be provided for in the Constitution itself on the analogy of the provisions in respect of the Chief Justice and Judges of the Supreme Court. Pending such Election measures being taken, a parliamentary law should be enacted for achieving the object'.

The Commission time and again in its various correspondence and reports has expressly opined that the current wording of Article 324(5) is 'inadequate' and requires an amendment to bring the removal procedures of Election Commissioners on par with the CEC to provide them with the 'same protection and safeguard[s]' as the Chief Election Commissioner.

Even the Supreme Court in 1995, in the case of T.N. Seshan, Chief Election Commissioner of India v. Union of India (UOI) and Ors. 1995 (4) SCALE 285, has held that the CEC is not superior to the Election Commissioners rather is at the same position as the other Election Commissioners by stating:

'As pointed out earlier, the scheme of Article 324 clearly envisages a multi-member body comprising the CEC and the ECs. The RCs may be appointed to assist the Commission. If that be so the ECs cannot be put on par with the RCs. As already pointed out, ECs form part of the Election Commission unlike

the RCs. Their role is, therefore, higher than that of RCs. If they form part of the Commission it stands to reason to hold that they must have a say in decision-making. If the CEC is considered to be a superior in the sense that his word is final, he would render the ECs non-functional or ornamental. Such an intention is difficult to cull out from Article 324 nor can we attribute it to the Constitution-makers. We must reject the argument that the ECs' function is only to tender advise to the CEC'.

Reason for the proposed reform

The reason for giving protection to a Chief Election Commissioner as enjoyed by a Supreme Court Judge in matters of removability from office was in order to ensure the independence of Commission from external pulls and pressure. However, the rationale behind not affording similar protection to other Election Commissioners is not explicable. The element of 'independence' sought to be achieved under the Constitution is not exclusively for an individual alone but for the whole institution. Thus, the independence of the Commission can only be strengthened if the Election Commissioners are also provided with the same protection as that of the Chief Election Commissioner.

Law Commission's Recommendation

The Law Commission in its 255th Report (2015) endorsed the view of the Commission and suggested the following changes to be brought in Article 324:

- In sub-section (5), delete the words 'the Election Commissioners and' appearing after the words 'tenure of office of'.
- In the first proviso to sub-section (5), after the words 'Chief Election Commissioner' appearing before 'shall not be removed', add the following words, 'and any other Election Commissioner'; also, after the words 'conditions of service of the Chief Election Commissioner', add the following words, 'and any other Election Commissioner'.
- In the second proviso to sub-section (5), after the words 'provided further that', delete the words 'any other Election Commissioner or' occurring before 'a Regional Commissioner'.

9.8.2 Matters Related to Electoral Roll

(a) **Use of common electoral rolls:** Article 324(1) of the Constitution of India empowers the Election Commission to, inter alia, supervise, direct, and control the preparation and revision of electoral rolls for all the elections to Parliament and State Legislatures, which is done by the Commission by the virtue of powers under The Representation of the People Act, 1951. Similarly, under Articles 243K and 243ZA and the relevant State laws, the State Election Commission supervises, directs, and controls the preparation and revision of electoral rolls for elections to the local bodies. There is no uniform law or procedure for State Election Commission to prepare these electoral rolls. Some States adopt the rolls prepared by the Commission while some prepare their rolls separately for elections. A proposal has been made by the Commission in this regard to bring in a reform with respect to use of common electoral rolls prepared by the Commission.

Reasons for the reform proposed

There is a non-uniformity of practice amongst States which causes duplication of essentially the same task between two different constitutional bodies, that is, the Election Commission of India and the State Election Commissions that entails the same effort and expenditure again by the States. Further, it creates a confusion amongst the voters, since they may find their names present in one roll, but absent in another. Thus, the use of common electoral rolls will overcome the issue of duplication and confusion and will also save the unnecessary effort and wastage of money. By virtue of common electoral rolls, the Parliamentary and Assembly rolls can be used in the local body elections, saving time, effort and expenditure, with the requisite modifications based on the wards or polling areas of the local bodies.

Law Commission's Recommendation

The Law Commission endorses the above suggestions of the Election Commission regarding introduction of common electoral rolls for Parliamentary, Assembly and local body elections. However, given that introducing common electoral rolls will require an amendment in the State laws pertaining to the conduct of local body elections, the Central Government should write to the various states in this regard.

(b) **Section 60 of the Representation of the People Act, 1950:** Under section 20A of The Representation of the People Act, 1950, Indian citizens living abroad owing to employment, education or otherwise, and have not acquired citizenship of another country, are entitled to be enrolled as elector in the native constituency in India in which his/her home address falls. Persons enrolled in the electoral roll under this section are called 'overseas electors'. The overseas electors have not been given any special voting facility which means that they can vote in person in the polling station concerned in the constituency in which they are enrolled.

Reason for the proposed reform:

Voting in person is not a viable option for the overseas electors as they cannot be expected to travel to India for voting. A Committee appointed by the Commission to consider alternative voting options for the overseas electors recommended the facility of voting through proxy or voting through postal ballot paper with one-way electronic transmission of the postal ballot paper (from Returning Officer to elector) as alternative voting options for the overseas electors.

(c) **Section 14(B) of the Representation of the People Act, 1950:** Under section 14(b) of The Representation of the People Act, 1950, the qualifying date for eligibility for enrolment in the electoral roll of a particular year is 1st of January of that year. Thus, a person who turns 18 after 1st January remains deprived of enrolment and becomes entitled only when the roll is revised next year.

Section 14 (b) is as follows:

(b) 'qualifying date', in relation to the preparation or revision of every electoral roll under this Part, means the 1st day of January of the year in which it is so prepared or revised:] [Provided that 'qualifying date', in relation to the preparation or revision of every electoral roll under this Part in the year 1989, shall be the 1st day of April, 1989.]

Reasons for the proposed reform:

Having only one qualifying date means that a large number of young persons who complete 18 years after 1st January would have to wait for next year for enrolment and would not be able to participate in elections held in the meanwhile. The Commission suggested that the law may be amended so that a person can be enrolled in the roll the day he or she turns 18. By such amendment, the principle of universal adult franchise is also respected and no person is deprived from enrolment for a period of one year.

9.8.3 Issues Related to Election Management

(a) **Making any false statement or declaration before authorities punishable:** Section 31 of The Representation of the People Act, 1950 makes a person who in connection with preparation, revision or correction of an electoral roll or in connection with inclusion or exclusion of an electoral roll makes a statement or declaration in writing which is false, be punishable with imprisonment extending to one year or with fine or with both.
However, there is no parallel provision in The Representation of the People Act, 1951, to penalise a person making a false declaration in connection with conduct of elections.

Reasons for the proposed reform:
There would be several cases of false statements before election authorities in connection with conduct of elections. In order to discourage motivated false statements before the election authorities, it would be useful to have a provision in The Representation of the People Act, 1951, similar to section 31 of the 1950 Act.

(b) **Proposal regarding filing of false affidavit:** Currently, a candidate to any National or State Assembly elections is required to furnish an affidavit, in the shape of Form 26 appended to The Conduct of Elections Rules, 1961, containing information regarding their criminal antecedents, if any, their assets, liabilities, and educational qualification. Section 125A of The Representation of the People Act, 1951 provides for the penalty for filing false affidavit. The offence is punishable by up to 6 months, or with fine, or with both.

Reason for proposed reform:
The Commission time and again has stressed on the importance of filing of true information by the candidates standing for elections in their affidavits. The filing of false affidavits in matters of election can have extremely serious consequences as it affects the purity of elections. The elector in order to make an informed choice has the right to know the correct information of the candidates. This view was also taken in the case of Krishnamoorthy v. Siva Kumar (2009) 3 CTC 446 pertaining to panchayat elections where the Court held that failure to disclose complete information may amount to undue influence, and that incorrect or false information interferes with the free exercise of the electoral right of the voter. Filing of false declaration about the background of the candidate undermines the very basic value of candidate disclosure, in turn affecting the right of the electors to know the antecedents of candidate. Therefore, it is necessary to enhance the punishment for filing false affidavit.

Law Commission's recommendation: The Law Commission in its 244th Report on 'Electoral Disqualifications' gave the following recommendations endorsing the view of the Election Commission:

(i) Introduce enhanced sentence of a minimum of two years under section 125A.
(ii) Include conviction under section 125A as a ground of disqualification under section 8(1) of The Representation of the People Act, 1951.
(iii) Set up an independent method of verification of winners' affidavits to check the incidence of false disclosures in a speedy fashion.

(iv) Include the offence of filing a false affidavit as a corrupt practice under section 123 of The Representation of the People Act, 1951.

(c) **Section 126 of the Representation of the People Act, 1951**
Under the criminal jurisprudence any person can set the law into motion unless specifically excluded by an express provision under a statute. In **The Representation of the People Act, 1951, section 32 clause (3) provides that no court shall take cognizance of any offence punishable under sub-section (1) unless there is a complaint made by order of or under authority from, the Election Commission or the Chief Electoral Officer of the State concerned.** However, no such provision is found under section 126 of the 1951 Act.

Reasons for proposed reform:
The proposal of the Commission is that section 126 of The Representation of the People Act, 1951 may be given a relook and in particular, necessary amendments may be made by adding a clause in section 126 stating that 'no court shall take cognizance of any offence under section 126(1)(b) unless there is a complaint made by order of or under the authority from the Commission or the CEO of the State concerned as in the case of section 32 of the 1951 Act. Another amendment that is required to be made in the Act is to include 'print media' under the present provision since the current framework only includes display by electronic media.

(d) **Adjournment of poll or countermanding of election on the ground of bribery:** Article 324 of the Constitution vests in the Election Commission the superintendence, direction and control of the preparation of the electoral rolls for, and the conduct of, all elections to Parliament and to the Legislature of every State and of elections to the offices of the President and Vice President held under the Constitution. The powers conferred thereunder are of widest amplitude as held by the Hon'ble Supreme Court in Mohinder Singh Gill v. Chief Election Commissioner (1978 SC851).

It was observed in M.S Gill's case that the framers of the Constitution took care to leave the scope of residuary power to Commission, foreseeing the infinite variety of situations that may emerge from time to time in such a large democracy as ours. Section 58A was inserted in The Representation of the People Act, 1951 to empower the Commission to countermand an election in the event of booth capturing in the constituency.

In S.Subramaniam Balaji v. Govt. of Tamil Nadu & Ors (2013) 9 SCC 659, the case relating to distribution of free gifts by the political parties (popularly known as 'freebies'), the Hon'ble Supreme Court observed that 'although, the law is obvious that the promises in the election manifesto cannot be construed as 'corrupt practice' under section 123 of The Representation of the People Act, the reality cannot be ruled out that distribution of freebies of any kind, undoubtedly, influences all people. It shakes the root of free and fair elections to a large degree'.

Reason for proposed Reform:
Over the period of time, especially in the recent years, money has played a key role in influencing the 'decision making' at the polls. There have been several instances of seizure of large amount of cash, liquor, gift items etc. from the candidates and their agents during the elections. In some cases, following large-scale instances of bribing of electors by candidates and workers of political parties, the Commission, using its plenary powers under Article 324 resorted to cancellation of the election process.

9.8.4 Issues Related to Logistics and Election Officials

(a) **Section 13CC of the Representation Of The People Act, 1950 And Section 28a of the Representation Of The People Act, 1951:** Section 13CC of the Representation of the People Act, 1950 states that:

'Chief Electoral Officers, District Election Officers, etc., deemed to be on deputation to Election Commission – The officers referred to in this Part and any other officer or staff employed in connection with the preparation, revision and correction of the electoral rolls for, and the conduct of, all elections shall be deemed to be on deputation to the Election Commission for the period during which they are so employed and such officers and staff shall, during that period, be subject to the control, superintendence and discipline of the Election Commission'.

Section 28A of the Representation of the People Act, 1951 states that

'Returning officer, presiding officer, etc., deemed to be on deputation to Election Commission – The returning officer, assistant returning officer, presiding officer, polling officer, and any other officer appointed under this Part, and any police officer designated for the time being by the State Government, for the conduct of any election shall be deemed to be on deputation to the Election Commission for the period commencing on and from the date of the notification calling for such election and ending with the date of declaration of the results of such election and accordingly, such officers shall, during that period, be subject to the control, superintendence and discipline of the Election Commission'.

Reasons for the reforms proposed

Transfer of election officials on the eve of elections can disturb the election preparedness.

(b) **Empowering the District Election Officer to requisition:** Section 159(1) of The Representation of the People Act, 1951 states that

'Staff of certain authorities to be made available for election work- (1) The authorities specified in subsection (2) shall, when so requested by a Regional Commissioner appointed under clause (4) of article 324 or the Chief Electoral Officer of the State, make available to any returning officer such staff as may be necessary for the performance of any duties in connection with an election'.

Reasons for proposed reforms

Section 26 of The Representation of the People Act, 1951 empowers the District Election Officers to appoint Presiding Officers and Polling Officers for polling stations falling in his district. Further, under section 20A of the 1951 Act, the District Election Officer is required to coordinate and supervise all work in the District in connection with conduct of elections. Therefore, for convenience, there should be express provisions empowering the District Election Officers to requisite staff for conduct of election under section 159 of the 1951 Act.

9.8.5 Issues Related to Nomination of Candidates

(a) **Section 33(7) of the Representation of the People Act, 1951 – Restriction on the number of seats from which one may contest:** As per the law of India, as it stands today, a candidate is permitted to contest an election from two different constituencies in a general election or a group of byelections or biennial elections. **Subsection (7) of**

section 33 of The Representation of the People Act, 1951, allows a person to contest a general election or a group of byelections or biennial elections from a maximum of two constituencies whereas section 70 of the 1951 Act, species that if a person is elected to more than one seat in either House of Parliament or in the House or either House of the Legislature of a State (some states have a Legislative Council or Vidhan Parishad as well, along with the Vidhan Sabha), then he/she can only hold on to one of the seats that he/she won in the election. Sub-section (7) was introduced through a 1996 amendment, prior to which there was no bar on the number of constituencies from which a candidate could contest.

The Election Commission proposed amendment of section 33(7) in the year 2004 to provide that a person cannot contest from more than one constituency at a time. However, in case the existing provisions are to be retained, a candidate contesting from two seats should bear the cost of the byelection to the seat that the contestant decides to vacate in the event of him/her winning both seats. The amount in such an event could be ₹5,00,000 for State Assembly and Council Election and ₹10,00,000 for election to the House of People (as proposed at that point of time).

In the year 2014, a writ petition was led before the Hon'ble Supreme Court, by the Voter's Party (a registered political party) challenging the constitutional validity of sub-sections (6) and (7) of section 33 and 70 of The Representation of the People Act, 1951. The petition is pending.

Reasons for the proposed reform

When a candidate contests from two seats, it is imperative that he has to vacate one of the two seats should he win both. This, apart from the consequent unavoidable financial burden on the public exchequer and the manpower and other resources for holding byelection against the resultant vacancy, would be an injustice to the voters of the constituency which the candidate is quitting from.

(b) **Disqualifications under Chapter III of the Representation of the People Act, 1951:** In the judgement dated 7th August, 2015, the Hon'ble Delhi Court has directed the Election Commission to consider the possibility, if any, of putting an impediment on a defaulter of public dues contesting election in order to ensure quick recovery of the said dues. In pursuance of the said judgement, the Commission has recommended amending provisions for disqualifications laid down in Chapter III of The Representation of the People Act, 1951so as to provide for disqualification in the event of defaulting in clearing public dues.

Direction of the Delhi High Court: The High Court made the following observations in its judgment:

- According to the report by India Today, the politicians and political parties in occupation of government accommodation allotted to them were in default of payment of electricity, water and telephone charges with respect thereto and no steps were being taken by the municipal and other governmental agencies for recovery of the said public dues. It was further reported that some politicians and political parties also owed money to five-star hotels run by India Tourism Development Corporation Ltd. (ITDC), a Public Sector Corporation, for events, functions held therein or for use thereof and that the ITDC, run and managed by bureaucrats under the control of the said politicians had also not taken any action for recovery of the said dues which were again public money.

- The zeal with which the public bodies try to recover dues from ordinary citizens was found to be totally missing in the case of politicians and political parties and which in fact had resulted in the accumulating arrears. There is a total lack of will on the part of governmental agencies to whom dues are owed, to recover the same from the politicians and political parties.
- The possibility of having the recoveries effected through the Lok Sabha and Rajya Sabha Secretariats by virtue of Rule 23 of the Members of Parliament (Travelling and Daily Allowances) Rule, 1957 also proved to be futile since the amounts due being very huge could not be recovered by way of deduction from the salaries.
- Neither the persuasion by the Supreme Court of the governmental agencies to whom dues are owed could prompt them for recovery nor did the different avenues explored by the Court for recovery have any substantial success due to the reluctance on the part of the governmental agencies to treat the political masters equally, as they treat other citizens.
- The defaulter politicians and political parties are found to have misused their position of power for their own benefit and gain which is against the simple premise of law that the public offices shall not be the workshops of personal gain.
- This calls for issue of directions to ensure that the MPs, MLAs and the political parties, taking advantage of the clout enjoyed by them over the officials of the municipal, electricity, water, telephone and other facilities agencies, are not able to escape without paying the dues.

Thus, the High Court under Paragraph 13 (reproduced below) issued, among others, the following directions:

- The ECI to, as directed in the earlier orders in this petition, continue to insist upon the candidates desirous of contesting an election to Parliament or to Legislative Assembly, along with their nomination form furnishing an affidavit of their being not in arrears of any public dues and if such candidate is in occupation of or in the past ten years been in occupation of any government accommodation to furnish a No Dues Certificate from the agency providing electricity, water and telephone to the said accommodation.
- The ECI to also within six months consider the possibility if any of putting any impediment to a defaulter of public dues contesting election, to ensure quick recovery of the said dues.

9.8.6. Issues Related to Decriminalisation of Politics

(a) **Decriminalisation of politics:** Section 8 of the Representation of the People Act, 1951 deals with disqualification on conviction for certain offences. Under this Section, disqualification arises only on conviction and there is no disqualification prior to conviction even if a person is facing several serious charges.

The Election Commission proposed in its set of proposals of 1998 and 2004 that Section 8 of the Representation of the People Act, 1951 should be amended to disqualify those persons from contesting election who are accused of an offence punishable by an imprisonment of 5 years or more even when trial is pending, given that the Court has framed charges against the person. To prevent misuse of the provision by the ruling party, the Commission suggested a compromise whereas only cases led prior to six months before an election would lead to disqualification of a candidate. In addition, the Commission proposed that candidates found guilty by a Commission of Enquiry should stand disqualified.

Some Important Judgements

In 2002, the Hon'ble Supreme Court gave a historic ruling in Union of India (UOI) v. Association for Democratic Reforms and Anr. With People's Union for Civil Liberties (PUCL) and Anr. v. Union of India (UOI) and Anr. (2002) 5 SCC 294 that every candidate, contesting an election to the Parliament, State Legislatures or Municipal Corporation, has to declare their criminal records, financial records and educational qualifications along with their nomination paper.

In 2005, the Supreme Court in Ramesh Dalal v. Union of India held that a sitting Member of Parliament (MP) or Member of State Legislature (MLA) shall also be subject to disqualification from contesting elections if he is convicted and sentenced to not less than 2 years of imprisonment by a court of law.

In Lily Thomas v. Union of India 2000 (4) SCALE 176, the Court held that Section 8(4) of The Representation of the People Act, 1951 is unconstitutional which allows MPs and MLAs who are convicted to continue in office till an appeal against such conviction is disposed off.

Further in 2013, the Hon'ble Supreme Court has requested the 20th Law Commission of India vide letter dated 16th January, 2013 to consider the matter again under two grounds, viz. disqualifications on the ground of framing of charges by the court or upon the presentation of the report by the investigating officer under Section 173 of Code of Criminal Procedure Code and disqualification on the ground of filing false affidavit under Section 125A of the Act of 1951. As per the concerns of the court, the Law Commission has suggested recommendations titled 'Electoral disqualifications' in its 244th report on Electoral Reforms.

The Hon'ble Supreme Court in Krishnamoorthy v. Sivakumar & Ors. (2015) case, while observing that the crucial recognised ideal which is required to be realised is eradication of criminalisation of politics and corruption in public life decided that 'disclosure of criminal antecedents of a candidate, especially, pertaining to heinous or serious offence or offences relating to corruption or moral turpitude at the time of filing of nomination paper as mandated by law is a categorical imperative and concealment or suppression of this nature deprives the voters to make an informed and advised choice as a consequence of which it would come within the compartment of direct or indirect interference or attempt to interfere with the free exercise of the right to vote by the electorate, on the part of the candidate'.

Reasons for the proposed amendment

Persons with criminal background, accused of serious offences contesting election sends very negative signals about our electoral process. Many of such persons facing charges of grave nature end up winning election and enter our temple of democracy namely the Houses of Parliament and State Legislature which is highly undesirable and the issue needs to be addressed.

The Commission while making the proposal is fully conscious of the general principles of criminal jurisprudence that a person is deemed to be innocent until proven guilty. But the proposed amendment will be in the larger national interest which should take precedence over the interests of the individuals.

Recommendation by Law Commission

Expediting trials in relevant courts where a case is led against a sitting MP/MLA and to conduct the trial on a day-to-day basis with an outer limit of completing the trial in one year. If the trial cannot be completed within the said time period or the charge is not quashed in the said period, the trial judge shall give reasons in writing to the relevant High Court.

Once the said period expires, two consequences may ensue: (i) The person may be automatically disqualified at the end of the said time period

(ii) The right to vote, remuneration and prerequisites of office shall be suspended at the end of the said period up to the expiry of the House.

Retroactive application from the date the proposed amendments come into effect, all persons with criminal charges (punishable by more than five years) pending on that date are liable to be disqualified subject to certain safeguards.

The punishment for filing false affidavits under Section 125A be increased to a minimum of two years, and that the alternate clause for fine be removed.

Conviction under Section 125A should be made a ground for disqualification under Section 8(1) of the RPA, 1951.

The filing of false affidavits should be made a corrupt practice under Section 123 of the RPA.

(b) **Use of religion in the name of electoral gain:** Elections are the manifestations of popular consent in a democratic society. History assents that it has significant repercussions on the making of a nation's governance and the nature of its policies. The framers of the Indian Constitution were concerned about the control that religion might exercise over the selection of government. A lot of dialogue and debate was made in the Constitutional assembly debates regarding the inclusion of word 'secularism'. The Forty-second Amendment of the Constitution of India, officially known as The Constitution (Forty-second amendment) Act, 1976 was in the following lines 'The democratic institutions provided in the Constitution are basically sound and the path for progress does not lie in denigrating any of these institutions. However, there could be no denial that these institutions have been subjected to considerable stresses and strains and that vested interests have been trying to promote their selfish ends to the great detriment of public good. It is, therefore, proposed to amend the Constitution to spell out expressly the high ideals of socialism, secularism and the integrity of the nation, to make the directive principles more comprehensive and give them precedence over those fundamental rights which have been allowed to be relied upon to frustrate socio-economic reforms for implementing the directive principles...... In the Preamble to the Constitution,-(a) for the words 'SOVEREIGNDEMOCRATIC REPUBLIC' the words 'SOVEREIGNSOCIALIST SECULAR DEMOCRATIC REPUBLIC' shall be substituted; and (b) for the words 'unity of the Nation', the words 'unity and integrity of the Nation' shall be substituted.

An Amendment Bill, [Representation of the People (Second Amendment) Bill, 1994] was introduced in the Lok Sabha to provide provision(s) to question the acts of misuse of religion by political parties before the Hon'ble High Court. However, the same lapsed in 1996 with the dissolution of 10th Lok Sabha. The Commission has forwarded the recommendation again on 2010.

Earlier Goswami Committee in its report in 1990 on Electoral Reforms had suggested parallel recommendation, which read as follows: 'Election Commission shall have the power to make recommendations to the appropriate authority to (a) refer any matter for investigation to any agency specified by the Commission and (b) prosecute any person who has committed an electoral offence under this Act or (c) appoint any special court for the trial of any offence or offences under this Act (RP Act 1951)'.

The above recommendations were included in the Representation of the People (Amendment) Bill, 1990 introduced in the Rajya Sabha. However, the said Bill was withdrawn by the government in December 1993, stating the Govt. would come up with a revised bill.

In the 255th report of the Law Commission on Electoral Reforms, recommendations were made to maintain internal democracy in the political parties, drawing a comparative study of electoral regulations in Germany, Portugal and Spain.

Reasons for the proposed reform

The Ministry of Home affairs referred to the Commission the relevant part of the Report of the Liberhans Ayodhya Commission of Inquiry, in 2010, for action on some recommendations for action by the Election Commission against the parties which misuse religious sentiments.

The proposal was to initiate swift action against those persons who attempt to misuse religious sentiments or making appeals to voters through the mode of their piety by holding disguised religious rallies in places of worship as political supplication, to strengthen the existing provisions in the Codes of Conduct and other election-related laws.

Under the existing law, that is, section 123(3) and (3A) of the Representation of the People Act, 1951, appeal on grounds of religion, race etc. and promotions of feelings of enmity between different classes of religion constitute corrupt practice and the same can be questioned only by way of an election petition. Further the same cannot be a subject of enquiry before the Commission when the election is in progress. Ironically these provisions will have application only during the period of election and there is no provision to challenge the corrupt practice of the candidate who lost the election.

(c) **Making bribery in elections a cognizable offence:** The phenomenon of bribing of voters with money and essential commodities and buying out local representatives has always plagued Indian elections. Section 123(1) of The Representation of the People Act 1951 defines 'Bribery' as any gift, offer or promise by a candidate or his agent or any other person with the consent of a Candidate or his election agent giving gratification, to any person whomsoever, with the object, directly or indirectly of inducing

(i) A person to stand or not to stand as, or to withdraw or not to withdraw from being a candidate at an election.
(ii) An elector to vote or refrain from voting at an election.
(iii) An elector for having voted or refrained from voting.

Section 171B of IPC also describes Bribery broadly in the lines that, if a person advances a gratification to any person with the object of inducing him or any other person to exercise their electoral right or of rewarding any person for having exercised any such right or accepts either for himself or for any other person any gratification as a reward for exercising any such right or for inducing or attempting to induce any other person to exercise any such right; commits the offence of bribery.

Section 171C of IPC talks about undue influence at elections as whoever voluntarily interferes or attempts to interfere with the free exercise of any electoral right commits the offence of undue influence at an election by threatening any candidate or voter, or any person in whom a candidate or voter is interested, with injury of any kind, or by inducing a candidate or voter to believe that he or any person in whom he is interested will become or will be rendered an object of Divine displeasure or of spiritual censure.

In 2012 the Election Commission recommended to the Home Ministry to amend the existing law to make bribery during elections (both cash and kind) a cognizable offence, enabling police to arrest the violators without a warrant and to enhance the punishment up to two years. The Home Ministry has conveyed to the Election Commission that it has initiated the process to amend the Sections 171B and 171E of the Code of Criminal Procedure (CrPC), 1973 for the same.

Reasons for the proposed reform

The change in law have become necessary as there have been increasing incidents of bribery being detected in all elections, from local body polls to Lok Sabha elections. This is because, currently, bribery is a bailable offence attracting only minimal punishment.

Moreover, the experience on the ground has shown that the law enforcing authorities feel handicapped in apprehending the culprits because they cannot proceed without a warrant issued by a competent Magistrate under Section 200 of the Code of Criminal Procedure Code, 1973 on being moved under section 155 of the said Act, to search or arrest any person even on specific information about the corruptive practice. These provide the violators an opportunity to evade legal action.

9.8.7 Issues Related to Reforms in Political Parties

(a) **Deregistration of political parties:** Section 29A of The Representation of the People Act, 1951 empowers the Election Commission of India to register associations and bodies as political parties. However, there is no constitutional or statutory provision that gives power to the Election Commission to de-register political parties.

The Supreme Court, in Indian National Congress (I) v. Institute of Social Welfare and Ors., (2002) 5 SCC 685, held that the law does not empower the Commission to de-register a political party on the grounds of violation of any provisions of constitution or any undertaking given to the Commission. It further held that

'34. However, there are three exceptions where the Commission can review its order registering a political party. First is where a political party obtained its registration by playing fraud on the Commission, Second, it arises out of Sub-section (9) of Section 29A of the Act and third, any like ground where no enquiry is called for on the part of the Election Commission, for example, where the political party concerned is declared unlawful by the Central Government under the provision of the Unlawful Activities (Prevention) Act, 1967 or any other similar law.

35. Coming to the first exception, it is almost settled law that fraud vitiates any act or order passed by any quasi-judicial authority even if no power of review is conferred upon it. In fact, fraud vitiates all actions. In Smith v. East Ellis Rural Distt. Council - (1956) 1 All E.R. 855 it was stated that the effect of fraud would normally be to vitiate all acts and order. In Indian Bank v. Satyam Fibres (India) Pvt. Ltd. - MANU/SC/0657/1996 : AIR1996SC2592, it was held that a power to cancel/recall an order which has been obtained by forgery or fraud applies not only

to courts of law, but also to statutory tribunals which do not have power of review. Thus, fraud or forgery practised by a political party while obtaining a registration, if comes to the notice of the Election Commission, it is open to the Commission to de-register such a political party.

36. The second exception is where a political party changes its nomenclature of association, rules and regulation abrogating the provisions therein conforming to the provisions of Section 29A(5) or intimating the Commission that it has ceased to have faith and allegiance to the Constitution of India or to the principles of socialism, secularism and democracy, or it would not uphold the sovereignty, unity and integrity of India so as to comply the provisions of Section 29A(5). In such case, the very substratum on which the party obtained registration is knocked off and the Commission in its ancillary power can undo the registration of a political party. Similar case is in respect of any like ground where no enquiry is called for on the part of the Commission. In this category of cases, the case would be where a registered political party is declared unlawful by the Central Government under the provisions of Unlawful Activities (Prevention) Act, 1967 or any other similar law. In such cases, power of the 'Commission to cancel the registration of a political party is sustainable on the settled legal principle that when a statutory authority is conferred with a power, all incidental and ancillary powers to effectuate such power are within the conferment of the power, although not expressly conferred. But such an ancillary and incidental power of the Commission is not an implied power of revocation. The ancillary and incidental power of the Commission cannot be extended to a case where a registered political party admits that it has faith in the Constitution and principles of socialism, secularism and democracy, but some people repudiate such admission and call for an enquiry by the Election Commission. Reason being, an incidental and ancillary power of a statutory authority is not the substitute of an express power of review.

41. It may be noted that the Parliament deliberately omitted to vest the Election Commission of India with the power to de-register a political party for non-compliance with the conditions for the grant of such registration. This may be for the reason that under the Constitution the Election Commission of India is required to function independently and ensure free and fair elections. An enquiry into non-compliance with the conditions for the grant of registration might involve the Commission in matters of a political nature and could mean monitoring by the Commission of the political activities, programmes and ideologies of political parties. This position gets strengthened by the fact that on 30th June, 1994 the Representation of the People (Second Amendment) Bill, 1994 was introduced in the Lok Sabha proposing to introduce Section 29-B where under a complaint to be made to the High Court within whose jurisdiction the main office of a political party is situated for cancelling the registration of the party on the ground that it bears a religious name or that its memorandum or rules and regulations no longer conforming the provisions of Section 29-A(5) or that the activities are not in accordance with the said memorandum or rules and regulations. However, this bill lapsed on the dissolution of the Lok Sabha in 1996'.

The recommendation by Department Related Parliamentary Standing Committee on Personnel, Public Grievances, Law and Justice in 61st Report on Electoral Reforms-Code of Conduct for Political Parties & Anti Defection Law states:

'Under Section 29 (A) Representation of People Act, 1951, the Election Commission of India has been given power to register political parties but the power of de-registration of political parties has not been given to Election Commission of India under that law. However, the Election Commission of India has assumed the power under para 16 A of the Election

Symbol (Reservation and Allotment) Order, 1968 to de-recognise the political parties in the event of violation of Model Code of Conduct. The net effect of de-recognition of political party makes that party almost dysfunctional as its symbol is taken away. The Committee, therefore, recommends that the power to de-recognise political parties on account of violation of Model Code of Conduct may be incorporated in the Representation of People Act, 1951 itself'.

Reasons for the proposed reforms

Many political parties get registered, but never contest election. Such parties exist only on paper. The possibility of forming political parties with an eye on availing the benefit of income tax exemption also cannot be ruled out. It would only be logical that the Commission which has the power to register political parties is also empowered to de-register in appropriate cases.

(b) **Tax relief for political parties:** Section 13A of the Income-tax Act, 1961 confers tax-exemption to political parties for income from house property, income by way of voluntary contributions, income from capital gains and income from other sources. In other words, only income under the head salaries and income from business or profession are chargeable to tax in the hands of political parties in India. Political parties registered with the Election Commission of India are exempted from paying Income Tax under section 13A of Income Tax Act, 1961 as long as the political parties comply with the proviso to section 13A, that is, if they file their Income Tax Returns every assessment year along with their audited accounts, income/expenditure details and balance sheet.

In 2003, sections 29B and 29C were inserted in The Representation of the People Act, 1951 making provisions regarding receiving of donations/contributions by political parties from individuals and companies (other than govt. companies). Section 29C provides that for contribution in excess of ₹20,000 in a year, the treasurer/authorised person of the party shall prepare a report of such contributions. The report is required to be submitted on an annual basis to the Commission before the due date for furnishing the return of its income, and failure to do so would render the party ineligible for any tax relief under the Income Tax Act notwithstanding any provisions therein.

Reason for the proposed reform

There could be cases where political parties could be formed merely for availing of provisions of income tax exemption if the facility, that are at the expense of the public exchequer, is provided to all political parties.

(c) **Compulsory maintenance of accounts by political parties:** Section 13A(a) of the Income Tax Act, 1961 requires the political parties to keep and maintain 'such books of account and other documents as would enable the Assessing Officer to properly deduce its income therefrom'. Section 13A(a) of the Income Tax Act, 1961 states that the accounts of such political party must be audited by an accountant as defined in the Explanation below sub-section (2) of section 288.

Section 29C of The Representation of the People Act, 1951 states that the treasurer of a political party or any other person authorised by the political party in its behalf shall, in each financial year, prepare a report declaring the donations received from persons or non-government companies in that financial year. Section 29C (3) states that the said report must be submitted before the due date for furnishing a return of its income of that financial year under section 139 of the Income Tax Act, 1961 to the Election Commission.

Section 29C (4) provides that tax exemption under section 13A of the Income Tax Act will not be availed to a political party which fails to submit the said report.

The 'Guidelines and Application Format for Registration of Political Parties under section 29A of The Representation of the People Act' by the Election Commission of India requires the parties seeking registration to maintain their accounts on accrual system and to be annually audited by Auditor on the panel of Comptroller and Auditor General of India. It further states that the audited annual accounts should be submitted to the Election Commission within 6 months of the end of financial year.

Reason for the proposed reform

Political parties are major stakeholders in a democracy and they should be accountable to the public. This will ensure transparency and empower people to make informed decisions about electing their representatives.

(d) **Accounting and auditing report of political parties:** There is no legislation or regulation or rule which prescribes either (a) standard financial accounting and reporting framework, or (b) auditing framework for financial statements of political parties in India.

Reason for the proposed reform

Accounting and auditing standards would help political parties to maintain uniformity in presentation of financial statements, proper disclosure and transparency of their accounts.

(e) **Prohibition on anonymous donations:** There is no constitutional or statutory prohibition on receipt of anonymous donations by political parties in India. But there is an indirect partial ban on anonymous donations through the requirement of declaration of donations under section 29C of The Representation of the People Act, 1951.

Reason for the proposed reform

Although section 29C of The Representation of the People Act, 1951 requires the political parties to declare their donations, however such declaration is mandated only for contributions above ₹20,000.

(f) **Cap on expenditure by political party on a candidate for election campaign:** The ECI issued transparency guidelines under Article 324 of the Constitution of India bearing No. 76/PPEMS/Transparency/2013 dated 29th August, 2014 with effect from 01st October, 2014 stating that although there is no cap on expenditure by political parties for propagating their program, parties are required to adhere to the cap prescribed in section 77(3) of The Representation of the People Act, 1951 and Rule 90 of the Election Rules while providing 'financial assistance' to candidates in their election campaigns. These amounts should be paid only by a crossed account payee cheque or draft or bank transfer, and not by cash.

Reason for the proposed reform

This amendment will ensure accountability and place a check on election expenditure by candidates.

(g) **Ceiling of campaign expenditure by political parties:** There is no limit on the campaign expenditure by political parties.

Law Commission of India report on Electoral Reforms, Report No. 255 (12th March, 2015) observed:

'2.28.3 Furthermore, Section 77 of the RPA only regulates the election expenses of candidates. Political parties are free to spend any amount as long as it is for the general party propaganda, and not towards an independent candidate. Thus, there is no ceiling on party expenditure. It is recommended that the law on this point does not change, namely that there are no caps on party expenditure under the RPA given that it would be very difficult to fix an actual, viable limit of such a cap and then implement such a cap. In any event, as the experience with section 77(1) discussed above reveals, in the 2009 Lok Sabha elections, on average candidates showed election expenditures of 59% of the total expenses limit. There is no reason why the same phenomenon of under-reporting will not transpire amongst parties.

2.28.4 Placing legislative ceilings on party expenditure or contributions will not automatically solve the problem, especially without putting in place a viable alternative of complete state funding of elections (which in itself is next to impossible right now). Our previous experience in prohibiting corporate donations in 1969 did not lead to a reduction in corporate donations. Instead, in the absence of any alternative model for raising funds, it greatly increased illegal, under the table and black money donations.

2.28.5 Although the problem of black money and under-reporting will remain under the existing regime of no caps on individual contribution and party expenses, it has to be tackled through a stricter implementation of the anti-corruption laws and RTI and improved disclosure norms. It might be desirable to regularly re-examine the 7.5% profit cap on company's contributions in light of the intended rationale, since the former can become a meaningless limit in the context of big companies'.

Reason for the proposed amendment

The limit on campaign expenditure will ensure level-playing field for all political parties and curb the menace of unaccounted money in elections. Further it will also control the money power used during election by political parties and their allies.

(h) **Limitation on the number of star campaigners:** As per section 77 of The Representation of the People Act, 1951, the expenditure incurred by the leaders of a political party on account of travel by air or by any other means shall not be deemed to be expenditure in connection with the election incurred or authorised by a candidate. Explanation (2) of the section defines political parties to include 40 persons of a recognised political party and 20 persons of a party other than the recognised political party, that is, registered unrecognised parties, whose names have been communicated to the Chief Electoral Officer and Election Commission of India within a period of 7 days from the date of notification. Such political leaders as communicated to the CEO and the Election Commission are known as Star Campaigners.

There is no prescribed number of star campaigners for byelections.

Reason for the proposed reform

The maximum number of star campaigners should be prescribed for byelections to ensure level playing field and for smoother election management.

9.8.8 Issues Related to Election Campaign and Advertisement

(a) **Ban on exit polls and opinion polls:** Opinion poll, sometimes simply referred to as a poll, is a kind of human research survey which is conducted to find out the public opinion before the elections. It is a way in which through a scientific survey the views of a particular group of people can be ascertained. Unlike Opinion Poll, Exit Poll is a post-election poll which is conducted when an elector walks out after casting his or her vote. These kinds of polls aim at predicting the actual result on the basis of the information collected from the voters.

The Representation of the People Act under section 126A bans conducting and disseminating results of exit polls during the period starting from commencement of polls till the completion of polls in all phases. According to the present scheme of The Representation of the People Act, 1951, section 126(1) (b) which prohibits the display of any election matter during the period of 48 hours before the hour fixed for conclusion of poll, is only limited to display by means of 'cinematograph, television or other similar apparatus'; and does not deal with the independence and robustness of the opinion polls themselves. However, there exists a lacuna as a ban on publishing such election matters in electronic media does not extend itself to print media. New sections 126A and 126B for the restriction on publication and dissemination of result of exit polls. However, in the present framework there is no restriction on conducting opinion polls or disseminating results of opinion polls even in phased elections.

The Commission has been of the view that there should be some restriction or regulation on the publishing/dissemination of the results of opinion polls also. The Commission had issued certain guidelines in this regard in 1998 which were subsequently challenged before the Courts. Later, on the observation of the Hon'ble Supreme Court that the Commission did not have the power to enforce these guidelines, the same were withdrawn.

Reasons for the proposed reform

The Commission recommends that there should be a restriction on publishing the results of such poll surveys before the elections and reiterates its view that like the Exit Polls, there should also be some restriction on conducting and disseminating the results of Opinion Polls right from the day of the first notification of an election till the completion of the poll in all the phases where a general election is held at different phases.

Law Commission's Recommendation

The Law Commission in its Report in the year 2015 endorsed the view of the Commission and has called for the regulation of opinion polls so as to ensure that first, the credentials of the organisations conducting the poll is made known to the public; second, the public has a chance to assess the validity of the methods used in conducting the opinion polls; and third, the public is made adequately aware that opinion polls are in the nature of forecasts or predictions, and as such are liable to error.

(b) **Ban on government-sponsored advertisement before elections:** In politics, there exists use of advertising campaigns to influence political debate, and ultimately the voters. Presently, there is a trend wherein the Central and various State Governments embark upon 'election advertising' in the guise of providing information to the public. Such kind of an advertisement released with an eye on the election contain material intended or likely to affect voting in an upcoming election.

Reasons for the proposed reform

The advertisements highlighting the achievements made by the government are understandably incurred from the public exchequer and are given or created with a view to influence the electorate in favour of the ruling party.

The Item VII clause (iv) of the Model Code of Conduct for the Guidance of Political Parties and Candidates, prohibits the issue of advertisement at the cost of public exchequer in the newspapers and other media. The misuse of official mass media during the election period for partisan coverage of political news and publicity regarding achievements with a view to furthering the prospects of the party in power is also prohibited under the said Item

VII. However, the problem arises as the Model Code of Conduct comes into operation only from the date on which the Commission announces an election and the advertisements released prior to the announcement of elections are not prohibited under the Model Code of Conduct.

(c) **Section 126 of the Representation of the People Act, 1951**
The section 126 of The Representation of People Act, 1951 prohibits electioneering activities by way of public meetings, public performance, processions, advertisements through cinematograph, television or similar apparatus during the period of 48 hours, the time fixed for conclusion of poll. The advertisements in TV and Radio are also prohibited during these 48 hours under the above-mentioned provision. However, due to the existing gap in the Act, the political parties and candidates issue advertisements in the newspapers during this period including on the day of polling and also indulge in house to house visits.

A distorted advertisement in print media on the poll day leaves the other candidates with no remedy to undo the damage.

Reasons for the proposed reform
The Commission is of the view that such activities need to be prohibited and therefore, proposes that section 126 must be amended in the interest of fair and free elections to prohibit publication of advertisements by political parties in print media also (as in electronic media) during the period of 48 hours before the polling to allow the voters to arrive at an unprejudiced opinion.

(d) **Paid news in connection with elections:** Free and fair elections is the foundation of any democracy and this can only be achieved when there is an absence of influence by money in corrupting the electoral process. According to a study conducted by the Commission, during the assembly elections held in the period 2011–2013 there have been 1987 cases where a notice for paid news were issued to the candidates and 1727 cases where the practice of paid news were confirmed by the District/State Level Committees appointed for the purpose.

The problem of 'paid news' especially during election campaign is a widespread phenomenon. This phenomena of paid news and its equivalent, political advertising being presented as news, are issues that cannot be treated separately. The Press Council of India also, in its report regarding paid news cases had recommended that paid news may be made a corrupt practice.

Reasons for proposed reforms
The general public attaches great value in news report as distinguished from advertisements by political parties and candidates. This makes the news items a very important source of information concerning the political parties or candidates. On the contrary, paid news is masquerading as news and publishes advertisements in the garb of news items, totally misleading the electors. This raises potential concerns relating to the truth or falsity of claims and the possible defamatory effects of such news items and advertisements. The right to know, that is, right to have accurate information is a necessity to make an informed choice for the electors. However, paid news have a tendency to influence this choice in a negative manner.

To make the matter worse, the whole exercise of publishing paid news involves use of unaccounted money and under reporting of election expenses of the candidates indulging in the malpractice. The influence of money also has the potential in resulting in uneven elections between people with dissimilar financial statures. Thus, in order to have 'fair' election in a democracy, a level playing field is paramount. This can only be achieved by mitigating the influence of money in elections.

(e) **Section 125A of the Representation of the People Act, 1951**
Section 125A of The Representation of the People Act, 1951 has been inserted in the statute book in the year 2002 after the 170th Report of the Law Commission of 1999 in order to deter the candidates from filing false affidavits before the Returning Officer. The above-mentioned section provides with punishment with imprisonment for a term which may extend to six months, or with fine, or with both.

Reasons for proposed reforms
Despite the introduction of Section 125A to the 1951 Act, there are several complaints about false affidavits filed by candidates. The wilful concealment of information and furnishing of false information needs to be curbed in the interest of free and fair elections.

Thus, for the purpose of effectively dealing with this issue and to tackle the menace of wilful concealment of information or furnishing of false information and to protect the right to information of the electors, the Commission recommended that the punishment under section 125A must be made more stringent.

9.8.9 Issues Related to Election Expenses and Election Petitions

(a) **Sections 78, 81 and 84 of the Representation of the People Act, 1951**
Section 78 of The Representation of the People Act, 1951:

Lodging of account with the district election officer: (1) Every contesting candidate at an election shall, within thirty days from the date of election of the returned candidate or, if there are more than one returned candidate at the election and the dates of their election are different, the later of those two dates, lodge with the district election officer an account of his election expenses which shall be a true copy of the account kept by him or by his election agent under Section 77'.

Section 123(6) of The Representation of the People Act, 1951 provides that incurring or authorising of expenditure in contravention of section 77 is a corrupt practice.

As per Section 80 read with Section 81 of the 1951 Act, no election can be called into question except by way of election petition led before the High Court within 45 days from the date of election of the returned candidate.

Reason for the proposed reform
The period of filing election petition is 45 days and the time period of filing accounts is 30 days. This leaves only a small period for a person to analyse expenditure statement of candidates and decide whether an election petition needs to be led. Hence, the time period for filing of accounts needs to be reduced. So that more time is available to analyse the accounts.

Further, there is no provision for filing an election petition against a candidate who has lost the election but is guilty of corrupt practice under Section 123 of the 1951 Act.

(b) **Election expenditure in case of adjournment of poll under Section 52 of the Representation of the People Act, 1951**
Section 52 of the Representation of the People Act, 1951 provides for adjournment of poll in case of death of a candidate of a recognised political party.

Reason for the proposed reform

Subsequent to the death of a candidate of a recognised party, the Election Commission calls upon the recognised political party, whose candidate has died, to nominate another candidate for the said poll within seven days of issue of such notice to such recognised political party. In order to ensure parity between the new candidate and the other contesting candidates, latter should be permitted to further incur election expenditure.

(c) **Appointment of additional judges in the High Courts:** Article 224 of the Constitution of India states:

'(1) If by reason of any temporary increase in the business of a High Court or by reason of arrears of work therein, it appears to the President that the number of the Judges of that Court should be for the time being increased, the President may appoint duly qualified persons to be additional Judges of the Court for such period not exceeding two years as he may specify'.

The judges to people ratio is low in India and there is a need to appoint additional judges to clear the backlog of cases. The Commission has proposed that appointment of additional Judges in High Courts for trying election petitions to ensure their speedy disposal should be considered.

9.8.10 Other Such Issues Related to Election

(a) **Form 26 under Rule 4A of the Conduct of Elections Rules, 1961:** Presently, the existing Form 26 (the format in which the candidates are required to submit affidavit) does not contain any clause requiring information with respect to the sources of income of the candidate

Reason for the proposed reform

Declaring the source of income of the candidate and spouse would serve the interests of transparency and the right of electors to obtain information about their candidates for them to make an informed choice of their representative.

(b) **Rule-making authority to be vested in Election Commission:** The present framework of **The Representation of the People Act 1950 and 1951 under Section 28 and 169**, respectively empowers the Central Government to make rules after consultation with the Election Commission. However, the Central Government is not bound to accept such views or recommendations of the Commission.

Reasons for the proposed reform

Since the Central Government is not bound to accept the views and recommendations of the Commission, there are instances when rules opposed to the specific recommendations of the Commission have been framed. On several other occasions, rules framed or amended have not been in line with the recommendations of the Election Commission.

9.9 RECENT LANDMARK JUDGEMENTS OF THE SUPREME COURT

In the discharge of its constitutional responsibility of conducting free, fair and peaceful elections in the country, the hands of the Election Commission have been strengthened by the Supreme Court of India, by its several landmark judgements, pronouncing upon the provisions of the Constitution of India, and the laws relating to the elections. These judgements of the Supreme Court are the guiding stars not only for the Courts, but also for the Election Commission, its electoral machinery, Governments at the Centre and in the states, political parties and the candidates contesting elections.

Together with the Election Commission, the Supreme Court had played a commendable role in making the political arena clean from corrupts and criminals. To begin with, let us have a look at the two important developments that took place in 1996. The first was the Supreme Court's notices to political parties in January to file returns required by the Income Tax and Wealth Tax Acts by 20 February, in response to a public interest petition filed by a private citizens' group, after the parties did not respond to notices issued by the Income Tax Department. This forced parties, none of which had filed for all the years since 1979 as required, to do so. (However they did this only for 1994–1995).

The second important development was the Supreme Court's order of 4 April, 1996, shortly before the general elections, interpreting Explanation 1 of Section 77(1) of the RPA such that election expenditure by a political party would not be clubbed with that of a candidate for the purposes of the spending ceiling only if the party had submitted audited accounts of its income and expenditures, something that no party had done. This constrained conspicuous party spending on behalf of the candidate during the 1996 campaign.

On 2nd May, 2002, the Supreme Court by upholding a PIL made by Association for Democratic Reforms, held that the right to information – the right to know antecedents, including the criminal past, or assets of candidates – was a fundamental right under Article 19(1) (a) of the Constitution and that the information was fundamental for survival of democracy. In its judgement, it directed the Election Commission to call for information on affidavit from each candidate seeking election to Parliament or the State Legislature as a necessary part of the nomination papers on: Whether the candidate has been convicted/acquitted/discharged of any criminal offence in the past – if any, whether the candidate was accused in any pending case of any offence punishable with imprisonment for two years or more, and in which charge was framed or cognizance taken by the court of law. If so, requires the details thereof; the assets (immovable, movable, bank balance, etc.) of a candidate and of his/her spouse and that of the dependents; liabilities, if any, particularly of any overdue of any public financial institution or Government dues; educational qualifications of the candidate.

The Election Commission then proposed amendment of statutory rules and the format of nomination papers, to give effect to this judgment of the Supreme Court. But political parties believed that the Election Commission and the judiciary were overstepping their powers. At the all-party meeting, held on 8th July, 2002, representatives of 21 political parties decided that the Election Commission's order should not be allowed to be implemented. The Supreme Court again came out as a guardian of the citizen's right to information. The Apex Court gave its judgment on 13th March, 2003, basically asserting its previous June 2002 decision, which required full disclosure by all candidates. The order made it clear that failing to furnish the relevant affidavit shall be considered as a violation of the Supreme Court's order and as such the nomination papers shall be liable to be rejected by the Returning Officer. Furnishing of wrong or incomplete information shall result in the rejection of nomination papers, apart from inviting penal consequences under the Indian Penal Code. The 2004 General Elections were conducted under these rules.

The above order is an effective step to make democracy healthy and unpolluted. Citizens have every right to know about the persons whom they prefer as their representatives. The EC has directed all Returning Officers to display the copies of nomination papers and affidavits filed by candidates to the general public and representatives of print and electronic media, free of cost.

One has to notice two things here. One is that, this judgement was given way back in 2002, when the country did not have Right to Information Act (which makes Government officials liable for punishment if they fail to respond to people within a stipulated timeframe). The Act was enacted only in 2005. The other is that some of the parties would be able to draw advantage from the Supreme Court order because they already have efficient watchdog systems and batteries of lawyers in place that would permit them to file counter-affidavits and challenge nominations of opposing candidates within hours of their being filed.

With regard to the reformation of Election Commission, there was a longstanding demand to make the EC a multi-member body. The Supreme Court in the S.S. Dhanoa v. Union of India case, 1991 had observed: '*When an institution like the Election Commission is entrusted with vital functions and is armed with exclusive and uncontrolled powers to execute them, it is both necessary and desirable that the powers are not exercised by one individual, however wise he may be. It also conforms to the tenets of democratic rule*'. With the 1993 Constitution Amendment Act, the Election Commission was made a multi-member body. The Act provided that the decision of three members 'shall, as far as possible, be unanimous'. But in case of difference of opinion among three members, the matter 'shall be decided according to the opinion of the majority'.

In a landmark judgement that may lead to decriminalisation of politics, the Supreme Court on 10th July, 2013 struck down the provision viz., Section 8(4) of RP Act 1951.

The following are some of the recent landmark judgements delivered by the Supreme Court of India.

(a) **Subramaniam Swamy v. Election Commission of India [CA No. 5803 of 2008], Supreme Court:** The Appellant filed the Appeal for striking down paragraph 10A of the Symbols Order as it denies equality before the law that is violative of Article 14 of the Constitution of India.

The appellant alleged that the provisions of Para 10A of the Election Symbols (Reservation and Allotment) Order, 1968, as amended pre 2001, suffers from the vice of arbitrariness and amounts to an undemocratic act which does not pass the acid test of equality before law under Article 14 of the Constitution – symbol reserved for a party is an intellectual property that could not be taken away by a legislation, and in addition seeking a direction to the Commission to amend the said Para 10A suitably.

The Court held that Symbols Order promulgated by the Election Commission on 31/08/1968 in exercise of powers conferred by Article 324 read with Section 29A of the R.P. Act, 1951 and Rules 5 and 10 of the Conduct of Elections Rules, 1961 to provide for reservation, choice and allotment of symbols at elections in Parliamentary and Assembly Constituencies, for recognition of political parties and for matters connected therewith, is perfectly in consonance with the democratic principles.

The concept of recognition of political party is no doubt inextricably connected with the concept of symbol of that party but only a political party having substantial following has a right for a reserved symbol. A party which remains only in the records can never be equated and given the status of a recognised political party in a democratic set up.

With regard to the challenge to the constitutionality of Para 10A of the Symbols Order providing for concession to candidates set up by an unrecognised party, which was earlier recognised as a National or State Party not earlier than six years from the date of notification of the election, for allotment of the symbol reserved earlier for it, it was held that the rationale for providing six years period in para 10A is perfectly reasonable as it gives the party opportunity to prove its continued following in the fresh elections within six years.

The Court did not agree to read down the provisions of clause 10A so as to avoid the mention of six years as that would amount to absurdity vis-a-vis paras 5 and 6 of the Symbol

Order. Provisions of Para 10A has to be read and interpreted in terms of other connected provisions in Paras 5, 6, 6A, 6B and 6C and also the objects on the Preamble to the Symbols Order.

It further held that a symbol may be an outcome of intellectual exercise but it does not become an 'intellectual property' of the party for which it is reserved and the Commission has every right to deprive a particular party with a dismal performance of that reserved symbol. Election Symbol is only the insignia which is associated with the particular political party that helps millions of illiterate voters to properly exercise their right to franchise in favour of candidate of their choice belonging to a particular party.

With regard to the prayer of the appellant to freeze the symbol of a recognised political party after the party loses eligibility criteria for such recognition as per Symbols Order, the Apex Court observed that though there is no such provision of freezing of any particular symbol in the said Order the issue can be considered by the Commission in case the issue is raised before it by the appellant party.

(b) **DMDK & Another v. Election Commission of India [WP (C) No. 532 of 2008], Supreme Court 176:** A bunch of writ petitions and SLPs were filed to challenge the constitutional validity of the amendment made by the Commission in para 6 of the Election Symbols (Reservation and Allotment) Order, 1968, vide Notification dated 1st December, 2000, to prescribe that in order to be recognised as a State Party in the State, a political party would have to secure not less than 6% of the total valid votes polled in the State and should also have returned at least 2 members to the Legislative Assembly of the State.

The petitioner political party 'DesiyaMurpokkuDravidaKazharam', a registered unrecognised political party under Sec.29A of the R.P. Act, 1951, was refused recognition as a 'State Party' by the Election Commission despite having secured 8.33% of the valid votes polled and returning 1 (one) candidate to the Assembly during the general election to the Tamil Nadu Legislative Assembly, 2006, on the ground that it did not qualify the bench mark of returning at least two members to the Legislative Assembly in addition to securing the minimum percentage of votes of 6% prescribed under the amended para 6A of the Symbols Order 1968. It was contended that the classification of parties into recognised and unrecognised parties on the basis of the seats won during an election and the percentage of votes polled, is unreasonable and arbitrary, having no nexus with the purpose sought to be achieved. It causes hardship to political parties as it imposes two conditions clubbed with other conditions that are highly anomalous and therefore liable to be struck down. It further contended that denying a common election symbol to the candidates of unrecognised political parties vis-a-vis recognised political parties' results in hostile discrimination by the Commission.

It was also contended that the symbol in the context of an illiterate electorate is absolutely necessary for a free and fair election and equating established parties with newly-formed parties is a disadvantage to the newly formed parties and thus violative of Article 14 and was, therefore, liable to be struck down.

The Supreme Court (a Three-Judge Bench and the judgment by a majority decision) rejected the challenge to the vires of the Election Symbols Order, 1968, and held that the constitutional validity of the 1968 Order and the power of the Commission under para 15 of that order to settle issues relating to claims of splinter groups of recognised political parties to be the original party has been decided by a three-judge bench of the Supreme Court in Sadiq Ali's case 40 years ago.

It further held that in order to gain recognition as a political party and to become entitled to the allotment of a common symbol, a party has to prove itself to establish its credibility as a serious player in the political arena of the state by achieving the benchmark laid down by the Commission under the Symbols Order, 1968, after taking into account the ground realities of conducting a state-wide poll.

(c) **S. Subramaniam Balaji v. Govt. of Tamil Nadu & Others [CA No. 5130 of 2013], Supreme Court 273:** In the manifestos released by the two recognised State political parties in the State of Tamil Nadu, namely, Dravida Munnetra Kazhagam (DMK) and All India Anna Dravida Munnetra Kazhagam (AIADMK) during the general election to the Legislative Assembly of Tamil Nadu held in the year 2006, promises/offer of several articles to the electorate were made. The Appellant in the above referred cases, Shri S. Subramanian Balaji, filed complaint seeking initiation of action in respect of the said promises on the ground that such promises of 'freebies' amount to bribery within the meaning of section 123 (1) of the Representation of the People Act, 1951 and Section 171-B of the IPC.

He also filed two writ petitions Nos. 9013 of 2006 and 1071 of 2007 before the Madurai Bench of the High Court of Madras challenging the propriety of the expenses incurred by the state government out of the state exchequer for fulfilling the promises of distribution of several household articles, such as, colour television sets, etc. made in their election manifestos to woo the gullible electorate with an eye on their votes. It was alleged that this amounted to corrupt practice and was unauthorised, impermissible and ultra vires the Constitutional mandates. The Madras High Court by its Order dated 25th June, 2007 dismissed both the writ petitions holding that the action of the state government in distributing free colour TVs could not be branded as a waste of public money.

The Appellant preferred an Appeal by way of SLP (C) No.21455 of 2008 before the Supreme Court being aggrieved by the judgment passed by the Madurai Bench of the High Court of Madras in the said two writ petitions filed by the Appellant. During the pendency of the SLP, the schedule of next general election to the Tamil Nadu Legislative Assembly due in the year 2011 was announced.

Both the parties, DMK and AIADMK, again released their election manifestos with a volley of promises of supply of articles like, grinders, mixies, electric fans, laptop computers, 4-gm gold thalis, ₹50,000 cash for girl's marriage, green houses, 20 kg rice, etc. to the people if they come to power.

The appellant separately filed a complaint dated 22nd March, 2011 before the Election Commission seeking initiation of action in respect of the above freebies as corrupt practices under Section 123 of the RP Act, 1951 and requested to disqualify all such candidates on the ground that such promises amount to bribery within the meaning of Section 123(1) of the 1951 Act and Section 171-B of the IPC.

The Appellant also filed complaint before the Comptroller and Auditor General of India and Accountant General of Tamil Nadu against the transfer of consolidated fund of the state for fulfilling the promises of freebies made in the election manifestos. The Appellant again challenged the promises of freebies by filing another Writ Petition No.17122 of 2011 on 19th July, 2011, before the High Court of Judicature at Madras on the same ground that such promises are unauthorised, impermissible and ultra vires the Constitutional mandates.

The Hon'ble High Court directed the Commission to dispose of the representations made by the Petitioner.

The Commission informed the complainant/appellant on the basis of the existing legal provisions that commission of a corrupt practice by a candidate under Section 123(1) of R.P. Act, 1951 can be raised only before the High Court in an election petition and such candidate can be disqualified only on being found guilty by the High Court and not otherwise. Likewise, any person committing the offence of bribery under Section 171 (B) of IPC can be disqualified only on conviction by the competent court and not otherwise. It was also informed that declaration of public policy or promise of public action, is neither a corrupt practice nor electoral offence under proviso (b) to clause (2) of Section 123 of R.P. Act, 1951 and proviso to Section 171B(1) and Section 171C(2) of IPC. The Commission also conveyed its feeling that the promise of such freebies at government cost could disturb the level playing field and vitiate the electoral process and expressed its willingness to implement any directions or decision of the Court in this regard.

The Supreme Court vide its judgment dated 5th July, 2013 held that promises in the election manifesto do not constitute a corrupt practice under Section123 of the RP Act, 1951. It held that the Directive Principles of State Policy enshrined in the Constitution enjoin upon the State to frame various welfare measures for the citizens and therefore there can be no objection to the promise of such welfare measures in election manifestos. As long as the schemes come within the realm of public purpose and money is withdrawn by passing suitable Appropriation Bill, they are in consonance with Article 14 of the Constitution. The Supreme Court dismissed the petition de hors the jurisdiction issue raised verbally by the respondent State Government of Tamil Nadu at the time of hearing.

The Court, however, observed that even though framing of manifestos is the right of the political parties, it cannot overlook the undesirable impact of some of the promises and offers on the conduct of free and fair elections and maintaining level playing field for all political parties and candidates. It advised the political parties to avoid making those promises which are likely to vitiate the purity of the election process or exert undue influence on the voters in exercising their franchise.

Accordingly, it directed the Election Commission to frame guidelines with regard to the contents of election manifestos in consultation with all the recognised political parties. It also laid down the following guiding principles for framing of such guidelines:

(i) Although the law is obvious that the promises in the election manifesto cannot be construed as 'corrupt practice' under Section 123 of RP Act, the reality cannot be ruled out that distribution of freebies of any kind, undoubtedly, influences all people. It shakes the root of free and fair elections to a large degree.

(ii) The fountainhead of the powers under which the Commission issues these orders is Article 324 of the Constitution which mandates the Commission to hold free and fair elections. The Election Commission, in order to ensure level playing field between the contesting parties and candidates in elections and also in order to see that the purity of the election process does not get vitiated, has in the past been issuing instructions under the Model Code of Conduct.

(iii) The fact that generally political parties release their election manifesto before the announcement of election date, in that scenario, strictly speaking, the Election Commission does not have the authority to regulate any act which is done before the announcement of the date of election. Nevertheless, an exception can be made in this regard as the purpose of election manifesto is directly associated with the election process.

[Note: Pursuant to the Supreme Court's above order, the Election Commission framed guidelines, in consultation with political parties, and inserted them as Part VIII of the Model Code of Conduct by its letter No.437/6/Manifesto/2013 dated 19th February, 2014]

(d) **Lily Thomas v. Union of India & Others [WP (C) No. 490 of 2005], Supreme Court:** These writ petitions were filed as Public Interest Litigations for mainly declaring sub-section (4) of Section 8 of the Representation of the People Act, 1951, giving special protection to sitting members of Parliament and State Legislature from immediate disqualification on conviction for offences under sub-sections (1), (2) or (3) of said Section 8 until three months from the date of conviction or, if within that period an appeal or application for revision is brought in respect of the conviction or the sentence, until that appeal or application is disposed off by the Court and ultra vires the Constitution being in contravention of the provisions of Articles 101 and 190 of the Constitution. Petitioners contended that persons to be elected as members of Parliament or a State Legislature stand on the same footing as sitting members of Parliament and State Legislature so far as disqualifications are concerned and sitting members of Parliament and State Legislature cannot enjoy special privilege of continuing as members even after conviction for offences under sub-Sections (1), (2) and (3) of Section 8 of the Act. The Parliament lacks legislative powers to enact sub-section (4) of Section 8 of the RP Act, 1951.

It was held by the Hon'ble Supreme Court that the provisions of Article 101(3)(a) and 190(1)(a) of the Constitution expressly prohibit Parliament to defer the date from which the disqualification is attracted in case of a sitting member of Parliament or State Legislature. The Parliament, therefore, exceeded its powers in enacting sub-section (4) of Section 8 of the Representation of the People Act, 1951 and accordingly declared sub-section (4) of Section-8 of the Act and ultra vires the Constitution. The Court held that

'......We also hold that the provisions of Article 101(3) (a) and 190(3)(a) of the Constitution expressly prohibit Parliament to defer the date from which the disqualification will come into effect in case of a sitting member of Parliament or a State Legislature. Parliament, therefore, has exceeded its powers conferred by the Constitution in enacting sub-section (4) of Section 8 of the Act and accordingly subsection (4) of Section 8 of the Act ultra vires the Constitution ……..... (para)

However, if any sitting member of Parliament or a State Legislature is convicted of any of the offences mentioned in sub-sections (1), (2) and (3) of Section 8 of the Act and by virtue of such conviction and/or sentence suffers the disqualifications mentioned in sub-sections (1), (2) and (3) of Section 8 of the Act after the pronouncement of this judgment, his membership of Parliament or the State Legislature, as the case may be, will not be saved by sub-section (4) of Section 8 of the Act which we have by this judgment declared ultra vires the Constitution notwithstanding that he files the appeal or revision against the conviction and/or sentence'.

(e) **Resurgence India v. Election Commission of India & Another [WP (C) No. 121 of 2008], Supreme Court:** The writ petition was filed under Article 32 of the Constitution of India for issuance of appropriate writ/direction including writ of mandamus to effectuate meaningful implementation of the judgments rendered by the Supreme Court in Union of India v. Association for Democratic Reforms and Another (2002) 5 SCC 294 and People's Union for Civil Liberties (PUCL) and Another v. Union of India &Anr. (2003) 4 SCC 399, and for that purpose to direct the respondents to make it compulsory for the Returning Officers to ensure that the affidavits filed by the contestants are complete in all respects and to reject the affidavits having blank particulars.

Pursuant to the Order of the Supreme Court in Union of India v. Association for Democratic Reforms and Another (Supra), the Election Commission, vide order dated 28th June, 2002, issued directions to the candidates to furnish a duly sworn affidavit to declare full and complete information relating to his/her criminal antecedents, if any, information regarding assets of the candidate as well as of his/her spouse and that of dependants, liability, if any, and educational qualification of the candidate, to enable electors to know the background of the candidates. It was also directed that non-furnishing of the affidavit by any candidate or furnishing of any wrong or incomplete information or suppression of any material information of substantial character, found by the Returning Officer after summary enquiry at the time of scrutiny of nomination papers, will result in the rejection of the nomination paper, apart from inviting penal consequences under the Indian Penal Code, 1860.

Subsequently, in People's Union for Civil Liberties (PUCL) and Another v. Union of India & Anr. (Supra), while reaffirming the aforementioned decision, the Apex Court, however, held that the direction to the Returning Officer to reject the nomination papers for furnishing wrong information or concealing material information and verification of assets and liabilities by means of a summary inquiry at the time of scrutiny of the nominations by the Returning Officer should not be enforced.

Accordingly, the Election Commission, issued revised order dated 27th March, 2003, inter alia, clarifying that its earlier order with regard to verification of assets and liabilities by means of summary inquiry and rejection of nomination papers on the ground of furnishing wrong information or suppression of material information shall not be enforceable.

Subsequently, the Commission, vide letter dated 02nd June, 2004 directed the Returning Officers that where any complaint regarding furnishing of false information by any candidate is submitted by anyone, supported by some documentary evidence, the concerned Returning Officer should initiate action to prosecute the candidate concerned by filing formal complaint before the appropriate authority. The Supreme Court held that right to know about the candidate is a universally recognised natural right flowing from the concept of democracy and is an integral part of Article 19(1)(a) of the Constitution. To effectuate the fundamental right of the citizens, the candidates are supposed to disclose their antecedents at the time of filing of nomination paper and for that purpose, the Returning Officer can very well compel a candidate to furnish the relevant information.

It accordingly held that in the affidavits filed by candidates along with their nomination paper, the candidates must fill up all columns therein and no column can be left blank. Therefore, at the time of filing of affidavit, RO has to check whether all columns of the affidavit filed with the nomination paper are filled up. If not, the RO shall give a reminder to the candidate to furnish information against blank columns and for that purpose one more column be incorporated in the standard Check List already prescribed by the Commission to ensure filing of all documents required to be filed by a candidate along with the nomination paper. In case no information is to be furnished against any item, appropriate remarks such as 'NIL' or 'Not Applicable' or 'Not Known' as may be applicable shall be indicated in such column by the candidate. No column can be left blank. If a candidate fails to fill the blanks even after reminder, the nomination paper will be liable to be rejected by the Returning Officer at the time of scrutiny of nomination papers.

It further clarified that even though filing of affidavit with blanks will attract the penal provisions of Section 125A(i) of the RP Act, however, as the nomination paper itself is rejected by the Returning Officer, it would not be necessary to prosecute the candidate again for the same act.

(f) **People's Union for Civil Liberties & Another v. Union of India & Another [WP (C) No. 161 of 2004], Supreme Court:** This writ petition was filed before the Hon'ble Supreme Court under Article 32 of the Constitution of India challenging the constitutional validity of Rules 41(2) & (3) and 49-O of the Conduct of Elections Rules, 1961, to the extent these provisions violate the secrecy of voting required to be maintained as per Section 128 of the Representation of the People Act, 1951, and Rules 39 and 49-M of the 1961 Rules in the case of voter who decides not to cast his vote at an election for any of the contesting candidates in fray.

The Apex Court held that casting of vote is a facet of the right of expression of an individual and the said right is provided under Article 19(1)(a) of the Constitution of India and any violation of the said right gives the aggrieved person the right to approach the Supreme Court under Article 32 of the Constitution. Right to vote as well as right not to vote have been statutorily recognised under Section 79(d) of the RP Act, 1951 and Rules 41 (2) & (3) of the CE Rules, 1961. The fundamental right under Article 19(1)(a) read with statutory electoral right granted under Section 79 (d) of the RP Act, 1951 is violated unreasonably if the right not to vote effectively is denied and secrecy is breached.

It was held that secrecy of ballot is a privilege granted in public interest to an individual. The Apex Court directed the Election Commission to provide **'None of the Above' (NOTA)** option on the EVM and ballot papers so that the electors who do not want to vote for any of the candidates can exercise their option in secrecy. It was also held that the provisions of Rules 41(2) and 49-O under which an elector not wishing to vote for any candidate had to inform the Presiding Officer about his decision, ultra vires Article 19(1)(a) of the Constitution and Section 128 of the Representation of the People Act, 1951.

(g) **Subramaniam Swamy v. Election Commission of India [CA No. 9093 of 2013], Supreme Court:** The appellant filed writ petition before High Court of Delhi seeking writ of Mandamus directing Election Commission of India to incorporate a system of 'Paper trail/Paper Receipt' in the Electronic Voting Machines (EVM) as a convincing proof that the EVM has rightly registered the vote cast by a voter in favour of a particular candidate. The petition was dismissed by the High Court. Hence, other writ petition under Article 32 also prayed for writ of Mandamus directing the respondents to effect the necessary modifications in the EVMs so as to allow the voters to verify their respective votes and attach printers to EVMs with a facility to print the running record of the votes. The petitioner also prayed for a direction to frame guidelines and to effect necessary amendments in the Conduct of Elections Rules, 1961.

The stand of the Election Commission was that the apprehension that EVMs could be tampered with, is baseless as the technology employed is such that it cannot be manipulated in any manner. There has been no instance of tampering with EVMs by anyone since its introduction. However, to make the voting procedure more transparent the Commission has been in the process of exploring the possibility of incorporating a viable Voter Verifiable Paper Audit Trail (VVPAT) system with EVMs. Ultimately, the design of VVPAT system was finalised on 19th January, 2013 and the relevant rules of the Conduct of Elections Rules, 1961 were modified to enable use of VVPAT with EVMs and Notified in the Gazette of India on 14th August, 2013.

The Commission thereafter decided to use the VVPAT system for the first time in the byelection from 51-Noksen (ST) Assembly Constituency in the State of Nagaland. In order to ascertain the efficacy of the newly introduced VVPAT system the Commission decided on its own to manually count paper slips of VVPAT besides electronic count of EVM. No discrepancy was found between both the electronic and paper count. The report was placed before the Court.

The Supreme Court observed that it is necessary to set up EVMs with VVPAT system because vote is nothing but an act of expression which has immense importance in democratic system. It permitted the ECI to introduce the system in gradual stages in the coming general elections and directed the Government of India to provide required financial assistance for procurement of required number of units of VVPAT for conduct of general elections all over India.

The Appeal and the Writ Petition were disposed with the above directions.

(h) **Ashok Shankarrao Chavan v. Dr.Madhavrao Kinhalkar & Others [CA Nos. 5044, 5045 & 5078 of 2014], Supreme Court:** The main issue in the case was whether the Election Commission has been empowered under Section 10A of the R.P. Act, 1951 to hold an enquiry to ascertain the correctness or otherwise of the account of election expenses incurred by a returned candidate as maintained under Sections 77(1) and (2) and lodged with the District Election Officer (DEO) under Section 78 of the 1951 Act for the purposes of deciding the question of disqualification under Section 10A of the 1951 Act, either at the instance of any candidate who also contested in the said election or by any other person or based on any other information received by the Commission through some reliable sources, especially after a decision is rendered by the High Court in the Election Petition preferred by one of the contesting candidates under Section 80 of the 1951 Act.

Ultimately, the Supreme Court dismissed the SLP filed by Shri Ashok Chavan vide its order dated 5th May, 2014 and gave its seal of approval to the decision of the Election Commission as upheld by the High Court to the effect that Section 10A clothes the Election Commission with the requisite power and authority to enquire into the allegations relating to failure to submit the accounts of election expenses in the manner prescribed and as required by or under the Act, is perfectly justified and declined to interfere with the same.

The Apex Court observed that an order of disqualification under Section 10A of the 1951 Act in respect of an elected candidate by the Election Commission does not amount to setting aside the election of the candidate. It emphasised that the scope of an Election Petition to be tried by a High Court and scope of an order of disqualification to be passed under Section 10A are different and one does not conflict with the other. The enquiry to be held under Section 10A is not to examine any allegation of corrupt practice falling under Section 123(6) of the Act. The only area of examination is with regard to correctness of account of election expenses maintained as per the provisions of sub-sections (1) and (2) of Section 77 of the 1951-Act. It did not agree with the contention that once the Election Petition has been rejected for want of particulars, a complaint under Section 10A cannot be pursued.

It was held that the power to hold an enquiry before passing an order of disqualification under Section 10A has been invested with the Election Commission. As per the provisions of sub-rule (5) and (6) of Rule 89 along with Section 10A, the Commission has to necessarily issue a show cause notice, consider whether the account lodged was in the manner as required by or under the Act and only thereafter, pass an order of either disqualification or otherwise.

It was further held that the enquiry under Section 10A would be more or less of a civil nature and, therefore, the principles of preponderance of probabilities alone would apply and that even after the order of disqualification, if any, is passed under Section 10A, after following the requirement of issuance of show cause notice, receipt of reply, etc., there is a further remedy available to the contesting candidate under Section 11 by which the aggrieved candidate can demonstrate before the Election Commission as to how the order of disqualification cannot stand and that it has to be varied. Further, the Constitutional remedy under Articles 32 and 226 is always available to question the correctness of any order that may be passed by the Commission under Sections 10A and 11 of the Act.

The Court held that the maintenance of account of the election expenses is not an empty formality and that the Court cannot turn a blind eye and state that Section 77(1) and (3), as well as 78 of the Act would be relevant only for the purpose of ascertaining the corrupt practices under Section 123(6) of the Act. In fact, it was held that ascertainment of the requirement under Section 77(3) of the Act, viz. the expenses incurred, should not exceed the limit prescribed and that it should be for both the purpose of an enquiry under Section 10A of the Act, as well as in the event where candidates exceed the limit through corrupt practices for the purpose of invalidating the election. Therefore, the requirement under Section 77(3) of the Act has got twin objectives to be fulfilled. Carrying on from this, the Court condemned 'paid news'.

(i) **Kisan Shankar Kathore v. Arun Dattatray Sawant & Others [CA No. 4261 of 2007], Supreme Court:** The Appellant, Shri Kisan Shankar Kathore, was elected from 56-Ambernath Assembly Constitueney, Maharashtra at the general election to the Maharashtra Legislative Assembly held in October, 2004. An election petition under Section 100(1)(d) (i) and (iv) of the RP Act, 1951 was filed before the Hon'ble High Court of Judicature at Bombay by Shri Arun Dattatray Sawant, who was a voter of the said assembly constituency, on the ground that in the nomination paper the Appellant had suppressed information about his dues payable to the Government, assets of his spouse and assets of a partnership firm of which he was a partner. It was contended that the appellant's nomination had been improperly accepted by the Returning Officer (RO) and the election was void due to non-compliance of the provisions of the Constitution of India, the Representation of the People Act, 1951 as well as Rules and Orders framed under the Act.

The Hon'ble Bombay High Court allowed the election petition and set aside the election of the appellant by treating non-disclosure of certain information about assets and liabilities in the affidavit, filed with the nomination paper, as material defect that amounted to non-compliance of the order passed by the Election Commission under Article 324 of the Constitution of India, which is founded on the law declared by the Apex Court under Article 141 of the Constitution of India, within the meaning of Section 100(1)(d)(iv) of the Representation of the People Act, 1951. The nomination form of the Appellant was thus improperly accepted by the Returning Officer and the election result was also materially affected because of non-disclosure of vital information to the electorate.

Aggrieved by the Order of the High Court, the present appeal was filed before the Supreme Court. The Appellant's contention was that the nature of information given in the nomination form ought to have been treated as substantial compliance.

The Hon'ble Supreme Court of India agreeing with the aforesaid findings of the Bombay High Court, held that the election of the returned candidate would be void when a Court finds at a later stage during the trial of an election petition, that there was a case of misinformation or suppressing of material information in the affidavit filed with the nomination paper by treating it as a case of improper acceptance of the nomination paper by the RO, holding that when the information is given by a candidate in the affidavit filed along with the nomination paper and objections are raised thereto questioning the correctness of the information or alleging that there is non-disclosure of certain important information, it may not be possible for the returning officer at that time to conduct a detailed examination. Summary enquiry may not suffice. Present case is itself an example which loudly demonstrates this. At the same time, it would not be possible for the Returning Officer to reject the nomination for want of verification about the allegations made by the objector. In such a case, when ultimately it is proved that it was a case of non-disclosure and either the affidavit was false or it did not contain complete information leading to suppression, it can be held at that stage that the nomination was improperly accepted. Learned senior counsel appearing for the Election Commission, rightly argued that such an enquiry can be only at a later stage and the appropriate stage would be in an election petition as in the instant case, when the election is challenged. The grounds stated in Section 36(2) are those which can be examined there and then and on that basis the Returning Officer would be in a position to reject the nomination. Likewise, where the blanks are left in an affidavit, nomination can be rejected there and then. In other cases where detailed enquiry is needed, it would depend upon the outcome thereof, in an election petition, as to whether the nomination was properly accepted or it was a case of improper acceptance. Once it is found that it was a case of improper acceptance, as there was misinformation or suppression of material information, one can state that question of rejection in such a case was only deferred to a later date. When the Court gives such a finding, which would have resulted in rejection, the effect would be same, namely, such a candidate was not entitled to contest and the election is void. Otherwise, it would be an anomalous situation that even when criminal proceedings under Section 125A of the Act can be initiated and the selected candidate is criminally prosecuted and convicted, but the result of his election cannot be questioned. This cannot be countenanced.

The Hon'ble Supreme Court dismissed the appeal being devoid of any merit.

(j) **Election Commission of India v. Bajrang Bahadur Singh & Others [SLP (C) No. 8850 of 2015], Supreme Court:** The Petitioner in the transferred case filed a writ petition before the Allahabad High Court on 13th March, 2015 challenging the legality of the Order passed by the Governor on 29th January, 2015 under Article 192(1) of the Constitution declaring the petitioner disqualified from continuing to be a member of the Uttar Pradesh Legislative Assembly on the ground that he had entered into a contract with the Government after having been elected as a Member of the Assembly on 6th March, 2012 and executed the contract thereby incurring disqualification contemplated under Article 191 (1) (e) read with Section 9A of the Representation of the People Act, 1951.

The Secretariat of the Uttar Pradesh Legislative Assembly issued a notification on 17th February, 2015 declaring the seat held by the Petitioner from the 315-Pharenda assembly constituency as vacant. The Election Commission thereafter announced the schedule for filling up the casual vacancy by issuing a press Note on 10th March, 2015 and issued the notification under Section 150(1) of the 1951 Act to notify the byelection from 315-Pharenda assembly constituency as per schedule announced by it.

The High Court of Allahabad passed an interim order on 20th March, 2015 and stayed the process of the byelection from 315-Pharenda assembly constituency that had already been notified by the Commission.

The Election Commission filed this SLP before the Supreme Court being aggrieved by the impugned interim order issued by the Allahabad High Court to stay the process of byelection in view of the constitutional bar to interference by Courts in electoral matters under Article 329 (b) of the Constitution.

The main contention of the petitioner in the writ petition before the Allahabad High Court was that disqualifications prescribed under Sections 8,9, 10A of the RP Act, 1951 run for a statutorily fixed time frame and for any disqualification under Section 9A of the RP Act, 1951 the period of disqualification is co-terminus with subsistence of the contract. The moment the contract ceases to subsist the disqualification also ceases to exist. The language of Article 191(1) also does not specify whether such disqualification is attracted subsequent to the election.

The Supreme Court held that though the period of disqualification prescribed under Section 9A for subsisting contract with the appropriate government for supply of goods to, or for the execution of any works undertaken by that government and under Section 10 for holding an office under Government Company is co-terminus with the currency of the disqualifying event, in the case of a sitting Member of Parliament or State Legislature the seat held by that Member falls vacant forthwith by operation of law as enunciated under sub-clause (3) of Article 190 of the Constitution. The Court thus rejected the submission of the petitioner and dismissed the transferred writ petition filed before the Allahabad High Court.

The Court further clarified that a person incurring disqualification under Sections 9A and 10 of the 1951 Act is not debarred from contesting any election, including a byelection arising as a direct consequence of his vacating the seat if the event of disqualification ceases to subsist by the relevant date.

On the question of jurisdiction of the High Court to intercept in the election process already set in motion by issuance of notification in view of the prohibition contained in Article 329(b) of the Constitution, the Supreme Court held that the interim order granted by the Allahabad High Court was justified as the primary challenge in the writ petition filed before the High Court was not to challenge the electoral process but the decision of the Governor disqualifying the petitioner that resulted in the vacancy for which a byelection was notified by the Election Commission. The interference in the process of byelection by the High Court under Article 226 arose out of an absolute necessity.

The Supreme Court observed that the extraordinary situation arose apparently due to conflicting constitutional obligations of High Court to adjudicate on any legality of Governor's decision under Article 192 and Election Commission's obligation to conduct bye-election within a period of six months from the date of occurrence of the vacancy under Section 150 of the RP Act, 1951.

By this judgment the Apex Court laid down that the Order of the Governor under Article 192 (though said to be final) can be called in question on limited grounds as explained by the Supreme Court in the cases of Kihoto Hollahan [1992 Supp (2) SCC 651] and Mahachandra Prasad Singh [(2004) 8 SCC 747]. The Supreme Court also prescribed the period of limitation for initiating proceedings before the High Courts against a decision of the Governor under Article 192 on the question of disqualification of a sitting member as eight (8) weeks from the date of the decision of the Governor and final disposal by the High Court within a period of eight weeks from the date of initiation without fail. The Apex Court further directed that such petitions should be heard by a Division Bench of the High Court comprising at least two judges and the Chief Justices of the High Courts have been directed to make appropriate arrangements for compliance within the limitation period.

(k) **Election Commission of India v. Praful & Another [CA No. 178 of 2016], Supreme Court:** The appeal was filed by the Election Commission against impugned final judgment and Order dated 20th December, 2007 passed by the High Court of Bombay at Aurangabad in writ petition No. 6084 of 2007, whereby it struck down one of the clauses [Clause 5(f)] of the public Notice dated 01st October, 2007 issued under Rule 31(1) of the Registration of Electors Rules, 1960, by the Electoral Registration Officers of Nagpur, Pune and Aurangabad Division Graduates' constituencies, in the form devised by the Election Commission, inviting applications in prescribed statutory Form 18 appended to the Registration of Electors Rules, 1960, from electors eligible for inclusion of their names in the electoral roll of these Graduates' constituencies with reference to 1st November, 2007 as the qualifying date. In para 5(f) of that notice, it was stated that a mere reference to an entry in the earlier roll relating to the applicant shall not be taken into account for determining the eligibility for enrolment in the electoral rolls and the applicant will have to produce his degree or certificate, in original, for verification by the Designated Officer.

The High Court had struck down the above clause as being without any legal authority or sanction. It held that the relevant Act and Rules do not confer jurisdiction or power on the Election Commission to order for preparation of electoral rolls afresh every time an election is held to Graduates'/Teachers' constituencies. It directed the Commission not to ask for documents from the electors, already enrolled in the electoral rolls of Graduates'/Teachers' constituencies.

The Apex Court considered the question as to whether in matters of revision of the electoral roll for graduates'/teachers' constituencies a fresh roll is to be prepared or the existing roll is to be revised and published after inviting claims and objections. It held that the clear legislative intent of the provisions of Sections 21 and 22 of the Representation of the People Act 1950 and Rule 31 of the Registration of Electors Rules, 1960, in the context of revision of electoral roll for graduates' and teachers' constituencies, is that it shall be prepared afresh after every six years as per the procedure embodied in Rule 31 of the 1960 Rules.

It further held that the requirement of an eligible voter to submit fresh application in prescribed Form 18 in case of Graduates' constituency and in Form 19 in case of Teachers' constituencies every six years adequately takes care of the requirement spelt out by Section 22 of the 1950 Act that an eligible voter shall not be deleted from the electoral roll without an opportunity.

The Apex Court thus upheld the validity of Clause 5 (f) of the impugned notice as being in conformity with the requirements of sub-rule (4A) of rule 31 of 1960 Rules. Any contrary view taken would be erroneous.

The Appeal was allowed and the order of the High Court was set aside with the observation that the High Court had fallen into error in taking the contrary view.

9.10 Q & A REGARDING ELECTIONS AND ASSOCIATED PROCESSES

1. **What is the minimum age for becoming a candidate for Lok Sabha (House of People) or Vidhan Sabha (Legislative Assembly) election?**
   Ans. Not less than 25 Years of age on the date of scrutiny of nomination papers. (As per : Article 84 (b) of Constitution of India and Article 173 (b) of the Constitution read with Sec. 36 (2) of the Representation of People Act, 1951.)

2. **Can anyone not registered as a voter in any constituency contest Election?**
   Ans. No one has to be registered as a voter in the current electoral roll to contest election. (As per: Sec. 4 (d) and Section 5 (c) of Representation of People Act, 1951)

3. **A person is a member of schedule caste in a particular state. Can he contest election from any other State for Lok Sabha (House of People) from a seat reserved for scheduled castes?**
   Ans. Yes. He can contest election from any other state from a seat reserved for scheduled caste. (As per : Sec. 4 of the Representation of People Act, 1951)

4. **A person is a member of schedule tribe in a particular state. Can he contest election from any other State for Lok Sabha (House of People) from a seat reserved for scheduled tribes?**
   Ans. Yes. He can contest election from any other state from a seat reserved for scheduled tribes except Lakshadweep, other than those in autonomous Districts of Assam and excluding the tribal areas of Assam. (As per: Sec. 4 of the Representation of People Act, 1951)

5. **A person is an elector in a particular State. Can he contest election for a seat in the Vidhan Sabha (Legislative Assembly) of any other state?**
   Ans. No. (As per: Sec. 5 of the Representation of People Act, 1951)

6. **A person is registered as a voter in a particular state but he is a member of schedule caste of other state. Can he contest election from a seat reserved for scheduled castes for Vidhan Sabha (Legislative Assembly) in which he is a voter?**
   Ans. No. (As per: Sec. 5 of the Representation of People Act, 1951) (Similar case holds good for the Schedule Tribe also).

7. **A person is a member of scheduled caste or scheduled tribe community. Can he contest an election from a general constituency?**
   Ans. Yes. (As per: Sec. 4 & 5 of the Representation of People Act, 1951)

8. **A person is convicted for some offence and is sentenced to imprisonment for 2 years. Can he contest elections?**
   Ans. No. (As per: Section 8 (3) of Representation of People Act, 1951)

9. **Supposing such person is on bail, disposal of his appeal pending, can he contest the election?**
   Ans. No. Even if a person is on bail, after the conviction and his appeal is pending for disposal, he is disqualified from contesting an election as per Supreme Court's decision. But if his conviction is also stayed, then he can contest.

10. **Can a person confined in jail, vote in an election?**
Ans. No. Such person cannot vote at any election if he is confined in a prison, whether under a sentence of imprisonment or transportation or otherwise, or is in the lawful custody of the police. (As per: Section 62(5) of the Representation of the People Act, 1951)

11. **Is a person subjected to preventive detention under any law entitled to vote in an election?**
Ans Yes. He is entitled to vote by postal ballot paper (As per: Proviso to Section 62(5) of the Representation of the People Act, 1951and Rule 18 (a) (iv) of Conduct of Elections Rules 1961).

12. **Can an overseas elector contest the election?**
Ans. Yes. An overseas elector whose name has been enrolled in the electoral roll has the right to contest elections, subject to the fulfilment of other requirements of the law. One of the essential qualifications prescribed under the law is that the candidate should make and subscribe an oath or affirmation in the prescribed form, before a person authorised by the Commission on its behalf.

13. **When does a candidate lose the deposit?**
Ans. A defeated candidate who fails to secure more than one-sixth of the valid votes polled in the constituency will lose his security deposit. (As per: Section 158(4) of Representation of People Act. 1951.)

14. **Can a person contest election to Lok Sabha (House of People)/Vidhan Sabha (Legislative Assembly) from as many constituencies as he likes?**
Ans. No. A person cannot contest from more than two constituencies at a general election for Lok Sabha (House of People)/Vidhan Sabha(Legislative Assembly). (As per: Section 33 (7) of Representation of People Act, 1951)

15. **Who allots the election symbols to contesting candidates?**
Ans. Returning Officer. [As per: The Election Symbols (Reservation and Allotment) Order, 1968]

16. **How reserved election symbol is allotted to candidate of a recognised National or State Party?**
Ans. For allotment of reserve symbol, the candidate has to declare in his nomination form that he has been setup by the concerned recognised party and has to submit prescribed declaration in Form B from the authorised office bearer of the party to the effect that he has been setup by that party. The declaration in Form B should be duly signed by the office bearer of the Party whose specimen signatures have been communicated in Form A subject to condition that both the forms have been delivered to Chief Electoral Officer of the State and Returning Officer before 3 P.M on the last date of making nominations. [As per: Paras 8 and 13 the Election Symbols (Reservation and Allotment) Order, 1968.]

17. **What are the duties of polling agents?**
Ans. The main duty of polling agents is to see that interests of the candidates, who have appointed them, are safeguarded at the polling stations by helping the Presiding Officer to detect and prevent impersonation of voters by challenging persons whose identity

as real elector is doubtful and to see that EVM is properly secured/sealed before, during and after the close of poll and mock poll is conducted in their presence and poll proceedings conducted in accordance with the procedure laid down by the Election Commission.

18. **Whether there is any restriction for plying of vehicles for electioneering purposes?**
Ans. Yes. one can ply any number of vehicles (all mechanised/motorised vehicles including 2 wheelers) for the purpose but one has to seek prior approval of the Returning Officer for plying such vehicles and must display permit issued by Returning Officer in original (not photocopy) prominently on the wind screen of the vehicle. The permit must bear the number of the vehicle and name of the candidate in whose favour it is issued. The expenditure incurred on this will be booked against the person.

19. **Whether there is any restriction for use of educational institutions including their grounds (whether Government-aided, Private or Government) for political campaigns and rallies?**
Ans. Use of educational institutions including their grounds (whether Government-aided, Private or Government) for political campaigns and rallies are not allowed.

20. **What is the deadline after which no public meetings and processions can be taken out?**
Ans. Public meetings cannot be held after 10 PM and before 6.00 AM. Further, one cannot hold public meetings and processions during the period of 48 hours ending with the hour fixed for the conclusion of poll. Suppose, poll day is 12th June, 2009 (Friday) and hours of poll are from 8.00A.M to 5.00 P.M., the public meetings and processions shall be closed at 5.00 P.M on the 10th June, 2009 (Wednesday). (As per: Sec. 126 of Representation of People Act, 1951).

21. **Is there any restriction on the presence of political functionaries in a constituency after campaign period is over?**
Ans. Yes After the closure of campaign period (starting from 48 Hrs. before closure of poll), presence of political functionaries etc. who have come from outside the constituency and who are not voters of the constituency should not continue to remain present in the constituency. Such functionaries should leave the constituency immediately after campaign period is over.

22. **Is wearing of special accessories like cap, mask, scarf etc. permitted during the campaigning? (Modi's Face mask during the election campaign)**
Ans. Yes, provided they are accounted for in the election expenses of the candidate concerned. However, supply and distribution of main apparels like saree, shirt, etc. by party/candidate is not permitted as it may amount to bribery of voters.

23. **Is there any restriction on use of places of worship as forum for election propaganda**
Ans. Yes. The provisions of Model Code of Conduct prohibit the use of places of worship as forum for election propaganda in any manner. The religious institutions

(prevention of Misuse) Act 1988 prohibits use of religious institutions or funds of religious institutions for the promotion or propagation of any political ideas or political activity or for benefit of any political party.

24. **Is there any restriction of canvassing in or near polling station?**
Ans. Yes. Canvassing for votes etc. within a distance of one hundred meteres of polling station is prohibited on the day of poll. (As per: Section 130 of Representation of 1951)

25. **Whether videography or photography is done inside the polling stations to monitor the poll proceedings by the election authority?**
Ans. In deference to the suggestions of Supreme Court, contained in its judgment dated 11th January, 2005 in Civil Appeal No. 9228 of 2003 – (Janak Bingham v. Das Rai and other), the photography by the official videographer has been allowed to be carried inside the polling stations to photograph electors and cover poll proceedings without compromising the secrecy of voting in certain identified polling stations assessed as critical on various factors.

26. **Is there any option for an elector not to vote for any of the candidates? What is meant by NOTA?**
Ans. Yes. The electors who do not wish to vote for any of the candidate can exercise their right not to vote for any candidate without violation of the secrecy of their decision. A ballot panel with the words 'None of the Above: NOTA' will be available after the panel containing the name and particulars of the last candidate on the ballot paper, there shall be a panel below the said last panel for the benefit of those electors who may wish to exercise the option of not voting for any of the candidates in the fray.

27. **Whether it is possible for an elector to know to which candidate he has cast his vote. What is meant by VVPAT?**
Ans: Election commission has ordered that a printer with drop box of such design, as may be approved by the Election Commission may also be attached to a voting machine for printing a paper trial of vote, in such constituency or constituencies or parts thereof as the commission may direct. In respect of such polling booths where printer for paper trial with drop box is used by pressing the balloting button, the electors shall be able to view the printed paper slip showing the serial number, name and the symbol of the candidate for whom he cast his vote before such paper slip gets cut and drop in the drop box through the transparent window of the printer.

28. **Who is responsible for the counting of votes and declaration of result of an election?**
Ans. The Returning Officer (as per: Sections 64 and 66 of Representation of People Act, 1951)

29. **How it is ensured that Control Unit of EVM has not been tampered with? (Recent allegations made by AAP)**
Ans. Before votes recorded in the EVM are counted, the carrying case and control unit of EVM are placed on the counting table for the inspection and checking of seals thereon by the candidate or their agents present at the counting table. If control unit is found to have been tampered with, votes recorded in that machine are not counted and matter is reported to the Commission for further direction.

30. **Can a candidate ask for a recount?**
Ans. Yes. By a written application stating the grounds on which recount is asked for. Such application can be made to the Returning Officer, who prepares and signs Final Result Sheet (Form 20).

31. **Is a candidate free to spend as much as he likes on his election?**
Ans. No. A candidate is not free to spend as much as he likes on his election. The law prescribes that the total election expenditure shall not exceed the prescribed maximum limit for the constituency concerned. (As per: Rule 90 of the Conduct of Election Rules, 1961 and Section 123 (6) of Representation of People Act, 1951.)

32. **Are the candidates required to file any account of election expenses?**
Ans. Yes. Every candidate at an election to the House of the People or State Legislative Assembly is required to keep, either by himself or by his election agent, a separate and correct account of all expenditure in connection with the election incurred or authorised by him or his election agent between the date on which he has been nominated and the date of declaration of result, both dates inclusive. Every contesting candidate has to lodge a true copy of the said account within 30 days of result of the election. (As per: Sections 77 & 78 of the Representation of People Act, 1951). The account of election expenses shall be lodged by a contesting candidate with the District Election Officer of the district in which the constituency from which he contested lies. (As per : Section 78 of the Representation of People Act, 1951)

33. **What is the penalty if a candidate does not file his account of election expenses?**
Ans. If the Election Commission is satisfied that a person has failed to lodge an account of election expenses within the time and in the manner required by or under the Representation of People Act,1951 and he has no good reason or justification for the failure, it has the power to disqualify him for a period of 3 years for being chosen as, and for being, a member of either House of Parliament or the Legislative Assembly or Legislative Council of a State. (As per: Section 10A of the Representation of People Act, 1951)

34. **Whether the expenditure incurred for preparation of campaigning materials prior to the date of nomination be accounted for in the election expenditure.**
Ans: Yes. The candidates, while maintaining their register of accounts of election expenditure, should also account for all expenditure including those incurred prior to the date of nomination for preparation of campaign materials etc. which are actually used during the post nomination period/in connection with the election.

35. **Whether the expenditure incurred by a political party on advertisements be accounted for in the account of the candidates.**
Ans. Yes. The expenditure incurred by a political party on advertisements, in connection with any election could be categorised into the following: (i) Expenditure on general party propaganda seeking support for the party and its candidates in general, but, without any reference to any particular candidate or any particular class/group of candidates (ii) Expenditure incurred by the party, in advertisements etc. directly seeking support and/or vote for any particular candidate or group of candidates. (iii) Expenditure incurred by the party which can be related to the expenditure for promoting the prospects of any particular candidate or group of candidates. In the case of any advertisement by political parties, whether

in print or electronic or any other media, falling in category (i) above, which is not relatable to the election of any particular candidate or a given group of candidates, the expenditure may be treated as expenditure of the political party on general party propaganda. In the cases of expenditure falling in categories (ii) and (iii) above, that is, cases where the expenditure is relatable to the election of a particular candidate or a group of candidates, the expenditure shall be treated as expenditure authorised by the candidates concerned and such expenditure shall be accounted for in the election expenses accounts of the candidates concerned. In those cases where the expenditure is incurred by the party for the benefit of a given group of candidates, the expenditure is to be apportioned equally among the candidates.

36. **What is an Electronic Voting Machine? In what way its functioning is different from the conventional system of voting?**
Ans. An Electronic Voting Machine consists of two Units – a Control Unit and a Balloting Unit – joined by a three-meter cable. The Control Unit remains with the Presiding Officer or a Polling Officer and the Ballot Unit is placed inside the voting compartment. Instead of issuing a ballot paper, the Polling Officer in charge of the Control Unit will press the Ballot Button. This will enable the voter to cast his vote by pressing the blue button on the Balloting Unit against the candidate and symbol of his choice.

37. **What are the unique features of EVMs?**
Ans. It is a simple machine that can be operated easily by both the polling personnel and the voters. It is sturdy enough to withstand rough handling and variable climatic conditions. Being a standalone machine without any network connectivity, nobody can interfere with its programming and manipulate the result.

38. **What are the features of Control Unit?**
Ans. The Control Unit is the main unit which stores all data and controls the functioning of EVM. The program which controls the functioning of the control unit is burnt into a microchip on a 'one time programmable basis'. Once burnt, it cannot be read, copied out or altered. The EVMs use dynamic coding to enhance security of data transmitted from ballot unit to control unit. The new EVMs have also got real-time clock and date-time stamping facility which enables them to record the exact time and date whenever key is pressed. After the voting is completed and the close button is pressed, the machine does not accept any data or record any vote. Through the press of 'total' button, the control unit can display the number of votes recorded till that time which can be cross checked with the register of voters in Form 17-A. The display system of the control unit shows the total number of votes polled in a polling station and the candidate-wise votes polled in the machine when the 'result' button is pressed by the counting staff in the presence of counting agents at the counting center. The control unit can also detect any physical tampering made with the connecting cable and indicate the same in the display unit.

39. **What are the features of Balloting Unit?**
Ans. It holds the ballot paper containing the names and symbols of candidates. When pressed, the candidate button on the ballot unit sends a signal to the control unit where this is recorded in a non-volatile memory which can store the poll data indefinitely even without a battery backup.

40. **Can booth capturing be prevented by the use of EVMs?**
Ans. By booth-capturing, if one means, taking away or damaging of ballot boxes or ballot papers, this evil cannot be prevented by the use of EVMs as EVMs can also be forcibly taken away or damaged by miscreants. But if one looks at booth capturing as a case of miscreants intimidating the polling personnel and stamping the ballot papers on the symbol and escaping in a matter of minutes, this can be prevented by the use of EVMs. The EVMs are programmed in such a way that the machines will record only five votes in a minute. As recording of votes has necessarily to be through Control Unit and Balloting Unit, whatever be the number of miscreants they can record vote only at the rate of 5 per minute. In the case of ballot papers, the miscreants can distribute all the 1000 odd ballot papers assigned to a polling station, among themselves, stamp them, stuff them into the ballot boxes within a few minutes and run away before the police reinforcements reach. In EVMs, in half-an–hour, the miscreants can record only a maximum of 150 votes by which time, chances are the police reinforcement would have arrived. Further, the presiding Officer or one of the Polling Officers can always press the 'close' button as soon as they see some intruders inside the polling station. It will not be possible to record any vote once the 'close' button is pressed and this will frustrate the efforts of the booth capturers.

41. **What are the advantages in using EVMs?**
Ans. The first and most important advantage is that the printing of millions of ballot paper scan be dispensed with, as only one ballot paper is required for fixing on the Balloting Unit at each polling station instead of one ballot paper for each individual elector. This results in huge savings by way of cost of paper, printing, transportation, storage and distribution. Second, counting is very quick and the result can be declared within 2 to 3 hours as compared to 30–40 hours, on an average, under the conventional system. Third, there are no invalid votes under the system of voting under EVMs. The importance of this will be better appreciated, if it was remembered that in the past in several cases, the number of invalid votes is more than the winning margin between the winning candidate and the second candidate, in a number of constituencies. To this extent, the choice of the electorate will be more correctly reflected when EVMs are used.

9.11 CONCLUSION

DEMOCRACY MUST, IN ESSENCE, MEAN THE ART AND SCIENCE OF MOBILISING THE ENTIRE PHYSICAL, ECONOMIC AND SPIRITUAL RESOURCES OF ALL THE VARIOUS SECTIONS OF THE PEOPLE, IN THE SERVICE OF THE COMMON GOOD OF ALL. - MAHATMA GANDHI

In a democratic country, the word 'election' symbolises the active and direct participation of the people of a nation to form a Government. It is universally accepted that for a democracy to work as one, its citizens elect their representatives and, in turn, rule themselves. The elections represent the general will of the people, as expressed in their votes. The voting population expresses its choice of candidate, political party and Government through exercising their franchise at regular intervals. The votes of the electors crystallise into the mandate of the people. Elections are held in our country every five years (the only exception is the six-year term of the Jammu and Kashmir Legislative Assembly).

By exercising their franchise, voters express their changing expectations and convictions regarding the kind of government they want.

The voters are the main stakeholders in a democracy and they vote with the belief that the Government, as the main arbiter of the future of the country and its people, will provide every citizen the best possible policies to build a better country, a better community, and a better life.

They also believe that it will work in the most efficient way to further their economic and social welfare, alleviate poverty and reduce the gap between the rich and the poor, build infrastructure, and formulate and implement policies that will ultimately improve the quality of life of every citizen, reduce the existing differences between different sections of society to make the social order as egalitarian as possible, maintain law and order, and protect the legal rights and civil liberties of the citizens.

The legitimacy of the entire democratic system of governance depends on the efficacy and effective working of the electoral mechanism. If the verdict of the people, which forms the basis of the propriety and legitimacy of the political system, is vitiated by unethical methods, the faith of the people in the electoral system gets eroded and ultimately destroys the very foundations of democracy.

In elections, voting is a primary manifestation of democratic behaviour. It creates and preserves the authenticity and credibility of democracy.

An electorate of informed and politically and socially aware citizens, determined to exercise their right to vote wisely, are equipped to build the right environment for a free and fair elections.

Democracy and elections are inextricable. In the Indian context, the emphasis has always been on creating a social order in which the people, by casting their vote without any coercion or inducement, make decisions about their government.

Electoral integrity is concerned with open dialogue, debate and information-sharing among leaders and the public. This depends on public confidence in electoral and political processes. Inclusiveness, transparency and accountability are tenets fundamental to developing the confidence of the voters in the electoral process. The four main tenets of a fair election process are:

1. Universal suffrage
2. Periodicity of election (i.e., prefixed term of the Lok Sabha/Legislative Assembly)
3. Independent election management bodies (EMBs)
4. Free, fair and transparent electoral process

Thus, the Representation of People Acts help to achieve a fair, periodic, independent and transparent election process which is the hallmark of democracy.

10

Role of Civil Services in a Democracy

LEARNING OBJECTIVES

In this Chapter, you will learn about:

- Introduction
- The Need for Public Administration (Civil Service)
- Meaning of Public Administration
- Characteristics of Public Administration (Civil Service)
- Significance of Public Administration (Civil Service)
- Theories Relating to Bureaucracy (Civil Service)
- Generalist vs Specialist Debate
- Minister-Civil Servant Relationship
- Concept of Ministerial Accountability to Parliament
- Anonymity of Civil Servants
- Civil Service Neutrality
- Problems of Bureaucratisation
- Administrative Reforms

The term of Public Administration, bureaucracy, civil service all has the common thread connecting them and in various context they reflect and have a similar meaning. The term public administration though has a wider meaning, which includes both the elected and permanent executive, while the term bureaucracy has come to denote the administration and hence the civil service and Civil Service is the body of permanent government officials who are appointed to run the country. In this Chapter we will be using terms Public Administration, Bureaucracy and Civil Service and they all refer to the same- the Public official appointed to the government with the mandate to serve the nation with public interest.

10.1 INTRODUCTION

Civil service refers to the body of government officials who are appointed to the civil occupations that are neither political nor judicial.

The term bureaucracy has a wider meaning, it refers to the body of employees in a large-scale organisation. More specifically it is related to the body of such employees having authority relationship within the organisation. Thus, every large business has its bureaucracy. In the government there are two types, the civil and military bureaucracies.

In the literature of public administration, the term civil bureaucracy has wider meaning than that of civil service. Thus, the employees of an autonomous corporation come under the concept of bureaucracy but they are not considered to be civil servants. It should be noted that the bureaucracy do not refer to the elected politicians, they refer only to the appointed officials.

In common usage, the term bureaucracy refers to the routine and delay in authorised work, while public administration do take these into account, it generally refers bureaucracy only to the appointed officials.

Hence, civil service essentially means the appointed government official, though bureaucracy has a negative connotation to it, it has been used to refer generally to the public servants, the term public administration has a wider meaning, which brings together the civil servants, the so called bureaucracy, and also the elected representatives of the people. The subject of public administration deals with the effective management of the resources-finance, human, intellectual etc. to deliver services to the people. The term 'Public' is important as regards to the public administration, though civil service does not explicitly mention it. It has to adhere to the public service values as elaborated by understanding of public administration.

10.2 THE NEED FOR PUBLIC ADMINISTRATION (CIVIL SERVICE)

The modern life is filled with complexity and hence the importance of public administration in such a scenario is increasing. This is because the need of the state to intervene in day-to-day activities of its citizens. There is no aspect of the life of citizen which is out of purview from the administration. The citizen comes in contact with some of the government agencies in their daily activities.

During the ancient times, the needs of the citizen were limited. They could therefore, live in a village, self-sufficiently, without any intervention by the state. But the scientific and the industrial revolution changed this scenario. The industrial products that are mass produced require specialised operation to manufacture them. Hence, the community started to live together in big cities. The means of production too has become complex and requires a much greater effort to organise them effectively.

Many a number of such activities now cannot be organised by citizens themselves privately, or as a village, or as even a community in cities. Thus the National, State and local governments have come forward to organise, and provide necessary infrastructure facilities, provide for effective production as well as facilitate the community-type living.

For example, railways has been built for the transport of the raw materials and also to distribute the finished goods. This also apart from facilitating manufacturing, helps in movement of people over long distances, that is an important facet of modern day living.

Similarly, communication facilities like telecommunication, microwave transmissions, satellite communication etc. all have to be provided for meeting the need and requirements of the modern communities. And all these require massive men and material investment, which is impossible to be provided by a small village community.

Such huge investments are made by the National governments and is implemented and administered with help of the local governments. Financing such projects alone is not the issue here, organising such large scale projects within the specified timeline is important.

Hence the point of contact between the citizen and the government has increased tremendously. And the importance of Public Administration has been keeping pace with such developments.

In this modern era, the Public Administration is seen as the face of the government. They are the vital link connecting the people with the government. Their role has been completely transformed to suit the modern day needs. In the chapter we will be discussing about modern day impact and the importance and the role played by the Civil Service in the modern day democracy.

10.3 MEANING OF PUBLIC ADMINISTRATION

The concept of Public Administration if part of the wider term of "administration". To understand the meaning of Public Administration we need to first understand what administration means.

10.3.1 Administration Defined

The term *administer* is derived from the Latin word *administrate*, which means to care or to look after the people and manage their affairs. Hence according to this wide definition, almost every human activity involves some kind of administration. Even in the primitive societies, activities such as hunting, gathering etc. require some form of organisation.

The decision has to be made regarding who will be doing what. Certain norms of behaviour had to be laid down to decide the distribution of work among the members of the community. But administration in such a scenario is simple as it involves less complex operations and lesser number of people.

But with increase in complexity in modern day life, the administration of both public and public life has become more complex.

The following are some of the definitions given by prominent scholars for *Administration.*

E.N. Gladden: "Administration is a long and slightly pompous word, but it has a humble meaning, for it means, to care for or look after people, to manage affairs… is determined action taken in pursuit of a conscious purpose."

F.M. Marx: "Administration is a determined action taken in pursuit of a conscious purpose. It is the systematic ordering of affairs and the calculated use of resources aimed at making those things happen which one wants to happen and foretelling to the contrary."

Felix A. Nigro: "Administration is the organisation and use of men and materials to accomplish a purpose."

Herbert A. Simon: "In its broadest sense, administration can be defined as the activities of groups cooperating to accomplish common goals."

John A. Veig: "Administration is determined action taken in pursuit of conscious purpose. It is the systematic ordering of affairs and the calculated use of resources, aimed at making those things happen which we want to happen and simultaneously preventing developments that fail to square with our intentions. It is the marshalling of available labour and materials in order to gain that which is desired at the lowest cost in energy, time and money."

Keith Henderson: "Administration is the arrangement of men and materials in the rational carrying out of purposes."

Pfiffner: "Administration is the organisation and direction of human and material resources to achieve desired ends."

L.D. White: "The art of administration is the direction, coordination and control of many persons to achieve some purpose or objective."

D. Waldo: "Administration is a type of cooperative human effort that has a high degree of rationality."

Brooks Adams: "Administration is the capacity of coordinating man and often conflicting social energies in a single organism, so adroitly that they shall operate as a unity."

Ordway Tead: "Administration is a variety of component elements which, together in action, produce the result of a defined task done. Administration, primarily, is the direction of people in association to achieve some goal temporarily shared. It is the inclusively process of integrating human efforts so that a desired result is obtained." He further adds, "Administration is the central power house of the motivational impulsion and spirit which makes the institution drive to fulfil its purpose."

James McCanny: "Administration is the organisation and use of men and materials to accomplish a purpose. It is the specialized vocation of managers who have skills of organizing and directing men and materials just as an engineer has the skill of building structures or a doctor has the skill of understanding the human ailments."

Luther Gulick: "Administration has to do with getting things done; with the accomplishment of defined objectives." George E. Berkley: "Administration is a process involving human beings jointly engaged in working towards common goals."

From the above definitions it is clear that administration is essentially a group activity which involves coordination and cooperation between the members to achieve desired results. This also means that administration is carried on with an element of rationality. Hence administration is a rational action, an attempt to maximise the results achieved by a group of people. While administration is a collective activity, and not all such collective activities are considered to be administration.

10.3.2 Public Administration Defined

Administration is a common term defining both public and private activities. Public Administration is that part of administration which is concerned with the activities of the government.

It is also called as governmental administration because the word 'public' in Public administration essentially points to 'government'. Hence the focus of public administration is on public bureaucracy, that is, governmental bureaucratic organisation.

The following are definitions of Pubic Administration as given by various scholars.

Woodrow Wilson: "Public Administration is detailed and systematic execution of law. Every particular application of law is an act of administration." He further says: Administration is the most obvious part of government; it is the government in action; it is the executive, the operative, the most visible side of the government."

L.D. White: "Public Administration consists of all those operations having for their purpose the fulfillment or enforcement of public policy."

Luther Gulick: "Public Administration is that part of the science of administration which as to do with government and thus concerns itself primarily with the executive branch where the work of government is done, though there are obviously problems in connection with the legislative and judicial branches."

H.A. Simon: "By Public Administration is meant in common usage, the activities of the executive branches of the national, state and local governments."

Pfiffner: "Public Administration consists of doing the work of the government whether it be running an X-ray machine in a health laboratory or coining money in the mint... Public Administration consists of getting the work of government done by coordinating the efforts of the people so that they can work together to accomplish their set tasks."

E.N. Gladden: "Public Administration is concerned with the administration of the government." H. Walker: "The work which the government does to give effect to a law is called Public Administration."

Willoughby: "The term administration may be employed in Political Science in two senses. In its broadest sense it denotes the work involved in the actual conduct of governmental affairs, regardless of the particular branch of government concerned. It is, thus, quite proper to speak of the administration of the legislative branch of the government, the administration of justice or judicial affairs, or the administration of the executive branch as well as the administration of the affairs of the administrative branch of the government, or the conduct of the affairs of the government generally. In its narrowest sense, it denotes the operations of the administrative branch only. As students of Public Administration we are concerned with the narrowest meaning of the term."

D. Waldo: "Public Administration is the art and science of management as applied to the affairs of the State." He further observes. "The process of public administration consists of the actions involved in affecting the intent or desire of a government. It is thus, the continuously active," business part of a government, concerned with carrying out the law as made by legislative bodies (or other authoritative agents) and interpreted by the courts, through the process of organisation and management. The field of study – putatively a science or discipline – of public administration focuses upon public administration as a process."

M. E. Dimock: "Public Administration is the fulfillment or enforcement of public policy as declared by the competent authorities. It deals with the problems and powers of the organisation and techniques of management involved in carrying out the laws and policies formulated by the policy-making agencies of government. Public administration is the law in action. It is the executive side of a government."

F.A. Nigro: "Public Administration

(i) is a cooperative group effort in a public setting;
(ii) covers all the three branches – executive, legislative and judicial, and their inter-relationship;
(iii) has an important role in the formulation of public policy and is thus part of the political process;
(iv) is different in significant ways from private administration; and
(v) closely associated with numerous private groups and individuals in providing services to the community."

J.S. Hodgson: "Public Administration comprises all activities of persons or groups in government or their agencies, whether these organisations are international, regional or local in their scope, to fulfill the purposes of these governments or agencies."

Ridley: "Public Administration in the public sector...It is administration by the state... Public Administration is governmental administration...It is administration by public authorities...Public authorities are authorities which administer according to the rules of public administration. Public administration should be the study of administration, descriptive, theoretical and normative."

M. RuthnaSwamy: "When administration has to do with the affairs of a state or minor political institutions like a Municipal or County Council, or District Board, it is call Public Administration." Dimock and Dimock: Like the study of politics, the study of public administration is a study of what people want through government and how they go about getting it. In addition, administration is the area of study and practice where law and policy are recommended and carried out."

J. Greenwood and D. Wilson: "Public Administration is an activity, a set of institutions and a subject of study." Rosenbloom: "Public Administration does involve activity, it is concerned with politics and policy-making, it tends to be concentrated in the executive branch of government, it does differ from private administration, and it is concerned with implementing law." He further adds, "Public Administration is the use of managerial, legal and political theories and processes to fulfill legislative, executive and judicial governmental mandates for the provision of regulatory and service functions for the society as a whole or for some segments of it."

M. Marx: "Public Administration has come to signify primarily the organisation, personnel, practices and procedures essential to effective performance of the civilian functions entrusted to the executive branch of government."

To sum up, Public Administration:

- Deals with the ends of the state, the interest of the public and law, and of the sovereign will;
- Provides for regulatory and other service related functions to the people in order attain good life;
- Differs significantly from private administration, as it emphasis on 'publicness';
- It covers all three branches in a democracy, although it may be tend to be viewed under the executive branch;
- Is a non-political bureaucratic system operating within a political system; and
- Is the business side of the government and is concerned with the policy-making and its execution.

10.4 CHARACTERISTICS OF PUBLIC ADMINISTRATION (CIVIL SERVICE)

The following are the characteristics of Public Administration, they are not exclusive and exhaustive. Some of the following may be available only in the public field and others may relate to administrative efficiency.

1. **Anonymity:** anonymity is an important characteristic of a public servant. He should maintain anonymity while carrying out the services for the public. The official acts are not carried out in their personal capacity, rather they are the agents of the government and carry out acts by virtue of the post they hold.

2. **Consciousness of Community Service:** the Public administrator works for the 'public'. The act is carried out for the betterment of the community and not for deriving financial benefits out of them.
3. **Public Responsibility:** the administrators have to be held publicly responsible for their acts and actions. They have to be questioned by the public regarding such aspects which will help the administration function on the right path. In India and Britain this is achieved with the help of **Ministerial Responsibility** and other such facilities which let people, the press and the representatives of the people question the actions of the administrators.
4. **Monopoly:** such conditions of monopoly are usual in the sphere of the government. From this characteristic raise other characteristic because of lack of competition in the administrative process.
5. **Large-Scale Organisation:** it is the usual character of a government organisation, as it deals with numerous issues concerned with the state and its subjects. Numerous problems arise because of this characteristic of administration. And this is not an essential character of administration. Though smaller organisation exists, they exist within the larger organisation of the state.
6. **Consistency of treatment:** this is an essential characteristic as the public official should not render unequal or favoured treatment to a section of people. Everyone should be treated equally and without discrimination. Unlike private service, favoured treatment cannot be accorded. The public administration should follow the law and principles laid down by the Constitution in all aspects.
7. **Public Information:** if the character of public responsibility has to work, then the public should have access to information regarding all such acts and functions of the administrators. The secrecy is considered to be intolerable in a democratic setup, and hence the administrators have to take special steps to provide information to the public even without them demanding for such information. Public administration is held to be everybody'd business.

10.5 SIGNIFICANCE OF PUBLIC ADMINISTRATION (CIVIL SERVICE)

In the contemporary age, which has witnessed the raise of 'Administrative state' has seen growth of role of the public administration. The functions it has been assigned to perform has grown in scope and function, and it is continuously increasing. Many of such functions relate to the essential requirement of human life, such as education, health, social security, sanitation etc. All these functions are over and above the basic regulatory function of the administration. The view point of eminent scholars below reflect the significance of the public administration.

Woodrow Wilson: "Administration is the most obvious part of the government; it is the government in action, it is the executive, the operative and the most visible side of the government."
Brooke Adams: "Administration is an important human faculty because its chief function is to facilitate social change and to cushion the stock of social revolution."
Paul H. Appleby: "Administration is the basis of government. No government can exist without administration. Without administration government would be a discussion club, if indeed, it could exist at all."

According to **Gerald Caiden** Public administration has taken up the following crucial roles in the modern contemporary society:

- Preservation of polity;
- Maintenance of stability and order;
- Management of large scale commercial services;
- Ensuring growth and economic development;
- Institutionalisation of Socio-economic changes;
- Formation of public opinion;
- Influencing public policies; and
- Formation of public opinion.

The significance of public administration can be studied under the following heads,

(i) **Public Administration (Civil Service) as an Instrument of Governance**
The most important function of the government is to govern, that is, maintain the peace, law and order, to ensure the safety and security of the people in the country. The government also has to uphold the contracts concluded between the people and settle any disputes arising between them. During the initial stages of the evolution of the government, this was probably the basic functions carried out by the administration.

As the government evolved and developed, many other important functions have been taken over by the administration, but the basic function remained the same. It is impossible to bring in development if peace is not maintained in the society. This function is highly essential and necessary, and without it civilised life is impossible.

The regulatory function of the public administration has not remained static. It has been growing in complexity as the government evolved. New methods have been developed to effectively distribute the goods for the public, new technologies have been incorporated by the administration for effective public service delivery.

(ii) **Public Administration (Civil Service) as an Instrument of development and Change**
The public administration has a very significant role to play as an instrument of change and development. The public administration embodies within itself the desires, qualities and aspirations of the people, it also reflects the intellect of its people. The public administration is an important tool in achieving development, and without it development is not possible.

Manpower is need to run the colleges, schools and other technical institutions. Manpower is also need to build infrastructures such as roads, bridges, buildings etc. and to run the industrial machinery. Scientific manpower is needed to carry out research and development. And only a well-developed and established public administration can make all this a reality.

Though a part of the contribution is made by the private sector, it cannot complete the task in full. The private may not be willing to contribute towards establishing the basic and essential infrastructure. For example, country-wide rail connectivity, telecommunication systems, roads, basic research etc. all have to be organised by the government.

In several developmental areas the initial thrust has be given by the government, without its support development in these sectors is not possible. And this is not possible without a well-established system of public administration. This aspect was highlighted by the western governments and the aid agencies which sought to help develop the south, that is, the developing nations.

It was contended that the aid will not be of use unless an effective system of public administration is established with skilled manpower. Financial assistance cannot be transformed into productive schemes. Thus the initial task of the developing countries, is therefore, to develop adequate and necessary administrative machinery to take up diverse tasks relating to development.

The administrative support relates not only to aspects related to economic development. In the developing countries, the public administration is also an instrument of social change. A number of welfare schemes have to be taken up. New laws to bring in development have to be enacted and enforced. For examples, laws relating to dowry, untouchables, protection of SCs, STs, rights of minorities, Children, labour, women etc. Though the impetus for development comes from the political class, it is the administration that drafts and enforces them. This is the fundamental task of the public administration.

(iii) **Public Administration (Civil Service) as an instrument of Welfare State**

In a modern democratic state, the government has to carry out several welfare functions for the people. This includes various aspects related to provision of schooling, medical facilities and other social security related issues. With the breaking down of the joint-family system, the responsibility of taking care the elderly and the infants, orphans and the widows fall upon the shoulders of the government. With the economic slowdown, the government now has to lookout for the unemployed youths also.

The development may raise up new problems such as those of creation of urban slums, pollution, juvenile delinquents etc. The state therefore has to identify all these problems and device necessary solutions addressing them. The formulation of such schemes and implementing them is another important function of the Public Administration.

The Public administration is thus not only the protector of the rights of the citizens, they have also become the provider of services for the people. The welfare of the people is now dependent on how effective the public administration functions. And because of this, the modern state is called as an "*Administrative State.*" Prof. V.V.Donham had stated, "*If our civilisation fails, it will be mainly because of administration.*"

(iv) **The Stabilising role of Public Administration (Civil Service) in society**

According to Prof. Paul Pigors of the Massachusetts Institute of Technology, the primary function of the public administration is that of stabilising the social institutions. The administrative function ensures the continuity of existing order with minimal effort and risk. Its fundamental aim is to "carry on" rather than venturing into new and untried avenues. Administrators are, therefore, the stabilizers of the society and the guardians of the tradition.

They are stabilizers in both positive and negative sense. In the positive sense, they help in the continuity of the system and help in preserving its principles. But they also act in other ways to frustrate new ideas and developments to change and reform the existing system. They resist change and slow down the rate of experimentation.

(v) **Public administration (Civil Service) as a key to modern society**

Modern society is considered to be a great society, as it consists as many groups connected together to achieve common objective. Every institution in a great society, and even the great society rests upon the administration. The state, like that of the private enterprises also rest upon the administration. And hence whatever the future might hold, the administration will be an essential instrument in service delivery.

(vi) **Public administration (Civil Service) as a mechanism for promoting culture in the society**

Public administration is not just an instrument of governance, it is also an important instrument used for promoting and preserving the culture of the society. The ideals and the values of the state may be high, and its impact on the lives of the people can only be measured only if these values are put in actual practice. Thus the public administration becomes an important instrument to implement the values and the ideals of the state. By becoming the part of social and cultural life of the people, it has become a permanent force in determining the character and activities of the state itself. Hence, Waldo calls administration as, "*part of the cultural complex which is not only acted upon but which also acts.*"

(vii) **Public administration (Civil Service)– a fourth branch of government**

Till the 19th century the role of state was of regulatory nature, and public administration did not play vital role in the lives of the people. It acted as an instrument of coercion and control rather than doing public service.

Because of the increase in complexity of society, the role of the State has changed, there is increase in nature and volume of functions concerning the social change and development. Welfare of the people is now considered to be paramount.

The era of *lassiez faire* state has come to an end, and now a positivist-interventionist welfare state has emerged in its place. This therefore has enhanced the importance of public administration. Hence scholars related to the public administration gave a separate status to the public administration, they not just separated it from the politics, but they called it as the *fourth branch* of government along with the executive, legislature and the judiciary.

(viii) **Increasing role of public administration (Civil Service) in policy making**

The modern welfare state has added new dimensions of role to public administration. Thus the nature of role played by the bureaucracy in policy making is changing slowly. The **concept of neutrality** of civil servants is also losing its significance.

The public administration is playing an important role in policy making in various way. It helps the executive in identifying the areas for policy making, they prepare the policy proposals, analyse various alternative and solutions available, dividing the major policy into various sub-policies, formulating programmes of actions and various modifications required in the existing policies.

The public administration is the only possible and effective instrument that could be used to formulate and implement the policies which the modern government is called upon to address. In the present era, the chief function of an administrator is considered to be policy making.

10.6 THEORIES RELATING TO BUREAUCRACY (CIVIL SERVICE)

10.6.1 Hegel's Theory

Hegel in his book *Philosophy of Right* talks about the nature of state, and the philosophical basis of existence of state. He talks about the system which exists outside the formal state setup, that is, the family and the civil society. And according to Hegel the civil servants carry the value of the society from which they come from. They have affinity towards the family and also become member of the civil society and finally raise to be a civil servant. The class division in the society integrates the society and not divides it. Hegel places the civil servants into the middle class, and he considers the middle class to be balancing factor in the society, and calls it the 'pillar of the state'.

1. Hegel acknowledges the importance of division of labour and power in a public authority.
2. He states about the important role played by the civil servants in the government.
3. He ruler shall be aid and advised by the ministry and civil service, and all these member should satisfy the educational requirements.
4. According to Hegel the society is divided into three classes based on the division of labour.

    a. The agriculture- substantial or immediate class
    b. The business- reflecting or formal class
    c. The civil servants- universal class

    Such a membership is essential for gaining status and recognition in a civil society.
5. The Civil servants or the bureaucracy is considered to be a "universal class" because it concerns with the universal interests of the society.
6. As members of the bureaucracy they are paid salary by the state. They have to be highly educated and must qualify for the appointment to government posts on the basis of merit. They are also provided with safety of tenure and hence are independent of immediate political pressure.
7. The state according to Hegel is the march of god. It is a rational and ethical entity. The Constitutional law according to Hegel is divided into three,

    a. The legislature- establish universal law making
    b. The executive- universal administering of the laws
    c. The Crown- the ultimate decision maker and units the other two arms of the state.

    The executive consists of the civil servants and the other higher advisory officials.
    The government has its own division of labour whereby the administration is divided into various departments managed by special officials.
    The appointment is made on the basis of knowledge and ability. The tenure is conditional and based on effective fulfilment of their duties. The offices of the civil servants are open to all class and categories of citizens.
8. The executive does not remain unchecked, to quote Hegel, *"The security of the state and its subjects against the misuse of power by ministers and their officials lies directly in their hierarchical organization and their answerability; but it lies too in the authority given to societies and corporations ...."*
9. The qualities of the civil servants will be, being dispassionate, upright and polite. This is because of their proper education in thought and ethical conduct.
10. The civil servants are universal class because

    a. They subsume all the particular classes under the universal class, and therefore reflect universal interest;
    b. Show a disposition of mind, which shuns selfish ends for effective discharge of public functions to achieve universal public good.

The Hegelian concept of bureaucracy is identical to that of Weber's Ideal type conception.

a. Tenured system of bureaucracy
b. Motivated to the service of the commonwealth and the people
c. Recruited on basis of merit
d. Paid according their performance
e. Autonomy and independent from other spheres
f. Acts as a break on the civil society

10.6.2 Weber's Bureaucracy

Max Weber was the first scholar to make a systematic analysis of bureaucracy as a system of organisation. The credit for systematic formulation of bureaucratic theory goes to him. His classic study provides for the starting point for the analysis of bureaucracy. As already seen, we have studied the formulation as given by Hegel, but his he has not explicitly mentioned about bureaucracy and his theory generally was not about bureaucracy. Hence Max Weber was the first person the separate the sphere of bureaucracy from the political system and study it.

10.6.3 Characteristics of Bureaucracy given by Weber

Weber identified the bureaucracy with the legal-rational authority. According to Weber the essence of bureaucracy is its rational character, that is, it is governed by a set of rules which is easily understood. He saw bureaucracy as an impersonal system operating on the basis of known rules and implemented by full-time appointed officials. Hence the Weberian model of bureaucracy excludes the elected political executives. He regarded the bureauracy based on the legal-rational authority as the most effective basis of an organisation. He saw it as the most efficient organisation form for the administrative purposes.

Weber developed the legal-rational idea type bureaucracy to explain its defining features. The following are the characteristics of the bureaucracy as given by Weber:

1. In a legal sense, each office has a clearly defined sphere of authority.
2. The officials all receive fixed salary in money according to their rank in the hierarchy. They are also eligible to receive a fixed pension.
3. The job is the primary occupation of the official, he has full concentration on it.
4. The official is subject to strict and systematic control and discipline in his conduct in the office.
5. There is a proper career structure, where the promotion is based on the merit and/ or seniority. The basis of promotion depends on the judgment of the superior officer.
6. The employees of the bureaucratic organisation are personally free and are subject to restrictions with regard to their impersonal official duties.
7. The administrative offices are arranged hierarchically; that is, each higher office controls and supervises the lower office below it.
8. The officials, are appointed, and not elected, on basis of a free contract. The official is always free to resign.
9. The officials are selected on the basis of technical qualifications as required by each post.
10. The official does not own his/her office and the means of administration. They cannot appropriate their position.

These ten feature constitute Weber's world renowned ideal, pure or most legal rational type bureaucracy. This concept of ideal type bureaucracy is applicable to both private and private administrative systems.

10.6.4 Attributes of Bureaucracy

According to Weber, "*Bureaucracy is by far the most efficient instrument of large scale administration which has ever been developed and the modern social order has become overwhelming dependent on it.*" He was of the opinion that a purely bureaucratic form of organisation had the chance and capability to attain the highest level of efficiency.

The following are the important elements of Weber's legal-rational type system.

1. **Hierarchy- a formal structure of well-defined authority:**
   It is the basic feature in the organisation which defines the position. It is the ranking of various positions in a descending order from the top to the bottom. It is a separation between the superior and the subordinate offices. Each level controls a level below them and in turn is controlled by the level above them. Weber gives greater importance to this characteristic of bureaucracy, "the organisation of offices follows the principle of hierarchy, that is, each lower office is under the control and supervision of a higher one." Thus no office is left uncontrolled in the system. It serves as a line of control and also as delegation of authority.
2. **Division of Labour-**
   The functioning is divided based on the specialisation. The organisation is thus broken down in basis of such specialised functions. Each employee is given a specific function, and thus becomes a master of it. The area of competence is demarcated. This raises the overall productivity and efficiency of the organisation. Each official thus knows what is function is and what to perform and also what not to perform that is not to encroach upon the functions of others. Another important aspect of division of labour is that it makes sure that no area is left uncovered.
3. **Rules-**
   The official function is carried out on basis of the rules. And these rules operate in reference only to the official job only. The emphasis is laid upon the rules in order to avoid the arbitrariness, personal favour etc. which may hinder the working of the organisation. The rules enable the decision taken at higher levels get implemented at the lower levels. The rules help in maintaining the uniformity and also in coordination of the efforts in the organisation. Thus rules help in stability, continuity and probability of the system, and each one knows the outcome of their action.
4. **Impersonality-**
   Irrational sentiments have to be avoided in any organisations, especially a public organisation such as Bureaucracy. The officials should discard their personal likes, dislikes etc. while performing their official duty. There has to be no bias while performing such tasks for the government. Every employee and the other people should be treated equally on par with each other. Thus decisions, should be governed by rational factors and not personal factors. And impersonality helps in dealing with people both within and outside the organisation.
5. **Official Records-**
   Another important feature of Weberian Bureaucracy is that everything is recorded in writing. The official records are therefore maintained. All the decisions and activities of the

organisation are recorded in writing and it is preserved for future reference. The filing system helps in preserving such records.

6. **Differentiation of Public and Private ends-**
   Personal interests and private ends are kept separate from the public purpose and the function. One's personal interest should never interfere with his official work. The rationality should always be maintained in the organisation. They are paid employees of the organisation, their tenure is determined by official rules and regulations, and they should not have any exclusive interest in the organisation.

These are thus the characteristics of the Bureaucracy as elaborated by Weber. These are not any regular characteristic, but are of an organisation which is 'ideal' which means that it doesn't exist in reality. The characteristics such as **precision, discipline, strictness, continuity and reliability** are the underlining feature of the bureaucracy. These characteristics technically make bureaucracy the most efficient organisation.

10.6.5 Reasons for Growth of Bureaucracy (Civil Service)

Weber was the first person to identify the reasons for the growth of bureaucracy in the West. He identified the following reasons:

1. **Money Economy:** the development of money economy as the important and foremost reason for the birth and development of bureaucratic system. To quote Weber, "*The development of money economy, in so far as the pecuniary compensation of the official is concerned, is a presupposition of bureaucracy.*" Weber observed that the bureaucratic organisation would only survive if the money economy develops and a steady economic growth is maintained.
2. **Emergence of mass democracy:** the emergence of larger middle class who are demanding the benefits of the mass democracy, such as the social and economic equality in another important reason for growth of bureaucracy. The impersonal bureaucracy operating based on rules was associated with the negation of practice of according special privilege to a specific group of persons.
3. **Protestant ethic:** according to Weber Protestant social ethic contributed to the development and ascendency of bureaucracy. This concept was opposed to traditionalism, old-age customs and methods. It called for working on fullest potential of an individual, not for greed or pursuit of pecuniary gain. Such new kind of ethos helped in modernisation of the economy, increase in production and productivity. This ethics also developed rational planning, personal discipline, technology and finally the bureaucratic organisation.
4. **Capitalist system:** the system based on ruthless competition played an important role in the development of bureaucracy. A system of highly effective bureaucracy was needed to maintain the competition in the free market economy. The bureaucracy was the most efficient instrument which could be used to achieve the organisational goals.

Thus all these factors were responsible for the growth and development of bureaucracy in the modern age.

10.6.6 Comparison between Weber and Hegel

The following is the comparison made between the philosophy of Weber and Hegel as presented to the CHEIRON: International Society for the History of the Social Sciences, by Gordon A. Welty.

There are more in common between the conception made by Weber and Hegel, though their fundamental basis differed. Both call that bureaucracy is an effective system. But Weber's rational type development goes beyond Hegel's view, and following is the few comparison of concepts of Weber and Hegel.

Weber	Hegel
There is a principle of fixed and official jurisdictional areas, which are generally ordered by rules, by laws or administrative regulations.	Division of labor occurs in the business of the executive (or the chief official of the State and his administration)… the business of government shall be divided into its abstract (or rule-bound) branches manned by special officials as different centres of administration…
Methodical provision is made for the regular and continuous fulfilment of (bureaucratic) duties and for the execution of the corresponding rights; only persons who have the generally regulated qualifications to serve are employed.	Between an individual and his (bureaucratic) office there is no immediate natural link. Hence, individuals are not appointed to office on account of their birth or native personal gifts. The objective factor in their appointment is (their) knowledge and proof of (their) ability.
The principles of office hierarchy and of levels of graded authority … offers the governed the possibility of appealing the decision of a lower office to its higher authority …	The security of the State and its subjects against the misuse of power by ministers and their officials (i.e. the bureaucracy) lies directly in their hierarchical organization and their answerability…
Once established and having fulfilled its task, an office tends to continue in existence…	… while the actions of the officials (or bureaucrats) are the fulfillment of their duty, their office is also a right exempt from contingency (i.e. exempt from arbitrary intervention from above).
The management of the modern office is based upon written documents, "the files," which are preserved in their original or draft form.	(A decision based on) the content of current affairs of state or the legal provisions required to meet existing needs (requires) their objective aspects, i.e. the grounds on which (the) decision is to be based, the relative laws, circumstances, etc. (This implicates what Weber calls "the files").
…bureaucracy segregates official activity as something distinct from the sphere of private life.	…The assured satisfaction of particular needs (the bureaucrat's subjective ends) removes the external compulsion which may tempt a man to seek ways and means of satisfying (his subjective ends, his particular needs) at the expense of his official duties.
Office management … usually presupposes thorough and expert training.	(The education of the bureaucrat consists of) direct education in thought and ethical conduct. Such an education is a mental counterpoise to the mechanical and semi-mechanical activity involved in acquiring the so-called "sciences" of matters connected with administration (administrative science).
When the office is fully developed, official activity demands the full working capacity of the official …	The state does not count on optional, discretionary services… casual servants may fail for private reasons to fulfill their duties completely …

The management of the office follows general rules, which are more or less, stable, more or less exhaustive and which can be learned.	The nature of the executive functions (as expressed in a bureaucracy) is that they are objective and that in their substance they have been explicitly fixed by previous decisions.

10.6.7 Marxian Criticism

The concept of bureaucracy was not central to Marx's thoughts. But he made a detailed study about the bureaucratic system in his "Critique of Hegel's Philosophy of Right". He had devoted an entire section on bureaucracy. He had expressed his views on the structure, function and the relationship of bureaucracy with the state and the society. He analysed the system as a set of relationships that arise because of the prevailing socio-economic context. Hence the conceptualisation of Marx's bureaucracy has to be understood within his general framework of his theory of class conflict, crisis of capitalism and the advent of communism.

Marx introduced the idea of bureaucracy in his criticism of Hegel's conception of executive authority of the state. Marx rejected the positive picture of state as presented by Hegel. According to Marx, the state does not represent the general interest of the people, rather it projects and serves only the interest of the dominant class in the society. And in the capitalist system, the state was the handmaiden of the dominant capitalist class.

Hence according to Marx,

- Bureaucracy is an instrument of domination used by the dominant class to exercise control over the lower class in the society.
- Interest of the bureaucracy is linked to that of the dominant class and the state.
- The bureaucracy is not functional as said by Hegel, it arises from the pathological division of labour in the society. It is an instrument of perpetual exploitation of the weaker sections of the society.
- In a capitalist society, the bureaucracy works to support and consolidate the class division and domination.
- The bureaucracy constitutes a particular, closed group within the state. It has its own interest which it defends against the other classes in the society.
- It uses the power to promote and sustain its own private ends. It does not act to achieve general interest of the society.
- The true purpose and intention of the state is cloaked in secrecy, mechanist action, and the faith in the authority.
- The objective of the bureaucracy becomes, securing higher position in the hierarchy, and making a better career. Hence the bureaucrats treat state as their private property.
- The information and other resources are manipulated to serve the interests of the dominant group.
- Another important character of bureaucracy is the hierarchy, according to Marx, "*....its hierarchy is a hierarchy of knowledge. The top entrusts the understanding of detail to the lower levels, whilst the lower levels credit the top with understanding of the general, and so, all are mutually deceived. Comprehensive knowledge is not possible in such a situation where knowledge is deliberately split up.*"
- Another important characteristic of bureaucracy is its secrecy. It carries out all its actions in secrecy to achieve its objective of privatising the civil society. Political consciousness is considered to be a treason. The spirit of mystery is preserved internally

through hierarchy and externally through the nature of closed society. As Marx states, the truth is that bureaucracy captures and hold the substance of the state.

- The bureaucracy becomes autonomous and an oppressive force.
- The bureaucracy contributes to the alienation of the people. According to Marx, "*even the paper qualification of the bureaucrat are a mark of separation from the rest of the society*."
- Incompetence is another feature of bureaucracy. It is in opposition to Hegel's view that bureaucracy is the most competent authority in the society.
- According to Marx, the bureaucracy leads a parasitic existence. It does not occupy an organic position in the society divided between the exploiter and the exploited. He simply calls it a 'parasitic body' used to maintain the status quo and privileges of the dominant class in the society.
- Bureaucracy is inseparable from the state. And it is integral part of the exploitative system. And hence it will not exist in a communal system of governance.

10.6.8 Comparison of Views of Hegel and Marx

Below is the views on bureaucracy as taken by Marx and Hegel. Marx developed his criticism based on the works of Hegel and hence views of Marx are in opposition to that of Hegel.

Marx	Hegel
Bureaucracy is not the will of the universal, it does not serve the general interest. It serves the private interest and reinforces the private spirit.	Bureaucracy is the will of the universal, and it serves the general interest of the people.
Bureaucracy leads to alienation of the people.	Bureaucracy is an integrating force which links the civil society and the state.
Bureaucracy owes its origin to the division of society into exploiters and exploited.	It arises from the opposition between the particular interest of the civils society and the general interest of the state.

Marx thus views bureaucracy as an oppressive force, the instrument of the capitalist system, which is used to exploit the weaker section of the society. This form of thinking of including bureaucracy within the social setup influenced other scholars who studied bureaucratic system, this includes Max Weber also.

10.7. GENERALIST VS SPECIALISTS DEBATE

The generalists and specialists are two important formulation of civil service in India. The proper relationship between them is essential for effective functioning of the civil service. But there has always undying issues between these two since the days of independence.

10.7.1 Meaning of the Term

A generalist civil servant does not possess a specialised qualification but is well equipped with the administrative procedures, rules and regulations and hence can be appointed to any administrative field.

He belongs to the managerial class, and performs activities such as planning, organising, coordinating, budgeting, staffing, directing, supervising and controlling.

Thus the civil servant who makes policies, coordinates, supervises and controls the administration is called as **generalists**. An IAS officer is a generalist civil servant par excellence.

As R.B.Jain observed, "*In his professional capacity a generalist possess the skill and techniques of the manager and a kind of politician. As a manager he is responsible for getting things done, and as a politician, he is responsible for interpreting the minds of the people to the complex social, economic and even political problems of the state within the constraints of the administrative system.*"

A specialised civil servant on the other hand, is the one who holds special knowledge or skill in a particular area. He is a professional expert in that area. Thus like a generalist, he is not an all-rounder. The specialist areas include that of the engineers, doctors, educationists, economists, police, agriculturalists etc.

10.7.2 Categorisation of Civil Service in India

The civil service in India can be categorised into technical and non-technical fields. The recruitment for the specialised services takes place based on basis of such specialised and professional qualifications. Hence the technical services need subject and professional experts from that particular field. The following are some of the services that require professional expertise,

- Indian Economic Service;
- Indian Statistical Service;
- Indian Forest Service;
- Central Engineering Service;
- Central Meteorological Service and so on.

The non-technical services are those for which the recruitment are carried out on basis of general educational qualifications. It is open to all candidates who have the necessary minimum qualification. These services include the following,

- Indian Administrative Service;
- Indian Foreign Service;
- Indian Police Service;
- Indian Revenue Service;
- Indian Audit and Account Service and so on.

These non-technical services can be further classified into functional and general purpose services. For the functional services the people get selected and remain in their service throughout their career all other services except the IAS falls into the category of functional non-technical service.

Hence IAS is the only general purpose service. The members of this cadre occupy all the top most administrative positions in the country. There is no separate functional field of occupation for the IAS cadre.

10.7.3 Areas of Controversy

The controversy between the generalists and the specialists relate to the following aspects,

- The entry to top posts are generally denied to the members of specialist service. Most of these top posts are occupied by members of the IAS, which is a generalist service.

- At the regional level specialised posts such as the Divisional Commissioner, Command Area Development Commissioner Etc. are all occupied by generalists.
- The generalists enjoy more proximity to the political heads than the specialists.
- The district is headed by the Collector, who is a 'generalist civil servant par excellence'. At the district level there are number of other institutions which are headed by specialists. Hence generalist heads team of specialists.
- The specialists are hence considered to be the subordinates of the generalists. The views, opinions and advice are not taken by the IAS- generalist service from the specialists.
- There is wide possibility of inter-organisational mobility by the generalists, than that of the specialists. The IAS officers can move from one department to another, or to a public enterprise, or local government etc. while there is no such scope for the generalists who can only move within their own departments.
- The pay and service conditions of the generalists are much more attractive than that of the specialists. This is the most important grievance of the specialists.
- Below the secretariat level, the departments are generally manned by the specialists, but sometimes, a generalist is appointed as the head of a technical department, such as Director of Health, Animal Husbandry etc.
- The generalists have a quicker and better chance of promotion and career development than the specialists.
- All the performance appraisal of the specialists is carried out by the generalist IAS officers.

Hence the abovementioned controversy has led to discontentment amongst the services. And thus has affected the morale and efficiency.

10.7.4 The Case for the Generalists

The following points are in support of the generalists,

a. The tenure system in the secretariat whereby, on rotation the people with the field experience are appointed, requires generalist administrators.
b. A generalist can act as a mediator between the political head and the specialist, between the government and the people, between the pressure groups and public interest.
c. The specialists are narrow-minded and are experts only in a particular field. They "know more and more about less and less". As Paul H. Appleby stated, "the price of specialisation of every kind is parochialism". Hence the generalist, on the other hand, have a broader outlook and flexibility in their approach.
d. The generalists are suited to higher management positions are they are much more experienced, and have high calibre, ability to manage things.
e. There has to be a generalist civil servant at all positions to carry on managerial functions.

10.7.5 The Case for Specialists

The following is in support and favour of specialist entry and greater role in the field of administration,

a. The IAS officers are considered to be the "Jack of all and Master of none". They are not equipped to deal with technical aspects related to administration.
b. In the present setup, the political head is deprived of technical and subject matter advice.
c. The generalists are not aware of the realities in the field, hence the policies formulated by them are unrealistic and un-implementable. Only the specialists know the difficulty of implementing and the problems faced by the people in the field.
d. The earlier era of 'intelligent amateur theory' does not hold good in the present times. The functions related to administration has become much more complex, technical and subject specific, hence only a specialist can deal with them effectively.
e. The generalists are not suitable for policy making as they do not have sufficient knowledge and understanding required to resolve the problems plaguing the society.

10.7.6 ARC Recommendations

The First Administrative Reforms Commission in 1969, in its Report on Personnel Administration made the following recommendations to resolve the generalist and specialist controversy.

Need for specialization: The first ARC recognized the need for specialization as the functions of Government had become diversified. A method of selection for senior management posts in functional areas and outside functional areas was laid down.

Unified Grading structure: A unified grading structure based on qualifications and nature of duties and responsibilities was suggested.

The first ARC had set out its philosophy on domain expertise as follows:

- Devising a rational basis to fill policy-making positions with those possessing required qualifications and competence. This would involve an optimum use of different Services for secretariat assignments as also the adoption of special measures to build necessary specializations in the secretariat.
- Selecting senior management personnel from all relevant sources – generalist and specialist. For the purpose, talent should be identified and nurtured in all the services, especially among those who have not so far been inducted into the higher management positions in the secretariat.
- Providing greater opportunities to talented personnel to move to higher positions in the civil services on the basis of competence and performance.

The first ARC classified higher civil service posts into two categories: (a) posts in the field, and (b) posts at headquarters. The field posts were held by the members of the 'functional' services which included not only the various engineering services but also services such as accounts and income tax. The first ARC noted that the only service that was not functional but occupied most of the higher posts in the civil services was the IAS. The ARC recommended that the IAS should be converted into a functional service.

Consistent with its philosophy of organizing the administrative machinery along functional lines and inducting talent from all sources, the ARC recommended eight broad areas of specialization:

- Economic Administration
- Industrial Administration
- Agricultural and Rural Development Administration

- Social and Educational Administration
- Personnel Administration
- Financial Administration
- Defence Administration and Internal Security
- Planning

The first ARC recommended a scheme of reforms to enable entry into middle and senior management levels in the Central Secretariat from all Services on the basis of knowledge and experience in the respective areas of specialization. The ARC also indicated, in broad terms, the knowledge and specialization required for staffing posts in each of these areas. The selection of personnel to the eight areas of specialization was to be made through a mid-career competitive examination. All Class I officers belonging to the All-India and Central Services with experience of eight to twelve years in the functional areas would be eligible. The selection process would consist of a written test to be administered by the UPSC and an interview to be conducted by a committee consisting of the Chairman, UPSC and two senior Secretaries of the Government of India.

The first ARC recommended a **unified grading structure** so that posts entailing similar qualifications, difficulties and responsibilities are grouped in the same grade. The principle of equal pay for equal work was sought to be recognized for the entire country for both the Union and the State Governments and even the local bodies. It was of the view that in the absence of a careful evaluation of the work content of jobs at certain levels and the matching of scales of pay thereto, the principle of equal pay for equal work cannot be implemented. The imbalance in remuneration attached to headquarters posts and field posts and the multiplicity of pay scales for different groups was sought to be addressed by this unified grading system. For grading, it recommended that the following considerations be taken into account:

- In services that provide for postings in the secretariat and at the field level, the liability for service all over the country should be reflected in the grading system.
- For services that provide only for field postings or postings only in secretariats but not in both, the grades would have to be related to the duties and responsibilities of these posts.
- The fact that the members of the State civil services are required to work only within the State and not outside, should be reflected in their grades.
- Posts involving higher research should be graded high, even though such posts carry little or no administrative responsibility.

The Commission recommended that the number of grades should range between 20 and 25.

10.7.7 Steps Taken

The government of India has taken the following steps to resolve the generalist-specialist conflict,

1. It created the Central Secretariat Service in 1948. This created a separate cadre of permanent secretariat officers.
2. It created the Central Administrative Pool in 1957 for appointments to the higher positions in the central secretariat.
3. It created the Indian Forest Service in 1966. It is a specialist all-India cadre service.

4. It has not been including the specialists in the board of management of the public sector undertakings.
5. It had also appointed many specialists in the erstwhile planning commission.
6. It created the Indian Economic Service and Indian Statistical Service, these are both specialised central service.
7. It has been appointing specialists to the senior administrative posts, such as, the Secretary, Additional Secretary, Joint Secretary and so on.

10.8 MINISTER-CIVIL SERVANT RELATIONSHIP

The Second ARC Report in its 10th Report states the following regarding the Minister-civil servant relationship, A healthy working relationship between Ministers and civil servants is critical for good governance. While the principles governing the roles and responsibilities of Ministers and civil servants are well defined in political theory, in the actual working of this relationship this division of responsibility becomes blurred with both sides often encroaching upon the other's sphere of responsibility. In any democracy, Ministers are responsible to the people through Parliament and therefore the civil servants have to be accountable to the Minister. However, an impartial civil service is responsible not only to the government of the day but to the Constitution of the land to which they have taken an oath of loyalty. At the same time, implementing the policies of the duly elected government is a core function of civil servants. That is why the division of responsibility between the civil servants and ministers needs to be more clearly defined. A framework in which responsibility and accountability is well defined would be useful.

10.8.1 Constitutional Provisions in India

The Indian Constitution provides for separation of powers between the legislature, executive and judiciary with well-defined roles and responsibilities for each one of them. Since India is a parliamentary democracy, there is an interface between the legislature and the executive at the level of the Council of Ministers, which is collectively responsible to the legislature. In terms of Articles 53 and 154, the executive power of the Union and the States vests in the President or Governor directly or through officers subordinate to him. These officers constitute the permanent civil service and are governed by Part XIV of the Constitution.

The Rules of Business of Government do provide for the Secretary to the Government to advise his/her Minister about the course of action proposed in a particular matter and to submit to him a note which tells him about the propriety or legality of his/her orders and suggest that either such orders not be given or that they be suitably modified. The relationship between the Secretary and the Minister is organic. The Minister has the mandate of the people to govern, but the Secretary has an equivalent constitutional mandate to advise the Minister. Once his/her advice has been suitably considered, unless the Minister passes an illegal order, the Secretary is bound to implement it. The Minister, on his/her part, is required to support the Secretary who is implementing his/her order. Once a law is framed or rules and regulations are approved, they apply to everyone, whether a member of the political executive or of the permanent civil service. **A civil servant is required to implement the orders of government without bias, with honesty and without fear or favour**. It is precisely in this area that a degree of a difference of opinion often occurs between the political executive and the civil servants.

10.8.2 Civil Service in Post Independent India

In the initial years after Independence, relations between Ministers and civil servants were characterized by mutual respect and understanding of each other's respective roles, with neither encroaching upon the other's domain. However, in subsequent years, matters started changing for the worse. While some civil servants did not render objective and impartial advice to their Ministers, often some Ministers began to resent advice that did not fi t in with short-term political interests. There was also a tendency for some Ministers at the Union and the State levels to focus more on routine administrative matters such as transfers in preference to policy making. At the same time, some civil servants learnt the art of 'manoeuvring' for favours in return for pliability in their decision making. This trend was further accentuated by rising materialism and acquisitiveness in society as well as decline in values across the board. As a result, 'political neutrality' which was the hallmark of the civil service in the pre-Independence era as well as in the period right after Independence, was gradually eroded. These trends led to the phenomenon of 'politicisation of the civil service' in India.

10.8.3 Areas of Friction

The areas of potential conflict in the relationship between the political executive and the permanent civil service can be identified as follows:

a. The concept of neutrality
b. Advisory role of civil servants in policy making
c. Statutory role of the civil servants
d. Discharge of delegated functions
e. Transfers and postings of civil servants

a. **The concept of Neutrality**
Sardar Patel had made the following observations in the Constituent Assembly to support the continuance of the pre-independence civil service structure:-

> "*It needs hardly to be emphasized that an efficient, discipline and contended civil service assured of its prospects as a result of diligent and honest work, is a sine-qua non of sound administration under democratic regime even more than under an authoritarian rule. The service must be above party and we should ensure that political considerations, either in its recruitment or in its discipline and control, are reduced to the minimum if not eliminated altogether.*"

Unfortunately, this vision of civil service neutrality no longer holds good. Changes in governments particularly at the state level often lead to wholesale transfer of civil servants. Political neutrality is no longer the accepted norm with many civil servants getting identified, rightly or wrongly, with a particular political dispensation. There is a perception that officers have to cultivate and seek patronage from politicians for obtaining suitable positions even in the Union Government. As a result, the civil services in public perception are often seen as increasingly politicized.

The Commission is of the view that the political neutrality and impartiality of the civil services needs to be preserved. The onus for this lies equally on the political executive and civil servants. The Commission in its Report on "Ethics in Governance" while examining the ethical framework for Ministers has recommended that a code of ethics for Ministers should inter-alia include the following:

> *"Ministers must uphold the political impartiality of the civil service and not ask the civil servants to act in any way which would conflict with the duties and responsibilities of the civil servants."*

As observed by Paul Appleby civil servants should not confuse 'political neutrality' with 'programme neutrality'. At the stage of policy formulation, the role of civil servants is to render free and frank advice which should not be coloured by any political considerations. Once a policy or programme has been approved by the elected government, it is the duty of the civil servant to faithfully and enthusiastically see to its implementation. Not carrying out this task in the right spirit would amount to misconduct inviting appropriate sanctions.

b. **Advisory role of civil servants in Policy making**
Rendering policy advice to the political executive is the most important "staff function" of the civil servant. Policy making is the ultimate responsibility of the Minister. After a policy is approved by the elected government, it is duty of the civil servant to implement such policy in the right earnest whether he/she agrees with it or not. At the same time, it is the duty of the civil servant to provide the factual basis, thorough analysis of all possible implications of any measure under consideration and free and frank advice, without fear or favour, at the stage of policy formulation. It is unfortunate that at times senior civil servants get bogged down in routine administrative decision making and are unable to contribute adequately to this crucial aspect of their functions. However, for civil servants to be able to provide appropriate policy inputs, they must acquire the necessary combination of a broad perspective of the sector as well as of the Government as a whole, combined with conceptual clarity and requisite knowledge.

If a policy that is being formulated is perceived by the civil servant to be against public interest, his/her responsibility is to convince the political executive about the adverse implications of such a policy. However, if the political executive does not agree with such an advice, there is little that the civil servant can do other than putting his/her views clearly on record. It is for the other institutional mechanisms such as Parliament, the CAG, Judiciary and ultimately the electorate to hold the political executive to account for bad policy

c. **Statutory role of the Civil Servants**
Civil servants are required to discharge statutory functions under various legislative enactments which may sometimes be quasi-judicial in nature. The role of the executive magistrate under the Cr. PC, the role of an Assessing Officer under the Income Tax Act and of the SHO under the Cr.PC and the respective Police Acts are some examples of such functions. It has been observed that there is an increasing trend on the part of the senior functionaries both in the civil services as well as elected representatives including Ministers to interfere in such statutory functions. Acquiescence in the face of such interference is primarily the fault of the officer who has been entrusted with these statutory functions although those bringing such extraneous pressures should also be held to account.

d. **Discharge of Delegated Functions**
In a democracy, the ultimate executive authority for all purposes lies with the political executive which is accountable to the people through Parliament. However, like in

any large organization, Government also has to function through a hierarchy of functionaries to carry out defined tasks at different levels and in different locations. This necessitates on practical considerations the delegation of authority and responsibility to the civil servants at different levels in government. Such delegation is in line with the principles of subsidiarity which helps to take government closer to the people. The principles of sound management demand that authority and responsibility should go hand-in-hand.

It has been observed that there is an increasing tendency in government departments to centralize authority and also after having first delegated authority downwards, to interfere in decision making of the subordinate functionaries. This is an unfortunate trend and it is for those holding leadership positions in government both in the political executive and in the civil services to correct it since such centralization leads to inefficiencies and poor service delivery. It is also for the legislature to correct this trend by means of legislative enactments in certain critical areas as has been done for local bodies through Constitutional amendments (73rd and 74th) followed by State laws.

e. **Postings and Transfers of Civil Servants**

The National Commission to Review the Working of the Constitution made the following observations regarding transfers and postings of civil servants:

> *"Arbitrary and questionable methods of appointments, promotions and transfers of officers by political superiors also led to corrosion of the moral basis of its independence. It has strengthened the temptation in services to collusive practices with politicians to avoid the inconvenience of transfers and to gain advantages by ingratiating themselves to political masters. They would do the politicians' biddings rather than adhere to rules. Lest the situation becomes more vicious, it is necessary that a better arrangement be conceived under the Constitution. The question of appointments, transfers and placements is not to be left to the discretion of the politicians or administrative bosses but be entrusted to independent and autonomous boards. The Commission, therefore, recommends that the questions of personnel policy including placements, promotions, transfers and fast-track advancements on the basis of forward-looking career management policies and techniques should be managed by autonomous Personnel Boards for assisting the high level political authorities in making key decisions. Such civil service boards should be constituted under statutory provisions. They should be expected to function like the UPSC. Reputed management experts from institutes of management, well known for their excellence, should be inducted into these boards to provide a broad based pool of expertise. The principle is not to take politics out of personnel policy but to make knowledge and information institutionally available to the political decision-makers on the basis of appropriate parliamentary legislation under Article 309. The sanctity of parliamentary legislation under Article 309 is needed to counteract the publicly known trends of the play of unhealthy and destabilizing influences in the management of public services in general and higher civil services in particular."*

Arbitrary and motivated transfers of government servants which are not in public interest and good governance have become a matter of great concern particularly in some States although the position is somewhat better at the Union Government level.

10.8.4 Minister Vs Civil Servant

Pfiffner has elaborated about the difference in activities of the Minister and the Civil servant, they are as follows,

Minister	Civil Servant
He is an amateur	He is a professional expert
He is a non-technical person	He is a technical and a subject matter and administrative expert.
He is partisan towards the interest of this party, the community to which he belongs, and the region from where he hails from.	He is non-partisan and carry out acts in a neutral manner as specified by the minister.
He is the face to the public, and hence has no contact with the public.	They work in the back ground. People do not know their faces and hence they have less people contact.
They are more involved in the formulation of the policy in order to implement the electoral promises made in their manifesto.	They have no such obligation, their involvement is less compared to the ministers, and they have other vital roles to play.
They are involved in more in the decision making process. They are the final authority to take decisions.	Their role is more advisory in nature. They render advice to the ministers regarding various aspects
Their position is of temporary nature. Their membership lasts only for a tenure of 5 years and has to be re-elected in order to gain membership again.	They hold a permanent seat. They are recruited through merit and they raise in the organisation via promotion. They only retire when they attain their super annulation.

10.9 THE CONCEPT OF MINISTERIAL ACCOUNTABILITY TO PARLIAMENT

The Public Service Committee in the Britain recommended the following as a working definition of Ministerial Accountability:

> *Ministers owe a fundamental duty to account to Parliament. This has, essentially, two meanings. First, that the executive is obliged to give an account—to provide full information about and explain its actions in Parliament so that they are subject to proper democratic scrutiny ….*
>
> *Second, a Minister's duty to account to Parliament means that the executive is liable to be held to account: it must respond to concerns and criticisms raised in Parliament about its actions because Members of Parliament are democratically elected representatives of the people. A Minister's effective performance of his functions depends on his having the confidence of the House of Commons….*

The Committee also considered that, as part of ministers' obligation to explain their actions to Parliament, they should make civil servants available to committees.

The following is the Resolution recommended on ministerial accountability:

1. Ministers have a duty to Parliament to account, and be held to account, for the policies, decisions and actions of their Department and Next Steps Agencies;
2. It is of paramount importance that Ministers give accurate and truthful information to Parliament, correcting any inadvertent error at the earliest opportunity. Ministers who

knowingly mislead Parliament will be expected to offer their resignation to the Prime Minister.

3. Ministers should be as open as possible with Parliament, refusing to provide information only when disclosure would not be in the public interest, which should be decided in accordance with relevant statute and the Government's Code of Practice on Access to Government Information (Second Edition, January 1997);
4. Similarly, Ministers should require civil servants who give evidence before Parliamentary Committees on their behalf and under their directions to be as helpful as possible in providing accurate, truthful and full information in accordance with the duties and responsibilities of civil servants as set out in the Civil Service Code (January 1996).

It can be seen that the resolution gives civil servants duties toward Parliament only in carrying out the requirements of their ministers.

As the Committee concluded "*it is not possible absolutely to distinguish an area in which a minister is personally responsible, and liable to take blame, from one in which he is constitutionally accountable. Ministerial responsibility is not composed of two elements which have a clear break between the two*".

10.10 ANONYMITY OF CIVIL SERVANTS

The word anonymity means that the Civil Servants work behind the curtain without taking any praise or blame. Mohit Bhattacharya States, "*Anonymity meant that the civil servant would merely advice the politician from behind and would be protected from being exposed to the din and fury of the politics.*"

The concept of anonymity requires that the Minister answer for the actions of the civil servants working under him in the parliament, and thus protect him from the criticism from the parliamentarians. **This means that the minister assumes total responsibility for all the acts of omissions and commissions of the civil servant working under him**.

The minister is the head of the ministry/department concerned and is politically responsible for its acts. He is mainly concerned with the policy making and consults his secretary on these aspects. The course of action is the prerogative of the minister. Hence he is completely responsible for the positive or negative results of the policy and not the secretary.

Therefore, the concept of anonymity is counterpart to the concept of Ministerial responsibility. This means that both these concepts go hand in hand together.

India and Britain follow the Parliamentary form of government. The concept of collective responsibility is the bedrock of the existence of parliamentary democracy. This means that the executive are responsible to the Parliament for all their acts and functions. Hence the principle of Ministerial Responsibility states that the Minister has to be responsible for the policy decisions he takes and should protect the civil servant from being exposed to the questions in the Parliament.

This concept of anonymity functions only in cases of legal and proper acts carried out by the civil servant. And thus does not protect in cases of illegal and improper acts. The Minister has to thus protect the civil servant who has acted to implement the policy within the legal boundaries. He need not protect those who are guilty of abuse of authority for personal ends or other illegal or criminal acts. In all such cases the civil servant is guilty and is held personally responsible for his actions.

As the civil service is governed by the concept of anonymity it is not accountable to the Parliament. But it is accountable to its political executives. The minister since he is answerable to the parliament, makes the civil servant answerable to him. The scheme of accountability is so distributed that, the Minister is accountable to the Parliament and the Civil servant is accountable to the Minister.

The Chagla Commission was constituted after the Mundhra Scandal to enquire into the issue concerning the Life insurance Corporation of India made to by private shares. The commission held in its report that, "*constitutionally the minister is responsible for the action taken by his secretary. He cannot take shelter behind them nor can he disown their actions.*" Thus the Chagla commission upheld the principle of Ministerial Responsibility and the concept of anonymity of civil service.

10.11 CIVIL SERVICE NEUTRALITY

Neutrality implies political impartiality or non-political nature of the civil service. It means that the civil servants should remain poltially neutral and be non-political and serve the government of the day impartially. They should render free and frank advice to the executives without any consideration. They should be,

- Objective
- Apolitical
- Dispassionate
- Non-partisan
- Professional

And should do their job with efficiency, loyalty, integrity and dedication.

According to Mohit Bhattacharya, neutrality means, 'a kind of political sterilisation, the bureaucracy remaining unaffected by the changes in the flow of politics....There might be changes in political leadership, but the civil servant would be unfailingly offering "technical" advice to the political master keeping himself aloof from the "politics" of the day.'

According to R.B.Jain, "*Political neutrality not only meant the absence of political activity or bias on the part of the individual member of the bureaucracy but also that the bureaucracy would respond to the will of the government, no matter what its political complexion be.*"

10.11.1 Assumptions Based on which Neutrality is Envisaged

The following are the assumptions based on which the political neutrality is advocated.

a. In a liberal democracy having multi-party system, the government and the party governing changes generally after every elections. Hence under these circumstances, the neutrality of civil service is precondition for the efficient functioning of the government. Thus it helps in serving the government of the day with same vigour and enthusiasm.
b. The neutrality rests on the basic principle of merit system. As the civil servants are recruited through a formal system, they do no owe their allegiance to any political party. This helps them to remain neutral, non-partisan and serve the government effectively.

c. According to Gerald E. Caiden, the merits of the neutral bureaucracy, viz. continuity, permanency, professionalism, and reliability far outweigh the disadvantages such as, incrementalism, conservatism and reluctance to change.
d. According to Masterman Committee, "*the public interest demands, maintenance of political impartiality in the civil service and of confidence in that impartiality as an essential part of the structure of the government.*"
e. The 'spoils system' and the 'politicised bureaucracy' are not the desirable alternatives of a 'neutral bureaucracy', which is permanent and laudable.
f. According to the UN handbook, political neutrality, "*is an essential complement to the merit system, for it guarantees that the career officials…will give the government, whatever its political make up, absolutely impartial advice, criticism and assistance in any matter which concerns it.*"

10.11.2 Breakdown of The Concept of Neutrality

The concept of neutrality is presently not in vogue. Though it was thought to be an essential characteristic, a number of factors have caused for it to change. According to R.B.Jain the following are the reasons for the breakdown of the concept of neutrality in civil service:

1. The decision making in the policy initiatives is not the prerogative of the political executives alone, the civil servants play an important role in such decision making process.
2. The civil servants are involved in the sphere of politics via policy formulations, implementations, its execution and legislation, these acts are generally political and is difficult to distinguish it from non-political acts.
3. Civil servants being humans is difficult to be remain neutral in all scenarios, issues and problems. There is always some degree of subjective bias in issues affecting them, which cannot be eliminated from their judgments.
4. During the performance appraisal of the top-civil servants an element of political assessment comes in.
5. The civil servant assume the role of the leadership, and this is especially so in the developing countries which are engaged in socio-economic upliftment and restructuring.

10.12 PROBLEMS OF BUREAUCRATISATION

Though the bureaucracy leads to efficiency, it also on the other hand leads to other problems. The following are some of the problems that arise because of the bureaucratisation:

- Bureaucratisation results in emphasis of routine and detail in work, this results in red tape or delay.
- The bureaucracy has a tendency to keep on expanding, and hence in course of time the funding to a large extent goes for the payment of the bureaucrats instead of meeting the developmental objectives.
- In developing countries, since other organs of governance, such as the civil society, pressure groups etc. are not well established, hence the bureaucracy acts without any restraint with no one to control or question them.
- The politicians are amateurs and often have to heed the advice of the much experienced and knowledgeable civil servants.

- The aim of the politicians generally is to formulate the policy for the people and they are responsible for them, the civil servants on the other hand have no such compulsion, they are thus work for their own self-aggrandizement.
- It is generally understood that the bureaucracy has to be under the control of the elected representatives. But in the developing countries the bureaucracy is more powerful and holds the political office below them.
- In some of the countries, the military and the civil servants remove the democratically elected government and assume power themselves and start ruling the country. Such dictatorship can be seen in some developing countries.
- Lack of professionalism and poor capacity building
- Inefficient incentive systems that rewards the corrupt and the incompetent and not the upright and honest.
- Outdated rules and procedures that limit the civil servant from performing effectively.
- Systemic discrepancies in promotion and empanelment
- Lack of proper transparency and accountability procedures - there is also no safety for whistle blowers
- Arbitrary and capricious transfers – insecurity in tenures impedes institutionalization
- Political interference and administrative submission
- A gradual erosion in values and ethics
- Patrimonialism

10.13 ADMINISTRATIVE REFORMS

The following are the reforms given in the Second Administrative reform commission as compiled by FICCI in its handbook on 2nd ARC.

10.13.1 Strengths and Weaknesses of Indian Administration

The reasonably swift and efficient response of our administration to a series of major natural calamities – the Tsunami of December 2004, the Mumbai floods of July, 2005, and the recent earthquake in Jammu & Kashmir - demonstrates that in times of crisis we are able to marshal our resources effectively. All these and competent election management show that we have an impressive administrative infrastructure and it responds well when objectives are clearly defined, resources are made available and accountability is surely enforced.

69. In general there is high degree of dissatisfaction in society on account of unfulfilled expectations and poor delivery. One reason why we are not able to overcome our weaknesses is the incapacity to institutionalize the best practices from our own country and elsewhere. For this, a conscious effort not only to identify and document best practices but also build policy and create new structures and institutions to allow mass replication needs to be made.

In general, the positive power to promote public good seems to be severely restricted, making it difficult for even the most conscientious and competent functionaries to deliver optimal results. The systemic rigidities, needless complexity and over centralization have made most elected politicians and appointed public servants ineffective and helpless. But the negative power of abuse of authority in pursuit of pelf, privilege and patronage, or harassment of public through flagrant violation of law, petty tyranny and nuisance value is virtually unchecked. This imbalance in the exercise of power is at the heart of the crisis of governance. As a result most agencies of government are functioning sub-optimally, and government programmes have not yielded the desired results. At most levels authority is divorced from accountability, leading to a system of realistic and plausible alibis for non-performance. Most functionaries are thus caught in a vicious cycle.

10.13.2 Priority Action Areas

There are two fundamental, interrelated objectives, which need to be achieved in the coming decades. The first is the fulfilment of human and national potential. This entails prevention of avoidable suffering and ensuring human dignity, access to justice and opportunity to all Indians so that every citizen is a fulfilled and productive human being. Only then can we realize our potential fully and play our rightful role in the global arena, protecting the vital interests of present and future generations, and promoting global peace, stability and prosperity.

Human development takes place through access to good quality education and healthcare to make every citizen productive and fulfilled. Despite our long-standing commitment to these goals, the results are uneven and far from satisfactory. Allocation of resources is undoubtedly inadequate leading to huge unmet demand. Even what is spent is not very productive in outcomes. Most of the nation's gene pool is wasted because of inadequate and poor quality of school education. Higher education too is not very successful in promoting excellence of producing service providers, leaders, managers and wealth creators, for the future. The public health system has also been unsatisfactory and inadequate, private health expenditure, which already accounts for about 80% of total expenditure, is growing (14% per annum) much faster than GDP. The resultant high cost and poor access seriously undermines human development.

The third broad area is infrastructure and sustainable natural resource development. While the economic aspects of these are well-recognized, the governance challenges are not adequately addressed. For instance, effective land administration is crucial to capital formation in agriculture and soil conservation. Energy plantation and biofuel production would require great administrative innovation and grassroots coordination. Urban management involves much more than resource allocation for infrastructure and poses formidable challenges of governance. Power distribution management through local people's involvement and ownership in a consumer-friendly way is more a governance issue than an economic or tariff problem. We need to create innovative modes of governance in dealing with such challenges.

Another area which needs special attention is the changing nature of federalism. The last decade has witnessed significant maturing of our federalism. The states are increasingly empowered to determine their own policies and programmes, and the union is ever more sensitive to local needs. However, the role of the Union is expanding in a substantial measure in recent years in new ways. Education, healthcare, rural and urban development and social security are either state subjects, or largely under state jurisdiction. And yet, the services are increasingly driven by union policies and funds. Paucity of resources at state level, need for standardization of services, compulsions of reducing regional disparities, and the imperatives of meeting the challenges of a growing economy in the modern world have necessarily enlarged the Union's role in these sectors. However, we need to carefully design mechanisms to monitor these programmes and enforce accountability at the local level, even as the desired outcomes are achieved, and the constitutional scheme of division of powers is fully respected.

- Propensity to centralize has been the dominant feature of our administration.
- We need to truly redesign government on the basis of the principle of subsidiary.

- A task which can be performed by a small unit should never be entrusted to a large unit.
- Only when economies of scale and technical complexity demand entrustment to the larger tier should it be done so.
- All the financial devolution and personnel transfer should match functional domain determined on this basis.
- The citizen will thereofore see the link between his vote and public good, and monies can be traced to services delivered.
- The structure of local governments envisaged in the 73rd and 74th Constitutional amendments is now in place, but the soul of self-governance and empowerment is largely missing.
- Hence because of the economic reform process, the states have come into their own, and yet the Union has in recent years discovered a more meaningful and strategic role for itself.
- Local government empowerment need not mean weakening of states. States must be enabled to discover their vital role in providing strategic inputs and leadership even as local governments deliver most of the basic services.

Pervasive corruption is the most disturbing element of our governance. Happily, recent years witnessed encouraging trends in certain sectors. Wherever competition, choice, transparency and technology have been introduced, corruption has dramatically declined. However, in other core sectors where the state's role is critical, corruption continues unchecked. There are signs of growing corruption in some of these state controlled sectors, indicating a shift from the traditional forms of corruption. Police, criminal justice system, healthcare delivery, public procurement and contracting, transfers and postings of officials, tax collection and land administration are areas, which are by nature fully or substantially state-controlled. Corruption is either continuing or growing in these sectors, as the inexhaustible demand for illegitimate funds in our governance system continues unabated. Clearly far-reaching political and electoral reforms to transform our political culture and alter the nature of incentives in public life are the need of the hour.

10.13.3 Good Governance

Governance is admittedly a weak link in our quest for prosperity and equity. We have an impressive governance infrastructure and significant successes to our credit. But we need to refashion the instruments to suit the emerging challenges. The quest for good governance - governance which is efficient, citizen centric and is rooted in a sound value system, is based on three inter-related fundamental ideas.

- The first is rule of law. Rule of law requires that laws and their implementation should be transparent, predictable and credible, and that those who make and implement laws should be accountable for their decisions. While the government of the day is accountable to the legislature, at the operating levels of administrations this accountability is often lacking. A steady pulse in the recommendations of the Commission is thus the emphasis on accountability at each level of administration and minimization of unfettered discretion in decision making. From accountability of decision making flows credibility, predictability and transparency.
- The second fundamental idea is to put the citizen first. All too often the relationship between the State and the citizen is a master client relationship, with the citizen reduced to the status of a supplicant.This has to go. Systemic changes along with information technology makes it possible to reduce, if not eliminate altogether, the time and trouble

involved in the citizen's contact with the State. It also makes it possible to introduce automaticity in decision making. The State has no look upon itself as a service provider, and, as in many cases the State is a natural monopoly, the Commission has made a number of recommendation to curtail monopolistic behaviour by State agencies.

- The third most important idea is the citizen's participation in decision making. In our scheme of things the Union Government being the furthest removed from the day-today life of the citizen represents the principle of rationality. The State Governments, because of the sheer size of constituencies also tends to be removed from the daily concerns of the citizen. It is the third tier of governance, the panchayats and the municipal bodies, which is the closest to the citizen and can represent the principle of concern. Hence, it is necessary that there is greater devolution of powers, from the Union to the State Governments and from the State Governments to local bodies, and that the local bodies function in appropriate units that allow participation of every citizen in decision making. This devolution will not weaken either the Union or the States: in fact it will strengthen them by enabling them to focus on matters they are uniquely equipped to address.

The 2nd ARC has noted the need for real decentralization of power with effective institutional checks for greater control by citizens on how they are governed. Judicial and police reforms need to ensure speedy, efficient and accessible justice and swift, sure and severe punishment for abuse of office. Self-regulatory mechanisms to uphold standards in professional groups are another area that requires urgent attention in the changing context. Finally, measures of accountability including the recently enacted Right to Information, well-designed citizen's charters with penalties for nonperformance, independent and effective anti-corruption agencies, citizen involvement in the fight against graft and leakages will surely expose corruption much more easily and enforce compliance with acceptable norms of public conduct.

10.13.4 Political and Executive Capability

Political direction of the administration is the essence of democracy and the 73rd and 74th amendments to the Constitution have expanded the scope of political decision making. This casts a great responsibility on the political parties, to educate and train their functionaries in administrative decision making.

Every State has it 'establishment', which is usually its civil service. From 1858 onwards the civil services have provided the 'establishment' of the Indian State, often through difficult and trying times. The structured merit-based recruitment and placement of civil servants in different cadres was seen as one of the methods of unifying the country after Independence. Today there is considerable managerial talent available outside the civil services. Ministers can draw upon a very large base of intellectual expertise not available in the Government. The Commission has made several suggestions on nurturing talent for the 'establishment' of the Indian State from an early age, sustaining their morale and skills, upgrading the Services throughout their career and the induction of fresh talent at appropriate stages.

10.13.5 Functional Review and Rationalization

Efficient discharge of government business is hampered by horizontal and vertical dispersal of decision making. Single or strongly related subjects are often administered in different ministries. The resultant narrow focus of Ministries entail that coherent points of view, or policy, emerges only after extensive and prolonged consultations. Such delay could be avoided by having Ministries that can take a holistic view of the subject. This would also result in governments which are more compact and in which coordination is quicker and easier. In the existing government structure issues are examined at too many levels, and the contribution of some of them is minimal. These levels need to be reduced to a rational number. The commission has made suggestions on internal working of ministries and departments. The Commission has also recommended creation of effective Executive Agencies with well-defined role and functions. This would facilitate the Ministries to focus more on policy making and analysis while the projects/programmes are implemented by the Executive Agencies.

10.13.6 Budgeting and Audit

Budgeting and Audit are critically important tools of governance. The mis-match between plan and budget classification needs to be ironed out to permit rigorous monitoring of expenditure. An expert group needs to look at accrual based budgeting. Ministries need to be realistic in making their estimates of expenditure so that large unspent balances do not remain at the end of the year. A multi-year perspective would be helpful in dealing with this. Audit is often seen as an adversarial exercise, which it need not be. While Auditors have to be sensitive to administrative compulsions, Ministries and Department need to understand that audit is an instrument for enhancing administrative efficiency. There is a need for better understanding and synergy between auditor and auditee for improved accountability and audit impact.

(a) PC Hota Committee Report on Civil Services Reforms (Extracts of some important recommendations from the committee report)

Introduction

The Civil Services, in India, is widely recognized has steel frame of administration because of their indispensible contribution towards the consolidation and administration of our country. Civil Service Reform in India is a difficult exercise considering the great diversity of our population, language, culture, infrastructure and the institutions of governance. We are the world's largest democracy with an area about 3.2 millon sq.km. and over a billion people. Civil service reforms also have to take into account constitutional provisions governing the distribution of powers between the Union, the States and the institutions of local government.

There have been several studies in the past on civil services reform, few of them, before Independence, are royal commission on public service in India (1912-1915) and Royal Commission on superior civil service in India (1923-1924). After Independence the Secretariat Re-organization Committee under the chairmanship of Sir Girijashankar Vajpayee (1947); the Committee on Reorganization of Government of India headed by Shri Gopalaswami Aiyangar, the Report on Public Administration (1951) by Shri A.D. Gorwala and the reports of 1953 and 1956 by Paul Appleby.

Continuing with the legacy, the Government of India on 03 February 2004 with comprehensive terms of reference to examine the whole gamut of civil service reforms and to submit our Report within a period of six months. The terms of reference are as follows:

(i) Making the Civil Service
- responsive and citizen-friendly
- transparent
- accountable
- ethical in its (a) actions and (b) interface with the people,

(ii) Making the civil service egovernance friendly.
(iii) Putting a premium on intellectual growth of civil servants and on upgrading their domain knowledge
(iv) Protecting the civil service against wrongful pressure exerted by
   a. administrative superiors
   b. political executive
   c. business interests
   d. other vested interests.

(v) Changes, if any necessary, in the various All India Services Rules and Central Civil Rules to provide a statutory cover to the proposed civil service reforms.

Term of Reference One: Making the Civil Service Responsive, Transparent, Accountable and Ethical

There is no formal arrangement by which Departments and Ministries of Government of India validate their programmes from the point of view of the common man or the beneficiary. To make the civil service citizen-friendly, each office/Department/Ministry must identify the points of citizen interface in their programmes. In other words, services to the common people, which are expected to be delivered by the office/Department/Ministry, need to be identified in consultation with the beneficiaries. The office/Department/Ministry will also have to benchmark the quality of services and the period within which services can be delivered. The grievance redressal mechanism should be strengthened and held accountable so that a common citizen will know the officer he can contact if he has a grievance and the time required to attend to the grievance.

1. To mould young entrants for the higher civil service through training, government may go back to the period from 1948 till 1971 when the age of eligibility was 21-24 years for general candidates (as against 21-30 years for general candidates at present) with five years age concession for members of the Scheduled Castes/Scheduled Tribes. Age concession for candidates of the Other Backward Classes may be three years as at present.
2. As no competitive examination will be proof against selection of a few unsuitable candidates, Directors of Training Academies may invoke the Probation Rules to weed out unsuitable officer-trainees.
3. Officers must have Annual Performance Plans. Invariably an Annual Performance Plan will be a component of the Action Plan/Vision Statement of the Department/Ministry and its strategic long-term plan. Wherever possible, performance targets must be quantified. If it is not possible to quantify the targets, some other mode of target setting be done to ensure that an officer is held strictly accountable for performance.
4. After 15 years of service, a rigorous review be carried out of performance of civil servants based on the earlier quinquennial review of performance. If an officer is not

honest and performance-oriented, he be weeded out of service on completion of 15 years on proportionate pension. An officer should also have the option to retire on proportionate pension after 15 years of service. A similar review be carried out subsequently at periodic intervals to determine if performance level of an officer has fallen sharply/if there are allegations against an officer's integrity.

5. Each Department/Ministry should be required to identify the points of citizen interface, benchmark the quality of services and strengthen the existing grievance redressal mechanism.
6. Officers of the higher Civil Service must supervise work of junior functionaries by regular visits and inspections. All officers of the higher Civil Service must put on the website/print media their contact telephone numbers during office hours. Every Ministry/Department/ Office having large public interface must have a few toll free telephone numbers with voice mail facility.
7. Junior officers at the cutting edge level of administration should be given training in customer service, attending to phone calls and resolving public grievances.
8. Rules under the Freedom of Information Act 2002 be notified immediately. The implementation of the Act be reviewed after three/four years by an independent Task Force.
9. The Official Secrets Act be modified to cover only the essential minimum requirements of national security, public order and individual privacy.
10. All officers having a public interface to wear name badges while on duty.
11. The duties, functions and responsibilities of all senior posts be laid down and publicized.
12. After every five to seven years in service, a civil servant should spend at least two months with a non-government organization, academic institution or the private sector.
13. ISO 9000 be introduced for government offices.
14. A full time officer should be posted in the Information and Facilitation Centre and each Department should attend to public grievances.
15. Annual Property Return of all public servants be put on the website.
16. Rules be framed under the Benami Transactions (Prohibition) Act 1988 for attachment/forefeiture of benami/ill-gotten property of corrupt public servants.
17. Article 311 of the Constitution be amended to enable President/Governor to dismiss/remove public servants summarily in case of corrupt practice/having assets disproportionate to known source of income. The officer concerned may be given post decisional hearing to prove his innocence. To ensure natural justice, such post-decisional hearing has been held to be constitutionally valid by the Supreme Court of India.
18. Under the overall control of the Central Vigilance Commission, committees of experts be set up in various Departments to scrutinize cases of officers before initiating departmental action for corrupt 96practices/launching prosecution against them under the Prevention of Corruption Act 1988. Such a reform will encourage honest officers to take bold commercial decisions in the public interest without the lurking fear of a vigilance/CBI inquiry.

19. Section 13 (1) (d) (iii) of the Prevention of Corruption Act 1988 be amended so that civil servants are not incriminated for taking bona fide commercial decisions in the public interest.
20. Every programme of government should specify the deliverables in terms of services. Functioning of government offices having large interface with the common man should be assessed once in three/four years by independent organizations.
21. Citizen Centres should be set up to build capability for analyzing and suggesting changes in government policies. The civil service training institutes should perform the nodal role in this behalf.
22. Each Department of the Government should develop an internal evaluation mechanism on the basis of clearly laid down parameters. The result of such evaluation should be part of the Annual Administration Report. Departments should be held accountable for outcomes and there should be a sharp focus on service delivery.
23. A State of Governance Report should be brought out evaluating the performance of each State on the basis of a set of parameters of good governance.

Term of Reference Two: Making the Civil Service e-Governance Friendly

'e-Government' is the use of Information and Communication Technologies (ICT) to transform government by making it more accessible, effective and accountable. e Government includes: (a) Providing greater access to information in government; (b) Promoting participation in government by enabling members of the public to interact with government officials; (c) Making government more accountable by making its operations more transparent and thus reducing opportunities for corruption; and (d) Providing development opportunities, especially benefiting rural and traditionally under-served communities.

24. Points of public interface in government should be identified for focused attention and improvement. Within a period of two years the procedures in the areas of public interface should be simplified and electronic service 97 delivery for the common people be introduced. Each Department/Ministry may lay down a time schedule to extend service delivery through electronic means.
25. To provide a clean, honest and transparent government, antiquated rules and procedures in Government must be discarded and new simplified ones be put in place. Such an exercise is absolutely essential for introduction of e-governance.
26. e-Governance can augment efficiency and ensure transparency in government. The Andhra Pradesh experiment of identifying officers as Chief Information Officers to be trained in the Indian Institute of Management, Ahmedabad, in e-Governance is a noteworthy initiative. New entrants to the Civil Service have adequate hands – on experience with computers and the internet and they could be sent periodically for further training in application of e-Governance.
27. Each Department should identify skill gaps keeping in view its functions and take steps to train the required number of people.
28. The National Informatics Centre (NIC) should function as a vehicle for disseminating best practices across the country.
29. Officers posted as Chief Executive of e-governance projects should be given reasonable tenure and held accountable for results.

30. The administrative and financial flexibility required for introducing innovative e-governance measures should be identified and operationalised.
31. The Minimum Agenda for e-Governance should be carried forward and each Department is required to identify specific activities which will be e-enabled in the next 12 months.
32. Departmental examination should include a practical test on the ability to use and apply computers.
33. Each Department/Ministry should have its own website of basic information relating to the Department/Ministry and the website be available for registering public grievances.

Term of Reference Three: Putting a Premium on Intellectual Growth

During public consultations, the committee was approached by several Group 'A' services including the Indian Information Service, the Indian Trade Service and the Indian Economic Service, who highlighted what they described as the less than ideal conditions under which their cadres are being managed. It was pointed out that apart from the stagnation at various levels, some of these services no longer serve the purposes for which they were set up. Their services are no longer being utilized optimally, leading many officers to leave the service or seek premature retirement. It may be true that the requirements of the Departments have changed and the service concerned is no longer in a position to meet them. If it is decided that a particular service is no longer required or requires a different set of skills, steps should be taken to either upgrade the skills of the existing incumbents or modify the recruitment processes to achieve the desired outcome. Continuing with a set of demoralized and demotivated group of senior civil servants is neither in the interest of the government nor that of the officers concerned.

34. Each Department/Ministry should undertake a review of the particular service of which it is the Cadre Controlling Authority to ensure that officers of the service are used optimally, promotion prospects for them are adequate and skill levels of officers are upgraded periodically. Each Department/Ministry should undertake a skill needs assessment to identify required skills and upgrade skill levels.
35. Civil servants should be encouraged to move laterally to non-government organizations.
36. Government should actively support and encourage outstanding work done by civil servants through National/State awards and commendations.
37. The initiative taken by the Department of Personnel and Training to provide funds to the Indian Institute of Management, Bangalore to develop a two-year course for officers of the IAS at mid-career level is a worthwhile experiment. Similar training programmes be devised for the Indian Police Service, the Indian Forest Service and other Central Services.

Term of Reference Four and Five: Protecting Civil Servants Against Wrongful Pressure and Changes in All India Service Rules and Central Civil Service Rules

Article 309 of the Constitution provides that "Acts of the appropriate Legislature may regulate the recruitment, and conditions of service of persons appointed to public services and posts in connection with the affairs of the Union or of any State, provided that it shall be competent for the President, or such person as he may direct, in the case of services and posts in connection with the affairs of the Union, and for the Governor of a State, or such person as he may direct, in the case of services and regulating the recruitment, and the conditions of service of persons appointed, to such services and posts until provision in that behalf is made by or under an Act of the appropriate Legislature under this article, and any rules so made shall have effect subject to the provisions of any such Act."

38. In the proposed Civil Service law, the highest political executive shall continue to be the final authority to order transfer of any officer before his tenure is over; but he will be expected to give due consideration to Report of the Administrative Inquiry/views of the Civil Service Board/Establishment Board and record reasons on the need for premature transfer of an officer. It is reiterated that the political executive shall have the final authority to transfer an officer at any stage in the public interest. An officer aggrieved by order of premature transfer can agitate the matter before a three-Member Ombudsman, who may, where suitable, award monetary compensation to the aggrieved officer. The constitution of the Ombudsman will be the same as the Ombudsman proposed for the Disputes Redressal Council. The President/Governor shall receive reports from the Ombudsman and shall lay an Annual Report on such transfers on the table of the Legislature. There should be a suitable provision in the law to enable States to adopt it and make it applicable in the States without going through the long process of drafting a law and get it passed in the Legislature.
39. The proposed comprehensive law on the Civil Service shall incorporate, inter alia, a Code of Ethics and a statutory minimum tenure in a post to an officer. Under the proposed law, if an officer is sought to be transferred before his tenure, there would be an expeditious administrative inquiry by a designated senior officer to be earmarked for this purpose. This can be dispensed with if the transfer is on promotion/deputation/foreign training. In all other cases, the Report of Inquiry with the views of the Civil Service Board/Establishment Board would be put up to the Chief Minister if officers of the All India Service/other civil services work in the States, or the Appointments Committee of the Cabinet if the officers work under the Central Staffing Scheme. For the officers of the other Central Services 100 working in Ministries/Departments but not under the Central Staffing Scheme, the new law will prescribe a tenure with a provision for administrative inquiry before an officer is sought to be transferred except on specified grounds.
40. The recommendation of the Surinder Nath Committee (July 2003) for increasing the domain knowledge of IAS officers be implemented. Similar exercise be undertaken to increase domain knowledge of officers of the other two All India Services and officers of the Central Services.
41. Officers of the All-India Service on deputation to their home State must invariably report back to their parent cadres on expiry of their periods of deputation. Only one term of deputation for an officer of the All India Service be allowed to the home State and that too to attend to urgent personal problem. The exemption at present available for officers of the North-East/Jammu & Kashmir cadres in matters of deputation may continue. Any violation of this stipulation will attract a major penalty proceeding and also be taken into account while considering the officer's empanelment/promotion. Such a stipulation would also be applicable to officers of the Central Service who go

on deputation to different State governments and to officers who go on deputation to international agencies/foreign governments.

42. Introduction of sophisticated technology alone would not make the administration people-friendly unless higher civil servants' have a proactive attitude and reach out to the common people. They must spend much more time in field visits, inspections, tours and night halts in remote and rural areas.
43. As officers of State Services appointed to All India Services by promotion also have to play leadership roles, they should face an Interview by the Selection Board. The Interview will not be a test of knowledge but will be only a test of leadership qualities.
44. The selection for promotion to All India Service will be made on an overall assessment of suitability of officers on basis of record of service and the Interview Test, Not more than 50% of the officers in a batch should make it to the Senior Administrative Grade. 30% should be the upper limit for Higher Administrative Grade and 20% for the highest grade of Secretaries to Government of India.
45. As there are large number of senior officers of the All India Service in different cadres, in selected districts, senior officers of the rank of Commissioners/Deputy Inspector Generals of Police/Conservators of Forests may be considered for posting as District Magistrates/Senior Superintendents of Police/ Divisional Forest Officers. The practice of posting very senior/Commissioner level officers in districts was prevalent before Independence and even for a few years after Independence. It is still prevalent in some States.
46. If the Establishment Board, after giving the views of the Minister in charge, who is a Member of the ACC, its utmost consideration, fails to change its original recommendation regarding the posting of an officer under the Central Staffing Scheme, the Cabinet Secretary may send the proposals of the Board with observations of the Minister in charge through the Home Minister, who is a Member of the ACC, to the Prime Minister, who heads the ACC for a final decision.
47. Steps be taken to reduce the number of officers who are empanelled for senior posts under the Central Staffing Scheme.
48. A member of the higher Civil Service would be debarred from being appointed as a Private Secretary or Officer on Special Duty to a Cabinet Minister / Minister of State in Government of India or in a State subject to certain stipulations. Ministers may have one of the officers of the civil service in their Department/Ministry to function as Private Secretary for a continuous period of two years only. The stipulation that no officer of a Civil Service can be Private Secretary of a Minister in the States or in the Central Government for more than two years may provide for an exception in case of the Prime Minister and the Chief Ministers.
49. Members of the All India Services and the Central Services, who are regular recruits through competitive examinations and who are unable to get promoted to the higher levels in their respective service due to non availability of posts, may be allowed the next higher grade as personal to them a year before retirement on superannuation. Such up gradation shall be available only to officers with proven record of efficiency and integrity.
50. Suspension from service of All India Service officers by the State Government will be invalid if not confirmed by the Government of India within a period of 60 days.

51. Under the new Civil Service law, a member of the higher civil service should not be appointed to any statutory commission or a constitutional authority after his retirement on superannuation. To insulate him from the temptation of post-retirement assignment, he should be appointed to such statutory bodies/Constitutional Authority only when he is not over 55 years of age so that he can demit office from these Commissions and Authorities after serving for five to six years.
52. There is a case for better compensation package for members of the higher civil service. Such compensation must bear a reasonable comparison with compensation for executives in the private sector. Issues related to a better package of compensation to the higher Civil Services may be referred to the next Central Pay Commission.
53. There should be a cooling off period of at least two years after resignation/retirement before a civil servant can join a political party and contest elections to any political office. No civil servant can be appointed to the high constitutional office of Governor of a State unless a period of two years elapses between his resignation/ retirement and his appointment as a Governor.
54. The recommendations of the National Police Commission relating to tenure of senior police officers, independent review of the work of police departments and streamlining the powers of arrest should be implemented. The recommendations of the Malimath Committee on criminal justice system be also implemented.
55. The procedure for reimbursement of medical expenses of civil servants should be simplified so that quality medical services are available from recognized private hospitals without having to report to the CGHS on each occasion of ailment. The facilities available at the CGHS hospitals also need to be strengthened.
56. To increase the representation of women in the civil service, it is prposed that within 15 years, at least 25 percent members of the higher civil service should be women as against 12 to 13 percent women at present. Women in the higher civil service be given four years of leave with full pay in their entire service career over and above the leave due to them under the normal leave rules. Such facility will enable them to balance their roles as officers with their roles as mothers/housewives.

Term of Reference Six: Changes in Rules Governing the Disciplinary Proceedings

The rules provide different procedures for imposing major or minor penalty on the Charged Officer. The decision to initiate major or minor penalty procedure is taken by the administrative Department/competent authority in consultation with the CVC in case of any allegation of malpractice/lack of integrity. In many cases, major penalty proceedings are resorted to even in cases where minor penalty proceedings would suffice. We feel that Administrative Department/ Disciplinary Authority may scrutinize the allegations more carefully and resort to minor penalty proceedings where the circumstances involve minor infringements of rules or procedural irregularities. Minor penalty proceedings can be concluded expeditiously as the Disciplinary Authority can take a decision regarding guilt of the charged official only on receipt of his explanation to the charge-sheet whereas a major penalty proceeding requires adherence to very elaborate procedure with appointment of an Inquiring Authority, examination and cross examination of witnesses, and scrutiny of documents produced as exhibits in the inquiry by either the Presenting Officer or the charged official.

57. To eliminate delay in disposal of a disciplinary inquiry, the Union Public Service Commission need not be consulted in case of a civil servant facing charges of corrupt practice and whose case has been referred to the Central Vigilance Commission for the first stage/second stage advice. If however the officer is penalized in the inquiry and prefers an appeal, the case may be referred to the UPSC for advice on the appeal petition.
58. Where minor disciplinary proceedings are sufficient to meet the end of justice, major penalty proceedings which are lengthy and time-consuming should not be initiated.
59. An Inquiry Officer should be relieved from his normal duties for a sufficient period to enable him to complete the departmental inquiry expeditiously and submit the report.
60. A database on disciplinary cases should be maintained to keep track of their progress.

Term of Reference Seven: Any Other Matter

61. An Employees Health Insurance Scheme on the pattern of defence forces should be introduced for the civil service.
62. A high level Selection Committee having a representation of the Chairman, Union Public Service Commission be established to prepare a panel of two names for appointment of one of them as a member of the State Public Service Commission by the Governor of a State. Similar High Level Selection Committee be constituted to recommend a panel of two names for appointment of one of them as a Member of the Union Public Service Commission by the President. Similar Committees be constituted to recommend panel of suitable names for other high level statutory and constitutional appointments such as Securities and Exchange Board of India, Telecom Regulatory Authority of India, Insurance Regulatory Authority, the Election Commission, the Comptroller & Auditor General to which retired civil servants are usually appointed.
63. To minimize litigation on service matters, in every Department/ Ministry there would be a Dispute Resolution Council (DRC) comprising a retired official as Chairman and tow serving officers as members. The decision of the DRC shall be invariably implemented. In case of disagreement orders of Core Group of Scretaries/Cabinet Secretary be obtained before DRC's report is acted upon. Similar Dispute Redressal Councils be set up by State Governments.
64. To ensure that the issued relating to the civil service get focused attention at the highest political level, the Empowered Sub-Committee on Governance of the National Development Council should go into the policy issues of the civil service and make suitable recommendations.

(b) **Central Civil Services (Conduct) Rules, 1964 (Updated)**

General

1. Every Government servant shall at all times--

    (i) maintain absolute integrity;
    (ii) maintain devotion to duty; and
    (iii) do nothing which is unbecoming of a Government servant.
    (iv) Commit himself to and uphold the supremacy of the constitution and democratic values: defend and uphold the sovereignty and integrity of India, the security of the State, public order, decency and morality;

(v) maintain high ethical standards and honesty;
(vi) maintain political neutrality;
(vii) promote the principles of merit, fairness and impartiality in the discharge of duties;
(viii) maintain accountability and transparency;
(ix) maintain responsiveness to the public, particularly to the weaker section;
(x) maintain courtesy and good behaviour with the public;
(xi) take decisions solely in public interest and use or cause to use public resources efficiently, effectively and economically;
(xii) declare any private interests relating to his public duties and take steps to resolve any conflicts in a way that protects the public interest;
(xiii) not place himself under any financial or other obligations to any individual or organisation which may influence him in the performance of his official duties;
(xiv) not misuse his position as civil servant and not take decisions in order to derive financial or material benefits for himself, his family or his friends;
(xv) make choices, take decisions and make recommendations on merit alone;
(xvi) act with fairness and impartiality and not discriminate against anyone, particularly the poor and the under-privileged sections of society;
(xvii) refrain from doing anything which is or may be contrary to any law, rules, regulations and established practices;
(xviii) maintain discipline in the discharge of his duties and be liable to implement the lawful orders duly communicated to him;
(xix) maintain confidentiality in the performance of his official duties as required by any laws for the time being in force, particularly with regard to information, disclosure of which may prejudicially affect the sovereignty and integrity of India, the security of the State, strategic, scientific or economic interests of the State, friendly relation with foreign countries or lead to incitement of an offence or illegal or unlawful gain to any person;
(xx) perform and discharge his duties with the highest degree of professionalism and dedication to the best of his abilities.

2. (i) Every Government servant holding a supervisory post shall take all possible steps to ensure the integrity and devotion to duty of all Government servants for the time being under his control and authority;
(ii) No Government servant shall, in the performance of his official duties, or in the exercise of powers conferred on him, act otherwise than in his best judgement except when he is acting under the direction of his official superior;
(iii) The direction of the official superior shall ordinarily be in writing. Oral direction to subordinates shall be avoided, as far as possible. Where the issue of oral direction becomes unavoidable, the official superior shall confirm it in writing immediately thereafter;
(iv) A Government servant who has received oral direction from his official superior shall seek confirmation of the same in writing as early as possible, whereupon it shall be the duty of the official superior to confirm the direction in writing.

Promptness and Courtesy

No Government servant shall

a. in the performance of his official duties, act in a discourteous manner;
b. in his official dealings with the public or otherwise adopt dilatory tactics or wilfully cause delays in disposal of the work assigned to him.

Observance of Government's Policies

Every Government servant shall, at all times-

(i) act in accordance with the Government's policies regarding age of marriage, preservation of environment, protection of wildlife and cultural heritage;
(ii) observe the Government's policies regarding prevention of crime against women.

Prohibition of Sexual Harassment of Working Women

1. No Government servant shall indulge in any act of sexual harassment of any woman at any work place.
2. Every Government servant who is incharge of a work place shall take appropriate steps to prevent sexual harassment to any woman at the work place.

Employment of Near Relatives of Government Servant in Companies or Firms

1. No Government servant shall use his position or influence directly or indirectly to secure employment for any member of his family in any company or firm;
2. (i) No Class I Officer shall, except with the previous sanction of the Government, permit his son, daughter or other dependant, to accept employment in any company or firm with which he has official dealings or in any other company or firm having official dealings with the Government:
3. No Government servant shall in the discharge of his official duties deal with any matter or give or sanction any contract to any company or firm or any other person if any member of his family is employed in that company or firm or under that person or if he or any member of his family is interested in such matter or contract in any other manner and the Government servant shall refer every such matter or contract to his official superior and the matter or contract shall thereafter be disposed of according to the instructions of the authority to whom the reference is made.

Taking Part in Politics and Elections

1. No Government servant shall be a member of, or be otherwise associated with, any political party or any organisation which takes part in politics nor shall he take part in, subscribe in aid of, or assist in any other manner, any political movement or activity.
2. It shall be the duty of every Government servant to endeavour to prevent any member of his family from taking part in, subscribing in aid of, or assisting in any other manner any movement or activity which is, or tends directly or indirectly to be, subversive of the Government as by law established and where a Government servant is unable to prevent a member of his family from taking part in, or subscribing in aid of , or assisting in any other manner, any such movement or activity, he shall make a report to that effect to the Government.
3. No Government servant shall canvass or otherwise interfere with, or use his influence in connection with or take part in an election to any legislature or local authority:

Provided that -

(i) a Government servant qualified to vote at such election may exercise his right to vote, but where he does so, he shall give no indication of the manner in which he proposes to vote or has voted;

(ii) a Government servant shall not be deemed to have contravened the provisions of this sub-rule by reason only that he assists in the conduct of an election in the due performance of a duty imposed on him by or under any law for the time being in force.

Explanation: The display by a Government servant on his person, vehicle or residence of any electoral symbol shall amount to using his influence in connection with an election within the meaning of this sub-rule.

Joining of Associations by Government Servants

No Government servant shall join or continue to be a member of, an association the objects or activities of which are prejudicial to the interests of the sovereignty and integrity of India, or public order or morality.

Demonstration and Strikes

No Government servant shall -

(i) engage himself or participate in any demonstration which is prejudicial to the interests of the sovereignty and integrity of India, the security of the state, friendly relations with foreign States, public order, decency or morality, or which involves contempt of court, defamation or incitement to an offence, or

(ii) resort to or in any way abet any form of strike or coercion or physical duress in connection with any matter pertaining to his service or the service of any other Government servant.

Criticism of Government

No Government servant shall, in any radio broadcast, telecast through any electronic media or in any document published in his own name or anonymously, pseudonymously or in the name of any other person or in any communication to the press or in any public utterance, make any statement of fact or opinion -

(i) which has the effect of an adverse criticism of any current or recent policy or action of the Central Government or a State Government:

Provided that in the case of any Government servant included in any category of Government servants specified in the second proviso to sub-rule (3) of rule 1, nothing contained in this clause shall apply to bonafide expression of views by him as an office-bearer of a trade union or association of Government servants for the purpose of safeguarding the conditions of service of such Government servants or for securing an improvement thereof; or

(ii) which is capable of embarrassing the relations between the Central Government and the Government of any State; or

(iii) which is capable of embarrassing the relations between the Central Government and the Government of any foreign State;

Gifts

1. Save as provided in these rules, no Government servant shall accept, or permit any member of his family or any other person acting on his behalf to accept, any gift.
   Explanation.- The expression "gift" shall include free transport, boarding, lodging or other service or any other pecuniary advantage when provided by any person other than a near relative or personal friend having no official dealings with the Government servant.
   Note (1) - A casual meal, lift or other social hospitality shall not be deemed to be a gift -
   Note (2) - A Government servant shall avoid accepting lavish hospitality or frequent hospitality from any individual, industrial or commercial firms, organisations, etc., having official dealings with him.
2. On occasions such as weddings, anniversaries, funerals or religious functions, when the making of gift is in conformity with the prevailing religious and social practice, a Government servant may accept gifts from his near relatives or from his personal friends having no official dealings with him, but shall make a report to the Government, if the value of such gift exceeds;-
   (i) rupees twenty five thousand in the case of a Government servant holding any Group 'A' post;
   (ii) rupees fifteen thousand in the case of a Government servant holding any Group 'B' post;
   (iii) rupees seven thousand five hundred in the case of a Government servant holding any Group 'C' post; and
3. In any other case of a Government servant shall not accept any gift without sanction of the Government if the value thereof exceeds.
   (i) rupees one thousand five hundred in the case of a Government servant holding any Group 'A' or Group 'B' post; and
   (ii) rupees five hundred in the case of a Government servant holding any Group 'C' or Group 'D' post.
4. Notwithstanding anything contained in sub-rules (2), and (3) a Government servant, being a member of the Indian delegation or otherwise, may receive and retain gifts from foreign dignitaries if the market value of gifts received on one occasion does not exceed rupees one thousand. In all other cases, the acceptance and retention of such gifts shall be regulated by the instructions issued by the Government in this regard from time to time.
5. A Government servant shall not accept any gifts from any foreign firm which is either contracting with the Government of India or is one with which the Government servant had, has or is likely to have official dealings. Acceptance of gifts by a Government servant from any other firm shall be subject to the provisions of sub-rule (3).]

Dowry

No Government servant shall-

(i) give or take or abet the giving or taking of dowry; or
(ii) demand directly or indirectly, from the parent or guardian of a bride or bridegroom, as the case may be, any dowry.

Explanation: For the purposes of this rule, 'dowry' has the same meaning as in the Dowry Prohibition Act, 1961(28 of 1961).

Public Demonstrations in Honour of Government Servants

No Government servant shall, except with the previous sanction of the Government, receive any complimentary or valedictory address or accept any testimonial or attend any meeting or entertainment held in his honour; or in the honour of any other Government servant:

Private Trade or Employment

1. Subject to the provisions of sub-rule (2), no Government servant shall, except with the previous sanction of the Government-
   a. engage directly or indirectly in any trade or business, or
   b. negotiate for, or undertake, any other employment, or
   c. hold an elective office, or canvass for a candidate or candidates for an elective office, in any body, whether incorporated or not, or
   d. canvass in support of any business of insurance agency, commission agency, etc., owned or managed by any member of his family, or
   e. take part except in the discharge of his official duties, in the registration, promotion or management of any bank or other company registered or required to be registered, under the Companies Act, 1956 (1 of 1956) or any other law for the time being in force, or of any co-operative society for commercial purposes.
   f. participate in or associate himself in any manner in the making of-
      (i) a sponsored media (radio or television) programme; or
      (ii) a media programme commissioned by Government media but produced by a private agency; or
      (iii) a privately produced media programme including video magazine:

Provided that no previous permission shall be necessary in case where the Government servant participates in a programme produced or commissioned by Government media in his official capacity.

2. A Government servant may, without the previous sanction of the Government,-
   a. undertake honorary work of a social or charitable nature, or
   b. undertake occasional work of a literary, artistic or scientific character, or
   c. participate in sports activities as an amateur, or
   d. take part in the registration, promotion or management (not involving the holding of an elective office) of a literary, scientific or charitable society or of a club or similar organisation, the aims or objects of which relate to promotion of sports, cultural or recreational activities, registered under the Societies Registration Act, 1860 (21 of 1860), or any other law for the time being in force, or
   e. take part in the registration, promotion or management (not involving the holding of elective office) of a co-operative society substantially for the benefit of Government servants, registered under the Co-operative Societies Act, 1912 (2 of 1912), or any other law for the time being in force:

Provided that:

(i) he shall discontinue taking part in such activities, if so directed by the Government; and
(ii) in a case falling under clause (d) or clause(e) of this sub-rule, his official duties shall not suffer thereby and he shall, within a period of one month of his taking part in such activity, report to the Government giving details of the nature of his participation.

Investment, Lending and Borrowing

1. No Government servant shall speculate in any stock, share or other investment:
   Provided that nothing in this sub-rule shall apply to occasional investments made through stock brokers or other persons duly authorised and licensed or who have obtained a certificate of registration under the relevant law.
   Explanation - Frequent purchase or sale or both, of shares, securities or other investments shall be deemed to be speculation within the meaning of this sub-rule.
2. (i) No Government servant shall make, or permit any member of his family or any person acting on his behalf to make, any investment which is likely to embarrass or influence him in the discharge of his official duties. For this purpose, any purchase of shares out of the quotas reserved for Directors of Companies or their friends and associates shall be deemed to be an investment which is likely to embarrass the Government servant.

   (ii) No Government servant who is involved in the decision making process of fixation of price of an Initial Public Offering or Follow-up Public Offering of shares of a Central Public Sector Enterprise shall apply, either himself or through any member of his family or through any other person acting on his behalf, for allotment of shares in the Initial Public Offerings or Follow-up Public Offerings of such Central Public Sector Enterprise.
3. If any question arises whether any transaction is of the nature referred to in sub-rule (1) or sub-rule(2), the decision of the Government thereon shall be final.
4. (i) No Government servant shall, save in the ordinary course of business with a bank or a public limited company, either himself or through any member of his family or any other person acting on his behalf,-
   a. lend or borrow or deposit money, as a principal or an agent to, or from or with, any person or firm or private limited company within the local limits of his authority or with whom he is likely to have official dealings or otherwise place himself under any pecuniary obligation to such person or firm or private limited company; or
   b. lend money to any person at interest or in a manner whereby return in money or in kind is charged or paid;

   Provided that a Government servant may, give to, or accept from a relative or a personal friend, a purely temporary loan of a small amount free of interest, or operate a credit account with a bona fide tradesman or make an advance of pay to his private employee;
   Provided further that nothing in this sub-rule shall apply in respect of any transaction entered into by a Government servant with the previous sanction of the Government.

   (ii) When a Government servant is appointed or transferred to a post of such nature as would involve him in the breach of any of the provisions of sub-rule (2) or sub-rule (4), he shall forthwith report the circumstances to the prescribed authority and shall thereafter act in accordance with such order as may be made by such authority.

Insolvency and Habitual Indebtedness

A Government servant shall so manage his private affairs as to avoid habitual indebtedness or insolvency. A Government servant against whom any legal proceeding is instituted for the recovery of any debt due from him or for adjudging him as an insolvent, shall forthwith report the full facts of the legal proceedings to the Government.

Note. - The burden of proving that the insolvency or indebtedness was the result of circumstances which, with the exercise of ordinary diligence, the Government servant could not have foreseen, or over which he had no control, and had not proceeded from extravagant or dissipated habits, shall be upon the Government servant.

Movable, Immovable and Valuable Property

1. (i) Every Government servant shall on his first appointment to any service or post submit a return of his assets and liabilities, in such form as may be prescribed by the Government, giving the full particulars regarding -
    a. the immovable property inherited by him, or owned or acquired by him or held by him on lease or mortgage, either in his own name or in the name of any member of his family or in the name of any other person;
    b. shares, debentures and cash including bank deposits inherited by him or similarly owned, acquired, or held by him;
    c. other movable property inherited by him or similarly owned, acquired or held by him; and
    d. debts and other liabilities incurred by him directly or indirectly.

Restrictions in Relation to Acquisition and Disposal of Immovable Property Outside India and Transactions with Foreigners, etc.

Notwithstanding anything contained in sub-rule (2) of Rule 18, no Government servant shall, except with the previous sanction of the prescribed authority, -

a. acquire, by purchase, mortgage, lease, gift or otherwise, either in his own name or in the name of any member of his family, any immovable property situated outside India;
b. dispose of, by sale, mortgage, gift or otherwise or grant any lease in respect of any immovable property situated outside India which was acquired or is held by him either in his own name or in the name of any member of his family;
c. enter into any transaction with any foreigner, foreign Government, foreign organisation or concern,-
    (i) for the acquisition, by purchase, mortgage, lease, gift or otherwise, either in his own name or in the name of any member of his family, any immovable property;
    (ii) for the disposal of, by sale, mortgage, gift or otherwise, or the grant of any lease in respect of any immovable property which was acquired or is held by him either in his own name or in the name of any member of his family.

Explanation.- In this rule "prescribed authority" has the same meaning as in Rule 18.

Restriction Regarding Marriage

1. No Government servant shall enter into, or contract, a marriage with a person having a spouse living; and
2. No Government servant, having a spouse living, shall enter into, or contract, a marriage with any person:

Provided that the Central Government may permit a Government servant to enter into, or contract, any such marriage as is referred to in clause (1) or clause(2), if it is satisfied that-

a. such marriage is permissible under the personal law applicable to such Government servant and the other party to the marriage; and (b)there are other grounds for so doing.

3. A Government servant who has married or marries a person other than of India Nationality shall forthwith intimate the fact to the Government.

Consumption of Intoxicating Drinks and Drugs

A Government servant shall

a. strictly abide by any law relating to intoxicating drinks or drugs in force in any area in which he may happen to be for the time being;
b. not be under influence of any intoxicating drink or drug during the course of his duty and shall also take due care that the performance of his duties at any time is not affected in any way by the influence of such drink or drug; refrain from consuming any intoxicating drink or drug in a public place
c. not appear in a public place in a state of intoxication;
d. not use any intoxicating drink or drug to excess.

Explanation: For the purposes of this rule, 'public place' means any place or premises (including a conveyance) to which the public have, or are permitted to have, access, whether on payment or otherwise.

Prohibition Regarding Employment of Children Below 14 Years of Age

No Government servant shall employ to work any child below the age of 14 years.

(c) Fourth Report – Ethics in Governance

Second Administrative Reforms Commission (Extracts from the Report on Ethics in governance)

1. *Coalition and Ethics*

The Constitution should be amended to ensure that if one or more parties in a coalition with a common programme mandated by the electorate either explicitly before the elections or implicitly while forming the government, realign midstream with one or more parties outside the coalition, then Members of that party or parties shall have to seek a fresh mandate from the electorate.

2. *Ethical Frame Work for Ministers*

In addition to the existing Code of Conduct for Ministers, there should be a Code of Ethics to provide guidance on how Ministers should uphold the highest standards of constitutional and ethical conduct in the performance of their duties.

Dedicated units should be set up in the offices of the Prime Minister and the Chief Ministers to monitor the observance of the Code of Ethics and the Code of Conduct. The unit should also be empowered to receive public complaints regarding violation of the Code of Conduct.

The Prime Minister or the Chief Minister should be duty bound to ensure the observance of the Code of Ethics and the Code of Conduct by Ministers. This would be applicable even in the case of coalition governments where the Ministers may belong to different parties.

An annual report with regard to the observance of these Codes should be submitted to the appropriate legislature. This report should include specific cases of violations, if any, and the action taken thereon.

The code of ethics, the code of conduct and the annual report should be put in public domain.

An office of ethics commissioner may be constituted by each house of parliament. This offers, functioning under the speaker/chairman, would assist the committee on ethics in discharge of its functions, and advise members, when required, and maintain necessary records.

In respect of states the commission recommend the following,

All states legislature may adopt a code of ethics and a code of conduct for their members.

Ethics Committees may be constituted with well-defined procedures for sanctions in case of transgressions, to ensure the ethical conduct of legislatures.

Registers of members interest may be maintained with the declaration of interest by members of the state legislatures.

Annual reports providing details including transgressions may be placed on the table of the representatives houses.

An office of ethics commissioner may be constituted by each house of state legislatures. The offers would function under Speaker/Chairman, on the same bases as suggested for Parliament.

3. *Office of Profit*

a. The Law should be amended to define office of profit based on the following principles:-

   All officers in purely advisory bodies where the experience, insights and expertise of a legislator would be inputs in governmental policy, shall not be treated as offices of profit, irrespective of the remuneration and perks associated with such an office.

   All offices involving executive decision making and control of public funds, including positions on the governing boards of public undertakings and statutory and non-statutory authorities directly deciding policy or managing institutions or authorizing or approving expenditure shall be treated as offices of profit, and no legislator shall hold such offices.

   If a serving Minister, by virtue of office, is a member or head of certain organizations like the Planning Commission, where close coordination and integration between the Council of Ministers and the organization or authority or committee is vital for the day-to-day functioning of government, it shall not be treated as office of profit.

   (The use of discretionary funds at the disposal of legislators, the power to determine specific projects and schemes, or select the beneficiaries or authorize expenditure shall constitute discharge of executive functions and will invite disqualification under Articles 102 and 191, irrespective of whether or not a new office is notified and held.)

b. Schemes such as MPLADS and MLALADS should be abolished.

c. Members of Parliament and Members of State Legislatures should be declared as 'Public Authorities' under the Right to Information Act, except when they are discharging legislative functions.

4. *Disqualification of Peoples Representatives*

The issue of disqualification of members on grounds of defection should be decided by the President/Governor on the advice of the Election Commission.

Section 8 of the Representation of the People Act, 1951 needs to be amended to disqualify all persons facing charges related to grave and heinous offences and corruption, with the modification suggested by the Election Commission.

5. ***Code of Ethics for Civil Servants***

'Public Service Values' towards which all public servants should aspire, should be defined and made applicable to all tiers of Government and parasternal organizations. Any transgression of these values should be treated as misconduct, inviting punishment.

Conflict of interest should be comprehensively covered in the Code of Ethics and in the Code of Conduct for officers. Also, serving officials should not be nominated on the Boards of Public undertakings. This will, however, not apply to non-profit public institutions and advisory bodies.

6. ***Ethical Frame Work for Judiciary***

A National Judicial Council should be constituted, in line with universally accepted principles where the appointment of members of the judiciary should be by a collegium having representation of the executive, legislature and judiciary. The Council should have the following composition:

- The Vice-President as Chairperson of the Council
- The Prime Minister
- The Speaker of the Lok Sabha
- The Chief Justice of India
- The Law Minister
- The Leader of the Opposition in the Lok Sabha
- The Leader of the Opposition in the Rajya Sabha

In matters relating to the appointment and oversight of High Court Judges, the Council will also include the following members:

- The Chief Minister of the concerned State
- The Chief Justice of the concerned High Court

a. The National Judicial Council should be authorized to lay down the Code of Conduct for judges, including the subordinate judiciary.
b. The National Judicial Council should be entrusted with the task of recommending appointments of Supreme Court and High Court Judges. It should also be entrusted the task of oversight of the judges, and should be empowered to enquire into alleged misconduct and impose minor penalties. It can also recommend removal of a judge if so warranted.
c. Based on the recommendations of the NJC, the President should have the powers to remove a Supreme Court or High Court Judge.
d. Article 124 of the Constitution may be amended to provide for the National Judicial Council. A similar change will have to be made in Article 217. Also, since the Council is to have the authority to oversee and discipline judges, further changes will need to be made to Article 217 (Clause 4).
e. A Judge of the Supreme Court should be designated as the Judicial Values Commissioner. He/she should be assigned the task of enforcing the code of conduct. Similar arrangement should also be made in the High Court.

7. ***The Prevention of Corruption Act, 1988***

The following should be classified as offences under the Prevention of Corruption Act:

- Gross perversion of the Constitution and democratic institutions amounting to wilful violation of oath of office.

- Abuse of authority unduly favouring or harming someone.
- Obstruction of justice.
- Squandering public money.

Section 7 of the Prevention of Corruption Act needs to be amended to provide for a special offence of 'collusive bribery'. An offence could be classified as 'collusive bribery' if the outcome or intended outcome of the transaction leads to a loss to the state, public or public interest.

a. In all such cases if it is established that the interest of the state or public has suffered because of an act of a public servant, then the court shall presume that the public servant and the beneficiary of the decision committed an offence of 'collusive bribery'.

The punishment for all such cases of collusive bribery should be double that of other cases of bribery. The law may be suitably amended in this regard.

10.13.7 Sanctions for Prosecution

a. Prior sanction should not be necessary for prosecuting a public servant who has been trapped red-handed or in cases of possessing assets disproportionate to the known sources of income.
b. The Prevention of Corruption Act should be amended to ensure that sanctioning authorities are not summoned and instead the documents can be obtained and produced before the courts by the appropriate authority.
c. The Presiding Officer of a House of Legislature should be designated as the sanctioning authority for MPs and MLAs respectively.
d. The requirement of prior sanction for prosecution now applicable to serving public servants should also apply to retired public servants for acts performed while in service.
e. In all cases where the Government of India is empowered to grant sanction for prosecution, this power should be delegated to an Empowered Committee comprising the Central Vigilance Commissioner and the Departmental Secretary to Government. In case of a difference of opinion between the two, the matter could be resolved by placing it before the full Central Vigilance Commission. In case, sanction is required against a Secretary to Government, then the Empowered Committee would comprise the Cabinet Secretary and the Central Vigilance Commissioner. Similar arrangements may also be made at the State level. In all cases the order granting sanction for prosecution or otherwise shall be issued within two months. In case of refusal, the reasons for refusal should be placed before the respective legislature annually.

10.13.8 Liability of Corrupt Public Servant to Pay Damage

In addition to the penalty in criminal cases, the law should provide that public servants who cause loss to the state or citizens by their corrupt acts should be made liable to make good the loss caused and, in addition, be liable for damages. This could be done by inserting a chapter in the Prevention of Corruption Act.

8. *Protection to Whistleblowers*

Legislation should be enacted immediately to provide protection to whistleblowers on the following lines proposed by the Law Commission:

- Whistleblowers exposing false claims, fraud or corruption should be protected by ensuring confidentiality and anonymity, protection from victimization in career, and other administrative measures to prevent bodily harm and harassment.
- The legislation should cover corporate whistleblowers unearthing fraud or serious damage to public interest by willful acts of omission or commission.

Acts of harassment or victimization of or retaliation against, a whistleblower should be criminal offences with substantial penalty and sentence.

9. *The Lokpal*

a. The Constitution should be amended to provide for a national Ombudsman to be called the Rashtriya Lokayukta. The role and jurisdiction of the Rashtriya Lokayukta should be defined in the Constitution while the composition, mode of appointment and other details can be decided by Parliament through legislation.
b. The jurisdiction of Rashtriya Lokayukta should extend to all Ministers of the Union (except the Prime Minister), all state Chief Ministers, all persons holding public office equivalent in rank to a Union Minister, and Members of Parliament. In case the enquiry against a public functionary establishes the involvement of any other public official along with the public functionary, the Rashtriya Lokayukta would have the power to enquire against such public servant(s) also.
c. The Prime Minister should be kept out of the jurisdiction of the Rashtriya Lokayukta because the Prime Minister is unchallenged authority along with leadership provides stability to our constitutional scheme. The Prime Minister is accountable to parliament and if he is opened to formal scrutiny by extra parliamentary authorities. The Government viability will be eroded and parliamentary supremacy will be in jeopardy . This would in turn undermine governance and public interest.
d. The Rashtriya Lokayukta should consist of a serving or retired Judge of the Supreme Court as the Chairperson, an eminent jurist as Member and the Central Vigilance Commissioner as the ex-officio Member.
e. The Chairperson of the Rashtriya Lokayukta should be selected from a panel of sitting Judges of the Supreme Court who have more than three years of service, by a Committee consisting of the Vice President of India, the Prime Minister, the Leader of the Opposition, the Speaker of the Lok Sabha and the Chief Justice of India. In case it is not possible to appoint a sitting Judge, the Committee may appoint a retired Supreme Court Judge. The same Committee may select the Member (i.e. an eminent jurist) of the Rashtriya Lokayukta. The Chairperson and Member of the Rashtriya Lokayukta should be appointed for only one term of three years and they should not hold any public office under the government thereafter, the only exception being that they can become the Chief Justice of India, if their services are so required.
f. The Rashtriya Lokayukta should also be entrusted with the task of undertaking a national campaign for raising the standards of ethics in public life.

10. *The Lokayukta*

a. The Constitution should be amended to incorporate a provision making it obligatory on the part of State Governments to establish the institution of Lokayukta and stipulate the general principles about its structure, power and functions.

b. The Lokayukta should be a multi-member body consisting of a judicial Member in the Chair, an eminent jurist or eminent administrator with impeccable credentials as Member and the head of the State Vigilance Commission as ex-officio Member. The Chairperson of the Lokayukta should be selected from a panel of retired Supreme Court Judges or retired Chief Justices of High Court, by a Committee consisting of the Chief Minister, Chief Justice of the High Court and the Leader of the Opposition in the Legislative Assembly. The same Committee should select the second Member from among eminent jurists/administrators. There is no need to have an Up-Lokayukta.
c. The jurisdiction of the Lokayukta would extend to only cases involving corruption. They should not look into general public grievances.
d. The Lokayukta should deal with cases of corruption against Ministers and MLAs.
e. Each State should constitute a State Vigilance Commission to look into cases of corruption against State Government officials. The Commission should have three Members and have functions similar to that of the Central Vigilance Commission.
f. The Anti Corruption Bureaus should be brought under the control of the State Vigilance Commission.
g. The Chairperson and Members of the Lokayukta should be appointed strictly for one term only and they should not hold any public office under government thereafter.
h. The Lokayukta should have its own machinery for investigation. Initially, it may take officers on deputation from the State Government, but over a period of five years, it should take steps to recruit its own cadre, and train them properly.
i. All cases of corruption should be referred to Rashtriya Lokayukta or Lokayukta and these should not be referred to any Commission of Inquiry.

11. *Ombudsman at Local Level*

A local bodies Ombudsman should be constituted for a group of districts to investigate cases against the functionaries of the local bodies. The State Panchayat Raj Acts and the Urban Local Bodies Act should be amended to include this provision.

The local bodies Ombudsman should be empowered to investigate cases of corruption or maladministration by the functionaries of the local self governments, and submit reports to the competent authorities for taking action. The competent authorities should normally take action as recommended. In case they do not agree with the recommendations, they should give their reasons in writing and the reasons should be made public.

12. *Promoting Transparency*

The Commission recommends encouragement of the mechanism of 'integrity pacts'. The Ministry of Finance may constitute a Task Force with representatives from Ministries of Law and Personnel to identify the type of transactions requiring such pacts and to provide for a protocol for entering into such a pact. The Task Force may, in particular, recommend whether any amendment in the existing legal framework like the Indian Contract Act, and the Prevention of Corruption Act is required to make such agreements enforceable.

13. *Reducing Discretion*

a. All government offices having public interface should undertake a review of their activities and list out those which involve use of discretion. In all such activities, attempt should be made to eliminate discretion. Where it is not possible to do so, well-defined regulations should attempt to 'bound' the discretion. Ministries and Departments should be asked to coordinate this task in their organizations/offices and complete it within one year.

b. Decision-making on important matters should be assigned to a committee rather than individuals. Care has to be exercised, however, that this practice is not resorted to when prompt decisions are required.
c. State Governments should take steps on similar lines, especially in local bodies and authorities, which have maximum 'public contact'.

14. ***Ensuring accessibility and Responsiveness***

a. Service providers should converge their activities so that all services are delivered at a common point. Such common service points could also be outsourced to an agency, which may then be given the task of pursuing citizens' requests with concerned agencies.
b. Tasks, which are prone to corruption, should be split up into different activities that can be entrusted to different persons.
c. Public interaction should be limited to designated officers. A 'single window front office' for provision of information and services to the citizens with a file tracking system should be set up in all government departments.

15. ***Vigilance Network***

A national database containing the details of all corruption cases at all levels should be created. This database should be in the public domain. Identified authorities should be made responsible for updating the database regularly.

16. ***Protection the Honest Civil Servant***

a. Every allegation of corruption received through complaints or from sources cultivated by the investigating agency against a public servant must be examined in depth at the initial stage itself before initiating any enquiry. Every such allegation must be analyzed to assess whether the allegation is specific, whether it is credible and whether it is verifiable.

   Only when an allegation meets the requirements of these criteria, should it be recommended for verification, and the verification must be taken up after obtaining approval of the competent authority. The levels of competent authorities for authorizing verifications/enquiries must be fixed in the anti- corruption agencies for different levels of suspect officers.

b. In matters relating to allegations of corruption, open enquiries should not be taken up straightaway on the basis of complaints/source information. When verification/ secret enquiries are approved, it should be ensured that secrecy of such verifications is maintained and the verifications are done in such a manner that neither the suspect officer nor anybody else comes to know about it. Such secrecy is essential not only to protect the reputation of innocent and honest officials but also to ensure the effectiveness of an open criminal investigation. Such secrecy of verification / enquiry will ensure that in case the allegations are found to be incorrect, the matter can be closed without anyone having come to know of it. The Inquiry/Verification Officers should be in a position to appreciate the sensitivities involved in handling allegations of corruption.

c. The evaluation of the results of verification/enquiries should be done in a competent and just manner. Much injustice can occur due to faulty evaluation of the facts and the evidence collected in support of such facts. Personnel handling this task should not only be competent and honest but also impartial and imbued with a sense of justice.
d. Whenever an Inquiry Officer requires to consult an expert to understand technical/complex issues, he can do so, but the essential requirement of proper application of mind has to take place at every stage to ensure that no injustice is caused to the honest and the innocent.
e. Capacity building in the anti-corruption agencies should be assured through training and by associating the required experts during enquiries/investigations. Capacity building among public servants who are expected to take commercial/financial decisions should be built through suitable training programmes.
f. The supervisory officers in the investigating agencies should ensure that only those public servants are prosecuted against whom the evidence is strong.
g. There should be profiling of officers. The capabilities, professional competence, integrity and reputation of every government servant must be charted out and brought on record. Before proceeding against any government servant, reference should be made to the profile of the government servant concerned.
h. A special investigation unit should be attached to the proposed Lokpal (Rashtriya Lokayukta)/State Lokayuktas/Vigilance Commission, to investigate allegations of corruption against investigative agencies. This unit should be multi-disciplinary and should also investigate cases of allegations of harassment against the investigating agency. Similar units should also be set up in states.

17. *Appoint of the Chief Election Commissioner/Commissioners*

A collegium headed by the Prime Minister with the Speaker of the Lok Sabha, the Leader of Opposition in the Lok Sabha, the Law Minister and the Deputy Chairman of the Rajya Sabha as members should make recommendations for the consideration of the President for appointment of the Chief Election Commissioner and the Election Commissioners.

18. *Expediting Disposal of Election Petitions*

Special Election Tribunals should be constituted at the regional level under Article 323B of the Constitution to ensure speedy disposal of election petitions and disputes within a stipulated period of six months. Each Tribunal should comprise a High Court Judge and a senior civil servant with at least 5 years of experience in the conduct of elections (not below the rank of an Additional Secretary to Government of India/Principal Secretary of a State Government). Its mandate should be to ensure that all election petitions are decided within a period of six months as provided by law. The Tribunals should normally be set up for a term of one year only, extendable for a period of 6 months in exceptional circumstances.

19. *Grounds of Disqualification for Membership*

Appropriate legislation may be enacted under Article 102(e) of the Constitution spelling out the conditions for disqualification of membership of Parliament in an exhaustive manner. Similarly, the States may also legislate under Article 198 (e).

20. *Immunity Enjoyed by Legislatures*

a. The Commission, while endorsing the suggestion of the National Commission to Review the Working of the Constitution, recommends that suitable amendments be effected to Article 105(2) of the Constitution to provide that the immunity enjoyed by Members of Parliament does not cover corrupt acts committed by them in connection with their duties in the House or otherwise.
b. The Commission also recommends that similar amendments may be made in Article 194(2) of the Constitution in respect of members of the state legislatures.

21. *Strengthening Investigation and Prosecution*

a. The State Vigilance Commissions/Lokayuktas may be empowered to supervise the prosecution of corruption related cases.
b. The investigative agencies should acquire multi-disciplinary skills and should be thoroughly conversant with the working of various offices/ departments. They should draw officials from different wings of government.
c. Modern techniques of investigation should also be deployed like electronic surveillance, video and audio recording of surprise inspections, traps, searches and seizures.
d. A reasonable time limit for investigation of different types of cases should be fixed for the investigative agencies.
e. There should be sustained step-up in the number of cases detected and investigated. The priorities need to be reoriented by focusing on 'big' cases of corruption.
f. The prosecution of corruption cases should be conducted by a panel of lawyers prepared by the Attorney General or the Advocate General in consultation with Rashtriya Lokayukta or Lokayukta as the case may be.
g. The anti-corruption agencies should conduct systematic surveys of departments with particular reference to highly corruption prone ones in order to gather intelligence and to target officers of questionable integrity.
h. The economic offences unit of states need to be strengthened to effectively investigate cases and there should be better coordination amongst existing agencies.

22. *Citizens Initiative*

a. Citizens' Charters should be made effective by stipulating the service levels and also the remedy if these service levels are not met.
b. Citizens may be involved in the assessment and maintenance of ethics in important government institutions and offices.
c. Reward schemes should be introduced to incentivise citizens' initiatives.
d. School awareness programmes should be introduced, highlighting the importance of ethics and how corruption can be combated.

23. ***Role of Media***

a. It is necessary to evolve norms and practices requiring proper screening of all allegations/complaints by the media, and taking action to put them in the public domain.
b. The electronic media should evolve a Code of Conduct and a self regulating mechanism in order to adhere to a Code of Conduct as a safeguard against malafide action.
c. Government agencies can help the media in the fight against corruption by disclosing details about corruption cases regularly.

24. ***Social Audit***

Operational guidelines of all developmental schemes and citizen centric programmes should provide for a social audit mechanism.

25. ***Supervisions***

a. The supervisory role of officers needs to be re-emphasised. It bears reiteration that supervisory officers are primarily responsible for curbing corruption among their subordinates, and they should take all preventive measures for this purpose.
b. Each supervisory officer should carefully analyze the activities in his/her organization/office, identify the activities which are vulnerable to corruption and then build up suitable preventive and vigilance measures. All major instances of loss caused to the government or to the public, by officials by their acts of omission or commission should be enquired into and responsibility fixed on the erring officer within a time-frame.
c. In the Annual Performance Report of each officer, there should be a column where the officer should indicate the measures he took to control corruption in his office and among subordinates. The reporting officer should then give his specific comments on this.
d. Supervisory officers who give 'clean certificates' to subordinate corrupt officers in their Annual Performance Reports should be asked to explain their position in case the officer reported upon is charged with an offence under the Prevention of Corruption Act. In addition, the fact that they have not recorded adversely about the integrity of their subordinate corrupt officers should be recorded in their reports.
e. Supervisory officers should ensure that all offices under them pursue a policy of suo motu disclosure of information within the ambit of the Right to Information Act.

26. ***Monitoring Compliance***

a. All offices having large public interface should have an online complaint tracking system. If possible, this task of complaint tracking should be outsourced.
b. There should be an external, periodic mechanism of 'audit' of complaints in offices having large public interface.
c. Apart from enquiring into each complaint and fixing responsibility for the lapses, if any, the complaint should also be used to analyse the systemic deficiencies so that remedial measures are taken.

27. *Audit*

a. It should be prescribed that as soon as any major irregularity is detected or suspected by the audit team, it should be immediately taken note of by government. A suitable mechanism for this may be put in place. It shall be the responsibility of the head of the office to enquire into any such irregularity and initiate action.
b. Audit teams should be imparted training in forensic audit.
c. Each office should make an annual public statement regarding pending audit queries.

28. *Promoting Competitions*

a. Each Ministry/Department may undertake an immediate exercise to identify areas where the existing 'monopoly of functions' can be tempered with competition. A similar exercise may be done at the level of State Governments and local bodies. This exercise may be carried out in a time bound manner, say in one year, and a road map laid down to reduce 'monopoly' of functions. The approach should be to introduce competition along with a mechanism for regulation to ensure performance as per prescribed standards so that public interest is not compromised.
b. Some Centrally Sponsored schemes could be restructured so as to provide incentives to states that take steps to promote competition in service delivery.
c. All new national policies on subjects having large public interface (and amendments to existing policies on such subjects) should invariably address the issue of engendering competition.

29. *Using Information Technology*

a. Each Ministry/Department/Organisation of government should draw up a plan for use of IT to improve governance. In any government process, use of Information Technology should be made only after the existing procedures have been thoroughly re-engineered.
b. The Ministry of Information and Technology needs to identify certain governmental processes and then take up a project of their computerization on a nationwide scale.
c. For computerization to be successful, computer knowledge of departmental officers needs to be upgraded. Similarly, the NIC needs to be trained in department specific activities, so that they could appreciate each other's view point and also ensure that technology providers understand the anatomy of each department.

30. *Proactive Vigilance on Corruption*

Taking proactive vigilance measures should primarily be the responsibility of the head of the office.

31. *Intelligence Gathering*

Supervisory officers should assess the integrity of his/her subordinates based on his/her handling of cases, complaints and feedback from different sources. This could then become an important input for risk profiling of officers.

(d) The ASPA Code of Ethics – 1994

The American Society for Public Administration (ASPA) exists to advance the science,processes, and art of public administration. The Society affirms its responsibility to develop thespirit of professionalism within its membership, and to increase public awareness of ethicalprinciples in public service by its example. To this end, we, the members of the Society, commitourselves to the following principles.

I. *Serve the Public Interest*

Serve the public, beyond serving oneself. ASPA members are committed to:

1. Exercise discretionary authority to promote the public interest.
2. Oppose all forms of discrimination and harassment, and promote affirmative action.
3. Recognize and support the public's right to know the public's business.
4. Involve citizens in policy decision-making.
5. Exercise compassion, benevolence, fairness and optimism.
6. Respond to the public in ways that are complete, clear, and easy to understand.
7. Assist citizens in their dealings with government.
8. Be prepared to make decisions that may not be popular.

II. *Respect the Constitution and the Law*

Respect, support, and study government constitutions and laws that define responsibilities ofpublic agencies, employees, and all citizens. ASPA members are committed to:

1. Understand and apply legislation and regulations relevant to their professional role.
2. Work to improve and change laws and policies that are counterproductive or obsolete.
3. Eliminate unlawful discrimination.
4. Prevent all forms of mismanagement of public funds by establishing and maintain-ingstrong fiscal and management controls, and by supporting audits and investigative activities.
5. Respect and protect privileged information.
6. Encourage and facilitate legitimate dissent activities in government and protect thewhistle blowing rights of public employees.
7. Promote constitutional principles of equality, fairness, representativeness, responsiveness and due process in protecting citizens' rights.

III. *Demonstrate Personal Integrity*

Demonstrate the highest standards in all activities to inspire public confidence and trust in public service. ASPA members are committed to:

1. Maintain truthfulness and honesty and to not compromise them for advancement, honor, or personal gain.
2. Ensure that others receive credit for their work and contributions.
3. Zealously guard against conflict of interest or its appearance: e.g., nepotism, improper outside employment, misuse of public resources or the acceptance of gifts.
4. Respect superiors, subordinates, colleagues and the public.

5. Take responsibility for their own errors.
6. Conduct official acts without partisanship.

IV. ***Promote Ethical Organizations***

Strengthen organizational capabilities to apply ethics, efficiency and effectiveness in serving thepublic. ASPA members are committed to:

1. Enhance organizational capacity for open communication, creativity, and dedication.
2. Subordinate institutional loyalties to the public good.
3. Establish procedures that promote ethical behavior and hold individuals and organizations accountable for their conduct.
4. Provide organization members with an administrative means for dissent, assurance of due process and safeguards against reprisal.
5. Promote merit principles that protect against arbitrary and capricious actions.
6. Promote organizational accountability through appropriate controls and procedures.
7. Encourage organizations to adopt, distribute, and periodically review a code of ethics as a living document.

V. ***Strive for Professional Excellence***

Strengthen individual capabilities and encourage the professional development of others. ASPAmembers are committed to:

1. Provide support and encouragement to upgrade competence.
2. Accept as a personal duty the responsibility to keep up to date on emerging issues and potential problems.
3. Encourage others, throughout their careers, to participate in professional activities and associations.
4. Allocate time to meet with students and provide a bridge between classroom studies and the realities of public service.

11

E-Governance

LEARNING OBJECTIVES

In this Chapter, you will learn about:

- Introduction
- Types of Interactions in e-Governance
- E-Governance Brings SMART Governance
- Benefits of e-Governance
- Limitations of e-Governance
- Recent e-Governance Initiatives
- Critical Conditions for Success of e-Governance
- Steps Needed to Be Taken
- Practice Questions

11.1 INTRODUCTION

According to the World Bank, 'E-Governance refers to the use by government agencies of information technologies (viz., wide area networks, the Internet, and mobile computing) that have the ability to transform relations with citizens, businesses and other arms of government. These technologies can serve a variety of different ends: better delivery of government services to citizens, improved interactions with business and industry, citizen empowerment through access to information or more efficient government management. The resulting benefits can be less corruption, increased transparency, greater convenience, revenue growth and/or cost reductions'.

11.1.1 e-Governance as per UNESCO

Governance refers to the exercise of political, economic and administrative authority in the management of a country's affairs, including citizens.

11.2 TYPES OF INTERACTIONS IN E-GOVERNANCE

As per the second administrative reforms committee's report, e-Governance facilitates interaction between different stakeholders in governance. It states that there are four types of interactions in e-Governance as follows:

(i) Government to citizens (G2C)
(ii) Government to business (G2B)

(iii) Government to government (G2G)
(iv) Government to employees (G2E)

These interactions may be described as follows:
G2G (Government to Government): With this mode of interaction, besides restructuring the governmental processes involved, information technology and communication (IT&C) helps in improving the flow of information and services within and between the different stakeholders involved, such as, departments within and across ministries. The interaction can happen in both horizontal and vertical directions. The key objective and outcome of e-Governance in this relationship is the need to increase efficiency, performance and productivity.

G2C (Government to Citizens): The purpose of any initiative that would improve governance will result in better delivery of services to citizens. In this respect, e-Governance enables the creation of a digital liaison between the government and citizens. This will enable the latter to benefit from efficient delivery of a wide range of public services. In addition to expanding the availability and accessibility, e-Governance also improves the quality of services as well. It seeks to make the government citizen-friendly. Additionally, it also raises the credibility of government in the minds of people.

Through e-Governance, citizens have several advantages as follows:

a. They can access services round-the-clock over the Internet.
b. They have a variety of access points, such as common service centres, e-kiosks or from their home/workplace.

G2B (Government to Business): The ease of doing business is a critical element in the healthy development of a country. For this purpose, it becomes imperative that the government–business interactions are maintained in a seamless manner. Reduction of red tape, time consumption, operational costs and the need for transparency are the most essential requirements to enable a competitive and congenial business environment. Transactional interactions, such as licensing, permits, procurement and revenue collection, etc., can be accelerated through the deployment of e-Governance initiatives. Such measures are sure to aid businesses to perform better and expand their operations.

G2E (Government to Employees): Every government depends highly on its workforce. Thus, it is vitally important to interact with its employees on a regular basis. This interaction has to happen on a two-way basis. On one hand, the government can send its circulars, notifications and memoranda to its employees across departments, with the push of a button. Similarly, by using IT&C tools, the government can also get to know and address the needs and concerns of its employees, on a faster and efficient manner, thereby satisfying them, which will lead to a much better functioning of the government machinery.

11.3 E-GOVERNANCE BRINGS SMART GOVERNANCE

The purpose of implementing e-Governance is to raise the level of performance and ensure the proper delivery of services to all who deserve them. This will be possible through five main characteristics of e-Governance SMART system.

11.3.1 S Implies Simple

What was carried out through several forms and documents would now be reduced and simplified with the help of IT&C tools. Through e-Governance, citizens will feel more comfortable to approach the government authorities to avail their services.

11.3.2 M Implies Moral

The entry of a novel system will instil a new system of ethical values in the administrative machinery. Through the implementation of technology, the scope for mismanagement or corruption could be greatly reduced.

11.3.3 A Implies Accountable

By imparting a robust framework in the management of information and processes, the performance at both individual and departmental levels can be effectively monitored. This results in a sense of accountability among the functionaries concerned.

11.3.4 R Implies Responsive

The streamlining of service delivery makes the system more responsive.

11.3.5 T Implies Transparent

Information that was until now confined to archives of the government department will now be available in the public domain through e-Governance. This will ensure transparency and will practically lessen the threshold for corruption.

11.4 BENEFITS OF E-GOVERNANCE

1. Citizens will be able to access information easily and can receive a higher quality of service.
2. E-governance would bring in timely and reliable information on the different aspects of governance and administrative actions.
3. It helps in reducing time, effort and money by automating processes and establishing online accessibility of public services. By bringing in short turnaround times, the organization and its processes can be controlled and managed much more effectively.
4. It helps in the simplification and rationalization of processes, which leads to efficient and accountable governance.
5. It provides an interface for the people to interact with the government. Such measures that enable participation will reinforce the faith of the people in democracy.
6. E-governance can provide effective solutions to end red tape, unwarranted delay, etc., by using modern tools, techniques and instruments of e-Governance.
7. E-governance assists in reaching out to the corners of the country, even to places where it is physically impossible to reach in person.
8. By following a 'citizen-first policy', e-Governance empowers them.
9. It will open up innovative methods in service delivery.
10. Within the governmental departments, it will help in:
    a. avoiding duplication
    b. reduction of transaction costs
    c. simplify procedures
    d. better communication and coordination
    e. secure information management

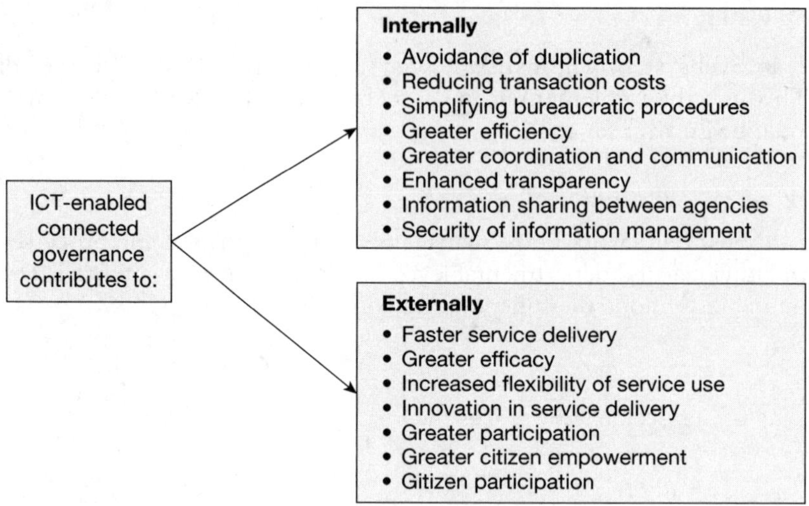

FIGURE 11.1 Benefits of e-Governance

11.5 LIMITATIONS OF E-GOVERNANCE

1. At present, there is no institutional agency to oversee the speedy and effective implementation of the scheme.
2. There is a lack of universal e-Governance architecture at the national level, which could cause problems in the universal implementation of certain central-sector schemes among two or more states at the same time.
3. Integration of sections of users and institutions becomes difficult, when there is no common model.
4. Adequate training to officials is a must, while introducing any new system in governance. A lack in this domain will result in an incomplete effort, thereby defeating the purpose of the process.
5. E-governance initiatives are not receiving a warm welcome from the employees of government organizations.
6. Most of the time, e-Governance initiatives are done with a process-centric mind set instead of a citizen-centric approach.
7. In countries such as India, there is a limited penetration of electronic communication. A sizable proportion of the population is yet to get access to computers or electronic gadgets in their villages and towns. Mere setting up of service centres in these areas would help little towards making it a success. Also the very knowledge base for accepting this new system of governance has not been prepared. People know little about how electronic devices work and would certainly feel difficult to adapt to the new system.
8. Proper e-Governance functioning requires a complete revamp of the conventional process. Retrofitting technological devices to existing workflows alone would entail inefficient output.

9. The limited Internet connectivity at present means that a large section of the population will not be able to access public services.
10. Resources are scarce and unavailable at right time.

11.6 RECENT E-GOVERNANCE INITIATIVES

1. Computerisation of Land Records (Department of Land Resources, Government of India)

A Conference of the Revenue Ministers of States/UTs had advocated such computerization as early as in 1985. Based on the recommendation, the Union Ministry of Rural Development selected eight districts in eight states for a pilot project on Computerization of Land Records, which was 100% centrally-sponsored. From 1994 to 1995 and afterwards, it was implemented in collaboration with the NIC.

The main objectives of the scheme were as follows:

(i) Ensuring that landowners get computerized copies of ownership, crop and tenancy and updated copies of Records of Rights (RoRs) on demand.
(ii) Realizing low-cost and easily-reproducible basic land record data through reliable and durable preservation of old records.
(iii) Ensuring accuracy, transparency and speedy dispute resolution.
(iv) Facilitating fast and efficient retrieval of information for decision making.
(v) According legal sanctity to computer-generated certificates of land records after authentication by the authorized revenue official.
(vi) Setting up a comprehensive land information system for better land-based planning and utilization of land resources.
(vii) Focusing on citizen-centric services related to land and revenue administration.

Due to the unsatisfactory implementation of the scheme, the Union Ministry for Rural Development constituted a Committee to suggest practical steps to implement the scheme. The Committee on Computerisation of Land Records submitted its Report in April 2005.

This Report suggested that the following:

(i) In addition to computerizing Records of Rights, all States must computerize the details of crops, cultivation, soil classification, irrigation, etc. Scanning of basic land records and digitization of cadastral maps/village maps may also be taken up under the Scheme of CLR.
(ii) Village/cadastral maps/tippan should be digitized under the scheme of CLR for integration, updation and preservation of maps, which will enable a landowner to get a computerized copy of the Records of Rights along with plot boundaries. Due to variations in the system of maintenance of cadastral map, States may adopt the strategy suitable to their requirements. However, priority for digitization should be given to those districts, which have successfully completed computerisation of textual land records.
(iii) Integration of computerisation of land records and computerisation of land registration should be initiated at the earliest on pilot basis in some States

without waiting for amendments suggested in the provisions of the Registration Act, 1908.

Funds for setting up of computer centre in the office of the Sub-Registrar may be given under the scheme of CLR equivalent to funds provided to sub-divisions. (The Committee also suggested making amendments to the Registration Act, 1908, to simplify registration and its integration with the land records).

(iv) There should be a time frame for the implementation of this scheme.

(v) According legal sanctity to computer-generated certificates of land records after authentication by the authorized revenue official.

(vi) Setting up a comprehensive land information system for better land-based planning and utilization of land resources.

(vii) Focusing on citizen-centric services related to land and revenue administration.

Lessons:

(i) The scheme failed to address the main problem in case of land records in India, that is, the land records do not reflect the factual ground reality.

Computerisation of existing land records without corroborating it with the actual field position only led to perpetuation of existing loopholes and errors.

(ii) Complex e-Governance projects have various components all of which need to be implemented for which a holistic approach is needed during implementation.

2. Admission to Professional Colleges—Common Entrance Test

With the rapid growth in the demand as well as supply of professional education, the process of admission to these institutions became a major challenge in the early 1990s. Recourse was then taken to Information and Communication Technology (ICT) to make the process of admission transparent and objective. One of the pioneering efforts was made by Karnataka. The State Government decided to conduct a common entrance test (CET) based on which admission to different colleges and disciplines was made. The allocation of seats in different colleges/disciplines is done through a process of 'computerized counselling' where the student can choose the discipline he/she wants, based of course on merit. Use of ICT in the admission process has helped in making the admission process totally transparent, fair and objective. Many institutions have now switched over to similar ICT-based admission process.

Lesson:

(i) ICT initiatives which bring tangible benefits to citizens are always sustainable.

3. Digital India

Digital India scheme which intends to transcend India into a digital economy has the following features:

(i) Governance and services on demand: Seamlessly integrated departments, services through online/mobile, services for ease of doing business, making financial transactions electronics and cashless, leveraging Geographic Information System (GIS).

(ii) Infrastructure as a core utility to citizens: High-speed Internet, Cradle to Grave Digital Identity, mobile phone and bank account, common service centres, private space on public cloud, safe and secure cyber space.
(iii) Digital empowerment of citizens: Universal digital literacy, universally accessible digital resources, digital resources in Indian languages, collaborative digital platform, citizens not required to submit physical documents.

Components of digital India:

Online Service Component

(i) Aadhaar
(ii) Digital Locker
(iii) E-Sign

Financial

a. PayGov
b. Jan Dhan Yojana

Mobile Enablement

a. Mobile Seva
b. Mobile-Based Digital Identity

E-participation

(i) E-Taal, MyGov, e-Sampark and Social Media

Mission Mode Projects

(i) Delivering more than 400 million e-Transactions per month.
(ii) CSCs, e-Districts, IncomeTax, MCA21, eBiz, Road Transport, eCourts, etc.

Open Data Initiatives

(i) National Portal of India Details India in e-Governance Development Index.

Telecommunication Infrastructure Component

(i) Public Internet Access Programme
(ii) NOFN and BharatNet
(iii) Mobile Connectivity

Human Capital Component

(i) National Digital Literacy Mission
(ii) e-Bhasha

4. Digital Locker

Objectives:

(i) Providing online facility for government and other agencies to send the electronic documents of citizens, storing legacy government certificates/documents.

(ii) Providing accessibility from anywhere and at any time basis, verification from the source in case of government-issued documents.
(iii) Providing facility to share the documents with service providers.
(iv) Getting rid of physical possession of documents and physical visits for availing services .
(v) Safe and secure authentication through Aadhaar (UID).
(vi) Coverage e-District, Educational Certificates.

E-Sign

Digital Signature Certificate treated on par with physical signature as per IT Act, 2000.

Gap in Operational Aspects of Digital Signature Certificate:

(i) Dongle based
(ii) Time-bound validity
(iii) Prone to misuse like impersonation
(iv) Limited adoption

Advantages with E-sign:

(i) Safe and secure and biometric-based authenticated.
(ii) Lifelong, issued each time.
(iii) Cannot be impersonated
(iv) Hassle free as it cannot be misplaced, misused or lost
(v) Cost effective as business model could be based on transaction.

11.7 CRITICAL CONDITIONS FOR SUCCESS OF E-GOVERNANCE

(a) *Adequate Infrastructure*

For reaching the benefits of e-Governance, more e-Governance projects have to be implemented by building adequate e-infrastructure particularly in rural and backward regions. Dependence on ICT has increased compared to other instruments of service delivery for the obvious reasons of cost effectiveness, equity, participation and increased responsiveness and accountability of the service providers. As dependence has increased, we need to have 'e-readiness' for promoting effective e-Governance.

World Economic Forum Consultation Report on e-readiness defines as the ability of the ICT networks to effectively adopt itself to the social and economic advancement can be achieved through building adequate e-infrastructure, bringing awareness among the leaders of government, civil society and market organizations. By building adequate e-infrastructure and initiating more rural-centric e-Governance projects keeping in mind the requirements of the larger section of the population, e-Governance can be promoted more effectively in India.

(b) *Sound Policy and Legal Framework*

New regulations and laws are essential with regard to the application of ICT in promoting governance to ensure accountability and supply of quality goods and services by the private and public sectors without harming the larger society. Removal of obsolete laws and discretionary powers, simplification of procedures to avoid administrative bottlenecks and constitution of single windows ensure speedy disposal of cases. For the successful application of electronic governance, a range of legislative regulations is required covering the aspects of electronic signatures, electronic archiving, data matching, freedom of information, data protection, computer crime and intellectual property rights. Already the Government of India has IT Act and Convergence Bill. The following policy and legal initiatives are to be taken for strengthening e-Governance in India.

(i) Accountability law for making public servants accountable and responsive for non-performance and malfunctioning of their departments
(ii) Law for privacy ensuring that the information about the citizen is not misused
(iii) A law in the line with the US Government Paper Elimination Act (GPEA) to promote use of electronic media
(iv) Amendments to Consumers Protection Law, Tariffs and Taxation Laws, Intellectual Property Regulations, etc., are required
(v) Preparing guidelines for content, technological standards, electronic payments
(vi) Setting standards for electronic publishing, archiving, e-mails, etc.

(c) *Socially Relevant Technologies and Integrated Management*

Lack of peoples' participation, fractured relationship between government agencies and citizens, lack of availability of local resources, limited integration with local Civil Society Organizations (CSO) and exogenous social and economic environment are the reasons which failed ICT to deliver the full range of services in governance matters.

Updating of data in local languages, standardization in all areas, such as encoding, application logic for common applications, user interfaces, preparing data dictionaries, making appropriate cyber laws, procedural and legal changes in the decision and delivery making processes as well as in the institutions, encouraging private–public partnerships can facilitate the successful application of the e-Governance projects in India.

Efforts are needed to incorporate local languages and local content in Internet in a massive way. Accessing Internet using keyboard may limit the use of Internet. So there is a need of developing voice-enabled Internet service with Indian languages, and applications should emerge out of India way of life.

(d) *Public–Private Partnership*

It is a fact that India needs huge amount of fund for the implementation of e-Governance projects. The governments do not have such huge amount of funds. In this regard, encouraging private investment seems to be the possible answer. Public Private Partnership (PPP) model can be encouraged to initiate the projects in order to meet the needs of the rising population. The Gujarat check post Project is an example of PPP model for promoting e-Governance in India.

(e) *Political and Administrative Leadership*

State governments with committed political and administrative leadership are mainly responsible for promoting e-governance in some states in spite of poor communication infrastructure facilities. State governments like Andhra Pradesh and Karnataka under the leadership of Chandrababu Naidu (in Andhra Pradesh) and S. M. Krishna, respectively, have taken major initiatives in popularizing e-Governance in the improving the quality of administration. They were able to overcome many barriers in implementation of e-Governance projects through a focussed and strategic approach aiming specified targets and allowing reasonable time frame for attaining them. Specialized agencies have also come up within government to initiate innovative experiments. It is sometimes argued that given the low level of development of communication infrastructure in most Indian stats, the prospects of E-governance is bleak. Even in situations where the initial conditions for trying out e-Governance appear to be non-existent in terms of inadequate skilled personnel or weak infrastructure, a gradual, flexible and reflective approach can bring about drastic positive changes.

(f) *Role of Civil Society*

The Civil society bodies like citizens groups, associations and social activists are playing an active role in extending ICT for the empowerment of citizens and effective delivery. In a project of Cyber Grameen, a non-profit organization set up by Krishna Prasad Tripuraneni, a telecom entrepreneur in Chennai, wireless technology is used to offer digital entertainment, distance learning, tele-medicine and government services. NGOs are also making officials responsive and accountable through e-Governance projects. The Online Complaint Monitoring System (OCMS) in Mumbai Municipal Corporation (BMC) with the active involvement of an NGO, named Praja Foundation, to redress citizens grievances, can be mentioned in this regard. It enables the citizens to register complaints and receive information on the complaint status quickly and easily, without the need to visit or call the ward offices at restricted timings.

Scholars attribute the ineffective utilization of installed ITC potential to the absence of links with the civil society. And its participation in e-Governance projects initiated by the governments is, however, not encouraging. Civil society and its representatives have been kept out in most of the programmes. Even in cases where such participation is sought, the linkages are either weak or notional. The CARD experience of Andhra Pradesh suggests that until and unless civil society bodies are active in the delivery of services, the situation will not improve.

(g) *Human Resources Development and Capacity Building*

Non-availability of proper human resources and lack of appropriate strategy are some of the roadblocks in the path of using ICT in the governance purposes. The fragmented approach in implementing the e-Governance programmes and computerization has led to excessive expenditure without delivering desired results. ICT has failed to promote desired results in facilitating governance because of organizational technical and human reasons. Information systems are not technical systems, rather these are social systems and there is a need to emphasize at the operational level in their social perspective. Some studies point out that the official mismanagement, lack of favourable attitude and orientation on the part of the officials hinder the progress of the application of e-Governance in India. Some projects were not effectively managed due to the lack of skills and motivations among the administrative staff.

Training for imparting skills (computer operation and content assessment) and including motivation among the officials are very essential for the effective utilization of ICT in governance. For instance, senior officers in Andhra Pradesh were trained in the Indian Institute of Management, Ahmadabad, for 4 months in hardware, software and special problems related to implementation of IT in government deportments with practical orientation. The government has been investing more than ₹2,50,000 to train each functionary. It spent ₹70 million on a 4.5 month training programme designed by the Indian Institute of Management, Ahmadabad, to train 20 officers to function as chief information officers. The programme covered a wide array of interdisciplinary topics, such as technology assessment, process re-engineering, change management, information analysis and project management. The programme was offered as a sandwich of classroom training alternated with hands-on project work. Similar training programme should be undertaken for capacity building of the bureaucrats for better application of ICT in service delivery.

11.8 STEPS NEEDED TO BE TAKEN

Going with the information given above, we can infer that e-Governance has a huge potential to promote efficient, prompt, responsive, citizen-friendly services to the people. It is cost-effective and has the potential to serve citizens at their doorsteps. Most importantly, it can be used as a tool to minimize corruption. While it is certain that people have to be trained to use the respective interfaces when implemented, it will help in the long run in avoiding long queues at government offices and secretariats. The very characteristic of digitization ensures limited scope to deny or delay services by the concerned service providers.

(i) Public–private partnership can be forged to address fund constraints. This will help in funding the required e-infrastructure and training for government officers across the country.
(ii) Proper orientation training to the officials have to be provided through seminars, conferences, workshops, etc. This should be followed up with proper legislation on electronic governance, maintaining the required e-readiness, awareness programs targeting the general public, etc.

When the required ecosystem is created as above, it will be helpful in assessing the effectiveness of e-Governance in terms the level of interactions between government and citizens. This could be done by calculating the percent of citizens reached, the turn-around time for delivery of services, costs incurred for providing services, availability of services, citizen satisfaction, etc.

The following parameters are a must while delivering services through IT and e-Governance:

1. Swift response by civil servants to queries
2. Improved communication between the officials and beneficiaries
3. Online accessibility to administrative structure, chart, form
4. Online accessibility to reports and documents of the government
5. Provisions for the people to share opinions on legislation and budgeting
6. Online accessibility of government's budgets and expenditure reports
7. Delivering services to a larger proportion of the population
8. Improved responsiveness, accountability and transparency in the administrative institutions
9. Availability of online applications for recruitments
10. Online process of tendering, procurement, open to public access
11. Availability of electronic documentation and record keeping
12. Availability of online redressal of grievances through e-Ombudsman

Government officials have to be sensitized about the challenges posed by socioeconomic development. E-Governance can impact civil service in a positive way, and it may lead to excellence in the delivery of basic and essential services. That said, the primary issue that needs attention is the development of a system that is clear, transparent, responsive and sensitive to the socioeconomic conditions of the public.

It would surely reduce the amount of time spent in addressing requests, thereby reducing red-tapism. While being cost-effective, it makes the delivery of public services quicker and efficient by introducing competition amongst delivery channels and departments.

With respect to the attitude among people to use e-Governance services, efforts should be taken to make e-channels accessible and visible, with proper training and demonstration. In fact, not all services need to be made electronic from day one. Gradual introduction of e-Governance in certain areas will help in people getting attuned to the systems easily.

11.9 PRACTICE QUESTIONS

1. 'In developing countries like India, e-Governance cannot entirely replace manual governance, but even its limited applications in several areas can bring enough changes'. Explain with relevant examples with regard to prospective application of E-governance in our system.
2. The potential of e-Governance is limited in Indian administrative system. Analyse the reasons.
3. e-Governance is a panacea to alleviate the evils associated with the Indian administrative processes. Illustrate.
4. 'Good governance is at its core as a structural concept containing several components without which it would be inchoate and shapeless'. Discuss how e-Governance would help to bring about good governance in India.
5. 'The latest limitation of e-Governance in India is not technological but e-literacy'. Explain the statement and suggest measures to rectify the remedy.
6. Bring out the various e-Governance initiatives undertaken in Digital India programme.

12

Right to Information

LEARNING OBJECTIVES

In this Chapter, you will learn about:

- Introduction
- RTI Activists Who Lost Their Life for RTI
- The Struggle for Right to Information
- Evolution of Right to Information (India)
- Significance of Right to Information
- Right to Information and Administrative Reforms
- Important Provisions of the Act
- Exemptions and Exclusions
- Implementing Issues of the Act
- ART – II Recommendations
- Political Parties under Right to Information
- Judiciary under Right to Information
- NGOs under Right to Information
- 10 Years of Right to Information
- Steps to Improve Right to Information Act
- Success Stories of Right to Information
- Conclusion
- Practice Questions

12.1 RIGHT TO INFORMATION

"*The Right to Information Law of 2005 signals a radical shift in our governance culture and permanently impacts all agencies of state. The effective implementation of this law depends on three fundamental shifts: from the prevailing culture of secrecy to a new culture of openness; from personalized despotism to authority coupled with accountability; and from unilateral decision-making to participative governance*".

—Second Administrative Reforms Commission

12.2 RTI ACTIVISTS WHO LOST THEIR LIFE FOR RTI

In the last few years, the following are some of those who laid down their lives fighting against corruption in public life. Do we know how many more unsung heroes are there?

- **Sathyendra Kumar Dubey:** Director Planning, National Highways Dept, murdered for exposing corruption in the Golden Quadrilateral project in Gaya, Bihar.
- **Amith Jethwa:** A Prominent RTI Activist and 'Green Crusader' was campaigning against alleged illegal mining in the Gir Sanctuary areas in Gujrat, which is backed by some politicians. He was shot at by unidentified assailants.
- **Sathish Shetty:** Famous in Pune for boldly invoking RTI Act to bring to light corruption in land dealings, killed while on his morning walk.
- **Arun Sawant:** Shot dead for exposing corruption in Badalpur Municipality.
- **Sola Ranga Rao:** Paid his life as he had filed RTI application in the Mandal Parishad Development Office regarding funds disbursement.
- **Venkatesh:** Died in his fight against encroachment of government lands.
- **Shanmugam Manjunath:** An IIM graduate; murdered for exposing sale of adulterated petrol.

12.3 THE STRUGGLE FOR RIGHT TO INFORMATION

Right to Information (RTI) is an integral component of a liberal democracy. This principle is widely accepted and it can be understood by the fact that most modern states have enacted their own versions of the law. The Indian version of RTI is considered to be the most soundly drafted among its peers, as the United Nations Development Programme (UNDP) in its appeal 'Eliminate Corruption, Enable Better Living' has hailed it as the best, in practice.

Like many other acts that empower the citizenry, this act had its own share of hurdles that it encountered through its years of drafting and formation. Thousands of activists put themselves through a relentless struggle to ensure that this act came into being. It began with the relentless fight by the civil society groups for People's Rights in Rajasthan that finally in 1997 resulted in the enactment of RTI Act in the state.

It was alleged during the 1990s that there was a rampant spread of corruption and malpractices in the implementation of poverty alleviation schemes in Rajasthan. The malpractices were brought to light by The Mazdoor Kisan Shakthi Sangathan (MKSS), a social movement in the state, which was initially seeking to understand the reasons behind the non-payment of minimum wages for workers in Rajasthan. It was when reports or information was denied to them, they realized that people were not being given a responsible and transparent administration. MKSS functionaries involved themselves in an extensive groundwork, which revealed a slew of malpractices in poverty alleviation schemes of the state. This made the public realize that they have to be informed of the policies, plans and administrative activities of the government. Thus was born a remarkable movement, which resulted in the creation of the first RTI law in the country, in the state of Rajasthan.

The movement was spearheaded by renowned social activists, Aruna Roy, Nikhil Dey and Changan Singh of the MKSS, with the extensive support of the common masses. It led to the Government of Rajasthan proclaiming in the assembly that they will come up with a law to provide access of information to the public on request.

After more than a year since the proclamation, the law was yet to materialize. Therefore, in April 1996, MKSS began a relentless struggle demanding the government to implement their prior proclamation in the Assembly. The demonstration was massive, with people from various walks of life participating in it. The government had no other option than passing the law and finally obliged in the year 2000. This became a shot in the arm for MKSS, as they began the process to realize the enactment of RTI throughout India.

MKSS paved the way for the formation of the National Campaign for Peoples Right to Information (NCPRI). Many organizations and human rights movements aligned themselves with NCPRI to bring about RTI Act.

In 2002, during the NDA Government headed by Sri Atal Bihari Vajpayee, a Bill on Freedom of Information Act 2002 was introduced in the Parliament. But it did not become an Act.

In 2004, the UPA headed by Manmohan Singh included RTI Act in its election manifesto; when it formed the government, it started taking steps to fulfil its promise.

In August 2004, the National Advisory Council, the NCPRI and the commonwealth Human Rights Initiative (CHRI) together made some changes in the 2002 RTI Bill and submitted the core document. On the basis of the core document, in December, the new Bill on RTI Act was introduced in the Parliament.

The Bill was approved by the Lok Sabha on 11 May 2005 and by the Rajya Sabha on12 May. The Indian President's approval was obtained on 15 May, and the Bill formally became an Act. It was published in the *Government Gazette* on 22 June, and from 12 Oct 2005, it was implemented.

Everyone has the right to freedom of opinion and expression; this right includes freedom to hold opinions without interference and to seek, receive and impart information and ideas through any media and regardless of frontiers.

12.4 EVOLUTION OF RIGHT TO INFORMATION (RTI) (INDIA)

- The Constitution of India does not provide for the RTI as a fundamental right. However, it is inherent, within the scope of Article 19(1)(a) and Article 21.
- As a party to the Universal Declaration on Human Rights, India acknowledges Article 19 of the declaration, which talks of the right to receive and impart information.
- Supreme Court in various cases, such as state of UP vs Raj Narain, SP Gupta vs UOI, Dinesh Trivedi vs. UOI, Bhopal gas leak case, has asserted that the idea of 'Right to Know' is a fundamental right.
- Mathew Commission (1982): Emphasized the Right to know.
- 5th Pay Commission (1994–97): Recommended the abolition of the Official Secrets Act and introduction of RTI Act.
- 1995: The Press Council of India brought out the first blueprint of a model RTI Act.
- 1997: Shourie Committee – another draft on RTI.
- 2000: Rajasthan and Karnataka enacted their own RTI Acts.
- 2001: Delhi enacted its RTI Act
- 2002: Maharashtra and Assam enacted their own RTI Acts.
- 2002: Freedom of Information act was introduced and enacted, but it was never notified.
- 2005: RTI finally enacted and got notified and came into force.

12.5 SIGNIFICANCE OF RIGHT TO INFORMATION (RTI)

1. RTI reinforces the idea of popular sovereignty.
2. It promotes openness, transparency and accountability in governance.
3. It is one of the viable weapons to combat corruption.

4. The proper use of RTI will check the arbitrary nature or high-handedness of officials.
5. It bridges the gap between providers and recipients of public services.
6. It paves the way for a participative democracy by including the citizens in the decision making process.
7. By enhancing participation, RTI strengthens grassroots democracy.
8. It serves as a device to access to other rights provided by law.
9. It creates an amicable ambience for transparency in government organizations.
10. Results in effective functioning of the government thereby enhancing predictability.
11. Access to information can empower the poor and the weaker sections of society to demand and get information about public policies and actions, thereby leading to their welfare.
12. Promotes administrative reforms by exposing weaklings and voids in the system.

12.6 RIGHT TO INFORMATION (RTI) AND ADMINISTRATIVE REFORMS

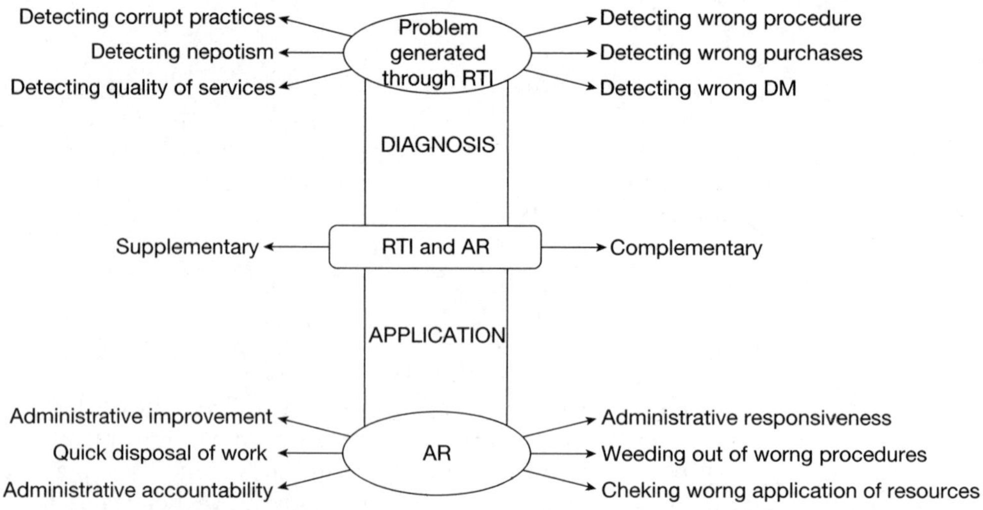

RTI and administrative reforms go hand-in-hand towards assuring good governance:

1. RTI ensures transparency, accountability and efficiency, which are themselves goals of administrative reforms.
2. RTI helps in revealing the shortcomings of the system, which leads to further administrative reforms.
3. RTI is a novel measure that cannot be successfully executed until and unless supported by structural and procedural reforms.
4. Constant requests for information under RTI can help civil servants to reduce the possibilities for errors and therefore can ensure better performance from the government machinery.

12.7 RIGHT TO INFROMATION ACT (2005)

The Act specifies that citizens have a right to:

- Request any information (as defined).
- Take copies of documents.

- Inspect documents, works and records.
- Take certified samples of materials of work.
- Obtain information in form of printouts, diskettes, floppies, tapes, video cassettes or in any other electronic mode or through printouts.

12.7.1 Information Defined

According to the law, the term '*Information*' has been defined as any material in the form of records, documents, memos, e-mails, opinions, advices, press releases, circulars, orders, logbooks, contracts, reports, papers, samples, models, data in any electronic form and information relating to any private body which can be accessed by a public authority under any other law for the time being in force.

12.7.2 Process

Under the Act, all authorities covered must appoint a Public Information Officer (PIO) within their organization. Any person may submit a request to the PIO for information in writing. It becomes the PIO's duty to provide information to the person who has requested for the information. If the request involves or pertains to another public authority, it will be the concerned PIO's responsibility to transfer/forward the request to a PIO of the concerned organization, within 5 days of receipt. In addition, every public authority is required to designate Assistant Public Information Officers (APIOs) to receive RTI requests and appeals for forwarding to the PIOs of their public authority. The citizen making the request is not obliged to disclose any information except his/her name and contact particulars.

The Act specifies time limits for replying to the request:

1. If the request has been made to the PIO, the reply is to be provided within 30 days of receipt.
2. If the request has been made to an APIO, the deadline gets an additional 5 days, and thus the reply is to be given within 35 days of receipt.
3. If the PIO transfers the request to another public authority (better concerned with the information requested), the time allowed to reply is 30 days but computed from the day after it is received by the PIO of the transferee authority.
4. For information concerning corruption and human rights violations by scheduled security agencies (those listed in the second schedule to the act), responses have to be provided within 45 days post the approval of the Central Information Commission.
5. However, if the life or liberty of any person is involved, the PIO is expected to reply within 48 hours.

If the information is not provided within the required period, it can be treated as a deemed refusal of information. Refusal with or without reasons may be ground for appeal or complaint. Further, information not provided within the time prescribed is to be provided free of charge.

12.8 EXEMPTIONS

The following things are exempted from disclosure:

1. Sensitive information, disclosure of which would prejudicially compromise the sovereignty and integrity of India; the security; strategic, scientific or economic interests of the State; relation with a foreign State or which may lead to the incitement of an offence.

2. Information which has been forbidden to be published by any court of law or tribunal or any disclosure that would constitute to contempt of court.
3. Information, the disclosure of which would cause a breach of privilege of Parliament or the State Legislature.
4. Information including commercial confidence, trade secrets or intellectual property, the disclosure of which would harm the competitive position of a third party, unless the competent authority is satisfied that larger public interest warrants the disclosure of such information.
5. Information available to a person in his/her fiduciary relationship, unless the competent authority is satisfied that the larger public interest warrants the disclosure of such information.
6. Information received in confidence from foreign Governments.
7. Information, the disclosure of which would endanger the life or safety of any person(s) or identify the source of information or assistance given in confidence for law enforcement or security purposes.
8. Information which would impede the process of investigation or apprehension or prosecution of offenders.
9. Cabinet papers including records of deliberations of the Council of Ministers, Secretaries and other officers.
10. Information which relates to personal information, the disclosure of which has no relationship to any public activity or interest, or which would cause unwarranted invasion of the privacy of an individual. However, such information, which cannot be denied to the parliament or a state legislature, is not exempted under this purpose.

Notwithstanding any of the exemptions listed above, a public authority may allow access to information, if public interest in disclosure outweighs the harm to the protected interests.

12.8.1 Exclusions

The following investigation and intelligence agencies are exempted from the purview of this law:

Central Intelligence any Security agencies specified in the Second Schedule like IB, RAW, Central Bureau of Investigation (CBI), Directorate of Revenue Intelligence, Central Economic Intelligence Bureau, Directorate of Enforcement, Narcotics Control Bureau, Aviation Research Centre, Special Frontier Force, BSF, CRPF, ITBP, CISF, NSG, Assam Rifles, Special Service Bureau, Special Branch (CID), Andaman and Nicobar, The Crime Branch-CID-CB, Dadra and Nagar Haveli and Special Branch, Lakshadweep Police, Agencies specified by the State Governments through a notification will also be excluded.

This exclusion is however not absolute and these organizations are required to provide information, when accused of corruption and/or human rights violations.

12.9 IMPLEMENTING ISSUES OF THE ACT AND THE SOLUTIONS

1. Appointment of Central Information Commissioners and State Information Commissioners should be done in a bipartisan manner involving the leader of opposition. Chief Justices of SC and HC may also be included.
2. Despite a legal obligation to constitute State Information Commissions, five states: Jharkhand, Manipur, Sikkim, Andhra Pradesh and Mizoram have not appointed them yet.

3. The Central Information Commission should be geographically dispersed across the country with at least four regional offices headed by an official in the ranks of commissioner. This is in addition to the regional offices of State Information Commissions.
4. Information commissions should be constituted by adequately representing different sections of society, instead of having a preponderance of Civil Servants. It is advisable to have at least half of the members as non-civil servants.
5. Private institutions that enjoy natural monopoly, or whose functions impinge on citizens lives substantially, must come under RTI.
6. Definition of 'Substantially Financed' has been taken variously. So commission has defined it:

   Organizations that have received 50% of annual operating costs or a sum more than ₹1 crore during any of preceding 3 years, should come under RTI.

7. NGOs and RTI
   NGOs having the following characteristics should come under the purview of RTI:
   - Substantially financed by government authorities.
   - NGOs having natural monopoly, impinging on citizens lives.
   - Any information, if it were held by government, subject to RTI disclosure, when transferred to NGO will continue to be subject to disclosure.
8. National Coordination Committee (NCC) should be created and be headed by Central Information Commissioner – this committee will monitor the implementation of RTI.
9. Application of RTI to legislature:
   - There should be a tracking mechanism so that action taken by executive branches on CAG reports and other enquiry commission reports is available to the public and legislators.
   - Working dynamics of Legislative Committees should be thrown open to the public.
10. Application of RTI Act to Judiciary
    - Records at district court and subordinate courts should be stored in a scientific manner and uniform way.
    - Administrative processes in district and subordinate courts should be computerized in a time bound manner.
11. Information provided by government departments are mystified and too technical. This should be addressed by providing information that will add value to the applicant.
12. Maintenance of information is not automated and therefore not efficient. Proper IT infrastructure should be installed in order to record day to day actions of the concerned departments.
13. Suo moto disclosure of information mandated under the Act is not being done properly.
14. Awareness of the law is very low among masses. More and more publicity is required to educate the people regarding the law.
15. Costs of accessing information through RTI are high.
16. Official Secrets Act promotes a culture of secrecy, which acts as a deterrent to RTI. It should be judiciously applied, without hindering the scope of RTI.
17. Officials need to be properly sensitized and trained with respect to transparency and accountability concerns of RTI.

18. Other acts, rules, manuals have not been amended to make them congruent with the RTI spirit.
19. RTI has not been able to create a climate of transparency as a norm. Rather RTI is being used to pet small work done or to threaten or harass.
20. Right to privacy has not been provided under the Act.
21. Bureaucratic pre-eminence in Information Commissions results in promotion of traditional bureaucratic ethos of secrecy and lack of accountability.
22. Many High Courts have made rules exempting themselves from RTI.

12.10 RECOMMENDATIONS OF SECOND ADMINISTRATIVE REFORMS

1. The Official Secrets Act, 1923 should be repealed, and substituted by a chapter in the National Security Act, containing provisions relating to official secrets.
2. Relevant provisions of Indian Evidence Act, 1872, civil procedure code needs to be amended.
3. A. As an affirmation of the importance of transparency in public affairs, Ministers on assumption of office may take an oath of transparency along with the oath of office and the requirement of administering the oath of secrecy should be dispensed with. Articles 75(4) and 164 (3), and the Third Schedule should be suitably amended.
   B. Safeguard against disclosure of information against the national interest may be provided through written undertaking by incorporation of a clause in the national security law dealing with official secrets.
4. Civil Services Rules of all states may be reworded in such a manner that disclosure of full and accurate information under RTI is a duty in good faith.
5. A. Section 12 of the Act may be amended to constitute the Selection Committee of CIC with the Prime Minister, Leader of the Opposition and the Chief Justice of India. Section 15 may be similarly amended to constitute the Selection Committee at the State level with the Chief Minister, Leader of the Opposition and the Chief Justice of the High Court.
   B. The GOI should ensure the constitution of SICs in all States within 3 months.
   C. The CIC should establish four regional offices of CIC with a Commissioner heading each. Similarly regional offices of SICs should be established in larger States.
   D. At least half of the members of the Information Commissions should be drawn from non-civil services background. Such a provision may be made in the Rules under the Act, by the Union Government, applicable to both CIC and SICs.
6. All ministries/departments/agencies/offices with more than one PIO have to designate a nodal APIO with the authority to receive requests for information on behalf of all PIOs. Such a provision should be incorporated in the Rules by appropriate governments.
   All public authorities may be advised by the Government of India that along with the PIOs they should also designate the appellate authority and publish both, together.
7. Suo moto disclosures should also be available in the form of printed, priced publication in the official language, revised periodically (at least once a year).
8. All government functionaries should be imparted at least one day training on RTI within a year.
9. Awareness campaigns may be entrusted to credible non-profit organizations at the State level.

10. The CIC and the SICs may be entrusted with the task of monitoring effective implementation of the RTI Act in all public authorities. (An appropriate provision could be made under Section 30 by way of removal of difficulties).
11. A National Coordination Committee (NCC) may be set up under the chairpersonship of the Chief Information Commissioner with the nodal Union Ministry, the SICs and representatives of States as members. The National Coordination Committee would:
    a. Serve as a national platform for effective implementation of the Act,
    b. Document and disseminate best practices in India and elsewhere,
    c. Monitor the creation and functioning of the national portal for RTI,
    d. Review the Rules and Executive orders issued by the appropriate governments under the Act,
    e. Carry out impact evaluation of the implementation of the Act; and
    f. Perform such other relevant functions as may be deemed necessary.
12. States may be advised to set up independent public grievances redressal authorities to deal with complaints of delay, harassment or corruption
13. A. Organisations which perform functions of a public nature that are ordinarily performed by government or its agencies, and those which enjoy natural monopoly may be brought within the purview of the Act.
    B. Norms should be laid down that any institution or body that has received 50% of its annual operating costs, or a sum equal to or greater than ₹1 crore during any of the preceding 3 years should be understood to have obtained 'substantial funding' from the government for the period and purpose of such funding.
    C. Any information which, if it were held by the government, would be subject to disclosure under the law, must remain subject to such disclosure even when it is transferred to a non-government body or institution.

ARC-II has called RTI Act the master key to good governance.

12.10.1 Change in Archaic Laws, Procedures and Practices

1. Official Secrets Act should be repealed and should be substituted by a chapter in the National Security Act.
2. Indian Evidence Act, 1872, should be amended to aid disclosure of officially classified information.
3. Civil Service Rules of all states to be reworded: Civil Servant shall communicate all information applicable under RTI to public.
4. Manual of official procedure to be reworded on same line.

12.11 POLITICAL PARTIES UNDER RIGHT TO INFORMATION (RTI)

Over the years and through its various judgments, the Supreme Court has consistently ruled in favour of the citizen's right to know. In State of UP vs Raj Narain (1975), the apex court declared that right to freedom of speech and expression guaranteed by Article 19(1)(a) included the right to know every public act, everything that is done in a public way and by their public functionaries.

In S.P. Gupta vs UOI and Anr (1981), the Supreme Court reiterated that right to know is implicit in right of free speech and expression, and disclosure of information regarding the functioning of the government must be the rule. In People's Union of Civil Liberties vs UOI (2004), the RTI was further elevated to the status of a human right, necessary for making governance transparent and accountable. It also emphasised that governance must be made participatory.

Political parties act as the vocal chords of the people, both within and outside the government. Through policy making and debates in legislatures, politicians voice the demands of citizens, acting as a liaison between the people and the government. In order to ensure that they truly serve the above purpose, it is necessary that they have a good level of transparency in their functioning. In the Indian political scenario, parties are scattered across various camps based on ideology, affiliation and several other divisions. However, it is quite strange to note that they stand united, when it comes to keeping their organizations away from eyes of RTI. In fact, the NDA government led by Prime Minister Narendra Modi went to the extent of filing a counter-affidavit before the Supreme Court in 2015, saying that including political parties under the RTI would adversely affect their internal working and political functioning. As a contention, political parties say that they already exhibit a good level of transparency by filing their income tax returns and reporting on their donations to the Election Commission of India. However, it is to be noted that until the financial year 2016–17, these returns only included donations above ₹20,000.

Considering this, it is evident that national political parties have for long been resisting the RTI to conceal obscurities in their sources of funding. This has also proved how the existing laws have miserably failed in bringing complete transparency in the funding of political parties, creating the need for an overhaul in the mechanism for political funding.

The current pattern of funding, which shows the control and influence exerted by the big corporates and the business houses, pose an important question about the status of autonomy of the political parties in representing people and shaping up the policies, and RTI would help in exposing such links.

12.12 JUDICIARY UNDER RIGHT TO INFORMATION (RTI)

There are three substantial questions of law regarding RTI for Judiciary. These are as follows:

1. Whether the independence of judiciary be affected by the information sought.
2. Whether such disclosure of information would threaten the reliability of the decisions and expression of honest opinion by all the constitutional bodies.
3. Whether non-disclosure is protected under Section 8(1)(j) of the RTI Act.

There are indeed some valid and effective arguments for the judiciary to feel the need for secrecy. For example, collegium discussions can cover a lot of areas, which includes the discussion of courtroom corridor gossip and private life of the judges, the examination intelligence reports given by the government and the expression of personal opinions of the judges.

Credibility and reputation is hugely important especially for those who are occupying the highest seat of Judiciary, and many feel that even the slightest tarnish to this could be debilitating and prevent judges from doing their job.

And this is especially important in the case of Judges who are rejected by the collegium but still continue to serve in their respective posts in the High Courts. It is a legitimate fear among the Judges that few overenthusiastic advocates may dig the dirt on the Judges and take it out of context in order to have some leverage in the Courtroom, by asking for their recusal or otherwise, questioning their independence while hearing a case.

And ultimately, many judges are people too, and by tradition and necessity, deeply private ones at that.

Therefore, being completely subject to RTI is perhaps deeply uncomfortable to some of them at a deeper level.

So, can anything be done to solve this issue?

There is no one easy solution, and it is difficult to find one when there is a standoff between the Apex Court and the Government about reform of judicial appointments.

12.13 NGOS UNDER RIGHT TO INFORMATION (RTI)

The definition of public authority under Section 2(h) of the Act is as follows:

'Public authority' means any authority or body or institution of self- government established or constituted:

- by or under the Constitution;
- by any other law made by the Parliament;
- by any other law made by a State Legislature;
- by notification issued or order made by the appropriate Government, and includes any:
  (i) body owned, controlled or substantially financed;
  (ii) non-Government organization substantially financed, directly or indirectly by funds provided by the appropriate Government;
  (iii) NGO that is substantially financed, directly or indirectly by the government is under RTI review.

In Thalapalam Service Co-operative Bank Ltd. v. Union of India (2013), the Supreme Court clarified that:

- 'controlled': a control of substantial nature over the management and affairs of the body and not just mere supervisory or regulatory control.
- 'financed directly or indirectly': receiving grants-in-aid, governmental funds, benefits from government schemes (for land, etc.).

Any NGO that qualifies the above is under the purview of the RTI Act, 2005.

Comptroller and Audit General (CAG) Shashi Kant Sharma directed social audits on NGOs and panchayat bodies directly funded by the government, state information commission has ordered all state government-funded NGOs to come under the ambit of RTI Act.

The order states transparency and accountability should be maintained by NGOs which receive annual funding of ₹50,000 and above by government. NGOs must come under section 4 (1) (b) of RTI Act, 2005, which demands proactive disclosure of information by an organization.

12.14 10 YEARS OF RIGHT TO INFORMATION (RTI)

In 2015, the RTI act completed 10 years, though amidst mixed opinions evaluating its journey so far. On one hand, there is a sense of rejoice for its role in establishing citizens' right to seek information from public authorities. On the other hand, inaction on reforms needed for efficient implementation of the act have raised doubts over how far things have practically changed at the ground level. The reality of RTI act's implementation lay somewhere in the middle of these two standpoints. In its decade-long existence, the act has managed to bring transparency by exposing slew of corruption cases running into thousands of crores such as CWG, 2G and

Adarsh society scam. But, accountability in the routine working of the public authorities is yet to take roots as majority of common citizens still find access to information difficult due to delays, supply of insufficient information and limited reach of the act.

12.14.1 Issues in the Existing Act's Implementation

Citizen's participation in everyday governance entails supply of information in due time. According to a study, pendency of cases in 23 Information Commissions (ICs) across India is 1,98,7391. And, it takes at least a year for an appeal to come up for hearing before an IC. The resultant delay in accessing information undermines citizens' right to know and redress individual grievances, access entitlements such as ration cards and pensions, investigate government policies and decisions, and expose corruption. One of the main reasons for high pendency of appeals with ICs is ineffective process of information supply at the level of Public authorities (PAs) during first application and subsequent first appeal.

The information Seeker Survey found that '75% of the citizens are dissatisfied with the quality of the information provided by PAs'. Even the process of first appeal does not yield substantial result. Except for first appeals filed with the central government or Delhi government, there is less than 4% chance of getting any information by filing a first appeal4. The reason behind such state of affairs is not only bureaucratic resistance to transparency but inefficient information collection and management system within government agencies. As the files and information are dispersed across several offices of one department for lack of digitisation of records, it becomes difficult to provide information completely and timely on the part of PAs.

Along with it, suppliers of information, the PIOs are not properly equipped or trained to handle the responsibility of supplying information. According to a study, 45% of the PIOs have not undergone any form of training related to the RTI act. Thus, lack of comprehensive capacity-building efforts make it difficult for them to process the bulky information held by government agencies into legible one sought by citizens. The IC report also observed that many cases may not have been brought up for adjudication if well-informed PIOs had resolved the issue earlier.

Lack of ownership of the act by state governments has also resulted in scarcity of financial resources for the functioning of the act. Union Government, on the recommendation of the 2nd Administrative Reform Commission had advised state governments to earmark 1% of the funds meant to implement major welfare schemes towards necessary reforms such as digitization of records and buying necessary infrastructure to provide information over a period of 5 years.

12.15 STEPS TO IMPROVE RIGHT TO INFORMATION (RTI) ACT

12.15.1 Creation of RTI Implementation Cell by Appropriate Governments

To ensure coordination between the appropriate Government and the Information Commission in discharging the duties mandated under the RTI Act, it is recommended that there should be an RTI Implementation Cell under the appropriate Government. This Cell should be under the leadership of a senior-level bureaucrat. This Cell is expected to set up implementation measures to promote compliance by the public authorities and oversee the status of implementation. The Chief CIC or Chief SIC may be an invitee in the meetings of the proposed Cell to help the appropriate Government in carrying out the responsibilities mandated under the Act.

12.15.2 Strengthening Implementation Set-up at Public Authority

'RTI readiness Plan' needs to be prepared to assess the status of current preparedness and to plan for the next 3 years. On basis of this report, a project plan needs to be developed to identify basic activities, which should be carried out for effective implementation of the RTI Act; assess the quality of record keeping and ensure good standards of records management; • coordinate and arrange adequate training for required staff in the authority; and identify areas for proactive disclosure. It will have to ensure the proactive disclosure is updated and linked to the needs of the citizens; plan for proper infrastructure, systems and processes are developed for implementation of RTI.

12.15.3 Annual Self-Assessment by Nodal Departments

It is suggested that the Centre/State Nodal Departments should carry out an annual self-assessment exercise. This self-assessment is to assess initiatives taken by the State Government towards implementation of the Act and also capture various outcomes. This exercise is intended to identify a comprehensive list of activities, which are needed to be taken by the Nodal Departments.

12.15.4 Massive Awareness Campaign

A massive awareness campaign is necessary to educate the citizens about the RTI Act and encourage citizen involvement. The awareness program must especially target the vulnerable categories of citizens such as:

(i) women;
(ii) farmers and rural families; and
(iii) middle and working class, for whom most of the social benefit schemes of the Government are targeted.

For this purpose, RTI awareness and education needs to be aggressively pursued using the appropriate medium of communication. Also adequate budget needs to be allocated by the appropriate Governments for this initiative. The main objectives of the campaign should be to (i) increase public knowledge and awareness; (ii) encourage citizen involvement and debate; and (iii) increase transparency within Government through informed citizenry.

12.15.5 Alternative Channels for Submission of RTI Requests

In order to facilitate citizens in filing RTI requests/appeals, the following alternate channels should be designated as APIOs (provided for under section 5(2)):

- Citizen Service Centres (CSCs) facilitating citizens in filing RTI applications
- Department of Posts to assist in drafting and forwarding the application/appeals
- RTI call centres
- RTI portal
- RTI resource centre in each district headquarter

RTI Call Centre: The RTI call centre could be a single nodal point used by citizens for filing RTI applications/appeals/complaints over the telephone. Additionally, it could also serve as a centralized database of all the RTI applications received and the respective responses. The following figure 3.3 depicts some of the mechanisms involved in the functioning of the call centre. The call centre can be developed on the lines of the 'Jankari' RTI call centre in Bihar. Through this initiative, the citizens can file information requests under the RTI Act through telephonic channel.

12.15.6 Creating Enabling Environment and Capacity Building

Recommendations:

1. Creation of a Knowledge Resource Centre.
2. Capacity building for training.
3. Making Record Keeping 'RTI Friendly'.
4. Development of Web-based applications for PAs and Information Commissions.
5. Improve Motivation of PIOs.
6. Earmarking budget for implementing the recommendations.

12.15.7 Improving Efficiencies at Information Commission Recommendation

Improving the disposal rate of complaints/appeals by information commission through following recommendations:

- Creation of more offices and using video conferencing for hearings.
- Passing order on merit of the case without hearing (to be used only when the order is in favour of appellant).
- Composition of Information Commissions.
- Induction Period for new Commissioners.
- Usage of Standard Templates for passing order.

12.16 SUCCESS STORIES OF RIGHT TO INFORMATION (RTI)

Success Story I

Attendance of the Village School Teacher

In a pre-middle school in Panchampur village, situated 70 km away from the District Headquarters of Banda, a teacher was appointed for the school. However, the teacher was absent for most of the times. The workers and volunteers from Delhi-based organisations like Kabir and Parivartan, along with the local workers from the Chingari Sangathan under the 'Action Research Villages' Campaign, propagated the use of the RTI. Finally, the villagers witnessed a ray of hope when they learned that they could question the Government and ask for information related to the attendance records, leave records and medical records of the absconding village school teacher. Fifteen villagers drafted an application regarding the same and filed a number of applications with the Primary Education Officer at the Banda District Head Quarters. They asked for the records of the teacher but also questioned the Primary Education Department about the department's role and responsibilities in such situations. Immediate action was taken on the issue by the department. The Primary Education Officer summoned the teacher the very next day and asked for an explanation. Living up to his accountability and responsibility, the officer appointed a new school teacher for the village school. The school was opened on the next day itself and regular teaching began in the school. An enquiry was ordered against the teacher and he was asked to report to the school instantly. The villagers were overwhelmed with the fact that their use of RTI could reap such instant results (Source: *PACS Report*).

Success Story 2

Campaign Report to the District Magistrate, Banda

Another interesting facet of the campaign was the process of filing RTI applications in Banda (UP). A group of 10 volunteers and villagers went to various offices for submitting their RTI applications. None of the applications could be filed easily. Most of the offices were ill-equipped for the task. One of the major problems faced during the filing process was that the clerks, and sometimes even the officers, appeared non-conversant and at times completely ignorant about the RTI Act itself. The applications were filed after a lot of trepidation, struggle and running around the offices. These experiences were submitted in the form of a report to the District Magistrate of Banda District, which had the desired effect and considerably improved the situation in most of the offices (Source: *PACS Report*).

Success Story 3

Transparency in Public Distribution System for BPL Families

The 'Mere Gaon Ke Sawaal' Campaign volunteers noticed that the residents of Nai Basti (Bahraich, UP) were also facing the same problems as the other economically backward villages of the region. The 'Kotedar' had been apathetic towards their requests. The use of RTI by the villagers, the women being in majority, was successful in curbing the corruption that had seeped in the Public Distribution System to some extent. When the campaign volunteers saw the BPL ration cards of the villagers, they found that no entries had been made during February 2006 to December 2006. It was evident that the villagers had not received any ration in the said time period. Immediately, 51 village residents agreed to file group RTI applications on the issue and demanded information regarding the acquisition and the distribution of the ration and also asked for copies of the ration records. The applications were filed by the applicants personally after a lot of difficulty at the District Supply Office. Exactly within a fortnight, the Kotedar reached the village and narrated a long sob story, which moved few of the innocent villagers so much that they even agreed to take back their RTI applications. They very next day, the Kotedar brought a minibus to the village along with 'pooris' made with 1 quintal flour and asked the villagers to come to the SDM's office and take back their RTI applications. But, the women of the forest village rights forum refused to do so. This initiative by the women of the village encouraged the other villagers and they also refused to take back their RTI applications. The Kotedar trying another of his tactics one day announced in the village that all those who requested for information can collect it from him. When few villagers reached to take the information, they were forced to make thumb imprints on a blank paper. The Dehat Sanstha volunteers immediately reported this scam to the SDM. Finally, the Kotedar was suspended (Source: *PACS Report*).

12.17 CONCLUSION

RTI is a landmark legislation as it was enacted after a sustained demand and struggle from the grassroots level. It empowers ordinary citizens to question government accustomed to function in unbreachable secrecy. Where people and activists have been able to make use of RTI, results have been rewarding—from uncovering human rights violations in Hashimpura, to bringing transparency in IIT-JEE entrance exams and making MNREGA (Mahatma Gandhi National Rural Employment Guarantee act)-related information public.

Yet, a lot remains to be done to make transparency and accountability a regular feature of governance in India. The urban–rural divide in its access contradicts its foremost objective of bringing information and thus, empowerment to the masses at grassroots level. The lack of reforms denies citizens the opportunity to make governance people-centric. Given that the weakness of the RTI lies in its weak implementation, the next phase of RTI act needs to focus on increasing the authority of implementing agencies, especially SICs, of the act in order to set in motion the practical regime of RTI by ensuring much needed compliance from government agencies.

12.18 PRACTICE QUESTIONS

1. 'The major assumption behind a new style of governance is the citizen's access to information. Much of common man's distress and helplessness could be traced to his lack of access to information and lack of knowledge of decision-making processes'. In the light of this statement, discuss the need for RTI and the modes in which they can be brought.
2. The RTI Act, 2005 has unleashed enormous expectations and aspirations among the citizens. Discuss.
3. Accountability is the question of democracy. In the light of this statement, evaluate the effectiveness of RTI Act.
4. RTI act is a major breakthrough in our democratic polity. Elucidate its effectiveness in our administrative system.
5. What arrangements are required to give protection to the whistle-blowers, as a part of RTI Act?
6. Is there a need to rationalize exemptions under RTI?
7. Bring out the lacunae affecting RTI act in its effective implementation.

13 Citizen's Charter

LEARNING OBJECTIVES

In this Chapter, you will learn about:

- Basic Concept of Citizen's Charter
- Objectives Behind Citizen's Charter
- Six Principles of the Citizen's Charter
- Rationale of a Citizen's Charter
- Significance of Citizen Charters
- International Context
- Citizen's Charter in India
- Components of a Citizen's Charter
- Implementation of the Citizen's Charter
- Inadequacies and Ground Realities Adversely Affecting the Effectiveness of Citizen's Charters
- Lessons Learnt in Quality Assurance from Examples Worldwide
- Assessment of Citizen's Charter
- Suggestions for Strengthening Citizen's Charter for More Effective Governance
- Second ARC on Citizen's Charter
- The Sevottam Model
- The ARC Seven-Step Model for Citizen Centricity
- Right to Service Acts
- Model Citizen's Charter
- Practice Questions

13.1 BASIC CONCEPT OF CITIZEN'S CHARTER

In any liberal democratic society, the quality service provided by the government is one of the key principles that ensure an inclusive, sustainable and equitable development. When such service is provided with unparalleled levels of transparency, accountability and responsiveness, it enables the citizens to cooperate in the developmental process towards achieving effective growth. It is here that the concept of Citizen's Charter plays a vital role. The prime objective of issuing a Citizen's Charter by an organisation is to improve the quality of services offered.

The Citizen's Charter is not legally enforceable and, therefore, is non-justiciable. However, it acts as a tool for facilitating the delivery of services to citizens with specified standards, quality and time frame, etc., with commitments from the Organisation and its clients. By clarifying the citizens of the process involved in delivering public services besides providing other similar information, the Citizen's Charter assists the government in its efforts to provide more responsive and citizen-friendly governance.

13.2 OBJECTIVES BEHIND CITIZEN CHARTERS

1. Appropriate statement of service standards based on public expectations.
2. Simplification of rules, regulations, guidelines and working norms for better delivery of services.
3. Time bound grievance redressal of citizens.
4. Established network with functionaries promoting service group participation.
5. Incorporating a culture of transparency within the organization.
6. Wide publicity of standards of organization.
7. More independent and impartial grievance redressal.
8. Consistent and continual improvement in quality of services to the beneficiaries
9. Clarifications of the objectives of organization functionaries.
10. Developing better responsiveness and reciprocity of the organization.
11. Modification in services to account to the changing needs of the people or service group.

13.3 SIX PRINCIPLES OF THE CITIZEN'S CHARTER

The six principles of the Citizen's Charter movement as originally framed were as follows:

(i) **Quality:** Improving the quality of services
(ii) **Choice:** To be offered wherever possible
(iii) **Standards:** Specifying what to expect and how to proceed if standards are not met
(iv) **Value:** For the taxpayers' money
(v) **Accountability:** Individuals and Organisations
(vi) **Transparency:** Rules/Procedures/Schemes/Grievances

13.4 RATIONALE OF A CITIZEN'S CHARTER

Citizen's Charter is a written, voluntary declaration made by organizations about service standards, choice, accessibility, non-discrimination, transparency and accountability. However, wide the range of services may be, it should be in accordance with the expectations of citizens. Therefore, it becomes one of the most efficient ways of defining the nature of services offered and standards of service delivery.

Citizens are entitled to expect a minimum quality of service as they fund the government either directly or indirectly through taxes. They would like to be assured that the price they pay is reasonably compensated with the quality and quantity of services provided. A Citizen's Charter serves this purpose as it acts as the meeting point of the expectations of the citizen and the level of service provided by the organizations. Another major significance of Citizen's Charters is that it helps in instilling a sense of duty into the minds of public officials, rather than being tyrants who hold power.

The role of Citizen's Charters should not be restricted to remain as simple documents of assurances or policy frameworks. Instead, it should be an organic set of initiatives and ideas to elevate the level of standards and service delivery and increase public participation in the best way possible.

If successfully implemented, the Charter can enable the following:

- Improved service delivery
- Greater responsiveness of officials towards the public
- Greater public satisfaction with services

13.5 SIGNIFICANCE OF CITIZEN CHARTERS

The advent and growth of Citizen's Charters was the result of a number of countries opting for globalization, privatization and liberalization as the base of their fiscal policy. As this made the government from being the only provider to becoming one of the providers in the market, there was a need for better efforts to ensure service delivery with the best standards. With the entry of multiple service providers, the citizen's status elevated from being a mere beneficiary to becoming a consumer, who was provided with opportunities for comparative decision making. It therefore becomes essential for the governments to bring in reforms into its mode of operations to improve service quality and service delivery. In India, the Right to Information (RTI) Act recommends the provision of Citizen's Charter in all government service outlets. Though it is not a legally binding requirement, it helps in conveying the message of transparency and accountability within the organization.

13.6 INTERNATIONAL CONTEXT

As mentioned earlier, the United Kingdom was the first country to introduce the Citizen's Charter initiative. Following suit, many other countries started implementing similar programmes. Though they featured specific regional customizations, the principle of transparency and accountability was common among all of them.

1. Australia - Service Charter, 1997
2. Belgium - Public Service Users' Charter, 1992
3. Canada - Service Standards Initiative, 1995
4. France - Service Charter, 1992
5. India - Citizen's Charter, 1997,
6. Malaysia - Client Charter, 1993,
7. Portugal - The Quality Charter in Public Services, 1993
8. Spain - The Quality Observatory, 1992.

13.7 CITIZEN'S CHARTER IN INDIA

The concept of Citizen's Charter made its entry into India in 1997. It was introduced at the conference of chief ministers, 1997, held at Delhi. One of the outcomes of the conference was the decision to formulate Citizen's Charters, especially in those sectors that have a large public interface (e.g., Railways, Telecom, Posts, Public Distribution Systems, etc.).

13.8 COMPONENTS OF A CITIZEN'S CHARTER

A good Citizen's Charter should have the following components:

(i) Vision and Mission Statement of the Organisation
(ii) Details of business transacted by the organisation
(iii) Details of 'Citizens' or 'Clients'
(iv) Statement of services including standards, quality, time frame, etc., provided to each citizen/client group separately and how/where to get the services
(v) Details of Grievance Redress Mechanism and how to access it
(vi) Expectations from the 'citizens' or 'clients'
(vii) Additional commitments such as compensation in the event of failure of service delivery.

13.9 IMPLEMENTATION OF THE CITIZEN'S CHARTER

It was decided that the Citizen's Charter project would be done on a pilot basis initially and taken across the country later. For this purpose, the banking sector was chosen, because of its customer service orientation and its advantage in terms of speeding up the process of incorporation, owing to its information technology infrastructure.

The pilot study was done in three major National level banks (e.g., Punjab National Bank, Punjab & Sind Bank and Oriental Bank of Commerce). The assessment of their implementation revealed the following inadequacies.

13.10 INADEQUACIES AND GROUND REALITIES ADVERSELY AFFECTING THE EFFECTIVENESS OF CITIZEN'S CHARTERS

1. At times, Citizen's Charter implementation was not pragmatic because of field functionaries and their awareness.
2. Inadequacies in capacity building among functionaries.
3. Lack of change in orientation, education even among the service groups.
4. Inadequacies in bringing changes in the work culture of the organization.
5. Rigidity of law and some legal hurdles and lack of proper modification of legal environment account to the new environment.
6. Gaps in the perception of field reality by drafters and the lack of effective participation of field level functionaries in the formulation process.
7. Lack of impartial and independent or effective ombudsman system.
8. Prevailing culture of corruption, non-transparent, procedural control and bureaucratic control.
9. Formulation of Charters without following a consultative process.
10. Lack of knowledge on the philosophy, goals and main features of the Charter, among service providers.
11. Poor publicity given to the Charters.
12. Poor allocation of funds for awareness generation on Citizen's Charter or for orientation of the staff on various components of the Charter.
13. Poor design and content.

14. Inadequate ground work in terms of assessment and reforming its processes to deliver the promises made in the Charters.
15. Lack of public awareness of the concept of Citizen's Charter.
16. Charters are rarely updated, revised or reviewed.
17. Lack of precision on standards and commitments in several cases.
18. In some cases, Charters have become a one-time exercise, frozen in time.
19. On the commitment front, the Charter programme has been throttled on account of poor planning and resource commitment for publicity.
20. Citizen Charters have still not been adopted by all ministries/department.

13.11 LESSONS LEARNT IN QUALITY ASSURANCE FROM EXAMPLES WORLDWIDE

(i) Involve customers in the creation of guarantees, standards, redress policies, complaint systems, and customer service agreements.
(ii) Educate customers about the services that an organisation provides, so they will have realistic ideas of the services that are available and will understand their own responsibilities.
(iii) Keep pressure on from outside the organization to create meaningful guarantees, standards, redress policies and complaint systems.
(iv) Create an external review process to approve guarantees, standards, redress policies, complaint systems, and the performance measurement processes associated with them.
(v) Publicize your standards, guarantees, redress policies, complaint systems, and results.
(vi) Involve frontline employees in creating standards and other tools – and in figuring out how to meet them – to help them buy in.
(vii) Empower frontline staff to make decisions.
(viii) Use standards, guarantees, complaints, and customer councils to redesign, reengineer and restructure.
(ix) Study other organizations including private companies, to see how you might rethink, redesign and reengineer.
(x) Back up your quality assurance approach with training, mentoring, learning networks and other support for employees.
(xi) Do not create a separate unit to do this; integrate customer quality assurance into your strategic and performance management systems.
(xii) Make sure your executive leadership is seriously committed.

13.12 ASSESSMENT OF CITIZEN'S CHARTER

A Government of India-sponsored assessment of Citizen's Charter in 2008 made following observations, which may be noted in the context of the Charters which were reviewed for their content:

a. Most of the Charters under review failed to communicate effectively the 'vision' of the organisation. 'Vision' statement was missing from nearly 60% of the reviewed Charters.

b. The articulation of the 'mission' was also not found in nearly 40% of the reviewed Charters.
c. The client groups/stakeholders/users were not identified at all in nearly 30% of the Charters reviewed. The identification was, at best, partial in case of many others.
d. Service standards and timelines have been neglected in the Charters of most organisations. The service delivery standards were not mentioned in about 43% of the Charters reviewed. The service quality standards were missing from about 38% of them.
e. As high as 40% of the Charters reviewed failed to give information about the processes of obtaining service benefits.
f. Nearly 62% of the Charters reviewed did not offer any clue regarding the system for obtaining suggestions from the client groups/stakeholders/citizens. None of the Charters gave information about time frame for review of the suggestions.
g. Almost 41% of the Charters under consideration did not indicate any timeframe for redress of public grievances.
h. None of Charters reviewed gave any indication of a system of resolution offered to the client groups/stakeholders/citizens if the organisations or any of its levels failed to fulfil their commitments.
i. Even a mention of an essential Charter component like Information Facilitation Counters (IFC) was missing from nearly 62% of the Charters and as high as 72% of them remained silent about the functions performed by the IFC and the facilities available therein.
j. Nearly 77% of the Charters reviewed remained silent about the RTI Act and about 94% of them failed to even mention the Information Handbook brought out under the RTI Act.
k. None of the Charters reviewed gave any indication regarding the periodicity for a review of the Charter. The commitment to review itself was rare.

13.13 SUGGESTIONS FOR STRENGTHENING CITIZEN'S CHARTER FOR MORE EFFECTIVE GOVERNANCE

1. Involving stakeholders in fixing standards.
2. Creating awareness among people.
3. Wide publicity about Citizen's Charter.
4. Clear channel of hierarchy to be mentioned for effective grievance redressal.
5. Independent and impartial Ombudsman for grievance redressal.
6. Appropriate modification with passage of time.
7. Changing legal procedures.
8. To change the culture of organization to training them in client orientation and participatory management.
9. Performance audit with Citizen's Charter.
10. Active HRD in organization, effective personnel policies to get rid of incompetent.
11. Linking performance, service delivery with performance appraisal.
12. The need for citizens and staff to be consulted at every stage of formulation of the Charter.
13. Orientation of staff about the salient features and goals/objectives of the Charter; vision and mission statement of the department; and skills such as team building, problem solving, handling of grievances and communication skills.

14. The need for creation of database on consumer grievances and redress.
15. The need for wider publicity of the Charter through print media, posters, banners, leaflets, handbills, brochures, local newspapers, etc., and also through electronic media.
16. Earmarking of specific budgets for awareness generation and orientation of staff.
17. Replication of best practices in this field.

13.14 SECOND ARC ON CITIZEN'S CHARTER

13.14.1 Making Citizen's Charters Effective: An Agenda for Reform

The Commission has briefly dealt with the issue of Citizen's Charters in its Fourth Report on 'Ethics in Governance'. The Commission observed that in order to make these Charters effective tools for holding public servants accountable, the Charters should clearly spell out the remedy/penalty/compensation in case there is a default in meeting the standards spelt out in the Charter. It emphasized that it is better to have a few promises which can be kept than a long list of lofty but impractical aspirations.

13.14.1.1. Internal Restructuring Should Precede Charter Formulation

As a meaningful Charter seeks to improve the quality of service, mere stipulation to that effect in the Charter will not suffice. There has to be a complete analysis of the existing systems and processes within the organization and, if need be, these should to be recast and new initiatives adopted. Citizen's Charters that are put in place after these internal reforms will be more credible and useful than those designed as mere desk exercises without any system re-engineering.

13.14.1.2. One Size Does Not Fit All

This huge challenge becomes even more complex as the capabilities and resources that governments and departments need to implement Citizen's Charters vary significantly across the country. Added to these are differing local conditions. The highly uneven distribution of Citizen's Charters across States is clear evidence of this ground reality. For example, some agencies may need more time to specify and agree upon realistic standards of service. In others, additional effort will be required to motivate and equip the staff to participate in this reform exercise. Such organizations could be given time and resources to experiment with standards, grievances redressal mechanisms or training. They may also need more time for internal restructuring of the service delivery chain or introducing new systems. Therefore, the Commission is of the view that formulation of Citizen's Charters should be a decentralized activity with the head office providing broad guidelines.

13.14.1.3. Wide Consultation Process

Citizen's Charters should be formulated after extensive consultations within the organization followed by a meaningful dialogue with civil society. Inputs from experts should also be considered at this stage.

13.14.1.4. Firm Commitments to be Made

Citizen's Charters must be precise and make firm commitments of service delivery standards to the citizens/consumers in quantifiable terms wherever possible. With the passage of time, an effort should be made for more stringent standards of service delivery.

13.14.1.5. Redressal Mechanism in Case of Default

Citizen's Charter should clearly lay down the relief which the organization is bound to provide if it has defaulted on the promised standards of delivery. In addition, wherever there is a default in the service delivery by the organization, citizens must also have recourse to a grievances redressal mechanism. This will be discussed further in the next chapter on grievances redressal mechanisms.

13.14.1.6. Periodic Evaluation of Citizen's Charters

Every organization must conduct periodic evaluation of its Citizen's Charter preferably through an external agency. This agency while evaluating the Charter of the organisation should also make an objective analyses of whether the promises made therein are being delivered within the defined parameters. The result of such evaluations must be used to improve upon the Charter. This is necessary because a Citizen's Charter is a dynamic document which must keep pace with the changing needs of the citizens as well as the changes in underlying processes and technology. A periodic review of Citizen's Charter thus becomes an imperative.

13.14.1.7. Benchmark Using End-User Feedback

Systematic monitoring and review of Citizen's Charters is necessary even after they are approved and placed in the public domain. Performance and accountability tend to suffer when officials are not held responsible for the quality of a Charter's design and implementation. In this context, end-user feedback can be a timely aid to assess the progress and outcomes of an agency that has implemented a Citizen's Charter. This is a standard practice for Charters implemented in the United Kingdom.

13.14.1.8. Hold Officers Accountable for Results

All of the above point to the need to make the heads of agencies or other designated senior officials accountable for their respective Citizen's Charters. The monitoring mechanism should fix specific responsibility in all cases where there is a default in adhering to the Citizen's Charter.

13.14.1.9. Include Civil Society in the process

Organizations need to recognize and support the efforts of civil society groups in preparation of the Charters, their dissemination and also facilitating information disclosures. There have been a number of States where involvement of civil society in this entire process has resulted in vast improvement in the contents of the Charter, its adherence as well as educating the citizens about the importance of this vital mechanism.

13.15 THE SEVOTTAM MODEL

Sevottam is a Service Delivery Excellence Model which provides an assessment-improvement framework to bring about excellence in public service delivery. The need for a tool like Sevottam arose from the fact that Citizen's Charters by themselves could not achieve the desired results in improving quality of public services. Besides, the absence of a credible grievances redressal mechanism within organizations was also becoming a major impediment in improving service delivery standards. Thus, it was felt that unless there is a mechanism to assess the outcomes of various measures, the reform initiatives would not yield the desired results. The Sevottam model works as an evaluation mechanism to assess the quality of internal processes and their impact on the quality of service delivery.

The Sevottam model has *three* modules.

1. The first component of the model requires effective Charter implementation, thereby opening up a channel for receiving citizens' inputs into the way in which organizations

determine service delivery requirements. Citizen's Charters publicly declare the information on citizens' entitlements thereby making citizens better informed and hence empowering them to demand better services.

2. The second component of the model, 'Public Grievance Redress' requires a good grievance redressal system operating in a manner that leaves the citizen more satisfied with how the organization responds to complaints/grievances, irrespective of the final decision.
3. The third component 'Excellence in Service Delivery' postulates that an organization can have an excellent performance in service delivery only if it is efficiently managing well the key ingredients for good service delivery and building its own capacity to continuously improve service delivery.

13.16 THE ARC SEVEN-STEP MODEL FOR CITIZEN CENTRICITY

This model draws from the principles of the IS 15700:2005, the Sevottam model and the Customer Service Excellence Model of the United Kingdom. Each organization should follow a step-by-step approach, which would help it in becoming increasingly more citizen centric. This approach should be followed not only by the top management but also by each unit of the organization that has a public interface (i.e; top management has the dual responsibility of setting standards for itself as well as guiding the subordinate offices in setting their own standards).

a. *Define* all services which you provide and identify your clients.
b. *Set* standards and norms for each service.
c. *Develop* capability to meet the set standards.
d. *Perform* to achieve the standards.
e. *Monitor* performance against the set standards.
f. *Evaluate* the impact through an independent mechanism.
g. *Continuous improvement* based on monitoring and evaluation results.

13.17 RIGHT TO SERVICE ACTS

In India, the *Right to Public Services Acts* have been legislated by states to guarantee time-bound delivery of services in both 'Government to citizen (G2C)' and 'Government to Business (G2B)' relationships. The laws also provide for the mechanism to punish officials, who fail to do so on time. Similarly, the Right to Service acts are meant to reduce corruption among government officials and to increase transparency and public accountability. Madhya Pradesh became the first state in India to enact Right to Service Act on 18 August 2010.

The recent trend of Right to Public Service Acts can be tracked back to the Citizen's Charter movement of the late 1990s and early 2000s. Though these Charters detailed what citizens could expect from the government, it was felt that these Charters lacked the precision necessary to be effective.

To address these perceived failures, the Right to Public Service Acts require that the services are clearly defined and must either be completed or denied (with explanation) within a specific timeframe. Failing which they will be required to pay a monetary penalty. In stacking a monetary penalty against officials who fail to provide service, the Right to Service Acts take inspiration from the RTI Act, 2005. It is believed by many that the RTI Act's threat of a triggered monetary penalty was a vital part of its perceived success.

13.18 MODEL CITIZEN'S CHARTER

Agriculture Insurance Company of India Ltd.

Citizens' Charter

Our Mission

- To provide comprehensive risk solution through various agricultural and allied insurance products to the farming community
- To be the most preferred service provider of agricultural and allied insurance products and global leader in this segment

Our Values

- Highest priority to customer needs
- High standards of public conduct
- Transparency in operations

Our Commitments

- To respond to all commercially viable crop insurance requirements of the farmers, within three months of receipt of completed information
- To ensure availability of the relevant information about insurance products to prospective customers in a lucid manner
- To promote customer awareness of various crop insurance products through various media
- To obtain, wherever necessary, a written proposal from the customer and to issue the insurance document accordingly
- To issue all necessary insurance documents, within fifteen days of receiving completed information
- To settle all claims within thirty days of receiving subsidy towards premium/claims and completion of all requirements
- To set up Customer Service Desks in all Regional Offices and to spread awareness about the same; also to guide the customers about the procedure and status of his claims
- To set up a Grievance Redressal mechanism in every Regional Office; also to guide the customers about the same
- To provide all the above services to the citizens without any gratification

13.19 PRACTICE QUESTIONS

1. Discuss the Purpose motive and mechanism existing in India to enforce 'Sevottam Model'.
2. 'An empirical evaluation of implementation Citizen's Charter in India is not much encouraging'. In the light of the statement discuss the hurdles in Implementation of Citizen's Charter and suggest remedies.
3. 'Citizen's Charter is not a ritual, it is a democracy intensifying concept'. In the light of the above statement analyse Citizen's Charter, with special reference to improve them.
4. 'he Citizen's Charter does not by itself create new legal rights, but it surely helps in enforcing existing rights'. Comment.
5. Explain Citizen Charter and examine its position in India with the examples of few best practices in use.
6. Discuss the various factors that should be considered before formulating Citizen's Charter in any organization.

14

Welfare Schemes for the Vulnerable Section of the Population

LEARNING OBJECTIVES

In this Chapter, you will learn about:

- Human Resource
- Education
- Health and Family Welfare
- Poverty Alleviation
- Food Security and Hunger Elimination
- Welfare Initiatives for Women (MCWD)

14.1 HUMAN RESOURCE

14.1.1 Introduction

The Government is committed to provide equitable access to quality education to all, across all levels from primary to university level, for which reforms are undertaken in the education sector as a continuous and ongoing process. The 42nd Constitutional Amendment, 1976, brought about a fundamental change by transferring education from the State List to the Concurrent List recognizing the federal structure of our country and giving equal responsibility to both the Central and State Governments to promote education. Recognizing the centrality of states both in policy formulation and effective implementation of education reforms, the Ministry of HRD has been regularly convening meetings of the Central Advisory Board on Education (CABE), which is a composite body and is also the highest advisory body on education. All the schemes implemented by the Government of India are in consultation with the States which meet regularly through the meetings of CABE. Similarly, all reform initiatives are also through consensus evolved between the Centre and the States through the CABE.

Presently, various initiatives, such as, the Right of Children to Free and Compulsory Education (RTE) Act, 2009, Sarva Shiksha Abhiyan (SSA), Rashtriya Madhyamik Shiksha Abhiyan (RMSA), ICT in Schools, Centrally Sponsored Scheme on Teacher Education (CSSTE), Shaala

Siddhi, Rashtriya Avishkar Abhiyan are being implemented which envisage significant reforms in the elementary education and secondary education. In higher education also, Rashtriya Uchchatar Shiksha Abhiyan (RUSA), Global Initiative for Academics Network (GIAN), Impacting Research, Innovation & Technology (IMPRINT), Technical Education Quality Improvement Programme(TEQIP), Pandit Madan Mohan Malviya National Mission on Teachers and Teaching (PMMMNMTT), Study Webs of Active-Learning for Young Aspiring Minds (SWAYAM), National Digital Library, Campus Connect Programme, Uchhatar Avishkar Abhiyan, Unnat Bharat Abhiyan are being implemented to improve the quality of higher education in the country. A number of initiatives are also undertaken by UGC and AICTE for quality improvement in higher and technical education. With a view to improving the competitiveness of the higher educational institutions, the National Institutional Ranking Framework (NIRF) has been launched.

The recent budget announcements refer to reforms in UGC for promoting greater administrative and academic autonomy and revised framework for outcome-based accreditation and credit-based programmes; leveraging Information Technology and launching 350 online courses through SWAYAM platform; and establishing a National Testing Agency to conduct all entrance examinations for higher education institutions.

It is to be noted that necessary budgetary allocations are provided both for effective implementation of the schemes and also for the proposed reform initiatives.

Currently, the process of formulating a New Education Policy is underway which may propose several reforms in examinations, governance, regulation, school standards, teachers & faculty, literacy and lifelong learning, skills and employability, quality assurance, internationalization, research, curricula, innovation, etc., so as to build an education system that promotes equitable access to quality education to all sections of the society.

14.1.2 Making Higher Education Relevant to the Needs of Society and Industry

The UGC has informed that it has launched the following schemes for making higher education relevant to the needs of the society and industry, namely: Career Oriented Courses (COC), Community Colleges (CC), introduction of degrees in vocational subjects and Pandit Deen Dayal Upadhyaya Knowledge Acquisition and Upgradation of Skilled Human Abilities and Livelihood (KAUSHAL) centres in line with National Skills Qualifications Framework (NSQF). The UGC, through collaboration with National Mission on Education thought ICT (NMEICT), has undertaken e-content development of postgraduate programmes called e-PG Pathashala.

The University Grants Commission (UGC) undertakes maintenance of standards in teaching and research and quality assurance in Universities, Deemed to be Universities and Colleges through the following mechanisms, namely: framing regulations and schemes and; disbursing grants to the eligible institutions. The UGC has notified several regulations with the objective of sustenance and improvement in the quality of higher education and for undertaking academic reforms. The regulations are available at http://www.ugc.ac.in/page/UGC-Regulations.aspx. In order to encourage research and development in the country, UGC has laid out schemes, awards, fellowships, chairs and programmes under which financial assistance is provided to institutions of higher education as well as faculty members working therein to undertake quality research, covering areas of knowledge across disciplines, including revival and promotion of indigenous languages. These schemes are at http://www.ugc.ac.in/page/XII-Plan-Guidelines.aspx.

The Central Government has launched several initiatives, such as, National Institutional Ranking Framework (NIRF), Impacting Research, Innovation & Technology (IMPRINT),

Uchchtar Avishkar Yojna (UAY), Global Initiative of Academic Networks (GIAN) in the field of education for the qualitative development of education in the country. Under the NIRF, Educational Institutions will be ranked by an independent ranking Agency for which objective criteria has been developed. They shall be ranked separately in fields such as Engineering, Management, Pharma, Architecture, etc. Under the IMPRINT initiative, the Government has taken the initiative to address major engineering challenges through the collaborative efforts of the Indian Institutes of Technology (IITs) and Indian Institute of Science (IISc). Under this, a roadmap is finalised to pursue engineering challenges in 10 technology domains that have large social impact. The objectives of UAY scheme are to promote innovation in IITs addressing issues of manufacturing industries; to spur innovative mindset; to coordinate action between academia and industry and to strengthen labs and research facilities. GIAN scheme is for facilitating partnership between higher educational institutions of the country and other countries. The scheme is aimed at tapping international talent pool of scientists and entrepreneurs.

The Central Government is also implementing the Centrally Sponsored Scheme of Rashtriya Uchchatar Shiksha Abhiyan (RUSA) for strategic funding and reforms in the State Higher Education sector.

14.1.3 Initiatives of Ministry of Human Resource Development

One of the major achievements, which Ministry of Human Resource Development accomplished during the year 2015, includes achievement of 100% target of completion of construction of separate toilets for boys and girls in schools under Swachch Vidyalaya Abhiyan within 1 year of the announcement made by the Prime Minister, Shri Narendra Modi on August 15, 2014. The year will also be known for technical advancement made by the Ministry by laying emphasis on ICT, leading to launch of a number of initiatives like e-pathshala, Saransh, Shala Siddhi, Shaala Darpan, availability of NCERT books on mobile app, etc.

The year 2015 also saw the Government of India's sincere efforts towards bringing out a New Education Policy to meet the changing dynamics of the population's requirement with regard to quality education, innovation and research, aiming to make India a knowledge superpower by equipping its students with the necessary skills and knowledge and to eliminate the shortage of manpower in science, technology, academics and industry. New Education Policy is being framed after a gap of 23 years.

For the first time, the Government of India is embarking on a time-bound grassroots consultative process, which will enable the Ministry of Human Resource Development to reach out to individuals across the country through over 2.75 lakh direct consultations while also taking input from citizens online.

The year will also be remembered because of the Indian Institute of Science, Bangalore, cracking the top 100 in world University ranking as per *Times High Education* ranking for 2015–16 and IIT, Delhi, also figuring in the top 200 list of QS. It has sent a strong message to other Indian Technical Institutes to better their performance in the key areas of academics research and faculty enrichment. A glimpse of major achievements and initiatives of the Department of Higher Education and the Department of School Education & Literacy is given as follows:

DEPARTMENT OF SCHOOL EDUCATION & LITERACY

A number of flagship schemes were launched by the Department of School Education and Literacy in the current year.

Padhe Bharat Badhe Bharat: It is a sub-programme of Sarva Shiksha Abhiyan launched in August, 2014, with special focus on improving language development and to create interest in mathematics. The two tracks of Padhe Bharat Badhe Bharat are: Early reading and writing with comprehension (ERWC) and early mathematics (EM).

As a follow-up to the foundational programme, in 2015–16 a programme called the *National Reading Initiative* was launched to develop and promote the habit of reading among students in elementary schools, thereby extending the programme up to Class 8. States were provided token funds to plan and implement innovative activities to promote reading. States have designed specific interventions targeting children in Classes 1 and 2 to improve learning outcomes. There are a variety of focussed programmes being currently implemented across the country.

Children with Special Needs: With the active support by Sarva Shiksha Abhiyan, over 25 lakh children with special needs have been enrolled in elementary education. In order to equip teachers to facilitate classroom transaction and teaching learning of children with special needs, material on curricular adaptations for inclusive classrooms has been developed by NCERT. This material in the form of two handbooks has been developed for teachers both at the primary and upper primary level. All teachers across the country are being oriented in practising such classroom adaptations through teacher training.

Rashtriya Madhyamik Shiksha Abhiyan: The RMSA guidelines provide for augmenting secondary school infrastructure through construction of additional classrooms, laboratories, toilet blocks, drinking water, libraries, etc. Till date, 10,513 new schools have been approved under the scheme. The RMSA Scheme has been revised to subsume the schemes of ICT @schools, Vocationalisation of Secondary Education, Inclusive Education for Disabled at Secondary Stage, and Girls Hostels from the financial year 2014–15. The Integrated RMSA scheme extends the benefit to aided Secondary schools (excluding infrastructure support and teachers and staff salaries) for quality interventions.

The Teacher Education Bureau is focusing on the following main components for improving the quality of teacher education:

1. **National Curriculum Framework of Teacher Education (NCFTE 2009):** The National Council of Teacher Education (NCTE) has prepared the National Curriculum Framework of Teacher Education (NCFTE 2009). This framework has been prepared in the background of the NCF, 2005, and the principles laid down in the Right of Children to Free and Compulsory Education Act, 2009.
2. **In-STEP: Capacity Building Program of Teacher Educators:** Ministry of Human Resource Development (MHRD) and USAID have formulated the In-STEP programme (India Support to Teacher Education Program) under which 110 teacher educators from the eastern and northeastern part of the country have undergone a 3-month fellowship at Arizona State University with the clear purpose of understanding issues related to teacher education.

   In addition, the **TESS-India** is another programme for Teacher Educators with collaboration between Department for International Development (DFID) and Ministry of HRD with UK's Open University as the implementing agency.
3. The **Centrally Sponsored Scheme on Teacher Education** (CSSTE) puts emphasis on monitoring of the process and outcome parameters in respect of each level of institution, and for the purpose a comprehensive monitoring mechanism has been

developed thereof. Joint Review Mission is a part of this monitoring mechanism. Joint Review Missions consisting of experts in Teacher Education have been sent to majority of the states to ensure effective implementation of the Centrally Sponsored Scheme for Teacher Education.

New activities/initiatives under CSSTE Scheme are as follows:

(i) **Enhanced use of E-Governance** in Teacher Education by National Council for Teacher Education (NCTE) for better regulation of the sector.
(ii) **Accreditation for Teacher Education Institutions (TEIs)** by National Council for Teacher Education for better management and improved quality of teacher education.
(iii) **Mapping of Teacher Education Institutions (TEIs)** by NCTE to identify the gap areas for effective future planning.

Digital Gender Atlas for Advancing Girls' Education in India: It was launched on 8th March 2015. The tool will help identify low-performing geographic pockets for girls, particularly from marginalised groups.

Udaan: This Scheme is dedicated to the development of girl child education, so as to promote the admission of girl students. It seeks to enhance the enrolment of girl students in prestigious technical education institutions through incentives and academic support.

"Beti Bachao, Beti Padhao" programme, launched on January 20, 2015, has ushered in to encourage education among girl children. The programme is a joint initiative of Ministry of Women and Child Development, Ministry of Health and Family Welfare and Ministry of Human Resource Development.

Saransh: The CBSE Board has launched an on-line facility titled 'Saransh' for affiliated and CBSE schools on 2nd November, 2014. It helps the schools to look at their performance at an aggregate level and at the level of each student. It is an online self-review tool for schools affiliated to the Central Board of Secondary Education (CBSE). It allows schools to identify areas of improvement in students, teachers and curriculum and take necessary measures to implement change. It also provides schools with a view of overall and individual student's performance in academic and extracurricular activities.

Curriculum for yoga from classes VI to X was released on the occasion of *International Yoga Day in June 2015.*

Rashtriya Avishkar Abhiyan was launched on 9th July 2015. This programme is directed towards creating interest among school-going students from classes I to XII in sciences. Model labs would be created all over the country for this purpose. The key activities under this programme include mentoring of elementary and secondary schools by institutions of higher education; forming Maths and Science clubs for children at school and professional development of teachers in order to make teaching of Maths and Science interesting for students. The activities/components of RAA are funded under Sarva Shiksha Abhiyan and Rashtriya Madhyamik Shiksha Abhiyan.

National Conference on ICT in School Education – The Conference was held on 7th November 2015. During the Conference, e-Pathshala, Saaransh, and National Programme on School Standards and Evaluation Framework (Shala Siddhi) were launched. All these are web portal/mobile app. These apps promise to make learning more interesting, school bags lighter and books available on the go.

The first phase of **"Shaala Darpan Project"** to cover all the 1,099 Kendriya Vidyalayas was launched in June 2015. This programme will be made available as a mobile app which will keep the parents informed of their ward's progress in schools.

The National Programme on School Standards and Evaluation (NPSSE)–Shaala Siddhi: In a step towards comprehensive school evaluation as central to improving quality of school education in India, National Programme on School Standards and Evaluation has been initiated by National University of Educational Planning and Administration (NUEPA), under the aegis of Union Ministry of Human Resource Development. The School Standards and Evaluation Framework (SSEF) has been developed as an instrument for evaluating school performance. This will enable the school to evaluate its performance against the well-defined criteria in a focused and strategic manner.

E-pathshala: As a part of the Digital India Campaign, the Ministry of HRD has launched 'e-pathshala' which is a single-point repository of e-resources containing, NCERT textbooks and various other learning resources. CBSE prescribes textbooks published by National Council of Educational Research and Training (NCERT) for classes IX to XII. For classes I to VIII, CBSE although approves syllabus as per pattern of syllabus given by NCERT, it does not prescribe any textbooks for these classes. **The National Curriculum Framework, 2005 (NCF)** stipulates that region-specific books take care of the local context, culture and resources and therefore different books for different regions better relate to the daily lives of the local students.

Mid-Day Meal Scheme: The IVR (Interactive Voice Response System) to monitor the daily implementation of Mid-Day Meal scheme was showcased this year during the National Conference on ICT in School Education. There are two recent interventions, such as Tithi Bhojan and Social Audit designed to attract community participation and channelize it for enrichment of Mid-Day Meal Scheme. The Central Government has requested the States to consider the concept of **Tithi Bhojan** for mid-day meals in a suitable manner, to encourage local community participation the programme. **Social Audit**, another intervention under this Scheme, means is a process in which people collectively monitor and evaluate the planning and implementation of the Scheme. It is viewed as an ongoing process of public vigilance. Bihar, Karnataka, Maharashtra, Odisha and Punjab have completed Social Audit. Social Audit is under progress in Madhya Pradesh, Rajasthan, and Uttar Pradesh and Tamil Nadu.

The Central Government notified 'Mid-Day Meal Rules, 2015', on September 30th, 2015. The Rules inter alia provide for temporary utilization of other funds available with the school for MDM in case school exhausts MDM funds for any reason; Food Security Allowance to be paid to beneficiaries in case of non-supply of meals for specified reasons; and monthly testing of meals on a random basis by accredited Labs to check its quality. These rules and their effective compliance by implementing agencies in the States will ensure better regularity in serving mid-day meals in schools.

Kala Utsav: A unique initiative of the Government of India was launched with the theme of 'Beti Bachao, Beti Padhao'. It provides an opportunity to learn about the art, culture and language of various States and UTs of the country at one place. About 1,400 students from across the country participated in this cultural programme. Teachers, parents and members of jury were also a part of this unique programme.

Kala Utsav seeks to enhance the life skills of the participants and prepare them as ambassadors of Indian culture besides integrating art in education.

DEPARTMENT OF HIGHER EDUCATION

A number of schemes related to Department of Higher Education were also launched during the year.

IMPRINT INDIA was released on 5th November 2015. It is a Pan-IIT and IISc joint initiative to develop a roadmap for research to solve major engineering and technology challenges in ten technology domains relevant to India. **IMPRINT INDIA** aims at direct research in the premier institutions into areas of social relevance. Under this, 10 domains have been identified which could substantially impact the living standards of the rural areas: (1) Health care technology, (2) Energy security, (3) Rural urban housing design, (4) Nanotechnology, (5) Water/river system, (6) Advanced materials, (7) Computer science and ICT, (8) Manufacturing technology, (9) Advanced security and (10) Environment/climate change. The research in each of these areas is being coordinated by one IIT. http://imprint-india.org/

Global Initiative for Academics Network (GIAN), was launched as an initiative to attract the best foreign academics to Indian Universities of Excellence. The programme has been launched to facilitate the partnership between Higher Education Institutions of India and other foreign universities. Under this, (352) courses are being offered by foreign faculty from 38 Countries. The cost of the travel and honorarium ranging from $8,000–$12,000 is being met from the scheme funds. These courses are being looked at as a starting point of long-term research collaboration between Indian Institutions and the other Global institutions; and therefore signal a major chapter in the higher education system.

National Institutional Ranking Framework (NIRF) has been launched by the Ministry of Human Resource Development on 29th September 2015. The ranking framework evaluates each higher education institution on five broad parameters, namely teaching/learning resources, research, graduation outcomes, outreach/inclusive nature and the public perception. The ranks will be declared on the first Monday of April every year. An independent body is being proposed to undertake this work based on objective and verifiable criteria.

So far, 2,500 institutions covering engineering, management, pharma, architecture and universities have registered for participation in the ranking and are submitting data. Participation in the NIRF would help the Indian educational institutions participate in the world rankings with greater confidence.

Study Webs of Active-Learning for Young Aspiring Minds (SWAYAM), is a Web portal where Massive Open On-line Courses (MOOCs) will be available on all kinds of subjects. SWAYAM is the Indian electronic e-education platform which proposes to offer courses from the high school stage to postgraduate stage in an interactive electronic platform. The IT platform for SWAYAM was built and become operational by March 2016 with a capacity to host nearly 2,000 courses. This would provide the best quality education to more than three crore students across the country. The system would allow 10 lakh students using the system concurrently. Once it becomes operational, students from the backward rural areas can access teaching from the best institutes in the country electronically, thereby, raising the overall standards of higher education in the country. SWAYAM-MOOCs project is intended to address the needs of school level 9–12 to undergraduate and postgraduate students, covering all disciplines.

Launch of the **Credit framework for Skills and Education** as per the National Skills Qualification framework paved the way for certification of skills through the formal system and allows for multiple exits and entrance into the education system with scope for vertical and lateral mobility. The CBCS will enable students to take courses of their choice, learn at their own pace, undergo additional courses and acquire more than the required credits, and adopt an interdisciplinary approach to learning. Approval by UGC of the Guidelines for **Choice-Based Credit Framework** provides for more choices for students to opt for employable courses through a system of flexible credits for foundational, elective and core courses. The **status of CBCS** is as follows:

1. All 39 Central Universities are implementing the CBCS system from 2015 to 16.
2. Major State Universities, like Madras University, Chennai; Bharathiar University, Coimbatore; Bharathidasan University, Tiruchirapalli; Osmania University, Hyderabad; University of Bombay, Mumbai; SNDT Women's University, Mumbai; M.S. University of Baroda, Vadodara; Lucknow University, Lucknow; Guru Nanak Dev University, Amritsar; Himachal Pradesh University, Shimla and Gauhati University, Guwahati, are also going to implement CBCS from the next academic session.

Saksham Scholarship Scheme: The All India Council for Technical Education (AICTE) is implementing Saksham scholarship scheme to provide support to differently abled students to pursue technical education.

Launch of the **Know Your College portal** is to provide informed decision-making opportunity for students along with complete availability of all e-learning resources. A portal called **Know Your College** (KYC) has been started in which the data declared by all the educational institutions is being placed in a public portal and also made available through a mobile application so that the stakeholders can verify the same. It will also work as one-stop shop for all educational resources. More than 40,000 higher educational institutions are already mapped under the KYC.

Under **Campus Connect** programme, all the Central Universities in the country are going to be connected through WIFI network at a cost of approximately ₹320 crores. Under this, all the classrooms, libraries, laboratories, hostels and places frequented by the students would be connected through a secured WIFI hotspots providing access to the educational and information resources to the students on 24×7 basis. This project completed by June 2016 and implemented by ERNET.

Promoting Start-ups: Thirty-seven new start-up parks/research parks would be set up this year with the coordination of Dept of Science and Technology (fund sharing on 50:50 basis) covering all the IITs, NITs and some IIITs/Central Universities. These would incubate the start-ups and hand-hold them till they reach the stage of commercialization, normally for a period of 5 years. IIT Madras Research Park has already become fully functional (it is ready for inauguration by the Prime Minister).

Unnat Bharat Abhiyan was launched for connecting higher education and society to enable technology and its use for development of rural areas. Under this, all technical and higher education institutions have been asked to adopt five villages each; identify technology gaps and prepare plans for innovations that could substantially increase the incomes and growth in the rural areas.

Ucchtar Aavishkar Abhiyaan: For promotion of innovation, All the IITs have been encouraged to work with the industry to identify areas where innovation is required and come up with solutions that could be brought up to the commercialization level. For this purpose, it is proposed to launch a scheme **Ucchtar Aavishkar Abhiyan** by investing ₹250 crores every year on identified projects proposed by IITs and NITs. Participation of industry in part-funding the project would be mandatory

Engineering skills to unemployed youth: An initiative as a part of the PMKVY is being launched to encourage all the 10,000 technical institutions (engineering and polytechnic) to provide engineering skills (through part-time courses of 6 to 8 months duration) to at least 100 unemployed youths using their infrastructure after college-hours. The training costs would be met by the central government, and the placement of the trained youth is the responsibility of the institution. This is expected to provide high-quality skilled persons required for the Make in India campaign.

Comprehensive Language Policy: An Expert Committee on Language was constituted on 29.12.2014 for preparation of Comprehensive Language Policy for the country and it met four times so far.

Matribhasha Diwas: Matribhasha Diwas was celebrated on 21.2.2015 to sensitize people about the need of greater use of mother tongues and other Indian Languages for development and progress of the Nation. Hon'ble HRM has inaugurated the programme at Chennai organized by CIIL, Mysore.

On the International front too, addressing The Leaders' Forum on an official visit to UNESCO Headquarters at Paris on 17th November, 2015, then Minister of Human Resource Development Smt Smriti Irani reaffirmed India's commitment to the ideals of UNESCO and to furthering its role and activities. In this context, she recalled the words of Mahatma Gandhi when in 1947 he had expressed the deep Indian interest in the efforts of UNESCO to "secure peace through educational and cultural activities".

Conference of Commonwealth Education Ministers: During the 19th Conference of Commonwealth Education Ministers at the Bahamas from 22 to 26 June, 2015, the Ministry of Human Resource offered the following: to set up the Malviya Commonwealth Chair for Cross-Border Teacher Education which will focus on issues pertaining to curriculum development, pedagogy, student assessment, pre-service and in-service teacher training and capacity development; Commonwealth Consortium for Research which can function in collaboration with the Commonwealth Education hub and provide cross funding for research projects which member nations deem appropriate; Strengthening of public institutions to bring about qualitative improvements in education at all levels; Providing e-Learning platform, SWAYAM to host e-courseware developed by Commonwealth of Learning; and Posting of digitized materials of Commonwealth countries on its soon to be established national e-Library.

Finally, the above flagship programmes, new schemes and innovations of the Ministry of HRD prove beyond doubt that it is playing a significant role in building strong foundations in education. While the Department of School Education & Literacy has its eye set on the universalization of Education and making better citizens out of the country's young brigade, the Department of Higher Education is engaged in establishing world class institutes of learning and providing ample opportunities for research and skill development to ensure that we create the world's largest workforce.

14.1.4. Rashtriya Uchchatar Shiksha Abhiyan (RUSA)

About

- Centrally Sponsored Scheme (CSS)
- Launched in 2013 under Ministry of Human Resources Development

Aim

- Providing strategic funding to eligible stable higher educational institutions.

Objectives

(i) Improve the overall quality of state institutions by ensuring conformity to prescribed norms and standards and adopt accreditation as a mandatory quality assurance framework.

(ii) Under transformative reforms in the state higher education system by creating a facilitating institutional structure for planning and monitoring and the state level, promoting autonomy in state universities and improving governance in institutions.
(iii) Ensure reforms in the affiliation, academic and examination system.
(iv) Ensure adequate availability of quality faculty in all higher educational institutions and ensure capacity building at all levels of employment.
(v) Create an enabling atmosphere in the higher education institutions to devote themselves to research and innovations.
(vi) Expand the institutional base by creating additional capacity in existing institutions and establishing new institutions in order to achieve enrolment targets.
(vii) Correct regional imbalances in access to higher education by setting up institutions in unserved and underserved areas.
(viii) Improve equity in higher education by proving adequate opportunities of higher education to SC/STs and socially and educationally backward classes; promote inclusion of women, minorities and different by abled persons.

Components

(i) Create new universities through upgradation of existing autonomous colleges and conversion of colleges in a cluster.
(ii) Create new model degree colleges, new professional colleges and provide infrastructural support to universities and colleges.
(iii) Faculty recruitment support, faculty improvements programmes and leadership development of education administrators.
(iv) In order to enhance skill development, the existing central scheme of polytechnics has been subsumed under RUSA
(v) A separate component to synergies vocational education with higher education also been included in RUSA.
(vi) RUSA also supports reforming, restructuring and building capacity of institutions in participating state.

Funding Pattern

- Central Funding – 60:40 for General category States 90:10 for Special category States 100% for UTs
- Based on norm based and outcome dependent
- Fund flow from central ministry through the state Govts/UTs to the state higher education councils before reaching identified institutions.
- On the basis on critical appraisal of state Higher Education Plans.

14.1.5 Pandit Madan Mohan Malaviya National Mission on Teachers & Teaching (PMMMNNMTT)

About

- A central sector scheme
- Commence in 2014–15 for a period of 3 years, that is, from 2014–15 to 2016–17 during XII Plan

Goals

- To ensure a coordinate approach so as to holistically address the various shortcoming relating to teachers and teaching across the education spectrum ranging from school education to higher education, including technical education; using the best international practices for excellence.
- To create and strengthen the institutional mechanisms at the centre and in the states, for augmenting training and discipline-wise capacity building of faculty and their periodic assessment for excellence.

14.1.6 National Initiative for Setting Up of Design Innovation Centres, Open Design School and National Design Innovation Network

Objectives

- To promote a culture of innovations and creative problem solving.
- To promote knowledge sharing and collaboration amongst industry, academia, Government Instructions, research laboratories, etc.
- To serve as a location for the industrial collaborators to encourage their new product development in the campus using in house facilities.
- To serve as a place that imparts design-based education and practice systematic design through projects.
- To enhance interdisciplinary design-focused innovation and creativity.
- To facilitate interdisciplinary design-focused education research and entrepreneurial activities in order to create commercial opportunities and build partnerships between academics and industry.
- To promote nurture and advance the culture of design and innovation in the country leading to significant contributions and break through impacting quality of human life.
- To create an ecosystem facilitating students, faculty to take their innovative ideas from classrooms/labs to market people.
- To facilitate evolution of new models of academia industry interactions as well as academia social interactions and develop institutional neutrals for innovations in the thematic areas.
- To promote innovations which are both inclusive and disruptive.
- To build a flagship programme in the areas of design and innovation which can be replicated in other institutes/universities in our country.
- To promote all forms of innovations in the complete value chain form process to product, including innovation as a discipline itself.
- To promote increase interactions/collaborations with institutes/organization worldwide working in the areas of design and innovation.

Components of the Scheme

(i) Design Innovation Centres(DICs)
(ii) Open Design School (ODS)
(iii) National Design Innovation Network

Financial Support

- Each of the DICs would be provided financial support to the extent of ₹10 crores during 12th plan.

- Out of this, non-recurring grant will be released in a period of 2 years.
- Recurring grant will be available annually, up to 3 years.

14.1.7 Scheme for Incentivizing State Governments for Expansion of Higher Education Institutions

Aim

- Introduced for incentivizing states for establishing new higher education institutions/ expanding existing higher education institutions.

Funding Pattern

- Provide central assistance to the state governments in the ration of 1:2 (1:1 for special category states) for establishing new higher educational institutions / expanding existing higher educational institutions.

Physical Targets

- XI & XII Plan include view universities, colleges, engineering colleges as well as expansion of existing colleges.

New central Sector Scheme of Interest Subsidy on Educational loans taken by taken by students from economically backward sections to pursue technical, professional education in India under the educational loan scheme of the Indian Bank's Association.

About

- A view central sector scheme of provide full interest subside during the period of moratorium on loans taken by students belonging to economically weaker sections from scheduled banks under the educational loan scheme of the Indian Bank's Association for pursuing any of the approved courses of studies in technical and professional streams from recognized institutions in India.

14.1.8 National Research Professorship (NRP)

About

- Started in 1949 to honour distinguished academics and scholars in recognition of their contribution to knowledge.

Beneficiaries and Eligibility

- Persons of real eminence, who have attained the age of 65 years of have made outstanding contributions in their respective fields and are still capable of productive research are considered for appointment as National Research Professor.

14.1.9 National Institutional Ranking Framework (NIRF)

The National Institutional Ranking Framework (NIRF) was approved by the MHRD and launched by Honourable Minister of Human Resource Development on 29th September 2015.

This framework outlines a methodology to rank institutions across the country. The methodology draws from the overall recommendations broad understanding arrived at by a Core Committee set up by MHRD, to identify the broad parameters for ranking various universities and institutions. The parameters broadly cover "Teaching, Learning and Resources," "Research and Professional Practices," "Graduation Outcomes," "Outreach and Inclusivity," and "Perception".

India Rankings – 2016 based on this framework were released on 4th April 2016.

For India Rankings – 2017, the main ranking parameters remain the same. However, there are a few significant changes in a few sub-parameters. Also, this year every large institution will be given a common overall rank as well as a discipline specific rank as applicable.

14.1.10 Parameters

Teaching Learning & Resources
These parameters are related to the core activities of any place of learning...

Research and Professional Practice
Excellence in teaching and learning is closely associated with the scholarship...

Graduation Outcome
This parameter forms the ultimate test of the effectiveness of the core teaching/learning...

Outreach & Inclusivity
The Ranking framework lays special emphasis on representation of women...

Perception
The ranking methodology gives a significant importance to the perception of the institution…

14.2 EDUCATION

14.2.1 Elementary Education

14.2.1.1 Sarva Siksha Abhiyan (SSA)

About

- SSA has been operational since 2000–01 to provide for a variety of interventions for universal access and retention bridging of gender and social category gaps in elementary education and improving the quality of learning.

SSA Interventions

- Inter alia, opening of new school and alternate schooling facilities, construction of schools and additional classrooms, toilets and drinking water, provisioning for teachers, regular teacher in service training and academic resource support, free text books and uniforms and support for improving learning achievement levels/outcome.

SSA-RTE Act

- The committee under Shri Anil Bordia, former Union Education secretary submitted a report, entitled "Implementation of RTE Act and resultant revamp of SSA" in April 2010, was guided by following principles.

  1. Holistic view of education.
  2. Equity
  3. Access
  4. Gender concern
  5. Centrality of teacher
  6. Moral compulsion
  7. Convergent and integrated system of education management.

1. **Holistic view of education**, as interpreted in the National Curriculum Framework 2005, with implications for systemic revamp of the entire content and process of education with significant implications for curriculum teacher education, educational planning and management.
2. **Equity**, to mean not only equal opportunity, put also creation of conditions in which the disadvantaged sections of the society-children of SC, ST, Muslim minority, landless agricultural workers and children with special needs, etc., can avail of the opportunity.
3. **Access**, not be confined to ensuring that a school becomes accessible to all children within specified distance but implies an understanding of the educational needs and predicament of the traditionally excluded categories SC, ST and other sections of the most disadvantaged groups, Muslim minority, girls in general and children with special needs.
4. **Gender concern**, implying not only an effort to enable girls to keep pace with boys but to view education in the perspective spelt out in the National Policy on Education 1986–92, that is, a decisive intervention to bring about a basic change in the status of women.
5. **Centrality of teacher**, to motivate them to innovate and create a culture in the classroom that might produce an inclusive environment for children, especially for girls from oppressed and marginalized backgrounds.
6. **Moral Compulsion** is imposed through RTE Act on parents, teachers, educational administrations and other stakeholders, rather than shifting emphasis on punitive processes.
7. **Convergent and integrated system of education management** is pre-requisite for implementation of RTE law. All states must move in that direction as speedily as feasible.

14.2.1.2 Mid-Day Meal Scheme (MDM)

About

- MDM was introduced for disadvantaged children in Madras Municipal Corporation.
- By the mid-1980s, three states (Gujarat, Kerala and Tamil Nadu) and Union Territory of Puducherry with their resources for children studying at the primary stage.

- By 1990–91, the number of states implementing the MDM programme with their own resources on a universal or large scale had increased to 12 states.

Two-Pronged Strategy

1. To lower the widespread incidence of malnutrition primarily among children of poor families.
2. To increase their access to education.

Aim

- To boost primary school attendance.
- To allow children of parents living below subsistence levels.
- To attain basic literacy levels, rather than being pushed into workforce at an early age.

Beneficiaries

- A centrally sponsored scheme to school children studying in classes I–VIII of government, government-aided schools, special training centres (STC) and madras's and Macaulay supported under SSA.

Requirement

- To provide cooked mid-day meal with *450 calories and 12g of protein to every child at primary level. *700 calories and 20g of protein at upper primary level.

14.2.1.3 Strengthening of Teacher's Training Institutes

About

- Originally, the government launched the scheme of restructuring and re-organisation of teacher education in 1987.

Aim

- To create a sound institutional infrastructure for pre-service and in-service training of elementary and secondary school teachers.
- For provision of academic resource support to elementary and secondary schools.

Components

1. Setting up of District Institutes of Education and Training (DIETs).
2. Strengthening of secondary teacher's education.
3. Institutions into colleges of teacher education (CTEs) and Institutes of advanced study in education (IASEs)
4. Strengthening of state councils of educational research and training (SCERTs).

Main Objectives

Revised under Xth plan.

1. Speedy completion of DIET/CTE/IASE/SCERT projects which have been sanctioned but not completed up to the end of the XI plan period.
2. Making DIETs, CTEs, IASEs, sanctioned (and SCERTs strengthened) up to IX Plan period, optionally functional and operational.
3. Sanction and implementation of from DIET/CTE/IASE/SCERT projects to the extent necessary.

4. Improvement in the quality of programmes being undertaken by DIETs, etc.
5. Scheme for infrastructure development private aided/unaided minority institutes (IDMS) (Elementary secondary)

Senior Secondary Schools

Objective

- To facilitate education of minorities by augmenting and strengthening school infrastructure in minority institutions (elementary/secondary/senior secondary schools) in order to expand facilities for formal education to children of minority communities.
- To encourage educational facilities for girls, children with special needs and those who are most deprived educationally amongst minorities.

Coverage

- Entire country.
- Preference to eligible minority institutions (private aided/unaided elementary/secondary/senior secondary schools) located in districts, blocks and towns having a minority population above 20% based on available census data.

Financial Pattern

- 75% fund for infrastructure development of beneficiaries especially preference to eligible minority institutions.
- Maximum 50 lakh primary schools for other infrastructural activities.

Eligible Conditional

- Voluntary organisations/societies/trusts running institutes/schools that are recognized by central or state governments.

Implementation

- Through state government.

14.2.1.4 Mahila Samakhya Programme:

About

- Launched in 1988.
- To pursue the objectives of the national policy on education, 1986.
- Recognized education as an effective tool for women's empowerment.

Parameters Concerned

1. Enhancing self-esteem and self-confidence of women.
2. Building a positive image of women by recognizing their contribution to the society, policy and the economy.
3. Developing ability to think critically.
4. Fostering decision making and action through collective processes.
5. Enabling women to make informed choices in areas like education, employment and health (especially reproductive health).

6. Providing information, knowledge and skill for economic independence.
7. Ensuring equal participation in developmental processes.
8. Enhancing access to legal literacy and information relating to their rights and entitlements in society with a view to enhance their participation on an equal footing all areas.

14.2.1.5 Entral Sponsored Scheme for Providing Quality Education in Madrasa (SPQEM)

- The scheme for providing quality education in madrasas has been recent after taking into account the inputs of the expert committee of national monitoring committee for minorities education (NMCME) XIth Five-Year Plan.

Objectives

1. To encourage traditional institutions like madrasas and maktahs by giving financial assistance to introduce science, mathematics, social studies, Hindi and English in their curriculum so that academic proficiency for classes I–VII is attainable for children studying these institutions.
2. To provide opportunities to students of these institutions to acquire education comparable to the National Education System especially for secondary and senior secondary levels.
3. To provide opportunities for vocational training for children studying in Madrasas opting for assistance above 14 years of age, to enhance their opportunities for entering the job market and encourage entrepreneurship.
4. To strengthen the state madrasa boards opting assistance, by enabling them to monitor the madrasa modernization programme and enhance awareness about education among the Muslim community.
5. To address in-service training of teachers appointed under scheme to improve their pedagogical skills.

Coverage

- SERPEM is a demand-driven scheme.
- To cover a total of 4,500–6,000 madrasas and provide honorarium to about 13,500–18,000 teachers in madrasas during 11th plan period.

Funding Pattern

- The central government will provide 100% funding during 11th plan.

Implementation

- The scheme will be implemented by the state governments.

14.2.2. Secondary Education

14.2.2.1 Rashtriya Madhyamik Shiksha Abhiyan (RMSA)

About

- Launched in March, 2009.
- The implementation of the scheme started from 2009 to 2010.

- It is envisaged to achieve an enrolment rate of 75% from 52.56% in 2005–06 at the secondary stage of implementation of the scheme by providing a secondary school within a reasonable distance of any habitation.

Objectives

1. To enhance access to secondary education.
2. To improve its quality of education imparted at secondary level through making all secondary schools conform to prescribed norms, removing gender, socioeconomic disability barriers.

Target

- To provide universal access to secondary level education by 2017, that is, by the end of 12th Five-Year Plan. To achieve universal retention by 2020.

Provisions

1. Quality interventions.
2. Equity interventions.
3. Physical facilities.

Implementation

- Implemented by state government societies.

Funding Pattern

- The central share is released to the implementing agency directly.

Adolescence Education Programme

Aim

- To empower young people with accurate, age appropriate and culturally relevant information.
- To promote healthy attitudes.
- To develop skills to enable them to respond to real-life situations in positive and responsible ways.

Co-ordination and Implementation

- NCERT (National Council of Educational Research and Training) coordinates the programme and works through both curricular and co-curricular formats to contribute towards holistic development of young people in pursuance of the National Curriculum Framework, 2005.
- NCERT is the coordinate agency of AEP supported by UNFPA.
- Implemented by six national agencies.

  1. NCERT
  2. Council of Boards of School Education (COBSE)
  3. National Institute of Open Schooling (NIOS)
  4. Central Board of Secondary Education (CBSE)

5. Kendriya Vidyalaya Sangathan (KVS)
6. Navodaya Vidyalaya Samiti (NVS)

14.2.2.2 National Popular Education Programme (NPEP)

Aim

- It develops awareness and positive attitude towards population and development issues leading to responsible behaviour among students and teachers and indirectly among parents and community at large.

Objective

- To impart authentic knowledge to learners about Adolescent Reproductive and Sexual Health (ARSH) concerns.
- To inculcate positive attitude.
- To develop appropriate life skills for responsible behaviour.

Fact

- NPEP is being implemented in 30 states and UTs.

Coordinating Agency

- NCERT is the coordinating agency.

14.2.2.3. National Scheme of Incentives to Girls for Secondary Education

About

- Launched in May 2008.
- Centrally sponsored scheme.

Objectives

- To promote enrolment of girl child in the age group of 14–18 at secondary stage, especially those who passed Class VIII.
- To encourage the secondary education of such girls.

Coverage

1. All SC/ST girls who pass Class VIII and girls who pass Class VIII examination from Kasturba Gandhi Balika Vidyalayas (irrespective of whether they belong to SC/ST) and enrol for class IX in state/UT government aided or local body schools.
2. Girls should be below 16 years of age (as on 31st march) on joining Class IX.
3. Married girls, girls studying in private un-aided schools and enrolled in schools run by central government, like NVS, KVS and CBS-affiliated schools are excluded.

Funding

- A sum of ₹3,000/- is deposited in the name of eligible girls as fixed deposit.
- The girls are entitled to withdraw the sum along with interest thereon on reaching 18 years of age and on passing 10th class examination.

E-governance

- The proposals/list of beneficiaries for the academic year submitted/uploaded on-line over national scholarship portal.

14.2.2.4 Financial Assistance for Appointment of Language

About

- The scheme has three parts. It provides for,
    1. Hindi teachers in the non-Hindi speaking states. This programme has been continuing since the second Five-Year Plan.
    2. Urdu teachers in the schools of those districts that have significant minority population. This scheme has been in place since 1999.
    3. Providing of modern Indian language teachers to teach a third language in those schools of the Hindi speaking states/UTs that demand them.
- The scheme has been introduced in 1993–94 and brought together in the Xth plan.

Aim

- To increase linkages among three parts.
- To improve better administrative efficiency.

Funding

- 100% funding provided to the state government by the central government.

Objective

- To encourage usage of Hindi, Urdu and one modern Indian language, other than English among school-going children under its three language formula.
- To fulfil the requirement of language teachers in government schools.
- To encourage propagation of the national language as well as Urdu and other modern Indian languages, like Kannada, Malayalam, Tamil and Telugu in the country.

14.2.2.5 Mission Mode Project on School Education

About

- GoI launched National e-Governance Plan (NeGP) comprising 27 mission mode projects and 8 components on 18th may 2006.

Result

- Four new e-Governance initiatives in different areas including the area of education.

Core Focus

- On "anytime anywhere" basis,
    1. Services for students could include registration for admission, attendance, transfer, scholarship, grievances and certificates.
    2. Services for teachers such as process of recruitment, rationalisaion, pay-role management, training schedules, administrative grievance redressal.
    3. National MIS platform for efficient school governance/administration.
    4. Services for design and development of digital learning resources and its dissemination.
    5. Services for central and state/UT departments for implementation of the schemes.
    6. Generation of integrated reports and any other common services.

14.2.2.6 National Means-cum-Merit Scholarship Scheme (MMMSS)

About

- It is proposed to award 100,000 scholarships to the gifted or meritorious students whose parental income is not more than ₹1,50,000/- per annum from all sources.
- Each state/UT shall have fixed quota of scholarship which will be decided on the basis of enrolment of students in Classes VII and VIII in the state/UT concerned and population of children of concerned age group of Classes VII and VIII.
- Provide reservation to different categories of students as for the state/UT norms as different states/UTs have their own norms of reservation.
- The total number of scholarships to a particular state/UT may be restricted to the allocation made by central government.
- NMMSS launched in May 2008 is a centrally sponsored scheme.

Objective

1. To award scholarships to meritorious students of EWS to arrest their dropouts at class VIII.
2. To encourage them to continue the study at secondary stage.

Financial Assistance

- Scholarship of ₹6,000/- per annum (₹500/- per month) per student in classes from IX to XII in state government, government-aided local body schools.

Eligibility

- Students whose parental income from all sources is not more than ₹1,50,000/-.

Not Eligible

- Students studying in "Kendara Vidyalayas" and Jawahar Navodya Vidyalas are not entitled to get scholarship.
- Students studying in Residential schools run by the state government institutions, where facilities like boarding, lodging and education are provided are not eligible.
- Students studying in private schools are not eligible.

14.2.2.7. Model School Scheme

About

- The model school scheme has been delinked from the support of GoI.
- The scheme stands transferred to states/UTs for further appropriate action.

Aim

- To provide quality education to talented rural children through setting up of 6,000 model schemes at the rate of one school per block as benchmark of excellence.

Objectives

1. To have at least one good-quality senior secondary school in every block.
2. To have a pace setting role.

3. To try out innovative curriculum and pedagogy.
4. To be a model in infrastructure, curriculum, evaluation and school governance.

Implementation

- Envisages setting up, 3,500 schools in as many educationally backward blocks (EBBs) through state/UT governments and remaining 2,500 schools under public private partnership (PPP) mode in blocks which are not educationally backward.

14.2.3 Adult Education

14.2.3.1 Saakshar Bharat

About

- A CSS of department of school education and literacy (DSEC), MHRD, GoI on international literacy day, 8th September 2009. A new variant of national literacy mission.

Aim

- To further promote and strengthen Adult Education, specially for women, by extending educational options to those adults who have lost the opportunity of access to formal education.
- To promote Adult Education for those whose crossed the standard age for receiving such education.
- To impart functional literacy to non-literates in the age group of 15–35 years in a time-bound manner.

Coverage

- Covers all adults in the age group of 15 and beyond, though its primary focus will be on women.

Objectives

1. Impart functional literacy and numeracy to non-literate and non-numerate adults.
2. Enable the neo-literate adults to continue their learning beyond basic literacy and acquire equivalency to formal education system.
3. Impart non- and neo-literates relevant skill development programmes to improve their earning and living conditions.
4. Promote a learning society by providing opportunities to neo-literate adults for continuing education.

Targets

- The principle target is to impart functional literacy to 70 million adults in the age group of 15 years and beyond.
- To minimize inter- and intra-regional/state disparities.

14.2.3.2 State Resource Centre (SRCs)

About

- To provide academic and technical resource support to adult.

- To continue education through development and production of material and training modules.
- To conduct motivational and environmental building, action research and evaluation and monitoring.

Categorization

- Based on workload size of their programme in area of their jurisdiction, there are two categories: Category A and B.

Financial Assistance

- SRCs are provided an annual recurring grant for programme, emoluments and office expenses in the ration of 45:45:10.

Planning, Monitoring, Evaluation and Capacity Building

- Directorate of Adult education, department of school education and literacy, MHRD is responsible for all these in SRCs.

14.2.3.3 Jan Shikshan Sansthan (JSSs)

Aim

- JSSs are established to provide vocational training to non-literate, neo-literate as well as school dropouts be identifying skills as would have market in the region of their establishment.

Categorization

- Category A , B and C

Financial Assistance

- CSS scheme so 100% financial assistance.

Monitoring and Evaluation

- Directorate of Adult Education, department of school education and literacy, ministry of Human resources, GoI, National Literacy Mission is responsible.

14.2.4 Teacher Education

14.2.4.1 Centrally Sponsored Scheme on Teacher Education

About

- As envisaged in the National Policy on Education (NPE), 1986 and its Programme of Action (POA), acss of restructuring and reorganization of teacher education was launched in 1987.
- To create a sound institutional infrastructure for pre-service and in-service training of elementary and secondary school teachers.
- For provision of academic resource support to elementary and secondary schools.
- The scheme has been revised under Xth Five-Year Plan.

Main Components of Revised Scheme

1. Modification in centre–state financing sharing pattern, from the existing 100% central assistance to sharing pattern in the ratio of 75:25 for all states/UTs (90:10 for NER states, including Sikkim).
2. Contribution of support to SCERTs/SIEs.
3. Strengthening and restructuring of SCERTs.
4. Training for educational administrators, including head teachers.
5. Orientation/induction training to teacher educators.
6. Continuation of support to CTEs and establishment of new CTEs.
7. Continuation of support to IASEs and establishment of new IASEs.
8. Continuation of support and restructuring of DIETs.
9. Establishment of Block institutes of teacher education (BITEs) for augmenting teacher education capacity in SC/ST and minority concentration areas.
10. Professional development of teacher educators.
11. Technology in teacher education.
12. PPP in teacher education monitoring mechanism.

14.2.5 New Education Policy Draft

14.2.5.1 Report of the Committee for Evolution of the New Education Policy

The Committee for Evolution of the New Education Policy (NEP) (Chair: Mr. T. S. R Subramanian) submitted its report on May 7, 2016. The Committee was constituted under the Ministry of Human Resource Development (MHRD) in October, 2015. The report proposes an Education Policy, which seeks to address challenges faced by the current education system. Key features of the proposed Policy are summarised below

- **Broad objectives of NEP:** The proposed Policy seeks to improve the quality and credibility of education by addressing the implementation gaps.
- **Early Childhood Care and Education (ECCE):** The Committee observed that the implementation of ECCE was inconsistent across states. It emphasised the need for all government schools to have facilities for pre-primary education. Hence, it recommended that ECCE for children from 4 to 5 years of age be declared as a right. This would facilitate pre-school education by the government instead of the private sector until children reach 6 years of age.
- **The Right to Education (RTE) Act, 2009:** Currently, the norms for infrastructure and quality have been laid down only for private schools. The Committee recommended that the RTE should be amended to provide uniform norms for recognition of both, government and private schools.
- It also recommended extending the RTE provision of common curriculum to minority institutions, which are currently exempted.
- **School exam reforms:** The Committee recommended the usage of scaled scores and percentiles instead of the traditional marking scheme. It suggested that students should be given the choice to pick the difficulty level of the Mathematics and Science exams in Class 10. To reduce the stress levels of students, the Committee proposed online on-demand board exams as opposed to year end exams.

- In addition, the Committee recommended that the policy of no detention should be upheld only till Cass 5 (age 11 years). This would reverse the existing policy of no detention till Class 8 (age 14 years).
- **Teacher Management:** The Committee observed that there has been a steep rise in teacher shortage, absenteeism and grievances. It recommended setting up of an Autonomous Teacher Recruitment Board. It also recommended that teaching license should be subject to renewal every 10 years. For teacher training, a 4-year integrated B.Ed. course should be implemented.
- **ICT in Education:** The Committee noted that the integration of information technology (IT) and the education sector was inadequate despite Computer literacy and studies in schools. It recommended IT be taken up for teacher training, adult literacy, remedial education and as a learning tool in higher education. This would also include developing online skill-based courses.
- **Vocational education and training:** The Committee recommended scaling up the existing National Skills Qualification Framework to include more students. It recommends expanding and revising the choice of vocational courses in accordance with local opportunities and resources. It also emphasised the need for formal certification by the various Boards of Education for vocational education at par with conventional education.
- Other institutional recommendations:

    (i) **All India Education Service(IES):** It would be established as an all India service;
    (ii) **National Higher Education Promotion and Management Act (NHEPMA):** NHEPMA would replace the existing separate laws governing individual regulators in higher education and redefine the role of existing regulatory bodies like UGC and AICTE; and
    (iii) **National Accreditation Board (NAB):** The NAB will subsume the existing accreditation bodies of National Assessment and Accreditation Council and the National Board of Accreditation and set standards for accreditation. The Committee also recommended mandatory accreditation for technical and medical institutions.

14.3 HEALTH AND FAMILY WELFARE

14.3.1 Pradhan Mantri Swasthya Suraksha Yojana (PMSSY), 2003

Objectives

- Correcting regional imbalances in the availability of affordable, reliable tertiary health care services and also the augment facilities for quality medical education in the country.

Components

- Setting up AIIMS (All India Institute of Medical Sciences)-like institutions.
- Upgradation of government medical college institutions.

Set up AIIMS-like institutions

Totally six, in the each state of,

- Bihar (Patna)
- Chhattisgarh (Raipur)
- Madhya Pradesh (Bhopal)
- Odisha (Bhubaneshwar)
- Rajasthan (Jodhpur)
- Uttaranchal (Rishikesh) under PMSSY Scheme

Major Facilities at 6 AIIMS

(i) Hospital with total bed strength of 960 beds with specialty/superspecialty departments.

(ii) Six basic science departments

- Anatomy
- Physiology
- Biochemistry
- Pharmacology
- Community medicine
- Forensic medicine

(iii) Other departments such as physical medicine and rehabilitation (PMR) department and AYUSH facilities.

(iv) Specialty departments (18) and superspecialty departments (15).

These are to be done in a phased manner.

Funding Pattern

- Approved cost of each new AIIMS in the first phase was ₹820 crores.

1. ₹620 Crores: Cost of construction.
2. ₹200 crores: Procurement of medical equipment and modular operation theatres.

14.3.2 Health Minister's Discretionary Grant (HMDG)

Division: Grants Section.
Funding Pattern: Budgetary provisions are made to fund the HMDG scheme.

Beneficiaries and Eligibility Criteria

1. Only those having annual family income up to ₹1,25,000/- and below are eligible for financial assistance from HMDG.
2. To defray a part of the expenditure on hospitalization/treatment in government hospitals in cases where free medical facilities are not available.

Types of Benefits

- Financial Assistance towards treatment in government hospitals including superspecialty government hospitals/institutes, as per guidelines.

14.3.3 Health Minister's Cancer Patient Fund (within Rashtriya Arogya Nidhi (RAN))

Division: Grants Section.

Funding Pattern

- Health minister's cancer patient fund (HMCPF) within RAN has been set up for providing financial assistance to the poor patients suffering from cancer.
- A corpus fund of ₹100 crore has been setup which has been placed in fixed deposit.
- Interest accrued thereon is utilized to provide the financial assistance.

Beneficiaries and Eligibility Criteria

- Patients suffering from cancer and living below poverty line, prescribed from time to time.

Type of Benefits

- Financial assistance towards treatment for cancer ailments is provided to the patients having treatment in 27 regional cancer centres (RCCs) as per guidelines.

14.3.4 Rashtriya Swasthya Bhima Yojana (RSBY) (2008)

Genesis

- Social security and healthcare assurance—motto of GoI.
- Unorganized workers social security act (2008) provide social security and welfare to the unorganized workers.
- Recommends providing social security schemes to mitigate riddles due to disability, health shocks, maternity and old age faced by unorganized workers.
- Two-third of expenditure on health is through out of pocket (OOP).
- Supply-side financing on health found to be not successful in reducing OOP expenditure on health.
- So, to test the demand side financing approach GoI, decided to introduce RSBY—a health insurance scheme for BPL families.

Objectives: For BPL Families

- To reduce OOP expenditure on health.
- Increase access to health care.
- Now extended to other defined categories of unorganized workers (11 categories defined in the list)

Funding Pattern

- Premium cost for enrolled beneficiaries is shared by GoI and the State governments.

Target

- To cover 70 million households by the end of 12th year plan (2012–2017).

Main Service-Delivering Model

- Demand financing
- Freedom of choice among accredited government and private hospitals.

- Cashless service reimbursable to provide on a pre-determined package rates on a family floater basis.

Fact

- Since 1st April 2015, RSBY has been transferred to ministry of health and family welfare on "as is where is" basis.

Two Fold Objectives

- To provide financial protection against catastrophic health costs by reducing out.
- To improve access to quality health care for BPL households of pocket expenditure for hospitalization and other vulnerable groups in the unorganised sector.

Implementation

- Beneficiaries under RSBY are entitled to hospitalization coverage up to ₹30,000/- per annum on family floater basis, which requires hospitalization.
- Benefits will be available under defined diseases in the package list.
- No age limit.
- Pre-existing conditions are covered from day one.
- Coverage extends to maximum 5 members of family, including head of household, spouse and up to three dependents. Central and state government pays the premium as per their sharing ratio to the insurer selected by the state government on the basis of a competitive bidding.
- At every state, the state government sets up a state nodal agency (SNA) responsible for implementing monitoring supervision and part-financing of the scheme by coordinating with insurance company, hospital, district authorities and other local stakeholders.

Unique Features of the Scheme

1. Empowering the beneficiary.
2. Business model of all stakeholders.
3. Information technology (IT) intensive.
    - First-time IT applications being used for social sector scheme on a large scale.
    - A biometric enabled smart card containing their fingerprints and photographs issued to every beneficiary family.
4. Safe and fool proof.
5. Portability.
6. Cashless and paperless transactions.
7. Robust monitoring and evaluation.

Beneficiaries

- Any BPL family, whose information is included in the district BPL list prepared by state government.
- Any family falling into 11 defined categories,
    1. Building and other construction workers registered with the welfare boards
    2. Licensed railway porters

3. Street vendors
4. MNREGA workers who have worked for more than 15 days during the preceding financial year (FY).
5. Beedi workers
6. Domestic workers
7. Sanitation workers
8. Mine workers
9. Rickshaw pullers
10. Rag pickers
11. Auto/Taxi driver

14.3.5 Revised National TB Control Program (RNTCP)

About

- Started in 1997 (RNTCPI)
- Then expanded across India until the entire nation was covered by RNTCP in March 2006 (RNTCP II)
- RNTCPII was designed to consolidate the gains achieved in RNTCP I
- To initiate the services to address TB/HIV MDR-TB to extend RNTCP to the private sector.
- RNTCP uses WHO recommended directly observed treatment short course (DOTS) strategy and reaches over a billion people in 632 districts/reporting units.

Initial Objectives

- To achieve and maintain a TB treatment success rate of at least 85% among new sputum positive (NSP) patients.
- To achieve and maintain detection of at least 70% of the estimated new sputum positive people in the community.

14.3.6 Pradhan Mantri Surakshit Matritava Abhiyan

The Pradhan Mantri Surakshit Matritva Abhiyan has been launched by the Ministry of Health & Family Welfare (MoHFW), Government of India to provide fixed-day, assured, comprehensive and quality antenatal care universally to all pregnant women on the 9th of every month.

As part of the campaign, a package of antenatal care services are to be provided to pregnant women in their second/third trimesters, by OBGY specialists/radiologist/physicians at government health facilities, with support from private sector doctors to supplement the efforts of the government.

One of the critical components of the Abhiyan is identification and follow-up of high-risk pregnancies. These services will be provided in addition to the routine ANC at the health facility/outreach at identified public health facilities in both urban and rural areas.

BGY specialists/radiologist/physicians working in the private sector are encouraged to volunteer for the campaign and various mechanisms have been developed to facilitate participation of private doctors.

Private doctors willing to volunteer can register for the programme via

- Toll-free number
- Toll-free SMS
- PMSMA portal
- Register using the 'Volunteer Registration' Section of the Mobile Application

As per the information available through the PMSMA portal, till date 1612 volunteers have registered for the programme across States/UTs including 54 volunteers in Rajasthan.

14.4 POVERTY ALLEVIATION

14.4.1 Pradhan Mantri Awas Yojana—Housing For All (Urban)

About

- Ensuring housing for all in urban areas
- Launched on 25th June 2015 to be implemented during 2015–2022
- Estimated housing shortage is in the order of ₹2 crores.

Components of PMAY

Mission Has 4 Verticals

(i) "In-situ" slum Redevelopment with participation of private developers using land as resource for providing housing to eligible slum dwellers.
(ii) Credit-linked subsidy scheme for providing interest rate relate to Ews/LIG beneficiaries.
(iii) Affordable housing in partnership with public and private sectors.
(iv) Beneficiary-led individual house construction/enhancement.

Rajiv Awas Yojana (subsumed in PMAY–HFA(U) Mission.

14.4.2 Credit-linked Subsidy Scheme under PMAY

- The beneficiaries of EWS (Economically Weaker Section) having household annual income up to 3 lakh and low Income Group (LIG) having household annual between ₹3 lakhs and up to ₹6 lakhs subject to their being otherwise eligible under scheme, can avail of interest subsidy at the rate of 65% on focusing ________ up to ₹6 lakhs from banks, Housing Finance Companies and other institutions for a tenure of 15 years or actual tenure of loan which ever in earlier.
- The net present value of the interest subsidy will be calculated at a discount of rate of 9%.
- The carpet areas of houses being acquired, constructed or enhanced should be up to 30 m^2 and 60 m^2 for EWs and LIG, respectively, in order to avail of credit-linked subsidy.
- Housing and urban Development Corporation Ltd., (HUDCO) and National Housing Bank (NHB) have been designated as Central Nodal Agencies (NAs) to ________ the subsidy to primary lending Institutions (PLIs).
- The PLIs include scheduled commercial Banks, Housing Finance Companies (HFCs), Regional Rural Banks (RRBs).

- State cooperative banks, urban cooperative banks or any other institutions as may be identified by the Ministry.
- Preference under the scheme, subject to beneficiaries being from EWS/LIG segments, would be given to:
    - Manual scavengers
    - Women (with overriding preference to widows)
    - Persons belonging to SCs/STs/OBCs, minorities, persons with disabilities and transgender people.

14.4.3 The Deen Dayal Antyodaya Yojana–National Rural Livelihood Mission (DAY-NRLM)

The Deen Dayal Antyodaya Yojana–National Rural Livelihood Mission (DAY-NRLM) is making a difference to the lives and livelihoods of over 3.6 crore households from where women have joined Self-Help Groups (SHGs). The collectives of women under SHGs, Village Organisations (VOs) and Cluster Level Federations (CLFs) has evolved transformational social capital that is changing gender relations, access to services and participation in Gram Sabhas and Panchayati Raj Institutions (PRIs). The programme has given confidence to women to seek Bank loans for economic activity after developing skills and competencies through a sustained Community Resource Person (CRP) led handholding for livelihood diversification. A total of 1.50 lakh women Community Resource Persons (CRPs) who have themselves come out of poverty are today the greatest agents of change in promoting sustainable agriculture, providing banking services, developing a cadre of Para Vets for animal care, bookkeepers and accountants to women's collectives, and most importantly an agent for social transformation of villages.

Since the inception of the programme in 2011, women members of SHGs have accessed ₹1.06 lakh crore as Bank credit. From ₹20,000 crore Bank linkage in 2014–15, SHGs got more than ₹30,000 crore as credit in 2015–16. Till February 2017 over ₹29,000 crore had already been disbursed and it is expected that about ₹35,000 crore to ₹38,000 crore will be mobilised as credit in the Financial Year 2016–17. Analysis of Bank linkage in 2016–17 shows the remarkable increase in credit linkage in States like Assam, Bihar, Odisha, Rajasthan and West Bengal. There is a clear National spread in Bank linkage as SHGs become vibrant and stronger institutions of the poor in many Northern Indian States as well. They are already strong and vibrant in the Southern Indian States.

Under the DAY-NRLM, over 30 lakh women farmers have been supported under Mahila Kisan Sashaktikaran Pariyojana (MKSP) to promote sustainable agricultural practices. Women SHG led Custom Hiring Centres (CHCs) for agricultural implements, power tillers, etc., have come up in some States. Vermi Compost/NADEP pits have also come up through the efforts of these women SHG farmers besides the promotion of pesticide free agriculture and multi-tier cropping in rain-fed regions for fodder, food, forest, fruits and fibre.

The DAY-NRLM programme has reached nearly 1/3rd of the Gram Panchayats of the country and efforts for its consolidation and expansion are being continuously made. During 2017–18, 52 lakh households through 4.5 lakh new SHGs were added to DAY-NRLM. Start-up Village Entrepreneurship Programme (SVEP) to develop 84,000 micro enterprises was started in 17 States covering 47 Blocks. Solid Waste Management initiative through convergence was done in 11,000 (nearly 90%) villages of Tamil Nadu through their women SHGs. The successful initiative has been initiated by DAY-NRLM in 6 other States. DAY-NRLM published a

Compendium of successful Business Models for Livelihood Diversification and also developed a Best Practice Volume based on National awards and recognition to the best SHGs during the year.

To facilitate diversification of livelihoods, skill development for Placement Based Wage Employment and self-employment was promoted on a large scale through the Deen Dayal Upadhyaya Grameen Kaushalya Yojana (DDUGKY) and Rural Self Employment & Training Institutes (RSETIs) respectively under DAY-NRLM. 1.60 lakh youth were trained and 79,400 placed under DDUGKY besides 4 lakh youth being trained in 585 RSETIs for self-employment in 2016–17. Twelve new Champion Employers were selected under DDUGKY for high quality training and committed placements. Some of the Champion Employers are Cafe Coffee Day, Apollo Mediskills, Team lease, etc. Training of drivers was also started at a large number of RSETIs during the year.

The first National evaluation of DAY-NRLM has been completed recently by the Institute of Rural Management Anand (IRMA). The draft report recognises the social capital developed through women's collectives at village level. The evaluation finds that the NRLM strategy has led to greater demand expression of rural poor not just through their weekly meetings but also through collective action in production as well as on social issues. Transforming lives through an even larger-scale diversification and development of livelihoods is clearly the way forward to reach the Mission Antyodaya objective of poverty-free gram panchayats.

14.4.4 Deen Dayal Antyodaya Yojana-National Urban Livelihoods Mission (Day-NULM)

About

- To reduce poverty and vulnerability of the urban poor households by enabling them to access gainful self-employment and skilled wage employment opportunities, resulting in appreciable improvements in their livelihoods on a sustainable basis, through building strong grass roots level institutions of the poor.

Aim

- To provide shelter equipped with essential services to the urban homeless in a phased manner.
- To address livelihood concerns of the urban street vendors by facilitating access to suitable spaces, institutional credit, social security and skills to the urban street vendors for accessing emerging market opportunities.

Constitutional Relevance

- As per the constitution (74th amendment) Act, 1992, urban poverty alleviation is the legitimate function of the urban Local Bodies (ULBs).

Values

(i) Ownership and productive involvement of the urban poor and their institutions in all processes.
(ii) Transparency in programme design and implementation, including institution building and capacity strengthening.

(iii) Accountability of government functionaries and the community.
(iv) Partnerships with industry and other stakeholders.
(v) Community self-reliance, self-dependence, self-help and mutual help.

Strategy

(i) Building Capacity of the urban poor their institutes and the machinery involved in the implementation of livelihoods development and poverty alleviation programmes through handholding support.
(ii) Enhancing and expanding existing livelihoods options of the urban poor.
(iii) Building skills to enable access to growing market-based job opportunities offered by emerging urban economies.
(iv) Training for and support to the establishment of micro-enterprises by the urban poor self and group.
(v) Cater to the needs of especially vulnerable segments of the urban homeless like the dependent children, aged, disabled, mentally ill and recovering patients, etc., by creating special sections within homeless shelters and provisioning special service linkages from them.
(vi) Ensure availability and access for the urban homeless population to permanent 24 hour shelters, including the basic infrastructural facilities like water supply, sanitation safety and security. To establish strong rights-based link water supply, sanitation, safety and security.
(vii) To establish strong rights-based linkages with other programmes which cover the right of the urban homeless to food, health care, education, etc., and ensure access for homeless populations to various entitlements, including to social security pensions, PDS, ICDS, feeding programmes, drinking water, sanitation, identity financial inclusion, school admission, etc., and to affordable housing.
(viii) To address livelihood concerns of the urban vendors by facilitating access to suitable places, institutional credit, social security and skills to the urban street vendors for accessing emerging market opportunities.

V. NULM Mission cities and Target population

(i) In the 12th Five-Year plan, NULM will be implemented in all district headquarter towns and all other cities with a population of 100,000 or more as per 2011 Census. Other towns may be allowed in exceptional cases on request of the states.
(ii) The primary target of NULM is the urban poor, including, urban homeless.
(iii) The socioeconomic and caste census (SECC), 2011 for identification of urban poor is currently under progress.

Interim Measure

- Urban population identified presently as below poverty line population in urban areas by states/UTs.

Broadening the Coverage

- Families of disadvantages groups like SCs, STs, women, minorities, disabled, etc., subject to a maximum of 25% of the above urban poor population.

Key/Main Components

1. Social Mobilization and Institution Development (SM & ID)
2. Capacity Building and Training (CB & T)
3. Employment through skills training and placement)
4. Self-employment programme (SEP)
5. Support to urban street vendors
6. Innovative and Special Projects

Funding Pattern

(i) Northeastern and Special category states (Arunachal Pradesh, Assam, Manipur, Meghalaya, Mizoram, Nagaland, Tripura and Sikkm; Uttarakhand, Himachal Pradesh, Jammu and Kashmir)—90:10 (Central share: State share)
(ii) All other states and UTs—75:25

Implementation

- At state level, a two-tier structure is followed:

  (i) Governing council chaired by CM of the state
  (ii) Executive committee chaired by Chief Secretary of the State.

14.4.5 Scheme of Shelter for Urban Homeless (SUTT)

Ministry of Urban and Poverty Alleviation.

Objective

- To provide shelter and all other essential services to the poorest of the poor segment of urban societies

About

- The shelters should be permanent all weather 24x7 shelters for the urban homeless.
- It is under NULM Mission.

Facts

- For every one lakh population, provisions should be made for permanent community shelters for a minimum of one hundred persons.
- Depending upon local conditions, each shelter caters to between 50 and 100 persons.
- For shelter planning purposes, a space of 50 ft^2 or 4.645 m^2 or say 5 m^2 per person may be taken as minimum space to be provided.

Facilities Provided

- Basic common facilities/amenities such as water, sanitation, electricity, kitchen/cooking space, common recreation space may be provided at the shelters for dignified human living.
- Linkage to Anganwadi, PHC childcare facilities and other social assistance programme is ensured.

Priorities

- Cities with population above 1 million in census of 2011.
- Other cities, towns identified by GOI/State governments to be of special social, historical or tourist importance Implementation.
- Each implementing organization shall set up a shelter management committee (SMC) comprising preferably caretakers and persons nominated from amongst residents of the shelter.
- Such an SMC be responsible for daily management, upkeep, cleanliness and disciplines at the shelter funding pattern.
- Government of India would fund 75% of cost of construction of shelters of 25% be the state contribution.
- In case of special category states (Arunachal Pradesh, Assam, Manipur, Meghalaya, Mizoram, Nagaland, Sikkim, Tripura, Jammu and Kashmir, Himachal Pradesh and Uttarakhand), this ratio will be 90:10.
- To bring in land is the responsibility of state government.

14.4.6 Rajiv Rinn Yojana (RRY)

About

- The Ministry of Housing and Urban Poverty Alleviation (MoHUPA) has designed an interest subsidy scheme for housing titled Rajiv Rinn Yojana (or) Rajiv Loan Scheme.
- As instrument to address the housing needs of the EWS and LIG segments in urban areas, through enhanced credit flow.
- Formulated to channelize institutional credit to the poorer segments of the society and increasing home ownership in the country along with addressing housing shortage.

Background

- RRY has been formulated by modifying the Interest Subsidy Scheme for Housing the Urban Poor (ISHUP) piloted in the 11th plan period with enhanced scope and coverage.
- Central sector scheme applicable in all the urban areas.
- Effective from October 1, 2013

Funding

- RRY provides for interest subsidy of 5% (500 basis points) on loans granted to EWS and LIG categories to construct their houses or extend the existing ones.
- Upper limit of the loan is ₹5 lakh for EWS and ₹8 lakh for LIG
- Interest subsidy be limited to the first ₹5 lakh of the loan amount in case the loan exceeds this amount.
- National Housing Bank (NHB) and Housing & Urban Development Corporation (HUDCO) designated as central Nodal Agencies (CAN) for the scheme.

Beneficiaries

- Below poverty line (BPL)
- Economically weaker section (EWS)
- Low-income group (LIG)

Target

- RRY is a target-driven scheme.
- Overall target for the 12th plan period is 1 million dwellings across the country, including slum and non-slum dwellers.
- The targets for the states for the current FYC are periodically fixed and conveyed to the concerned department(s).

14.4.7 Credit Risk Guarantee Fund Scheme (CRGFT)

About

- With a view to improve access to loans for EWS/LIG persons, CRGFT with a corpus of ₹1,000 crore in the 12th Five Year Plan has also been created under RAY (Rajiv Awas Yojana).
- The ceiling of housing loan limit eligible under the GRGFT scheme has been increased from ₹5 lakh to ₹8 lakh with effective from 1st October 2014.
- The guarantee cover would be available up to ₹5 lakh only as per the scheme to individual borrowers.
- Sixty-one banks and HFCs have signed MoU with CRGF Trust Fact.
- So far, CRGFT covers 1,366 housing loan accounts for loan amount of ₹36.98 crore provided to EWS/LIG households.

14.4.8 Prime Minister's New 15-Point Programme for the Welfare of Minority Communities

About

- Prime Minister's new 15-point programme for the welfare of minorities (Prime Ministers 15-PP) is administered by Ministry of Minority Affairs (MoMA).

Aim

- To ensure the benefits of various government schemes flow equitable by to the minority communities.
- Whenever possible, 15% of targets and outlays under various schemes should be earmarked for minorities.
- MoMA advised the ministries/Departments implementing PM's 15-PP to capture socioreligious communities (SRCs)-wise data in respect of their schemes.

Schemes Covered under PM's New 15-PP

a. Schemes in 15PP considered amenable to earmarking for minority.
   (i) Swarn Jayanti Shahari Rojgar Yojana (SJSRY) restructured as NULM.
b. Schemes in 15PP for which flow of fund to minority concentration areas is quantified.
   (i) Integrated Housing and Slum Development Programme (IHSDP)
   (ii) Basic Services Urban Poor (BSUP)

Aim

- BSUP and IHSDP comprise submissions of erstwhile JnNURM which was launched in 2005 initially for 7 years.

- No new projects have been sanctioned after March 31, 2012 Beneficiaries of BSUP/ IHSDP.
- A total of 15% of the central allocation is to be earmarked for the minority communities.
- State/UTs were requested to give priority to cities/slums, predominantly inhabited by minority communities where minority population is 25% or more), while submitting detailed project reports (DPRs).

14.4.9 Mahatma Gandhi National Rural Employment Guarantee Act (MGNREGA)

Mahatma Gandhi National Rural Employment Guarantee Act (MGNREGA) has come a long way since its inception and has become a lifeline to millions. The Act was notified on 7th September, 2005 to provide minimum of 100 days of guaranteed wage employment in a financial year to every rural household whose adult members volunteer to do unskilled manual work. Social inclusion, gender parity, social security and equitable growth are the founding pillars of Mahatma Gandhi NREGA.

Achievements

During Financial Year (FY) 2015–16, 235 crore person days were generated which was the highest compared to the previous five years. During FY 2016–17 so far, 4.8 crore households were provided employment in 142.64 lakh works. In the process, 200 crore person-days of employment were generated. Out of the total employment, 56% have been generated for women. This is the highest ever participation of women since inception of the programme.

Total expenditure in the programme since its inception is ₹3,76,546 crore and ₹48,000 crore is the allocation of fund for FY 2017–18, which is the highest ever allocation for MGNREGA. The expenditure in FY 2016–17 so far is ₹51,902 crore and is the highest since inception.

On an average, 25 to 30 lakh works were completed every year (till FY 2013–14). On the contrary, 51.3 lakh works have been completed so far in current FY 2016–17.

For the first time since inception of the programme, Consolidated Guidelines for Water Conservation were drafted. Mission Water Conservation—Planning and monitoring Framework for Natural Resource Management (NRM)-related works under MGNREGA in convergence with Pradhan Mantri Krishi Sinchayee Yojana (PMKSY) and Integrated Watershed Management Programme (IWMP) has been prepared for scientific planning and execution of water management works with the use of latest technology is the focus area of the Ministry.

In FY 2016–17 (so far), 63% of total expenditure is on NRM (Natural Resource Management) works. Expenditure on agriculture and allied sector works in FY 2016–17 is nearly 70%, which was only around 48 % in FY 2013–14.

GeoMGNREGA is a path-breaking initiative that uses space technology for geo-tagging all assets created under MGNREGA for improved planning, effective monitoring, enhanced visibility and greater transparency. The initiative was implemented in FY 2016–17, and so far, nearly 65 Lakh assets have been geotagged and made available in the public domain.

Direct Benefit Transfer

To further streamline the fund flow mechanism and bring down delay in payment of wages, the Ministry of Rural Development has implemented National Electronic Fund Management System (NeFMS) in 21 States and 1 Union Territory. Around 96% of the wages are being paid electronically into the bank/post office accounts of MGNREGA workers through Electronic Fund Management System (eFMS). In FY 2013–14, only 37% of the wages were paid electronically.

A total of 8.9 crore active workers have their Aadhaar numbers seeded in NREGASoft-MIS so far, while the number was merely 76 Lakh in January 2014. As of now, 4.25 crore workers have been enabled for aadhaar-based payment system (ABPS).

Good Governance Initiatives

Job card verification and updation was taken up during FY 2016–17, and 75% of active job cards have been updated/verified in campaign mode.

Initiative has been taken to simplify MGNREGA through issuance of Annual Master Circular (AMC) for FY 2016–17 by superseding 1039 circulars/advisories issued earlier. The AMC for FY 2017–18 will be issued.

Reduction in number of registers being maintained at Gram Panchayat level to 7 simplified Registers from an average of 22 Registers has been implemented. So far, 2.05 lakh Gram Panchayats have already adopted it.

The programme is progressing towards a more independent and empowered system of Social Audit and Internal Audit to ensure growth with accountability through a trained community cadre of social auditors drawn from women SHGs.

New Initiatives

The Ministry has taken up skill development of the MGNREGA workers through initiatives like Bare Foot Technicians and Project LIFE (Livelihood In Full Employment) in order to move them up the skilling ladder.

The Ministry initiated Inter State Exchange Programmes, a process ensuring sharing of ideas and good practices. So far, Tamil Nadu, Rajasthan, Meghalaya, Jharkhand, Andhra Pradesh and Chhattisgarh have already been visited by various States during FY 2016–17.

For the first time, guidelines for Non-PMGSY Roads were developed based on PMGSY Guidelines for basic layer. The asset will be durable with a possibility of upgradation to PMGSY standards in future.

The Performance Outcome Report of MGNREGA was for the first time published during FY 2015–16 and will be published for FY 2016–17.

14.5 FOOD SECURITY AND HUNGER ELIMINATION

14.5.1 Public Distribution System (PDS)

About

- Evolved as a system of management of scarcity and for distribution of food grains at affordable prices.
- Operated under joint responsibility of the central and state governments.
- The central government through Food Corporation India (FCI) has assumed the responsibility of the following:
    - Procurement
    - Storage
    - Transportation
    - Bulk allocation of foods to state governments.

State Government's Role

Operational responsibility including:

- Allocation within state.
- Identification of families below the poverty line (BPL)
- Issue of ration cards
- Supervision of the functioning of fair price shops (FPS) rest with state governments.

Commodities

- Wheat, rice, sugar, kerosene to state/UTs for distribution.
- Additional items of mass consumption like cloth, pulses, salt and tea, etc., by some states/UTs.

Contribution

- Containment of rise in food grains prices.
- Ensure access of food to urban consumers

Fact

- After the Green Revolution, the outreach of PDS was extended to trial blocks and areas of high incidence of poverty in 1970s and 1980s.

14.5.2 Revamped Public Distribution System (RPDS)

About

- Launched in June 1992 in 1775 block throughout the country.

Aim

1. To strengthen and streamline the PDS.
2. To improve its reach in the for flange, hilly, remote and inaccessible fair price (FPS) in identified areas.

Improvement of PDS infrastructure

Specific programmes

- Drought-Prone Areas Programme (DPAP)
- Integrated Tribal Development Project (ITDP)
- Dearth Development Programme (DDP)
- Designated Hill Areas (DHA) in consultation with state government for special focus.

Fact

- Food grains for distribution in RPDS areas issued to the states at 50 paise below central issue

Price

- The scale of issues was up to 20 kg per card.

14.5.3 Targeted Public Distribution System (TPDS)

About

- After failure of PDS (Criticisms).
- To serve the population BPL, its urban bias, negligible coverage in the states with the highest concentration of rural poor and lack of transport and accountable arrangements for delivery.
- With effect from June 1, 1997.

Allocation and Beneficiaries

- Under TPDS, GoI allocates food grains (rice and wheat) at the rate of 35 kg per family per month to states/UTs for 6.52 crore.
    - About 2.43 crore Antyodaya Anna Yojana (AAJ) families.
    - For distribution at subsidized prices through FPS.

Fact about APL

- Above Poverty Line (APL) families are also made depending upon the availability of food grains in the central pool and past off take.
- Allocation of food grains to APL families ranges between 15 and 35 kg per family per month.

14.5.4 Antyodya Anna Yojana (AAY)

About

- Centrally sponsored scheme for ten million of the poorest families.
- Launched by NDA government in December 2000.

Target

- Lookout for the poorest of the poor by providing them 35 kg of rice and wheat at ₹3 and ₹2 per kg, respectively.

Objective

1. To ensure food security to the poorest of the poor.

Status

- Originally, each beneficiary was given 25 kg per month at the state of ₹3 per kg.
- Increased to 35 kg of rice per card per month at the rate of ₹2 per kg through FPD from November 2006 onwards.

14.5.5 Annapurna Scheme

About

- Launched by GoI with effect from April, 2000.

Aim

- To provide food security to meet the requirement of those senior citizens who, though eligible, have remained uncovered under the National Old Age Pension Scheme (NOAPS).

Beneficiaries

- The age of the applicant male or female should be 65 year or above.
- Under Annapurna scheme, 10 kg of food grains per month to be provided "free of cost" to the beneficiary.

Extension

- GoI decided to extend this scheme to another 10 lakh old people but give them only 10 kg of food grain, either wheat or rice free of charge every month.

14.5.6 National Old Age Pension Scheme (NOAPS)

About

- Introduced as a 100% CSS on 15th August, 1995.
- About 60 lakh old people get monthly pension ranging from 100 to 250 per month.

Fact

- About one-third of the beneficiaries were found to be neglected by their offspring or were living above and another one-third were found to have a dependent (mostly spouse) and in remaining cases, the beneficiaries did not have a regular source of income.
- In some states, the benefits were distributed once in 2 months and in some others there was no fitted frequency for distribution.

14.5.7 Mid-Day Meal Scheme (MDMS)

About

- The National Programme of Nutritional support to primary education (NP-NSPE) was launched as a CSS in 1955.
- Commonly referred to as MDMS

Aim and Target

1. To enhance enrolment, retention, attendance of children in schools apart from improving their nutritional levels.
2. Extended to upper primary class (VI to VIII) children in 347 economically backward blocks (EBBs) in 2007.
3. Universalized at elementary level in 2008.

Implementation

1. Through states/UTs
2. Managed and implemented by:
    - School management/village education committees.
    - Panchayat Raj Institutions.
    - Self-Help Groups

- Now includes Madrasas and Maktaks supported under SSA as well as children under National projects.

Details

- Calorific value, protein inclusion, additional nutritional supplements and vitamins.

Special Attention

- Poor-performing districts (144)
  - 17 in left-wing extremism (LWE)
  - 11 in northeastern states (Tripura, Meghalaya, Assam)
  - 17 in tribal districts
  - 13 in hilly areas (Jammu and Kashmir and Uttarakhand)

14.5.8 Integrated Child Development Scheme (ICDS)

About

- Launched in 1975—a nationwide programme for overall development of children below 6 years and of the expectant and nursing the others.

Package

It contains six services:

1. Supplementary feeding
2. Immunization
3. Health check-ups
4. Referral services
5. Pre-school education
6. Health and nutrition education for its beneficiaries

Beneficiaries

- Children below 6 years of age.
- Expectant and nursing mothers.

Funding Pattern

- As it is a CSS scheme, 100% financial assistance to states/UTs.

14.5.9 Entire Country Gets National Food Security Act Coverage

Kerala and Tamil Nadu have also rolled out the National Food Security Act (NFSA). With this, now the Act has been implemented in all the States and Union Territories. As a result, now 81.34 crore persons will get wheat at ₹2/kg and rice at ₹3/kg. Being an important initiative for ensuring food security of the people, the Government of India actively pursued with all the States/UTs for its early implementation.

Now the centre will focus on further reforms in PDS, which will include end to end computerization of the system for which States/UTs are being technically and financially assisted. This is important for bringing in transparency in the functioning of the public distribution system (PDS), which is vital feature of NFSA, in order to check leakages and diversion of food grains.

Highlighting other initiatives taken by the Centre to make the PDS leakage proof, the beneficiary's database has been digitized in all the 36 States/UTs, wherein, information is available right up to beneficiary level and is in the public domain. Online allocation of food grains is being done in 28 States/UTs, and the entire food grain supply chain has been computerized in 18 States/UTs. A 100% linkage of Ration Cards with Aadhaar, which is 71% at the moment, will be achieved. Food grain losses of FCI have been brought down to 0.04% and major FCI depots have been made online.

In another significant step towards better targeting and leakage-free distribution of food grains, direct benefit transfer is being carried out in two different modes. In the first mode, food subsidy is being transferred in cash into the bank account of beneficiaries, who then have the choice to buy food grains from the open market. This has been started in UTs of Chandigarh, Puducherry and urban areas of Dadra & Nagar Haveli. The second mode involves automation of fair-price shops, for distribution of food grains through an electronic point of sale (e-PoS) device which authenticates beneficiaries at the time of distribution and also electronically captures the quantum of food grains distributed to the family. As of 31 Jan 2016, e-PoS devices are operational in 1,61,854 fair-price shops.

For smooth functioning of PDS, State Governments are also being provided Central assistance for meeting expenditure of intra-State transportation and handling of food grains and fair-price shop dealer's margin. The assistance for fair-price shop dealers' margin also contains a component of assistance for installation and operation of PoS devices at fair price shops. So far, ₹1,874 crore has been released to State Governments by the Government of India in 2016–17.

At this current coverage, monthly allocation of food grains to States/UTs under the Act is about 45.5 lakh tons, with subsidy implication of about ₹11,726 core per month or about ₹1,40, 700 crore per year.

14.6 WELFARE INITIATIVES FOR WOMEN (MCWD)

14.6.1 Beti Bachao Beti Padhao Scheme

- To address the issue of decline in CSR (Child Sex Ratio) in 100 gender-critical districts (now extended to 61 more districts).

Objectives

1. Prevent gender-biased sex-selective elimination.
2. Ensure survival and protection of the girl child.
3. Ensure education of the girl child.

Two Major Components

1. Mass communication campaign.
2. Multi-sectoral action in 100 selected districts (as pilot) with adverse CSR, covering all states and UTs).

Multi-sectoral intervention

1. Ministry of women and child development
2. Ministry of Health and family welfare
3. Ministry of Human Resource Development

One-stop Centre Scheme

- Centrally sponsored scheme.
- A sub-scheme of umbrella scheme for National Mission for Empowerment of women including Indira Gandhi Mattritav Sahyog Yojana. Established across the country to provide integrated support and assistance under one roof to women affected by violence, both in public and private places in a phased manner.
- Girls under 18 years of age are referred to centre, served in coordination with authorities, institutions established under Juvenile Justice (Care and Protection of children) Act, 2000 and Protection of children from sexual offence act, 2012.
- Women help line to give assistance in
    - Medical
    - Police
    - Shelter
    - Psycho-social support/counselling
    - Legal aid/ counselling
    - Video-conferencing facility

Funding Pattern

- Centrally sponsored scheme funded through Nirbhaya fund.
- Central government will provide 100% financial assistance to the state government/UT administrations.
- Day-to-day implementation and administrative matters would be responsibility of the state government, both social audit and audit would be done.
- Social audit and audit would be done.
- Social audit by civil society groups.
- 12th working plan group recommended this one-stop crisis centre.

14.6.2 Universalization of Women Helpline Scheme (1091)

- With respect to Article 21 of the constitution.

Objectives

- Provide toll-free 24 hours telecom service to women affected by violence seeking support and information.
- Facilitate crisis intervention through referral to police/hospital/ambulance services.
- Provide information about the appropriate support services available to the woman affected by violence, in her particular situation within the local area in which she resides or is employed.
- Creation and maintenance of a comprehensive referral database by the helpline within its local area.

Key Stakeholders

- Ministry of communications and IT and Department of telecommunications.
- Ministry of Home Affairs/state/district
- Ministry of Health and family affairs/state/district.

14.6.3 Ujjawala Scheme

- A comprehensive scheme for prevention of trafficking and rescue, rehabilitation and re-integration of victims of trafficking and commercial sexual exploitation.

Objective

- To prevent trafficking of women and children for commercial sexual exploitation through social mobilization and investment of local communities, awareness generation programmes, generate public discourse through workshops, seminars and such events and any other innovative activity.
- To facilitate rescue of victims from the place of their exploitation and place them in safe custody.
- To provide rehabilitation services of both immediate and long term to the victims by providing basic amenities/needs, such as shelter, food, clothing medical treatment, including counselling, legal aid and guidance and vocational training.
- To facilitate reintegration of the victims into the family and society at large.
- To facilitate repatriation of cross-border victims to their country of origin.

Target Group/Beneficiaries

- Women and children who are vulnerable and victims of trafficking for commercial sexual exploitation. **Implementing Agencies**

1. Social welfare/women and child welfare department of state government.
2. Women's development corporations.
3. Women's development centres.
4. Urban local bodies.
5. Reputed public/private trust or voluntary organisation. These organization must have adequate experience in the field of trafficking, social defence, dealing with women and children in need of care and protection, children in conflict with law, etc.

Components of Scheme

1. Prevention
2. Rescue
3. Rehabilitation
4. Re-integration
5. Repatriation

The implementing agency should bear the 10% cost of the project.

Funding Pattern

- Release of funds will be shared between central government states and implementing agencies in the ratio 60:30:10 except northeastern and Himalayan states where the applicable sharing ration shall be 80:10:10, respectively.
- In case of UT, sharing ratio will be 90:10 between the central government and implementing agency.

- Funds to the states/UT will be released in two instalments.
    1. First instalment: 50% of allocated grant in the beginning of financial year after deducting any unspent balance available with state/UT.
    2. Second instalment released after 60% of the first instalment has been utilized. State government/UTs are required to furnish half-yearly statement of expenditure to MCWD.

14.6.4 Working Women Hostel

Objectives

- To promote availability of safe and conveniently located accommodation for working women, with day-care facility for their children, wherever possible, in urban or even rural areas where employment opportunity for women exist.

Beneficiaries

1. Working women, who may be single, widowed, divorced, separated married but where husband or immediate family does not reside in the same city/area.
2. Particular preference may be given to women from disadvantaged sections of the society.
3. Provision for reservation of seats for physically challenged beneficiaries.
4. Women under training for job provided the total training period does not exceed 1 year on the condition: vacancy available after accommodated working women. (WW)
5. Number of women under training for job should not exceed 30% of the total capacity.
6. Girls up to age of 18 years and boys up to age of 5 years, accompanying working mothers will be provided accommodation, with their mothers.

Financial Assistance Components

1. 75% of the cost of construction of building of working women hostel only on public land.
2. Financial assistance for hostels to be run in rented premises.

Funding Pattern: For Construction of Hostel Building

- For new hostel construction, the ratio 50:40:10 in three instalments.

14.6.5 Rajiv Gandhi National Crèche Scheme for the Children of Working Mothers

Objective

- To provide day-care facilities for children (6 months to 6 years) of working mothers in the community.
- To improve nutrition and health status of children.
- To promote physical, cognitive, social and emotional development (holistic development) of children.
- To educate and empower parents, caregivers for better childcare. **Services**
- Day-care facilities, including sleeping facilities.
- Early stimulation for children below 3 years and pre-school education for 3 to 6 years old children.

- Supplementary nutrition (to be locally sourced).
- Growth monitoring
- Health check-up and immunization.

Target Group

- Focus on children of 6 months to 6 years of working women in rural and urban areas who are employed for a minimum period of 15 days in a month or in year.

Implementing Agencies

- Through the existing mother NGOs and CSWB.
- If required, these organisation could implement scheme through other suitable voluntary/NGOs
- Run the crèches as per the Standard Operating Procedure (SoP).

Funding Pattern

- NGOs/organisation will get themselves registered with the implementing agencies, that is, CSWB/mother NGOs from whom they are seeking grants-in-aid for running the crèches.
- They should also have the Aadhaar number of key functionaries of the crèche and beneficiaries (i.e., children).
- Released on quarterly basis to implementing agencies/mother NGOs on receipt of request and requisite documents.
- No grants, in case the no. of children in particular months falls below 10.
- In case of number of children for a particular month is less than 25 but more than 9, supplementary nutrition cost will be provided on pro rata basis coordination and convergence.
- Ensure linkages with local PHC/such centre, government hospital in area for immunization and basic health check-up of children.
- Ensure convergence with other schemes and programmes like ICDS, SSA and MGNREGA within the vicinity.
- Arrangements for doctor's visit for medical check-up of children should be ensured; unwillingness of qualified doctors to visit far-flung crèche centres in rural areas needs to be adequately compensated.

14.6.6 SWADHAR GREH—A Scheme for Women in Difficult Circumstances

Vision

- A supportive institutional framework for women victims of difficult circumstances so that they could lead their life with dignity and conviction.

Objectives

1. To cater to the primary need of shelter, food, clothing, medical treatment and care of women in distress and who are without any social and economic support.
2. To enable them to regain their emotional strength that gets hampered due to their encounter with unfortunate circumstances.

3. To provide them with legal aid and guidance to enable them to take steps for their readjustment in family/society.
4. To rehabilitate them economically and emotionally.
5. To act as a support system that understands and meets various requirements of women in distress.
6. To enable them to start their life after dignity and conviction.

Swadhar Greh will be set up in every district with capacity of 30 women.

Strategies

- Temporary residential accommodation with provision of food, clothing, medical facilities, etc.
- Vocational and skill upgradation timings for economic rehabilitation of such women.
- Counselling, awareness generation and behavioural trainings.
- Legal aid and guidance.
- Counselling through telephone.

Beneficiaries

Availed by Women alone 18 Years of Age Who Are:

- Deserted and without any social and economic support.
- Survivors of natural disasters who have been rendered homeless and without any social and economic support.
- Prisoners released from jail and without family, socioeconomic support.
- Victims of domestic violence, family tension or discord who are made to leave their homes without any means of subsistence and no special protection from exploitation and/or facing litigation on account of martial disputes.
- Trafficked women/girls rescued or runaway from brothels or any other places where they face exploitation and women affected by HIV/AIDS who do not have any social or economic support. However, such women/girls should first seek assistance under UJJAWALA scheme in areas where it is in operation.

Funding Pattern

- MWCD provide 100% funding as grant-in-aid to the state governments and UT administrations for release to implementing agencies.

Implementing Agencies

- State government agencies including women development corporate established by them
- Central/state autonomous bodies
- Municipal bodies
- Cantonment boards
- Panchayat Raj Institutions and cooperative institutions
- Departments of women and child development/social welfare of the state governments
- Public trusts registered under any law for the time being in force.
- Civil society organisations such as NGOs

Components of the Scheme

1. Construction grant for construction of building will be admissible to state governments, municipal corporations, cantonment boards and panchayat raj institutions only. Land for this purpose is to be provided by the IA free of cost
2. Rent for SWADHAR Greh, if run in a rented building
3. Assistance for recurring and non-recurring expenditure for management of Swadhar Greh
4. Provision for food, shelter, clothing, medical care, pocket expense for residents and children.
5. Provision of counselling, legal aid, vocational training and guidance

14.6.7 STEP—Central Sector Scheme Since 1986–1987

About

- Support to training and employment programme for women (STEP) aims to provide skills that give employability to women and to provide competencies and skills that enable women to become self-employed/entrepreneurs.

Beneficiaries

- Intended to benefit women who are in the age group of 16 years and above across the country and not exceed 200.

Funding Pattern

- Grant under the scheme is given to an institution/organisation directly including NGOs and not the states/UTs. 90% by GoI and remaining 10% by IA from assistance.
- Any sector for imparting skills related to employability and entrepreneurship, including but not limited to the agriculture, horticulture, food processing, handlooms, tailoring, stitching, embroidery, zari, etc., handicrafts, computer and IT enable services along with soft skills and skills for the work place such as spoken English, gems and jewellery, travel and tourism, hospitality as identified by MSDE (Ministry of skill development and entrepreneurship).

Objectives

a. To provide skills that give employability to women.
b. To provide competencies and skills that enable women to become self-employed/ entrepreneurs.

Scope

- GoI set an ambitious plan training 500 million individuals by 2022 which translates to training 42 million a year.

Project Approval

- By project appraisal committee (PAC).

14.6.8 Nari Shakti Puraskar (National Award for Women)

- Awarded for outstanding work preferably in exceptional circumstances to individual men or women/groups academic institutions/NGOs/ villages, etc., in the broad, disaggregated areas/activities coming under the promotion of economic empowerment, social empowerment, effective implementation of women related legislates and gender mainstreaming.

Objectives

- Strengthening their legitimate place in the society for women.
- Provide an opportunity to the current generation to understand the contribution of women in building of society and the nation.

Recipients

- Drawn from institutions and individuals

Nominations

- Invite nominations from state government, UT-concerned central ministries, NGOs, universities, institutions, private and public sector undertakings working for empowerment of women.
- 20 Nari Shakti purashkars shall be conferred every year.
- Declared every year on 20th February and awards conferred on 8th March on the occasion of International Women's Day (IWD)
- Certificate and Cash amount

14.6.9 Indira Gandhi Matritiva Sahyog Yojana (IGMSY)— A Conditional Maternity Benefit Scheme

Objectives

1. Promoting appropriate practices, care and service utilization during pregnancy, safe delivering and location.
2. Encouraging the women to follow (optimal) ICYF practices, including early and exclusive breast feeding for the first 6 months.
3. Contributing to better enabling environment by providing cash incentives for improved health and nutrition to pregnant and lactating mothers.

About Implementation

- Implemented through ICDS Scheme.
- Focal point of implementation would be Anganwadi centre (AWC) at the village.

Target Group

- Pregnant women of 19 years of age and above, for first two live births (benefit for still births would be as per the guidelines of scheme).
- All government and PSUs (Central and State) employees would be excluded from the scheme as they are entitled for paid maternity leave.

Financial Assistance

- Financial assistance to state governments would be given in two instalments by MoWCD.
- MoWCD transfers the funds to the consolidated account of the concerned state government.

14.6.10 Women Transforming India

NITI Aayog launches 'Women Transforming India' campaign, in partnership with the UN in India and MyGov - #WomenTransform.

Celebrating women doers, leaders and change makers from across the country, NITI Aayog—Government of India's premier think tank—has launched the 'Women Transforming India' initiative on, March 8, International Women's Day, in partnership with the UN in India and MyGov.

As a policy think tank, NITI Aayog seeks to engage directly with women leaders from across urban and rural areas of India. 'Women Transforming India' is, therefore, our effort at putting our ear to the ground to gather successful stories of change heralded by women at the grassroots level, within communities.

Through the initiative, NITI Aayog is seeking for entries in the form of written essays/stories (not exceeding 500 words), preferably accompanied by photographs that set a context to the narrative. These stories should reflect new ground broken by women in empowering themselves/others, or of challenging stereotypes.

Winning entries will receive a certificate of appreciation from NITI Aayog and the UN in India. Change makers may also have a chance to interact directly with policy makers in the Government of India to enable affect positive policy action.

We seek to encourage and recognize women who have made a difference, particularly, by demonstrating leadership in the economic, sociocultural and environmental front. Stories of change fostered through the setting up of small businesses/enterprises to generate livelihood opportunities for communities, challenging discriminatory practices/norms, or preserving the environment and responding to challenges of climate change are encouraged. Successes in leading change could have been achieved either through the use of technology or by employing innovating on-ground methods.